BRITISH
COLUMBIA

ANDREW HEMPSTEAD

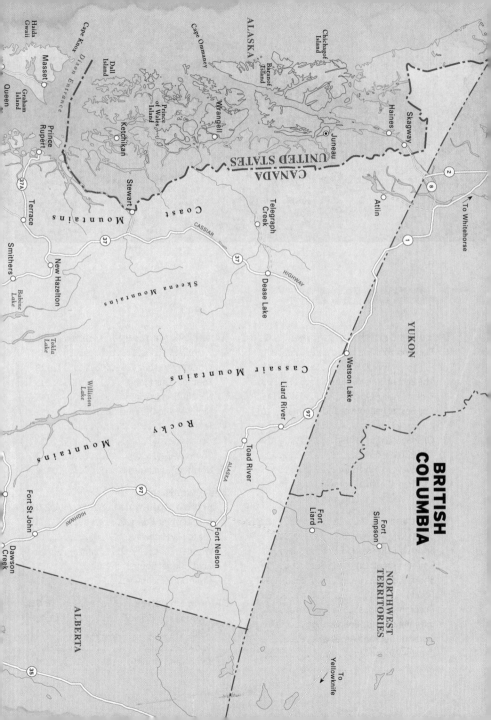

Contents

DISCOVER

British Columbia

British Columbia, the westernmost province of Canada, stretches from the Pacific Ocean to the towering heights of the Rocky Mountains. Sandwiched between is some of this planet's most magnificent scenery: an enormous variety of terrain, including towering mountain ranges, ancient glaciers, endless rivers, crystal clear lakes, old-growth temperate rainforests, rugged coastline, hundreds of islands, and even a desert. Wildlife is abundant: The forests provide a home for bears, moose, deer, and elk, while the ocean is alive with whales, dolphins, and all manner of other sealife.

Settled by Europeans just over 200 years ago, this landscape has been home to civilization for thousands of years. World-class facilities such as the Museum of Anthropology at UBC and the Royal BC Museum preserve the culture of the First Nations, which can also be experienced by visiting abandoned villages, tasting indigenous dishes, and learning about meaningful art, such as colorful totem poles.

Clockwise from top left: Vermilion River in Kootenay National Park; waterfalls in Fraser Valley; Indian paintbrush; Yukon shopfront; wagon wheel on Historic Hat Creek Ranch; kayaking on Vancouver waterway.

The province's largest city is Vancouver, a splendid conglomeration of old and new architectural marvels, parks and gardens, and sheltered beaches. Just across the Strait of Georgia is the provincial capital, Old World Victoria. But the soul of British Columbia lies away from the cities, in the surrounding vastness. Continuing north along the Alaska Highway through the Yukon Territory, the wilderness grows wilder and more remote.

British Columbia is one of the most beautiful, exciting, and inspirational places on this planet. You have to experience it for yourself.

Clockwise from top left: Sherbrooke Lake in Yoho National Park; grizzly bear; powder skiing in Whistler; gold panner statue.

Planning Your Trip

Where to Go

VANCOUVER

Dramatic **snowcapped mountains** rise high above a modern city clinging to the coastline. A downtown core of **century-old buildings** and **steel-and-glass skyscrapers** overlooks busy waterways. Sandy beaches and rocky shorelines fringe manicured suburbs. Magnificent **old-growth forests** and **brilliant flower gardens** overflow with color. And residents in love with the outdoors eagerly take advantage of its magnificent natural surroundings.

VICTORIA AND VANCOUVER ISLAND

The elegant capital of British Columbia couldn't be more different from its much larger neighbor, Vancouver. **Well-preserved buildings** line the streets. **Totem poles** sprout from shady parks. Restored historical areas house trendy shops, offices, and exotic restaurants. Meanwhile, **double-decker buses** and **horse-drawn carriages** compete for the summer tourist trade. Beyond city limits, the rest of Vancouver Island beckons, with outdoor experiences ranging from hiking the rugged **West Coast Trail** to whale-watching at **Telegraph Cove.**

SOUTHWESTERN BRITISH COLUMBIA

Exploring southwestern BC is like taking three very different vacations. The **Sunshine Coast** spreads out to the north, attracting families, scuba divers, and sun-loving Canadians. The Sea to Sky Highway leads to **Whistler,** an upscale, outdoorsy resort town of epic proportions. Traveling east from Vancouver, the road forks—head upstream through the scenic **Fraser River Canyon** to central British Columbia or to a winding mountain highway through **Manning Provincial Park.**

If You Have...

- **A WEEKEND:** Spend your time in Vancouver.
- **ONE WEEK:** Add Whistler and Vancouver Island.
- **TWO WEEKS:** Add the Okanagan Valley, the Kootenays, and the Canadian Rockies.
- **THREE WEEKS:** Add Central and Northern British Columbia and Yukon.

view from the top of the Sea to Sky Gondola

OKANAGAN VALLEY

Around 180 kilometers (110 miles) from end to end, the gorgeous Okanagan Valley is dotted with **orchards and wineries,** the latter a major attraction. But if the only thing you know about wine is that you like it, no worries—wine-tasting in the Okanagan Valley is a completely unsnobby affair. The entire valley brims with **bustling tourist towns, world-class golf courses, marvelous resorts,** and enough **warm lakes** to keep the kids busy for an entire vacation.

THE KOOTENAYS

Named for its original inhabitants, the Kootenay region is monotonous—in an

The Yukon

NORTHWEST TERRITORIES

0   100 mi

0   100 km

ALASKA

Northern British Columbia

ALBERTA

Central British Columbia

Canadian Rockies

Southwestern British Columbia

Victoria and Vancouver Island

The Kootenays

Vancouver   **Okanagan Valley**

© AVALON TRAVEL

overwhelmingly beautiful, mountain-and-lakes kind of way. Alpine snowfields feed mighty rivers and massive lakes, creating a **recreational playground** for anglers, canoeists, and kayakers. Several parks merit special attention: **White Grizzly Wilderness** for the opportunity to view grizzly bears, **Kokanee Creek** to watch fish spawning along a shallow creek bed, and **Akamina-Kishinena** for its solitude.

CANADIAN ROCKIES

Welcome to the Canadian Rockies, a vast wilderness where wildlife is always abundant and hiking trails always scenic. The region is at its most breathtaking at **Lake O'Hara** in **Yoho National Park,** while adjacent **Kootenay National**

Park offers up more magnificent Canadian wilds, along with hot springs.

CENTRAL BRITISH COLUMBIA

Cutting a swath across the province, the central region of British Columbia is extremely diverse. To the east, a series of glaciated mountain ranges are protected by **Glacier** and **Mount Revelstoke National Parks,** which offer accessible adventure. The scenery changes dramatically west of **Salmon Arm,** as mountains recede into sagebrush-covered hills. In the heart of this desert landscape is **Kamloops** and the ranching country of the **Cariboo.**

NORTHERN BRITISH COLUMBIA

Northern BC is a long way from anywhere else. You won't see famous attractions. Instead, you'll find **lakes and forest** and lots of both. **Small towns** provide excellent access to outdoor activities, as well as a little bit of pioneering history. The coastline is mostly inaccessible, but where highways push down to the ocean, **Prince Rupert** and **Stewart** offer scenic rewards. For a real adventure, jump a ferry to **Haida Gwaii,** where totem-pole villages are slowly being reclaimed by nature.

THE YUKON

Linked to British Columbia by the **Alaska Highway,** the Yukon is a continuation of the forested wilderness. Many visitors pass right through on their way to Alaska, but it's worth lingering to explore the natural wonders of **Kluane National Park,** the modern frontier delights of **Whitehorse,** and the world's most famous gold rush town, **Dawson City.**

Mount Robson Provincial Park rainbow

Know Before You Go

When to Go

The high season is most definitely **summer,** or more precisely **July and August.** The parks come alive with campers, the lakes and streams with anglers, the mountains with hikers, the woods with wildlife, and the roadsides with stalls selling fresh produce.

While **April-June** is considered a shoulder season, in many ways the province is at its blooming best in spring. Crowds are at a minimum, the days are long, golfers hit the links in shirts and shorts, and lodging rates are reduced. **Fall** (Sept.-Nov.) can also be tremendous, particularly **September,** with lingering warm temperatures and a noticeable decrease in crowds.

Vancouver and Victoria can be visited **year-round,** with some outdoor activities—golfing, biking, hiking, and more—possible in the dead of winter on southern Vancouver Island. Alpine resorts throughout the province begin opening in December, with seasons extending through March.

Passports and Visas

To enter Canada, a **passport, passport card,** or **NEXUS card** is required by citizens and permanent residents of the United States. For further information, see the website http://travel.state.gov. For current **entry requirements** to Canada, check the Citizenship and Immigration Canada website (www.cic.gc.ca).

All other foreign visitors must have a valid passport and may need a visa or visitors permit, depending on their country of residence and the vagaries of international politics. At present, visas are not required for citizens of the United States, Commonwealth countries, or Western Europe. The standard entry permit is for six months, and you may be asked to show onward tickets or proof of sufficient funds to last you through your intended stay.

Transportation

Visitors to British Columbia have the option of arriving by **road, rail, ferry,** or **air.** The main gateway city for flights from North America is **Vancouver,** which is also the main Canadian gateway for flights originating in Asia and the South Pacific.

Driving, whether it be your own vehicle or a **rental car,** is by far the best way to get around, although all cities have airports and most towns are served by buses.

The Best of British Columbia

Two weeks in British Columbia allows the opportunity to travel throughout the province, including to the northern region. Of course, you can always add to your itinerary with more time in Vancouver and Victoria—but you'll find more adventure traveling farther afield.

Day 1

Arrive in **Vancouver** for a two-night stay. Spend the rest of your first day exploring **Gastown** and the waterfront area, including **English Bay.** Rent a bike for an evening ride around **Stanley Park.**

Day 2

Spend the day in the bustling resort town of **Whistler,** a 90-minute drive north of Vancouver along Highway 99, returning to Vancouver in time for dinner atop **Grouse Mountain.**

Day 3

Take the 90-minute ferry ride across to Vancouver Island and visit **Victoria** sights such as the **Royal BC Museum** and **Butchart Gardens,** then explore the urban oasis of **Goldstream Provincial Park.**

Day 4

Make **Tofino,** a three-hour drive from Victoria along Highways 1 and 4, your final destination on Day 4. Even with a visit to **Cathedral Grove** and a short walk along the driftwood-strewn beaches of **Pacific Rim National Park,** you will have time to enjoy a relaxing evening in Tofino.

Day 5

Rise early and make your way north up the island to **Telegraph Cove,** a four-hour drive from Tofino via Highways 4 and 19. Go **whale-watching** in the afternoon and continue north for 60 kilometers (38 miles) to **Port Hardy.**

Day 6

The morning ferry from Port Hardy gets into **Prince Rupert** in the late afternoon, linking up with the overnight ferry to Haida Gwaii.

Butchart Gardens

Mount Robson

Day 7

Even after 24 hours and two ferry trips, you'll be invigorated by the uniqueness of the First Nations history and total wilderness of **Haida Gwaii.**

Day 8

You have all day on the island to explore the beaches of **Naikoon Provincial Park** and First Nations attractions like the **Haida Heritage Centre.** Ferries depart Haida Gwaii for Prince Rupert in the evening (book a cabin to get a good night's rest on board).

Day 9

Arriving in **Prince Rupert** at dawn, take breakfast at the Cow Bay Cafe while waiting for the **Museum of Northern British Columbia** to open. Head west, stopping at '**Ksan Historical Village.** Aim for an overnight stay in Prince George—an eight-hour drive from Prince Rupert—but don't push it; the more driving you get done today, the quicker you will reach the mountains the following day.

Day 10

After the long haul across northern British Columbia, the first views of the Canadian Rockies, two hours' driving beyond Prince George, are a relief. As **Mount Robson** comes into view, you will be wowed. Short hikes to viewpoints and waterfalls will fill your afternoon.

Day 11

Drag yourself away from Mount Robson and head south on Highway 5 for four hours to the river city of **Kamloops,** then east along the Trans-Canada Highway to **Revelstoke.** Even if you're not a railway buff, **Craigellachie** (site of the last spike on the transcontinental railway) is a pleasant stop along this two-hour stretch of road.

Day 12

Drive the **Meadows in the Sky Parkway** near Revelstoke and continue east along the Trans-Canada Highway for two hours to **Yoho National Park.** This may be the night for a splurge at the **Emerald Lake Lodge** (at the very least, walk around this beautiful lake).

Best Photo-Ops

Photographers easily find inspiration in the stunning landscapes in British Columbia, but capturing the scenes successfully on your camera often provides a challenge. Here are a few ideas for maximizing the quality of images.

For Vancouver's classic city-and-mountain scene, head to the **Burrard Street Bridge** or **Kitsilano Beach** in the evening. On a clear morning, **Grouse Mountain** provides a view back south across downtown, which is especially appealing during winter, with the snow-covered slopes in the foreground. In Victoria, the boardwalk around the **Inner Harbour** encourages photographers to find different angles, whether it be kayakers passing in front of the **Fairmont Empress** or the **Parliament Buildings** illuminated at night.

Photographers will love the wilderness areas of **Vancouver Island,**

Wolves are one of the ultimate shots for photographers.

especially the sparkling waterways of **Goldstream Provincial Park,** the beaches of **Pacific Rim National Park,** and the old-growth forests of **Strathcona Provincial Park.** Other provincial highlights for nature-loving photographers are the **waterfalls** of southwestern British Columbia and the crystal-clear **lakes** of the Kootenays and Northern British Columbia. In Yoho National Park, **Emerald Lake** and the **Lake O'Hara** area are two of the most photogenic destinations in all of Canada.

The best opportunities for photographing wildlife include **whales** near Telegraph Cove, **bald eagles** at Brackendale, **bears** and **elk** in the Canadian Rockies, and **moose** in northern British Columbia.

While photography is simplest in good weather, don't pass up a morning basking in thick mist, whether it's the Vancouver skyline or a driftwood-strewn beach on **Haida Gwaii.** As bright sun illuminates the sky behind the thick clouds, the fog breaks apart gradually, and when it does, the sun radiates like a spotlight, illuminating the sparkling dampness that clings briefly to the landscape.

Day 13

Head south along Highway 95 for three hours through the Columbia Valley. Stop at the **Creston Valley Wildlife Management Area** before veering west along Highway 3 to the artsy city of **Nelson.**

Day 14

It's a seven-hour drive to **Vancouver** from Nelson via Highway 3. En route, the **wineries, golf courses,** and abundance of **water sports** in the **Okanagan Valley** will tempt you to linger a day or two longer.

The Best of Vancouver and Victoria

In British Columbia, metropolitan centers thrive alongside sublime wilderness. Start in Vancouver and ferry to its namesake island to enjoy the best of both worlds. This itinerary balances a little bit of everything: cities, mountains, and ocean.

Day 1
Head north from Vancouver airport and loop around Point Grey to the **Museum of Anthropology,** a wonderful introduction to the history of the Pacific Northwest. Duck through the old-growth forest behind the museum to get a feel for the city's natural splendor. Check in to your hotel and take an evening stroll through **Gastown** to the Water Street Café for dinner.

Day 2
Even if you hit **Stanley Park** as the sun first rises, you'll find that many locals have beaten you on their morning jog. Cross to the North Shore and take the **Grouse Mountain Skyride.** Drive Highway 99 to **Whistler,** which takes around 90 minutes. After dinner at award-winning Araxi, spend the evening exploring the resort village.

Day 3
Catch the ferry from Horseshoe Bay to **Nanaimo,** on Vancouver Island. Drive Highway 4 for the two-hour journey across the island to **Tofino,** making a stop at **Cathedral Grove.** Splurge by staying at the Wickaninnish Inn and dining in-house.

Day 4
Book a Tofino **whale-watching** tour for the morning, enjoy an outdoor lunch at Tacofino,

ocean scenery in Victoria

Victoria's parliament building at night

and then take a beach walk in **Pacific Rim National Park** before returning along Highway 4 to Nanaimo for the night.

Day 5

Heading south from Nanaimo along Highway 19 for 45 kilometers (28 miles), detour at Crofton Bay to catch a ferry to **Salt Spring Island.** Enjoy lunch at an outdoor café in Ganges, then make the short ferry hop to Swartz Bay, gateway to **Victoria** and home to the centrally located Magnolia Hotel and Spa.

Day 6

Make your way to the Inner Harbour on foot. The **Royal BC Museum** is a must-see, Market Square and the surrounding streets are interesting to explore, and the fish-and-chips at Barb's Fish & Chips is perfect for lunch. Still hungry? Head to **Oak Bay** for afternoon tea.

Day 7

Arrive at **Butchart Gardens** at opening time—before the bus-tour crowd arrives—then return to Vancouver by ferry. You'll get there in time for an afternoon flight home.

Family Fun

Bringing the kids? Not a problem—there are plenty of attractions suited to the needs of youngsters.

VANCOUVER

Stanley Park is a fantastic place for children, and many activities are free or almost free. Explore the forests, relax on the beaches, rent a bike and ride the seawall, or jump aboard the miniature railway. The park's world-class **Vancouver Aquarium** is a must (time your visit with the always entertaining dolphin show). Break up the day with a picnic lunch at **Third Beach** or a hot dog from Prospect Point Bar & Grill.

Distinctively shaped **Science World,** southeast of downtown on False Creek, contains hands-on displays that help those of all ages understand the wonderful world of science. **Granville Island Water Park** offers very wet fun, with pools, slides, geysers, and sprays. In the same area, the **Kids Market** offers 50-odd shops as well as a playground, daily shows, and birds to feed on the adjacent waterway.

Kids will be kids, so you may want to spend time with the tribe at an old-fashioned fun park. The best of these is **Playland,** in Hastings Park. Enjoy old-fashioned amusements like the merry-go-round, a wooden roller coaster, a Ferris wheel, an arcade, and a petting zoo.

VICTORIA AND VANCOUVER ISLAND

On the ferry trip between Victoria and Vancouver, find an outside seat on the starboard side and watch the Vancouver skyline and Coast Mountains disappear into the distance. Once in the provincial capital, a **double-decker bus tour** is popular with all ages. Catch a water taxi to **Fisherman's Wharf** for lunch, and hope that the resident seals make an appearance.

Beyond Victoria, family time on Vancouver Island should focus on the outdoors: the **beaches** of **Parksville** and **Qualicum,** the **trails** of **Pacific Rim National Park, ferry** rides through the **Southern Gulf Islands,** or, for older kids, surf lessons at **Tofino.** The **rooftop**

Fort Steele Heritage Town

goats at **Coombs** are a diversion from these more adventurous outings.

SOUTHWESTERN BC

In Whistler, don't miss a chance to ride on the **Peak 2 Peak Gondola.** At the top of the mountain, you'll find opportunities to snowshoe across areas of year-round snowpack. For a different sort of adventure, take the kids to the **Othello-Quintette Tunnels** near Hope. These huge tunnels run through a steep gorge of the Coquihalla River.

OKANAGAN VALLEY AND THE KOOTENAYS

In Vernon, family-run **Davison Orchards** offers wagon tours, a Critter Corral, a fruit and vegetable market, and—best of all—an ice cream stand. On Kootenay Lake, take the kids on the **world's longest free ferry ride.** Get an outside seat on the *Osprey,* which offers striking views of the lake-scape. Don't miss out on the 1880s-style theatrics at **Fort Steele Heritage Town,** near Cranbrook.

Okanagan Wine Tasting

The Okanagan Valley is a four-hour drive (or a short flight) from Vancouver, making it an ideal destination for a weekend getaway. Wineries are spread from one end of the valley to the other, so it's best to spend your time in just one or two of the following growing regions, taking winery tours, renting a bicycle for road touring, or simply doing nothing more than relaxing in one of the country's most appealing climates.

Osoyoos and Oliver

This arid region is at the south end of the Okanagan. Make reservations at **Spirit Ridge at Nk'Mip Resort,** a winery built along the shore of a beautiful lake. The sprawling complex includes upscale accommodations, multiple dining options, and a golf course.

North of Osoyoos, the town of Oliver is surrounded by more than 20 wineries, including **Burrowing Owl,** which also offers rooms for the night overlooking the vineyard. Another worthwhile stop is **Stoneboat Vineyards,** which offers a casual yet informative tour.

Naramata

Make reservations at the lakeside **Naramata Heritage Inn & Spa,** where you can pamper yourself with spa services and good food accompanied by local wines. Explore the wineries scattered along the road between Penticton and Naramata by bike, over two days. Break for lunch at the **Red Rooster** or **Hillside Estate** winery bistros, both with unforgettable lake views.

Kelowna

In the heart of the Okanagan, Kelowna is a sprawling city dotted with both wineries and golf courses, making it a good destination for those looking to combine interests. Stay near downtown at the waterfront **Hotel Eldorado** and enjoy dinner at restaurants such as **Krafty Kitchen + Bar** that showcase local product. As for the wineries themselves, local tour companies will do the driving for you. If you're hitting the winery circuit yourself, **Mission Hill, Quail's Gate,** and **Hainle** are three worthy stops (and all have restaurants open for lunch and dinner).

wine tasting in Okanagan Valley

Okanagan Valley grapes

snowboarding at Whistler Olympic Park

Ski and snowboard enthusiasts could spend an entire winter exploring British Columbia.

VANCOUVER

Suit up and head for Grouse Mountain, where the runs are lighted for night skiing and the views back down across British Columbia's largest city are breathtaking.

VANCOUVER ISLAND

Many visitors to Vancouver Island in winter are escaping the snow found elsewhere in Canada. But there's also skiing and snowboarding up island from Victoria at Mount Washington.

SOUTHWESTERN BRITISH COLUMBIA

Whistler Blackcomb is one of the world's premier alpine resorts, with 3,000 hectares (7,400 acres) of terrain on two mountains. Cross-country skiing at Whistler Olympic Park, heli-skiing in the surrounding mountains, and world-class shopping and dining add to the appeal.

OKANAGAN VALLEY

Three resorts—Apex Mountain Resort, Big White, and Silver Star—combine to make the valley an excellent choice for a ski getaway. Each has a self-contained village, with Silver Star being famous for its colorful gold rush-themed buildings.

KOOTENAYS AND CANADIAN ROCKIES

Hidden winter gems attract hard-core skiers and snowboarders looking for deep powder. At the top of the list are Red Mountain Resort at Rossland and Whitewater, near Nelson.

Family-friendly Panorama Mountain Village near Invermere and Golden's Kicking Horse Mountain Resort are equal to any resort in the province.

CENTRAL AND NORTHERN BRITISH COLUMBIA

Revelstoke Mountain Resort has undergone massive expansion in recent years, while adjacent Revelstoke is a quintessential ski town. Sun Peaks Resort, north of Kamloops, is a self-contained resort with slopes to suit all levels of experience. North of Prince George, Powder King lives up to its name with an annual average snowfall of 12 meters (40 feet).

Getaways to Adventure

Outdoors enthusiasts will love the varied opportunities for adventures in British Columbia. Some can be enjoyed in just a day (plus travel time), but many of the activities involve multiple days to complete. Mix and match from the following highlights to create your own adventurous getaway.

Hike the West Coast Trail
4-6 DAYS
Experienced backcountry hikers won't want to miss the rugged and remote **West Coast Trail** on Vancouver Island. This self-sufficient four- to six-day coastal trek starts west of Victoria and ends near the remote village of Bamfield. The majority of hikers leave their vehicles at one end of the trail and return to their starting point by scheduled shuttle. If you don't have the time for the famed West Coast Trail, get a taste for the adventure in **Juan de Fuca Provincial Park,** where short trails lead to wild coastal beaches or the **Wild Pacific Trail** day hike near Ucluelet.

Dive in the Strait of Georgia
1-2 DAYS
The shallow waters off **Nanaimo** are renowned for artificial reefs created by ships that have been sunk especially for **wreck diving.** Tell the experts at Ocean Explorers Diving that you want to try a dive, and let them choose a site that best suits your experience, whether it be the 442-foot-long *Saskatchewan* or the popular **snorkeling with seals** option. Nanaimo's **Buccaneer Inn** is the best divers' hangout.

Surf at Tofino
1 DAY
Surfing at the beaches off Tofino is made easy by Live to Surf, who will outfit you with a wetsuit and surfboard for an hour or so of fun in the local breakers. Take a lesson if you've never

Wasa Provincial Park

Tofino beach

surfed before. **Pacific Sands Beach Resort** is designed especially for outdoorsy types like yourself.

Camp in the Kootenays
4 DAYS

For camping adventure, concentrate on the Kootenays. Here, amid forests, mountains, and lakes are dozens of delightful provincial park campgrounds. My faves? **Gladstone** for its warm water, **Kokanee Creek** and **Wasa** for family-friendly beaches, and **Whiteswan Lake** for fishing and hot springs in their natural state.

Hike in the Canadian Rockies
3 DAYS

Many locals spend a lifetime hiking in the Canadian Rockies. Three days is just enough time to get a taste for the region, with a full day spent at **Lake O'Hara** and another on the lofty **Iceline Trail.** Spend the third day combining shorter hikes such as **Stanley Glacier** and **Emerald Lake.**

Kayak in Gwaii Haanas National Park Reserve
6 DAYS

Hop aboard a charter boat or floatplane to access this remote archipelago, famed for its abandoned **Haida villages** and fallen **totem poles.** Local outfitters supply kayaks and all the camping equipment you'll need.

Drive the Alaska Highway
10 DAYS

You could drive from **Dawson Creek** to the **Yukon** and back in under a week, but to fully experience this one-in-a-lifetime destination, 10 days is more appropriate. This allows time to explore the wilderness of **Kluane National Park** and the gold rush history of **Dawson City.** Stop for a soak in **Liard River Hot Springs** along the way.

The Trans-Canada Highway

Professional truckers make the trip between Calgary and Vancouver along the Trans-Canada Highway (Hwy. 1) in 12 hours or so. But you're on vacation, so plan on expanding the drive to a weeklong sojourn that will get you to Vancouver . . . eventually.

Day 1

Depart **Calgary** (Alberta) and try not to be tempted by the wonders of Banff National Park as you enter the mountains and cross the border into British Columbia at **Yoho National Park.** Explore the **Yoho Valley** by road, then head to **Emerald Lake** for an afternoon walk. If you don't feel like splurging on park accommodations, continue one hour west along the Trans-Canada Highway to **Golden.**

Day 2

Ride the **Kicking Horse Mountain Resort gondola,** then hit the highway for the one-hour drive to **Glacier National Park.** This park is spectacular even from the highway, so unless you're a keen hiker or it's getting late in the day, continue another hour along the Trans-Canada Highway to **Revelstoke.** After dinner at Woolsey Creek Bistro, take in an outdoor evening concert in Grizzly Plaza.

Day 3

Drive south 250 kilometers (156 miles) from Revelstoke along Highways 23 and 6 to **Nelson.** Break up the trip with a short detour to **Sandon,** British Columbia's best-known ghost town, and to watch spawning kokanee at

First Nations Highlights

U'Mista Cultural Centre

In the 12,000 years that anthropologists surmise human beings have inhabited what is now British Columbia, a variety of cultures have evolved, each with its own unique and distinguishing features. Today, visitors can immerse themselves in First Nations history at the following destinations and attractions:

- Vancouver's **Museum of Anthropology** at UBC is one of the best places in the world to learn about the earliest inhabitants of the Pacific Northwest.

- **Duncan** is a small town with a big collection of historic and contemporary totem poles.

- **Quadra Island** has been home to the Kwagiulth people for generations. You can learn about them at the Nuyumbalees Cultural Centre and then spend the night surrounded by their distinctive architecture at Tsa-Kwa-Luten Lodge.

- **Alert Bay** is home to a thriving community of Kwakwaka'wakw, who welcome visitors to the U'Mista Cultural Centre and the world's highest totem poles.

- **Kootenay National Park** has no sign of indigenous inhabitation, but visitors today can soak in hot springs used for generations by First Nations and then visit the Paint Pots, where ocher was used for ceremonial face painting.

- **'Ksan Historical Village** is a reconstructed Gitxsan village, complete with musical and dance performances.

- **Haida Heritage Centre at Kaay Llnagaay** brings both traditional and moderns arts and crafts of the Haida together under one roof.

- **Gwaii Haanas National Park** protects the ancestral home of the seafaring Haida people. Accessible only by boat or plane, the park's abandoned villages are the highlight.

Lake O'Hara in Yoho National Park

Kokanee Creek Provincial Park. Make dinner reservations at All Seasons Café.

Day 4

Driving through the **West Kootenays** to the **Okanagan Valley** is a delight, although a roller-coaster Highway 3 means the 260-kilometer (162-mile) trip takes around four hours. Stop for a swim in **Christina Lake** en route.

Day 5

Spend the day at your leisure in the Okanagan Valley. Near **Osoyoos, Nk'Mip Desert Cultural Centre** is an interesting stop, unless it's a super-hot day—then stay close to the water or visit the **Naramata wineries.** Spend the night in **Kelowna** at the Hotel Eldorado and dine at the hotel's lakefront bistro.

Day 6

A summer chairlift ride at **Silver Star Mountain Resort,** an hour's drive north from Kelowna on Highway 97, will leave you with pleasant memories of the Okanagan. Then allow 90 minutes to drive to Kamloops via Highway 97, stopping en route at **Historic O'Keefe Ranch** for a late lunch and a living history lesson. Spend the night in Kamloops, taking in a performance by **Western Canada Theatre.**

Day 7

Give the direct Coquihalla Highway a miss and allow three hours to travel down the **Fraser River Canyon** to **Hope.** Suburban Vancouver is approaching, so if you feel like stalling the inevitable onslaught of city traffic, take a walk through the **Othello-Quintette Tunnels.**

Vancouver

Look for ★ to find recommended
sights, activities, dining, and lodging.

Highlights

★ **Canada Place:** Its towering white sail-like architecture is a city landmark and takes pride of place along the Vancouver waterfront (page 32).

★ **Gastown:** The cobbled streets of Gastown make up Vancouver's main tourist precinct. The only official attraction is the steam clock, but there are many buildings of historical interest (page 33).

★ **Granville Island:** Interested in the arts? Want to learn about the history of fishing? Do you enjoy browsing through interesting market stalls? You'll find all this and more on bustling Granville Island (page 39).

★ **Stanley Park:** This massive chunk of downtown has been protected in its old-growth forested state for all time (page 41).

★ **Vancouver Maritime Museum:** With displays for all ages, this museum catalogs the city's rich and varied nautical past (page 45).

★ **VanDusen Botanical Garden:** Garden lovers will be in their element at this formal garden in the heart of one of Vancouver's most upscale neighborhoods (page 46).

★ **Museum of Anthropology:** Inspired by the longhouses of First Nations people, the Museum of Anthropology houses a stunning collection of totem poles and related arts and crafts (page 47).

★ **Grouse Mountain Skyride:** With views extending across the city to Mount Baker in Washington State, this gondola is a spectacular ride. A wealth of on-mountain activities make this a good half-day excursion (page 48).

During the 2010 Olympic Winter Games, a worldwide audience was captivated by Vancouver's scenic beauty and cosmopolitan charms.

Indeed, if you view this gleaming mountain- and sea-dominated city for the first time on a beautiful sunny day, you're bound to fall for it in a big way. See it on a dull, dreary day when the clouds are low and Vancouver's backyard mountains are hidden, and you may come away with a slightly less enthusiastic picture—you'll have experienced the "permagray," as residents are quick to call it with a laugh.

But even gray skies can't dampen the city's vibrant outdoorsy atmosphere. By day, the active visitor can enjoy boating right from downtown, or perhaps venture out to one of the nearby provincial parks for hiking in summer and skiing and snowboarding in winter. More urban-oriented visitors can savor the aromas of just-brewed coffee and freshly baked bread wafting from cosmopolitan sidewalk cafés, join in the bustle at seaside markets, sun on a local beach, or simply relax and do some people-watching in one of the city's tree-shaded squares. By night, Vancouver's myriad fine restaurants, hip nightclubs, and world-class performing-arts venues beckon visitors to continue enjoying themselves into the wee hours. No matter your taste, Vancouver holds an abundance of world-class attractions and many smaller gems that are easy to miss. The hardest part will be working out how to best fit all of the activities into your itinerary.

PLANNING YOUR TIME

Deciding how best to spend your time in Vancouver is a personal thing: Outdoorsy budget travelers will spend their days (and money) in different ways from a honeymooning couple looking to kick back and relax for a few days. But this is one of the true joys about visiting Vancouver—there really is something for everyone.

Regardless of whether you have a weekend or a full week scheduled for Vancouver, plan on rising early and heading out to **Stanley Park** for a walk or ride at least once. Visit the major museums—**Museum of Vancouver, Vancouver Maritime Museum,** and the **Museum of Anthropology**—in the

---

Previous: Vancouver skyline from Stanley Park; Burrard Inlet. **Above:** The suspension bridge in Lynn Canyon Park.

Vancouver

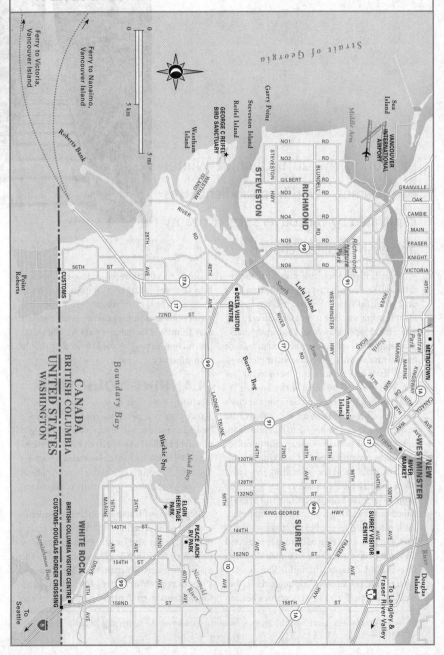

Strait of Georgia

Ferry to Victoria, Vancouver Island

Ferry to Nanaimo, Vancouver Island

Roberts Bank

Sea Island

VANCOUVER INTERNATIONAL AIRPORT

Middle Arm

Garry Point
Steveston Point
Steveston Island
Reifel Island
Westham Island

GEORGE C REIFEL BIRD SANCTUARY

STEVESTON

RICHMOND

NO1 RD
NO2 RD
STEVESTON
GILBERT BLUNDELL RD
NO3 HWY
NO4 RD
NO5 RD
NO6 RD

GRANVILLE
OAK
CAMBIE
MAIN
FRASER
KNIGHT
VICTORIA
49TH

Richmond Nature Park

99

91

WESTMINSTER HWY

Central Park

METROTOWN

NORTH ARM

MARINE WAY
MARINE DR
8TH AVE
KINGSWAY
1A
CANADA WAY

Point Roberts

56TH ST
AVE
48TH AVE

17A

DELTA VISITOR CENTRE

72ND ST
AVE

17

South Arm River

Lulu Island

99

17

Burns Bog

LADNER TRUNK

91

Annacis Island

17

NEW WESTMINSTER

RIVER MARKET

River Road

Fraser

CUSTOMS

CANADA
BRITISH COLUMBIA
UNITED STATES
WASHINGTON

Boundary Bay

Blackie Spit

Mud Bay

Semiahmoo Bay

WHITE ROCK

Nicomekl River

16TH AVE
24TH AVE
MARINE DRIVE
140TH ST
32ND ST
154TH AVE
158ND ST
8TH AVE

ELGIN HERITAGE PARK

PEACE ARCH RV PARK

40TH AVE

10

64TH AVE
120TH ST
128TH ST
132ND ST
56TH ST
144TH AVE
152ND AVE

72ND ST
80TH ST
88TH ST

KING GEORGE HWY

SURREY

99A

96TH AVE
104TH AVE
108TH AVE

SURREY VISITOR CENTRE

FRASER HWY

Douglas Island

To Langley & Fraser River Valley

158TH ST

1A

CUSTOMS—DOUGLAS BORDER CROSSING
BRITISH COLUMBIA VISITOR CENTRE

99

To Seattle

5

0 5 km
0 5 mi

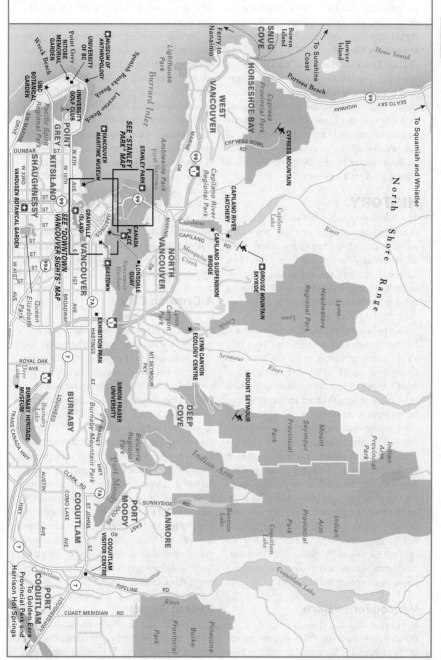

mornings. Leave the afternoons for outdoor pursuits that can be active (**kayaking** on False Creek), educational (**Capilano Salmon Hatchery**), or breathtaking (**Grouse Mountain Skyride**). Luckily, attractions such as **Canada Place** and **Gastown** are clustered around downtown, with others such as **Granville Island** and the city's three major museums farther out but easily reached by public transportation. Try to arrange your sightseeing schedule around the weather. If the forecast calls for a rainy day, concentrate on the museums, leaving the North Shore and Stanley Park for a sunny day.

HISTORY

The first Europeans to set eyes on the land encompassing today's city of Vancouver were gold-seeking Spanish traders who sailed through the Strait of Georgia in 1790. Although the forested wilderness they encountered seemed impenetrable, it had been inhabited by humans since becoming ice-free some 10,000 years earlier.

Not to be outdone, the Brits sent Captain George Vancouver to the area in 1792. Vancouver cruised through the Strait of Georgia in search of a northwest passage from Europe to East Asia, charting Burrard Inlet and claiming the land for Great Britain in the process. As stories of an abundance of fur-bearing mammals filtered east, the fur companies went into action. The North West Company sent fur trader and explorer Simon Fraser overland to establish a coastal trading post. In 1808, he reached the Pacific Ocean via the river that was later named for him, and he built a fur fort on the riverbank east of today's Vancouver. In 1827, the Hudson's Bay Company established its own fur fort on the Fraser River, 48 kilometers east of present-day Vancouver. Neither of these two outposts spawned a permanent settlement.

Vancouver Is Born

It wasn't until the discovery of gold up the Fraser River in the late 1850s that settlement really took hold in the area. The town of New

Westminster, just southeast of present-day Vancouver, was declared British Columbia's first capital in 1866.

The settlement of Vancouver began with the establishment of a brickworks ("Bricks? Why on earth make bricks when we've got all these trees?" said the Woodcutters' Union spokesman) on the south side of Burrard Inlet. Sawmills and related logging and lumber industries followed, and soon several boomtowns were carved out of the wilderness. The first was Granville (now downtown Vancouver), which the original settlers called Gastown after one of its earliest residents, notorious saloon owner "Gassy Jack" Deighton. In 1886 Granville, population 1,000, became the City of Vancouver. Not long thereafter, fire roared through the timber city. Just about everything burned to the ground, but with true pioneering spirit, Vancouver was rebuilt at lightning speed.

A Growing City

In 1887, the struggling city got a boost with the arrival of the first transcontinental railroad. Selected as the western terminus for the Canadian Pacific Railway, Vancouver suddenly became Canada's transportation gateway to Asia and an important player in the development of international commerce around the Pacific Rim. Additionally, the opening of the Panama Canal in 1915 created the perfect outlet for transporting the province's abundant renewable resources to North America's east coast and Europe, resulting in further development of the port facilities and a population boom. Granville Island and the far reaches of Burrard Inlet sprawled with industry, the West End developed as a residential area, the University of British Columbia grew in stature, and the opening of the Lions Gate Bridge encouraged settlement on the north side of Burrard Inlet.

Recent Times

From what began just 120 years ago as a cluster of ramshackle buildings centered around a saloon, Vancouver has blossomed into one of the world's greatest cities. While the city holds onto the largest port on North America's west coast, boasting 20 specialized terminals that handle more tonnage than any other port in Canada, it is now a lot less reliant on its traditional economic heart for its growth. Even after the technology bust, the high-tech industry continues as the fastest-growing sector of Vancouver's economy. This knowledge-based industry has both revitalized the local economy and created a major shift in government thinking. Tourism contributes over $6 billion annually to the local economy, with finance, real estate, insurance, and manufacturing also forming large slices of the local economic pie. Vancouver is also North America's third-largest movie-making center. Worth $1 billion annually to the city, this exciting industry employs up to 40,000 people on as many as 30 simultaneous productions.

Sights

As British Columbia's largest city, Vancouver holds an abundance of world-class attractions, as well as many smaller gems that are easy to miss. Whether you're interested in visiting museums or exploring mountain peaks, you will find plenty to do in Vancouver—the hardest part will be working out how to best fit them into your itinerary. Luckily, many attractions are clustered around downtown, with others such as Granville Island and the city's three major museums farther out but easily reached by public transportation. Try to arrange your sightseeing schedule around the weather. If the forecast calls for a rainy day, concentrate on the museums, leaving the North Shore and Stanley Park for a sunny day.

ORIENTATION

Vancouver isn't a particularly easy city to find your way around, although an excellent transit system helps immensely. **Downtown** lies on a spit of land bordered to the north and east by Burrard Inlet, to the west by English Bay, and to the south by False Creek, which almost cuts the city center off from the rest of the city. Due to the foresight of city founders, almost half of the downtown peninsula has been set aside as parkland.

The **City of Vancouver** officially extends south and west from downtown, between Burrard Inlet and the Fraser River, and encompasses the trendy beachside suburb of **Kitsilano** (known as "Kits" to the locals) and **Point Grey,** home of the University of British Columbia. To the east, the residential sprawl continues through the suburbs of **Burnaby, New Westminster,** and **Coquitlam,** which have a combined population of well over 400,000.

Farther south, the low-lying Fraser River delta extends all the way south to the U.S. border. Between the north and south arms of the river is **Richmond,** (pop. 200,000), home of Vancouver International Airport. South of the south arm is the mostly industrial area of **Delta** (pop. 100,000), as well as **Tsawwassen** (pop. 21,000), departure point for ferries to Vancouver Island.

Southeast of the Fraser River lies **Surrey,** another of those never-ending suburbs, this one with a population of 500,000. The sprawl continues east from Surrey. With Vancouver growing at an incredible rate, and as development to the south and north are restricted—by the international border and the Coast Mountains—there's nowhere to go but east. From Surrey, the Trans-Canada Highway passes through the Fraser River Valley and towns such as **Langley** (pop. 85,000), **Abbotsford** (pop. 145,000), and **Chilliwack** (pop. 85,000)—all now part of the city's sprawl.

Across Burrard Inlet to the north of downtown, **North Vancouver** (pop. 85,000) is a narrowly developed strip backed up to the mountains and connected to the rest of the city by the Lions Gate Bridge. To its west are **Horseshoe Bay,** departure point for Sunshine Coast and Vancouver Island ferries, and **West Vancouver** (pop. 43,000), an upscale suburb.

DOWNTOWN
★ Canada Place

The stunning architectural curiosity with the billowing 27-meter-high (88-foot) Teflon-coated fiberglass "sails" on Burrard Inlet—the one that looks as if it might weigh anchor and cruise off into the sunset at any moment—is **Canada Place,** a symbol of Vancouver and a city icon. Built as the Canada Pavilion for the city's 1986 World Exposition on Transportation and Communication, the World's Fair known as Expo '86, this integrated two-hectare (six-acre) waterfront complex is primarily a convention center and cruise-ship dock. The Vancouver Convention Centre, which makes up the bulk of the complex, has been expanded to triple its size at adjacent Burrard Landing, in a half-billion-dollar project that has changed the face of the downtown waterfront. The original complex at the foot of Burrard Street also houses the luxurious 405-room Pan Pacific Hotel (the glass marvel with a domed top), restaurants,

shops, and an IMAX theater. Start your self-guided tour near the main entrance, then allow at least an hour to wander through the complex. Don't miss walking the exterior promenade—3.5 city blocks long—for splendid views of the harbor, the North Shore, the Coast Mountains, and docked Alaska-bound cruise ships. At the far end of Canada Place is the entrance to **FlyOver Canada** (888/290-7343, 10am-9pm daily, adults $27, seniors $21, children $12), a stunning multimedia presentation showcasing the best of Canada on a massive spherical screen.

Vancouver Art Gallery

Francis Rattenbury, architect of Victoria's Empress Hotel and many other masterpieces, designed Vancouver's imposing neoclassical revival courthouse, which now houses the **Vancouver Art Gallery** (750 Hornby St., 604/662-4700, 10am-5pm Wed.-Mon., 10am-9pm Tues., adults $24, seniors $20, students $18, children $6.50). Initially, the courthouse faced Georgia Street, and although the exterior retains its original 1911 design, the main entrance is now on Robson Street. The gallery is scheduled to move to a new building near the library on Cambie Street in 2021.

The current gallery houses a large

Canada Place

Gastown Steam Clock

incorporated various art deco elements into its design and even a copper-colored roof similar to that of the nearby Hotel Vancouver.

Next door to Cathedral Place is the **Hongkong Bank** building, which features a massive 27-meter (88-foot) aluminum pendulum in the lobby. Next door again, on the corner of West Georgia and Burrard Streets, is **Christ Church Cathedral.** When built in 1895, it was in the heart of a residential area. Over the ensuing century, it was engulfed by modern developments and is today Vancouver's oldest church, attracting more sightseers than believers. Across West Georgia Street from these buildings is the **Fairmont Hotel Vancouver** (900 W. Georgia St.). Built in 1887, the original hotel on this site featured 200 rooms, half of which had private baths, unheard of in that day. It burned to the ground in 1932 and was replaced by the hotel that stands today, which reflects the heritage of Canadian Pacific Railroad-built hotels across the country with its distinctive château-style design topped by a copper roof.

★ Gastown

Three blocks east of Canada Place, Gastown is a marvelous place to spend a few hours. It was the birthplace of Vancouver, officially named Granville in 1870 but always known as Gastown, for saloon owner "Gassy Jack" Deighton. The Great Fire of 1886 destroyed almost all of Gastown's wooden buildings, but the district was rebuilt in stone and brick. By the 1960s, this historic district held nothing more than decrepit Victorian-era buildings and empty warehouses. A massive rejuvenation program commenced, and today historic Gastown is one of the city's most popular tourist attractions. Tree-lined cobblestone streets and old gas lamps front brightly painted restored buildings that are host to galleries, restaurants, and an abundance of gift and souvenir shops.

Most of the action centers along **Water Street,** which branches east off Cordova Street and slopes gently toward the site of Gassy Jack's original saloon (now the

collection of works by one of Canada's preeminent artists, **Emily Carr,** who was born on Vancouver Island in 1871 and traveled the world honing her painting and drawing skills before settling in Vancouver in 1906. Her style reflects the time she spent with First Nations people of the Pacific Northwest coast, but she was also influenced by techniques acquired during periods when she lived in London and Paris. Carr combined these influences to create unique works, and the gallery is well worth visiting for these alone. The Carr collection is on the third floor, along with the works of many other local artists. The gallery also holds pieces by contemporary artists from North America and Europe as well as an impressive collection of historical art.

Cathedral Place

Cathedral Place is worth visiting for an intriguing sculpture, *Navigational Device,* located in the lobby. The high-rise, built in 1991, replaced a classic art deco building. To placate opposition to the construction, architects

Downtown Vancouver

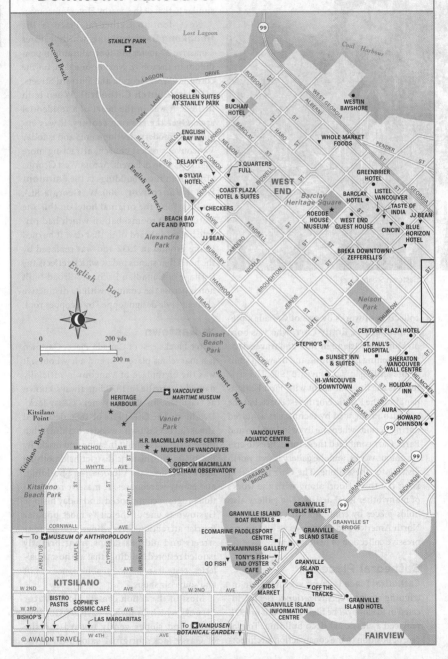

Lost Lagoon

Coal Harbour

99

STANLEY PARK ★

Second Beach

LAGOON   DRIVE

PARK   LANE

ROSELLEN SUITES
AT STANLEY PARK ■

BEACH

CHILCO   ENGLISH
               BAY INN ■

DELANY'S ■

SYLVIA
HOTEL ●

BEACH BAY
CAFE AND PATIO ■

CHECKERS ■

JJ BEAN ■

BUCHAN
HOTEL ■

BARCLAY   ST

HARO   ST

ALBERNI   ST

WEST GEORGIA

ROBSON   ST

WESTIN
BAYSHORE ■

WHOLE MARKET
FOODS ■

PENDER   ST

GILFORD   ST

NELSON   ST

COMOX   ST

3 QUARTERS
FULL

BIDWELL   ST

COAST PLAZA
HOTEL & SUITES

WEST
END

Barclay
Heritage Square

GREENBRIER
HOTEL ■

BARCLAY   ST   LISTEL
HOTEL ■   VANCOUVER ■

TASTE OF
INDIA ▼   JJ BEAN ■

GEORGIA   ST

English Bay Beach

Alexandra
Park

DENMAN   ST

DAVIE   ST

BURNABY   ST

ROEDDE
HOUSE
MUSEUM ★

WEST END
GUEST HOUSE ●

CINCIN ▼

BLUE
HORIZON
HOTEL ■

BREKA DOWNTOWN/
ZEFFERELLI'S ▼

CABRERO   ST

NICOLA   ST

PENDRELL   ST

BROUGHTON   ST

ST

ST

English   Bay

0   200 yds
0   200 m

Sunset
Beach
Park

HARWOOD   ST

BEACH   AVE

JERVIS   ST

BUTE   ST

Nelson
Park

THURLOW

ST

STEPHO'S ▼

CENTURY PLAZA HOTEL ■

ST. PAUL'S
HOSPITAL

SHERATON
VANCOUVER
WALL CENTRE ■

SUNSET INN
& SUITES ●

HI-VANCOUVER
DOWNTOWN ●

PACIFIC   AVE

Sunset   Beach

BURRARD   ST

DAVIE   ST

HELMCKEN

HOLIDAY
INN ■

HOWE   ST

DRAKE   HORNBY   ST

AURA ■

HOWARD
JOHNSON ●

99

Kitsilano
Point

Kitsilano Beach

HERITAGE
HARBOUR ★

VANCOUVER
MARITIME MUSEUM ★

Vanier
Park

H.R. MACMILLAN SPACE CENTRE ★
★ MUSEUM OF VANCOUVER

GORDON MACMILLAN
SOUTHAM OBSERVATORY

VANCOUVER
AQUATIC CENTRE ■

SEYMOUR   ST

RICHARDS   ST

99

99

MCNICHOL   AVE

WHYTE   AVE

CHESTNUT   ST

Kitsilano
Beach Park

CORNWALL   AVE

BURRARD ST
BRIDGE

HOWE

GRANVILLE

GRANVILLE ST
BRIDGE

99

To ★ MUSEUM OF ANTHROPOLOGY

ARBUTUS   ST

MAPLE   ST

CYPRESS   ST

BURRARD   ST

KITSILANO

W 2ND   AVE

W 3RD

BISHOP'S

BISTRO
PASTIS

SOPHIE'S
COSMIC CAFÉ

LAS MARGARITAS

W 4TH   AVE

W 2ND   AVE

ANDERSON   ST

GRANVILLE ISLAND
BOAT RENTALS ■

ECOMARINE PADDLESPORT
CENTRE ■

WICKANINNISH GALLERY ■

GO FISH ▼

TONY'S FISH
AND OYSTER
CAFE ▼

KIDS
MARKET

GRANVILLE
PUBLIC MARKET

GRANVILLE ST
BRIDGE

GRANVILLE
ISLAND STAGE ■

GRANVILLE
ISLAND
★

OFF THE
TRACKS ▼

GRANVILLE
ISLAND HOTEL ■

GRANVILLE ISLAND
INFORMATION
CENTRE

To ★ VANDUSEN
BOTANICAL GARDEN ↓

FAIRVIEW

© AVALON TRAVEL

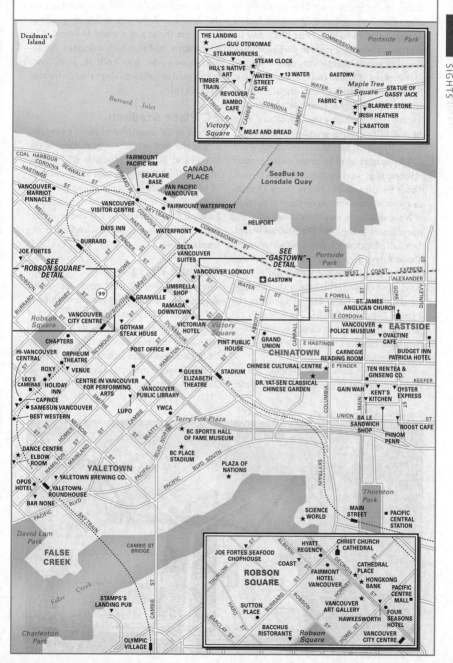

Alhambra Hotel). As you first enter Water Street, you're greeted by **The Landing,** a seven-story heritage building that has had its exterior restored to its former glory and its interior transformed from a warehouse to a shopping arcade. Continuing down the hill, on the corner of Water and Cambie Streets, is the **Gastown Steam Clock,** one of only two in the world (the other is a replica of this, the original one). Built by a local clock maker in the mid-1970s, it is powered by a steam system originally put in place to heat buildings along a 10-kilometer-long (6-mile) underground pipeline that snakes through downtown. Watch for the burst of steam every 15 minutes, which sets off steam whistles to the tune of Westminster chimes. Continue east along Water Street to the 1899 **Dominion Hotel,** then half a block south down Abbott Street to **Blood Alley,** the hangout of many infamous late-19th-century rogues. Most buildings still standing along Water Street were built immediately after the Great Fire of 1886, but the **Byrnes Block** (2 Water St.) is generally regarded as the oldest; it stands on the site of Deighton House, Gassy Jack's second and more permanent saloon.

Water Street ends at the cobbled **Maple Tree Square,** at the intersection of Water, Carrall, Powell, and Alexander Streets. A bronze **statue of Gassy Jack** watches over the square and the site of his original saloon from the top of a whiskey barrel. The **Alhambra Hotel,** which occupies the actual saloon site, was built in 1886 from bricks used as ballast in ships that sailed into Burrard Inlet.

BC Place Stadium

As host of the opening and closing ceremonies of the 2010 Winter Olympic Games, the 55,000-seat **BC Place Stadium** (777 Pacific Blvd., 604/669-2300) was seen by an audience of billions. Today, it comes alive for home games of the BC Lions, one of the Canadian Football League teams, and is the venue for major trade shows, concerts, and other big events.

Science World

The impressive, 17-story-high, geodesic-shaped silver dome (it's best known locally as "the golf ball") stands above the waters of False Creek on the southeast side of city center. Built as the Expo Preview Centre for Expo '86, it later housed restaurants, shops, and the world's largest Omnimax theater for a time. Today the Vancouver landmark is home to

Science World is known locally as "the golf ball."

Vancouver Views

Whenever I visit a city for the first time, I like to start off by finding a viewpoint that lets me see the layout of the city. In Vancouver, the obvious option to get your bearings is by taking a flightseeing trip in a helicopter or floatplane, but this also means paying out big bucks. Instead, consider one of the following less expensive options.

view of downtown from Stanley Park

DOWNTOWN

Vancouver Lookout: For immediate orientation from downtown, catch the high-speed, stomach-sinking glass elevator up the outside of 40-story **Harbour Centre** (555 W. Hastings St., 604/689-0421, 8:30am-10:30pm daily summer, 9am-9pm daily fall-spring, adults $17.50, seniors $14.50, students $12.50, children $9.50). The ride takes less than a minute and ends at the Observation Deck, an enclosed room 130 meters above street level, from where views extend as far away as Mount Baker, 140 kilometers (87 miles) south. Walk around the circular room for 360-degree views. Keep your receipt and you can return at any time during the same day (the top of the tower is a great place to watch the sun setting over the Strait of Georgia).

Down on the Waterfront: From Vancouver Visitor Centre, continue down Burrard Street to **Canada Place** and wander around the west side promenade for neck-straining views of the city close up, as well as North Vancouver and the rugged mountains beyond. For a look at the skyline and sparkling Canada Place from sea level, take the SeaBus from the adjacent Waterfront Station across Burrard Inlet to **Lonsdale Quay.**

Stanley Park: Drive, walk, or cycle Stanley Park's 10-kilometer (6-mile) **Seawall Promenade** to appreciate the skyline to the east, the busy shipping lanes of First Narrows to the north, and the sandy beaches of English Bay to the west. Sunsets from English Bay Beach, in the West End, are delightful.

NORTH SHORE

The best views from the north side of Burrard Inlet are gained by taking the **Grouse Mountain Skyride** (Nancy Greene Way, 604/980-9311, adults $45, seniors $41, youths $26, children $16, includes on-mountain activities) up the slopes of Grouse Mountain. The panorama extends back across the inlet to downtown and beyond to Mount Baker, in Washington State, and west to Vancouver Island. In summer, the gondola departs from the base station every 10 minutes 8:45am-10pm daily.

Head west along Highway 1 from the Grouse Mountain turnoff to Cypress Bowl Road. At the second switchback, there's a particularly good city skyline view. Continue west to Horseshoe Bay, then return to the city along Marine Drive, which parallels Burrard Inlet, providing many glimpses of the city skyline. At **Lighthouse Park,** along this route, English Bay, Stanley Park, and Kitsilano Beach are laid out in all their glory from Point Atkinson.

UPTOWN

South of downtown, the **Kitsilano foreshore** provides that well-known view of the city skyline backed by the Coast Mountains. The south side of the city is relatively flat. The high point is 152-meter (500-foot) **Little Mountain,** in Queen Elizabeth Park, where the city skyline and abruptly rising mountains contrast starkly with the residential sprawl of Vancouver.

Science World (1455 Quebec St., 604/443-7440, 10am-6pm daily, adults $23.25, seniors and students $18.50, children $15.25), a museum providing exhibitions that "introduce the world of science to the young and the young at heart." The three main galleries explore the basics of physics, natural history, and music through hands-on displays, while a fourth gallery holds an ever-changing array of traveling exhibits. The Science Theatre shows the feature *Over Canada*, a high-definition aerial tour of Canada accompanied by the sounds of Canadian musicians.

The most enjoyable way to get to Science World is aboard a False Creek Ferry from Granville Island or the Vancouver Aquatic Centre. If you don't want to take the ferry, you can drive to the west end of Terminal Avenue—plenty of parking is available—or take the SkyTrain to Main Street Station and then walk across the street.

CHINATOWN

The first Chinese immigrants came to Vancouver in the 1880s to work on rail line construction. In total, the Canadian Pacific Railway (CPR) employed 17,000 Chinese workers, and most settled around an area known as Shanghai Alley, at the west end of today's Chinatown. The Chinese cleared the surrounding land and began growing produce that was sold at markets around the intersection of Pender and Carrall Streets. Here you'll find the Dr. Sun Yat-Sen Classical Chinese Garden and the **Sam Kee Building** (8 W. Pender St., at Carrall St.), best known as **the world's narrowest office building.** When city developers widened surrounding streets in 1912, the Chinese consortium that owned the lot decided to proceed with its planned building, but simply made it narrower than first conceived. The result is a building 1.8 meters (6 feet) wide, noted in the *Guinness Book of Records* as the "narrowest building in the world."

The heart of Chinatown has moved eastward over the years and is now centered on the blocks bordered by Main, East Pender,

Gore, and East Georgia Streets. With a population exceeding 24,000, it is the second-largest Chinese community in North America and one of the largest outside Asia. Stroll through the neighborhood to admire the architecture—right down to the pagoda-roofed telephone booths—or to seek out one of the multitude of inexpensive restaurants. You'll find markets and genuine Cantonese-style cuisine east of Main Street and tamer Chinese-Canadian dishes along Main Street and to the west. The district's intriguing stores sell a mind-boggling array of Chinese goods—wind chimes, soy sauce, teapots, dried mushrooms, delicate paper fans, and much, much more. Along Main Street, several shops sell ginseng, sold by the Chinese ounce (38 grams). Cultivated ginseng starts at $10 per ounce, while wild ginseng goes for up to $400 per ounce. In addition to selling the herb, the staff at **Ten Ren Tea and Ginseng Co.** (550 Main St., 604/684-1566, 10am-6pm daily) explains ginseng preparation methods to buyers and offer tea tasting as well.

To get to Chinatown from downtown, catch bus 19 or 22 east along Pender Street. Try to avoid East Hastings Street at all times; it's Vancouver's skid row, inhabited by unsavory characters day and night.

Chinese Cultural Centre

The **Chinese Cultural Centre** (50 E. Pender St., 604/658-8850, 9am-6pm Tues.-Sun.) is the epicenter of community programs for the local Chinese population, but holds interest to outsiders. Around the corner from the main entrance, the distinctive museum and archives building (555 Columbia St., 604/658-8880, 11am-5pm Tues.-Sun., donation) catalogs the history of Chinese Canadians in Vancouver.

Dr. Sun Yat-Sen Classical Chinese Garden

Gardening enthusiasts won't want to miss this peaceful and harmoniously designed garden behind the Cultural Centre, the **Dr.**

Sun Yat-Sen Classical Chinese Garden (578 Carrall St., 604/662-3207, 9:30am-7pm daily summer, 10am-4:30pm daily fall-spring, adults $14, seniors $11, students $10). The garden features limestone rockeries, a waterfall and tranquil pools, and beautiful trees and plants hidden away behind tall walls. The buildings and other artificially constructed elements, including wood carvings and sculptures, were shipped from China. This was the first authentic classical Chinese garden built outside China, and it remains to this day the largest. Well worthwhile are the tours (free with admission) conducted up to eight times daily. Adjacent to the gardens is **Dr. Sun Yat-Sen Park**, where admission is free.

★ GRANVILLE ISLAND

Follow Granville Street southwest through downtown and cross False Creek by bridge or ferry to reach Granville Island. Regarded as one of North America's most successful inner-city industrial-site redevelopments, the jazzed-up island is *the* place to go on a bright sunny day—allow at least several hours or an entire afternoon for this hive of activity.

When Europeans first settled Vancouver, Granville Island was nothing more than a sandbar, but tons of fill transformed it into an island. It soon became a center of industry (its official name is Industrial Island), filled with factories and warehouses. Lacking space, city officials at one point proposed to reclaim all of False Creek, but in the end only a small section was filled—and Granville Island became joined to the mainland. By the end of the 1970s, the island and adjacent areas had become an industrial wasteland, so with a massive injection of funds from the federal government, the entire waterfront got a facelift.

You can spend the better part of a day just walking around the island looking at the marina, the many specialty businesses that reflect the island's maritime heritage, fresh food markets, gift shops, restaurants, and theaters. The highlight is colorful **Granville Island Public Market** (9am-7pm daily), a hub of activity from dawn to dusk and a lot more than a tourist attraction. Inside the market you'll find all kinds of things to eat—fresh fruit and vegetables, seafood from local waters, a wide variety of meats, specialty ingredients, and prepared ready-to-go meals—as well as unique jewelry and crafts, potted plants, and cut flowers.

To get to the island by boat, jump aboard

Granville Island Public Market

one of the small **False Creek Ferries.** The boats run regularly between the island, Vancouver Aquatic Centre at Sunset Beach ($3.50), and Vanier Park ($6). To get to the island by land, take a number 50 (False Creek) bus from Howe Street to the stop under Granville Street Bridge at the entrance to the island, or take a Granville Island bus from downtown. Parking on the island is almost impossible, especially on weekends when locals do their fresh-produce shopping. If you do find a spot, it'll have a three-hour maximum time limit.

ROBSON STREET AND THE WEST END

The West End (not to be confused with the West Side, south of downtown, or West Vancouver, on the north side of the harbor) lies west of the Central Business District, between Burrard Street and **English Bay Beach,** the gateway to Stanley Park. Wander down Robson or Denman Street and you'll soon see the appeal of the urban lifestyle afforded by life in the West End—the endless outdoor cafés, wide range of dining choices, fashionable boutiques, the sandy beaches of English Bay, and, of course, the proximity of Stanley Park.

Robson Street

What began as an enclave of European businesses had transformed itself into one of Vancouver's most fashionable shopping and dining precincts by the 1980s. Today, many of the designer boutiques and European cafés have been replaced by ubiquitous chain stores and restaurants, but it's still a popular shopping and dining precinct. The main concentration of shops is the few blocks northwest from Burrard Street. If anywhere in the city could be called "coffee row," then this would be it. From the intersection with Jervis Street, Robson Street begins its gradual descent to the West End.

Five blocks farther northwest is Denman Street. Turn left to make your way to English Bay Beach after passing through another restaurant-filled section of the West End; turn right to find bike-rental outlets catering to Stanley Park-bound cyclists.

Barclay Heritage Square

Most of the West End's early-1900s buildings are long gone, but a precinct of nine homes built between 1890 and 1908 has been saved and is preserved as Barclay Heritage Square, which looks much as it would have when the homes were first built around the turn of the

Barclay Heritage Square is a concentration of historic homes in the heart of the West End.

totem poles in Stanley Park

peninsula jutting out into Burrard Inlet, is a sight for sore eyes in any weather—an enormous peaceful oasis sandwiched between the city center's skyscrapers and the North Shore at the other end of Lions Gate Bridge. Unlike other famous parks, like New York's Central Park and London's Hyde Park, Stanley Park is a permanent preserve of wilderness in the heart of the city, complete with dense coastal forests and abundant wildlife. The biggest changes to the park since its dedication over a century ago have been the work of Mother Nature, including a devastating windstorm in December 2006 that destroyed hundreds of trees.

Walk or cycle the 10-kilometer (6-mile) **Seawall Promenade** or drive the perimeter via **Stanley Park Drive** to take in beautiful water and city views. Travel along both is one-way in a counterclockwise direction (those on foot can go either way, but if you travel clockwise you'll be going against the flow). For vehicle traffic, the main entrance to Stanley Park is at the beginning of Stanley Park Drive, which veers right from the end of Georgia Street; on foot, follow Denman Street to its north end and you'll find a pathway leading around Coal Harbour into the park. Either way, you'll pass a small information booth where park maps are available. Just before the booth, take Pipeline Road to access **Malkin Bowl,** home to outdoor theater productions; a **rose garden;** and forest-encircled **Beaver Lake.** Pipeline Road rejoins Stanley Park Drive near the Lions Gate Bridge, but by not returning to the park entrance you'll miss most of the following sights.

Vancouver Aquarium

In the forest on the east side of the park is Canada's largest aquarium, the **Vancouver Aquarium** (Avison Way., 604/659-3474, 9:30am-7pm daily summer, 10am-5pm daily fall-spring, adults $39, seniors and students $30, children $22), the third largest in North America. Guarding the entrance is a five-meter (16-foot) killer whale sculpture by preeminent First Nations artist Bill Reid. More than

20th century, right down to the style of the surrounding gardens.

The only one of the nine open to the public is **Roedde House Museum** (1415 Barclay St., 604/684-7040, tours 10am-4pm Tues.-Sun. June-Aug., 2pm-4pm Wed.-Fri. Sept. and May, adults $6, seniors $5, children $3). Built in 1893, this Queen Anne Revival-style home is a classic example of Vancouver's early residential architecture. Francis Rattenbury, architect of Victoria's Empress Hotel, designed the two-story residence for Gustav Roedde, Vancouver's first bookbinder. Typical of the era, it features a wide veranda, upstairs porch, and bay windows. It was restored using historical records to ensure accuracy—right down to the color of the walls and interior furnishings. The easiest way to get to the house is to take Broughton Street off Robson Street.

★ STANLEY PARK

Beautiful Stanley Park, a lush 405-hectare (1,000-acre) tree- and garden-carpeted

Stanley Park

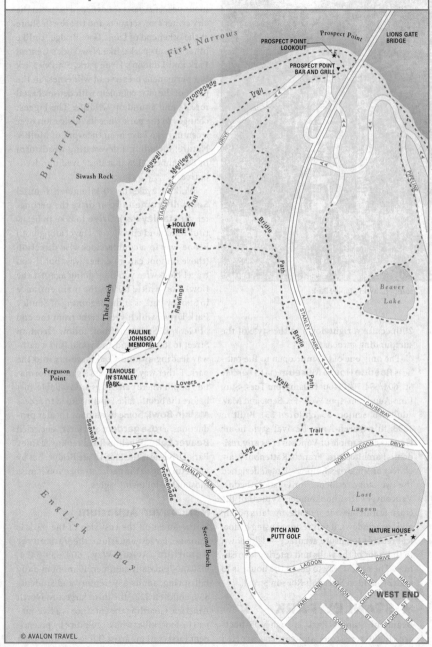

First Narrows

PROSPECT POINT
LOOKOUT

Prospect Point

LIONS GATE
BRIDGE

PROSPECT POINT
BAR AND GRILL

Burrard Inlet

Promenade

Trail

STANLEY PARK DRIVE

Seawall

Merilees

Trail

PIPELINE

Siwash Rock

Bridle

Path

Beaver
Lake

★ HOLLOW
TREE

Rawlings

Third Beach

PAULINE
JOHNSON
MEMORIAL

STANLEY PARK

Bridle

Path

Ferguson
Point

TEAHOUSE
IN STANLEY
PARK

Lovers

Walk

CAUSEWAY

Seawall

Lees

Trail

NORTH LAGOON DRIVE

STANLEY PARK

Lost
Lagoon

Promenade

DRIVE

PITCH AND
PUTT GOLF

NATURE HOUSE ★

Second Beach

English Bay

LAGOON

DRIVE

PARK LANE

NELSON

BARCLAY ST

CHILCO ST

HARO

WEST END

COMOX

ST

GILFORD ST

© AVALON TRAVEL

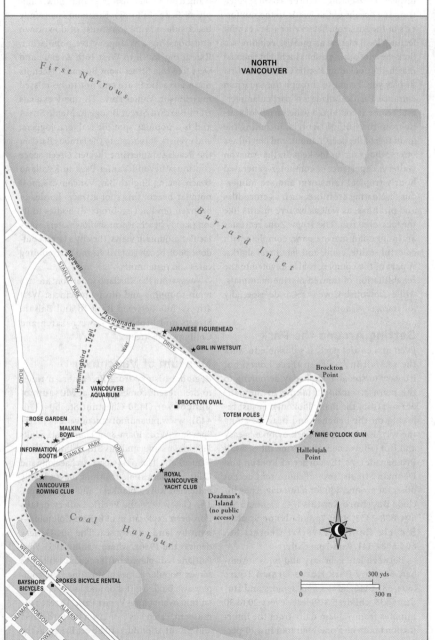

First Narrows

NORTH
VANCOUVER

Burrard Inlet

Seawall

STANLEY PARK

Promenade

DRIVE

Hummingbird Trail

AVISON WAY

★ JAPANESE FIGUREHEAD

★ GIRL IN WETSUIT

Brockton
Point

★ VANCOUVER
AQUARIUM

■ BROCKTON OVAL

TOTEM POLES ★

ROAD

★ ROSE GARDEN

★ MALKIN
BOWL

★ NINE O'CLOCK GUN

INFORMATION ■
BOOTH   ■ STANLEY PARK

DRIVE

Hallelujah
Point

★ VANCOUVER
ROWING CLUB

★ ROYAL
VANCOUVER
YACHT CLUB

Deadman's
Island
(no public
access)

Coal   Harbour

WEST GEORGIA   ST

■ BAYSHORE
BICYCLES

■ SPOKES BICYCLE RENTAL

DENMAN   ST
ROBSON   ST
ALBERNI   ST
BIDWELL   ST

0   300 yds

0   300 m

8,000 aquatic animals and 600 species are on display, representing all corners of the planet, from the oceans of the Arctic to the rainforests of the Amazon. The Steller's Bay exhibit features local marine mammals, including sea lions. Several other exhibits highlight regional marinelife, including Pacific Canada, the first display you'll come to through the aquarium entrance. Pacific Canada is of particular interest because it contains a wide variety of sealife from the Gulf of Georgia, including the giant fish of the deep, halibut, and playful sea otters who frolic in the kelp. In the Amazon Gallery, experience a computer-generated hourly tropical rainstorm and see numerous fascinating creatures, such as crocodiles and piranhas, as well as bizarre misfits like the four-eyed fish. The Tropic Zone recreates an Indonesian marine park, complete with colorful sealife, coral, and small reef sharks. A part of the complex is also devoted to the rehabilitation of injured marine mammals, while Clownfish Cove is set aside especially for younger visitors.

Getting Around the Park

Even at a casual pace, it's possible to walk the seawall in less than three hours, but it's easy to spend a whole day detouring to the main attractions, taking in the panoramas from the many lookouts, or just relaxing on the benches and beaches along the way. Exploring the park by bike is easy and fun (allow one hour to ride the Seawall Promenade). At the corner of Robson and Denman Streets, several shops rent decent bikes for around $30 for a full day. They include **Bayshore Rentals** (745 Denman St., 604/688-2453, 9am-7pm daily) or **Spokes Bicycle Rental** (1798 W. Georgia St., 604/688-5141, 9am-7pm daily).

Between late February and mid-November, **Stanley Park Horse-Drawn Tours** (604/681-5115, adults $40, seniors and students $38, children $19) leave every 20 to 30 minutes from 9:30am daily from the information booth on a one-hour tour in a 20-person carriage.

KITSILANO

Named for a Squamish chief and known simply as "Kits" to locals, Kitsilano is a trendy beachside suburb southwest of downtown and boasting a young, active population. Extending south to West 16th Avenue and west to Alma Street from Burrard Street, its main attractions are two not-to-be-missed museums in Vanier Park. This park extends from Burrard Street Bridge to Maple Street and is a popular spot for walkers, joggers, and cyclists. It is home to the famous Bard on the Beach summertime theater. Green space continues beyond Vanier Park to Kitsilano Beach, facing English Bay. Vancouver's most popular beach, this spot attracts hordes of bronzed (and not-so-bronzed) bodies to its long sandy beach, warm shallow waters, spectacular mountain views, the city's largest outdoor pool, beach volleyball, and surrounding cafés and restaurants.

Away from the Kitsilano waterfront are two main shopping and dining precincts: West 4th Avenue between Burrard and Balsam Streets and Broadway between Larch and Collingwood Streets.

Museum of Vancouver

Regional history from Precambrian times to the present comes to life at **Museum of Vancouver** (1100 Chestnut St., 604/736-4431, www.museumofvancouver.ca, 10am-5pm Sun.-Wed., 10am-8pm Thurs.-Sat., adults $19, seniors and students $16, children $9) in Vanier Park. The West Coast Archaeology and Culture galleries hold ravishing masks, highly patterned woven blankets, and fine baskets. The Gateway to the Pacific Gallery details European exploration of British Columbia—both by land and by sea. The 50s Gallery depicts the 1950s, where a shiny 1955 Ford Fairlane is displayed and black-and-white TVs screen popular shows of the time. The complex also holds a gift shop and a self-serve restaurant overlooking Vanier Park. To reach the museum, catch bus 2 or 22 on Burrard Street and get off after Burrard Street Bridge at the Cornwall and Cypress Street stop, or catch a ferry to Vanier Park from Granville Island or the Aquatic Centre at Sunset Beach. If you're driving, you'll find plenty of parking.

On the east side of the museum is the **City of Vancouver Archives** (1150 Chestnut St., 604/736-8561, 9am-5pm Mon.-Fri., free). This public facility holds around 500,000 photographs and 5,000 books, as well as a wealth of maps, documents, records, and reports that combine to tell the story of Vancouver's social, economic, and cultural history.

H. R. MacMillan Space Centre

Children especially will love the **H. R. MacMillan Space Centre** (1100 Chestnut St., 604/738-7827, 10am-5pm daily summer, 10am-3pm daily fall-spring, adults $15, seniors and students $10.75), in the same building as the Museum of Vancouver. The main features are displays related to planet Earth, the surrounding universe, and space exploration. Throughout the day, the GroundStation Canada Theatre shows 20-minute audiovisual presentations that explore the universe. Other highlights are Virtual Voyages, a flight simulator that makes a five-minute virtual reality journey through space, and the Cosmic Courtyard, a fun learning center.

Adjacent to the museum complex

is the **Gordon MacMillan Southam Observatory** (604/738-7827, donation), which is open for public stargazing 7pm-11pm Saturday when the skies are clear.

★ Vancouver Maritime Museum

Just a five-minute stroll from the Museum of Vancouver is the **Vancouver Maritime Museum** (1905 Ogden Ave., 604/257-8300, 10am-5pm Mon.-Sat., noon-5pm Sun. summer, 10am-5pm Tues.-Sat., noon-5pm Sun. fall-spring, adults $12.50, seniors and students $10), at the end of Cypress Avenue. Filled with nautical-themed displays that showcase British Columbia's seafaring legacy, exhibits chronicle everything from the province's first European explorers and their vessels to today's oceangoing adventurers, modern fishing boats, and fancy ships. Beyond the front desk is a historical Royal Canadian Mounted Police (RCMP) vessel, the *St. Roch,* which fills the first main room. Now a National Historic Site, the *St. Roch* was the first patrol vessel to successfully negotiate the infamous Northwest Passage. Beyond the vessel and easy to miss are the large black-and-white images of local waterways from 100 years ago—a real eye-opener as to how much and how quickly

Kitsilano Beach

Vancouver has grown. Children tend to gravitate toward the back of the museum to the Maritime Discovery Centre, where they can dress up as a fisherman, try their hand at navigation, and crawl through a pirate's cave

When you're finished inside the museum, wander down to the water to view a small harbor where a fleet of historical vessels is docked.

★ VanDusen Botanical Garden

In the mid-1960s, Shaughnessy residents lost their golf course to encroaching residential development but managed to save a plot of land that was later redeveloped as a public garden—the city's answer to Victoria's Butchart Gardens, albeit on a smaller scale. Today, the 22-hectare (54-acre) **VanDusen Botanical Garden** (5251 Oak St., at 37th Ave., 604/257-8335, 9am-8:30pm daily June-Sept., shorter hours Oct.-May, adults $11, seniors and students $8.25, children $5) is home to more than 7,500 species from every continent except Antarctica. It's the place to feast your eyes on more than 1,000 varieties of rhododendrons as well as roses, all kinds of botanical rarities, winter blossoms, and an Elizabethan hedge maze. Look for the display board near the front entrance to see what's best for the time of year in which you're visiting. The complex also includes a shop selling cards, perfumes, soaps, potpourri, and all kinds of gifts with a floral theme. At popular **Shaughnessy Restaurant** (604/261-0011), the light and airy decor, picture windows, and garden view bring the outside in. It's open for a reasonably priced lunch (11:30am-3pm daily) and for a more expensive, dressier dinner (5pm-9pm daily); reservations are recommended. To get there by bus, take number 17 south along Burrard Street. Oak Street runs parallel to Granville Street; access to the garden is on the corner of East 33rd Avenue.

Queen Elizabeth Park

Less than two kilometers (1.2 miles) from the VanDusen Botanical Garden, this 53-hectare (130-acre) park sits atop 152-meter (500-foot)

Bloedel Floral Conservatory

Little Mountain, the city's highest point, with magnificent views of Vancouver and the Coast Mountains. Now operated by the Vancouver Board of Parks and Recreation, the land was sold to the city by the CPR in 1929 and quarried for rock to build roads. The land today is a paradise of sweeping lawns, trees, flowering shrubs, masses of rhododendrons—a vivid spectacle in May and June—formal flower gardens including a rose garden in the park's southwest corner, sunken gardens in the old quarry pits, and mature plantings of native trees from across Canada. Public facilities include tennis courts and a pitch-and-putt golf course.

The highlight of the park is the magnificent **Bloedel Floral Conservatory** (604/257-8584, 9am-8pm Mon.-Fri. and 10am-8pm Sat.-Sun. summer, 10am-5pm daily fall-spring, adults $6.50, seniors $4.30, children $3.15). It's a glass-domed structure rising 40 meters (130 feet) and enclosing a temperature-controlled humid tropical rainforest. Inside you'll find a profusion of exotic flowering plants and a resident free-flying avian population, including multihued parrots. The park's main entrance is by the junction of 33rd Avenue West and Cambie Street; to get here from downtown, take bus 15 south on Burrard Street.

UNIVERSITY OF BRITISH COLUMBIA (UBC)

The UBC campus sprawls across **Point Grey,** the westernmost point of Vancouver and the southern extremity of Burrard Inlet. It enjoys a spectacular coastal location, surrounded by parkland laced with hiking trails. Many of the trails provide access to the beach. The campus encompasses more than 400 hectares (990 acres) and serves as many as 35,000 students at one time.

★ Museum of Anthropology

Containing the world's largest collection of arts and crafts of the Pacific Northwest First Nations, the excellent **Museum of Anthropology** (6393 NW Marine Dr., 604/827-5932, 10am-5pm daily summer, 10am-5pm Tues.-Sun. fall-spring, adults $18, seniors and students $16) should not be missed. Designed by innovative Canadian architect Arthur Erickson, the ultramodern concrete-and-glass building perches on a high cliff overlooking the Pacific Ocean and mimics the post-and-beam structures favored by the Coast Salish people.

The entrance is flanked by panels in the shape of a bent box, which the Salish believed contained the meaning of life. Inside, a ramp lined with impressive sculptures by renowned modern-day carvers leads to the Great Hall, a cavernous 18-meter (60-foot) room dominated by towering totem poles collected from along the coast and interspersed with other ancient works. A museum highlight is the collection of works by Haida artist Bill Reid, including *The Raven and the First Men,* which is carved from a four-ton chunk of yellow cedar, drenched in natural light, and raised above sand from Haida Gwaii. The surrounding seats are popular spots to sit and simply stare. Other displays include intricate carvings, baskets, ceremonial masks, fabulous jewelry, and European ceramics. Outside, a deliciously scented woodland path on the left side of the museum leads to a reconstructed Haida village and some contemporary totem poles with descriptive plaques.

If you have your own vehicle, make sure you have a fistful of change to park in the lot beside the museum ($3.50 per hour).

University Gardens

Just south of the Museum of Anthropology is the serene **Nitobe Memorial Garden** (1895 Lower Mall, 604/822-9666, 11am-4:30pm daily mid-Mar.-Oct., adults $7, seniors $5.50, children $4), named for and dedicated to a prominent Japanese educator. Spread over one hectare (2.5 acres), this traditional Japanese garden of shrubs and miniatures has two distinct sections: the Stroll Garden, laid out in a form that symbolizes the journey through life, and the Tea Garden, the place to contemplate life from a ceremonial teahouse. The garden is surrounded by high walls (which almost block out the noise of traffic from busy Marine Drive), making it a peaceful retreat. Outside of summer, the garden is open limited hours (10am-2:30pm Mon.-Fri.), but admission is by donation.

Also on campus is the delightful **UBC Botanical Garden** (6804 Marine Dr., 604/822-9666, 9am-4:30pm Mon.-Fri. mid-Mar.-mid-Oct., 9:30am-4:30pm Sat.-Sun. mid-Oct.-mid-Mar., adults $20, seniors $15, children $10). Set amid coastal forest, the 44-hectare (110-acre) garden dates to the turn of the 20th century and features eight separate sections, which hold around 10,000 species of trees, shrubs, and flowers. The various gardens have themes of specific regions or environments. Highlights include Canada's largest collection of rhododendrons; a Native Garden alive with the plants, flowers, and shrubs found along the Pacific Northwest coast; a display of mountain plants from the world's continents in the Alpine Garden; and medieval healing plants in the Physick Garden.

NORTH SHORE

North of downtown lie the incorporated cities of **North Vancouver** (pop. 85,000) and **West Vancouver** (pop. 44,000), both of which are dramatically sandwiched between the North Shore Range of the Coast Mountains and Burrard Inlet. The North Shore is accessible from downtown via the **Lions Gate Bridge,** but the SeaBus, which runs from Waterfront Station to **Lonsdale Quay,** offers a more enjoyable alternative to getting caught in bridge traffic. At the lively quay, a small information center (to the right as you come out of the SeaBus terminal) dispenses valuable information, and transit buses depart regularly for all nearby sights.

Capilano Suspension Bridge

Capilano Suspension Bridge (3735 Capilano Rd., 604/985-7474, 8:30am-8pm daily summer, 9am-5pm daily fall-spring, adults $43, seniors $39, youths $27, children $15) is one of Vancouver's most popular sights. The first bridge across the Capilano River opened in 1899. That remarkable wood-and-hemp structure stretched 137 meters (450 feet) across the deep canyon. Today, several bridges later, a wood-and-wire suspension bridge spans the canyon some 70 fearsome meters (230 feet) above the Capilano River. Allow at least two hours to walk the bridge, step out onto the numerous cantilevered decks, take the Treetops Adventure and the Cliffwalk over suspended walkways, and wander along the forested nature trails. Back near the main entrance, First Nations carvers display their skills in the Big House, and you'll find the requisite gift shop and eateries. To get there by car, cross Lions Gate Bridge, turn east onto Marine Drive and then immediately north onto Capilano Road, continuing to 3735 Capilano, on your left. If you don't want to drive, take the free shuttle from Canada Place; check the schedule at www.capbridge.com.

Capilano River Hatchery

This is my favorite North Shore attraction—and not only because it's free. If you've always wanted to know more about the miraculous life cycle of salmon, or want some facts to back up your fish stories, visit the **Capilano River Hatchery** (4500 Capilano Park Rd., 604/666-1790, 8am-8pm daily summer, 8am until dusk daily fall-spring, free) on the Capilano River, just upstream from the suspension bridge. Beside the rushing Capilano River and ensconced in cool rainforest, salmon are diverted through a channel and into artificially constructed spawning grounds. The channel is topped by a metal grate in one section and lined with glass windows in another. This allows up-close viewing of the salmon as they fight the current through their July to October run. In addition to the life-cycle displays, an exhibit on fly-fishing holds some interesting old tackle.

★ Grouse Mountain Skyride

Continuing north, Capilano Road becomes Nancy Greene Way and ends at the base of the **Grouse Mountain Skyride** (604/980-9311, adults $46, seniors $41, youths $26, children $16, parking $8), North America's largest aerial tramway. For an excellent view of downtown Vancouver, Stanley Park, the Pacific Ocean, and as far south as Mount Baker in Washington State, take the almost-vertical eight-minute ride on the gondola to the upper slopes of 1,250-meter (4,100-foot) Grouse Mountain. The gondola runs year-round, departing every 15 minutes 8:45am-10pm daily in summer.

The trip to the top is a lot more than a gondola ride—and it's easy to spend the best part of a day exploring the surrounding area and taking advantage of the attractions included in the price of the ride up. Of the many possible hikes, the one-kilometer (0.6-mile) **Blue Grouse Interpretive Trail** is the easiest and most enjoyable, winding around a lake and through a rainforest. Another trail leads to a fenced area where wolves and bears are rehabilitated after being orphaned. The best-known hike is the **Grouse Grind,** from the base of the gondola to the top. It's so named for a reason: The trail gains more than 1,000 meters (3,300 feet) of elevation in just 2.9 kilometers (1.8 miles). Thousands of locals make the trek daily as part of a self-imposed fitness program, with upward of 100,000 completing the trail each summer season. Once at the top, it costs $12 for a one-way ticket back down. Other summit activities include a fun but touristy logging show, chairlift rides, a First Nations longhouse with dancing and storytelling, and widescreen movie presentations of the outdoor wonders of British Columbia and local wildlife.

Lynn Canyon Park

On its way to Burrard Inlet, Lynn Creek flows through a deep canyon straddled by this 240-hectare (930-acre) park. Spanning the canyon is the "other" suspension bridge. The one here, built in 1912, is half as wide as its more famous counterpart over the Capilano River, but it's a few meters higher and, best of all, it's free. An ancient forest of Douglas fir surrounds the impressive canyon and harbors several hiking trails. At the bridge is the **Lynn Canyon Ecology Centre** (3663 Park Rd., 604/990-3755, 10am-5pm daily, donation), where displays, models, and free slide shows and films explore plant and animal ecology.

Lynn Canyon Park is seven kilometers (4 miles) east of the Capilano River. To get here by car, take the Lynn Valley Road exit off Highway 1, east of the Lions Gate Bridge. On public transportation, take the SeaBus to Lonsdale Quay, then buses 228 or 229.

Mount Seymour Provincial Park and Vicinity

Hikers and skiers flock to this 3,508-hectare (8,670-acre) park, 20 kilometers (12.4 miles) northeast of downtown. The park lies off Mount Seymour Parkway, which splits east off the Trans-Canada Highway just north of Burrard Inlet. The long and winding access road to the park climbs steadily through an ancient forest of western hemlock, cedar, and Douglas fir to a small facility area at an elevation of 1,000 meters (3,300 feet). From the parking lot, trails lead to the summit of 1,453-meter (4,770-foot) Mount Seymour; allow one hour for the two-kilometer (1.2-mile) trek.

If you continue along Mount Seymour Parkway instead of turning north toward the park, you end up in the scenic little village of **Deep Cove** on the west shore of Indian Arm (off the northeast end of Burrard Inlet)—an excellent spot for a picnic. Take your sack lunch to the waterfront park and watch the fishing and pleasure boats coming and going

Grouse Mountain Skyride

in the bay. More adventurous visitors can swim, kayak, or scuba dive.

Cypress Provincial Park

This 3,012-hectare (7,440-acre) park northwest of downtown encompasses a high alpine area in the North Shore Mountains. To get to the park, take the Trans-Canada Highway 12 kilometers (7.5 miles) west of Lions Gate Bridge and turn north onto Cypress Bowl Road (exit 8). Even the park access road up from the Trans-Canada Highway is worthwhile for the views. At the second switchback, the Highview Lookout provides a stunning panorama of the city, with interpretive panels describing the surrounding natural history. Just beyond the third switchback is another lookout, along with picnic tables. At the 12-kilometer (7.5-mile) mark, the road splits. Go straight ahead to reach Cypress Bowl ski area, which hosted freestyle skiing and snowboarding events during the 2010 Olympic Winter Games. From the main day lodge, well-marked hiking trails radiate out like spokes. One easy trail leads under the Black Chair (to the left as you stand in front of the day lodge) and passes a small alpine lake before ending after 1.3 kilometers (0.8 miles) at a lookout; allow one hour for the round-trip.

Lighthouse Park

On a headland jutting into Howe Sound, Lighthouse Park lies eight kilometers (5 miles) west of the Lions Gate Bridge. Trails lead through the park to coastal cliffs and a lighthouse (allow 15 minutes from the parking lot) that guides ships into narrow Burrard Inlet. Views from the lighthouse grounds are spectacular, extending west over the Strait of Georgia and east to Stanley Park and the Vancouver skyline.

Horseshoe Bay

The pretty little residential area of Horseshoe Bay offers plenty to see and do while you wait for the Vancouver Island or Sunshine Coast ferry. If you and your trusty vehicle are catching one of the ferries, buy your ticket at the car booth, move your automobile into the lineup, and then explore the town. Several restaurants, a bakery, a supermarket, a pub, and a couple of good delis cater to the hungry and thirsty. A stroll along the beautiful waterfront marina is a good way to dawdle away some waiting time.

Bowen Island

From Vancouver, this is the most accessible of hundreds of islands dotting the Strait of Georgia. The island is only a 20-minute ferry trip from Horseshoe Bay, but it seems a world away from the city. The ferry (250/386-3431, hourly 6am-9:45pm daily, adults $12.35, children $6.20, vehicles $34.85) docks at the island's main settlement, aptly named **Snug Cove,** where you'll find all the services of a small town. There's good swimming at Mannion Bay, near Snug Cove, and **Bowen Island Sea Kayaking** rents kayaks (604/947-9266, $45 for 3 hours) and offers twice-daily tours (3 hours, $75 pp). Island information is available at the **Bowen Island Visitor Centre** (432 Cardena Rd., 604/200-2399, www.tourismbowenisland.com, 9am-5pm daily summer).

TOURS

If you don't have a lot of time to explore Vancouver on your own, or just want an introduction to the city, consider taking one of the many tours available. They'll maximize your time and get you to the highlights with minimum stress.

Vancouver Trolley Company

From the main pickup point, a trolley-shaped booth at the top end of Gastown, the **Vancouver Trolley Company** (157 Water St., 604/801-5515 or 888/451-5581, www.vancouvertrolly.com) operates an old-fashioned trolley through the streets of downtown Vancouver. The two-hour City Attractions Tour stops at over 20 sites, from Stanley Park in the north to Science World in the south. Trolleys run 9am-4pm daily in summer, coming by each stop every half hour. A day pass is adults $42, seniors $38, children $22; reservations aren't necessary.

Harbor Cruises

From late April to September, **Harbour Cruises** (604/688-7246 or 800/663-1500, www.boatcruises.com) offers an hour-long tour (adults $35, seniors and students $28, children $15) of bustling Burrard Inlet on the paddle-wheeler MPV *Constitution*. Tours depart from the north foot of Denman Street up to four times daily. In the evening, the company offers a 2.5-hour Sunset Dinner Cruise (7pm daily May-early Oct., adults $83, children $69, includes dinner).

While puttering around False Creek on a small ferry is an inexpensive way to see this part of the city from water level, **False Creek Ferries** (604/684-7781) also offers a 40-minute guided tour of the historical waterway for just $18 pp. Departures (10am-5pm daily) are from Granville Island.

Flightseeing

Flightseeing tours of the city are offered by **Harbour Air** (604/274-1277 or 800/665-0212, www.harbourair.com) from its seaplane base on the west side of Canada Place. Options range from a 10-minute flight over downtown (adults $90, children $45) to a full-day trip to Victoria, including time at Butchart Gardens ($435 pp).

Sports and Recreation

PARKS
Stanley Park

Vancouver is not a particularly good city to explore on foot, but it does have one redeeming factor for foot travelers—Stanley Park, an urban oasis crisscrossed with hiking trails and encircled by a 10-kilometer (6-mile) promenade that hugs the shoreline. Along the way are many points of interest, benches, and interpretive plaques pointing out historical events. Allow three hours for the entire circuit. The promenade can be walked in either direction, but those on bikes and skates must travel counterclockwise. It is *always* packed, especially in late afternoon and on weekends.

Away from the Seawall Promenade, you'll find most trails a lot less busy. A good alternative to exploring one long section of the promenade is to ascend the steps immediately north of Lions Gate Bridge to Prospect Point (and maybe stop for a snack at the café), then continue west along the Merilees Trail, which follows the top of the cliff band to Third Beach. Along the way, an old lookout point affords excellent views of Siwash Rock and the Strait of Georgia.

The isthmus of land linking the park to the rest of the downtown peninsula is less than one kilometer (0.6 miles) wide, but it's mostly taken up by Lost Lagoon. A 1.5-kilometer (0.9-mile) trail (30 minutes round-trip) encircles this bird-filled body of water. In the heart of the park is Beaver Lake, a small body of water that is alive with birds throughout summer.

False Creek

From English Bay Beach, a promenade continues along English Bay to Sunset Beach and Vancouver Aquatic Centre. The small ferries that operate on False Creek, extending service as far west as the Aquatic Center, open up several walking combinations around the creek. Granville Island is a good starting point. No official trails go around the island, but if you walk east from the market, you pass a community of floating houses and go through a grassed area to Lookout Hill. Continue around the island and you'll come across a small footbridge leading to the mainland. From this point, it's seven kilometers (4.3 miles) around the head of False Creek, passing the Athletes' Village, Science World, and the Plaza of Nations, then closely following the water to the foot of Hornby Street for the short ferry trip back across to Granville Island; allow two hours without stopping.

Pacific Spirit Regional Park

This 762-hectare (1,880-acre) park on the Vancouver peninsula offers 35 kilometers (22 miles) of hiking trails through a forested environment similar to that which greeted the first European settlers more than 200 years ago. A good starting point is the **Pacific Spirit Regional Park Centre** (16th Ave. W., west of Blanca St., 604/224-5739, 8am-4pm Mon.-Fri.), which has a supply of trail maps. The entire park is crisscrossed with trails, so although getting seriously lost is impossible, taking the wrong trail and ending up away from your intended destination is easy. One good trailhead is opposite a residential area in the east of the park, at the junction of Imperial Road and King Edward Avenue. From this point, the Imperial Trail heads west through a forest of red cedar and fir, crosses Salish Creek, then emerges on Southwest Marine Drive, across the road from a plaque that notes the many explorers who contributed to opening up Vancouver to European settlement. From this lofty viewpoint, the view extends across the Strait of Georgia. This trail is 2.8 kilometers (1.7 miles) one-way; allow two hours for the round-trip.

BICYCLING

Stanley Park is a mecca for cyclists; among its network of bike paths is the popular Seawall Promenade, which hugs the coast for 10 kilometers (6 miles). Bike travel is in a counterclockwise direction. On the south side of English Bay, a cycle path runs from Vanier Park to Point Grey and the university, passing some of the city's best beaches on the way. On the north side of Burrard Inlet, hard-core mountain bike enthusiasts tackle the rough trails of Cypress Provincial Park and Grouse Mountain.

Near the entrance to Stanley Park, where Robson and Denman Streets meet, you'll find a profusion of bike-rental shops. These include **Bayshore Bicycles** (745 Denman St., 604/688-2453) and **Spokes Bicycle Rental** (1798 W. Georgia St., 604/688-5141).

GOLF

Vancouver has more than 50 golf courses, most of which are open to the public. It is often said that in Vancouver it is possible to ski in the morning and golf in the afternoon, and because most courses are open year-round,

looking across to downtown from the path around False Creek

this really is true. There's a pitch-and-putt golf course in **Stanley Park** (604/681-8847, 8am-6:30pm daily). With 18 holes under 100 yards each, the course makes a fun diversion. Greens fees are $14.25 per round, plus $2 per club for rentals. For serious golfers staying downtown, I'd recommend heading out to the **University Golf Club** (5185 University Blvd., Point Grey, 604/224-1818, greens fees $65), where the fairways are lined with mature trees and the clubhouse exudes Old World charm. In Richmond, south of downtown, water comes into play on 13 holes of the **Mayfair Lakes Golf & Country Club** (5460 No. 7 Rd., Richmond, 604/276-0505, greens fees $79), but the unique feature here is the salmon, which spawn in Mayfair's waterways. North of the city, **Furry Creek Golf and Country Club** (604/922-9461 or 888/922-9462, Mar.-Oct., greens fees $89), is bordered on one side by the driftwood-strewn beaches of Howe Sound and on the other by towering mountains, making it one of the most scenic courses in the Vancouver region.

WATER SPORTS
Swimming
All of Vancouver's best beaches are along the shoreline of English Bay; 10 have lifeguards on duty 11:30am-8:45pm daily in summer. Closest to downtown is **English Bay Beach,** at the end of Denman Street. Flanked by a narrow strip of parkland and a wide array of cafés and restaurants, this is *the* beach for people-watching. From English Bay Beach, the Seawall Promenade leads north to **Second** and **Third Beaches,** both short, secluded stretches of sand. To the south is **Sunset Beach,** which is most popular with families. On the south side of English Bay, **Kitsilano Beach** offers sweeping views back across the bay to downtown and the mountains beyond. Take a dip in the salted, outdoor, and heated **Kitsilano Pool** (2305 Cornwall Ave., 604/731-0011, 7am-8pm Mon.-Fri., 9am-8pm Sat.-Sun., adults $6, seniors $4.50, children $3), which is 137 meters (450 feet) long and was built in 1931.

Swimmers take note: Even at the peak of summer, the ocean water here only warms up to about 17°C (63°F), tops. If that doesn't sound enticing, head to **Vancouver Aquatic Centre** (1050 Beach Ave., 604/665-3424, 6:30am-9pm Mon.-Fri., 8am-9:30pm Sat., 10am-9:30pm Sun., adults $6, seniors $4.50, children $3). Inside is a 50-meter heated pool, along with saunas, whirlpools, and a small weight room.

Canoeing and Kayaking
Granville Island is the center of action for paddlers, and the calm waters of adjacent False Creek make the perfect place to practice your skills. For the widest choice of equipment, head to **Ecomarine Paddlesport Centre** (1668 Duranleau St., 604/689-7575, www.ecomarine.com, 9am-8pm daily summer, 10am-6pm daily fall-spring), which rents single sea kayaks (from $39 for 2 hours), double sea kayaks ($52 for 2 hours), and stand-up paddleboards (from $29 for 2 hours). This company also offers lessons and tours.

The **Indian Arm** of Burrard Inlet allows for a real wilderness experience, right on the city's back doorstep. This 22-kilometer (14-mile) fjord cuts deeply into the North Shore Range; the only development is at its southern end, where the suburb of Deep Cove provides a takeoff point for the waterway. **Deep Cove Kayak Centre** (2156 Banbury Rd., Deep Cove, 604/929-2268, www.deepcovekayak.com, Apr.-Oct.) rents kayaks for $39 for two hours for a single kayak or $39 for a stand-up paddleboard.

SKIING AND SNOWBOARDING
While Vancouver is the gateway to world-renowned Whistler-Blackcomb, the city boasts three other alpine resorts on its back doorstep. They don't offer the terrain or facilities of Whistler, and their low elevations can create unreliable conditions, but a day's skiing or boarding at any one of the three sure beats being stuck in the hustle and bustle of the city on a cold winter's day.

Grouse Mountain

Towering above North Vancouver, the cut slopes of the **Grouse Mountain resort** (604/980-9311, www.grousemountain.com, adults $61, youth and seniors $45, children $25) can be seen from many parts of the city, but as you'd expect, on a clear day views from "up there" are much more spectacular. To get there, take Capilano Road north from the Trans-Canada Highway, following it onto Nancy Greene Way, from which a gondola lifts you 1,000 vertical meters (3,280 feet) to the slopes. Four chairlifts and a couple of T-bars serve 24 runs and a vertical rise of 365 meters (1,200 feet). Advanced skiers and boarders shouldn't get too excited about a day on the slopes here—even the runs with names like Purgatory and Devil's Advocate are pretty tame—but schussing down the slopes of Grouse Mountain after dark is an experience you won't soon forget. Most runs are lighted and overlook the City of Vancouver, laid out in all its brilliance far below. Night skiing (4pm-10pm) costs adults $48, youths and seniors $40, and children $22.

Cypress Mountain

The eyes of the world were on the small **Cypress Mountain resort** (604/926-5612, www.cypressmountain.com, adults $64, seniors $44, children $28) on Vancouver's North Shore when it hosted the freestyle skiing and snowboarding events of the 2010 Olympic Winter Games. It offers about 34 runs across a vertical rise of 534 meters (1,750 feet). A quad chair and four doubles combine to open a wide variety of terrain on two mountain faces, most suited to beginners and intermediates. Spectacular views take in Howe Sound and Vancouver Island. Cypress also caters to cross-country skiers and snowshoers, with 16 kilometers (10 miles) of groomed and track-set trails, some of which are lighted for night skiing. A package of cross-country ski rentals, a lesson, and trail pass costs $80. Snowshoe rentals are $25 per day. To get to the resort, take

the Trans-Canada Highway 12 kilometers (7.5 miles) west from Lions Gate Bridge and turn north on Cypress Bowl Road.

Mount Seymour

Thanks to having the highest base elevation of Vancouver's three alpine resorts, the snow at **Mount Seymour** (604/986-2261, www.mountseymour.com, adults $56, seniors $40, children $26) is somewhat reliable, but the area's relatively gentle terrain will be of interest only to beginning and intermediate skiers and boarders. Four chairlifts serve 20 runs and a vertical rise of 365 meters (1,200 feet). You can also rent snowshoes ($27) and tramp along the resort's trail system, but the Saturday-night guided snowshoe walk ($59) is a real treat—and not only because of the chocolate fondue at the end. The resort is in Mount Seymour Provincial Park. To get there, head north off the Trans-Canada Highway 15 kilometers (9 miles) east of the Lions Gate Bridge, following the Mount Seymour Parkway to Mount Seymour Road.

SPECTATOR SPORTS

Vancouverites love their sports—not just being involved themselves, but supporting local teams. With a long season and outside activities curtailed by the winter weather, ice hockey—known in Canada simply as "hockey"—draws the biggest crowds (although the official national sport is lacrosse), but the city also boasts professional football, baseball, and soccer teams.

Hockey

In 1911 the world's second (and largest) artificial ice rink opened at the north end of Denman Street, complete with seating for 10,000 hockey fans. The local team, then known as the Vancouver Millionaires, played in a small professional league, and in 1915 Vancouver won its first and only Stanley Cup, the holy grail of professional ice hockey. The team of today, the **Vancouver Canucks** (604/899-7400, www.canucks.

com), plays in General Motors Place (across from BC Place Stadium on Griffith Way) between October and April; ticket prices range $80-240.

Football
The **BC Lions** (604/589-7627, www.bclions.com) are Vancouver's Canadian Football League (CFL) franchise. American football fans may be surprised by some of the plays because the rules are slightly different from those of the National Football League (NFL). And no, you're not imagining things: The playing fields are larger than those used in the game's American version. CFL teams have been competing for the Grey Cup, named for Earl Grey, a former governor-general of Canada, since 1909. Home games are played at BC Place Stadium (777 Pacific Blvd.), on the south side of downtown at the corner of Robson and Beatty Streets. The season runs June-November, with most games played in the evening; tickets range $40-95.

Soccer
Vancouver is a soccer stronghold, and with two professional teams and dozens of intra-city leagues, it is always well represented on the national team. The **Whitecaps** (604/899-9283, www.whitecapsfc.com), Vancouver's professional men's soccer team, play in the Major Soccer League, competing against teams across North America through the summer. Formerly known as the 86ers, the team was sold and renamed in 2001, and players today have the unenviable task of maintaining the team's record as one of the winningest in all of professional sports—the 86ers were undefeated for six entire seasons through the 1980s. Home games are played at BC Place Stadium (777 Pacific Blvd.). The season runs May-August, and game-day tickets are in the $20-45 range.

Entertainment

There's never a dull moment in Vancouver when it comes to nightlife. The city's unofficial entertainment district extends southwest along Granville Street from Granville Street Mall and south from this strip to False Creek. Cinemas line Granville Street Mall, and beyond the mall is a smattering of nightclubs, with the main concentration of these in Yaletown. Performing arts and concert venues are scattered throughout the city, but the three largest—Ford Centre for the Performing Arts, Queen Elizabeth Theatre, and BC Place Stadium—are south of Granville Street along Georgia Street.

For complete listings of all that's happening around the city, pick up the free *Georgia Straight* (www.straight.com). Friday and weekend editions of Vancouver's two daily newspapers, *The Province* and the *Vancouver Sun,* offer comprehensive entertainment listings.

As in all other major cities across Canada and much of the United States, **Ticketmaster** (604/280-3311, www.ticketmaster.ca) has a monopoly on advance ticket sales to major entertainment events; have your credit card ready. **Tickets Tonight** (in the visitors center, 200 Burrard St., 604/684-2787, www.ticketstonight.ca, 10am-6pm daily) sells half-price tickets the day of major performances.

BARS
Ever since "Gassy Jack" Deighton set up the city's first liquor outlet (a barrel of whiskey set atop a crude plank bar) in the area that became known as Gastown, Vancouver has had its favorite watering holes.

Gastown
In the historical building The Landing, **Steamworks Brewing Co.** (375 Water St.,

604/689-2739, 11:30am-midnight daily) is the perfect place to relax with a beer from the in-house brewery. The atmosphere is casual yet stylish, and you'll have great views across Burrard Inlet. Down the hill is stylish **131 Water** (131 Water St., 604/669-7219, 11am-11pm Sun.-Thurs., 11am-1am Fri.-Sat.), with a few tables street-side and a quieter courtyard out back.

At the far eastern end of Gastown, the lively **Blarney Stone** (216 Carrall St., 604/687-4322, 11am-2am daily) frequently resounds with rowdy Irish party bands. The evening crowd here is older and often single. In the same vein, across the road is the **Irish Heather** (212 Carrall St., 604/688-9779, 11:30am-midnight Sun.-Thurs., 11:30am-2am Fri.-Sat.), renowned for its Guinness on tap and wide selection of whiskeys.

Yaletown and Granville Island

Yaletown Brewing Co. (1111 Mainland St., 604/681-2739, 11:30am-midnight Sun.-Wed., 11:30am-1am Thurs., 11:30am-3am Fri.-Sat.) is the premier drinking hole for the hip population of inner-city Yaletown. The in-house brewery produces a variety of excellent beers, there's a great patio, and the food is of a high standard for a pub. Also in Yaletown, the **Opus Bar** (22 Davie St., 604/642-0557, 11:30am-midnight Sun.-Thurs., 11:30am-1am Fri.-Sat.) serves up creative cocktails and imported beer in a sizzlingly hip setting off the lobby of the Opus Hotel.

Walk back toward downtown from the Opus to **Doolin's Irish Pub** (654 Nelson St., 604/605-4343, 11:30am-2am daily), which dispenses mugs of Guinness and hearty food such as a ploughman's lunch ($10). The small but always lively **Wicklow Pub** (610 Stamp's Landing, 604/879-0821, 11:30am-midnight Mon.-Fri., 11am-midnight Sat.-Sun.) overlooks False Creek just east of Granville Island and a short ferry trip from Yaletown. Aside from beer and liquor, this joint offers delicious snacks to keep you going, live music on weekends, and great sunset views of the harbor.

West End

Toward the West End, **Joe Fortes Seafood and Chophouse** (777 Thurlow St., 604/669-1940, 11am-11pm daily) boasts a great bar, complete with a wide range of beers and a condensed menu from the adjacent restaurant. In the same part of town, at street level of the Best Western, **The Park at English Bay** (1755 Davie St., 604/682-1831, 11am-2am Mon.-Fri., 11am-2am Sat.-Sun.) is a popular lounge for a long list of regional wines and drink specials (4pm-6pm daily).

NIGHTCLUBS

Nightclubs change names and reputations regularly, so check with the free entertainment newspapers or the website www.clubzone.com for the latest hot spots. Naturally, weekends are busiest, with the most popular clubs having cover charges up to $20 and long lines after 9pm. During the rest of the week, cover charges are reduced and many places hold promotions with giveaways or discounted drinks.

Downtown nightclubs are concentrated at the southern end of downtown along and immediately south of Granville Street. In a converted movie theater toward the central business district, spacious **Venue** (881 Granville St., 604/646-0064, 10am-3am Fri.-Sat.) is highly regarded for its alternative live music scene midweek, while on weekends it offers more of a rave atmosphere with a DJ spinning house, trance, or whatever's hot in the music scene. Nearby, and also in a converted movie theater, **Caprice** (967 Granville St., 250/685-3288, 11pm-3am Wed., 10pm-3am Fri.-Sat.) combines a lounge and food service with a multilevel nightclub with a friendly vibe.

The stylish setting at **Aura** (1180 Granville St., 604/688-8889, 10am-3am Thurs.-Sun.) mimics the latest trends in the Las Vegas clubbing scene. The New York-style **Bar None** (1222 Hamilton St., 604/689-7000, 10am-3am Fri.-Sat.) attracts a young, single crowd for DJ-spun tunes. Drink prices at Bar None are higher than at most other local venues.

For serious dancing to electronic and hip hop away from the main entertainment district, check out **Red Room** (398 Richards St., 604/687-5007, 9am-2am Thurs.-Sun.), at the top end of Gastown.

LIVE MUSIC AND COMEDY

The world's biggest rock, pop, and country acts usually include Vancouver on their world tours, and the city's thriving local music industry supports live bands at a variety of venues. Most big-name acts play BC Place Stadium, the Orpheum, or Queen Elizabeth Theatre. Attracting a huge crowd every night of the week at the classic **Roxy** (932 Granville St., 604/331-7999, 8pm-3am daily), two house bands play rock-and-roll music from all eras to a packed house on weekdays, with imported bands on weekends. **Railway Stage & Beer Cafe** (579 Dunsmuir St., 604/564-1430, 11am-2am Sun.-Thurs., 11am-3am Fri.-Sat.) oozes historic charm and is the place for acts that range from rock to funk.

The **Coastal Jazz & Blues Society** (604/872-5200, www.coastaljazz.ca) maintains a listing of all the city's jazz and blues events on their website. Attracting acts from throughout Canada, **Lafflines** (530 Columbia St., New Westminster, 604/525-2262, 7pm-11pm Thurs., 7pm-midnight Sat.-Sun.) offers live comedy three nights a week. Vancouver Theatresports League performs improvised comedy at the **Improv Centre** (1502 Duranleau St., Granville Island, 604/738-7013, www.vtsl.com, from 7:30pm Wed.-Sun.), with a waterfront lounge providing an ideal destination for a preperformance drink.

THE ARTS
Theater

Vancouver boasts around 30 professional theater companies and more than 20 regular venues. The main downtown venues are owned and operated by the City of Vancouver, with the website www.vancouvercivictheatres.com detailing each one.

The **Centre in Vancouver for Performing Arts** (777 Homer St., 604/602-0616, www.centreinvancouver.com, matinees from $50, evening shows $60-100) hosts the biggest of musical hits. Designed by renowned architect Moshe Safdie, the modern wonder features a five-story glass lobby flanked by granite walls. The tri-level theater seats more than 1,800 and boasts North America's largest stage. A similar facility is the **Chan Centre for the Performing Arts** (6265 Crescent Rd., 604/822-9197, www.chancentre.com), comprising three stages, including the 1,400-seat Chan Shun Concert Hall. It's on the UBC campus in Point Grey.

One of the great joys of summer in the city is sitting around Malkin Bowl in Stanley Park watching **Theatre under the Stars** (604/734-1917, www.tuts.ca, 7pm Mon.-Sat. June-Aug.). Since 1934 these shows have drawn around 1,000 theatergoers nightly, with performances usually musically oriented. The setting itself, an open amphitheater surrounded by towering Douglas fir trees, is as much of an attraction as the performance. Tickets ($35-50) can be bought online and also go on sale at 2pm daily from a booth beside the bowl.

Arts Club Theatre (1585 Johnston St., 604/687-1644, www.artsclub.com, tickets $28-50) always offers excellent theater productions at the **Granville Island Stage.** Productions range from drama to comedy to improv. Another venue for the Arts Club is the restored **Stanley Industrial Alliance Theatre** (2750 Granville St.), south of the island at 12th Avenue.

For university productions, head out to **Frederic Wood Theatre** (6354 Crescent Rd., 604/822-2678, tickets $12-18) on the UBC campus. Performances run throughout the academic year.

Music and Dance

The **Queen Elizabeth Theatre** (630 Hamilton St., 604/665-3050) is the home of **Vancouver Opera** (604/683-0222, www.vancouveropera.ca, tickets $50-115). The theater also hosts a variety of music recitals and stage performances.

The historical **Orpheum Theatre** (Smithe St. and Seymour St.) dates to 1927 and houses its original Wurlitzer organ. Now fully restored, the theater provides excellent acoustics for the resident **Vancouver Symphony** (604/876-3434, www.vancouversymphony. ca) as well as for concerts by the professional **Vancouver Chamber Choir** (604/738-6822, www.vancouverchamberchoir.com), the amateur **Vancouver Bach Choir** (604/696-4290, www.vancouverbachchoir.com), and a variety of other musical groups. Renowned for its support of emerging musicians, the **Vancouver Recital Society** (604/602-0363, www.van-recital.com) presents piano, cello, and violin players at the Vancouver Playhouse and Chan Centre for the Performing Arts throughout its October-April season.

Ballet British Columbia (604/732-5003, www.balletbc.com, tickets $18-45) performs in the **Queen Elizabeth Theatre** (630 Hamilton St., 604/665-3050) throughout its winter season. Vancouver's other major dance venue is the **Dance Centre** (677 Davie St., 604/606-6400, www.thedancecentre.ca). Designed by Arthur Erickson, this stunning seven-story glass-enclosed building provides a home to around 30 professional and amateur dance companies.

CINEMAS

Cinemas are in all of the major shopping malls and elsewhere throughout the city. **Cineplex** (604/434-2463, www.cineplex.com, tickets $12-16) operates cinemas across the city. Call or check online for locations and screenings. For foreign and Canadian indie films, check out **The Cinematheque** (1131 Howe St., 604/688-8202, www.thecinematheque.ca, tickets $10-16).

FESTIVALS AND EVENTS

Festivals of some description take place in Vancouver just about every month of the year. Whether it's a celebration of local or international culture, the arts, sporting events, or just a wacky longtime tradition, there's always a reason to party in Vancouver. Tickets for most major events can be booked through **Ticketmaster** (www.ticketmaster.ca).

Spring

Vancouver International Wine Festival (various downtown venues, 604/872-6623, www.vanwinefest.ca, late Feb.) is one of North America's largest wine shows, bringing together representatives from more than 175 wineries and 14 countries. While the trade and wine connoisseurs are catered to, casual wine buffs enjoy a variety of events, including access to hundreds of wines from around the world.

The spring sports schedule kicks off with a blast from the starter's gun for the **Vancouver Sun Run** (604/689-9441, www. vancouversun.com/sunrun, 3rd Sun. in Apr., downtown), a 10-kilometer (6-mile) run (or walk) through the streets of downtown. Attracting over 50,000 participants, it is Canada's largest (and the world's third-largest) such run. A couple of weeks after the annual fun run, serious runners hit the streets for the **Vancouver Marathon** (downtown, 604/872-2928, www.bmovanmarathon.ca, 1st Sun. in May), an internationally accredited marathon and a qualifier for the Boston Marathon. Races are contested in different lengths, including the marathon, a half-marathon, and a five-miler. All begin and end at BC Place Stadium, with the marathon following the shoreline of False Creek, winding through the streets of downtown, then to Stanley Park, and crossing to Kitsilano.

Rodeo isn't usually associated with Vancouver, but each May cowboys from throughout North America descend on the city for the three-day **Cloverdale Rodeo and Country Fair** (Cloverdale, 604/576-9461, www.cloverdalerodeo.com, 3rd weekend in May). The rodeo—saddle bronc, bareback, bull riding, steer wrestling, and calf roping—takes place at 2:30pm and 7:30pm daily. Grandstand tickets cost from

$25. Other events include the agricultural show, a Western trade show, First Nations dancing and arts and crafts, and a parade. All of the action takes place at the Cloverdale Fairground, between Surrey and Langley.

Don't let your children tell you how bored they are if your family is in Vancouver on the third weekend of May. The **Vancouver International Children's Festival** (604/708-5655, www.childrensfestival.ca, adults $22, children $12.50) is a kid's paradise, with face painting, costumes, plays, puppetry, mime, sing-alongs, storytelling, and fancy-hat competitions. A large area of Granville Island is fenced off for the week.

Summer
The **Canadian International Dragon Boat Festival** (False Creek, www.vancouverdragonboatfestival.ca, 3rd weekend of June) attracts up to 2,000 competitors from as far away as Asia and Europe. In addition to the races, a blessing ceremony and cultural activities take place in and around the Plaza of Nations.

Throughout summer, **Bard on the Beach** (Vanier Park, 604/737-0625, www.bardonthebeach.org, mid-June-late Sept.) performs three favorite Shakespeare plays in two open-ended tents in Vanier Park, allowing a spectacular backdrop of English Bay, the city skyline, and the mountains beyond. Tickets are well priced at just $22-34 for 1pm and 3pm matinees and $45 for 7:30pm evening performances. They're sold in advance through Ticketmaster and on the night of the performance at the door.

Watching amateur variety acts at the **Kitsilano Showboat** (Kitsilano Beach, 604/734-7332, www.kitsilanoshowboat.com, mid-June-mid-Aug.) on a warm summer evening has been a Vancouver tradition since 1935. Today, amateur singers, dancers, and musicians take to the Showboat stage Monday, Wednesday, and Friday nights, entertaining more than 100,000 people throughout the 10-week season.

Vancouver taps its feet to the beat of the **Vancouver International Jazz Festival** (throughout the city, 604/872-5200, www.coastaljazz.ca, last week of June), when more than 1,500 musicians from countries around the world gather to perform traditional and contemporary jazz at 40 venues around the city. The festival kicks off with a free street party in historic Gastown, while other venues include the Orpheum Theatre, David Lam Park, Granville Island Market, Metrotown, and the Commodore Ballroom.

fireworks over the harbor on Canada Day

Canada Day (Canada Place and Steveston, July 1) is Canada's national day. The main celebrations—music, dancing, and fireworks—are held at Canada Place, but if you head out to the Steveston Salmon Festival (604/718-8094, www.stevestonsalmonfest.ca), you'll come across a massive salmon barbecue, art show, food fair, children's festival, drag racing, and more.

In addition to wonderful music, the Vancouver Folk Music Festival (Jericho Beach, 604/602-9798, www.thefestival.bc.ca, middle weekend of July, day pass from $60) features storytelling, dance performances, live theater, and a food fair. The beachside venue includes seven stages with the city skyline and mountains beyond as a backdrop.

Celebration of Light (English Bay, 604/733-7171, www.hondacelebrationoflight.com, late July-early Aug.) is the world's largest musical fireworks competition, filling the summer sky with color. Each year, three countries are invited to compete; each has a night to itself (last Sat. in July and the following Wed. and Sat.), putting on a 30-minute display at 10pm; on the final night (1st Sat. in Aug.), the three competing countries come together for a grand finale. The fireworks are set off from a barge moored in English Bay, allowing vantage points from Stanley Park, Kitsilano, Jericho Beach, and as far away as West Vancouver. Music that accompanies the displays can be heard around the shoreline; if you're away from the action, tune your radio to 101.1 FM for a simulcast.

The Vancouver Pride Parade (604/687-0955, www.vancouverpride.ca, first Sun. in Aug., downtown) culminates a week of gay pride celebration. It runs along Denman Street, ending at Sunset Beach, where there's entertainment and partying. Festivities during the preceding week include a picnic in Stanley Park, Gay Day at Playland, a ball at Plaza of Nations, art exhibitions, and nightclub parties.

Attracting more than 300,000 spectators, Abbotsford International Airshow (Abbotsford, 604/852-8511, www.

abbotsfordairshow.com, 2nd weekend of Aug., adults $30, children $12, camping $25), one of North America's largest airshows, is held at Vancouver's "other" airport, 70 kilometers (43 miles) east of downtown in Abbotsford. The highlight is a flyby of Canada's famous Snowbirds, but there's a full program of stunt and technical flying and an on-ground exhibition of military and civilian planes from all eras of aviation.

The country comes to the city for two weeks at the end of August for the Pacific National Exhibition (Hastings Park, 604/253-2311, www.pne.ca, late Aug., general admission $18), one of Canada's largest agricultural exhibitions. What began as a simple fair in 1910 has grown into a massive event, with live entertainment, multiple attractions, and special events at Playland. One of many highlights is the twice-daily Royal Canadian Mounted Police musical ride, a precision drill performed by Canada's famous "Mounties." Each day of the fair ends with Fire in the Night, a colorful extravaganza of lasers, dancers, and fireworks. The Pacific National Exhibition Grounds are six kilometers (4 miles) east of downtown along Hastings Street East where Highway 1 crosses Burrard Inlet.

Fall

The Vancouver International Fringe Festival (604/257-0350, www.vancouverfringe.com, 2nd week of Sept., $10-18) schedules over 500 performances by 80 artists from around the world at indoor and outdoor stages throughout Granville Island.

Running in early October, the Vancouver International Film Fest (downtown theaters, 604/683-3456, www.viff.org, early Oct.) features more than 300 of the very best movies from around 50 countries at theaters across downtown. The festival isn't as well known as other film festivals, but it has grown to become the third largest in North America.

After movie buffs have had their fill, literary types congregate on Granville Island for the **Vancouver International Writers Festival** (Granville Island, 604/681-6330, www.writersfest.bc.ca, late Oct.), a celebration of local and national literary talent. Most events are open to the public and include lectures, a festival bookstore, talks, and readings by around 100 leading writers, poets, and playwrights. They take place in island bookstores, the Granville Island Hotel, and on Granville Island Stage.

Winter

For the **Festival of Lights** (604/257-8666, www.vancouver.ca/vandusen), Central Vancouver's VanDusen Botanical Garden is transformed each December evening by more than 80,000 lights and seasonal displays such as the Nativity scene.

While most folks spend New Year's Day recovering from the previous night's celebrations, over 2,500 brave souls head down to English Bay Beach and go *swimming*. The **Polar Bear Swim** was started in the early 1900s by a local businessman, Peter Pantages, who took to the water every day of the year; to promote the fact that it was possible to swim year-round, he formed the Polar Bear Club. On the first day of 1920, a small group assembled at English Bay Beach, dove into the frigid waters, and began a tradition that continues to this day. It starts at 2:30pm.

During **Chinese New Year** (late Jan. or early Feb.), Chinatown comes alive for two weeks with a colorful parade, music, dancing, and a spectacular display of fireworks. The Chinese calendar is linked to the lunar New Year, which varies from late January to early February.

Shopping

Vancouver has shopping centers, malls, and specialty stores everywhere. Head to Gastown for First Nations arts and crafts, Robson Street for boutique clothing, Granville Street Mall for department stores, Granville Island for everything from ships' chandlery to kids' clothing, Yaletown for the trendy clothes of local designers, Eastside for army-surplus stores and pawnbrokers, Chinatown for Eastern foods, and the junction of Main Street and East 49th Avenue for Indian goods.

SHOPPING DISTRICTS

Despite looking pretty dowdy these days, **Granville Street Mall** nevertheless forms the heart of the downtown shopping precinct; the two-block stretch of Granville Street is closed to private vehicles, although buses and taxis still pass through. The mall's **Pacific Centre** features 165 shops, a massive food court, and a three-story-high waterfall.

Across Lions Gate Bridge in West Vancouver are a couple of shopping centers worth a mention. In a scenic location at Marine Drive and Taylor Way, **Park Royal Shopping Centre** holds almost 200 shops and three department stores. Also on the north side of Burrard Inlet is **Lonsdale Quay Market,** the terminus of the SeaBus from downtown. This bustling center features a great fresh-food market on the first floor and a range of boutiques and galleries on the second.

British Columbia's largest shopping complex, **Metrotown,** houses more than 200 shops. It's on the Kingsway in Burnaby; get there from downtown on the SkyTrain.

Gastown

Sandwiched between the many cafés, restaurants, and tacky souvenir stores along Water Street are other stores selling Vancouver's best selection of First Nations arts and crafts. One of the largest outlets, **Hill's Native Art** (165 Water St., 604/685-4249, 9am-9pm daily) sells $15 T-shirts, towering $12,000 totem poles, and everything in between, including genuine Cowichan sweaters and carved ceremonial masks. The **Inuit Gallery of Vancouver** (206 Cambie St., 604/688-7323, 10am-6pm Mon.-Sat., noon-5pm Sun.) exhibits the work of Inuit and British Columbian First Nations artists and sculptors.

Stanley Park

Within **Klahowya Village** (Pipeline Rd., 604/921-1070, 11am-4pm Mon.-Thurs., 11am-5pm Fri.-Sun. mid-June-Aug.) are the **Artisan Marketplace** and **Métis Trading Post,** both excellent places to purchase traditional First Nations arts and crafts. As a bonus, on weekends, you can watch the artisans at work.

Granville Island

Arts-and-crafts galleries on Granville Island include **Wickaninnish Gallery** (1666 Johnston St., 604/681-1057, 10am-7pm daily), which sells stunning First Nations art, jewelry, carvings, weavings, and original paintings, and **Gallery of BC Ceramics** (1359 Cartwright St., 604/669-3606, 10:30am-5:30pm daily), showcasing the work of the province's leading potters and sculptors.

Duranleau Street is home to many maritime-based businesses, adventure-tour operators, and charter operators. To buy a sea kayak, canoe, or stand-up paddleboard (from $1,100 secondhand), head to **Ecomarine Paddlesport Centre** (1668 Duranleau St., 604/689-7575, 9am-6pm Sun.-Thurs., 9am-9pm Fri.-Sat. summer, 10am-6pm daily fall-spring). The city's leading dive shop is **Rowands Reef Scuba Shop** (1512 Duranleau St., 604/669-3483, 10am-6pm daily), with sales, repairs, rentals, and plenty of information on local dive spots.

Commercial Drive

Extending south from East Hastings Street, Commercial Drive is a little rough around the edges, but it offers a wonderful collection of different shopping experiences. Known locally as "The Drive," it originally thrived as a center of Italian culture. You can still stop by and watch a game of European football at the welcoming **Abruzzo Cappuccino Bar** (1321 Commercial Dr., 604/254-2641, from 7am daily) with older locals, or choose from over 200 flavors at **La Casa Gelato** (1033 Venables St., 604/251-3211, 10am-6pm daily), but shopping is the main draw.

Stepping into **Wonderbucks** (1803 Commercial Dr., 604/253-0510, 10am-6pm daily) is like stepping back in time. If there were big-box homeware stores 40 years ago, this is what they would have looked like, complete with friendly service and a collection of items that is halfway between hip and eclectic. North toward downtown, **Dandelion Kids** (1206 Commercial Dr., 604/676-1862, 10am-9pm Mon.-Sat., 11am-6pm Sun.) is a kids' store for modern parents, complete with one-of-a-kind sculptures designed especially for baby bedrooms.

OUTDOOR AND CAMPING GEAR

A small stretch of West Broadway, between Main and Cambie Streets, holds Vancouver's largest concentration of outdoor equipment stores. The largest of these, and the largest in British Columbia, is **Mountain Equipment Co-op** (130 W. Broadway, 604/872-7858, www.mec.ca, 10am-7pm Mon.-Wed., 10am-9pm Thurs.-Fri., 9am-6pm Sat., 10am-6pm Sun.). Like the American REI stores, it is a cooperative owned by its members; to make a purchase, you must be a member (a one-time charge of $5). The store holds a massive selection of clothing, climbing and mountaineering equipment, tents, backpacks, sleeping bags, books, and other accessories.

BOOKSTORES

General independents are nonexistent in downtown Vancouver. The Canadian bookstore giant **Chapters Indigo** has multiple Vancouver stores, including one in the heart of the city, branded as **IndigoSpirit** (810 Granville St., 604/979-8899, 9:30am-9pm Mon.-Sat., 10am-8pm Sun.), and others in major shopping centers such as Burnaby's Metrotown, each stocking more than 100,000 titles.

UBC Bookstore (University of British

Columbia, 6200 University Blvd. at Westbrook Mall, 604/822-2665, 9:30am-5pm Mon.-Fri., 11am-5pm Sat.) has almost 100,000 titles on its shelves.

Vancouver has three excellent bookstores specializing in travel-related literature. **Wanderlust** (west of Cypress St. at 1929 W. 4th Ave., Kitsilano, 604/739-2182, www.wanderlustore.com, 10am-7pm Mon.-Fri., 10am-6pm Sat., noon-5pm Sun.) stocks general travel guides, maps, atlases, and a range of travel accessories. Farther west is **The Travel Bug** (2865 W. Broadway, 604/737-1122, www. travelbugbooks.ca, 9:30am-6pm Mon.-Sat., 11am-5pm Sun.), with an equally impressive collection of travel guides as well as more regional titles than you ever imagined existed. If you like maps, you'll love **International Travel Maps and Books** (12300 Bridgeport Rd., Richmond, 604/273-1400, www.itmb.com, 9:30am-5pm Mon.-Sat.), one of the world's most prolific cartography companies, whose title list includes over 400 maps covering offbeat destinations.

Food

With an estimated 4,000 restaurants and hundreds of cafés and coffeehouses, Vancouver is a gastronomical delight. The city is home to more than 60 different cultures, so don't be surprised to find a smorgasbord of international restaurants. The local specialty is west coast or "fusion" cuisine, which combines fresh Canadian produce, such as local seafood and seasonal game, with Asian flavors and ingredients, usually in a healthy low-fat way. Vancouver has no tourist-oriented San Francisco-style Fisherman's Wharf, but however and wherever it's prepared, seafood will always dominate local menus. Always ask if it's local—Pacific salmon, halibut, snapper, shrimp, oysters, clams, crab, and squid are all harvested in the ocean off Vancouver.

DOWNTOWN

Downtown Vancouver has so many good dining options that it is a shame to eat in a food court, but as in cities around the Western world, they are a good place for a fast, reliable, and inexpensive meal. The southwest corner of the Pacific Centre (Howe St. and Georgia St., diagonally opposite the art gallery) holds a glass-domed food court with many inexpensive food bars and seating indoors and out.

Cafés

I always struggle to find decent coffee in the heart of downtown, but Gastown does have a few good options. Some of the best coffee is ground and brewed at **Bambo Cafe** (301 W. Cordova St., 604/681-4323, 7am-7pm Mon.-Fri., 9am-6pm Sat.-Sun., lunch $8-13), which uses only organic free-trade beans, but is equally desirable for its freshly squeezed juices and inexpensive sandwiches, salads, and filled focaccia.

Although everyone has different coffee tastes, **Revolver** (325 Cambie St., 604/558-4444, 7:30am-6pm Mon.-Fri., 9am-6pm Sat.) is generally regarded as one of the best places in the city for coffee lovers. Although beans are not roasted in-house, the very best roasts are sourced from throughout North America and rotated weekly. In addition to coffee made to order, you can sample a flight of coffees brewed in different ways. Around the corner, **Timbertrain** (311 W. Cordova St., 604/915-9188, 7am-6pm Mon.-Fri., 8am-6pm Sat.-Sun.) gets rave reviews for its single-origin, brewed-to-order coffee.

At **Meat & Bread** (370 Cambie St., 604/566-9003, 11am-5pm Sun.-Wed., 11am-7:30pm Thurs.-Sat., sandwiches $7-10), the art of sandwich making is taken to a new level, without going over the top. Each sandwich is custom-made on a freshly baked ciabatta bun and filled with one of four daily choices, then served on a wooden cutting board.

Downtown Diners

"Quality Food, Snappy Service" is the catch-cry at **The Templeton** (1087 Granville St., 604/685-4612, 8:30am-11pm daily, $9-18), which has been serving downtown locals since 1934. Eat at the low counter or in the vinyl booths, each with a small jukebox, and enjoy traditional diner fare as well as more exotic creations, such as a chicken burger with pineapple salsa. Wash it down with a banana split.

The ★ **Elbow Room,** one block south of Granville Street (560 Davie St., 604/685-3628, 8am-3pm daily, lunch $8-14), is a Vancouver institution where portions are huge and the prices reasonable ($12 for the Lumberjack breakfast), but it's the service that you'll remember long after the meal. Feel like coffee? Get it yourself. A glass of water, maybe? "Get off your ass and get it yourself," a sign declares. The waiters take no nonsense, and the constant banter from the open kitchen, if not memorable, is at least unique. But it's all in good fun, and if you get abused you'll join a long list of celebrities whose photos adorn the walls. If you don't finish your meal, you must make a donation to a local charity; if it's a pancake you can't finish, you're advised to "just rub it on your thighs, because that's where it's going anyway!"

Pacific Northwest

At Gastown's busiest intersection, opposite the crowd-drawing steam clock, is ★ **Water Street Cafe** (300 Water St., 604/689-2832, 11:30am-11pm daily, $18-38), in the 1906 Edward Hotel. Unlike dining at most other Gastown eateries, you won't feel like you're in the touristy quarter of Vancouver. White linens, dark blue carpets, and lots of polished woodwork ooze style, while service is professional. Most important, the food is well priced and delicious, including many pasta dishes under $25.

Ensconced within the stylish Hyatt Regency Vancouver is the contemporary ★ **Mosaic Grille** (655 Burrard St., 604/639-4770, 6:30am-10pm daily, $23-45), which opens each morning with a healthy, well-prepared buffet, or choose from regional specialties such as Dungeness crab benedict and banana strawberry granola. In the evening, crab cannelloni and sweet corn bisque are both winners as starters. When it comes to a main, the choice is yours—from type of meat, portion size, and how it's cooked to accompanying starches and vegetables.

A few blocks north of the Hyatt Regency toward Burrard Inlet, sleek **Showcase** (1128 W. Hastings St., 604/639-4040, breakfast, lunch, and dinner daily, $19-35), at street level of the Vancouver Marriott Pinnacle, features floor-to-ceiling windows, contemporary styling, a split-level restaurant/bar layout, and a six-meter (20-foot) canvas hanging from the ceiling. Breakfast comprises all of the usual traditional North American choices ($30 for a full cooked breakfast, including coffee), but it's lunch and dinner that shine, with well-priced yet exotic dishes prepared using local seafood and game, simply and stylishly presented.

One of Vancouver's best restaurants is **Hawkesworth** (801 W. Georgia St., 604/673-7000, 6:30am-10:30am, 11:30am-2pm, and 5pm-10pm Mon.-Fri., 7am-2pm and 5pm-10pm Sat.-Sun., $44-52), owned and operated by David Hawkesworth, generally regarded as one of Canada's premier chefs. The elegant restaurant comprises four themed rooms at street level of the luxurious Rosewood Hotel Georgia. The setting, coupled with high-quality service, makes this a special place to dine. But it's the food that really shines—even the traditional cooked breakfast ($24). The rest of the day, it's classic presentations of west coast seafood and local game, or choose the tasting menu for $118 pp.

Seafood

Downtown Vancouver has a choice of upscale seafood restaurants, but nowhere to recommend serving simple fish-and-chips. If that's what you're after, head south to Granville Island.

One of Vancouver's finest seafood restaurants is ★ **YEW Seafood + Bar** (Four Seasons Hotel, 791 W. Georgia Ave.,

604/692-4939, 7am-2:30pm and 5pm-10pm daily, $32-52), a cavernous space within one of Vancouver's finest hotels. The casual decor is British Columbian all the way, while the menu swims with schools of piscatory pleasures. Wild salmon, papaya, and peanut salad is one of more than 20 appetizers, while traditionally prepared entrées, such as paella stuffed with the freshest local seafood, make up the main menu. The extensive wine list is especially strong on white wines—the perfect accompaniment for a feast of seafood.

At Canada Place is **Five Sails** (999 Canada Place, 604/844-2855, 5:30pm-10pm daily, $38-55), in the Pan Pacific Vancouver. The fabulous setting and harbor views are reflected in the prices. The menu features dishes originating in the chef's French homeland, but steers away from using the fusion techniques that are prevalent in many of Vancouver's better restaurants. For an appetizer, the Dungeness crab salad is an easy choice, while main dishes include roasted halibut char and olive-crusted rack of lamb.

Slick and chic, **Coast** (1054 Alberni St., 604/685-5010, 11am-11pm daily, $22-67) is a cavernous dining room that bristles with energy. It was formerly a warehouse, and the industrial feel has been softened with a light color scheme and modern furnishings. The menu of fresh seafood is a knockout from beginning to end: Start with clam chowder with smoked bacon, which comes with chunks of sourdough bread for dipping. Then move onto entrées such as tempura-battered halibut with aromatic spiced fries or one of the seasonal grill choices, which may include ahi tuna or wild salmon.

Steak

Steak lovers who feel like a splurge should consider **Gotham Steakhouse** (615 Seymour St., 604/605-8282, 11:30am-11pm Mon.-Fri., 4pm-11pm Sat.-Sun., $40-155). The cavernous room holding this restaurant is divided into a restaurant and a bar, meeting in the middle under a 13-meter-high (43-foot) arched ceiling. With furnishings of thick

leather seats, dark-colored hardwood tables, and plush velvet carpet, both sections exude the atmosphere of a private club. If the steak here isn't the best in Vancouver, servings are certainly the most generous, especially the signature dish, a $155 tomahawk ribeye, earning Gotham awards from city magazines such as the "Best Restaurant When Someone Else Is Paying."

European

La Pentola (322 Davie St., 604/642-0557, 7am-2pm and 5pm-10pm daily, $24-32), in the Opus Hotel, is a stylish, energetic bistro at the street level of Vancouver's hippest hotel. The northern Italian menu blends easily with the young money-to-burn crowd—and prices are not as outrageous as you may imagine. The lunch menu changes with the season, while à la carte choices include delicious osso buco.

Lupo (869 Hamilton St., 604/569-2535, 5pm-9pm Mon.-Fri., 5pm-9:30pm Sat.-Sun., $32-47) is extremely popular with those looking for contemporary Italian cooking in a stylish yet inviting setting. The breads and pastas are prepared daily, and Fraser River Valley produce such as free-range chicken is used whenever possible. The signature dish is roasted rack of lamb.

In Gastown, **L'Abattoir** (217 Carrall St., 604/568-1701, 10am-2pm Sat.-Sun., 5:30pm-10pm daily, $38-48) is within a historic building beside Blood Alley and has exposed wood beams and brick walls. The specialty is Canadian game and produce prepared and presently simply yet stylishly. Adding to the charm are generous portions.

Don't be put off by the address; **Salt Tasting Room** (45 Blood Alley, 604/633-6018, 4pm-11pm daily, $15) is another Gastown favorite. The concept is simple: choose between daily meat, cheese, and condiment choices to make up a charcuterie plate of your own choosing. There is no kitchen as such, just a tapas-style bar and long table in a historic Gastown space with exposed red-brick walls.

For Vancouver's finest French cuisine, go

to the small, intimate Le Crocodile (909 Burrard St., 604/669-4298, 11:30am-2:30pm Mon.-Fri., 5:30pm-10:30pm Mon.-Sat., $29-46), which has won innumerable awards over its three decades as one of Vancouver's premier restaurants. The smallish menu relies heavily on traditional French techniques, which shine through on appetizers (or *entrées*, as they are properly called at Le Crocodile), such as wild mushroom soup with truffle oil or frog legs sautéed in a chive butter sauce, and mains like roasted free-range chicken breast with shiitake mushroom risotto.

Japanese

Guu (375 Water St., 604/685-8682, 11:30am-11:30pm Mon.-Thurs., noon-midnight Fri.-Sat., noon-11:30pm Sun., $15-22) is a groovy Japanese restaurant with an energetic chef who oversees the needs of mostly young, always loud patrons. Known in Japan as *izakaya*-style dining, the atmosphere is informal, with a menu that encourages sharing. It's similar to a North American neighborhood pub, but instead of wings and nachos, choices include *harumaki* (spring rolls), *shiso age* (chicken and plum sauce wrapped in thin bread), and *maguro* (tuna with avocado and mango sauce).

CHINATOWN

Chinatown, east of downtown, centers on a three-block stretch of Main Street south of East Hastings Street. The precinct has lots of vendors selling fresh produce, as well as hole-in-the-wall places like Ba Le Sandwich Shop (638 Main St., 604/662-8108, 8am-6pm daily), with ridiculously inexpensive food to go.

Dining in Chinatown offers two distinct options: traditional eateries, where you'll find the locals, and the larger Westernized restaurants that attract non-Chinese and a younger Chinese crowd. A perfect combination of the two is Kent's Kitchen (232 Keefer St., 604/669-2237, 10:30am-7pm daily, $7-12), a modern café-style restaurant where the service is fast and efficient, the food freshly prepared, and the prices incredibly low. Two specialty dishes, rice, and a can of soda pop make a meal that costs just $10, with more unusual dishes such as pig's feet for $8, including rice. The most expensive combination is a large portion of shrimp and sweet-and-sour pork, which along with rice and soda pop is $12 (and could easily feed two people).

One of Chinatown's most popular restaurants is Phnom Penh (294 E. Georgia St., 604/682-5777, 10am-9pm Mon.-Thurs.,

Granville Island Market

10am-10pm Fri.-Sun., $8-16), an unremarkable dining room that is renowned for its delicious Cambodian-Vietnamese menu. English translations will help you choose a dish that suits your tastes—whether it's the signature crispy deep-fried chicken wings or something as adventurous as curried frog legs. No reservations are taken, and there's usually a lineup for a table.

Tiny **Gain Wah Restaurant** (218 Keefer St., 604/684-1740, 10am-11pm Tues.-Sun., $6-12) is typical of the many hundreds of noodle houses found in Hong Kong. The restaurant is best noted for congee, a simple soup extracted from boiling rice. A bowl of congee costs $2, with flavorings an additional $0.50-2. On the main menu, no dish except those containing seafood is over $10. The friendly staff is willing to describe the more unfamiliar dishes.

Uphill from Gain Wah, past the aforementioned Kent's Kitchen, **Oyster Express** (296 Keefer St., 604/684-3300, 5pm-10pm Tues.-Sat.) is another small space, but without Asian influence. A blackboard menu of oysters from around the world allows diners to order and taste the difference in varieties, including many local choices. Most oysters are in the $3-4 range, but at least one variety each night is sold for under $2. A 5pm-7pm daily happy hours also keeps costs down.

If I'm looking for street parking around Chinatown, I always head first to Gore Street, one block east of Main Street, and here you'll find **Roost Café** (789 Gore St., 778/953-1575, 7am-3pm Tues., 7am-10pm Wed.-Fri., 9am-11pm Sat., 7am-3pm Sun., breakfasts $9-16), a bright, simply decorated room with a few tables along the sidewalk. The draw is a combination of quality coffee and creative and well-presented breakfasts, such as avocado toast topped with pickled vegetables.

On the northern edge of Chinatown is the **Ovaltine Café** (251 E. Hastings St., 604/685-7021, 8am-11pm Mon.-Thurs., 8am-midnight Fri.-Sat., 8am-3pm Sun., $5-9), easily spotted by the classic neon sign hanging out front. This relic from the past is in a horrible part of the city, but if you can brave the unnerving crowd on the street out front, once inside you'll find a classic diner that has been serving up cheap chow since 1942.

GRANVILLE ISLAND
Market

Granville Island Market (Johnston St., 9am-7pm daily) bustles with locals and visitors alike throughout the day. In the tradition of similar European markets, shopping here is an unpretentious and practical affair, with lots of talking, poking, and inquiring at stalls selling fresh meats, seafood, fruit and vegetables, and cheeses and at specialty stalls stocked with prepackaged goodies to go. It is difficult to go past the **Stock Market** (604/687-2433, 8am-7pm daily, $6-8.50) when recommending a stall to grab lunch. Specializing in soups and broths to take home, a couple of soups are served steaming hot each day (try anything with wild salmon; you're in for a real treat).

Seafood

In the name of research, I have tried fish-and-chips at every place that sells it on Granville Island. My advice? Give the outlets within Granville Island Market a wide berth and search out **Tony's Fish and Oyster Cafe** (1511 Anderson St., 604/683-7127, 11:30am-8pm Wed.-Mon., $10-21), where the fish is fresh and the batter perfectly prepared. Two pieces of cod and chips is $13, but I'd suggest upgrading to the halibut (one piece and chips for $13). You can also order fish tacos, local oysters, or clam chowder. There are only around 20 seats in the café, but you can also order to go. Tony's is right at the entrance to Granville Island, on the left as you enter by road. Similarly, the emphasis at **Go Fish** (1505 W. 1st Ave., 604/730-5040, 11:30am-7pm Tues.-Fri., noon-7pm Sat.-Sun., $9-20) is on the very freshest seafood at reasonable prices. It's a takeout-only place, with a few outdoor seats, and often a lineup, so expect to wait for your order. To get here, walk off the island and take the harborside promenade to the right.

You'll pay more for a meal at the following two places, but the trade-off is that they are restaurants, with more seating and extensive menus. The distinctive yellow building on Granville Island's northern tip is **Bridges** (1696 Duranleau St., 604/687-4400, 11am-midnight daily, mains $18-25). With stunning water views, the restaurant's outside, absolute-waterfront eating area is very popular. The outside menu features typical wide-ranging bistro-style fare of hamburgers, salads, and pastas, as well as basic seafood dishes such as a platter to share for $38. The food is nothing special, but the views are unbeatable and the service professional. Inside, the bistro offers a similar menu, or eat in the upstairs dining room (dinner daily, mains $28-38), which is more formal and is open nightly for a seafood-oriented menu.

Under the Granville Street Bridge, **Sandbar** (1535 Johnston St., 604/669-9030, 11:30am-10:30pm daily, $16-42) is well worth searching out. Downstairs features an open kitchen and water views, a world away from the hustle and bustle of the nearby marketplace. The upstairs room features a private deck complete with its own elevated waterfront bar. The menu comprises mostly seafood, all reasonably priced.

Pacific Institute of Culinary Arts

★ **Bistro 101** (1505 W. 2nd Ave., 604/734-0101, 11:30am-1:15pm and 6pm-8:30pm Mon.-Fri.), within the Pacific Institute of Culinary Arts, by the entrance to Granville Island, is renowned for its state-of-the-art facilities and world-class teachers led by chef Julian Bond. Cuisine prepared by these budding chefs is served to the public in the institute's 50-seat dining room. The quality of the food is impossible to fault, and its presentation is also impeccable. The three-course set lunch ($23) and dinner ($35) are a bargain, and on the first Friday of every month it's an extravagant west coast seafood lunch ($28) and dinner ($38) buffet. Desserts and pastries produced by the institute's bakery classes are also tempting and are offered at the café-style bakery (9am-5pm Mon.-Sat.).

ROBSON STREET AND THE WEST END
Cafés and Coffeehouses

It's been said that Vancouver is addicted to coffee, and walking along Robson Street, it would be hard to disagree. The street harbors multiple outlets of the main coffeehouse chains, including six **Starbucks** (of 100 city-wide) and four of the city's 40-plus **Blenz** outlets. Another local chain is **JJ Bean,** which has grown since the 1990s to have cafés across the city, including one just off Robson Street (1188 Alberni St., 604/254-3724, 6am-8pm Mon.-Fri., 7am-8pm Sat.-Sun.) and another deep in the West End (1209 Bidwell St., 604/563-2439, 6am-8pm daily). JJ Bean's success is simple: pouring excellent coffee, with beans roasted daily, in a comfortable setting.

Breka Downtown (818 Bute St., 604/620-8200) is half a block off busy Robson Street. It's open 24 hours daily and is always busy—so much so that patrons often need to take a number and wait for service. The coffee is great, as are the freshly baked muffins and European-style breads. Salads and healthy sandwiches are also available.

At the west end of Robson Street, **Whole Foods Market** (1675 Robson St., 604/687-5288, 7:30am-10:30pm daily) is a cavernous store selling groceries and premade meals for the health-conscious. Whole Foods Market also has an in-house bakery, a deli, and a juice bar.

If you're hanging out on English Bay and looking to take a break from the beach, search out your favorite flavors from the strip of sidewalk eateries along the south end of Denman Street. At **Delany's** (1105 Denman St., 604/662-3344, 6am-7pm Mon.-Fri., 6:30am-7pm Sat.-Sun., lunch $6.50-10), part of a small local coffeehouse chain, the emphasis on fine coffee but you can also order the usual array of sandwiches and wraps. Kitty-corner to Delany's you'll find the unusual mix of excellent coffee and Taiwanese street food at **3 Quarters Full** (1789 Comox St., 778/865-5598, 9am-6pm Sun.-Thurs., 9am-8pm Fri.-Sat., lunch $9-13), which also offers a wide selection of sweet treats, including a

Taiwanese version of a cake roll and delicious cheesecake.

Seafood

Half a block off Robson, ★ **Joe Fortes** (777 Thurlow St., 604/669-1940, 11am-11pm daily, $26-50) is named after one of Vancouver's best-loved heroes, a Caribbean-born swimming coach and lifeguard at English Bay. This restaurant is a city institution and is always busy with the young and beautiful set. The comfortable interior offers elegant furnishings, bleached-linen tablecloths, a rooftop patio, and an oyster bar where you can relax while waiting for your table. Of the grilled fish on offer, try something different, like the delicately textured black cod or Arctic char, caught in Canada's northern waters. In warmer weather, request a table on the patio.

The outdoor seats at **Beach Bay Café and Patio** (1193 Denman St., 604/685-7337, noon-9pm Mon.-Thurs., noon-10pm Fri., 10am-10pm Sat., 10am-9pm Sun., $18-33) are the perfect place to dine on seafood such as steamed Salt Spring Island mussels followed by baked halibut, although many of the indoor tables at this minimalistic restaurant also have water views.

European

Self-described as a "dignified spaghetti joint," **Zefferelli's** (1136 Robson St., 604/687-0655, 11:30am-10pm Mon.-Fri., 5pm-10pm Sat.-Sun., $17-27) dishes up simple Italian fare in a stylish room featuring a wine rack along one entire wall.

One block west of Zefferelli's, and named for a traditional Italian toast, **CinCin** (1154 Robson St., 604/688-7338, 5pm-11pm daily, $16.50-37) is a Mediterranean-style restaurant with an extremely loyal local following. The centerpiece of the dining room is a large open kitchen, with a wood-fired oven and a rotisserie in view of diners. The heated terrace fills up quickly and is the place to watch the Robson Street action from above. The specialty is gourmet pizza, but the oven is also used to cook seasonal dishes like rack of lamb broiled in a rosemary marinade.

The atmosphere at **Tavola** (1829 Robson St., 604/606-4680, from 5pm daily, $16-28) is inviting and cozy, and the service is faultless, but the hearty Italian cooking is what really shines: The antipastos are delicious and the pastas and sauces are made from scratch in-house.

Indian

A Taste of India (1282 Robson St., 604/682-3894, 11am-midnight daily, $13-16) stands out along this strip of fashionable boutiques and trendy cafés. The decor—complete with plastic flowers—is nothing to write home about, but this restaurant is worth visiting for its wide selection of traditional Indian dishes at reasonable prices, including a classic made-from-scratch butter chicken for just $16.

STANLEY PARK

The simplest way to enjoy a meal in Stanley Park is by having a picnic—smoked salmon, a selection of cheeses, a loaf of sourdough bread—you know the drill. But for something a little more formal, three restaurants are all excellent alternatives.

The least expensive place to eat in Stanley Park is **Prospect Point Bar & Grill** (5601 Stanley Park Dr., 604/669-2737, 11am-6pm daily summer, shorter hours fall-spring, $15-18), near the south end of Lions Gate Bridge, with a large deck with over 100 seats, from which views extend across busy Burrard Inlet to the North Shore and beyond to the mountains. Fish-and-chips is the specialty, but you can also order dishes such as seafood spaghetti and a salmon burger. During the daily 3pm to 5pm happy hours, some drinks are $5 and starters are two for one. Off to one side is an ice cream outlet, or just stop by for a coffee.

Between Second and Third Beaches is the ★ **Teahouse in Stanley Park** (Ferguson Point, 604/669-3281, 11:30am-10pm Mon.-Fri., 10:30am-10pm Sat.-Sun., $22-42). Originally built as an officers' mess, the building of today contains an intimate restaurant of connected rooms with bright, elegant surroundings set among towering trees. Healthy, contemporary cooking is the order of the day. Look for starters such as carrot and ginger soup, dishes to share such as a smoked-salmon tasting board, and mains like sesame-crusted BC tuna.

KITSILANO AND VICINITY

The main concentration of restaurants on the south side of False Creek is in Kitsilano, along West 4th Avenue between Burrard and Vine Streets. This part of the city was the heart of hippiedom in the 1970s, and while most restaurants from that era are long gone, a few remain, and other, newer additions to the local dining scene reflect that period of the city's history.

Cafés and Healthy Eats

A standout in the local café scene is **The Only Cafe** (2678 W. 4th Ave., 778/379-3299, 10am-6pm Mon., 7:30am-8pm Tues.-Sat., 10am-8pm Sun.), where the emphasis is on just one thing—the very best coffee. Information is given about each bean, and options include traditional drip, European espresso, Australian flat white, and for true connoisseur, siphon coffee (the Royal Belgium Pot is the ultimate siphon coffee experience).

Retro-hip **Sophie's Cosmic Café** (2095 W. 4th Ave., at Arbutus St., 604/732-6810, 8am-2:30pm Mon.-Tues., 8am-8pm Wed.-Sun., $11-14) typifies the scene, with a definite cosmic look, but also provides a good value and fast, efficient service. Standard bacon and eggs is $9, and omelets are around $12. The rest of the day, check the blackboard above the food-service window for dishes such as a nut and herb burger ($14).

Whole Foods Market (2285 W. 4th Ave., 604/739-6676, 8am-10pm daily) is a large grocery-style store crammed with natural and organic foods. Off to one side is the Gourmet Deli & Bakery, with its own courtyard patio, where you can fill up at the salad bar or order anything from muffins to smoked salmon wraps.

A few blocks south of West 4th Avenue is West Broadway, where there are many more cafés, but they are more spread out. One of the best for coffee-lovers is **Pallet Coffee Roasters** (2002 W. Broadway, 604/736-2687, 7am-7pm Mon.-Fri., 8am-6pm Sat.-Sun., lunch $9-11), a slick space with quality coffee and small portions of healthy breakfasts and lunches, like avocado bruschetta.

Vegetarian

A throwback to the hippie era of the 1960s is ★ **Naam** (2724 W. 4th Ave., 604/738-7151, 24 hours daily, $10-14), at Stephens Street, a particularly good natural-food restaurant in a renovated two-story private residence. Naam boasts large servings, excellent service, and an easygoing atmosphere that has become legendary.

French

The much-lauded **Bishop's** (2183 W. 4th Ave., 604/738-2025, 5:30pm-10pm Tues.-Sun., $35-45) is very French in all respects. Owner and longtime Vancouver restaurateur John Bishop makes all diners feel special, personally greeting them at the door, escorting them to their table, and then describing the menu and wine list as required. Elegant surroundings, parched-white linen, and soft jazz background music complete the picture. The menu features French classics but changes as seasonal produce becomes available, such as salmon and halibut, Fraser River Valley vegetables, and fruits from the Okanagan Valley.

Bistro Pastis (2153 W. 4th Ave., 604/731-5020, 11:30am-2pm and 5:30pm-10pm daily, $22-40) is a modern yet casual city-style French bistro. Classic French main courses (don't dare call them "entrées" at this very French restaurant) change with the season. Wines offered are almost exclusively French.

Mexican

At Maple Street, **Las Margaritas** (1999 W. 4th Ave., 604/734-7117, 11:30am-10pm daily,

$14-20) boasts, "Mild or wild, we can add all the octane you wish." The decor is California-style south-of-the-border: white stucco walls, Mexican hats, a tile floor, tile-topped tables, and an outdoor deck. Throw back a couple of margaritas with your meal for the full effect. Farther west, near McDonald Street, **Topanga Cafe** (2904 W. 4th Ave., 604/733-3713, 11:30am-10pm Mon.-Sat., 3pm-8pm Sun., $12-24.50) also offers inexpensive California-style Mexican dishes in a home-style atmosphere.

Indian

Five blocks south of West Broadway is ★ **Vij's** (3106 Cambie St., 604/736-6664, from 5:30pm daily, $26-35), one of Vancouver's most acclaimed Asian restaurants. Vikram Vij, the owner, is a master at combining the intense flavors of his India homeland with the tastes of his Vancouver customers, thereby creating a unique menu that appeals to everyone. Presentation and service are of the highest standard, but the food really makes this restaurant stand out. No reservations are taken, and getting a table often involves waiting in the restaurant's lounge, which says something about a place in a nondescript building within a few blocks of a kilometer-long strip of other restaurants.

NORTH SHORE

If you've crossed Burrard Inlet on the SeaBus, visit **Lonsdale Market** (123 Carrie Cates Court, 9am-7pm daily) for around 80 shops and vendors, some selling local produce seafood fresh from the trawlers.

The pick of spots for breakfast or lunch in suburban West Vancouver, west of Lonsdale Quay and the Lions Gate Bridge, is **Savary Island Pie Company** (1533 Marine Dr., 604/926-4021, 6am-7pm daily, lunch $8-14). Join the line at this super-popular café and order a slice of focaccia pizza or a generous slab of chicken potpie, saving room for an oatmeal cookie or brownie.

Seafood

On the north side of Burrard Inlet, ★ **Salmon House on the Hill** (2229 Folkstone Way, West Vancouver, 604/926-3212, 5pm-10pm Mon.-Fri., 10:30am-2:30pm and 5pm-10pm Sat.-Sun., $29-45) offers a relaxed atmosphere while providing panoramic views across Burrard Inlet to Stanley Park and the city center from its elevated mountainside location. The cavernous interior is full of First Nations arts and crafts, including a dugout canoe suspended over the main dining area. For an appetizer, the seafood chowder is my recommendation. It's not a huge serving, but it is thick and delicious. The house specialty of salmon barbecued over an open-flame alderwood-fired grill is hard to pass up as a main. To get there, take the 21st Street exit off Upper Levels Highway to Folkstone Way, and turn left on Ski Lift Road.

Accommodations

Whether you're looking for a luxurious room in a high-rise hotel or a downtown dorm, Vancouver has accommodations to suit all budgets. Downtown hotel room rates fluctuate greatly depending on supply and demand, much more so than bed-and-breakfasts and motels in suburban locations. In Vancouver, demand is highest in summer and on weekdays, so if you're looking to save a few bucks, plan on being in town in the cooler months (May and September are my favorite times to be in Vancouver), or stay at a business hotel as part of a weekend package. The prices quoted below are **rack rates.** The vast majority of guests do not pay rack rates, especially at the larger chains. For example, while researching pricing for this edition, most of the properties listed below as charging $200-300 were offering rooms closer to $150 outside summer, and the Four Seasons was discounting rooms by 40 percent year-round just for booking 30 days in advance.

One word of warning: If you plan to have a vehicle, prepare yourself for parking fees up to $35 per day in the downtown area. Ask if weekend rates include free parking—they often do. The following recommendations reflect my favorites in various price categories throughout the city. You won't find every downtown hotel mentioned here, and outside downtown, only convenient and good-value choices are included.

DOWNTOWN
$50-100

As you may imagine, the only downtown accommodations in this price range are backpacker lodges. For those on a budget, they are a great way to stay in the heart of the action and to mingle with like-minded travelers from around the world.

HI-Vancouver Downtown (1114 Burnaby St., 604/684-4565, www.hihostels.ca, dorm members $37, nonmembers $43, private room $96-112 s or d) is typical of the new-look facilities operated by Hostelling International, the world's largest and longest-running network of backpacker accommodations. The complex offers a large kitchen, a library, a game room, public Internet access, a travel agency, bike rentals, bag storage, and laundry. The dormitories hold a maximum of four beds but are small. Rates include a light breakfast and wireless Internet.

HI-Vancouver Central (1025 Granville St., 604/685-5335, www.hihostels.ca, dorm members $39-49, nonmembers $43-54, private room $99-137 s or d) is renovated hotel complete with its own downstairs bar. As you'd expect, it's more of a party atmosphere than the HI hostel on Burnaby Street, and a *lot* more so than the hostel at Jericho Beach in Kitsilano.

Privately owned backpacker lodges in Vancouver come and go with predictable regularity. Many should be avoided. One

exception is **Samesun Vancouver** (1018 Granville St., 604/682-8226 or 877/972-6378, www.samesun.com, dorm $36, $96-110 s or d), which is excellent in all respects. Typical of inner-city hostels the world over, rooms in this old four-story building are small, but each has been tastefully decorated, and the communal lounge and kitchen areas serve guests well. Other facilities include a separate TV room and a rooftop patio.

C&N Backpackers (927 Main St., 604/682-2441 or 888/434-6060, www.cnn-backpackers.com, dorm $30, $80 s or d) has undergone some improvements in recent years, but conditions are still sparse. There's a sink in every dorm room and other bath facilities on every floor. The location is central to Pacific Central Station, but the neighborhood is among the worst in the city after dark.

Dating to the mid-1990s, the **YWCA** (733 Beatty St., 604/895-5830 or 800/663-1424, www.ywcahotel.com, $86-96 s, $98-143 d) is popular with those who don't want to spend a fortune on accommodations but don't like the "backpacker scene" at regular hostels. It's a few blocks from Vancouver's business core, but the modern facilities and choice of nearby restaurants more than compensate for the walk. More than 150 rooms are spread over 11 stories. Each room has a telephone, and the private rooms have televisions. Communal facilities include two kitchens, three lounges, and two laundries. Guests also have use of the nearby YWCA Health and Wellness Centre, which houses a pool and gym. The least expensive rooms share a bath.

$100-150

Rack rates in this price range remain in the domain of older hotels—mostly bad—but check major booking engines and you may find some of the mid-range chains discounted to $150. Outside summer, spending $100-150 per night will also get you a room in one of the older downtown motels, such as the **Comfort Inn Downtown** (654 Nelson St., 604/605-4333, www.comfortinndowntown.com).

$150-200

Of the older hotels, the ★ **Victorian Hotel** (514 Homer St., 604/681-6369 or 877/681-6369, www.victorianhotel.ca, $194-324 s or d) is one of the best choices. Guest rooms have only basic amenities, but they are comfortably furnished and light on the wallet. The central location and complimentary breakfast make them an even better value. Built as a guesthouse in 1898, the Victorian has rooms decorated in a regal color scheme, which complements the polished hardwood floors. Rooms that share baths are the least expensive, while those with en suite baths have lovely bay windows. Rates drop by around 20 percent outside summer.

$250-300

Least expensive of the central business district hotels is **Days Inn Vancouver Downtown** (921 W. Pender St., 604/681-4335 or 877/681-4335, www.daysinnvancouver.com, $259-349 s or d). The 85 rooms are small, and surrounding high-rises block any views. But each room is decorated in bright and breezy pastel colors, wireless Internet is free, and coffeemakers are provided; there's also an in-house restaurant and valet parking.

Although guest facilities at **Ramada Inn & Suites Downtown Vancouver** (435 W. Pender St., 604/488-1088 or 888/389-5888, www.ramadadowntownvancouver.com, $269-299 s or d) are limited compared to other properties in this price category, like the Days Inn, its location is central. As an old hotel, its 80 rooms are small, but they are well appointed and come with everything from blow-dryers to free wireless Internet.

Best Western Plus Chateau Granville (1100 Granville St., 604/669-7070 or 800/663-6575, www.chateaugranville.com, $255-325 s or d) is a good 10-minute walk from the Burrard Inlet waterfront, but has spacious, well-decorated rooms, many with balconies, as well as a restaurant and underground parking.

Two blocks closer to downtown is the seven-story, 245-room **Holiday Inn Hotel and Suites Vancouver Downtown** (1110 Howe St., 604/684-2151 or 800/663-9151, www.ihg.com, $260-600 s or d), featuring an indoor pool, a day spa, a kids' play room, a lounge, a café, and a restaurant. The guest rooms come in a variety of configurations, but all are well equipped, and as at Holiday Inns the world over, children stay and eat for free.

A colorful paint job and bright fabrics can do a lot to reinvent an old hotel, and you won't find a better example than the centrally located 110-room **Howard Johnson Hotel Downtown** (1176 Granville St., 604/688-8701 or 888/654-6336, www.hojovancouver.com, $262-322 s or d). The main downsides are thin walls.

The best reason to stay at the contemporary ★ **Century Plaza Hotel & Spa** (1015 Burrard St., 604/687-0575 or 800/663-1818, www.century-plaza.com, $269-329 s or d) is the Absolute Spa, a favorite haunt of movie stars working on location in Vancouver. Each of the 236 kitchen-equipped rooms is comfortable, but not as opulent as the spa facility. Other amenities include a café, a restaurant specializing in seafood and local produce, and a lounge. Decent weekly rates and spa packages are also available.

Over $300

Although not right downtown, modern ★ **Sunset Inn & Suites** (1111 Burnaby St., 604/688-2474 or 800/786-1997, www.sunsetinn.com, $309-409 s or d) provides excellent value just three blocks from Sunset Beach and English Bay. Each welcoming unit has a full kitchen, a balcony, a large screen TV, free wireless Internet, and a super-comfortable bed. Other pluses include free local calls, free parking, a light breakfast served daily in the lobby, laundry, and a fitness room. The more expensive units have separate bedrooms.

Generally regarded as one of the world's hippest hotels and last renovated in 2013, the ★ **Opus Hotel** (322 Davie St., Yaletown, 604/642-6787 or 866/642-6787, www.opushotel.com, $509-809 s or d) fills a distinct niche in the Vancouver scene as a mega-cool place to stay. This means vibrant colors, striking decor, clean-lined furnishings, 250-count linens, 27-inch flat-screen TVs, iPads, luxurious baths filled with top-notch bath products, valet-only parking, and upscale dining and drinking off the brightly minimalist lobby. Rooms are decorated in distinct themes and come in a variety of configurations, including one daring layout with the bath on the floor-to-ceiling windowed outer wall.

Delta Hotels and Resorts, Canada's largest chain of upscale hotels, has two downtown Vancouver properties, including **Delta Hotels by Marriott Vancouver Downtown Suites** (550 W. Hastings St., 604/689-8188 or 888/663-8811, www.marriott.com, $539-639 s or d), in the heart of downtown. None of the 225 suites is equipped with a kitchen, but each is spacious and has a separate bedroom and comfortable lounge area. Other guest facilities include a health club, an indoor pool, saunas and a whirlpool, and a street-level New York-style restaurant open for breakfast, lunch, and dinner.

Drawing a mix of upscale business travelers and international vacationers, the **Vancouver Marriott Pinnacle** (1128 W. Hastings St., 604/684-1128 or 800/207-4150, www.marriott.com, $569-964 s or d) is an excellent choice in the downtown core. This full-service property features 434 spacious rooms, each with stylish furniture, elegant baths, a writing desk full of office supplies, two telephones with voicemail, a coffeemaker, ironing facilities, and also an umbrella for Vancouver's occasional rainy days. Guests also enjoy complimentary use of the hotel's health club, which features a 17-meter (60-foot) indoor pool, a hot tub, a sauna, and a large outdoor patio area.

One block from the city end of Robson Street is the super-luxurious European-style ★ **Sutton Place Hotel** (845 Burrard St., 604/682-5511 or 866/378-8866, www.suttonplace.com, $670-930 s or d), one of only a handful of properties in North America to get a precious five-diamond rating from the American Automobile Association. This, Vancouver's most elegant lodging, features original European artwork in public areas and reproductions in the 396 rooms and suites. Rooms are furnished with king beds, plush bathrobes, ice dispensers, and two phone lines, and guests enjoy a twice-daily maid service, complete with fresh flowers. Vida Spa is an in-house fitness and health facility in the tradition of a luxurious European spa resort. Other facilities include a glass-enclosed pool, a business center, an English club-style lounge bar, and Boulevard Kitchen & Oyster Bar, an upmarket restaurant. Discounted weekend and off-season rates are around $300.

For all of the modern conveniences along with unbeatable city and harbor views, head for the sparkling **Pan Pacific Hotel Vancouver** (Canada Place, 604/662-8111 or 800/937-1515, www.panpacific.com, from $819 s or d). It garners a five-diamond rating from the American Automobile Association and is generally regarded as one of the world's top 100 hotels. It's part of the landmark Canada Place (the top 8 floors of the 13-story complex are guest rooms), whose Teflon sails fly over busy, bustling sidewalks and a constant flow of cruise ships. Each of the 504 spacious rooms boasts stunning views, contemporary furnishings, and a luxurious marble bath. Facilities include an outdoor swimming pool, a fitness room, Five Sails Restaurant, and the summer-only Patio Terrace, from where outstanding views extend across the water to Stanley Park.

Four Seasons Hotel (791 W. Georgia St., 604/689-9333 or 800/819-5053, www.fourseasons.com, $830-1,130 s or d) offers 372 luxuriously appointed guest rooms, with guests enjoying fresh flowers, a wide range of in-room amenities, and twice-daily housekeeping. Other guest facilities include an indoor-outdoor pool complex, a business center, and various eating establishments, including casual dining in a plant-filled atrium and the grandiose YEW restaurant. Somewhat surprisingly, the Four Seasons is kid-friendly, with children supplied with teddy bears and mini bathrobes.

Fairmont Hotels and Resorts, best known for landmark accommodations such as the Fairmont Banff Springs in Alberta, operates three properties in the downtown area. Most spectacular and newest is **Fairmont Pacific Rim** (1038 Canada Place, 604/695-5300 or 800/257-7544, www.fairmont.com, $1,350-2,300 s or d), across the road from the Vancouver Convention Centre and Burrard Inlet. Opening just prior to the 2010 Winter Olympic Games, the property boasts 377 rooms, many with sweeping views extending across the water to the North Shore Mountains. The rooms have an elegant yet earthy feel, while being outfitted with luxuries such as marble baths. Other amenities include spa services and three dining areas.

The copper-roofed **Fairmont Hotel Vancouver** (900 W. Georgia St., 604/684-3131 or 800/257-7544, www.fairmont.com, $1,000-1,300 s or d) is a downtown landmark—you can't help but notice the distinctive green copper roof, the gargoyles, and the classic Gothic château-style architecture of this grande dame. Today, with its former glory restored, the Hotel Vancouver is one of Canada's grandest accommodations, from the cavernous marble-lined lobby to the high ceilings and 556 elegantly furnished rooms. Facilities include restaurants, a comfortable lounge, an indoor pool, saunas, a weight room, health facilities, 24-hour room service, ample parking, and a large staff to attend to your every whim.

You'll be knocked out by the views at the **Fairmont Waterfront** (900 Canada Place Way, 604/691-1991 or 800/257-7544, www.fairmont.com, $1,100-1,800 s or d) rising 23 stories from beside Canada Place. The 489 rooms are all spacious, and more than half of them enjoy stunning harbor views. Guest facilities include a third-floor health club and outdoor pool, and rooms are equipped with luxurious bathrobes, a work desk, and remote checkout.

CHINATOWN
$50-100

The location of the 1914 **Budget Inn Patricia Hotel** (403 E. Hastings St., 604/255-4301, www.patriciahotel.ca, $80-159 s or d) isn't the best—it's separated from downtown by infamous East Hastings Street—but the price is right, parking is free, and downstairs is a popular pub with in-house brewery and decent food. Rooms are available in a variety of configurations; the smallest rooms share baths, while larger rooms come with basic baths and queen beds.

GRANVILLE ISLAND
Over $300

The only lodging on this bustling shopping and dining precinct south of downtown is the **Granville Island Hotel** (1253 Johnston St., 604/683-7373 or 800/663-1840, www.granvilleislandhotel.com, $399-469 s or d) enjoys a fabulous location on the island of the same name immediately south of downtown. The hotel is designed to attract a young, hip clientele. Contemporary and elegant, the rooms are spacious and furnished with Persian rugs, marble-floored baths, and modern necessities.

ROBSON STREET AND THE WEST END

Robson Street and the West End—with their sidewalk cafés, restaurants open until the wee hours, and fashionable boutiques—provides a great alternative to staying right downtown.

$50-100

A hostel for grown-ups, the three-story **Buchan Hotel** (1906 Haro St., 604/685-5354 or 800/668-6654, www.buchanhotel.com, $99-174 s or d) is in a quiet residential area one block from Stanley Park. It was built as an apartment hotel in 1926, and the atmosphere today is friendly, especially in the evenings, when guests gather in the main lounge. On the downside, the 61 guest rooms are small and sparsely decorated, and some share baths.

$100-150

Built in the 1920s, the European-style **Barclay Hotel** (1348 Robson St., 604/688-8850, www.barclayhotel.com, $89-209 s, $119-209 d) has 80 medium-size air-conditioned guest rooms, a small lounge, and an intimate restaurant. Renovated in 2017, the rooms are stylish in a slightly old-fashioned way; each holds a comfortable bed, a writing desk, couch, and a small wall-mounted television.

$150-200

The **Greenbrier Hotel** (1393 Robson St., 604/683-4558 or 888/355-5888, www.greenbrierhotel.com, $180-240 s or d) looks a bit rough on the outside, but each of the 33 units was refurbished for the 2010 Winter Olympic Games, and each has a large living area, flat-screen TV, and separate bedroom. Some rooms have a microwave and fridge, while others have a full kitchen. This three-story building has no elevator.

Overlooking English Bay and the closest beach to downtown, the old-style funky ★ **Sylvia Hotel** (1154 Gilford St., 604/681-9321 or 877/681-9321, www.sylviahotel.com, $199-279 s or d) is a local landmark sporting a brick and terra-cotta exterior covered with Virginia creeper vine. Built in 1912 as an apartment building, the eight-story Sylvia was the tallest building on this side of town until 1958. Today, it's popular with budget travelers looking for something a little nicer than a hostel (although the less expensive rooms are fairly small). The more expensive rooms feature fantastic views of English Bay, separate bedrooms, and full kitchens.

$250-300

In the heart of bustling Robson Street is the 214-room **Blue Horizon Hotel** (1225 Robson St., 604/688-1411 or 800/663-1333, www.bluehorizonhotel.com, $299-359 s or d). Facilities include an indoor lap pool, a fitness room, a sauna, and services for business travelers. The hotel is also home to the popular Inlets Bistro and a sidewalk café. All 214 rooms are large, brightly lit, and have a work desk, coffee-making facilities, wireless Internet, and an in-room safe. One quirk of the layout is that every room is a corner room, some with private balconies. To take advantage of this, request a room on floors 15-30.

Over $300

Listel Hotel Vancouver (1300 Robson St., 604/684-8461 or 800/663-5491, www.thelistelhotel.com, $305-370 s or d) is an elegant full-service lodging best known for its innovative use of original and limited-edition Northwest Coast artwork in many of the 130 rooms. Rooms are well appointed and highlighted by contemporary furnishings, goose-down duvets, and luxurious baths.

Coast Plaza Hotel & Suites (1763 Comox St., 604/688-7711 or 800/716-6199, www.coasthotels.com, from $345 s or d) is part of a mid-priced Pacific Northwest hotel chain. A couple of blocks from English Bay and surrounded by good dining choices, this full-service hotel comes with 267 rooms on 35 levels. As a former apartment tower, its rooms are spacious; all have balconies and most have kitchens. Amenities include a fitness center, an indoor pool, room service, a bistro (from 6:30am daily), and a lounge. Look for discounts of over 50 percent outside summer. (If you're traveling extensively in British Columbia, consider the Coast Hotels frequent traveler program—it's free to join and offers a variety of discounts.)

Built at the turn of the 20th century, public areas of the **West End Guest House** (1362 Haro St., 604/681-2889 or 888/546-3327, www.westendguesthouse.com, $350-430 s or d, includes breakfast) are decorated with photographs of early Vancouver and the Klondike gold rush taken by the original owners. The property has been lovingly refurbished in Victorian-era colors and furnished with stylish antiques to retain its original charm. Each of the seven guest rooms has a brass bed complete with cotton linens and a goose-down duvet, an en suite bath, a television, and a telephone. Guests can relax either in the comfortable lounge or on the outdoor terrace and have the use of bikes.

Families will especially like **Rosellen Suites at Stanley Park** (2030 Barclay St., 604/689-4807 or 888/317-6648, www.rosellen-suites.com, from $399 s or d), in a residential area right by Stanley Park. Each of the 30 extra-spacious units features modern furnishings, a separate living and dining area, a full kitchen, and modern conveniences such as personalized voicemail. Rates include access to a nearby fitness facility and indoor pool.

The 509-room **Westin Bayshore** (1601 W. Georgia St., 604/682-3377 or 888/625-5144, www.westinbayshore.com, from $520 s or d) is unique within the downtown peninsula in that it offers a distinctive resort-style atmosphere—the perfect haunt for families who are willing to pay for a prime location. Lying right on Coal Harbour and linked to Stanley Park by a waterfront promenade, it has undergone massive renovations since the infamous recluse Howard Hughes spent four months in his Westin suite in 1971. The hotel now features a large outdoor pool surrounded by outdoor furniture settings as well as a poolside lounge, a health club, and a yacht charter operation at the marina.

KITSILANO AND VICINITY
$50-100

If you're on a budget, visiting in summer, and don't need to stay right downtown, **HI-Vancouver Jericho Beach** (1515 Discovery St., Point Grey, 604/224-3208 or 866/762-4122, www.hihostels.ca, May-Sept., dorm $37, private room $95-145 s or d) is a good alternative choice. The location is fantastic—in scenic and safe parkland behind Jericho Beach, across English Bay from downtown, and linked to extensive biking and walking trails. Inside the huge white building are separate dorms for men and women, rooms for couples and families, a TV room, and a communal kitchen. Additional amenities include a large café operated by a local culinary school and bike rentals. To get here, take Northwest

Marine Drive off 4th Avenue West and turn right down Discovery Street.

NORTH SHORE
$150-200

Perfect as a jumping-off point for a ferry trip to the Sunshine Coast or Vancouver Island is the **Horseshoe Bay Motel** (6588 Royal Ave., 604/921-7454, www.horseshoebaymotel.ca, $158-178 s or d), 12 kilometers (7.5 miles) west of the Lions Gate Bridge, tucked below the highway in Horseshoe Bay and right by the BC Ferries terminal. Rooms are clean and comfortable, but you're paying for the location more than anything.

Gracious **Thistledown House** (3910 Capilano Rd., North Vancouver, 604/986-7173 or 888/633-7173, www.thistle-down.com, $195-295 s or d) has been restored to resemble a country-style inn. Each of the five guest rooms has been tastefully decorated and has its own character, a private bath and balcony, and many delightful touches, such as homemade soap. If you're going to splurge, request the Under the Apple Tree room, which features a king bed, a split-level sitting room, and a large bath complete with a whirlpool tub. Rates include a gourmet breakfast served in the dining room and afternoon tea served in the cozy lounge or landscaped gardens, depending on the weather.

Over $300

If you don't have transportation but don't want to stay downtown, the **Lonsdale Quay Hotel** (123 Carrie Cates Court, North Vancouver, 604/986-6111 or 800/836-6111, www.lonsdalequayhotel.com, $375-550 s or d) is a good choice. It enjoys an absolute waterfront location above lively Lonsdale Quay Market and the SeaBus Terminal, making it just 12 minutes to downtown by water. Each of the 70 rooms is equipped with modern furnishings and amenities that normally only come with a more expensive downtown room, such as granite baths. The hotel has a restaurant, but downstairs, spread throughout the market, are waterfront cafés, restaurants, and lounges. The standard rooms and executive rooms have limited views, but upgrade to a spacious Waterfront Executive Suite and you'll have a stunning view across Burrard Inlet to the panorama of downtown.

CAMPING

The closest campground to downtown is **Capilano RV Park** (295 Tomahawk Ave., North Vancouver, 604/987-4722, www.capilanorvpark.com, $64-83). To get there from downtown, cross Lions Gate Bridge, turn right on Marine Drive, right on Capilano Road, and right again on Welch Street. From Highway 1/99 in West Vancouver, exit south on Taylor Way toward the shopping center and turn left over the Capilano River. Amenities include a swimming pool, a big hot tub, a TV and games room, and a laundry facility. This campground is very popular in summer, so even though there are more than 200 sites, you'll need to book well ahead to ensure a place.

Information and Services

EMERGENCY SERVICES

For emergencies, call **911.** For medical emergencies, contact the downtown **St. Paul's Hospital** (1081 Burrard St., 604/682-2344), which has an emergency ward open 24 hours a day, seven days a week. Other major hospitals open 24 hours daily are **Vancouver General Hospital** (899 W. 12th Ave., 604/875-4111) and **Lions Gate Hospital** (231 E. 15th St., North Vancouver, 604/988-3131). **Seymour Health Centre** (1530 W. 7th Ave., 604/738-2151, 7:30am-6pm Mon.-Fri., 8am-5pm Sat.) is just off Granville Street south of downtown. For emergency dental help, call the **AARM Dental Group** (1156 Pacific Blvd., 604/629-0386; 8am-6pm Mon.-Sat.). For Vancouver's city police, call 911 or 604/264-3111.

INFORMATION

The city's main information center is **Vancouver Visitor Centre** (Plaza Level, 200 Burrard St., 604/683-2000, 9am-5pm daily), right downtown in the heart of the waterfront district one block from Canada Place.

COMMUNICATIONS
Postal Service

Vancouver's **main post office** (349 W. Georgia St., 604/662-5722) is open Monday-Saturday. **Postal Station A** (757 W. Hastings St.) and the branch at **Bentall Centre** (595 Burrard St.) are also open Monday-Saturday. Visitors can have their mail sent to them c/o General Delivery, Postal Station A, Vancouver, BC V3S 4P2, Canada. The West Hastings Street post office will hold the mail for two weeks and then return it to the sender.

Libraries

The **Vancouver Public Library** (350 W. Georgia St., 604/331-3600, 10am-9pm Mon.-Thurs., 10am-6pm Fri.-Sat., 11am-6pm Sun.) is a magnificent nine-story facility—a far cry from the city's first library, which opened with a grant of £250 back in 1887. Its elliptical facade contains a glass-walled promenade rising six stories above a row of stylish indoor shops and cafés. Once inside, you'll soon discover that the city also found enough money to stock the shelves; the library holds more than one million books. To help you find that one book you're searching for, use the self-guided tour brochure available at the information desk.

Newspapers and Periodicals

Vancouver's two newspapers are *The Province* (www.theprovince.com), published daily except Saturday, and the *Vancouver Sun* (www.vancouversun.com), published daily except Sunday. Both are published by the same company, Postmedia Network (www.canada.com), with *The Province* more tabloid-driven than the *Sun*. Both are available at newsstands and vending machines throughout the city for less than $1. Canada's two national dailies, the *Globe and Mail* and the *National Post,* are both based in Toronto but are readily available in Vancouver.

Many free publications are distributed throughout the city. The weekly *Georgia Straight* (www.straight.com) features articles on local issues, as well as a full entertainment rundown for the city. *Westender* (www.westender.com), also a weekly, spotlights downtown issues and has good restaurant reviews, while the monthly *Common Ground* (www.commonground.ca) is dedicated to health and personal development.

PHOTOGRAPHY

Print processing from your memory cards is offered by dozens of outlets throughout Vancouver. Two of the most reliable are **London Drugs** (604/872-8114 for locations), with branches throughout Metro Vancouver, and **Lens and Shutter** (2918 W. Broadway, 604/428-0838, 10am-6pm Mon.-Sat., noon-4pm Sun.). In the heart of downtown, **Leo's Cameras** (1055 Granville St., 604/685-5331, 9am-5pm Mon.-Sat.) has an excellent selection of new and used camera equipment, with knowledgeable staff on hand to answer any questions. Prices are competitive, especially for the newest camera models and accessories.

If you've arrived in Vancouver with a mobile phone—or, in fact, almost any electronic device from another country—you should be able to find parts, plugs, and adapters at **Foreign Electronics** (432 E. Broadway, 604/879-1189, 10am-6pm Mon.-Fri., 11am-5pm Sat.).

Getting There and Around

Most visitors arrive in Vancouver by air or road. For those driving, downtown Vancouver is 1,060 kilometers (653 miles) from Calgary along the Trans-Canada Highway (allow at least 12 hours), or a painful 4,530 kilometers (2,807 miles) across the country from Toronto. The sprawl of Vancouver extends right to the U.S. border; officially the driving distance between downtown Seattle and downtown Vancouver is 225 kilometers (140 miles), but allow plenty of time for traffic and border delays. Farther afield, it's 2,055 kilometers (1,277 miles) between Los Angeles and Vancouver and 4,785 kilometers (2,973 miles) from New York.

AIR

Vancouver International Airport (YVR; www.yvr.ca) is on Sea Island, 15 kilometers (9 miles) south of Vancouver city center. Over 16 million passengers pass through the terminal annually. The three-story international terminal and adjacent domestic terminal hold coffee shops and restaurants, car-rental agencies, a post office, currency exchanges, newsstands, gift shops, and duty-free shops. Numerous information boards provide a quick airport orientation, and an information booth on level 3 of the international terminal offers tourist brochures, bus schedules, and taxi information.

Airport Transportation

The **Canada Line** (www.translink.ca) is a 16-kilometer (10-mile) stretch of light rail line linking the airport to downtown Vancouver, with 19 stations en route. The journey to or from the airport takes around 30 minutes and costs $9. The service runs every 4-10 minutes between 5am and a little after midnight.

A cab from the airport to downtown takes at least 25 minutes and runs around $50. Cabs line up curbside on the arrival levels of both the international and domestic terminals 24 hours daily. All cabs that pick up from the airport must be accredited by the innovative YVR Taxi Program. Administered by the Vancouver Airport Authority, the program gives incoming visitors the peace of mind that their drivers will speak English, know their way around the city, load all baggage, accept credit cards, and accept U.S. dollars at a fair exchange rate.

RAIL

Vancouver is served by **VIA Rail** (416/366-8411 or 888/842-7245, www.viarail.ca) passenger trains from across the country and is the terminus for the **Rocky Mountaineer** (604/606-7245 or 800/665-7245, www.rockymountaineer.com). The Vancouver terminus of all VIA Rail services is **Pacific Central Station** (1150 Station St.), two kilometers (1.2 miles) southeast of downtown, a $12 cab ride, or just a few minutes on the SkyTrain from any of the four downtown stations. Inside the station you'll find a currency exchange, cash machines, lockers, a newsstand, information boards, and a McDonald's restaurant. Pacific Central Station is also the long-distance bus depot. The Rocky Mountaineer (1755 Cottrell St.) terminates behind Pacific Central Station off Terminal Avenue.

BUS

All long-distance Greyhound bus services terminate in Vancouver at **Pacific Central Station** (1150 Station St.). **Quick Shuttle** (604/940-4428 or 800/665-2122, www.quickcoach.com) operates a regular bus service to Pacific Central Station and major downtown Vancouver hotels from downtown Seattle (US$43 one-way) and Seattle's SeaTac Airport (US$59 one-way).

GETTING AROUND
TransLink

TransLink (604/953-3333, www.translink.ca) operates an extensive network of buses, trains, and ferries that can get you just about anywhere you want to go within Vancouver.

Buses run to all corners of the city 5am-2am daily. Transfers are valid for 90 minutes of travel in one direction. **SkyTrain** is a computer-operated (no drivers) light-rail transit system that runs along 65 kilometers (40 miles) of track from downtown Vancouver to Vancouver International Airport, through New Westminster, and over the Fraser River to suburban Surrey. The city-center stations are underground but are clearly marked at each street entrance. The double-ended, 400-passenger **SeaBus** scoots across Burrard Inlet every 15-30 minutes, linking downtown Vancouver to North Vancouver in just 12 minutes. The downtown terminus is Waterfront

The seaplane base is on the downtown waterfront.

Station, beside Canada Place and a five-minute walk from the Vancouver Visitor Centre.

On weekdays 5:30am-6:30pm, the city is divided into three zones, and fares vary by zone: adults $2.85-5.60 for each sector. Zone 1 encompasses all of downtown and Metro Vancouver; Zone 2 covers all of the North Shore, Burnaby, New Westminster, and Richmond; and Zone 3 extends to the limits of the TransLink system. At other times (including all weekend), travel anywhere in the city costs $2.85 one-way. Pay the driver (exact change only) for bus travel or purchase tickets from machines at any SkyTrain station or SeaBus terminal. Request a free transfer from the driver if required. A **DayPass** costs adults $10, seniors and children $7.75 (if purchased from the international airport, adults $15, seniors and children $12.75), and allows unlimited travel for one day anywhere on the TransLink system. Day passes are available at all SeaBus and SkyTrain stations as well as FareDealers (convenience stores such as 7-Eleven and Mac's) throughout the city.

Ferry

Apart from the SeaBus, the only other scheduled ferry services within the city are on False Creek. Two private companies, **False Creek Ferries** (604/684-7781) and **Aquabus** (604/689-5858), operate on this narrow waterway. From the main hub of Granville Island, 12- to 20-passenger ferries run every 15 minutes 7am-10pm daily to the foot of Hornby Street, and under the Burrard Street Bridge to the Aquatic Center (at the south end of Thurlow St.) and Vanier Park (Museum of Vancouver). Every 30-60 minutes, both companies also run down the head of False Creek to Stamp's Landing, the Plaza of Nations, and Science World. Fares with both companies are $3.50-6 per sector, or adults $16, seniors and children $12 for a full day of unlimited travel.

BIKE

Downtown Vancouver is not particularly bicycle-friendly, but nearby areas such as Stanley Park and the coastline west of Kitsilano are perfect places for pedal power. The main concentration of rental shops surrounds the corner of Robson and Denman Streets, two blocks from Stanley Park. Expect to pay from $10 per hour or $30 per day for the most basic mountain bike and $15 per hour or $50 per day for a suspension mountain bike. Most of the shops also rent in-line skates and tandem bikes. Near to Stanley Park, try **Bayshore Rentals** (745 Denman St., 604/688-2453, 9am-7pm daily) or **Spokes Bicycle Rental** (1798 W. Georgia St., 604/688-5141, 9am-7pm daily).

TAXI

Taxicabs are easiest to catch outside major hotels or transportation hubs. Fares in Vancouver are a uniform $3.20 flag charge plus $1.84 per kilometer (plus $0.30 per minute when stopped). Trips within downtown usually run around $12. The trip between the airport and downtown is $50. A 10-15 percent tip to the driver is expected. Major companies include **Black Top** (604/731-1111), **Vancouver Taxi** (604/871-1111), and **Yellow Cab** (604/681-1111). Several wheelchair-accommodating taxi cabs are available from Vancouver Taxi. The fares are the same as regular taxis.

Car

An excellent public transit system makes up for the fact that Vancouver isn't the world's most driver-friendly city, especially downtown, where congestion is a major problem, particularly during rush hour. West Georgia Street is a particular trouble spot, with traffic from all directions funneling onto Lions Gate Bridge to cross to the North Shore. Many downtown streets are one-way and lack left-turn lanes, adding to the congestion. On a larger scale, Vancouver lacks any real expressways, meaning a tortuous trip through downtown to get anywhere on the North Shore.

Downtown metered **parking** costs $2 to $3 per hour, but is often difficult to find during business hours. Meters take coins, or pay by phone or credit card. Most shopping centers have underground parking, and a few mul-tistory parking lots are scattered throughout the city core (including between Water and Cordova Streets in Gastown; access it from either side). These cost from $6 per hour and from $30 per day, with discounts for full-day parking for early arrivals. One place you'll be assured of finding parking is under the downtown hotels, which generally charge $8-15 per hour for nonguests. Guests at these same hotels pay up to $35 per 24-hour period for parking.

Greater Vancouver

When your plane touches down at Vancouver International Airport, it's landing on Sea Island. Several such islands are part of a massive alluvial fan formed over eons of time as silt and gravel have washed down the Fraser River and been deposited in the Strait of Georgia. The largest of these islands holds the city of Richmond, which is sandwiched between the north and south arms of the river. Across the South Arm are Delta and Tsawwassen, from which ferries depart for Vancouver Island. Across Boundary Bay from Tsawwassen is White Rock, a large residential area that sits right on the U.S.-Canada border.

When you leave Vancouver and head due east, you travel through the most built-up and heavily populated area of British Columbia, skirting modern commercial centers, residential suburbs, and zones of heavy industry. Metro Vancouver extends almost 100 kilometers (60 miles) along the Fraser Valley, through mostly residential areas. The main route east is the Trans-Canada Highway, which parallels the Fraser River to the south, passing through Burnaby and Abbottsford.

RICHMOND

The incorporated city of Richmond (population 200,000) sprawls across **Lulu Island** at the mouth of the Fraser River. Most visitors to Vancouver cross the island on their way north from the United States on Highway 99, or to and from the airport or Tsawwassen Ferry Terminal. Steveston is the main reason to visit Richmond, but on the way, consider escaping the suburban sprawl at **Richmond Nature Park** at the junction of Highways 91 and 99 (access is signposted from Westminster Hwy.). This 85-hectare (210-acre) park has been left in its natural state; the only development consists of trails leading to duck-filled ponds and fens. The park is open dawn to dusk daily, and there is a nature house (9am-5pm daily, free).

Steveston

On Lulu Island's southwestern extremity, the historical fishing village of Steveston is a lively spot worth a visit. In the 1880s it had more than 50 canneries and was the world's largest fishing port. Today, a redeveloped stretch of harborfront bustles with activity in summer. Casual visitors and local fishers mingle at fishing-supply outlets, shops selling packaged seafood products, boutiques, and restaurants. Below the main wharf, fishing boats sell the day's catch—halibut, salmon, ling cod, rock cod, crab, and shrimp—to the general public at excellent prices. The fisherfolk are friendly enough, chatting happily about their catch and how best to cook it up.

On the harborfront you'll find the **Gulf of Georgia Cannery National Historic Site** (12138 4th Ave., 604/664-9009, 10am-5pm daily, adults $7.80, seniors $6.55, children $3.90), a cannery that operated between 1894 and 1979. Much of the original cannery has been restored. In addition to canning line exhibits and demonstrations of the various machines, an audiovisual presentation is offered in the Boiler House Theatre, and the Discovery area is set aside for children.

Another historical site, the **Britannia**

Heritage Shipyard (5180 Westwater Dr., 604/718-8050, noon-5pm daily May-Sept., donation) is reached by following the signs east along Moncton Street. Dating to 1885, the actual Britannia Shipyard building is currently being restored, but it is surrounded by four already restored buildings from the same era, five others in various states of disrepair, and a variety of interesting wooden vessels. Another interesting Steveston attraction is **Steveston Museum** (3811 Moncton St., 604/718-8439, 9:30am-5pm Mon.-Sat., noon-4pm Sun., donation), in the old Royal Bank building, which profiles local history through displays such as a reconstructed general store. At the west end of Moncton Street is **Garry Point Park,** a windswept piece of land jutting into the Strait of Georgia, with views extending to the Southern Gulf Islands.

To get to Steveston, take Highway 99 to the Steveston Highway exit, then head west, passing by a magnificent Buddhist temple. Town center is south from the Steveston Highway along the No. 1 Road.

Accommodations

The following Richmond accommodations are good choices for those visitors who arrive late at night or have an early departure from the international airport. Also, if you arrive in Vancouver and want to head straight over to Vancouver Island, staying in this vicinity saves an unnecessary trip into downtown. All accommodations detailed in this section offer complimentary airport shuttles. As with downtown accommodations, rack rates quoted below are much higher than most guests pay, especially outside the busy July-August summer season.

$150-200

Three kilometers (2 miles) from the airport, the **Holiday Inn Express Vancouver Airport** (9351 Bridgeport Rd., 604/273-8080 or 877/660-8550, www.ihg.com, $184 s or d) is a typical modern multistory airport hotel, with large and comfortably furnished rooms.

$200-250

The **Coast Vancouver Airport Hotel** (1041 SW Marine Dr., 604/263-1555 or 800/716-6199, www.coasthotels.com, from $222-234 s or d) lies farther from the airport (toward the city) than the rest of the Richmond lodgings, but with free airport transfers, free long-term parking, and in-house dining, it is still aimed directly at airport travelers. No surprises with the rooms here; each has modern decor, a work desk, an ironing facility, a coffeemaker, and free local calls.

$250-300

Pacific Gateway Hotel (3500 Cessna Dr., 604/278-1241 or 866/382-3474, www.pacific-gatewayhotel.com, $260-318 s or d) is on Sea Island. This 382-room independent hotel offers the high standard of rooms and service expected of an international-style hostelry. Fitness facilities are adequate but limited, and there's a small outdoor pool. Dining options include a café, a lobby restaurant, and Pier 73, which overlooks the Fraser River.

OVER $300

Centrally located three kilometers (2 miles) from the main airport terminals and a short walk to the Canada Line transit system, the **Radisson Hotel Vancouver Airport** (8181 Cambie Rd., 604/276-8181 or 800/395-7046, www.radisson.com, $309-389 s or d) is a sprawling complex of 184 guest rooms, a fitness center, an indoor pool, and a bistro-style restaurant.

Hilton Vancouver Airport (5911 Minoru Blvd., 604/273-6336 or 800/445-8667, www.hilton.com, $459-639 s or d) is five kilometers (3 miles) south of the airport near the Richmond shopping district. The midsize rooms are each outfitted with a work desk, two phone lines, and a coffeemaker, and each has a private balcony. Other facilities include a fitness center, a heated outdoor pool, a whirlpool tub, two tennis courts, and an above-average restaurant specializing in west coast cuisine.

Right at the international airport, the **Fairmont Vancouver Airport** (3111 Grant McConachie Way, 604/207-5200 or 866/540-4441, www.fairmont.com, from $487 s or d) is the most convenient lodging for those flying home from Vancouver. The 392 rooms are equipped with remote-controlled everything, right down to the drapes; fog-free bath mirrors; and floor-to-ceiling soundproofed windows. Other more traditional hotel conveniences include a huge work center, a health club (where swimmers take to the self-adjusted current of a lap pool), and the Absolute Spa massage and treatment facility.

DELTA

Pass under the South Arm of the Fraser River via Highway 99 and the George Massey Tunnel and you'll emerge in the sprawling industrial and residential district of Delta (pop. 105,000).

George C. Reifel Migratory Bird Sanctuary

Take Highway 17 (exit 28) south from Highway 99 and turn right on Ladner Trunk Road, continuing through Ladner Village along River Road West to an old wooden bridge providing access **George C. Reifel Migratory Bird Sanctuary** (604/946-6980, 9am-4pm daily, adults $5, seniors and children $3), far enough from the city to be missed by most visitors. The 350-hectare (800-acre) sanctuary protects the northern corner of low-lying Westham Island, a stopover for thousands of migratory birds in spring and fall. The best time for a visit is during the spectacular snow goose migration, which runs from early November to mid-December. Otherwise, you'll see abundant migratory birdlife anytime between October and April. The island also serves as a permanent home for many bird species, including bald eagles, peregrine falcons, herons, swans, owls, and ducks.

Accommodations

Delta is an ideal place to stay if you're planning to get an early-morning jump on the

Blue herons are one of the many species at the George C. Reifel Migratory Bird Sanctuary.

crowds for the ferry trip over to Vancouver Island or if you're arriving from the United States and don't feel like tackling city traffic after a long day's drive.

$100-150

Delta Town & Country Inn (6005 Hwy. 17, 604/946-4404 or 888/777-1266, www.deltainn.com, $149 s or d) is at the junction of Highway 99 and Highway 17, halfway between the airport and the ferry terminal, but the setting is parklike and quiet, with most of the 49 rooms enjoying views over extensive gardens and a landscaped pool area. In addition to the large outdoor pool, facilities include tennis courts, a restaurant, and a sports bar.

$150-200

The closest lodging to the southern departure point for ferries to Vancouver Island is the **Coast Tsawwassen Inn** (1665 56th St., 604/943-8221 or 800/716-6199, www.tsawwasseninn.com, $160-180 s or d), four kilometers (2.5 miles) northeast of the ferry terminal back toward the city along Highway 17 and within walking distance of downtown Tsawwassen cafés and restaurants. The hotel comprises two separate sections, one containing 50 well-decorated guest rooms, an indoor and outdoor pool, a fitness center, a restaurant, and a lounge. The other part of the complex holds 89 much larger suites, each with a kitchen, a separate bedroom, and a private patio.

CAMPING
Peace Arch RV Park (14601 40th Ave., 604/594-7009, www.peacearchrvpark.ca, tents $38, hookups $48-52) sprawls over eight hectares (20 acres) between White Rock and Delta, 10 kilometers (6 miles) from the Douglas Border Crossing. Take exit 10—King George Highway—north from Highway 99, then the first right, 40th Avenue. Although filled with many permanent trailers, facilities include a heated pool, wireless Internet, a playground and mini-golf, a game room, coin-operated showers, and laundry.

SURREY
The city of Surrey is well within Metro Vancouver but is officially its own incorporated city—with a population of 500,000, it's British Columbia's second largest. Surrey sprawls from the Fraser River in the north to White Rock and the international boundary in the south and from Delta in the west to Langley in the east. Its first settlers were the Stewarts, who built a homestead beside the Nicomekl River in 1894. The original homestead is now the centerpiece of **Elgin Heritage Park** (13723 Crescent Rd., 250/543-3456, free), where the grounds are always open. To get there, take the King George Highway exit off Highway 99, then turn onto Elgin Road, which becomes Crescent Road.

WHITE ROCK
Named for a 400-ton glacial erratic that sits by the shoreline, this incorporated city of 20,000 lies right on the international border and surrounds the **Douglas Border Crossing.** It is the main border crossing for Vancouver-bound travelers heading north from Seattle on Highway 5 (north of the border, Highway 99). At the 24-hour checkpoint are duty-free shops and **Peace Arch Provincial Park,** where a stone archway symbolizes the friendly relationship enjoyed between Canada and the United States.

Take 8th Avenue west from the first interchange north of the border to reach downtown

Burnaby Lake Regional Park

White Rock. Marine Drive hugs the coastline for five kilometers (3 miles), lined almost the entire way with outdoor cafés, restaurants, old beach houses, and ocean-inspired condominiums. At around 149th Street is the main concentration of restaurants, an information center, and 470-meter-long (1,500-foot) **White Rock Pier,** which is a great place for a casual stroll. Although the entire strip bustles with activity on summer weekends, this section is super busy. The city's namesake, a remnant of the last ice age, lies above the high-tide mark just south of the pier. It is now painted bright white and impossible to miss. The beach is no Caribbean gem, but at low tide, locals flock to the wide expanse of sand to bake in the sun, wade in shallow water, play Frisbee, or skim-board across pools of water. After exploring White Rock's natural attractions, grab an ice cream at **Cones and Creamery** (14961 Marine Dr., 604/536-7644, 9am-11pm daily) or enjoy local seafood overlooking the ocean at **Charlie Don't Surf** (15011 Marine Dr., 604/538-1988, 11am-10pm daily, $15-29).

BURNABY

Immediately east of downtown, Burnaby (population 240,000) was incorporated as a city in 1992, but in reality it's part of Vancouver's suburban sprawl. It extends east from Boundary Road to Coquitlam, while Burrard Inlet lies to the north and riverside New Westminster to the southeast. The Trans-Canada Highway bisects Burnaby, but access is easiest via the SkyTrain, which makes four stops in the city. Among these stops is **Metrotown** (4700 Kingsway, 10am-9pm Mon.-Sat., 11am-7pm Sun.), which is Vancouver's largest shopping mall.

Sights

Burnaby Village Museum (6501 Deer Lake Ave., 604/297-4565, 11am-4:30pm Tues.-Sun. May-early Sept., free) lies in Deer Lake Park, on the south side of the Trans-Canada Highway; to get there take exit 33 south, then turn left onto Canada Way and right onto Deer Lake Avenue. The village is a reconstruction of how a BC town would have looked in the early 1900s, complete with more than 30 shops and houses, heritage-style gardens, and costumed staff.

Greater Vancouver's largest lake is Burnaby Lake, which is surrounded by **Burnaby Lake Regional Park,** immediately north of the Trans-Canada Highway. A 10-kilometer (6-mile) walking trail encircles the lake, but to focus on the most bird-rich corner of the park take exit 37 north from the Trans-Canada Highway and turn west off Gaglardi Way onto Winston Street, then south on Piper Avenue. Here, a boardwalk just into the lake and you may see grebes, swans, ducks, and sandpipers.

Burnaby Mountain Park, also north of the Trans-Canada Highway, surrounds the campus of **Simon Fraser University,** the province's second-largest campus, with a student population of 35,000. Centennial Way (off Burnaby Mountain Parkway) leads to the park's high point, where views extend down Burrard Inlet to North Vancouver and its stunning mountain backdrop. Also at the summit is a collection of totem poles, Japanese sculptures, and a rose garden. The university is worthy of inspection. Its unique design of quadrants linked by a massive fountain-filled courtyard is typical of architect Arthur Erickson, who was partly responsible for its design.

Accommodations

The Kingsway is a main thoroughfare linking downtown to Burnaby. It is lined with a smattering of inexpensive motels—perfect if you want to save a few dollars and like the convenience of being a short bus ride from downtown.

$100-150

One of the least expensive motels in Burnaby is the **Happy Day Inn** (7330 6th St., 604/524-8501 or 800/665-9733, www.happydayinn.com, $102-128 s or d). Each of the 32 rooms is brightly decorated and air-conditioned. Amenities include a small fitness facility and a sauna. To get here, take Edmonds Street northeast from the Kingsway to 6th Street.

On the western side of Burnaby, **2400 Motel** (2400 Kingsway, 604/434-2464 or 888/833-2400, www.2400motel.com, $112-164 s or d) is a classic roadside-style place with landscaped gardens, basic rooms, wireless Internet, and coffee and newspapers offered in the office each morning. It's near Nanaimo Street and within walking distance of the 29th Avenue SkyTrain station.

$150-200

Within walking distance of a SkyTrain station is the **Days Inn-Vancouver Metro** (2075 Kingsway, 604/876-5531 or 800/546-4792, www.daysinnvancouvermetro.com, $155-220 s or d), with 66 rooms opening to a quiet courtyard. The renovated rooms are typical of other Days Inn properties with a simple, contemporary feel, and each has amenities, such as wireless Internet, blow-dryers, and coffeemakers.

$250-300

Holiday Inn Express Vancouver Metrotown (4405 Central Blvd., 604/438-1881 or 877/660-8550, www.ihg.com, $264-324 s or d, includes breakfast) is part of Vancouver's biggest shopping complex and is connected to downtown by the SkyTrain. The 100 rooms are spread over six stories in this contemporary hotel. Other facilities include a wide range of recreational amenities, including an outdoor swimming pool, a tennis court, and a fitness center.

CAMPING

Adjacent to the east end of Burnaby Lake Regional Park, **Burnaby Cariboo RV Park** (8765 Cariboo Place, Burnaby, 604/420-1722, www.bcrvpark.com, tents $42-47, hookups $61-71) offers a wide range of facilities, including a large indoor heated pool, a fitness room, a whirlpool tub, a sundeck, a playground, a lounge, a barbecue area, a grocery store, and a laundry facility. The park is 17 kilometers (11 miles) east of downtown. To get there, take

exit 37 ("Gaglardi") from the Trans-Canada Highway, turn right at the first traffic light, and take the first left and then the first right into Cariboo Place.

NEW WESTMINSTER

"New West," as it's best known, is a densely populated residential area 15 kilometers (9 miles) southeast of downtown Vancouver. Due to its strategic location, where the Fraser River divides, it was declared the capital of the mainland colony in 1859 and then the provincial capital in the years 1866-1868. Only a few historic buildings remain, and the old port area has been totally overtaken by modern developments. **River Market** (810 Quayside Dr., 604/520-3881), along the riverfront and below the old main street, is open for very unmarket-like hours (not until 10am each day), but it holds an interesting selection of fresh produce, take-out food stalls, and specialty shops. Out front is the *Samson V,* built in 1937, and when it was retired in 1980, the last remaining paddle-wheeler on the river. It's now open for public inspection (noon-5pm daily July-Aug., noon-5pm Sat.-Sun. spring and fall, donation); call the local museum (604/527-4640) for details. Beside the market is the **Fraser River Discovery Centre** (788 Quayside Dr., 604/521-8401, 10am-4pm daily June-Aug., 10am-4pm Wed.-Sat. Sept.-May, free), which describes the river and its importance to the development of New Westminster.

INFORMATION AND SERVICES
South

If you approach Vancouver from the south on Highway 5 (Highway 99 in Canada), the first official information center you'll come to is the **Peace Arch Visitor Centre** (298 Hwy. 99, 604/541-4555, 8am-6pm daily summer, 9am-4pm daily fall-spring) immediately north of the border and right beside the highway. A currency exchange is on-site.

Continuing north, take the 8th Avenue exit east from Highway 99 to the **Surrey**

Visitor Centre (730 176th St., 604/531-6646 or 888/531-6646, www.discoversurreybc.com, 9am-5pm daily mid-May-Aug., 10am-4pm Mon.-Fri. Sept.-mid-May).

Those heading into the city may want to continue to the **Delta Visitor Centre** (6201 60th Ave., 604/946-4232, www.deltachamber.com, 9am-5pm Mon.-Fri. July-Aug., 8:30am-4:30pm Mon.-Fri. Sept.-June), which is well signposted from the main highway into the city.

Continuing out to the historic fishing village of Steveston, **Richmond Visitor Centre** (3811 Moncton St., 604/271-8280 or 877/247-0777, www.tourismrichmond.com, 9:30am-6pm Mon.-Sat., 10am-6pm Sun.) is in a restored residence one block back from the waterfront. It's operated by Tourism Richmond.

Vancouver International Airport (604/247-7540) has information booths on the arrival levels of the international and domestic terminals; both are open 8am-11:30pm daily.

North

A handy source of information north of the harbor is the small visitors center in the historical building beside **Lonsdale Quay,** which is open in summer 9am-6pm daily.

East

If you're approaching the city from the east along Highway 1, **Chilliwack Visitor Centre** (44150 Luckakuck Way, 604/858-8121 or 800/567-9535, www.tourismchilliwack.com, 8:30am-4:30pm daily summer, 8:30am-4:30pm Mon.-Fri. fall-spring) is a good place to stop, stretch your legs, and gather some local information.

Forty kilometers (25 miles) farther west toward the city, take exit 92 to reach the **Abbotsford Visitor Centre** (34561 Delair Rd., 604/859-1721, www.tourismabbotsford.ca, 9am-5pm daily).

On the west side of the Fraser River, Tourism New Westminster (604/526-1905, www.tourismnewwestminster.com) operates **New Westminster Visitor Centre** (777 Columbia St., 604/526-1905, 10am-5pm daily July-Aug., 10am-4pm Mon.-Fri. Sept.-June) in the museum building. This location is out of the way for highway travelers, but if you do make the detour, take Brunette Avenue south from exit 40 off the Trans-Canada Highway.

Approaching Vancouver from the east along Highway 7, **Mission Visitor Centre** (34033 Lougheed Hwy., 604/826-6914, www.missionchamber.bc.ca, 8am-5pm Mon.-Fri., 9am-5pm Sat.-Sun. June-Aug., 8am-4pm Mon.-Fri. Sept.-May), in the town of the same name, has a wealth of Vancouver information.

Coquitlam Visitor Centre (1116 Brunette Ave., 604/516-6151, www.tricitieschamber.com, 11am-5pm Tues.-Fri., 10am-4pm Sat.-Sun. summer) is north of Highway 7, within the Mackin House Museum. As well as Coquitlam and Port Coquitlam, the center represents Port Moody and the wilderness areas to the north.

Victoria & Vancouver Island

Look for ★ to find recommended
sights, activities, dining, and lodging.

Highlights

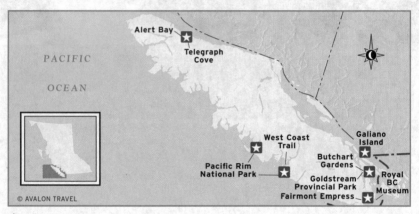

★ **Fairmont Empress:** You don't need to be a guest at this historical hotel to admire its grandeur. Plan on eating a meal here for the full effect (page 94).

★ **Royal BC Museum:** If you visit only one museum in Victoria, make it this one, where you can come face-to-face with an Ice Age woolly mammoth (page 95).

★ **Goldstream Provincial Park:** Laced with hiking trails, Goldstream Provincial Park is a great escape from the city. If you're visiting in late fall, a trip to the park is worthwhile to view the spectacle of spawning salmon (page 105).

★ **Butchart Gardens:** Even if you have only one day in Victoria, make time to visit one of the world's most delightful gardens (page 105).

★ **West Coast Trail:** Winding through 77 kilometers (48 miles) of old-growth forest, with

the Pacific Ocean close at hand, this ambitious trail is one of the world's great long-distance hikes (page 131).

★ **Galiano Island:** Each of the Southern Gulf Islands has its own personality, but Galiano Island is a favorite for kayakers (page 142).

★ **Pacific Rim National Park:** Canada isn't renowned for its beaches, but this park protects some magnificent stretches of sand (page 162).

★ **Alert Bay:** On Cormorant Island, Alert Bay is a hotbed of First Nations history. A cultural center and one of the world's tallest totem poles are highlights (page 193).

★ **Telegraph Cove:** It's worth the drive to Telegraph Cove just to wander around the postcard-perfect boardwalk village, but you'll also want to take a tour boat in search of orca whales (page 194).

Vancouver Island, the largest isle in North America's Pacific, stretches for more than 450 superb kilometers (280 miles) off the west coast of mainland British Columbia.

Victoria, the provincial capital, lies at the southern tip of the island. Its deeply entrenched British traditions make Victoria unique among North American cities.

The rest of the island draws scenery buffs, outdoor adventurers, wildlife-watchers, and students of Pacific Northwest culture. A magnificent chain of rugged snowcapped mountains, sprinkled with lakes and rivers and pierced by deep inlets, effectively divides the island into two distinct sides: dense, rain-drenched forest and remote surf- and wind-battered shores on the west, and well-populated, sheltered, beach-fringed lowlands on the east. Much of the lush, green island is covered with dense forests of Douglas fir, western red cedar, and hemlock. The climate, stabilized by the Pacific Ocean and warmed by the Japanese current, never really gets too hot or too cold, but be prepared for cloudbursts, especially in winter.

PLANNING YOUR TIME

Many visitors to Victoria spend a few nights in the city as part of a longer vacation that includes the rest of Vancouver Island. At an absolute minimum, plan on spending two full days in the capital, preferably overnighting at a character-filled bed-and-breakfast. Regardless of how long you'll be in the city, much of your time will be spent in and around the Inner Harbour, a busy waterway surrounded by the city's top sights and best restaurants. At the top of the must-see list is the **Royal BC Museum,** which will impress even the biggest museo-phobes. Victoria's most visited attraction is **Butchart Gardens,** an absolutely stunning collection of plants that deserves at least half a day of your time. **Goldstream Provincial Park** and the scenic waterfront drive between downtown and Oak Bay are two outdoor destinations you should figure into your schedule.

Exploring Vancouver Island beyond Victoria requires some advance planning

---

Previous: Strathcona Provincial Park; the Fairmont Empress on the harbor in Victoria. **Above:** a seaplane in Tofino.

Vancouver Island

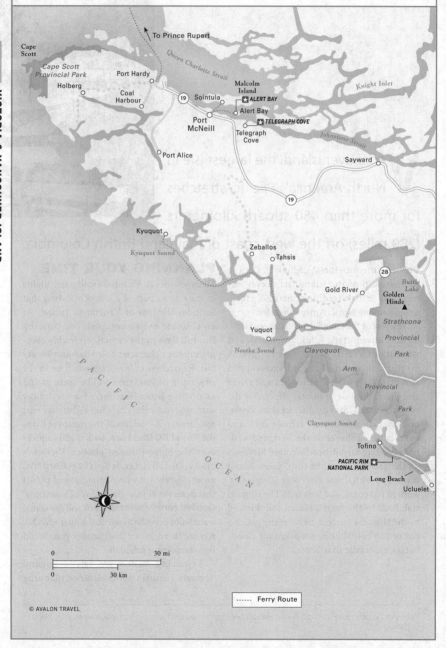

Cape Scott

Cape Scott Provincial Park

Holberg

Port Hardy

Coal Harbour

To Prince Rupert

Queen Charlotte Strait

19

Sointula

Malcolm Island

★ ALERT BAY

Alert Bay

Knight Inlet

Port McNeill

✚ TELEGRAPH COVE

Telegraph Cove

Johnstone Strait

Port Alice

Sayward

19

Kyuquot

Kyuquot Sound

Zeballos

Tahsis

28

Butte Lake

Gold River

Golden Hinde ▲

Strathcona

Yuquot

Provincial

Nootka Sound

Clayoquot

Park

Arm

Provincial

PACIFIC

Park

Clayoquot Sound

Tofino

OCEAN

PACIFIC RIM NATIONAL PARK ✚

Long Beach

Ucluelet

0   30 mi

0   30 km

© AVALON TRAVEL

······· Ferry Route

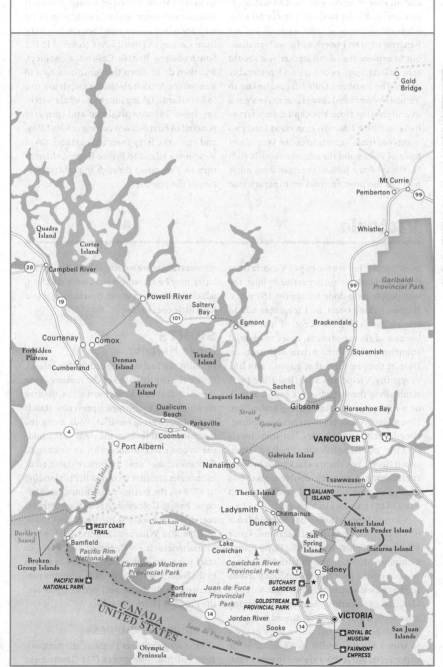

and an idea of where you want to end up. If you have just a day to spare, you can take the oceanside drive west from Victoria to Port Renfrew or travel north as far as Nanaimo, but to explore the island farther you should schedule at least two days and preferably more. The Southern Gulf Islands, linked to Victoria by ferry and floatplane, make a good overnight trip from the capital (my favorite is **Galiano Island**). Plan on at least two nights out from Victoria to do the West Coast town of Tofino and the adjacent **Pacific Rim National Park** justice. Incorporating other parts of the province into an itinerary that includes Vancouver Island is easy. The most obvious and useful option is to do your thing on Vancouver Island and then catch a ferry from Comox to Powell River (covered in the Southwestern British Columbia chapter), and then drive down the Sunshine Coast to Vancouver. A more ambitious loop is to drive to Port Hardy, taking time to go whale-watching from **Telegraph Cove** and immerse yourself in First Nations culture at **Alert Bay**, and catch the ferry from the northern tip of Vancouver Island to Prince Rupert, then return to Vancouver through the central portion of the province.

Victoria

Most people first see the city of Victoria from the Inner Harbour as they arrive by boat, the way people have done for almost 150 years. Ferries, fishing boats, and seaplanes bob in the harbor, with a backdrop of manicured lawns and flower gardens, quiet residential suburbs, and striking urban architecture. Despite the pressures that go with city life, easygoing Victorians still find time for a stroll along the waterfront, a round of golf, or a night out at a fine-dining restaurant. Discovering Victoria's roots has been a long-time favorite with visitors, but some locals find the "more English than England" reputation tiring. Yes, there's a tacky side to some traditions, but high tea, double-decker bus tours, and exploring formal gardens remain some of the true joys in Victoria.

Victoria (pop. 345,000) has an abundance of created and natural attractions. Once you've visited must-sees like the Royal British Columbia Museum and Butchart Gardens, you can devote your time to outdoor pursuits such as whale-watching, a bike ride through Oak Bay, or something as simple as enjoying afternoon tea in an old-fashioned tearoom. You will be confronted with oodles of ways to trim a bulging wallet in Victoria. Some commercial attractions are worth every cent, whereas others are routine at best, though the latter may be crowd-pleasers with children, which makes them worth considering if you have little ones in tow.

SIGHTS
Inner Harbour
Initially, the harbor extended farther inland; before the construction of the massive stone causeway that now forms the marina, the area on which the impressive Empress now stands was a deep, oozing mudflat. Walk along the lower level and then up the steps in the middle to come face-to-face with an unamused Captain James Cook; the bronze statue commemorates the first recorded British landing in 1778 on the territory that would later become British Columbia. Above the northeast corner of the harbor is the **Victoria Visitor Centre** (812 Wharf St., 250/953-2033, www.tourismvictoria.com), the perfect place to start your city exploration. Be sure to return to the Inner Harbour after dark, when the parliament buildings are outlined in lights and the Empress Hotel is floodlit.

★ FAIRMONT EMPRESS
Overlooking the Inner Harbour, the pompous 1908 **Fairmont Empress** (721 Government

St., 250/384-8111 or 800/257-7544, www.fairmont.com) is Victoria's most recognizable landmark. Its architect was the well-known Francis Rattenbury, who also designed the BC parliament buildings, the Canadian Pacific Railway (CPR) steamship terminal (now housing the wax museum), and Crystal Garden. It's worthwhile walking through the hotel lobby to gaze—head back, mouth agape—at the interior razzle-dazzle, and to watch people partake in traditional afternoon tea hosted in the Lobby Lounge. Browse through the conservatory and gift shops, and drool over the menus of the various restaurants.

★ ROYAL BC MUSEUM

Canada's most-visited museum and easily one of North America's best, the **Royal British Columbia Museum** (675 Belleville St., 250/356-7226, http://royalbcmuseum.bc.ca, 10am-5pm daily, adults $22, seniors and youths $16) is a must-see attraction for even the most jaded museum-goer. Its fine Natural History galleries are extraordinarily true to life, complete with appropriate sounds and smells. Come face-to-face with an Ice Age woolly mammoth, stroll through a coastal forest full of deer and tweeting birds, meander along a seashore or tidal marsh, and then descend into the Open Ocean exhibit via submarine—a very real trip that's not recommended for claustrophobics. The First Peoples galleries hold a fine collection of artifacts from the island's first human inhabitants, the Nuu-chah-nulth (Nootka). Many of the pieces were collected by Charles Newcombe, who paid the Nuu-chah-nulth for them on collection sorties in the early 1900s. More modern human history is also explored here in creative ways. Take a tour through time via the time capsules; walk along an early-1900s street; and experience hands-on exhibits on industrialization, the gold rush, and the exploration of British Columbia by land and sea in the Modern History and 20th Century galleries.

The Royal Museum Shop stocks an excellent collection of books on Canadiana, wildlife, history, and First Nations art and culture, along with postcards and tourist paraphernalia. The museum's **theater** (9am-8pm daily, additional charge) shows nature-oriented IMAX films.

SURROUNDING THE MUSEUM

In front of the museum, the 27-meter (89-foot) **Netherlands Centennial Carillon**

Fairmont Empress

Greater Victoria

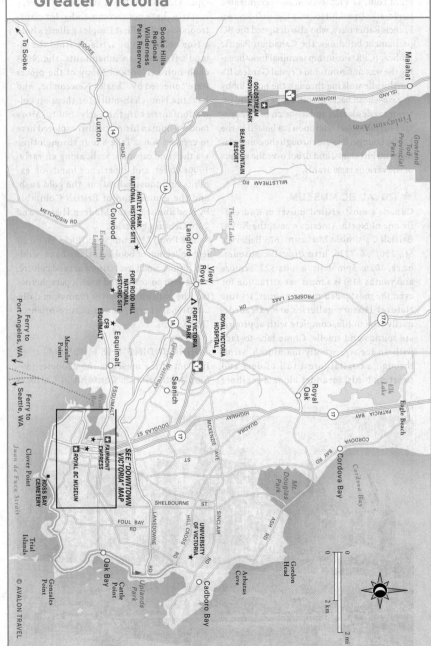

© AVALON TRAVEL

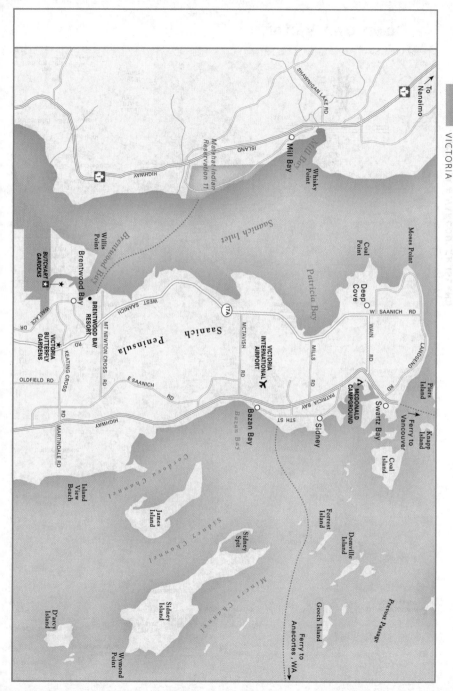

Downtown Victoria

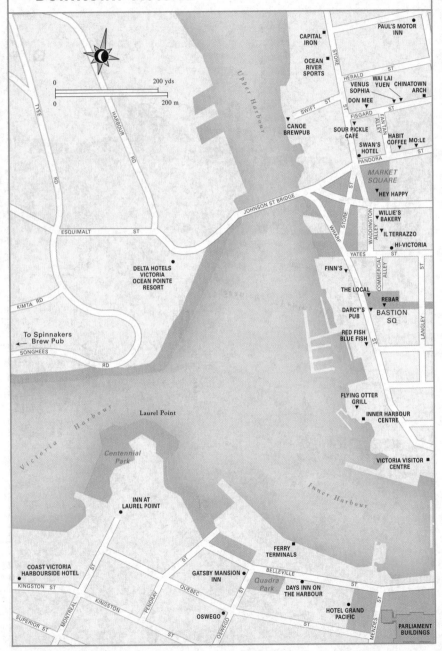

0   200 yds
0   200 m

Upper Harbour

PAUL'S MOTOR INN

CAPITAL IRON

STORE ST

OCEAN RIVER SPORTS

HERALD

WAI LAI YUEN

VENUS SOPHIA   CHINATOWN ARCH

SWIFT ST

DON MEE

FISGARD

FAN TAN ALLEY

CANOE BREWPUB

SOUR PICKLE CAFÉ

HABIT COFFEE   MO:LE

SWAN'S HOTEL

PANDORA

MARKET SQUARE

STORE ST

HEY HAPPY

WADDINGTON ALLEY

WILLIE'S BAKERY

IL TERRAZZO

WHARF

HI-VICTORIA

YATES

JOHNSON ST BRIDGE

ESQUIMALT   ST

HARBOUR   RD

TYEE   RD

FINN'S

COMMERCIAL ALLEY

DELTA HOTELS VICTORIA OCEAN POINTE RESORT

THE LOCAL

REBAR

DARCY'S PUB

BASTION SQ

LANGLEY

KIMTA RD

RED FISH BLUE FISH

To Spinnakers Brew Pub

SONGHEES

RD

Victoria Harbour

FLYING OTTER GRILL

INNER HARBOUR CENTRE

Laurel Point

VICTORIA VISITOR CENTRE

Centennial Park

Inner Harbour

INN AT LAUREL POINT

FERRY TERMINALS

COAST VICTORIA HARBOURSIDE HOTEL

GATSBY MANSION INN

BELLEVILLE

Quadra Park

DAYS INN ON THE HARBOUR

KINGSTON   ST

QUEBEC

PENDRAY

MONTREAL

KINGSTON

OSWEGO

HOTEL GRAND PACIFIC

SUPERIOR ST

OSWEGO

ST

MENZIES

PARLIAMENT BUILDINGS

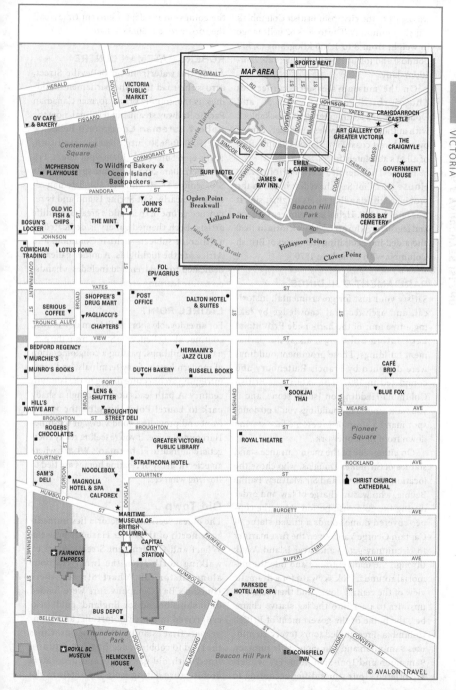

was a gift to the city from British Columbia's Dutch community. The tower's 62 bells range in weight from 8 to 1,500 kilograms (3,300 pounds) and toll at 15-minute intervals 7am-10pm daily.

On the museum's eastern corner lies **Thunderbird Park** (Belleville St. and Douglas St.), a small green spot chockablock with authentic totem poles intricately carved by northwest coast First Nations people. Best of all, it's absolutely free.

Beside Thunderbird Park is **Helmcken House** (10 Elliot St.), the oldest house in the province still standing on its original site. It was built by J. S. Helmcken, pioneer surgeon and legislator, who arrived in Victoria in 1850 and aided in negotiating the union of British Columbia with Canada in 1870.

PARLIAMENT BUILDINGS

Satisfy your lust for governmental, historical, and architectural knowledge by taking a free tour of the harborside **Provincial Legislative Buildings,** a.k.a. the parliament buildings. These prominent buildings were designed by Francis Rattenbury and completed in 1897. The exterior is British Columbia Haddington Island stone, and if you walk around the buildings you'll no doubt spot many a stern or gruesome face staring down from the stonework.

On either side of the main entrance stand statues of Sir James Douglas, who chose the location of Victoria, and Sir Matthew Baillie Begbie, who was in charge of law and order during the gold rush period. Atop the copper-covered dome stands a gilded statue of Captain George Vancouver, the first mariner to circumnavigate Vancouver Island. Walk through the main entrance and into the memorial rotunda, look skyward for a dramatic view of the central dome, and then continue upstairs to peer into the legislative chamber, the home of the government of British Columbia. Free guided tours (every 20 minutes 9am-noon and 1pm-5pm daily summer, 9am-noon and 1pm-5pm Mon.-Fri. winter) are offered. Tour times differ according to

the goings-on inside; for current times, call the **tour office** (250/387-3046).

ROBERT BATEMAN CENTRE

Along the waterfront on Belleville Street, across the road from the parliament buildings, is the grandly ornate former Canadian Pacific Railway steamship terminal, now the **Robert Bateman Centre** (470 Belleville St., 250/940-3630, http://batemancentre.org, 10am-6pm Sun.-Wed., 10am-9pm Thurs.-Fri. summer, 10am-5pm daily fall-spring, adults $10, seniors $8.50, children $6). Bateman resides on nearby Salt Spring Island and is renowned as one of the world's greatest wildlife artists. Each themed gallery is dedicated to a different subject—British Columbia and Africa are the highlights. Another gallery is dedicated to children and includes a hands-on nature learning area.

LAUREL POINT

For an enjoyable short walk from downtown, continue along Belleville Street from the parliament buildings, passing a conglomeration of modern hotels, ferry terminals, and some intriguing architecture dating to the late 19th century. A path leads down through a shady park to Laurel Point, hugging the waterfront and providing good views of the Inner Harbour en route. If you're feeling really energetic, continue to **Fisherman's Wharf,** where an eclectic array of floating homes are tied to floating wharves.

Old Town

The oldest section of Victoria lies immediately north of the Inner Harbour between Wharf and Government Streets. Start by walking north from the Inner Harbour along historical Wharf Street, where Hudson's Bay Company furs were loaded onto ships bound for England, gold seekers arrived in search of fortune, and shopkeepers first established businesses. Cross the road to cobblestoned **Bastion Square,** lined with old gas lamps and decorative architecture dating from the 1860s to the

CENTENNIAL SQUARE

Centennial Square, bounded by Government Street, Douglas Street, Pandora Avenue, and Fisgard Street, is lined with many buildings dating from the 1880s and 1890s, refurbished in recent times for all to appreciate. Don't miss the 1878 **City Hall** (fronting Douglas St.) and the imposing Greek-style building of the Hudson's Bay Company. In the heart of Centennial Square is **Spirit Square,** which is dedicated to First Nations people. Here you'll find two totem poles and a garden with native plants.

Chinatown

Continue down Fisgard Street into colorful **Chinatown,** Canada's oldest Chinese enclave (and second-oldest in North America behind San Francisco). Chinese prospectors and laborers first brought exotic spices, plants, and a love of intricate architecture and bright colors to Victoria in the late 1850s, and the exotic vibe continues to this day. The original Chinatown was much larger than today's and was home to more than 3,000 residents at its peak in the early 1900s. After being revitalized in the 1980s and being declared a National Historic Site of Canada in 1995, the precinct is now a popular visitor attraction. Its epicenter is Fisgard Street between Government and Store Streets, with the intricate **Gate of Harmonious Interest** providing the official entrance.

Today Chinatown is a delicious place to breathe in the aroma of authentic Asian food wafting from the many restaurants. Poke through the dark little shops along Fisgard Street, where you can find everything from fragile paper lanterns and embroidered silks to gingerroot and exotic fruits and veggies, then cruise Fan Tan Alley, the center of the opium trade in the 1800s.

South of the Inner Harbour
EMILY CARR HOUSE

In 1871, artist Emily Carr was born in this typical upper-class 1864 Victorian-era home, which now hosts visitors as the **Emily Carr**

Robert Bateman Centre

1890s. This was the original site chosen by James Douglas in 1843 for Fort Victoria, the Hudson's Bay Company trading post. At one time the square held a courthouse, a jail, and gallows. Today restored buildings house touristy restaurants, cafés, nightclubs, and fashionable offices.

MARITIME MUSEUM OF BRITISH COLUMBIA

Behind the Fairmont Empress, the **Maritime Museum of British Columbia** (634 Humboldt St., 250/385-4222, 10am-5pm daily summer, 10am-4pm Tues.-Sat. fall-spring, adults $10, seniors $8, under age 13 free) traces the history of seafaring exploration, adventure, commercial ventures, and passenger travel through displays of dugout canoes, model ships, Royal Navy charts, figureheads, photographs, naval uniforms, and bells. One room is devoted to exhibits chronicling the circumnavigation of the world, and another holds a small theater. The museum also has a nautically oriented gift shop.

House (207 Government St., 250/383-5843, 11am-4pm Tues.-Sat. May-Sept., adults $7, seniors and students $6, children $4.50). Carr moved to the mainland at an early age, escaping the confines of the capital to draw and write about the First Nations people of the west coast and the wilderness in which she lived. She is best remembered today for her painting, a medium she took up in later years.

BEACON HILL PARK

Known to Coast Salish people as Meeacan (a First Nations word for "belly"), for its resemblance to a man lying on his back, this large tract of land immediately south of downtown was protected as parkland in 1882. Today the 25-hectare (62-acre) park is an oasis of green that extends from the back of the Royal BC Museum along Douglas Street out to cliffs that offer spectacular views of Juan de Fuca Strait and, on a clear day, the distant Olympic Mountains.

Look for peacocks in Beacon Hill Park.

The park is geographically divided in two by Dallas Road. On the downtown side of the road are landscaped gardens protected by grand Garry oak trees, tennis courts, bowling greens, playgrounds, mini golf, bird-filled ponds, and even a cricket pitch.

Beacon Hill Childrens Farm (Circle Dr., 250/381-2532, 10am-4pm daily Apr.-Oct., adults $4, children $3) is home to chickens, pigs, donkeys, and goats. The farm was originally part of a much larger zoo complex that operated between 1883 and 1990. Although zoo animals have long since been removed, peacocks that were let loose upon its closure run free through the surrounding greenery.

Rockland

This historical part of downtown lies behind the Inner Harbour, east of Douglas Street, and is easily accessible on foot.

CHRIST CHURCH CATHEDRAL

Along Quadra Street, three blocks uphill from the Inner Harbour, **Christ Church Cathedral** (930 Burdett Ave., 250/383-2714) is the seat of the Bishop of the Anglican Diocese of British Columbia. Built in 1896 in 13th-century Gothic style, it's one of Canada's largest churches. Self-guided tours are possible (8:30am-5pm Mon.-Fri. and 7:30am-8:30pm Sun., free). Visit www.christchurchcathedral.bc.ca/events for a listing of musical performances hosted by the cathedral. The park next to the cathedral is a shady haven to rest weary feet, and the gravestones make fascinating reading.

ART GALLERY OF GREATER VICTORIA

From Christ Church Cathedral, walk up Rockland Avenue for four blocks through the historical Rockland district, passing stately mansions and colorful gardens on tree-lined streets. Turn left on Moss Street and you'll come to the 1889 Spencer Mansion and its modern wing, which together make up the **Art Gallery of Greater Victoria** (1040 Moss St., 250/384-4101, 10am-5pm Mon.-Wed. and Sat., 10am-9pm Thurs., noon-5pm Sun., adults $13, seniors $11, children $2.50). The gallery contains Canada's finest collection of Japanese art, a range of contemporary art, an Emily Carr gallery, and traveling exhibits, as well as a Japanese garden with a Shinto shrine. The Gallery Shop sells art books, reproductions, and handcrafted jewelry, pottery, and glass.

GOVERNMENT HOUSE

Continue up Rockland Avenue from the art gallery to reach **Government House,** the official residence of the lieutenant governor, the queen's representative in British Columbia. Open to the public throughout the year, the surrounding gardens include an English-style garden, a rose garden, and a rhododendron garden, along with green velvety lawns and picture-perfect flower beds. On the front side of the property, vegetation has been left in a more natural state, with gravel paths leading to benches that invite one to pause and take in the city panorama.

CRAIGDARROCH CASTLE

A short walk up (east) from the art gallery along Rockland Avenue and left on Joan Crescent brings you to the baronial four-story mansion known as **Craigdarroch Castle** (1050 Joan Cres., 250/592-5323, http://thecastle.ca, 9am-7pm daily summer, 10am-4:30pm daily fall-spring, adults $15, seniors $13.50, children $6). From downtown take bus 11 (Uplands) or 14 (University) to Joan Crescent, then walk 100 meters (110 yards) up the hill. The architectural masterpiece was built in 1890 for Robert Dunsmuir, a wealthy industrialist and politician who died just before the building was completed. For all the nitty-gritties, tour the mansion with volunteer guides who really know their Dunsmuir, and then admire at your leisure all the polished wood, stained-glass windows, Victorian-era furnishings, and the great city views from upstairs.

Scenic Route to Oak Bay

This driving starts south of the Inner Harbour and follows the coastline of Juan de Fuca Strait all the way to the University of Victoria. Allow around one hour to reach the university, but allow at least half a day if you plan multiple stops. If you don't have your own transportation, most city tours take in the sights along the route.

You can take Douglas Street south alongside Beacon Hill Park to access Juan de Fuca Strait, but it's best to continue east along the Inner Harbour to the mouth of Victoria Harbour proper along Belleville then Kingston Streets to Ogden Point, which is the official starting point of the Scenic drive (marked by small blue signs).

Gorge Waterway

This natural canal leads north from the Inner Harbour to Portage Inlet, a small saltwater lake beside Highway 1. At the far end of the waterway are **Craigflower Manor** and **Craigflower Schoolhouse,** two historically important buildings that are not open to the public but may be easily viewed from outside the grounds. They were built in the 1850s on what was the island's first farm. To reach Craigflower, take Gorge Road (Hwy. 1A) north from downtown to the Craigflower Bridge (around 4 kilometers/2.5 miles). The schoolhouse is on the left, and the manor is across the bridge on the right.

The best way to see the Gorge is from sea level, aboard a **Victoria Harbour Ferry** (250/708-0201). This company runs funky little 12-passenger vessels (round-trip tour adults $26, seniors $24, children $14) to a turnaround point at Gorge Park by the Tillicum Road Bridge.

POINT ELLICE HOUSE

Built in 1861, the restored **Point Ellice House** (2616 Pleasant St., 250/380-6506, 11am-5pm daily May to mid-Sept., adults $6, children $3) sits amid beautiful gardens along the Gorge on Point Ellice, less than 2 kilometers (1.2 miles) from the Inner Harbour. The house's second owner, Peter O'Reilly, a successful entrepreneur and politician, bought it in 1868 and entertained many distinguished guests here. Original Victorian-era artifacts clutter every nook and cranny of the interior, but the best reason to visit is to enjoy a traditional English afternoon tea (11am-3pm daily, $25 pp). To get here from the Inner Harbour, jump aboard a Victoria Harbour Ferry (10 minutes, $15 round-trip), or by road take Government or Douglas Streets north from downtown, turn left on Bay Street, and turn left again on Pleasant Street.

West of Downtown
CFB ESQUIMALT NAVAL & MILITARY MUSEUM

The small **CFB Esquimalt Naval & Military Museum** (250/363-4312, 10am-3:30pm daily summer, 10am-3:30pm Mon.-Fri. fall-spring, adults $2, seniors and children $1) lies within the confines of Canadian Forces Base (CFB) Esquimalt, on Esquimalt Harbour west of downtown. A couple of buildings have been opened to the public, displaying naval, military, and general maritime memorabilia. To get here from downtown, take the Johnson Street Bridge and follow Esquimalt Road to Admirals Road; turn north, then take Naden Way, and you're on the base; follow the museum signs.

HATLEY PARK NATIONAL HISTORIC SITE

Hatley Park National Historic Site (2005 Sooke Rd., 250/391-2666) protects a sprawling estate established over 100 years ago by James Dunsmuir, son of coal baron Robert Dunsmuir and then premier of British Columbia. The site has also been used as a military college and is currently part of Royal Roads University. Visitors are invited to walk through the classic Edwardian-style garden, a rose garden, and a Japanese garden, and to stroll through an old-growth forest that extends to Esquimalt Lagoon. Dunsmuir's imposing 40-room mansion is also open for guided tours (4 times daily Mon.-Fri. summer, adults $18, seniors $15.50, students $10.50).

FORT RODD HILL NATIONAL HISTORIC SITE

Clinging to a headland across the harbor entrance from CFB Esquimalt, the picturesque **Fort Rodd Hill National Historic Site** (603 Fort Rodd Hill Rd., Colwood, 250/478-5849, 10am-5:30pm daily mid-Feb.-Oct., 9am-4:30pm daily Nov.-mid-Feb., adults $4, seniors

Hatley Park National Historic Site

$3.50, children $2) comprises **Fort Rodd,** built in 1898 to protect the fleets of ships in the harbor, and **Fisgard Lighthouse,** which dates to 1873. The expansive grounds are an interesting place to explore; audio stations bring the sounds of the past alive, much of the original fortifications are open for exploration, workrooms are furnished as they were at the turn of the 20th century, and on a low rocky outcrop, the lighthouse has been fully restored and is open to visitors. To get here from downtown, take the Old Island Highway (Gorge Rd.) and turn left on Belmont Road and then left onto Ocean Boulevard. By bus, take bus 50 from downtown, then transfer to bus 52.

★ Goldstream Provincial Park

Lying 20 kilometers (12 miles) from the heart of Victoria, this 390-hectare (960-acre) park straddles the Trans-Canada Highway northwest of downtown on its loop around the south end of Saanich Inlet.

The park's most distinctive natural feature is the Goldstream River, which flows north into the Finlayson Arm of Saanich Inlet. Forests of ancient Douglas fir and western red cedar flank the river; orchids flourish in forested glades; and at higher elevations forests of lodgepole pine, western hemlock, and maple thrive.

SALMON VIEWING

Although Goldstream is a great place to visit any time of year, the natural highlight occurs late October through December, when mostly chum salmon—and limited numbers of cohos and chinooks—fight their way upriver through the park to spawn themselves out on the same shallow gravel bars where they were born four years previously. Bald eagles begin arriving in December, feeding off the spawned-out salmon until February. From the picnic area parking lot, two kilometers (1.2 miles) north of the campground turnoff, a trail leads 400 meters (440 yards) along the Goldstream River to **Freeman King Visitor Centre** (250/478-9414, www.goldstreampark. com, 9am-4:30pm daily, free), where the life cycle of salmon is described.

Saanich Peninsula

The Saanich Peninsula is the finger of land that extends north from downtown. It holds Victoria's most famous attraction, Butchart Gardens, as well as Victoria International Airport and the main arrival point for ferries from Tsawwassen. If you've caught the ferry over to Vancouver Island from Tsawwassen, you'll have arrived at **Swartz Bay,** on the northern tip of the Saanich Peninsula; from here it's a clear run down Highway 17 to downtown Victoria and the waterfront town of Sidney. If you're coming from Goldstream Provincial Park, head north, or from Nanaimo on Highway 1, head south, to reach **Mill Bay,** where a ferry departs regularly for **Brentwood Bay** on the Saanich Peninsula. (Brentwood Bay is home to Butchart Gardens.) Ferries run in both directions nine times 7:30am-6pm daily. Peak one-way fares for the 25-minute crossing cost adults $8, children $4, and vehicles $18.50. For exact times, contact **BC Ferries** (250/386-3431, www.bcferries.com).

★ BUTCHART GARDENS

Carved from an abandoned quarry, the delightful **Butchart Gardens** (800 Benvenuto Dr., Brentwood Bay, 250/652-4422, www. butchartgardens.com, 9am-10pm daily summer, 9am-4pm winter, varying close time spring and fall, summer adults $33, ages 13-17 $17, ages 5-12 $3, less in winter) are Victoria's best-known attraction. They're approximately 20 kilometers (12 miles) north of downtown.

A Canadian cement pioneer, R. P. Butchart, built a mansion near his quarries. He and his wife, Jennie, traveled extensively, collecting rare and exotic shrubs, trees, and plants from around the world. By 1904 the quarries had been abandoned, and the couple began to beautify them by transplanting their collection into formal gardens interspersed with concrete footpaths, small bridges, waterfalls, ponds, and fountains. The gardens now contain more than 5,000 varieties of flowers, and the extensive nurseries test-grow some 35,000 new bulbs and more than 100 new roses every year. Go there in spring, summer, or early autumn to treat your eyes and nose to a marvelous sensual experience (many gardeners would give their right hands to be able to work in these gardens). Highlights include the Sunken Garden (the original quarry site) with its water features and annuals; the formal Rose Garden, set around a central lawn; and the Japanese Garden, with views to Saanich Inlet. In winter, when little is blooming, the basic design of the gardens can best be appreciated. Summer visitors are in for a special treat on Saturday nights in July and August, when a spectacular fireworks display lights up the garden.

As you may imagine, the attraction is very busy throughout spring and summer. For this reason, try to arrive as early as possible, before the tour buses do. Once through the tollgate and in the sprawling parking lot, make a note of where you parked. On the grounds, pick up a flower guide and follow the suggested route. After you've done the rounds (allow at least two hours), you can choose from a variety of eateries. You'll also find a gift shop specializing in—you guessed it—floral items, as well as a store selling seeds.

VICTORIA BUTTERFLY GARDENS

In the same vicinity as Butchart Gardens, **Victoria Butterfly Gardens** (1461 Benvenuto Dr., 250/652-3822, www.butterfly-gardens.com, 9am-5pm daily summer, 10am-3pm daily fall-spring, adults $16.40, seniors and students $12, children $6) offers you the opportunity to view and photograph some of the world's most spectacular butterflies at close range. Thousands of these beautiful creatures—species from around the world—live here, flying freely around the enclosed gardens and feeding on the nectar provided by colorful tropical plants. You'll also be able to get up close and personal with exotic birds such as parrots and cockatoos.

TOURS
Carriage Tours

The classic way to see Victoria is from the comfort of a horse-drawn carriage. Throughout the day and into the evening, **Victoria Carriage Tours** (250/383-2207 or 877/663-2207, www.victoriacarriage.com) has horse carriages lined up along Menzies Street at Belleville Street awaiting passengers. A 30-minute tour (seating up to 6, $100) goes around the downtown waterfront precinct; there's also a 45-minute tour costs ($145) or

Butchart Gardens

take the 60-minute Royal Tour ($185). Tours run 9am-midnight daily in summer and bookings aren't necessary, though there's often a line.

Bus Tours

Big red double-decker buses are as much a part of the Victoria tour scene as horse-drawn carriages. These are operated by Gray Line (250/744-3566 or 800/663-8390, www.sightseeingvictoria.com) from beside the Inner Harbour. There are many tours to choose from, but to get oriented while also learning some city history, take the 90-minute Grand City Drive Tour (every 40 minutes, adults $40, students $28, children $18), departing from the harbor front. The most popular of Gray Line's other tours is the one to Butchart Gardens ($71.50, including garden admission).

Ferry Tours

Victoria Harbour Ferry (250/708-0201, www.victoriaharbourferry.com, late Feb.-late Oct.) offers boat tours of the harbor and Gorge Waterway. The company's funny-looking boats each seat around 20 passengers and depart regularly 9am-dusk from below the Fairmont Empress. The 45-minute loop tour (adults $26, seniors $24, children $14) allows passengers the chance to get on and off where they want, or travel pieces of the entire loop for $4-12 per sector.

SPORTS AND RECREATION

All of Vancouver Island is a recreational paradise, but Victorians find plenty to do around their own city. Walking and biking are especially popular, and from the Inner Harbour, it's possible to travel on foot or by pedal power all the way along the waterfront to Oak Bay. Commercial activities are detailed here, but the best place to get information on a wide variety of operators is the Inner Harbour Centre (950 Wharf St., 250/995-2211 or 800/575-6700, www.innerharbourcentre.com), based on a floating

dock just around the corner from the information center.

Hiking and Biking

If you're feeling energetic—or even if you're not—plan on walking or biking at least a small section of the Scenic Marine Drive, which follows the shoreline of Juan de Fuca Strait from Ogden Point all the way to Oak Bay. The section immediately south of downtown, between Holland Point Park and Ross Bay Cemetery, is extremely popular with early-rising locals, who start streaming onto the pedestrian pathway before the sun is up.

Out of town, Goldstream Provincial Park, beside Highway 1, offers the best hiking opportunities. Goldstream is worth visiting for its network of hiking trails. Starting from the visitors center, the 200-meter (220-yard) Marsh Trail will reward you with panoramic water views from the mouth of the Goldstream River. Another popular destination is Goldstream Falls, at the south end of the park. This trail leaves from the back of the park campground and descends to the picturesque falls in around 300 meters (330 yards). Noncampers should park at the campground entrance, from where it's 1.2 kilometers (0.7 miles) to the falls. One of the park's longer hikes is the Goldmine Trail, which begins from a parking lot on the west side of Highway 1 halfway between the campground and day-use area. This trail winds 2 kilometers (1.2 miles) one-way through a mixed forest of lodgepole pine, maple, and western hemlock, passing the site of a short-lived gold rush and coming to Niagara Falls, a poor relation of its eastern namesake but still a picturesque flow of water. Of a similar length, but more strenuous, is the trail to the summit of 419-meter (1,370-foot) Mount Finlayson, which takes about one hour each way and rewards successful summiteers with views back across the city and north along Saanich Inlet. The trail is accessed from Finlayson Arm Road.

The Galloping Goose Regional Trail follows a rail line that once linked Victoria and Sooke. For 55 kilometers (34 miles) it parallels residential back streets, follows waterways, and passes through forested parkland. The rail bed has been graded the entire way, making it suitable for both walkers and cyclists. The official starting point is the disused railroad station at the top end of downtown where Wharf and Johnson Streets merge, and from the end of the trail in Sooke, bus 1 will bring you back to the city. Obviously you can't walk the entire trail in a day, but even traversing a couple of short sections during your stay is worthwhile for the variety of landscapes en route.

For those keen on getting around by bike, it doesn't get much better than the bike path following the coastline of the peninsula on which Victoria lies. From downtown, ride down Government Street to Dallas Road, where you'll pick up the separate bike path running east along the coast to the charming seaside suburb of Oak Bay. From there, Oak Bay Road will take you back into the heart of the city for a round-trip of 20 kilometers.

You can rent bikes at **Sports Rent** (1950 Government St., 250/385-7368, www.sportsrentbc.com, 9am-5:30pm Mon.-Fri., 9am-5pm Sat., 10am-5pm Sun.), just north of downtown, starting at $12-15 per hour or $35-50 per 24 hours. Once you reach Oak Bay, stop by **Oak Bay Bicycles** (1990 Oak Bay Ave., 250/598-4111, www.oakbaybikes.com, 9am-5:30pm Mon.-Fri., 9am-5pm Sat., 10am-5pm Sun.) for an eye-popping selection of bikes for everyone, including kids, tandem, road, racing, and mountain. They also have a modern repair shop and rentals.

Whale-Watching

Heading out from Victoria in search of whales is something that can be enjoyed by everyone. Both resident and transient whales are sighted during the local whale-watching season (mid-Apr.-Oct.), along with sea lions, porpoises, and seals. Trips last two to three hours, are generally made in sturdy inflatable boats with an onboard naturalist, and cost $90-110 pp. Recommended operators departing

A Whale of a Time

Once nearly extinct, today an estimated 20,000 **gray whales** swim the length of the British Columbia coast twice annually between Baja Mexico and the Bering Sea. The spring migration (Mar.-Apr.) is close to the shore, with whales stopping to rest and feed in places such as Clayoquot Sound and Haida Gwaii. **Orcas,** best known as **killer whales,** are not actually whales but the largest member of the dolphin family. Adult males can reach 10 meters (33 feet) in length and up to 10 tons in weight, but their most distinctive feature is a dorsal fin that protrudes more than 1.5 meters (5 feet) from their back. Orcas are widespread in oceans around the world, but they are especially common in the waters between Vancouver Island and the mainland. Three distinct populations live in local waters: resident orcas feed primarily on salmon and travel in pods of up to 50; transients travel by themselves or in very small groups, feeding on marine mammals such as seals and whales; and offshore orcas live in the open ocean, traveling in pods and feeding only on fish.

from the Inner Harbour include **Orca Spirit Adventures** (250/383-8411 or 888/672-6722), **Great Pacific Adventures** (250/386-2277 or 877/733-6722), and **Prince of Whales** (250/383-4884 or 888/383-4884).

Kayaking and Stand-Up Paddleboarding

With a waterfront location within easy walking distance of downtown, **Ocean River Sports** (1824 Store St., 250/381-4233 or 800/909-4233, www.oceanriver.com, 9:30am-6pm daily) is the most convenient place to head for kayaking and stand-up paddleboarding (SUP). Single kayaks, SUPs, and canoes (2 hours $40, full-day $60) and double kayaks (2 hours $60, full-day $90) are available. Throughout summer, Ocean River offers a variety of guided paddles, including a relaxing 2.5-hour evening tour ($70 pp) and the more adventurous 3-hour SUP tour of the harbor ($75 pp).

Scuba Diving

Close to downtown Victoria lie several good dive sites, notably **Ogden Point Breakwater,** which since its construction in 1916 has become a haven for marinelife, including octopuses, eels, anemones, starfish, and schools of rockfish. The breakwater is home base for **Ogden Point Dive Centre** (199 Dallas Rd., 250/380-9119, www.divevictoria.com, 9am-6pm daily), which offers rentals, instruction, and a guided shore dives ($99, with a dry-suit $129). Other amenities include lockers and showers.

To access the great diving in the Straits of Georgia and Juan de Fuca, you'll need to charter a boat. One particularly interesting site is **Race Rocks,** a 25-minute boat ride from Victoria. Because of strong tides, this site is for experienced divers only, but those that do venture out have the chance of seeing sea lions, abalones, giant sea urchins, king crabs, and an abundance of fish. Farther north, off the Saanich Peninsula's north end, the 110-meter (360-foot) **HMCS _Mackenzie_** destroyer escort was scuttled especially for divers. Ogden Point Dive Centre leads guided dives (Sat.-Sun., from $160 pp) that require boat access.

Swimming

The best beaches and ocean swimming is east of downtown starting at Oak Bay and extending all the way up the Saanich Peninsula. Most of the summer crowds spend the day at these beaches sunbathing; although a few hardy individuals brave a swim, water temperature here tops out at around 17°C (63°F). **Willows Beach,** at Oak Bay, is popular with local residents, but doesn't have as much sand as points north.

At the south end of Arbutus Cove is **Hollydene Beach,** a short stretch of sand that is as soft as anything found in the Victoria region. Continuing north is **Cordova Bay Beach,** a wider stretch of sand with similar cool waters. Farther north still is **Island View**

Beach Regional Park, where a long stretch of sand is backed by piles of driftwood and a forested area.

Warmer than the ocean are lakes dotted throughout the region. I've swum in most places and found **Eagle Beach** on **Elk Lake** to have the warmest water. It's a large shallow lake with a mostly sandy bottom that warms the water through the day, plus the beach is backed by a row of grand old willow trees. To get here, follow Highway 17 north toward the ferry terminal; you'll see the lake off to the left of the highway before reaching Sayward Road, where you exit. At forest-encircled **Thetis Lake,** west of downtown along the Trans-Canada Highway, the water is cooler than Elk Lake, but the small stretch of sand is a pleasant spot to relax in the sun.

If the ocean water surrounding Victoria is a little cold for your liking (as it is for most people), head downtown to **Crystal Pool** (2275 Quadra St., 250/361-0732, 5:30am-11pm Mon.-Thurs., 5:30am-10pm Fri., 6am-4pm Sat., 8:30am-4pm Sun., adults $5.75, seniors $4.50, children $4), which has an Olympic-size pool, a water slide, two kids' pools, a sauna, and a whirlpool.

ENTERTAINMENT AND EVENTS
The Arts

Dating to 1914 and originally called the Pantages Theatre, the grand old **McPherson Playhouse** (known lovingly as the "Mac" by local theatergoers) went through hard times during the 1990s but has seen a recent revival of fortunes and now hosts a variety of performing arts. It's in Centennial Square, at the corner of Pandora Avenue and Government Street. The Mac's sister theater, the **Royal Theatre** (805 Broughton St.), across downtown, began life as a roadhouse and was used as a movie theater for many years. Today it hosts stage productions and musical recitals. For schedule information and tickets at both theaters, contact the **Royal & McPherson Theatres Society** (250/386-6121 or 888/717-6121, www.rmts.bc.ca).

Performing arts on a smaller scale can be appreciated at the **Belfry Theatre** (1291 Gladstone Ave., 250/385-6815, www.belfry.bc.ca, Oct.-Apr., $25-40), in a historical church, which offers live theater.

Pacific Opera Victoria (250/385-0222, www.pov.bc.ca) performs three productions each year (usually Oct.-Apr., $25-75) in the McPherson Playhouse. The **Victoria Operatic Society** (250/381-1021, www.vos.bc.ca) presents musical theater year-round at the McPherson Playhouse.

At the **Symphony Splash** (250/385-9771, www.victoriasymphony.ca) on the first Sunday of August, the **Victoria Symphony** performs on a barge moored at the Inner Harbour. This kicks off the performing arts season, with regular performances through May at the Royal Theatre and other city venues.

Nightlife

Although it's not cheap, enjoying a drink at **The Veranda** (721 Government St., 250/384-8111, 11am-10:30pm daily May-Sept.) is a memorable experience. With prime harborfront location from the covered veranda of the iconic Fairmont Empress, you can enjoy a wide variety of beers, wines, cocktails, and champagne.

Closer to the Inner Harbour and converted from an old grain warehouse is **Swans Brewery & Pub** (Swans Hotel, 506 Pandora St., 250/361-3310, 11am-1am Mon.-Sat., 11am-midnight Sun.), which brews its own beer. Unlike many other smaller brewing operations, this one uses traditional ingredients and methods, such as allowing the brew to settle naturally rather than filtering it. The beer is available at the hotel's bar, in its restaurants, and in the attached liquor store. The main bar is a popular hangout for local businesspeople and gets busy 5pm-8pm Monday to Friday.

A few blocks farther north and right on the water is the **Canoe Brewpub** (450 Swift St., 250/361-1940, 11:30am-11pm Sun.-Wed., 11:30am-midnight Thurs.-Sat.), housed in an 1894 redbrick building that was at one time

home to generators that powered Victoria's street lights. This place is popular with the downtown crowd and has a huge patio overlooking the harbor. It's also kid-friendly and has live music Thursday to Saturday nights with no cover charge.

The **Strathcona Hotel** (919 Douglas St., 250/383-7137) is Victoria's largest entertainment venue, featuring four bars, including one with a magnificent rooftop patio (with a volleyball court) and the Sticky Wicket, an English bar complete with mahogany paneling.

Also offering magnificent water views is **Spinnakers Brewpub** (308 Catherine St., 250/386-2739, 8am-11pm daily), across the Inner Harbour from downtown. Having opened in 1984 as Canada's first brewpub, Spinnakers continues to produce its own European-style ales, including the popular Spinnakers Ale. The original downstairs brewpub is now a restaurant while upstairs is now the bar. Most important, both levels have outdoor tables with water views. The classic Spinnakers combo is a pint of India Pale Ale ($7.50) and beer-battered halibut and chips ($21).

Victoria's many English-style pubs usually feature a wide variety of beers, congenial atmosphere, and inexpensive meals. The closest of these to downtown is the **James Bay Inn** (270 Government St., 250/384-7151, 11am-11pm daily). Farther out, **Six Mile Pub** (494 Island Hwy., 250/478-3121, 11am-11pm Mon.-Tues., 11am-noon Wed.-Sat., 10am-11pm Sun.) is a classic Tudor-style English pub that was established in 1885, making it the province's oldest pub. To get there, head west out of the city along Highway 1 and take the Colwood exit.

Most of Victoria's nightclubs double as live music venues attracting a great variety of acts. In the Strathcona Hotel, **Distrikt** (919 Douglas St., 250/383-7137), is a city hot spot. It comes alive with live rock-and-roll some nights and a DJ spinning the latest dance tunes on other nights. In the same hotel, **Big Bad John's** (919 Douglas St., 250/383-7137) is the city's main country music venue. At the bottom of Bastion Square, **Darcy's Pub** (1127 Wharf St., 250/380-1322, 11am-1am daily) is a great place for lunch or an afternoon drink, but after dark it dishes up live rock to a working-class crowd.

Victoria boasts several good jazz venues. The best of these is **Hermann's Jazz Club** (753 View St., 250/388-9166, 5pm-midnight daily). Check the **Victoria Jazz Society website** (www.jazzvictoria.ca) for a schedule of local jazz performances.

Festivals

Due to its mild climate, Victoria's outdoor festivals extend beyond the summer into spring and fall, with the first major event occurring in May. Visti www.tourismvictoria.com for an easy-to-navigate event schedule.

SPRING

Officially, of course, February is still winter, but Victorians love the fact that spring arrives early on the west coast, which is the premise behind the **Flower Count** (throughout the city, www.flowercount.com, last week in Feb.). For other Canadians summer is a long way off, but locals count the number of blossoms in their own yards, in parks, and along the streets. Totals in the tens of millions are tabulated and gleefully reported across the country.

The birthday of Queen Victoria has been celebrated in Canada since 1834 and is especially relevant to those who call her namesake city home. The Inner Harbour is alive with weekend festivities that culminate in the **Victoria Day Parade** (downtown, Mon. preceding May 25). The parade takes two hours to pass a single spot. Although Queen Victoria's actual birthday was May 24, the event is celebrated with a public holiday on the Monday preceding May 25.

Hosted by the Royal Victoria Yacht Club and with more than 60 years of history behind it, **Swiftsure International Yacht Race** (finishes at Inner Harbour, 250/592-9098, www.swiftsure.org, last weekend of May) attracts thousands of spectators to the shoreline

of the Inner Harbour to watch a wide variety of vessels cross the finish line in six different classes, including the popular pre-1970 Classics division.

SUMMER

At **Victoria International Jazzfest** (downtown, 250/388-4423, www.jazzvictoria.ca, last week of June), more than 300 musicians from around the world descend on the capital for this weeklong celebration at various city venues.

At **Symphony Splash** (Inner Harbour, 250/385-9771, www.victoriasymphony.ca, first Sun. in Aug.), the local symphony orchestra performs from a barge moored in the Inner Harbour to masses crowded around the shore. This unique musical event attracts upward of 40,000 spectators who line the shore or watch from kayaks.

The water comes alive during the **Victoria Dragon Boat Festival** (Inner Harbour, 250/704-2500, www.victoriadragonboat.com, mid-Aug.), with up to 100 dragon boat teams competing along a short course stretching across the Inner Harbour. Onshore entertainment includes the Forbidden City Food Court, classic music performances, First Nations dancing, and lots of children's events.

The **Victoria Fringe Theatre Festival** (throughout the city, 250/383-2663, www.intrepidtheatre.com, last week of Aug., $12-18) is a celebration of alternative theater, with more than 350 acts performing at venues throughout the city, including outside along the harbor foreshore and inside at the Conservatory of Music on Pandora Street.

SHOPPING

Victoria is a shopper's delight. Although the city doesn't have defined shopping precincts, the following descriptions provide an overview of shopping destinations within the downtown core. In the Inner Harbour, **Government and Douglas Streets** are the main strip of tourist and gift shops. The bottom end of Douglas, behind the Fairmont Empress Hotel, is where you'll pick up all those souvenir T-shirts and such. The touristy shops are all open Sunday.

All summer, the historical precinct of **Bastion Square** is filled with local artisans selling their wares at the **Bastion Square Public Market** (11am-5:30pm Thurs.-Sat.). Linking Broad and Government Streets (near View St.), the cobblestoned **Trounce Alley** is off most visitors' radar, but worth searching out for the spiritual gifts at **Instinct Art & Gifts** (622 View St., 250/388-5033, 10am-5:30pm Mon.-Sat., noon-5pm Sun.) and the 1862 men's clothing store **W&J Wilson** (1221 Government St., 250/383-7177, 10am-5:30pm Mon.-Sat., 11am-4pm Sun.). Cross under the arch across Fisgard Street and enter Chinatown, with vendors selling produce and Asian curios, and then wander down **Fan Tan Alley**, Canada's narrowest street, and through an eclectic array of shops and boutiques.

Fort Street between Cook and Quadra Streets has been branded **Mosaic Village** in recognition of the wide variety of local merchants in the area—antiques shops, art galleries, clothing boutiques, and cooking supply stores.

DOWNTOWN

Up Government Street, away from the Inner Harbour, are stylish shops, such as **Hill's Native Art** (1008 Government St., 250/385-3911, 9am-7pm daily), selling a wide range of authentic First Nations souvenirs including original prints, Inuit carvings, totem poles, and jewelry from the island's coastal communities.

Cowichan Trading (1328 Government St., 250/383-0321, 9am-6pm daily) specializes in Cowichan sweaters and other products handknitted by the Cowichan people of Vancouver Island. It also sells art and pewter.

Murchie's (1110 Government St., 250/381-5451, 7:30am-6pm daily) sells an incredibly diverse selection of teas from around the world as well as tea paraphernalia such as teapots, gift sets, and collector tins. Traditions also continue at **Rogers Chocolates** (913 Government St., 250/881-8771, 9:30am-7pm Sun.-Thurs., 9:30am-10pm Fri.-Sat.), which

is set up like a candy store of the early 1900s, when Charles Rogers first began selling his homemade chocolates to the local kids.

OLD TOWN

In Old Town, the colorful, two-story **Market Square** courtyard complex was once the haunt of sailors, sealers, and whalers who came ashore looking for booze and brothels. It's been jazzed up, and today shops here specialize in everything from kayaks to condoms.

In the vicinity, a few blocks to the north, **Capital Iron** (1900 Store St., 250/385-9703, 9am-6pm Mon.-Sat., 10am-5pm Sun.) is the real thing. Housed in a three-story building that dates to 1863, this business began in the 1930s by offering the public goods salvaged from ships. In the 80-plus years since, it has evolved into a department store stocking an eclectic variety of hardware and housewares, many of which are maritime-related.

BOOKSTORES

Don't be put off by the touristy location of **Munro's Books** (1108 Government St., 250/382-2464 or 888/243-2464, 9am-6pm Mon.-Wed., 9am-9pm Thurs.-Sat., 9:30am-6pm Sun.), in a magnificent neoclassical building that originally opened as the Royal Bank in 1909. It holds a comprehensive collection of fiction and nonfiction titles related to Victoria, the island, and Canada in general.

Munro's may be the grandest bookstore in town, but it's not the largest. That distinction goes to **Chapters** (1212 Douglas St., 250/380-9009, 8am-11pm Mon.-Sat., 9am-11pm Sun.). In seaside Oak Bay, **Ivy's Bookshop** (2188 Oak Bay Ave., 250/598-2713, 9:30am-6pm Mon.-Sat., noon-5pm Sun.) is a friendly little spot with a wide-ranging selection from local literature to current best-sellers.

Bibliophiles the world over are familiar with www.abebooks.com, a website devoted to helping book lovers find used and rare books. What they probably don't know is that the conglomerate had its humble roots in Victoria (the company was started by two local couples in 1996, one of whom owned a secondhand bookstore in the western suburb of Colwood). Ironically, the success of www. abebooks.com has led to the closure of many local used bookstores, as has happened the world over, but one that remains is **Russell Books** (734 Fort St., 250/361-4447, 9am-6pm Mon.-Sat., 11am-5pm Sun.), specializing in rare regional and nautical titles.

A suburban bookstore of note, this one specializing in general used books, is **James Bay Coffee and Books** (143 Menzies St., 250/386-4700, 8am-6pm Mon.-Fri., 8:30am-6pm Sat.-Sun.). A huge selection of used books is only part of the appeal, as you can order familiar breakfasts and lunches, surf the Internet for free, and enjoy live music on Friday evenings. To get there from downtown, follow Menzies Street south from the Inner Harbour for five blocks.

FOOD
Downtown

Although locals are often disdainful of the touristy restaurants clustered around the Inner Harbour and complain that both the quality of food and service don't justify the prices, these restaurants do have a couple of redeeming features—many have water views and all are handy to downtown accommodations. Additionally, because of the thriving tourist trade centered on the Inner Harbour, chances are you will find something to suit your tastes and budget close at hand—pub fare, seafood, Canadian, Asian, Italian, Mexican, and even Himalayan. Unlike many cities, and aside from the small Chinatown, international restaurants are not confined to particular streets. On the other hand, Fort Street east of Douglas has a proliferation of restaurants that are as trendy as it gets on Vancouver Island.

You will still find great interest in traditional English fare, including afternoon tea, which is served everywhere from motherly corner cafés to the grand Fairmont Empress. English cooking in general is much maligned but worth trying. For the full experience, choose kippers and poached eggs for breakfast, a ploughman's lunch (crusty bread, a chunk of cheese, pickled onions), and then roast beef with Yorkshire pudding (a crispy pastry made with drippings and doused with gravy) in the evening.

COFFEEHOUSES

While Victoria is generally associated with afternoon tea, there are some serious coffee lovers in the capital. The focus at minimalist **Habit Coffee** (552 Pandora St., 250/294-1127, 7am-6pm Mon.-Fri., 8am-6pm Sat.-Sun.) is most definitely the coffee, though it offers an eclectic collection of magazines to browse through. Walk through Market Square from Habitat to ★ **Hey Happy** (560 Johnson St., 250/590-9680, 7:30am-5:30pm Mon.-Fri., 9am-5pm Sat.-Sun.), a small brightly lit place with a few outdoor tables. Ordering coffee at Het Happy is part of the experience—beans are ground individually for each order, and the baristas make a show of each serving. Look for seasonal drinks, such as iced coconut milk lattes in summer. Also recommended by the caffeine crowd is **Serious Coffee** (1280 Broad St., 250/380-0272, 6:30am-8pm Mon.-Fri., 8am-8pm Sat., 8am-6pm Sun.), with lots of comfortable seating.

Shatterbox (916 Pandora Ave., 778/432-2121, 7:30am-2:30pm Mon.-Fri.), a few blocks east of City Hall, is a gathering spot for local regulars who gather here for a wide range of highly regarded coffee drinks and a friendly atmosphere. Similarly, a good percentage of locals consider **Moka House** as pouring the best coffee in the city. Although they don't have any downtown locations, outlets are within walking distance of Fisherman's Wharf (19 Dallas Rd., 250/298-8452, 6:30am-5:30pm Mon.-Fri., 8am-5pm Sat.-Sun.) and on the east side of Beacon Hill Park (345 Cook St., 250/388-7377, 6am-11pm daily). As a bonus, bagels are excellent and both cafés have a patio.

BAKERIES

In Old Town, **Willie's Café Bakery** (537 Johnson St., 250/381-8414, 8am-3pm

Afternoon Tea

Afternoon tea, that terribly English tradition that started in the 1840s as a between-meal snack, is one ritual you should definitely partake in while visiting Victoria. Many North Americans don't realize that there is a difference between afternoon tea and high tea, and even in Victoria the names are sometimes used in place of one another. Afternoon tea is the lighter version, featuring fine teas (no tea bags) accompanied by delicate crustless sandwiches, scones with clotted cream and preserves, and a selection of other small treats. High tea (traditionally taken later in the day, around 6pm) is more substantial—more like dinner in North America.

The best place to immerse yourself in the ritual is at one of the smaller tearooms scattered around the outskirts of downtown. You can order tea and scones at the **James Bay Tea Room** (332 Menzies St., 250/382-8282, 8am-4pm daily, $15-26), but apart from the faux-Tudor exterior, it's not particularly English inside. **White Heather Tea Room** (1885 Oak Bay Ave., 250/595-8020, 10am-5pm Tues.-Sat., $23-30) is a small, homey setting, with a great deal of attention given to all aspects of afternoon tea—right down to the handmade tea cozies.

If the sun is shining, a pleasant place to enjoy afternoon tea is **Point Ellice House** (2616 Pleasant St., 250/380-6506, 11am-4pm Thurs.-Mon. May-June, 11am-5pm daily July-early Sept., adults $25, children $13), a historical waterfront property along the Gorge Waterway. The price includes a tour of the property. As you'd expect, it's a touristy affair at **Butchart Gardens** (800 Benvenuto Dr., Brentwood Bay, 250/652-4422, noon-4pm daily, $36), with Cornish pasties, quiche, and more.

The **Fairmont Empress** (721 Government St., 250/389-2727, $75) offers the grandest of grand afternoon teas in their Lobby Lounge, but you'll pay for it. Still, it's so popular that you must book at least a week in advance through summer and reserve a table at one of 12 sitting times between 11am and 6pm.

Finally, **Murchie's** (1110 Government St., 250/381-5451, 7:30am-6pm daily), in the heart of the downtown tourist precinct, sells teas from around the world as well as tea paraphernalia such as teapots, gift sets, and collector tins. The adjacent café pours teas from all over the globe in a North American-style coffeehouse.

Mon.-Fri., 8am-4pm Sat.-Sun., lunch $6.50-9.50) is an old-style café offering full cooked breakfasts, cakes, pastries, and sodas, with a quiet cobbled courtyard in which to enjoy them. Ignore the dated furnishings at the **Dutch Bakery** (718 Fort St., 250/383-9725, 7:30am-5pm Mon.-Sat.) and tuck into freshly baked goodies and handmade chocolates.

Two blocks north from the Dutch Bakery, but a world apart in concept, **Fol Epi** (732 Yates St., 778/265-6311, 7am-6pm Mon.-Fri., 8am-6pm Sat.-Sun.) is renowned for its delicious breads, all prepared from scratch and sold though this modern café. Ciabatta, baguettes, and cranberry hazelnut whole-wheat loafs—you can't go wrong. Similarly, and nearby, **Wildfire Bakery** (1517 Quadra St., 250/381-3473, 7:30am-6pm Mon.-Fri., 8am-5pm Sat., 8:30am-5pm Sun., lunch $7-10) is best known for its hand-shaped, preservative-free breads that begin with in-house grinding of island-grown wheat. Wildfire also offers freshly made granola and tasty lunches.

CASUAL DINING

The Veranda (Fairmont Empress, 721 Government St., 250/384-8111, 11am-10:30pm daily May-Sept., $14-40) enjoys a prime location at the front of Victoria's best-know hotel, with unobstructed views across landscaped gardens to the Inner Harbour. Food prices are not as high as you may expect, with seafood chowder ($12), single-serve pizza ($20), and halibut and chips ($32) for the refined setting and wonderful location.

Sam's Deli (805 Government St., 250/382-8424, 7am-5pm Mon.-Fri., 7:30am-5pm Sat.-Sun., $7-12) also draws in tourists like a magnet from its central location right across from the information center. Many places nearby have better food, but Sam's boasts a superb location and a casual, cheerful atmosphere that makes it perfect for families. Try a seafood chowder and salad combo ($10.50) or sandwiches ($7-12): shrimp and avocado is an in-house feature.

Broughton Street Deli (648 Broughton St., 250/380-9988, 7am-4pm Mon.-Fri., 9am-3pm Sat., breakfast $10-13, lunch $6-9) occupies a tiny space at street level of a historical redbrick building two blocks back from the Inner Harbour. Soups ($6) are made from scratch daily, and sandwiches are just $8.

Heading north from the Inner Harbour, at the foot of Bastion Square, **The Local** (1205 Wharf St., 250/385-1999, 11:30am-10pm Sun.-Thurs., 11:30am-midnight Fri.-Sat., $12-18) offers a menu of simple, globally inspired cooking, although the outdoor tables are reason enough to stop by. The halibut burger, the tandoori chicken wrap, the ahi tuna tacos—it's all excellent.

A few blocks north of The Local, in Old Town, the small **Sour Pickle Café** (1623 Store St., 250/384-9390, 7:30am-3:30pm Mon.-Fri., 8:30am-3:30pm Sat.-Sun., lunch $7-13) comes alive with funky music and an enthusiastic staff. The menu offers bagels (from $3.80), full cooked breakfasts (from $9), soup of the day ($6), healthy sandwiches ($8-11), and delicious single-serve pizzas (around $13).

Well worth searching out, **Blue Fox** (919 Fort St., 250/380-1683, 7:30am-4pm Mon.-Fri., 8am-3pm Sat.-Sun., lunch $7-12) nearly always a line for tables. Breakfast includes Eggs Benedict Pacífico (with smoked salmon and avocado) and Apple Charlotte (French toast with apples and maple syrup). At lunch, try an oversize Waldorf salad or a curried chicken burger with sweet date chutney. Almost everything is under $12.

Downstairs in the James Bay Inn, south of downtown, **Art Deco Café Restaurant** (270 Government St., 250/388-9928, 7:30am-9pm daily, $12-25) has an art deco theme, friendly staff, and a predictable wide-ranging menu

that suits the tastes of in-house guests (who receive a 15 percent discount on their food) and hungry locals avoiding the waterfront area.

OLD-STYLE DINERS

Much as visitors flock to the cafés and restaurants of the Inner Harbour and Government Street, the area away from the waterfront remains the haunt of lunching locals. Reminiscent of days gone by, **John's Place** (723 Pandora Ave., 250/389-0711, 7am-9pm Mon.-Fri., 8am-4pm and 5pm-9pm Sat.-Sun., $11-20), just off Douglas Street, serves excellent value for those in the know. The food is good, the atmosphere casual, and the waiters actually seem to enjoy working here. It's breakfast, burgers, salads, and sandwiches throughout the week, but weekend brunch is busiest, when there's nearly always a line spilling onto the street.

Opposite Beacon Hill Park and in business since 1958, **Beacon Drive-In** (126 Douglas St., 250/385-7521, 7am-10pm daily, $5-11) dishes up the usual collection of cooked breakfasts and loaded burgers, with so-so milk shakes to wash it all down. Dating to the 1960s, **Paul's Motor Inn Restaurant** (1900 Douglas St., 250/382-9231, 7am-3pm Mon., 7am-8pm Tues.-Sun., $9-15) has no-frills cooked breakfasts (from $7), sandwiches and burgers ($9-12), and full meals such as meatloaf with a side of mashed potatoes (under $15).

SEAFOOD

Fish-and-chips is a British tradition, sold as such at a number of places around town. Most centrally located is **Old Vic Fish & Chips** (1316 Broad St., 250/383-4536, 11:30am-8pm Thurs.-Tues., $13-19), which has been in business since 1930. As at any island fish-and-chip joint, paying extra for halibut is worthwhile.

My favorite two places for fish-and-chips are away from the tourist-clogged streets of the Inner Harbour. For the very best quality, **Fairfield Fish & Chips** (1277 Fairfield Rd., 250/380-6880, 11:30am-7:30pm Tues.-Sat., $8-14) is a winner. Fish choices include halibut, haddock, cod, and rockfish, which are served with perfectly cooked chips. Other options include a halibut burger and deep-fried oysters. It's located along Fairfield Road at Moss Street, a few blocks north of Dallas Road.

The location alone makes ★ **Barb's Fish & Chips** (Fisherman's Wharf, foot of St. Lawrence St., 250/384-6515, 11am-8:30am daily Mar.-Oct., $12-23), a sea-level eatery on a floating dock, my other favorite. It's not a restaurant as such, but a shack surrounded by outdoor table settings, some protected from the elements by a canvas tent. The food is as fresh as it gets. Choose cod and chips, halibut and chips, or clam chowder, or splash out on a steamed crab. Adding to the charm are the surrounding floating houses and seals that hang out waiting for handouts. An enjoyable way to reach Barb's is by ferry from the Inner Harbour. Also on Fisherman's Wharf is **The Fish Store** (250/383-6462, 11am-6pm daily, longer hours in summer), which sells a wide variety of local seafood, as well as fish-and-chips, fish tacos, and other light meals.

Down on the docks below downtown, at the foot of Broughton Street, ★ **Red Fish Blue Fish** (1006 Wharf St., 250/298-6877, 11:30am-7pm daily mid-Feb.-Oct., $11-24) is a takeout place ensconced in a brightly painted shipping container. Unusual for a fish-and-chip joint, the emphasis is on wild, sustainable fisheries. Prices reflect the waterfront location (two pieces of halibut with chips for $20), but the quality of fish is excellent. Other choices include a grilled scallop burger and wild salmon fish tacos. Expect a line in summer.

Occupying a prime downtown location on a floating dock amid whale-watching boats, seaplanes, and shiny white leisure craft just south of Red Fish Blue Fish, the **Flying Otter Grill** (950 Wharf St., 250/414-4220, 11am-9:30pm Mon.-Fri., 11am-10pm Sat.-Sun., $14-22) is just steps from the main tourist trail, but it's far enough removed to make it a popular haunt for a quiet, casual waterfront meal. The setting alone makes the Flying Otter a winner, but the menu is a knockout. Choose crab cakes or pan-fried oysters or sweet chili chicken

wings to share, and then move on to mains like seafood paella. To get here, walk north along the harbor from the information center.

Touristy **Finn's** (1208 Wharf St., 250/360-1808, 11:30am-10pm daily, $17-40) is a bustling waterfront complex with a maritime theme and family atmosphere. Beyond the Wharf Street entrance is the main dining room and a two-story deck, where almost every table has a stunning water view. Seafood starters to share include prawn and pork dim sum and steamed mussels. Mains include everything from burgers to lobster tails, with lots of local seafood in between. Prices in this central location are higher than at other restaurants, but during happy hour (4pm-5:30pm daily), some drinks and food items are heavily discounted (half-price oysters, beer $4).

Spinnakers Brewpub (308 Catherine St., 250/386-2739, 8am-11pm daily, $13-29) was Canada's first in-house brewpub, and it's as popular today as when it opened in 1985. The crowds come for the beer but also for great food served up in a casual, modern atmosphere. British-style pub fare, such as a ploughman's lunch, is served in the bar, while west coast and seafood dishes such as sea bass basted in an ale sauce are offered in the downstairs restaurant.

CANADIAN

Of course, there's seafood on the menu at one of Victoria's best restaurants, **Agrius** (732 Yates St., 778/265-6312, 9am-2pm daily, 5pm-10pm Wed.-Sat., $32-36), a small 36-seat restaurant at the back of one of the city's best bakeries. But the main draw is the slow-food concept, with all dishes made from scratch using island and British Columbia suppliers—even the ketchup and sausages are prepared in the Agrius kitchen. Diners are offered a variety of breads to start, all made from scratch in-house, and can then choose between a strawberry salad or beef tartare, before moving on to mains such as pork chop, dry aged on the premises, accompanied by seasonal island vegetables.

CHINESE

Victoria's small Chinatown surrounds a short, colorful strip of Fisgard Street between Store and Government Streets. Generally the menus are filled with familiar Westernized Chinese choices. Near the top (east) end of Fisgard Street is **QV Café and Bakery** (1701 Government St., 250/384-8831, 6:30am-11pm daily, $7-12), offering inexpensive Western-style breakfasts in the morning and Chinese delicacies the rest of the day.

One of the least expensive places in the area is **Wah Lai Yuen** (560 Fisgard St., 250/381-5355, 10am-8pm Tues.-Sun., $8-15), a simply decorated, well-lit restaurant with fast and efficient service. The wonton soups are particularly good. Try the Szechwan prawns, or get adventurous and order salted squid. Out front is a bakery with offerings such as peanut-almond soft cake.

Down the hill a little and up a flight of stairs is **Don Mee Restaurant** (538 Fisgard St., 250/383-1032, 11am-10pm Mon.-Fri., 10am-10pm Sat.-Sun., $11-23), a vast dining room specializing in the cuisine of Canton. Although there is an emphasis on seafood, the Peking duck, served over two courses, is a highlight. Four-course dinners (under $25 pp) for two or more are a good deal.

OTHER ASIAN RESTAURANTS

Noodle Box (818 Douglas St., 250/384-1314, 11am-9pm daily, $9-14) started out as a street stall and now has multiple locations, including uphill from the back entrance to the Fairmont Empress. The concept is simple—an inexpensive noodle bar, serving up fare made to order (including spice level) and similar to what you'd find on the streets of Southeast Asia.

One of the best Thai restaurants in the city is **Sookjai Thai** (893 Fort St., 250/383-9945, 11:30am-9:30pm Mon.-Thurs., 11:30am-10:30pm Fri.-Sat., $11-19). The tranquil setting is the perfect place to sample traditional delights such as *tom yum goong* (a prawn and mushroom soup with a hint of tangy citrus), and baked red snapper sprinkled with spices

sourced from Thailand. The snapper is the most expensive main, and there are several inspiring vegetarian choices (around $12).

The Mint (1414 Douglas St., 250/386-6468, 5pm-2am daily, $14-23) is dark, richly decorated room downstairs on the main thoroughfare through downtown, so it's easy to miss. The menu blends Nepalese cooking styles with seafood and Western produce to create tasty and innovative dishes at reasonable prices, such as butter chicken poutine (under $10). The kitchen is open until 2am, making it a popular late-night haunt.

EUROPEAN

One of the most popular restaurants in downtown Victoria is **Pagliacci's** (1011 Broad St., 250/386-1662, 11:30am-10pm daily, $14-29), known for hearty Italian food, homemade bread, great desserts, and loads of atmosphere. Small and always busy, the restaurant attracts a lively local crowd, many with children; you'll inevitably have to wait for a table during the busiest times (reservations are not taken). Pasta options include a prawn fettuccine topped with tomato mint sauce.

The setting of **Il Terrazzo** (Waddington Alley, 250/361-0028, 11am-3pm Mon.-Fri., 5pm-10pm daily, $15-36), in a redbrick building in the historical Old Town precinct, is perfect for this traditional northern Italian dining room. The pasta is made in-house, and when combined with local seafood (think halibut baked with a peppercorn and blackberry demi-glace on a bed of three-cheese fusilli pasta), the combination is divine.

The energetic atmosphere at ★ **Café Brio** (944 Fort St., 250/383-0009, 5:30pm-9pm Tues.-Sat., $22-32) is contagious, and the food is as good as anywhere in Victoria. The Mediterranean-inspired dining room is adorned with lively artwork and built around a U-shaped bar, while out front are a handful of tables on an alfresco terrace. A creative menu combines local, seasonal produce with expertise and flair. The charcuterie, prepared in-house, is always a good choice to begin with, followed by wild salmon prepared however your server suggests. Order the sticky date toffee pudding, even if you're full.

VEGETARIAN

★ **Rebar** (50 Bastion Square, 250/361-9223, 11:30am-9pm Mon.-Fri., 9:30am-8pm Sat.-Sun., $8.50-17) is a cheerful, always-busy 1970s-style vegetarian restaurant with a loyal local following. Dishes such as the almond burger at lunch and Thai tiger prawn curry at dinner are full of flavor and made with only the freshest ingredients. Still hungry? Try the nutty carrot cake. Children are catered to with fun choices such as banana and peanut butter on sunflower-seed bread. It's worth stopping by just for juice: vegetable and fruit juices, power tonics, and wheatgrass infusions ($7) are made to order.

In the heart of Chinatown, **Venus Sophia** (540 Fisgard St., 250/590-3953, 10am-5:30pm Tues.-Sun., lunch $7-12) has been long known as a tea room, but a change in ownership in 2011 saw an expansion to include an extensive menu of simple yet creative vegetarian dishes, including a tasty brie and mango quesadilla.

Oak Bay

Oak Bay, east of downtown, is a picturesque seaside suburb with many grand homes and bustling shopping strip dotted with cafés. It's also the end of the scenic coastal drive from downtown. One of the most popular cafés in Oak Bay is **Discovery Coffee** (1964 Oak Bay Ave., 250/590-7717, 6:30am-6pm daily), which roasts its own coffee and is one of the only places in the city with a syphon coffeemaker. Just off Oak Bay Avenue, **Crumsby's** (2509 Estevan Ave., 250/595-2221, 8am-5pm Mon.-Sat., 9am-4pm Sun., lunch $8-11) has soups and salads, but it's the cupcakes that draw the most attention, with choices as varied as mini cupcakes and vegan chocolate.

Ottavio Italian Bakery (2272 Oak Bay Ave., 250/592-4080, 8am-6pm Tues.-Sat., lunch $8-12) has been operated by three generations of the same Italian family. The hand-rolled breads are baked daily, the very best imported oils and spices are reasonably priced, and the gelato is as good as anywhere in the city. At lunch, enjoy an antipasto platter or grilled panini on rosemary and olive oil focaccia.

Although the **Oak Bay Beach Hotel** (1175 Beach Dr., 250/598-4556) is a modern replacement for the historical hotel that once stood on this waterfront site, dining options remain similar to those enjoyed by generations of locals and visitors alike. **Snug Pub** (11am-midnight daily, $14-24) was a busy social hangout as early as the 1950s, and in the reinvented hotel it continues this role, with dishes such as fish-and-chips and steak and kidney pie, all best enjoyed with a pint of beer on the waterfront patio. Much of the exposed beam work and dark polished wood in **Kate's Café** (6am-5pm daily, lunch $9-14) was reclaimed from the original structure. The classic cooking offered in the upscale 32-seat **Dining Room** (7am-11am and 6pm-9pm daily, $24-42) has been impressing the genteel residents of Oak Bay for generations.

West of Downtown

If you are staying on Bear Mountain, head to **Bear Mountain Market** (1325 Bear Mountain Pkwy., 778/265-7108, 6am-9pm daily) for the best coffee on the mountain, as well as sandwiches and other light lunches made in-house. For a resort-like setting, head over to the nearby Westin Bear Mountain, where the **Pool Side Bar & Grill** (1999 Country Club Way, 250/391-7160, 11am-7pm daily July-Aug., lunch $14-17) is the perfect place to dine and dip on a warm afternoon. The sandwiches, wraps, and salads are all reasonably priced, and the setting can't be beat. The resort's main restaurant is **Bella** (1999 Country Club Way, 250/391-7160, 6:30am-11:30am and 5pm-10pm daily, $20-39), where the emphasis is on healthy breakfasts such as blueberry and orange pancakes and refined evening dining.

Heading north from Victoria toward Nanaimo, **Malahat Chalet** (Moon Water Lodge, 265 Trans-Canada Hwy., 778/432-4606,

8am-9pm Sun.-Thurs., 8am-10pm Fri.-Sat., $15-32) offers sweeping views across Saanich Inlet from a lofty location high above the water. Outdoor tables are the place to be on warm days, but inside is also cozy and inviting. You can stop by and enjoy the panorama over a coffee, but the food is good, much of it created using local seafood and produce. The Fisherman's Soup (halibut, salmon, prawns, and clams) is filling enough to suffice as a main, but if you're still hungry, the beer-battered halibut or grilled salmon doused in a maple-whisky glaze are both good choices.

Saanich Peninsula

Seahorses Cafe (799 Verdier Ave., Brentwood Bay, 250/544-1565, 10:30am-4pm Mon. and Wed.-Fri., 9:30am-4pm Sat.-Sun., lunch $11-18) has a prime waterfront location beside the ferry dock in Brentwood Bay, with lots of outdoor tables taking full advantage of the setting. In addition to the usual array of coffee drinks, the breakfast bun is a great way to start the day. Crab cakes, salmon burgers, and pulled pork wraps anchor the lunch menu. As a bonus, Seahorses has the least expensive kayak rentals ($20 for 2 hours) I have found on Vancouver Island.

Across the ferry dock from Seahorses Cafe is **Brentwood Bay Pub** (849 Verdier Ave., Brentwood Bay, 250/544-5102, 11:30am-11pm daily, $13-27), part of Brentwood Bay Resort, where the waterfront patio is extremely busy on weekends, but you can usually talk your way to a table with a view midweek. The menu is a step or two above typical pub fare, with healthy salads and mains such as garlic prawn linguine.

★ **Café Zanzibar** (1164 Stelly's Cross Rd., 250/652-1228, 9am-4pm Sun.-Mon., 7:30am-4pm Tues.-Wed., 7:30am-4pm and 5pm-10pm Thurs.-Fri., 8am-4pm and 5pm-10pm Sat., lunch $15-18) is in a delightful rural setting inland from Brentwood Bay (off West Saanich Rd.), with a patio draped in greenery providing the best seating on warmer days. Full English breakfasts using free-range local eggs and quality bacon draw morning diners,

but it is the global-inspired lunch and dinner menus that are the real star, with prices much lower than you'd pay in downtown Victoria. Tandoori chicken and mango salad, the lamb burger with apricot mango relish, or North African lamb shanks—it's hard to go wrong with anything on the Zanzibar menu.

ACCOMMODATIONS

Victoria accommodations come in all shapes and sizes. A couple of downtown hostels cater to travelers on a budget, but there are also a surprising number of convenient roadside motels with rooms for under $100, including one right off the Inner Harbour. Bed-and-breakfasts are where Victoria really shines, with more than 300 at last count. You'll be able to find bed-and-breakfast rooms for under $100, but to fully immerse yourself in the historical charm of the city, expect to pay more. In the same price range are boutique hotels, such as the Bedford Regency—that is, older hotels that have been restored and come with top-notch amenities and full service. Most of the upscale hotel chains are not represented downtown—the city has no Four Seasons, Hilton, Hotel Inter-Continental, Hyatt, Marriott, Radisson, or Regent. Finally, if you are looking for a splurge, the surrounding area is blessed with two lodges (Sooke Harbour House in Sooke and Brentwood Bay Resort) that regularly garner top rankings in the glossy travel magazine polls.

In the off-season (Oct.-May), the nightly rates quoted here are discounted up to 50 percent, but occupancy rates are high as Canadians flock to the country's winter hot spot. No matter what time of year you plan to visit, arriving in Victoria without a reservation is unwise, but especially in the summer months, when crowds of visitors compete for a relative paucity of rooms. As a last resort, staff at the **Victoria Visitor Centre** (Wharf St., 250/953-2022 or 800/663-3883, www. tourismvictoria.com) can offer help finding a room. Regardless of your budget, you can't go wrong staying at one of the following specially selected places.

Downtown

All but a couple of the venues in this section are within easy walking distance of the Inner Harbour. If you're traveling to Victoria outside summer, don't be put off by the quoted rates, because the downtown hotels offer the biggest off-season discounts. If you're simply looking for a motel room and don't want to pay for the location, check the British Columbia *Accommodations* guide for options along the routes leading into downtown from the north.

UNDER $50

Budget travelers are well catered to in Victoria, and although the choices in the capital are more varied than in Vancouver, no particular backpacker lodge stands out above the rest.

In the heart of the oldest section of downtown Victoria is **HI-Victoria** (516 Yates St., 250/385-4511 or 888/883-0099, www.hihostels.ca, dorm $35, nonmembers $38.50, private room $78-105 s or d). The 108-bed hostel enjoys a great location only a stone's throw from the harbor. Separate dorms and bath facilities for men and women are complemented by two fully equipped kitchens, a large meeting room, a lounge, a library, a game room, travel services, public Internet terminals, and an informative bulletin board. There are a limited number of private rooms.

$50-100

Housed in the upper stories of an old commercial building, **Ocean Island Backpackers Inn** (791 Pandora Ave., 250/385-1789 or 888/888-4180, www.oceanisland.com, dorm $35, private room $56-110 d) is just a couple of blocks from downtown. This party place—exactly what some young travelers are looking for, but annoying enough for some to generate letters to harried travel writers. On the plus side, the lodging is clean, modern, and welcoming throughout. Guests have use of kitchen facilities, a laundry room, and a computer for Internet access. There's also plenty of space to relax, such as a reading room, a music room (guitars supplied), a television room, and a street-level bar open until midnight.

Private rooms range from a super-small room with bunk beds ($56) to an en suite ($110) that sleeps a family of four.

$100-150

In the heart of the city center, the six-story 1913 **Strathcona Hotel** (919 Douglas St., 250/383-7137 or 800/663-7476, www.strathconahotel.com, $125-175 s or d) holds a variety of bars, including a couple of the city's most popular, as well as 86 guest rooms. They are sparsely furnished but clean and comfortable. It's worth upgrading to the much larger Premier Rooms. Rates include a light breakfast.

Paul's Motor Inn (1900 Douglas St., 250/382-9231 or 866/333-7285, www.paulsmotorinn.com, $135-175 s or d) is an older two-story motel set around a courtyard a 15-minute walk north of the Inner Harbour. Rates include parking and Internet access, and there's a diner-style restaurant onsite where most cooked breakfasts are under $10. The Executive Rooms are quite spacious and well suited to families with younger children who don't mind sleeping on a pull-out sofa bed.

In a quiet residential area immediately east of downtown, **The Craigmyle** (1037 Craigdarroch Rd., Rockland, 250/595-5411 or 888/595-5411, www.victoriahomestay.ca, from $125 s, $145 d) has been converted from part of the original Craigdarroch Estate—it stands directly in front of the famous castle. This rambling 1913 home is full of character, comfortable furnishings, and lots of original stained-glass windows. The 15 guest rooms include singles, doubles, and family suites; some share baths while others are en suite. An inviting living room with a TV, a bright sunny dining area, and friendly longtime owners make this a real home away from home. Check-in is 2pm-6pm.

Dating to 1911 and once home to artist Emily Carr, **James Bay Inn** (270 Government St., 250/384-7151 or 800/836-2649, www.jamesbayinn.com, $149-199 s or d) is five blocks from the harbor and within easy walking distance of all city sights and Beacon Hill

Park. From the outside, the hotel has a clunky, uninspiring look, but a bright and breezy decor and new beds in the simply furnished rooms make it a pleasant place to rest your head. All guests enjoy discounted food and drink at the downstairs restaurant and pub.

$150-200

One of the least expensive hotel options close to the Inner Harbour, but still just one block from Douglas Street, is the 1867 **Dalton Hotel & Suites** (759 Yates St., 250/384-4136 or 800/663-6101, www.daltonhotel.ca), Victoria's oldest hotel. Millions of dollars have been spent restoring the property with stylish wooden beams, brass trim and lamps, ceiling fans, and marble floors reliving the Victorian era. The restored boutique rooms ($165-215 s or d) are absolutely charming, with large beds and lovely baths. Some rooms at the Dalton haven't been renovated in years. Sold as standard rooms ($125-135 d) and not pictured on the website, they are a little overpriced. Tea and toast is included in all of these rates. The Dalton offers some attractive off-season meal-inclusive deals—just make sure you know which class of room you'll be in.

Just four blocks from the Inner Harbour, the 1905 ★ **Beaconsfield Inn** (988 Humboldt St., 250/384-4044 or 888/884-4044, www.beaconsfieldinn.com, $199-279 s or d) is exactly what a Victorian bed-and-breakfast should be. Original mahogany floors, high ceilings, classical moldings, imported antiques, and fresh flowers from the garden create an upscale historical charm throughout. Each of the nine guest rooms is individually decorated in Edwardian style. I stayed in the Emily Carr Suite, named for the renowned artist who spent her early years in the city, with a rich burgundy and green color scheme, Carr prints on the walls, a regal mahogany bed topped by a goose-down comforter, an oversize bath and jetted tub, and separate sitting area with a fireplace. After checking in, you'll be invited to join other guests for high tea in the library and then encouraged to return for a glass of sherry before heading out

for dinner. Breakfast, served in a formal dining room or a more casual conservatory, is a grand affair, with multiple courses of hearty fare delivered to your table by your impeccably presented host.

Every time I visit Victoria, I expect to see that the old **Surf Motel** (290 Dallas Rd. 250/386-3305, www.surfmotel.net, $165-195 s or d, Oct.-Mar. $125) has been demolished, but it's still here, offering priceless ocean and mountain views. It's south of the Inner Harbour; take Oswego Road from Belleville Street.

Yes, it's a chain hotel, but **Days Inn Victoria on the Harbour** (427 Belleville St., 250/386-3451 or 800/665-3024, www.daysinnvictoria.com, from $179 s or d) has a prime waterfront location that will make you feel like you're paying more than you really are. Befitting the location, rooms have a subtle nautical feel and, like all Days Inns, practical yet comfortable furnishings. In winter, you'll pay from just $120 for a suite with a view, with a light breakfast included. Year-round bonuses include free parking, in-room coffeemakers, and complimentary newspapers and bottled water.

In the oldest section of downtown, surrounded by the city's best dining and shopping opportunities, is the **Bedford Regency** (1140 Government St., 250/384-6835 or 800/665-6500, www.bedfordregency.com, $179-239 s or d), featuring 40 guest rooms of varying configurations. Stylish, uncluttered art deco furnishings and high ceilings make the standard rooms seem larger than they really are. A better deal are the deluxe rooms and suites, which provide more space and better amenities for only slightly more money.

If you're looking for a modern feel, centrally located ★ **Swans Suite Hotel** (506 Pandora Ave., 250/361-3310 or 800/668-7926, www.swanshotel.com, $195-355 s or d) is an excellent choice. Located above a restaurant-pub complex that was built in the 1880s as a grain storehouse, each of the 30 split-level suites holds a loft, a full kitchen, a dining area, and a bedroom. The furnishings are casual yet elegantly rustic, with West Coast artwork adorning the walls and fresh flowers in every room. In the off-season, all rooms are discounted up to 40 percent.

$200-250

Separated from downtown by Beacon Hill Park, **Dashwood Manor** (1 Cook St., 250/385-5517 or 800/667-5517, www.dashwoodmanor.com, $209-299 s or d), a 1912 Tudor-style heritage house on a bluff overlooking Juan de Fuca Strait, enjoys a panoramic view of the entire Olympic Mountain Range. The 12 guest rooms are elegantly furnished, and hosts Michael Dwyer and David Marshall will happily recount the historical details of each room. The Oxford Grand room ($249) holds a chandelier, a stone fireplace, and antiques.

Right on the Inner Harbour, **Gatsby Mansion Inn** (309 Belleville St., 250/388-9191 or 800/663-7557, http://huntingdonmanor.com, from $235 s, $245 d) has a central position across from the water. Dating to 1897, this magnificent property has been elegantly restored, with stained-glass windows, a magnificent fireplace, lots of exposed wood, crystal chandeliers under a gabled roof, and antiques decorating every corner. Afternoon tea is served in a comfortable lounge area off the lobby, and the restaurant has a nice veranda. Packages make staying at the Gatsby Mansion more reasonable, or visit in winter for as little as $160 s or $170 d.

$250-300

Very different from Victoria's traditional accommodations is the contemporary **Parkside Hotel & Spa** (810 Humboldt St., 250/940-1200 or 855/616-3557, www.parksidevictoria.com, from $259 s). Within walking distance of the Inner Harbour, the guest rooms have a contemporary ambience, and each has one or two bedrooms, a full kitchen with stainless-steel appliances, and large wall-mounted TVs. Rooms on the upper floors have city views. Other highlights include a fitness room, an indoor pool, a theater, a rooftop patio, and underground parking.

Similar in style and amenities is **Oswego** (500 Oswego St., 250/294-7500 or 877/767-9346, www.oswegohotelvictoria.com, from $265 s or d). Rooms on the upper floors have water views, including the two three-bedroom penthouse suites. Amenities include a fitness room, underground parking, and a contemporary bistro, all within walking distance of downtown.

Coast Victoria Hotel (146 Kingston St., 250/360-1211 or 800/716-6199, www.coasthotels.com, from $265 s or d) is the last of the string of accommodations along the south side of the harbor but is still within easy walking distance of downtown. Rates here fluctuate greatly. The rack rate for a harbor-view room with a very small balcony is $285 s or d, but book online and you'll get the same room with breakfast included for a nonrefundable $180. Rates include local calls, wireless Internet, a daily paper, and in-room coffee. The in-house Blue Crab Bar & Grill is notable for its extensive seafood menu.

In the same vicinity and sitting on a point of land jutting into the Inner Harbour, the **Inn at Laurel Point** (680 Montreal St., 250/386-8721 or 800/663-7667, www.laurelpoint.com, from $280 s or d) offers a distinct resort atmosphere within walking distance of downtown. Two wings hold around 200 rooms; each has a water view and private balcony, but well worth the extra money are the Terrace Suites. Amenities include an indoor pool, beautifully landscaped Japanese-style gardens, a sauna, a small fitness facility, Aura Restaurant, a lounge, and a gift shop.

Enjoying an absolute waterfront location right downtown is the **Victoria Regent** (1234 Wharf St., 250/386-2211 or 800/663-7472, www.victoriaregent.com, $279-349 s or d). The exterior of this building is nothing special, but inside, the rooms are spacious and comfortable. The best-value rooms at the Regent are the suites, which include a full kitchen, a balcony, wireless Internet, and a daily newspaper.

The ★ **Magnolia Hotel & Spa** (623 Courtney St., 250/381-0999 or 877/624-6654, www.magnoliahotel.com, from $279 s or d, off-season $169-209 s or d) is a European-style boutique hotel just up the hill from the harbor. It features an elegant interior with mahogany-paneled walls, Persian rugs, chandeliers, a gold-leaf ceiling, and fresh flowers throughout public areas. The rooms are each elegantly furnished and feature floor-to-ceiling windows, heritage-style furniture in a contemporary room layout, richly colored fabrics, down duvets, a work desk with cordless phone, and coffee-making facilities. Many also feature a gas fireplace. The baths are huge, each having marble trim, a soaker tub, and a separate shower stall. The hotel is also home to the Magnolia Spa and a stylish Mediterranean-themed restaurant. Rates include a light breakfast, a daily newspaper, passes to a nearby fitness facility, and unlike at most other downtown hotels, free parking.

In a prime waterfront position next to the parliament buildings is the **Hotel Grand Pacific** (463 Belleville St., 250/386-0450 or 800/663-7550, www.hotelgrandpacific.com, $289-389 s or d). Aside from more than 300 rooms, this modern property is also home to Spa at the Grand, a health club, spa services, restaurants and lounges, and a currency exchange. All rooms are well appointed, spacious, and have small private balconies.

OVER $300

Across the Inner Harbour from downtown, offering stunning city views, is the modern, upscale **Delta Hotels Victoria Ocean Pointe Resort** (100 Harbour Rd., 250/360-2999 or 888/236-2427, www.marriott.com, from $320 s or d). This hotel offers all of the services of a European-style spa resort with the convenience of downtown just a short ferry trip away. The rooms are simply yet stylishly furnished, with huge windows taking advantage of the views. Each comes with a work desk and high-speed Internet access, two phone lines, and plush robes. Facilities include a large health club, an indoor glass-enclosed pool, spa and massage services, tennis, a lounge, a seasonal outdoor terrace, and two restaurants.

The grand old **Fairmont Empress** (721 Government St., 250/384-8111 or 800/257-7544, www.fairmont.com, from $459 s or d) is Victoria's best-loved accommodation. With only magnificent gardens separating it from the Inner Harbour, it's also in the city's best location. Designed by Francis Rattenbury in 1908, the Empress is one of the original Canadian Pacific Railway hotels. The 464 guest rooms are offered in 90 different configurations, but as in other hotels of the era, most are small. Each is filled with Victorian period furnishings and antiques. The least expensive Fairmont Rooms start at $459 in summer, but if you really want to stay in this Canadian landmark, consider upgrading to a Fairmont Gold room. Although not necessarily larger, these rooms have harbor views, private check-in, nightly turndown service, and a private lounge with a patio where hors d'oeuvres are served in the evening; the $499-599 rates include a light breakfast. If you don't stay at the Empress, plan on at least visiting one of the restaurants or having a drink in the regal Bengal Lounge.

Oak Bay

East of downtown in the suburb of Oak Bay, the Tudor-style **Oak Bay Guest House** (1052 Newport Ave., 250/598-3812 or 800/575-3812, www.oakbayguesthouse.com, $165-210 s or d), one block from the waterfront, has been taking in guests since 1922. It offers 11 smallish antique-filled rooms, each with a private balcony and a bath. The Sun Lounge holds a small library and tea- and coffee-making facilities, while the Foyer Lounge features plush chairs set around an open fireplace. Rates include a delicious four-course breakfast.

West of Downtown

The small community of Malahat is strung out along the main route up the island

25 kilometers (16 miles) from downtown Victoria, making it a good place to spend the night for those who want to get an early start on northward travel. Along the way to Malahat, you'll pass by Bear Mountain.

$50-100

If you just need somewhere to spend the night, it's hard to go past the cozy cabins at **Malahat Bungalows Motel** (300 Trans-Canada Hwy., 250/478-3011, $85-115 s or d). No surprises here; expect fairly basic motel-style units spread around well-maintained grounds. There is no air-conditioning, but each room has wireless Internet and a flat-screen TV.

$250-300

The Westin Bear Mountain (1999 Country Club Way, 250/391-7160 or 888/533-2327, www.bearmountain.ca, from $279 s or d) is a small part of an ambitious real estate and recreational development that sprawls over the namesake mountain summit about 30 minutes' drive from downtown. Access is from Highway 1's exit 14, off Millstream Road. More than 150 rooms are spread through two buildings, and all have luxurious touches such as slate floors, deep soaker tubs, and super comfortable beds. The main lodge holds a spa facility and multiple dining options while a separate building is home to a health club, an outdoor heated pool, and more dining options. Rooms have balconies and many have full kitchens. Check online for golf packages (from $200 pp).

Moon Water Lodge (265 Trans-Canada Hwy., Malahat, 778/432-3123, $250-350 s or d) may be right beside the island's main highway, but you'd never know once inside the building, where views extend across the coastal forest to the protected waters of Saanich Inlet. Almost all rooms have water views and private balconies, while the in-house Malahat Chalet Restaurant, across the parking lot, also has a great outlook. The rooms are all well decorated and come with gas fireplaces, bathrobes, comfortable beds, and free calls within North America.

Saanich Peninsula

With the exception of the waterfront Brentwood Bay Resort, these accommodations are along Highway 17, the main route between downtown Victoria and the BC Ferries terminal at Swartz Bay. These properties are best suited to travelers arriving at or departing from the airport or ferry terminal but are also handy to Butchart Gardens.

$50-100

Right beside the highway, **Western 66 Motor Inn** (2401 Mt. Newton Cross Rd., 250/652-4464 or 800/463-4464, www.western66motorinn.com, $92-96 s or d) has a large variety of affordable rooms, English-style gardens, complimentary coffee in the lobby each morning, and an inexpensive family restaurant on the premises. Traveling families will want to upgrade to the ample family rooms ($160), which sleep up to six people.

$100-150

At the same intersection as the Western 66 is **Quality Inn Waddling Dog** (2476 Mt. Newton Cross Rd., 250/652-1146 or 800/567-8466, www.qualityinnvictoria.com, $135-155 s or d), styled as an old English guesthouse complete with an English pub. The Waddling Dog offers several well-priced packages that include meals and admission to Butchart Gardens.

OVER $300

You'll feel like you're a million miles from the city at ★ **Brentwood Bay Resort** (849 Verdier Ave., Brentwood Bay, 250/544-2079 or 888/544-2079, www.brentwoodbayresort.com, $329-589 s or d), an upscale retreat overlooking Saanich Inlet. It's one of only three Canadian properties with a Small Luxury Hotels of the World designation, and you will want for nothing. You can learn to scuba dive, take a water taxi to Butchart Gardens, enjoy the latest spa treatments, or join a kayak tour. The guest rooms take understated elegance to new heights. Filled with natural light, they feature contemporary West Coast styling (lots

Brentwood Bay Resort

through **Goldstream Provincial Park** (19 kilometers/11 miles from downtown, $33) and begins its up-island journey north. The southern end of the park holds 161 well-spaced campsites scattered through an old-growth forest—it's one of the most beautiful settings you could imagine close to a capital city. The campground rates include hot showers but there are no hookups. The park's interpretive center is farther north along the highway, and many trails lead off from the campground, including a 10-minute walk to photogenic Goldstream Falls. The campground is also within walking distance of a grocery store.

In Malahat, seven kilometers (4 miles) farther north along Highway 1, is **Cedar Springs Ranch** (230 Trans-Canada Hwy., 250/478-3332 or 844/578-3332, www.cedar-springsranch.com, mid-May-mid-Sept., tents $42, hookups $49-54), which has basic cabins ($92-114 s or d) that sleep four to six in bunk beds (bring your own bedding). Facilities include showers, an outdoor pool, a laundry room, a store, and a game room.

of polished wood and natural colors), the finest Italian sheets on king beds, and private balconies. Modern conveniences like DVD entertainment systems, wireless Internet, and free calls within North America are a given. Dining options include a beautiful restaurant specializing in Vancouver Island produce and local seafood and an upscale pub with a waterfront patio.

Camping
WEST OF DOWNTOWN
Fort Victoria RV Park (340 Island Hwy., 250/479-8112, www.fortvictoria.ca, $50) is six kilometers (4 miles) northwest of the city center on Highway 1A. This campground provides full hookups (including cable TV), free showers, laundry facilities, wireless Internet, and opportunities to join charter salmon-fishing trips.

NORTH ALONG HIGHWAY 1
Continuing west from the campgrounds west of downtown, Highway 1 curves north

SAANICH PENINSULA
Halfway between downtown Victoria and Sidney is **Island View Beach Regional Park** (Homathko Dr., 250/652-0548, late May-early Sept., $15-20, cash only), right on the beach three kilometers (2 miles) east of Highway 17.

INFORMATION AND SERVICES
Tourism Offices
Tourism Victoria runs the bright, modern **Victoria Visitor Centre** (812 Wharf St., 250/953-2033 or 800/663-3883, www.tourismvictoria.com, 8:30am-8:30pm daily May-Sept., 9am-5pm daily Oct.-Apr.), which overlooks the Inner Harbour. The friendly staff can answer most of your questions. They also book accommodations, tours and charters, restaurants, entertainment, and transportation, all at no extra cost; sell local bus passes and map books with detailed area-by-area maps; and stock an enormous selection of brochures. Also get the free *Accommodations*

publication and the free local news and entertainment papers—the best way to find out what's happening while you're in town.

Coming off the ferry from Vancouver, stop in at **Sidney Visitor Centre** (10382 Pat Bay Hwy., 250/656-0525, www.sidney.ca, 9am-5pm daily summer), which is just off the highway along the road leading into Sooke.

Emergency Services

In a medical emergency, call 911 or contact **Victoria General Hospital** (1 Hospital Way, 250/727-4212), northwest of downtown just off the Trans-Canada Highway. For cases that aren't urgent, a handy facility is **James Bay Medical Treatment Centre** (230 Menzies St., 250/388-9934, 11am-5:30 Mon.-Fri., 10am-3:30pm Sat.). For dental care, try the **Cresta Dental Centre** (3170 Tillicum Rd., at Burnside St., 250/384-7711, 8am-9pm Mon.-Fri., 9am-5pm Sat.-Sun.). You can fill prescriptions at **Shoppers Drug Mart** (1222 Douglas St., 250/381-4321, 6am-midnight Mon.-Fri., 9am-midnight Sat.-Sun.).

GETTING THERE AND AROUND
Air

Air Canada (604/688-5515 or 888/247-2262, www.aircanada.ca), **Pacific Coastal** (604/273-8666 or 800/663-2872, www.pacific-coastal.com), and **WestJet** (604/606-5525 or 800/538-5696, www.westjet.com) have scheduled flights between Vancouver and Victoria, but the flight is so short that the attendants don't even have time to throw a bag of peanuts in your lap. These flights are really only practical if you have an onward destination—flying out of Victoria, for example, with Los Angeles as a final destination.

Several companies operate seaplanes between downtown Vancouver and downtown Victoria. From Coal Harbour, on Burrard Inlet, **Harbour Air** (604/274-1277 or 800/665-0212, www.harbourair.com) has scheduled floatplane flights to Victoria's Inner Harbour. Expect to pay around $130 pp one-way for any of these flights.

VICTORIA INTERNATIONAL AIRPORT

Victoria International Airport (YYJ, www.victoriaairport.com), the island's main airport, is on the Saanich Peninsula, 20 kilometers (12 miles) north of Victoria's city center. Once you've collected your baggage from the carousels, it's impossible to miss the car-rental outlets (Avis, Budget, Hertz, and National) across the room, where you'll also find a currency exchange and an information booth. Outside is a taxi stand and the ticket booth for the shuttle bus. The modern terminal also houses a lounge, various eateries, and a profusion of greenery.

YYJ Airport Shuttle (778/351-4995 or 855/351-4995, www.yyjairportshuttle.com, adults $25, children $15 one-way) operates buses between the airport and major downtown hotels as well as **Capital City Station** (721 Douglas St.) every 30 minutes. The first departure from downtown to the airport is 5am. A **taxi** costs approximately $75 from the airport to downtown.

Ferry
FROM VANCOUVER

BC Ferries (250/386-3431 or 888/223-3779, www.bcferries.com) links Vancouver and Victoria with a fleet of ferries that operate year-round. Ferries depart Vancouver from **Tsawwassen,** south of Vancouver International Airport (allow one hour by road from downtown Vancouver) and **Horseshoe Bay,** on Vancouver's North Shore. They terminate on Vancouver Island at **Swartz Bay,** 32 kilometers (20 miles) north of Victoria. On weekends and holidays, the one-way fare on either route costs adults $17.20, ages 5-11 $8.60, and vehicles $57.50. Limited vehicle reservations ($15 per booking) are accepted online at www.bcferries.com.

In high season (late June-mid-Sept.), the ferries run about once an hour 7am-10pm daily. September to June, they run a little less frequently. Both crossings take around 90 minutes. Expect a wait in summer, particularly if you have an oversize vehicle: each ferry can accommodate far fewer large vehicles than standard-size cars and trucks.

Try to plan your travel outside peak times, which include summer weekends, especially Friday afternoon sailings from Tsawwassen and Sunday afternoon sailings from Swartz Bay. Most travelers don't make reservations but simply arrive and prepare themselves to wait for the next ferry if the first one fills. Both terminals have shops with food and magazines as well as summertime booths selling everything from crafts to mini doughnuts.

FROM WASHINGTON STATE

From downtown Seattle's Pier 69, **Clipper Navigation** (250/382-8110 or 800/888-2535, www.clippervacations.com, adults US$109 one-way, US$185 round-trip) runs passenger-only ferries to Victoria's Inner Harbour. In summer, sailings are made five times daily, with the service running fall-spring on a reduced schedule. Travel is discounted with seven days advance purchase, off-season, and year-round for seniors and children.

North of Seattle, Anacortes is the departure point for **Washington State Ferries** (206/464-6400, 250/381-1551, or 888/808-7977, www.wsdot.wa.gov/ferries, adults US$19.45, seniors and children US$9.70, vehicles with driver US$53.65) to Sidney, 32 kilometers (20 miles) north of Victoria on Vancouver Island, with a stop en route in the San Juan Islands. Make reservations at least 24 hours in advance.

The final option is to travel from Port Angeles to Victoria. The *MV Coho* (250/386-2202 or 360/457-4491, www.cohoferry.com, adults US$18.50, children US$9.25, vehicles with driver US$64) runs year-round, with up to four crossings daily in summer.

Bus

Capital City Station (721 Douglas St.) is behind the Fairmont Empress. **Pacific Coach Lines** (604/662-7575 or 800/661-1725, www.pacificcoach.com) operates bus service between Vancouver International Airport and downtown Victoria (6am-9pm daily summer, $55 one-way, includes ferry fare) via the Tsawwassen-Swartz Bay ferry. The trip takes 3.5 hours, but is made more comfortable with onboard restrooms and free wireless Internet.

Most central attractions can be reached on foot, but the **Victoria Regional Transit System** (250/385-2551, www.transitbc.com, $2.50 per ride, day pass $5) is excellent and easy to jump on and off to get everywhere you want to go. Pick up an *Explore Victoria* brochure at the information center for details on the buses needed to reach all the major sights, parks, beaches, and shopping areas.

Bike

Victoria has some excellent designated bike paths, including one that follows the coastline from the Inner Harbour to Oak Bay. For rentals ($12-15 per hour, $35-50 for 24 hours), **Sports Rent** (1950 Government St., 250/385-7368, www.sportsrentbc.com, 9am-5:30pm Mon.-Fri., 9am-5pm Sat., 10am-5pm Sun.) has a handy downtown location, and their website has links to all the best riding options. Or try **Oak Bay Bicycles** (1990 Oak Bay Ave., 250/598-4111, www.oakbaybikes.com, 9am-5:30pm Mon.-Fri., 9am-5pm Sat., 10am-5pm Sun.).

Taxi

Taxis operate on a meter system, charging $3.30 at the initial flag drop plus just over $2 per kilometer. Call **Blue Bird Cabs** (250/382-8294 or 800/665-7055), **Empress Taxi** (250/381-2222), or **Victoria Taxi** (250/383-7111).

Vicinity of Victoria

SOOKE

About 34 kilometers (21 miles) from Victoria, Sooke (with a silent "e") is a forestry, fishing, and farming center serving a surrounding population of 13,000. The town is best known for a lodge that combines luxurious accommodations with one of Canada's most renowned restaurants, but a couple of other diversions are worth investigating as well.

Sights and Recreation

The town spreads along the shore of Canada's southernmost Pacific harbor. The safe haven for boats is created by **Whiffen Spit,** a naturally occurring sandbar that extends for over one kilometer (0.6 miles). Take Whiffen Spit Road (through town to the west) to reach the spit. It's a 20-minute walk to the end, and along the way you may spot seals and sea otters on the shoreline.

Another natural attraction are the **Sooke potholes,** a series of intriguing geological features found alongside the Sooke River. To get here, turn north off Sooke Road onto Sooke River Road on the east (Victoria) side of the Sooke River.

Sooke Region Museum (2070 Phillips Rd., 250/642-6351, 9am-5pm daily, donation) is on the west side of Sooke River Bridge. When you've finished admiring the historical artifacts, relax on the grassy area in front or wander around the back to count all 478 growth rings on the cross-section of a giant spruce tree. The museum is also home to **Sooke Visitor Centre.**

Across the harbor is **East Sooke Regional Park,** protecting 1,422 hectares (3,512 acres) of coastal forest and rocky shoreline. It holds around 50 kilometers (30 miles) of trails leading along sea cliffs, to the open meadows of an abandoned apple orchard, and to lofty lookouts. Pick up a map from the visitors center to help find your way around the park. The main access is Gillespie Road, which branches south off Highway 14 on the east side of Sooke. One kilometer (0.6 miles) down Gillespie Road is a pullout on the left. Park here to access the Galloping Goose Trail. Linking downtown Victoria and Sooke, this stretch is a pleasant

East Sooke Regional Park

walk or bike through old-growth forest, with a spur to the left leading to a lookout above Roche Cove.

Food

The best place for a coffee in Sooke is **Stick in the Mud** (6715 Eustace Rd., 250/642-5635, 6am-5pm Mon.-Fri., 7:30am-5pm Sat.-Sun., $7.50-11), where the coffee beans are roasted in-house and all the baked goods and sandwiches are prepared daily. For a simple, old-fashioned diner-style meal, head to **Mom's Café** (2036 Shields Rd., 250/642-3314, 8am-8pm daily, $12-16), where breakfasts are all under $10 and halibut and fries is $13. Turn right onto Shields Road one block west of the Petro Canada gas station.

In addition to luxury accommodations, one of Canada's finest dining experiences can be had at **Sooke Harbour House** (1528 Whiffen Spit Rd., 250/642-3421, 5:30pm-9pm daily, 4 courses around $95 pp). The decor is country-style simple, not that anything could possibly take away from the food and ocean views. The menu changes daily, but most dishes feature local seafood, prepared to perfection with vegetables and herbs picked straight from the surrounding garden and specialties such as sea asparagus harvested from tidal pools below the restaurant. The cellar is almost as renowned as the food—it holds more than 10,000 bottles. Reservations are essential.

17 Mile House Pub (5126 Sooke Rd., 250/642-5942, 11am-11pm daily, $14-26) is a charming relic from the past. It dates from an era when travelers heading to Sooke would stop for a meal 17 miles from Victoria's City Hall. The walls of this 1894 building are decorated in a century's worth of memorabilia, and there's still a hitching post out back. The menu is typical pub fare, although one thing that definitely wasn't on the menu 100 years ago is a delicious jambalaya.

Accommodations

★ **Sooke Harbour House** (1528 Whiffen Spit Rd., 250/642-3421 or 800/889-9688, www.sookeharbourhouse.com, $329-559 s or d) combines the elegance of an upscale country-style inn with the atmosphere of an exclusive oceanfront resort. The restaurant attracts discerning diners from around the world, but the accommodations offered are equally impressive. The sprawling waterfront property sits on a bluff, with 28 guest rooms spread throughout immaculately manicured gardens. Each of the rooms reflects a different aspect of life on the west coast, and all have stunning views, a wood-burning fireplace, and a deck or patio. Off-season, rates are reduced up to 40 percent.

SOOKE TO PORT RENFREW

The road west from Sooke takes you past gray pebbly beaches scattered with shells and driftwood, past **Gordon's Beach** to **French Beach**, about 20 kilometers (12 miles) from Sooke. Here you can wander down through a lush forest of Douglas fir and Sitka spruce to watch Pacific breakers crashing up on the beach—and keep an eye open for whales and eagles. It's a great place for a windswept walk, a picnic, or camping (with pit toilets, $15). An information board at the park entrance posts detailed maps and articles on area beaches, points of interest, plants, and wildlife.

Continuing west, the highway winds up and down forested hills for another 12 kilometers (7.5 miles) or so, passing evidence of regular logging as well as signposted forest trails to sandy beaches. Along this stretch of coast are two great accommodations. The first, located three kilometers (2 miles) beyond French Beach, is **Point No Point Resort** (10829 West Coast Rd., 250/646-2020, www.pointnopointresort.com, $215-280 s or d), which features 28 cabins, each with ocean views, a full kitchen, and a fireplace. Explore the shore out front, relax on the nearby beach, or scan the horizon for migrating whales, with the Olympic Mountains as a backdrop. The in-house restaurant serves lunch daily and dinner (mains $29-42) Wednesday-Sunday.

Two kilometers (1.2 miles) farther west,

high upon oceanfront cliffs, **Fossil Bay Resort** (11033 West Coast Rd., 250/646-2073, www.fossilbay.com 2-night minimum weekends, $219-249 s or d) offers six modern cottages, each with a hot tub, a private balcony, a wood-burning fireplace, a king bed, a full kitchen, and Wi-Fi.

Sandcut Beach

Officially within Jordan River Regional Park, this scenic highlight was little known except to local residents until the creation of a park in 2010 (there was no signage along the highway, nor an official access trail). Today, a 10-minute walk through an old-growth forest leads to the beach. The highlight is an oceanfront waterfall, which to the east (left) as you emerge at the beach. In any other location, the cascade would be of little consequence, but tumbling over a sandstone cliff with the ocean and Olympic Mountains as a backdrop makes this spot a photographer's dream (late afternoon has the best light).

Jordan River

When you emerge at the small settlement of Jordan River, take time to take in the smells of the ocean and the surrounding windswept landscape. The town comprises only a few houses, a logging operation, and **Jordan River Regional Park.** The park lies on a point at the mouth of the Jordan River. It's not the best campground ($15, cash only) you'll come across, but some sites are right on the ocean, while others are scattered along the river mouth and in the open forest for more protection from the elements; surfers often spend the night here, waiting for the swells to rise and the long right-hand waves known as Jordans to crank up.

Juan de Fuca Provincial Park

Established in 1996, this 1,528-hectare (3,776-acre) park protects a narrow swath of Pacific coastline between China Beach, three kilometers (2 miles) west of Jordan River in the east, and Botanical Beach near Port Renfrew in the west. From Highway 14, there are four

Juan de Fuca Provincial Park

main access points, as well as the Juan de Fuca Marine Trail, which parallels the coast for the entire length of the park.

At the east side of the park, a 700-meter (0.4-mile one-way) trail leads down through towering Sitka spruce to **China Beach,** which is strewn with driftwood and backed by a couple of protected picnic sites. Between the driftwood and the ocean is a long stretch of sand that at low tide is also very wide. Vehicle-accessible camping ($18) is available back up by the highway. Continuing west, parking areas at Sombrio Beach and Parkinson Creek are trailheads for beach access, with the former a popular surfing spot and also home to an interesting moss-filled canyon. The fourth and westernmost access point is Botanical Beach.

HIKING

While the West Coast Trail gets most of attention from serious hikers, the 47-kilometer (29-mile) **Juan de Fuca Marine Trail** is more accessible for the average hiker, easier, and does not have the high cost associated with its more famous neighbor. The forest and ocean scenery is arguably equal to the West Coast Trail, although there are fewer long stretches of sand, and due to the accessibility, there is not the same solitude.

Stretching from China Beach (just west of Jordan River) in the east to Port Renfrew in the west, the trail can be completed in three days, but with two additional access points (Sombrio Beach and Parkinson Beach), it's possible to enjoy sections of the trail as a day hike. One of the busiest sections of the trail is at the Port Renfrew End, where you can hike from Botanical Beach for a short distance to get a feeling for the coastal wilderness.

Along the trail are six wilderness campgrounds (no reservations, $5 pp), four of which are simply designated areas along the back of driftwood-strewn beaches. **West Coast Trail Express** (250/477-8700, www.trailbus.com) picks up and drops off along the route so, for example, you could park at China Beach, hike to Port Renfrew, and then jump aboard the daily service to return to your vehicle ($30 pp).

Port Renfrew

This small seaside community clings to the rugged shoreline of Port San Juan, 104 kilometers (65 miles) west of Victoria along Highway 14. Best known as the starting point of the West Coast Trail, the town attracts both anglers and hikers, with tourist facilities for both.

Follow the signs through town to **Botanical Beach,** the town's main "official" sight. At this fascinating intertidal pool area, low tide exposes hundreds of species of marine creatures at the foot of scoured-out sandstone cliffs. The 2.7-kilometer (1.8-mile) loop trail from the end of the road passes the beach as well as Botany Bay, which is more of a rocky outlook than a beach. This is also the official end of the Juan de Fuca Marine Trail, a wilderness hiking trail extending back along the coast to China Beach.

San Juan Valley

If you don't want to return to Victoria along Highway 14, and you're eventually heading north up the island, consider traveling across the San Juan Valley 53 kilometers (33 miles) to Lake Junction and Lake Cowichan. The valley is forested with massive Douglas firs up to 800 years old. Be aware that this is an active logging area—logging trucks don't give way, *you* do. Make sure you have enough gas, and drive with your headlights on so the trucks see you from a good distance. You'll find rustic campgrounds (no hookups) at **Fairy Lake,** six kilometers (4 miles) from Port Renfrew, and **Lizard Lake,** 12 kilometers (7.5 miles) farther along the road. Lizard Lake is best suited for small tents, and both have excellent fishing.

★ WEST COAST TRAIL

The magnificent West Coast Trail meanders 75 kilometers (47 miles) along Vancouver Island's untamed western shoreline, through the West Coast Trail unit of **Pacific Rim National Park.** It's one of the world's great hikes, exhilaratingly challenging, incredibly beautiful, and very satisfying—many hikers come back to do it again. The quickest hikers can complete the trail in four days, but by allowing six or seven days, you'll have time to fully enjoy the adventure. The trail extends from the mouth of the Gordon River, five kilometers (3 miles) north of Port Renfrew to Pachena Bay, near the remote fishing village of Bamfield on Barkley Sound. Along the way you'll wander along beaches, steep clifftops, and slippery banks; ford rivers by rope, suspension bridge, or ferry; climb down sandstone cliffs by ladder; cross slippery boardwalks, muddy slopes, bogs, and deep gullies; and balance on fallen logs. But for all your efforts you're rewarded with panoramic views of sand and sea, dense lush rainforest of hemlock and cedar, waterfalls cascading into deep pools, all kinds of wildlife—gray whales, eagles, sea lions, seals, and seabirds—and the constant roar and hiss of the Pacific surf pummeling the sand.

Planning Your Hike

The first step in planning to hike the West Coast Trail is to do some research at the Parks Canada website (www.pc.gc.ca). The invaluable information covers everything you need to know, including an overview of what to expect, instructions on paying trail-user fees, a list of equipment you should take, a list of relevant literature, tide tables, and advertisements for companies offering trailhead transportation.

Permits

The West Coast Trail is open May through September, with a quota system in effect between mid-June and mid-September. During this period, only 52 hikers per day are issued permits to start down the trail, 26 from each end. Reservations (519/826-5391 or 877/737-3783, 8am-6pm daily) for 40 of the 50 slots are accepted starting in early January. The trail-use permit is $127.50 pp and the nonrefundable reservation fee is $24.50 pp, which includes a waterproof trail map. The remaining 10 spots (5 from each end, no reservation fee) per day are allocated on a first-come, first-served basis, but expect a wait of up to two days in summer. For one month before and after peak season, there is no quota. Once at Port Renfrew or Bamfield, all hikers must head for the registration office to pick up their trail-use permit, pay for the two ferry crossings (each $16 pp, cash only), and attend a 90-minute orientation session (9:30am, 1pm, and 3:30pm daily). The 3:30pm session is for those who want to head out on the trail early the following morning.

Hiking Conditions

The trail can be hiked in either direction. The first two days out from Port Renfrew traverse the most difficult terrain, meaning more enjoyable hiking for the remaining days. The first two days out from Pachena Bay are relatively easy, meaning a lighter pack for the more difficult section.

Hikers must be totally self-sufficient, because no facilities exist along the route. Go with at least one other person, and travel as light as possible. Wear comfortable hiking boots, and take a stove, at least 15 meters (50 feet) of strong light rope, head-to-toe waterproof gear (keep your spare clothes and sleeping bag in a plastic bag), a small amount of fire starter for an emergency, sunscreen, insect repellent, a first-aid kit (for cuts, burns, sprains, and blisters), and waterproof matches. Rainfall is least likely in the summer; July is generally the driest month, but be prepared for rain, strong winds, thick fog, and muddy trail conditions even then.

River Crossings

Along the trail are two river crossings that are made via ferry. One is at Gordon River outside Port Renfrew. The other, midway along the trail, crosses Nitinat Narrows, the treacherous mouth of tidal Nitinat Lake. Ferries run 9am-5pm daily through the hiking season. The ferry fees (each $16) are collected on behalf of private operators in conjunction with the trail permit. When there is no ferry service (Oct.-Apr.), the West Coast Trail is closed.

Information

Seasonal trail offices are beside the Gordon River, five kilometers (3 miles) north of Port Renfrew (Pachidah Rd., 250/647-5434) and Pachena Bay (250/728-3234). Maps of the West Coast Trail are sold at specialty map and outdoor stores in Victoria or Vancouver, as well as at the trail offices at each end of the trail. The cost of a trail-use permit includes a waterproof trail map, or purchase one at the trail offices for $8.

Getting There

Unless you plan on turning around and returning to the beginning of the trail on foot, you'll want to make some transportation arrangements. Getting to and from either end of the trail is made easier by **West Coast Trail Express** (250/477-8700 or 888/999-2288, www.trailbus.com), which departs Victoria daily in the morning to both ends of the trail. The fare between Victoria and Port Renfrew is $66 one-way, while between Victoria and Pachena Bay it's $85. Pickups are made along the way, including from Nanaimo and Port Alberni. Travel between the trailheads costs $95. West Coast Trail Express also rents camping and hiking gear.

Tip: If you leave your vehicle at the Port Renfrew end of the trail and return by bus, you won't have to shuttle a vehicle out to remote Bamfield.

DUNCAN

Duncan, self-proclaimed "City of Totems," lies along the Trans-Canada Highway about 60 kilometers (37 miles) north of Victoria. The small city of 5,000 serves the surrounding farming and forestry communities of the Cowichan Valley. In addition to the regular tourist services, it's worth planning a stop in Duncan to view the many totem poles dotted around downtown. Hockey fans may want to head to the local skating rink (Island Savings Centre, 2687 James St.), between the highway and downtown, home to the world's largest hockey stick and puck.

The historic downtown core lies west of the Trans-Canada Highway, beyond the sprawling malls. Here you'll find the majority of Duncan's 80 totem poles, including 42 that are part of a self-guided walking tour. Two distinctly different carvings stand side by side behind City Hall—a First Nations carving and a New Zealand Maori carving donated by Duncan's sister city in New Zealand, Kaikohe.

BC Forest Discovery Centre

A local attraction is the 40-hectare (98-acre) **BC Forest Discovery Centre** (2892 Drinkwater Rd., 250/715-1113, 10am-4:30pm daily June-Aug., 10am-4pm Thurs.-Mon. Apr.-May and Sept., adults $16, seniors $14, children $11), one kilometer (0.6 miles) north of town. You can catch a ride on an old steam train and puff back in time, through the forest and past a farmstead, a logging camp, and Somenos Lake. Then check out the working sawmill, restored planer mill, blacksmith's shop, and forestry and lumber displays. The main museum building holds modern displays pertaining to the industry, including hands-on and interactive computer displays and an interesting audiovisual exhibit. The grounds are a pleasant place to wander through shady glades of trees (most identified) or over to the pond, where you'll find a gaggle of friendly geese awaiting a tasty morsel.

Food

Always crowded with locals, **Duncan Garage Café & Bakery** (330 Duncan St., 250/748-6223, 7am-6pm Mon.-Sat., 8:30am-5pm Sun., lunch $7-10) is well worth searching out across from the museum in the historic heart of downtown. Within the same complex is a store specializing in local organic produce and a used bookstore.

Duncan's premier dining room is **Hudson's on First** (163 1st St., 250/597-0066, 11am-2pm Tues., 11am-9pm Wed.-Sat., 10am-2pm Sun., $20-39) in a beautifully restored heritage home near the center of downtown. The menu is dominated by modern European cooking, with most choices using Vancouver Island game and produce, including a delicious mussel main.

Accommodations and Camping

Along the highway north of downtown, **Thunderbird Motor Inn** (5849 York Rd., 250/748-8192, www.thunderbirdmotorinn.ca, $85-120 s or d) is a basic roadside motel with older but clean rooms, each with air-conditioning and wireless Internet.

★ **Sahtlam Lodge and Cabins** (5720 Riverbottom Rd. W., 250/748-7738 or 877/748-7738, www.sahtlamlodge.com, 3-night minimum, from $180 s or d) is beside the Cowichan River west of town. Three cabins are spread across the property, and each is equipped with an old-style fireplace, a woodstove, and a full kitchen. A breakfast basket delivered daily to your cabin is included. On the south side of the river, continue along Boys Road to **Riverside RV & Camping** (3065 Allenby Rd., 250/746-4352, $22-30), which has a mix

Carmanah Walbran Provincial Park

If you're looking for a day trip to escape the tourist-clogged streets of Victoria, you can't get any more remote than the **Carmanah Valley.** Eyed by logging companies for many years, the Carmanah and adjacent Walbran Valley were designated a provincial park in 1995, providing complete protection for the 16,450-hectare (40,650-acre) watershed. For environmentalists, creation of the park was a major victory because this mist-shrouded valley extending all the way to the rugged west coast holds an old-growth forest of absolute wonder. Many 800-year-old Sitka spruce and 1,000-year-old cedar trees—some of the world's oldest—rise up to 95 meters (300 feet) off the damp valley floor. Others lie where they've fallen, their slowly decaying moss- and fern-cloaked hulks providing homes for thousands of small mammals and insects.

The only way to reach the park is via Lake Cowichan, following the south shore of Cowichan Lake to Nitinat Main, a logging road that leads south to Nitinat Junction (no services). There, the road is joined by a logging road from Port Alberni. From this point, Nitinat Main continues south to a bridge across the Caycuse River. Take the first right after crossing the river. This is Rosander Main, a rough road that dead-ends at the park boundary. The park is signposted from Nitinat Junction, but the signs are small and easy to miss.

From the road's-end parking lot, a rough 1.3-kilometer (0.8-mile) hiking trail (30 minutes one-way) descends to the valley floor and Carmanah Creek. From the creek, trails lead upstream to the Three Sisters (2.5 kilometers/1.5 miles, 40 minutes), through Grunt's Grove to August Creek (7.5 kilometers/4.6 miles, 2 hours), and downstream through a grove of Sitka spruce (2.4 kilometers/1.5 miles, 40 minutes) named for Randy Stoltmann, a legendary environmentalist who first brought the valley's giants to the world's attention.

of shaded and sunny sites, including many riverside tent sites.

COWICHAN LAKE AND VICINITY
Lake Cowichan

Lake Cowichan (population 3,500) is the name of a sprawling town at the east end Cowichan Lake. (The etymological reason for the reversal in the order of the town's name has been lost to time.) Vancouver Island's second largest lake, Cowichan is a 32-kilometer-long (20-mile) inland waterway known as Kaatza (Land Warmed by Sun) to local Coast Salish people. Logging roads—mostly unpaved—encircle the lake for 75 kilometers (47 miles) round-trip and provide hikers access to the adjacent wilderness, which includes the legendary **Carmanah Valley** in Carmanah Walbran Provincial Park.

Cowichan Lake is popular for a variety of **water sports,** but you really need a boat to take full advantage of its extensive waters. Instead, plan on **tubing** down the Cowichan River—it's a fun, inexpensive activity that everyone can enjoy. The starting point is waterfront Saywell Park beside the visitors center, from where the Cowichan River flows slowly eastward for around one hour of easy float time; things then speed up slightly before reaching the recommended pullout point at Little Beach, 2.5 hours from the starting point.

Making the experience easy for everyone to enjoy is **The Tube Shack** (250/510-7433, www.cowichanriver.com, 10am-5pm daily summer), right at the put-in point. They charge $20 pp for tube rental and shuttle back from Little Beach to town. Families have the option of renting a larger tube for $60, which includes the shuttle.

A major draw for serious anglers, salmon-filled **Cowichan River** has its source at Cowichan Lake, draining into the Strait of Georgia near Duncan. Much of its length is protected by **Cowichan River Provincial Park,** which extends over 750 hectares (1,850 acres) and 20 kilometers (12 miles). There are three access points to the park, including

Skutz Falls (second access road), where salmon spawn each fall. Trails are well sign-posted and link into the Trans-Canada Trail, which follows the river west to Cowichan Lake.

If tubing is not your thing, wander through Saywell Park to **Kaatza Station Museum** (125 South Shore Rd., 250/749-6142, 10am-4pm daily summer, donation), at the end of a rail line that once linked the lake to the main line along Vancouver Island's east coast. In addition to the railway station, two school rooms are filled with artifacts, while outside, railway rolling stock includes a 1916 caboose.

On the waterfront is **Cowichan Lake Visitor Centre** (125 South Shore Rd., 250/749-3244, www.cowichanlake.ca, 9am-5pm daily summer, 10am-4pm daily fall-spring). The center is a good source of information on conditions along the logging roads lacing the valley.

NORTH TOWARD NANAIMO

Nanaimo is just 45 kilometers (28 miles) north of Duncan—less than 30 minutes along the di-vided highway—but several small towns invite short detours along the way.

Chemainus

Chemainus has always been a sleepy little mill town; its first sawmill dates back to 1862. In 1982, MacMillan Bloedel shut down the town's antiquated mill, which employed 400 people, replacing it a year later with a modern mill employing only 155 people. Not wanting their town to slip into oblivion, residents hired local artists to cover the walls of downtown com-mercial buildings with larger-than-life murals depicting the town's history and culture. The result was outstanding, and in 1983, the artsy project won a prestigious downtown revital-ization competition against towns and cities from around the world. Ironically, by 1985, the mill had been modernized and reopened, and today, the thriving town is also home to one of the island's major theater companies.

Follow the signs to downtown Chemainus from Highway 1 and park at **Waterwheel Park,** central to local activities and eater-ies, and a pleasant downhill walk to the wa-terfront. Once the site of a grand home built for the sawmill manager, the tree-shaded park has a historical themed playground, lots of flower beds, and a working replica of the wa-terwheel that powered the original 1862 saw-mill. Pick up a walking tour map of the murals at **Chemainus Visitor Centre,** located at the park, where you'll see the first enormous mu-ral—a street scene. From there you can ex-plore the rest of Chemainus on foot, following the yellow footprints into town.

Chemainus Theatre Festival (9737 Chemainus Rd., 250/246-9820 or 800/565-7738, www.chemainustheatrefestival.ca) is a professional theater with productions ranging from Canadian comedies to Broadway classics performed in a purpose-built 274-seat theater. Performances run Wednesday-Sunday with tickets ranging $30-70, or $55-95 with lunch or dinner. Purchase tickets online or at the onsite box office.

From beside the park, **Chemainus Tours** (250/246-5055, adults $15, children $7.50) operates horse-drawn carriage rides every 30 minutes through summer around town, pass-ing all of the murals along the route.

One of many inviting downtown cafés is **Owl's Nest Bakery Bistro** (9752 Willow St., 250/324-8286, 9am-4:30pm daily, lunch $8-12). Their coffee is the best in town, and the wraps, salads, seafood chowder, and grilled paninis are all healthy and delicious.

Ladysmith

The trim little village of Ladysmith, 88 kilo-meters (53 miles) north of Victoria, is set on a high point of land immediately west of the highway. The first of its two claims to fame is its location straddling the 49th parallel (a cairn is located in front of the post office on 1st Ave.), the invisible line separating Canada from the United States. After much bargain-ing for the 1846 Oregon Treaty, Canada got to keep all of Vancouver Island despite the 49th parallel bisecting the island. The second claim is a little less historically important— Ladysmith was the birthplace of actress Pamela Anderson, whose family operated a small cabin resort along the waterfront.

The town itself was laid out in 1904 by coal baron James Dunsmuir for his employees who worked in one of his mines north of the village. When the mine closed in 1936, logging took over as the most important local industry.

Southern Gulf Islands

Spread throughout the Strait of Georgia between mainland British Columbia and Vancouver Island, this group of islands is Canadian territory but linked geologically to the San Juan Islands, immediately south. Five of the islands—**Salt Spring, the Penders, Galiano, Mayne,** and **Saturna**—are populated, and each is linked to the outside world by scheduled ferry service.

The mild, almost Mediterranean climate, beautiful scenery, driftwood-strewn beaches, quaint towns, and wide-ranging choice of accommodations combine to make the islands popular in summer, when laid-back locals share their home with flocks of visitors. Still, there's plenty of room to get away from the hustle, with pockets of the archipelago protected by **Gulf Islands National Park,** mile after mile of remote coastline, and easily reached peaks beckoning to be explored. After kayaking, biking, or hiking, the best way to end the day is at one of the many island restaurants, feasting on salmon and crab brought ashore that morning.

Ferry Service

The main transportation provider is **BC Ferries** (250/386-3431 or 888/223-3779, www.bcferries.com), which operates scheduled year-round services to the Southern Gulf Islands from both Vancouver Island and Vancouver. The main departure points are Swartz Bay, 32 kilometers (20 miles) north of Victoria, and Tsawwassen, on the south side of Vancouver. All ferries take vehicles (including RVs), motorcycles, bicycles, canoes, and kayaks. It's important to check the timetables (online or posted at each terminal) because some ferries are nonstop and others make up to three stops before reaching the more remote islands. Also try to avoid peak periods, such as Friday and Sunday afternoons. Aside from that, simply roll up and pay your fare.

Regardless of the final destination, the round-trip fare from Swartz Bay (Victoria) to any of the Southern Gulf Islands is a reasonable adults $12.60, children $6.30, vehicles $36.90. Interisland travel is charged on a one-way basis: adults $6.75, children $3.40, vehicles $14.40. The fare system is designed to be flexible; for example, if you plan to travel to Galiano Island from Swartz Bay, with a stop on Salt Spring Island on the way out, you would pay the interisland fare departing Salt Spring and then use the return portion of the main ticket from Galiano.

From the mainland Tsawwassen terminal (south of downtown Vancouver), the fare is the same regardless of which island you travel to: one-way adults $19.80, children $9.80, vehicles $72.80. Operating a couple of times daily, this service stops at all but Saturna Island, with Salt Spring the final stop, two hours after departure from Tsawwassen.

SALT SPRING ISLAND

Largest of the Southern Gulf Islands, 180-square-kilometer (70-square-mile) Salt Spring (pop. 10,500) lies close to Vancouver Island, immediately north of Saanich Inlet. Ferries link the south and north ends of the island to Vancouver Island, and myriad roads converge on the service town of **Ganges.** The island is home to many artisans, along with hobby farmers, retirees, and wealthy

Southern Gulf Islands

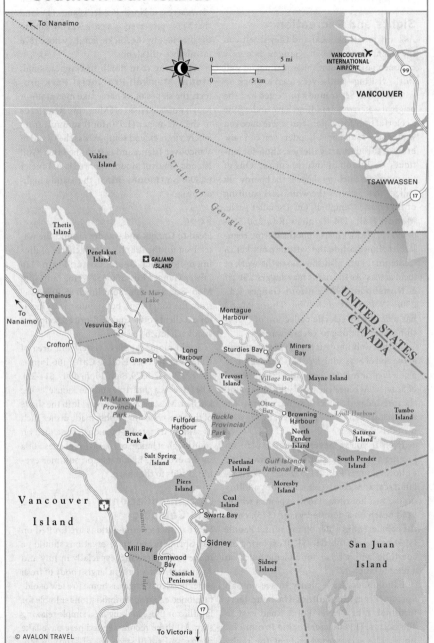

To Nanaimo

0   5 mi
0   5 km

VANCOUVER INTERNATIONAL AIRPORT

VANCOUVER

99

TSAWWASSEN

17

Valdes Island

Strait of Georgia

Thetis Island

Penelakut Island

★ GALIANO ISLAND

Chemainus

St Mary Lake

To Nanaimo

Vesuvius Bay

Crofton

Montague Harbour

UNITED STATES
CANADA

Long Harbour

Sturdies Bay

Miners Bay

Ganges

Prevost Island

Village Bay

Mayne Island

Mt Maxwell Provincial Park

Ruckle Provincial Park

Otter Bay

Browning Harbour

Lyall Harbour

Tumbo Island

Fulford Harbour

North Pender Island

Saturna Island

Bruce Peak

Salt Spring Island

Portland Island

Gulf Islands National Park

South Pender Island

Vancouver Island

1

Piers Island

Moresby Island

Saanich

Coal Island

Swartz Bay

San Juan Island

Mill Bay

Sidney

Brentwood Bay

Saanich Peninsula

Sidney Island

17

To Victoria

© AVALON TRAVEL

Vancouverites who spend their summers at private getaways.

Sights and Recreation

Ask any longtime local and they'll tell you the island's main town, Ganges, is overly commercialized. But it's still quaint, and well worth visiting—at the very least to stock up with supplies. Set around a protected bay, the original waterfront buildings have undergone a colorful transformation, and where once you would have found boat-builders you can now browse through art galleries, shop for antiques, or dine on innovative cuisine. One of the most eye-catching shops is the boardwalk gallery that features the whimsical painting of Jill Louise Campbell. On a smaller scale, **Mahon Hall** (114 Rainbow Rd., 250/537-0899) is filled with arty booths during regular art shows, while the Saturday market in Centennial Park also showcases the work of local artists. As the name may suggest, **Stuff & Nonsense** (2909 Fulford Ganges Rd., 250/653-4620, 11am-5:30pm Thurs.-Mon.) has a decidedly eclectic collection of everything from clothing to kitchen wares.

Within walking distance of the waterfront, at the end of Seaspring Drive, is **Mouat Park,** a quiet reprieve from the bustle. From the end of Seaview Avenue, trails lead into and around the forested park, which also has a fern-filled area set aside for disc golf (free; bring your own Frisbee).

Even if you've never kayaked, plan on joining a tour with **Island Escapades** (163 Fulford-Ganges Rd., 250/537-2553, www.islandescapades.com). Get a feel for paddling on the two-hour tour ($65), explore a white-sand beach on a deserted island ($75), enjoy the calm evening water on the Sunset Paddle ($75), or spend a full-day ($170) exploring the coastline, with a break for a picnic lunch on a remote beach.

Landlubbers have plenty to see on Salt Spring. From the Fulford Harbour ferry terminal, take Beaver Point Road east to 486-hectare (1,200-acre) **Ruckle Provincial Park.** The access road ends at the rocky headland of Beaver Point, from where trails lead north along the coastline, providing great views across to North Pender Island. The land that's now protected as a park was donated to the province by the Ruckle family, whose 1876 farmhouse still stands.

Along the road north to Ganges, small **Mount Maxwell Provincial Park** protects the slopes of its namesake mountain. A rough unsealed road off Musgrave Road leads to the 588-meter (1,930-foot) summit, from where views extend south across the island to Vancouver Island and east to the other Gulf Islands. South of Mount Maxwell is 704-meter (2,300-foot) **Mount Bruce,** the island's highest peak.

Food

Head to Ganges and wander around the waterfront for the island's widest choice of dining options. **T.J. Beans Coffee Shop** (110 Lower Ganges Rd., 250/537-1216, 7am-6pm Mon.-Sat., 8am-5pm Sun., lunch $6-9) is away from the waterfront, but popular with locals for excellent coffee and well-priced soup and sandwich lunch specials.

Right along the busy waterfront area of Ganges is ★ **Tree House Café** (106 Purvis Lane, 250/537-5379, 8am-10pm daily, $14-22). The "tree" is a plum tree and the "house" is the kitchen. Most people dine outside in the shade of the tree, choosing freshly made dishes such as salmon frittata for breakfast, tuna melt on sourdough at lunch, or roasted yam quesadilla in the evening. Live music on summer evenings adds to the charm.

Accommodations and Camping

Short-term accommodations are limited on Salt Spring Island, so reservations should be made before arriving, especially in July and August. St. Mary Lake, a largish body of fresh water north of Ganges, is home to a few of old-fashioned cabin accommodations suitable for families or those looking for a simple relaxing stay. All three recommended here have lake access and small stretches of sandy beach, while the lake itself holds a hungry population of bass and trout that can be caught right from the shoreline. Least expensive is **Lakeside Gardens** (1450 North End Rd., 250/537-5773, www.lakesidegardensresort.com, Apr.-Nov., $100-160 s or d), with rustic waterfront cabanas that share baths, and self-contained cottages.

Along the same stretch of lakeshore, **Cedar Beach Resort** (1136 North End Rd., 250/537-2205 or 888/537-4366, www.saltspring-accommodations.com, $131-241) has larger cabins, each with a full kitchen and up to two bedrooms. For me, the allure of the lodging at **Maple Ridge Cottages** (301 Tripp Rd., 250/537-5977, www.mapleridge-cottages.com, $165-199 s or d) is the location on St. Mary Lake, but the rustic charm of the wooden cottages brings families back year after year. Relax on the deck while your catch of the day cooks on the barbecue for the full effect. Free use of canoes and kayaks is a popular bonus.

My pick for lodging on the island is ★ **Spindrift Oceanfront Cottages** (255 Welbury Point Rd., southeast of Ganges, 250/537-5311, www.spindriftsaltspringisland.com, $150-290 s or d, Oct.-Apr. $120-210). The six cottages are spread around a private peninsula lightly forested with arbutus and fir trees. Trails lead to two sandy beaches and to a grassed area at the very tip of the peninsula. The cottages themselves each have a kitchen, a wood-burning fireplace, and a deck with water views.

Mineral Springs Resort (1460 North Beach Rd., 250/537-4111 or 800/665-0039, www.saltspringspa.com, $220-300 s or d) commands lots of attention for its spa services, but the accommodations are also noteworthy. Each spacious unit features lots of polished wood topping out in a vaulted ceiling, a modern kitchen, a fireplace, and a two-person spa tub filled with mineral water. Guests have use of rowboats, mountain bikes, a game room, and a barbecue area.

The campground ($18) in **Ruckle Provincial Park** conceals 78 sites in a forest of Douglas firs overlooking Swanson Channel. The camping area is a short walk from the parking lot, making this place unsuitable for RVs. With more facilities and within walking distance of downtown Ganges is **Garden Faire Campground** (305 Rainbow Rd., 250/537-4346, www.gardenfaire.ca, tents $25, hookups $35), set in an old-growth forest. Facilities are limited, but it's 10 minutes of easy walking through Mouat Park to town.

Information

Salt Spring Island Visitor Centre (121 Lower Ganges Rd., 250/537-5252 or 866/216-2936, www.saltspringtourism.com, 9am-5pm daily summer, 11am-3pm daily fall-spring) is in downtown Ganges, on the main road above the marina. Head to **Salt Spring Books** (104 McPhillips Ave., 250/537-2812, 9am-5:30pm Mon.-Sat., 10am-5pm Sun.) to pick up some holiday reading or check your email on the public-access computers.

Getting There

Salt Spring has two ferry terminals with year-round service to two points on Vancouver Island operated by **BC Ferries** (250/386-3431 or 888/223-3779, www.bcferries.com). If you're traveling up from Victoria, the Swartz Bay terminal is the most convenient departure point, with 10 to 12 departures daily for **Fulford Harbour,** a 20-minute drive south of Ganges. Sailings are even more frequent on the 20-minute run between Crofton, near the Vancouver Island town of Duncan, and **Vesuvius Bay,** at the island's north end. The round-trip fare on either of these routes is adults $12.60, children $6.30, vehicles $36.90, and you can depart from a different terminal than your arrival at no extra cost. Interisland ferries (adults $6.75, children $3.40, vehicles $14.40 one-way) depart from a third terminal, at **Long Harbour,** east of Ganges. From the mainland, daily sailings depart the Tsawwassen terminal (south of downtown Vancouver) bound for Long Harbour (adults $19.80, children $9.80, vehicles $72.80 one-way).

THE PENDERS

It's just a short hop by ferry from Salt Spring Island to **Otter Bay** on North Pender Island. Originally, North and South Pender Islands were joined, but in 1903 a canal was dredged between the two as a shipping channel. Today, a rickety wooden bridge forms the link. Between them, the two islands are home to around 2,000 people, most of whom live on North Pender.

The island has dozens of little beaches to explore, with public roads providing ocean access at more than 20 points. One of the nicest spots is **Hamilton Beach** on Browning Harbour, south of the ferry terminal.

Food

The commercial hub of the Penders is the **Driftwood Centre,** a city-like shopping mall overlooking cleared pastureland south of the ferry terminal. In addition to gas, groceries, booze, and a bank, there are several eateries, including a super-busy **Vanilla Leaf Bakery Cafe** (4605 Bedwell Harbour Rd., 250/629-6453, 7am-5pm Mon.-Sat., 8am-5pm Sun., lunch $7-10), which has excellent coffee and oversize cinnamon buns.

Northwest of Hope Bay, **Southridge Farms Country Store** (Port Washington Rd., 250/629-2051, 9:30am-5:30pm Mon.-Sat. 11am-5pm Sun.) is stocked with seasonal produce, perfect for taking back to your island lodging. Eggs, fruit and vegetables, and organic beef are all sourced from island farms. Within the store is a small café pouring great coffee and offering a range of simple bakery items.

Accommodations and Camping

The least expensive way to enjoy an overnight stay on North Pender Island is to camp at **Prior Centennial Campground** (mid-May-mid-Oct., $14), a unit of Gulf Islands National Park. The 17 campsites have no showers or hookups, but the location among ferns and towering cedar trees is excellent. To be assured of a site, make reservations through the Parks Canada Campground Reservation Service (877/737-3783, www.pccamping.ca) for a small additional fee. The campground is six kilometers (3.7 miles) south of the ferry terminal off Canal Road.

The north island's premier lodging is the **Oceanside Inn** (4230 Armadale Rd., 5 kilometers/3 miles from the ferry terminal, 250/629-6691 or 800/601-3284, www.penderisland.com, May-Oct., $150-200 s or d). Each room is elegantly furnished, and a wide balcony takes advantage of the waterfront location. Rates include a delicious cooked breakfast, use of an outdoor hot tub, and small luxuries such as fluffy bathrobes.

On South Pender Island, **Poet's Cove Resort** (9801 Spalding Rd., 250/629-2100 or 888/512-7638, www.poetscove.com, $269-499 s or d) is one of the largest resort complexes in the Southern Gulf Islands. Overlooking a protected cove it boasts a large freeform outdoor pool, a marina, canoe and kayak rentals, bike rentals, and spa services. Guest rooms come in three configurations—lodge rooms, cottages, and villas—with all units featuring comfortable furnishings and an abundance of natural materials throughout. Dining options include two restaurants and a waterfront café (7am-3pm daily).

Information

Pender Island Visitor Centre (250/629-6541, www.penderislandchamber.com, 9am-6pm daily summer) is a small booth up the hill from the ferry terminal.

Getting There

BC Ferries (250/386-3431 or 888/223-3779, www.bcferries.com) has up to eight sailings 6:30am-9:30pm daily between Swartz Bay and Pender Island (nonstop, 40 minutes, adults $12.60, children $6.30, vehicles $36.90 round-trip). Interisland sailings (adults $6.75, children $3.40, vehicles $14.40 per sector) are equally regular. From Tsawwassen, there is just a single direct sailing (adults $19.80, children $9.80, vehicles $72.80 one-way) each week, on Friday evening, with all other trips making at least one stop.

MAYNE ISLAND

Separated from North Pender and Galiano Islands by narrow channels, Mayne Island is just 21 square kilometers (8 square miles) in area. Its year-round population of fewer than 1,000 triples in summer, but the island never really seems crowded. Ferries dock at village-less **Village Bay.** All commercial facilities are at nearby **Miners Bay,** which got its name during the Cariboo gold rush, when miners used the island as a stopping point. From the ferry terminal, narrow roads meander to all corners of the island, including to **Georgina Point Lighthouse,** which was staffed between 1885 and 1997. Island beaches are limited to those at **Oyster Bay,** but visitors can enjoy interesting shoreline walks or take the winding road to the low summit of Mount Park for panoramic views. For something a little different, wander through **Dinner Bay Park,** where a small Japanese garden takes pride of place.

The best island kayaking originates from the sandy beach in Bennett Bay, which is within Gulf Islands National Park. This is the main departure point for tours led by **Kayaking Gulf Islands** (250/539-0864), with a three-hour paddling tour ($66) of this unit of Gulf Islands National Park.

Food

Head to the **Sunny Mayne Bakery Café** (472 Village Bay Rd., 250/539-2323, 6am-4pm daily, lunch $7-10) less than one kilometer (0.6 miles) east of the ferry terminal, for freshly baked breads, homemade soups, picnic hampers, sumptuous cakes and pastries, healthy sandwiches, ice cream, and the island's best coffee concoctions.

For something a little more substantial, continue across the island to **Bennett Bay Bistro** (494 Arbutus Dr., 250/539-3122, 11:30am-8pm Thurs.-Tues., 11:30am-3pm Wed., $12-19), with lots of outdoor seating on a tiled patio overlooking Bennett Bay. The menu is dominated by fresh, simple choices, none better than the $12 beer-and-burger lunch deal. If you're staying at Blue Vista Resort, you're within easy walking distance of this restaurant. No-frills short-order grills are the order of the day at the old **Springwater Lodge** (Village Bay Rd., 250/539-5521, breakfast, lunch, and dinner daily, $9-18).

Accommodations

The least expensive island lodging is **Springwater Lodge** (Village Bay Rd., 250/539-5521, www.springwaterlodge.com, $40-95 s or d), an old hotel overlooking Active Pass from Miners Bay. Rooms are basic at best and baths are shared, but for less than $50, you know what you're getting. Beside the hotel are four well-equipped cabins ($260 s or d). The inn also has a restaurant that's open daily for simple meals.

On the east side of the island, across the road from protected Bennett Bay, the emphasis at **Blue Vista Resort** (563 Arbutus Dr., 250/539-2463 or 877/535-2424, www.bluevistaresort.com, $115-165 s or d) is on outdoor recreation, with hosts Carmen and Andrew Pearson eager to share their love of the island with you by filling your day with activity ideas. Rooms and cabins are furnished practically, with separate bedrooms, wireless Internet, cooking facilities, and decks surrounded by native forest.

Camping at **Mayne Island Eco Camping** (359 Maple Dr., Miners Bay, 250/539-2667, www.mayneislandcamping.com, Apr.-Oct., $30 s or d, plus $10 per child) is pleasant but primitive, designed for tents only. Spread around the back of a short beach, some walk-in sites are right on the water, whereas others are dotted throughout the forest. Facilities include outhouses, a hot water-fed "tree" shower, and kayak rentals. Part of the same property is the two-bedroom **Seal Beach Cottage** ($215).

Information

The Mayne Island website (www.mayneisland.com) is loaded with useful information, including links to current weather conditions, accommodations, services, and, for those who fall in love with island living, real estate agents. Stock up on reading materials at **Miners Bay Books** (574 Fernhill Rd., 250/539-3112, 11am-4pm Thurs.-Tues. summer).

Getting There

BC Ferries (250/386-3431 or 888/223-3779, www.bcferries.com) has four nonstop 50-minute sailings daily between Swartz Bay and Mayne Island's Village Bay terminal (adults $12.60, children $6.30, vehicles $36.90, round-trip). Other sailings go via Pender Island, while the longest (2 hours) detour out to Saturna Island. Two or three ferries each day link Tsawwassen with Mayne (adults $19.80, children $9.80, vehicles $72.80 one-way), although most stop at Galiano Island en route. A regular stream of ferries arrive and depart from the other Southern Gulf Islands (adults $6.75, children $3.40, vehicles $14.40 per sector).

★ GALIANO ISLAND

Named for a Spanish explorer who sailed through the Strait of Georgia more than 200 years ago, this long, narrow island—27 kilometers (17 miles) from north to south but only a few kilometers wide—has some delightful beaches and good kayaking. Most of the 1,000 residents live in the south, within a five-minute drive of the ferry terminal at **Sturdies Bay.** While Montague Harbour Provincial Park gets most of the attention from visitors, the island is dotted with many less obvious ocean access points, many of which aren't even signposted. The beach below Active Pass Road is typical; look for the utility pole numbered 1038 and make your way down the steep trail to a protected cove. Ask at the information center or at your lodging for a full listing of similar spots.

Also worth visiting is **Bodega Ridge Provincial Park,** on the road to the island's northern tip. This park protects a high ridge that is home to rare peregrine falcons

(a walking trail traverses the ridgetop) and a string of intriguing sandstone cliffs accessible only by those kayaking or boating.

Montague Harbour Provincial Park

Climbing out of Sturdies Bay, roads tempt exploration in all directions. Take Porlier Pass Road to reach Montague Harbour Provincial Park, which protects an 89-hectare (210-acre) chunk of coastal forest and a beach of bleached-white broken seashells. You can walk out along the beach and return via a forested trail in around 20 minutes. At the end of the beach are middens, piles of empty shells that accumulated over centuries of indigenous people's feasts.

Recreation

The best way to explore local waterways is with **Galiano Kayaks** (250/539-2442), based at the marina in Montague Harbour. Three-hour guided tours ($55) leave either early in the morning or at sunset. Another tour takes in the local marinelife on a five-hour paddle ($85). Those with previous experience can rent a kayak ($58 single, $90 double per day).

Galiano Golf Club (24 St. Andrews Cres., 250/539-5533) is typical of the many courses on the Southern Gulf Islands, with nine holes open year-round, inexpensive greens fees ($25), a relaxed atmosphere, and a clubhouse offering rentals and basic meals.

Food

To immerse yourself in island life, plan on dining at the **Galiano Grand Public House** (2470 Sturdies Bay Rd., 250/539-9885, www. grandcentral.ca, 8am-2:30pm Wed.-Mon., lunch $10-15), which is decorated in lumberjack artifacts and has seating ripped from old buses. Free-range eggs are the prime ingredient in the omelets, which are huge (smoked salmon, cream cheese, and basil, $17). Sandwiches and burgers dominate the lunch menu. Check the website for occasional summer weekend openings, often with live music. While you're waiting for a ferry—or even if you're not—line up at the **Max & Moritz** food wagon, in front of the parking lot at the ferry terminal, for a combination of German and Indonesian dishes, such as *nasi goreng* and bratwurst.

The stellar food is reason enough to dine at the **Galiano Inn** (134 Madrona Dr., 250/539-3388, 8:30am-10am, noon-3pm, and 6pm-8:30pm daily June-Sept., $24-40), but the unobstructed water views cost no extra. Although the upscale dining room has a touch of Old World elegance, the cooking is healthy and modern, with a seasonal menu that uses fresh island produce and local seafood. Professional service and an impressive wine list round out what many regard as the finest restaurant on the Southern Gulf Islands. In summer, a sunken patio buzzes with activity as locals and visitors from outlying islands enjoy lunchtime treats such as pizza cooked in an outdoor wood-fired oven in a cultured garden setting.

Accommodations and Camping

Many of the travelers you'll meet on the ferry to Galiano will be staying for a week or more in an island cottage. If this style of vacation sounds ideal to you, check www.galianoisland.com for a choice of rentals, but do so well before planning your visit, because the best ones fill fast. **Paradise Rock Ocean Front Cottage** (310 Ganner Dr., 250/539-3404, www.cedarplace.com/paradise, $150-175 s or d) is typical in all respects—water views from a private setting, self-contained, and with a deck holding a propane barbecue—except that it can be rented for as few as two nights.

You'll see the magnificent gardens of the ★ **Galiano Inn** (134 Madrona Dr., 250/539-3388 or 877/530-3939, www.galianoinn.com, $249-399 s or d), at the head of Sturdies Bay, before the ferry docks. The elegant guest rooms infused with European charm come in three configurations, and all have views extending down the bay to Mayne Island. Other highlights include private balconies, very comfortable beds, plush robes, luxury baths

with soaker tubs, and extras such as CD players and coffeemakers. The inn is also home to the **Madrona del Mar Spa,** the place to get pampered with a soothing hot stone massage or to kick back in the seaside hot tub. Guests can also book a variety of tours aboard the inn's own motor cruiser, including wine-tasting on nearby Saturna Island.

The campground in **Montague Harbour Provincial Park** (reservations 519/826-6850 or 800/689-9025, www.discovercamping.ca, mid-Mar.-Oct., $25), 10 kilometers (6 miles) from the ferry, is one of the best in the Southern Gulf Islands. Sites are set below a towering forest of old-growth cedar and fir trees and open to a white shingle beach that aligns perfectly to watch the setting sun. As with most provincial park campgrounds, facilities are limited to picnic tables, pit toilets, and drinking water.

Information

Right at the ferry terminal is **Galiano Island Visitor Centre** (250/539-2233, www.galianoisland.com, 9am-5pm daily July-Aug.). The Southern Gulf Islands have a surprising number of bookstores, and none are better than **Galiano Island Books** (76 Madrona Dr., 250/539-3340, 10am-5:30pm daily), down the first left after exiting the dock area. Stop by for works by island writers as well as Canadiana, children's titles, and some great cookbooks that use local ingredients.

Getting There

Read the schedule carefully before planning your trip between Galiano Island and Swartz Bay, as many sailings make two stops en route, and some require a transfer at Mayne Island. Regardless of the number of stops, the fare between Swartz Bay and Galiano is adults $12.60, children $6.30, vehicles $36.90 round-trip. Ferries arrive and depart from the other Southern Gulf Islands throughout the day, with services to Mayne Island (adults $6.75, children $3.40, vehicles $14.40, per sector) all nonstop. Two or three ferries each day link Tsawwassen with Galiano, two of which are nonstop (adults $19.80, children $9.80, vehicles $72.80 one-way). As with service to the other Southern Gulf Islands, all ferries are operated by **BC Ferries** (250/386-3431 or 888/223-3779, www.bcferries.com).

If there's one island you don't take your vehicle, make it Galiano. The ferry docks in the south at Sturdies Bay, which is within walking distance of most accommodations, the island's premier dining spot, and the local bookstore. Or you can rent a moped or small boat from **Galiano Adventures** (300 Sticks Allison Rd., 250/539-3443, www.galianoadventures.com, May-Sept.).

SATURNA ISLAND

Most remote of the populated Southern Gulf Islands, 31-square-kilometer (12-square-mile) Saturna protrudes into the heart of the Strait of Georgia and features a long rugged northern coastline and around half its land area within **Gulf Islands National Park.** Although First Nations people visited the island seasonally, the first permanent settlers didn't arrive until the 1850s, and it was as recently as the 1970s that the island was linked to the outside world by a scheduled ferry service. The island's name comes from the *Saturnina,* a Spanish ship that passed by the island in the 1790s. Today, Saturna, with a year-round population of just 350, offers a couple of lodging and dining choices, but there are no banks, doctors, or pharmacies, and ferries only stop by a few times a day. From the ferry dock at **Lyall Harbour,** two roads head southeast for around 14 kilometers (9 miles). East Point Road hugs the northern coastline offering views across to Tumbo Island before ending at **East Point.** Here you can go swimming or simply admire the sweeping views across the border to the San Juans. Narvaez Bay Road parallels East Point Road, ending at its namesake **Narvaez Bay,** which is protected by Gulf Islands National Park. Here, a 1.7-kilometer (1-mile) trail continues west to an exposed headland surrounded by the calm blue waters of the Strait of Georgia. An alternate trail from this parking lot climbs along an old logging road to a viewpoint where the San Juan Islands are clearly visible across Boundary Pass; allow 40 minutes for this 2.5-kilometer (1.6-mile) loop.

The northern end of the island around peaceful **Winter Cove** is protected by another small unit of **Gulf Islands National Park.** Here, a 1.6-kilometer (1-mile) walking trail winds through a forest of Douglas fir before looping back beside a coastal salt marsh and along the shoreline.

Food

Right at the ferry dock, **Wild Thyme Coffeehouse** (109 East Point Rd., 250/539-5589, 6am-4pm Thurs.-Sun., lunch $6.50-10) is the polar opposite of your typical big-city coffeehouse. Here, a double-decker bus is permanently parked beside the road, with seating upstairs and out front. The coffee is locally roasted, the loose-leaf teas island-grown, and the delightful choice of soups, sandwiches, and pastries are all made on-site.

Also by the ferry dock, **Saturna Lighthouse Pub** (100 East Point Rd., 250/539-5725, noon-11pm daily, $15-23) has a fantastic deck with sweeping water views. The food, well-priced and delicious, includes choices such as the Surf and Turf Burger (prawns, bacon, and swiss cheese), halibut and chips, and a couple of simple pasta dishes. Off East Point Road, at **Saturna Café** (Narvaez Bay Rd., 250/539-2936, 9am-6pm daily, lunch $8-13.50) you can expect simple home-style cooking, casual ambience, and friendly service.

Accommodations and Camping

Overlooking Boot Cove and also within walking distance of the dock is **Saturna Lodge** (130 Payne Rd., 250/539-2254 or 866/539-2254, www.saturna.ca, May-Oct., $159-199 s or d, includes breakfast). Right on the water, this modern lodging offers six guest rooms, a hot tub, a lounge with a fireplace, and extensive gardens.

Saturna has no vehicle-accessible campgrounds. Affiliated with Saturna Lighthouse

Pub, **Arbutus Point Campground** (100 East Point Rd., 250/539-5725, www.saturna-pub.com, $30) has a few tent sites within walking distance of the ferry dock. With bike and kayak rentals available nearby, staying at this campground means you can leave your vehicle on the mainland. The only other campsites are accessible along the 1.7-kilometer (1-mile) walking trail out to **Narvaez Bay**. Here, within Gulf Islands National Park, is a small campground (mid-May-Sept., $6 pp) beside Little Bay.

Information and Services

The best source of pre-trip planning information is the website www.saturnatourism.com, and although there is no official visitors center on the island, any of the 300 full-time residents should be able to help you out. A few places have wireless Internet access, including **Saturna Point Store** (100 East Point Rd., 250/539-5726, 10am-5pm Mon.-Sat., 10am-4pm Sun. summer, 10am-5pm Mon. and Thurs.-Sat., 10am-4pm Sun. fall-spring), which also has a computer with Internet access, an ATM, and the island's only gas pump.

Getting There

BC Ferries (250/386-3431 or 888/223-3779, www.bcferries.com) has a direct evening sailing between Saturna Island and Swartz Bay (adults $12.60, children $6.30, vehicles $36.90 round-trip), but the three or four other daily sailings are routed through Mayne Island. The 40-minute trip between Mayne Island and Saturna is a nonstop service running three times daily. Regardless of whether Mayne or one of the other Southern Gulf Islands (connect through Mayne) is your final destination, the fare (adults $6.75, children $3.40, vehicles $14.40 one-way) is the same.

Nanaimo and Vicinity

Nanaimo (pronounced na-NYE-mo) sprawls lazily up and down the hilly coastal terrain between sparkling Nanaimo Harbour and Mount Benson, on the east coast of Vancouver Island 110 kilometers (69 miles) north of Victoria. With a population of 84,000, it's the island's second-largest city and one of the 10 largest cities in British Columbia. It's also a vibrant city enjoying a rich history, mild climate, wide range of visitor services, and a direct ferry link to both of Vancouver's ferry terminals.

SIGHTS

Downtown Nanaimo lies in a wide bowl sloping down to the waterfront, where forward thinking by early town planners has left wide expanses of parkland. Down near the water, the Civic Arena building makes a good place to park your car and go exploring on foot. Right in front of the Civic Arena is **Swy-A-Lana Lagoon,** a unique artificially constructed tidal lagoon full of interesting marinelife. A promenade leads south from the lagoon to a bustling downtown marina filled with commercial fishing boats and leisure craft. Beside the marina is a distinctive mast-like sculpture that provides foot access to a tiered development with various viewpoints. Up in downtown proper, many historical buildings still stand, most around the corner of Front and Church Streets and along Commercial Street. Look for hotels dating to last century, the Francis Rattenbury-designed courthouse, and various old commercial buildings. Up Fitzwilliam Street are the 1893 St. Andrew's Church and the 1883 railway station.

Nanaimo Museum

In the heart of downtown, the **Nanaimo Museum** (100 Museum Way, 250/753-1821, 10am-5pm daily summer, 10am-5pm Mon.-Sat. fall-spring, adults $2, seniors $1.75,

Nanaimo and Vicinity

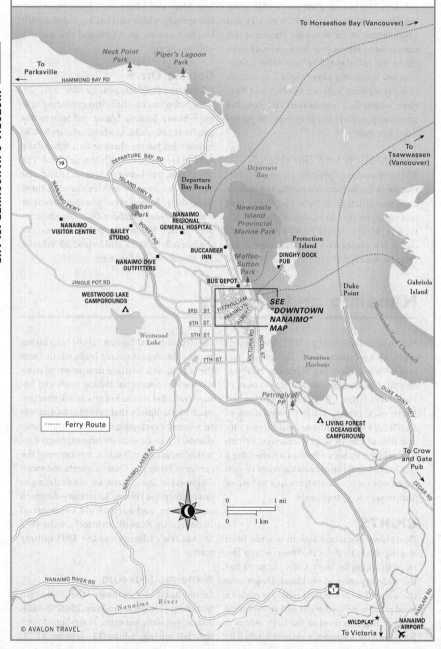

To Horseshoe Bay (Vancouver)

To Parksville

Neck Point Park

Piper's Lagoon Park

HAMMOND BAY RD

DEPARTURE BAY RD

ISLAND HWY N

NANAIMO PKWY

19

Beban Park

BOWEN RD

Departure Bay Beach

Departure Bay

Newcastle Island Provincial Marine Park

To Tsawwassen (Vancouver)

NANAIMO VISITOR CENTRE

BAILEY STUDIO

NANAIMO REGIONAL GENERAL HOSPITAL

Protection Island

NANAIMO DIVE OUTFITTERS

BUCCANEER INN

Maffeo-Sutton Park

DINGHY DOCK PUB

Duke Point

Gabriola Island

JINGLE POT RD

BUS DEPOT

3RD ST

FITZWILLIAM

FRANKLYN

ALBERT

VICTORIA RD

NICOL ST

SEE "DOWNTOWN NANAIMO" MAP

Northumberland Channel

WESTWOOD LAKE CAMPGROUNDS

4TH ST

5TH ST

7TH ST

Westwood Lake

Nanaimo Harbour

NANAIMO LAKES RD

Petroglyph PP

LIVING FOREST OCEANSIDE CAMPGROUND

DUKE POINT HWY

To Crow and Gate Pub

CEDAR RD

------ Ferry Route

0   1 mi

0   1 km

NANAIMO RIVER RD

HASLAM RD

Nanaimo River

© AVALON TRAVEL

WILDPLAY

To Victoria

NANAIMO AIRPORT

children $0.75) is a modern facility showcasing local and island history. Walk around the outside to appreciate harbor, city, and mountain views, as well as replica petroglyphs of animals, humans, and spiritual creatures. Then allow at least an hour for wandering through the displays inside, which focus on life in early Nanaimo and include topics such as geology, the First Nations, pioneers, and local sporting heroes. An exhibit on the coal-mining days features a realistic coal mine from the 1850s. Don't miss the impressive First Nations carvings by James Dick.

The Bastion

Overlooking the harbor at the junction of Bastion and Front Streets, and totally rebuilt in 2010, stands the Bastion, a well-protected fort built in 1853 by the Hudson's Bay Company to protect employees and their families against an attack by First Nations people. Originally used as a company office, arsenal, and supply house, today the fort houses the **Bastion Museum** (250/753-1821, 10am-3pm daily June-Aug., donation). A group of local university students dressed in appropriate gunnery uniforms and led by a piper parades down Bastion Street at 11:45am daily in summer. The parade ends at the Bastion,

where the three cannons are fired out over the water. It's the only ceremonial cannon firing west of Ontario. For a good vantage point, be here early.

Parks

Newcastle Island Provincial Marine Park is a magnificent chunk of wilderness separated from downtown Nanaimo by a narrow channel. It's mostly forested, ringed by sandstone cliffs and a few short stretches of pebbly beach. Wildlife inhabitants include deer, raccoons, beavers, and more than 50 species of birds.

A 7.5-kilometer (4.7-mile) walking trail (allow 2-3 hours) encircles the island, leading to picturesque Kanaka Bay, Mallard Lake, and a lookout offering views east to the snowcapped Coast Mountains. **Nanaimo Harbour Ferry** (877/297-8526, no reservations) departs for the island from Maffeo-Sutton Park every 20 minutes 9am-9pm daily summer, with fewer sailings in spring and fall. The round-trip fare is adults $9, seniors $8, children $5.

Along the Millstone River and linked by a trail to the waterfront promenade, 36-hectare (89-acre) **Bowen Park** remains mostly in its natural state, with stands of Douglas fir,

Nanaimo Harbour

Downtown Nanaimo

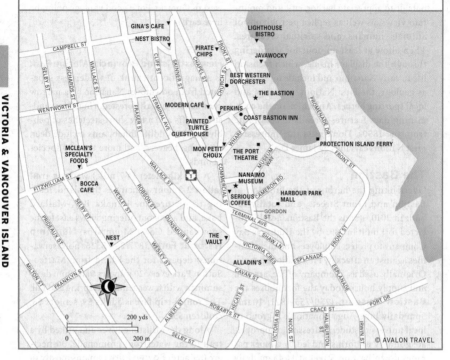

hemlock, cedar, and maple. It's home to beavers and birds, and even deer are occasionally sighted within its boundaries. Street access is from Bowen Road.

On the road into downtown Nanaimo from the south, two kilometers (1.2 miles) north of the Nanaimo Parkway intersection, **Petroglyph Provincial Park** features a short trail leading to ancient petroglyphs (rock carvings). Petroglyphs, found throughout the province and common along the coastal waterways, were made with stone tools, and they recorded important ceremonies and events. The designs at this park were carved thousands of years ago and are believed to represent human beings, animals (real and supernatural), bottom fish, and the rarely depicted sea wolf, a mythical creature that's part wolf and part killer whale.

West of downtown (take Wentworth St. and then Jingle Pot Rd. across the Nanaimo Pkwy.), 106-hectare (262-acre) **Westwood Lake Park** surrounds the crystal-clear waters of its namesake lake. Resident flocks of Canada geese and ducks, tame enough to snatch food from your fingers, inhabit the park. The lake's healthy population of cutthroat trout attracts anglers year-round.

Along Hammond Bay Road, north of downtown and beyond Departure Bay, is **Piper's Lagoon Park,** encompassing an isthmus and a rocky headland that shelter a shallow lagoon. A trail from the parking lot leads to the headland, with views of the mainland across the Strait of Georgia. Continuing north, more trails lead through **Neck Point Park** to rocky beaches and ocean-side picnic areas.

RECREATION
Diving

A great variety of dives can be accessed from Nanaimo, including several vessels that have been sunk especially for diving enthusiasts, such as the HMCS *Cape Breton* and HMCS *Saskatchewan*, both 120-meter (400-foot) Navy destroyer escorts. The much smaller *Rivtow Lion*, a rescue tug, was scuttled in the shallow waters of Departure Bay, making it a popular spot for novice divers. Marinelife is also varied, with divers mixing with harbor seals, anemones, sponges, salmon, and "tame" wolf eels. **Nanaimo Dive Outfitters** (2205 Northfield Rd., 250/756-1863, www.nanaimodiveoutfitters. ca, 10am-5:30pm Mon.-Fri., 9am-5pm Sat.) is a well-respected island operation, offering sales, equipment rentals, and charters aboard *The Shepherd*. For nondivers, there is an option to go snorkeling with the local seal population.

Bungee Jumping

Nanaimo is home to **WildPlay** (35 Nanaimo River Rd., 250/716-7874, 10am-6pm daily summer), North America's only bridge-based commercial bungee jump. People flock here from afar to have their ankles tied and connected to "Bungee Bridge" by a long elastic rope. Next they dive headfirst 42 meters (138 feet) down almost to the surface of Nanaimo River, rebounding until momentum dissipates. To receive this thrill of a lifetime you have to part with $130, and if you have any cash left over, you'll find must-have T-shirts, hats, posters, videos, stickers, and other souvenirs to prove to the world that you really did it. At the same facility, other adrenaline rushes can be had by taking the Primal Swing ($100 pp) or the Zip Line ($30). All of the above are thoroughly entertaining to watch, with good viewing areas and plenty of parking provided. The site is 13 kilometers (8 miles) south of downtown.

ENTERTAINMENT AND EVENTS
World Championship Bathtub Race

On the last Sunday of every July, the waters off Nanaimo come alive for the World Championship Bathtub Race (250/753-7223, www.bathtubbing.com), the grand finale of the annual **Nanaimo Marine Festival.** Originally, competitors raced across the Strait of Georgia between Nanaimo and Kitsilano Beach, Vancouver. Today, they leave from downtown Nanaimo, racing around Entrance and Winchelsea Islands to the finish line at Departure Bay in a modified bathtub fitted with a 7.5-horsepower outboard motor. The racers are escorted by hundreds of boats of the more regular variety, loaded with people just waiting for the competitors to sink. Every bathtubber wins a prize—a golden plug for entering, a small trophy for making it to the other side of the strait, and a silver plunger for the first tub to sink. These days, the sport and the festivities around it have grown enormously, attracting tens of thousands of visitors to Nanaimo. And "tubbing," as the locals call it, has spread to other BC communities, where preliminary races qualify entrants for the big one.

Nightlife

The best place in Nanaimo to enjoy a drink while soaking up harbor views is the **Lighthouse Pub** (50 Anchor Way, 250/754-3212, 11am-midnight daily), built out over the water in front of the main shopping district. At dock level is a restaurant, while the pub upstairs has nightly drink specials, a pool table, and a good selection of pub food (with the emphasis on seafood). Escape the pub atmosphere by requesting seating at the outside section of the restaurant.

Minnoz Lounge (11 Bastion St., 250/753-6601, 4pm-10pm daily), within the downtown Coast Bastion Hotel, brings a bit of class to the local drinking scene, with a long list of city-style cocktails and wines from around the world.

Longwood Brew Pub (5775 Turner Rd., 250/729-8225, 11am-midnight daily) is Nanaimo's only brewpub. There's a pub downstairs and a restaurant upstairs, but the lagers and traditional British ales brewed in-house can be enjoyed in either section. Tours, with the obligatory tasting, are offered at 3pm Saturday. Longwood's is around five kilometers (3 miles) north of downtown along Highway 19A (Island Hwy.); look for Turner Road on the right.

One of the most interesting places to go for a cold beverage on a warm summer day is **Dinghy Dock Pub** (Protection Island, 250/753-2373, 11:30am-8pm Sun.-Wed., 11:30am-10pm Thurs.-Sat.), accessible only from Nanaimo Boat Basin by ferry (every hour 9:10am-11:10pm daily, adults $9, children $5 round-trip). This floating restaurant is also a good place for a meal and hosts live entertainment on Friday and Saturday nights May to September.

The Arts

Lovers of the arts will find Nanaimo to be quite the cultural center, with the main focus being the **Port Theatre** (125 Front St., 250/754-8550, www.porttheatre.com). This magnificent 800-seat theater in an architecturally pleasing circular concrete-and-glass building opposite the harbor showcases theater productions, musicals, and music performances by a wide range of artists year-round. The **Nanaimo Theatre Group** (2373 Rosstown Rd., 250/758-7224, www.nanaimotheatregroup.ca) presents live performances at the Bailey Studio. The **Nanaimo Art Gallery** (150 Commercial St., 250/754-1750, 10am-5pm Tues.-Sat., donation) displays and sells works by a diverse range of island artists.

FOOD

Nanaimo has a remarkably wide choice of dining options, including a dozen or more cafés and restaurants offering everything from local seafood to Middle Eastern cuisine.

Cafés

If you're wandering along the harbor and looking for a spot to relax with a hot drink, you won't do better than **Javawocky** (90 Front St., 250/753-1688, 7am-8pm Mon.-Fri., 8am-7pm Sat.-Sun.), overlooking the harbor. It offers all of the usual coffee drinks, great milk shakes, inexpensive cakes and pastries, and light lunchtime snacks.

Downtown, Commercial Street is lined with cafés. **Serious Coffee** (60 Commercial St., 250/591-1065, 7am-7pm Mon.-Tues., 7am-9pm Wed.-Fri., 7am-7pm Sat., 8am-6pm Sun.), in the Nanaimo Museum complex, is one gathering spot for serious coffee lovers. Up the hill slightly, **Mon Petit Choux** (120 Commercial St., 250/753-6002, 8am-5pm Mon.-Sat., 9am-5pm Sun., lunch $6-8) seems to attract a slightly older crowd for in-house baking, such as delicious cheesecake brownies, while nearby **Perkins** (234 Commercial St., 250/753-2582, 7:30am-5pm Mon.-Fri., 8:30am-3pm Sat.-Sun.) serves up coffee and muffins to all types.

At **The Vault Café** (499 Wallace St., 250/591-0776, 8am-10pm Mon.-Tues., 9am-midnight Wed.-Sat., 10am-4pm Sun.), across the highway from Commercial Street, it's all about the coffee through the day, but the wide-ranging menu is also notable, and there's often live music in the evenings. This place has a distinct European vibe within a historic commercial building designed by Francis Rattenbury, of Empress Hotel fame.

Up Fitzwilliam Street from the center of town in the Old Quarter is a concentration of quality eateries, including **Bocca Cafe** (427 Fitzwilliam St., 250/753-1797, 7am-6pm Mon.-Fri., 8am-5pm Sat., 9am-4pm Sun., lunch $8-12), an inviting little space that is a favorite with locals looking for a little style. From the delicious coffee and muffins in the morning to freshly made sandwiches at lunch, everything is delightful. Tables lining a covered walkway are especially popular.

Buzz Coffee House (1861 Dufferin Cres., 250/591-8310, 7am-5pm Mon.-Fri., 8am-4pm Sat., 10am-4pm Sun., lunch $8-11) is in the northern suburbs of Nanaimo, but if you're heading that way well worth searching out for its friendly atmosphere, delicious breakfasts and lunches, and healthy smoothies. From downtown, take Comox Road west along the south side of Bowen Park for around three kilometers (2 miles) and look for Dufferin Crescent to the left.

Waterfront Dining

Dinghy Dock Pub (Protection Island, 250/753-2373, 11:30am-8pm Sun.-Wed., 11:30am-10pm Thurs.-Sat., $13-31) offers a unique dining experience; the floating restaurant is moored at nearby Protection Island. Well known for great food and plenty of seagoing atmosphere, the pub also hosts live entertainment on Friday and Saturday nights from May to September. To get to the restaurant, take a ferry (250/753-8244, hourly 9:10am-11:10pm daily) from Nanaimo Boat Basin.

In the seaplane terminal on the waterfront (below the Bastion), the **Lighthouse Bistro** (50 Anchor Way, 250/754-3212, 11am-10pm daily, $13-30) is built over the water and has a large heated outdoor deck. The salmon chowder is excellent, served with delicious bread. Also on the menu are tasty appetizers, salads, burgers, sandwiches, croissants, pasta dishes, and good daily specials. Upstairs is the **Lighthouse Pub,** with a similar menu and specials such as cheap wings on Wednesday.

Casual Dining

Near the top end of Commercial Street, **Modern Café** (221 Commercial St., 250/754-5022, 11am-11pm Tues.-Sun., 11am-9pm Sun., $12-23) has had a number of serious revamps since opening in 1946 that have seen changes to both the menu and decor, while leaving the distinctive neon sign out front in place.

Along the waterfront at the north end of downtown, ★ **Pirate Chips** (75 Front St., 250/753-2447, 11am-10pm Mon.-Thurs., 11am-midnight Fri.-Sat., 11am-8pm Sun., $8-16) is a funky little restaurant where you can load up hearty servings of fries with various

toppings, tuck into delicious seafood tacos, brave a peanut butter and bacon burger, and even try a deep-fried Nanaimo bar.

For some of the best Mexican food on Vancouver Island, head for **Gina's Mexican Cafe** (47 Skinner St., 250/753-5411, 11am-8pm Mon.-Thurs., 11am-9pm Fri., noon-9pm Sat., noon-8pm Sun., $13-22), behind the courthouse north of Pirate Chips. Although it's on a back street, the building itself, a converted residence, is hard to miss—the exterior is painted shades of purple and decorated with a fusion of Mexican and maritime memorabilia.

When I walked into brightly decorated **Aladdin's** (67 Victoria Cres., 250/716-1299, 11am-10pm Mon.-Sat., $14-18), across the highway from Commercial Street, right at closing time on a quiet weekday night, the staff were already closing for the night, and yet were welcoming and happy to take my order. The menu combines Greek and Middle Eastern favorites, portions are huge, and prices very reasonable. At lunch, you'll pay around $10 for wraps, donairs, and souvlaki.

Island Grown

★ **Nest Bistro** (77 Skinner St., 250/591-2721, 5pm-11:30pm Tues., 11:30am-3pm and 5pm-11:30pm Wed.-Fri., 5pm-11:30pm Sat., 5pm-10pm Sun., $14-26), one of Nanaimo's best restaurants, is a space that many visitors miss, yet is just a couple of blocks from the bustle of Commercial Street. The ambience is friendly and inviting, with the chef-owners always present. A great deal of effort goes into sourcing local seafood, game, and produce, which is found in dishes such as arugula salad, seafood risotto, and a variety of thin-crust pizzas.

Beyond Downtown

South of the city, **Crow & Gate Pub** (2313 Yellow Point Rd., 250/722-3731, 11am-11pm daily, $12-18) mimics an English country pub, complete with exposed beams, a large fireplace, and expansive landscaped gardens dotted with outdoor table settings. Go to the bar to order traditional dishes such as Ploughman's lunches and steak and mushroom pie, or stay local with pan-fried oysters and a shrimp sandwich. To get there from town, head south out to the Duke Point ferry terminal and turn south onto Cedar Road just beyond the bridge over the Nanaimo River. Cedar Road turns into Yellow Point Road and the pub is on the right after four kilometers (2.5 miles).

On the north side of the city, just south of where Highway 19A rejoins Highway 19 (Inland Island Hwy.), **Longwood Brew Pub** (5775 Turner Rd., 250/729-8225, 11am-midnight daily, $12-25) is a large modern facility with a menu filled with local produce and seafood. Eat downstairs in the pub or upstairs in the more formal dining room. Restaurant starters include fish tacos topped with pineapple and mango salsa while mains such as citrus-infused cedar plank salmon are all very good value. Longwood's filled up for brunch (10am-1:30pm Sun., $24 pp), where omelets are made to order and seafood abounds. From downtown, follow Highway 19A (Island Hwy.) north and turn left onto Turner Road after five kilometers (3 miles).

ACCOMMODATIONS
Under $50

A few of Nanaimo's older motels offer rooms for around $50 outside summer, but only **Painted Turtle Guesthouse** (121 Bastion St., 250/753-4432, www.paintedturtle.ca, dorms $30, $99 s or d) falls into this price range year-round. In a restored heritage building, this guesthouse enjoys a convenient location in the heart of downtown and just one block from the harbor front. The hostel operates year-round, providing four-bed dorms, private rooms (family rooms have a queen and bunk beds), a large and modern kitchen, laundry facilities, a lounge area, and friendly hosts. The property is a member of Hostelling International (www.hihostels.ca), so members can book through that website.

$50-100

On an island of overpriced accommodations, the two-story ★ **Buccaneer Inn** (1577 Stewart Ave., 250/753-1246 or 877/282-6337, www.buccaneerinn.com, $90-190 s or d) stands out as being an excellent value. Across from the waterfront and within easy walking distance of downtown and the Departure Bay ferry terminal, the Buccaneer is bedecked by a nautical-themed mural and colorful baskets of flowers and surrounded by well-maintained grounds, a sundeck, picnic tables, and a barbecue facility. The rooms are spacious and brightly decorated, and each has a desk, coffee-making facilities, a small fridge, and Internet connections. The smallest rooms are $80 s or d, while kitchen suites, some with gas fireplaces, start at $150 s or d. Friendly owner-operators provide a wealth of information on the local area, as does the motel website.

$100-150

As you'd expect, accommodations right downtown are more expensive than those farther out. A bit nicer than you'd expect from the bland exterior, the **Best Western Dorchester Hotel** (70 Church St., 250/754-6835 or 800/661-2449, www.dorchesternanaimo.com, $145-195 s or d) offers water views and a rooftop terrace from a central location. Rooms in this historical building won't win any design awards, but they are relatively modern, many have water views, and wireless Internet access is included. The hotel also has a rooftop patio, a lounge, and a restaurant with water views.

$150-200

Also right downtown, the **Coast Bastion Inn** (11 Bastion St., 250/753-6601 or 800/716-6199, www.coasthotels.com, from $169 s or d) is a full-service, 179-room contemporary hotel with an exercise room, a day spa, the contemporary Minnoz Restaurant and Lounge, water views from every room, and wireless Internet included.

Camping

Two commercial campgrounds are within 10 kilometers (6 miles) of the city center, but the nicest surroundings are in the provincial park out on **Newcastle Island** (www.newcastleisland.ca, $18), connected to downtown by regular passenger ferry service. The island isn't suitable for RVers, but it's ideal for those with a lightweight tent. Facilities include picnic tables and a barbecue shelter, while the island is also home to a restaurant open daily for dinner.

The closest of the commercial campgrounds to downtown is **Westwood Lake Campgrounds** (380 Westwood Rd., 250/753-3922, www.westwoodlakecampgrounds.com, tents $34, hookups $42, basic cabins $100-150 s or d), set on the edge of beautiful Westwood Lake. Amenities include a sandy beach with canoe rentals, a barbecue area, a game room, laundry facilities, and hot showers.

Living Forest Oceanside RV & Campground (6 Maki Rd., 250/755-1755, www.campingbc.com, $32-56) is on 20 hectares (49 acres) of coastal forest at the braided mouth of the Nanaimo River south of downtown. The location is delightful and facilities are modern, including a laundry room, a general store, a game room, and coin showers.

INFORMATION AND SERVICES

Nanaimo is promoted to the world by **Tourism Nanaimo** (250/751-1556, www.tourismnanaimo.com). The main **Nanaimo Visitor Centre** (Hwy. 19/Island Hwy. at Northfield Rd., 9am-5 daily summer) is in a small but architecturally eye-catching structure at the north entrance to town (if you're traveling up-island from Victoria, stay on the main highway north; the center is well signed). Another useful resource is the website www.gonanaimo.com.

The main **post office** is on Front Street in the Harbour Park Mall. For emergencies, head to **Nanaimo Regional General Hospital** (1200 Dufferin Cres., 250/754-2141). If you need a pharmacy, go to the **Pharmasave** (2000 N. Island Hwy., Brooks Landing Mall, 250/760-0771).

GETTING THERE AND AROUND

It's possible to get to Nanaimo by airplane or bus, but most people arrive by ferry from Vancouver, or by vehicle up Highway 19 from Victoria; allow 90 minutes for the 110-kilometer (68-mile) trip.

BC Ferries (250/386-3431 or 888/223-3779,

Nanaimo Visitor Centre is at the north entrance to town.

www.bcferries.com) operates regular services between Vancouver and Nanaimo along two different routes. Ferries leave Vancouver's Tsawwassen terminal up to eight times a day for the two-hour trip to Nanaimo's **Duke Point** terminal, 20 minutes south of downtown and with direct access to the highway that bypasses the city. Through downtown, at the north end of Stewart Avenue, is the **Departure Bay** terminal. This facility contains a large lounge area with a café and large-screen TVs. Ferries from Vancouver's Horseshoe Bay terminal leave up to 11 times a day for Departure Bay. Fares on both routes are the same: Peak one-way travel costs adults $17.20, children $8.60, vehicles $57.50. Limited reservations are taken via the website ($10-21 plus ferry fare).

Harbour Air (250/714-0900) flies daily between downtown Vancouver (just west of the convention center) and the seaplane base in downtown Nanaimo ($109 one-way). The **Greyhound** bus depot (Terminal Ave. and Comox Rd., 800/753-4371) is at the rear of the Howard Johnson hotel. Buses depart regularly for points north and south of Nanaimo and west to Port Alberni and Tofino.

Nanaimo Regional Transit System (250/390-4531) buses run daily. The main routes radiate from downtown's Prideaux Street Exchange north to Departure Bay, west to Westwood Lake, and south as far as Cedar. An all-day pass is $6.50. Rental car agencies in Nanaimo include **Avis** (250/716-8898), **Budget** (250/760-7368), **Discount** (250/729-2277), and **Hertz** (250/734-1964).

GABRIOLA ISLAND

From Nanaimo, visitors can jump aboard a ferry to the nearby rural oasis of Gabriola Island. Geologically linked to the Southern Gulf Islands, immediately to the south, Gabriola is partly residential, but it also holds large expanses of forest, abundant wildlife, and long stretches of unspoiled coastline. With an area of 57 square kilometers (22 square miles), it's one of the larger islands in the group and is separated from

Vancouver Island by a narrow straight south of Nanaimo.

Petroglyphs were carved on island cliffs by Snuneymuxw people who lived on the island for at least 1,000 years prior to Spanish explorers making landfall in 1791 and 1792. By the 1850s, European settlers arrived from Nanaimo and established farms. The island population remained low until the 1960s and 1970s, when the counterculture movement discovered the charms of Gabriola. The population has doubled in the last 30 years to 4,600 year-round residents.

Sights and Recreation

Many scenic spots invite you to pull off—at petroglyphs, secluded bays, and lookouts. The North and South Roads encircle the island, combining for a 30-kilometer (18.6-mile) loop that's perfect for a leisurely day-long bike ride.

Take Taylor Bay Road north from the ferry terminal to access the island's best beaches, including **Gabriola Sands Provincial Park**, a short stretch of fine white sand bookended by forest. Aside from a few picnic tables and restrooms, the park has no services—the beach is simply a wonderful place to spend a summer's day.

Drive out to the park's southern headland through stands of Garry oak and arbutus protected by **Drumbeg Provincial Park**. From the end of the road, walk out onto the grassy headland for sweeping views across Gabriola Passage present the opportunity for viewing whales, seals, and sea lions. On the loop back to the ferry dock, the South Road passes **Gabriola Island Golf Club** (825 South Rd., 250/247-8822, $25), a friendly little nine-hole set around Hoggan Lake. Facilities include rentals, a driving range, and a clubhouse with inexpensive meals.

Food and Accommodations

On the island's southeast coastline, **Page's Resort and Marina** (3350 Coast Rd., 250/247-8931, www.pagesresort.com, campsites $20-25, cabins $199-259 s or d) has a small campground surrounded by mature trees and a few comfortable one- and two-bedroom self-contained cabins. Down on the waterfront is a full-service marina, a grocery store, and a bookstore. Immediately north of the ferry dock, **Descanso Bay Regional Park** (595 Taylor Bay Rd., 250/247-8255, $17, cash only) offers 32 unserviced campsites sloping down to a rocky cove.

Basic services are available less than one kilometer (0.6 miles) uphill from the ferry terminal on North Road. Here you'll find gas, groceries, and **Mad Rona's Coffee Bar** (500 North Rd., 250/247-0008, 7am-4pm daily, $8-12), a modern café that opens to landscaped gardens. The food is typical island café fare—breakfast burritos, freshly made sandwiches, and mostly healthy pastries. Adjacent to Mad Rona's is ★ **Woodfire** (500 North Rd., 250/247-0095, 4pm-9pm daily, $16-27), a stylish dining room that is the perfect setting to enjoy gourmet pizza such as The Breakwater (crab, cilantro, and cherry tomatoes) or classic pastas with a side of wood-fired vegetables.

Information

Gabriola Visitor Centre (480 North Rd., 250/247-9332, www.gabriolaisland.org, 10am-6pm daily July-Aug., 10am-6pm Fri.-Sun. spring and fall) is less than one kilometer (0.6 miles) east of the ferry terminal.

Getting There

BC Ferries (250/386-3431) schedules 15 sailings daily between the terminal off Front Street in Nanaimo (downtown, across from Harbour Park Mall) and Gabriola Island. The trip takes 20 minutes one-way, and reservations are not taken. The peak round-trip fare is adults $11.45, children $5.75, vehicles $26.95. For a taxi on the island, call **Gabriola Island Cabs** (250/247-0049).

155

VICTORIA & VANCOUVER ISLAND
HIGHWAY 4 TO THE WEST COAST

Highway 4 to the West Coast

From Nanaimo, it's 35 kilometers (22 miles) northwest up Highway 19 to one of Vancouver Island's main highway junctions, where Highway 4 spurs west to Port Alberni and the island's west coast. The map shows a distance of 84 kilometers (52 miles) between the Nanaimo and Port Alberni along Highway 4, but it's a winding highway, with lots of slower truck traffic, so allow at least one hour. Follow Highway 4 to its end to reach **Pacific Rim National Park,** a long, narrow park protecting the wild coastal strip and some magnificent sandy beaches, and **Tofino,** a picturesque little town that makes the perfect base for surfing, sea kayaking, whale-watching, or fishing excursions.

ENGLISHMAN RIVER FALLS PROVINCIAL PARK

After turning off Highway 19 north of Nanaimo, make your first stop here, where Englishman River—full of cutthroat and rainbow trout—cascades down from high in the Beaufort Range over two photogenic waterfalls within an old-growth forest of Douglas fir, western red cedar, and hemlock. At the end of the park access road is a forested picnic area surrounded by lush ferns, easy hiking trails to both the upper and lower falls, and, downstream of the lower fall, a crystal-clear swimming hole. Back along the access road is a 94-site campground (no hookups or showers, May-Sept., $23) enclosed by the same forested setting. A short walking trail links the campground to the waterfalls. For campsite reservations, contact **Discover Camping** (800/689-9025, www.discover-camping.ca).

To get to the park, turn off Highway 4 on Errington Road, three kilometers (2 miles) west of the Highway 19 junction, and continue another nine kilometers (5.5 miles), following signs.

COOMBS

What started just over 30 years ago as a simple produce stand has grown into the **Old Country Market** (2310 Alberni Hwy., 250/248-6272, 9am-8pm daily), the life-blood of Coombs, along Highway 4A west of Highway 19. Before moving inside the market buildings, you'll want to stand out front and look upward, where several goats can be seen contentedly grazing along the roof line, seemingly oblivious to the amused, camera-clicking visitors. Inside the main building is a selection of goodies of epic proportions—a bakery, a deli, an ice cream stand, and a wealth of healthy island-made produce. Behind the main building and in an adjacent property are rows of arty shops selling everything from pottery to jewelry to kites.

On the west side of Coombs, at the junction of Highways 4 and 4A, is **Creekmore's Coffee** (2107 Alberni Hwy., 250/752-0158, 6:30am-6pm Mon.-Fri., 8am-6pm Sat.-Sun.), an unassuming place that pours freshly roasted coffee as good as any on the island.

LITTLE QUALICUM FALLS PROVINCIAL PARK

This 440-hectare (1,090-acre) park lies along the north side of the highway, 10 kilometers (6 miles) west of Coombs. The park's main hiking trail leads alongside the Little Qualicum River to a series of plummeting waterfalls, both upstream and downstream of the main day-use area. Stay the night in a sheltered riverside campsite (no hookups or showers, May-Sept., $23). The source of the Little Qualicum River is **Cameron Lake,** a large, deep-green, trout-filled body of water just outside the western park boundary.

CATHEDRAL GROVE

At the west end of Cameron Lake, Highway 4 dives into one of the last remaining easily accessible stands of old-growth forest remaining in British Columbia. The tallest trees are protected by **MacMillan Provincial Park.** Highway 4 through the park is extremely narrow, and traffic within Cathedral Grove can get extremely congested in summer, so take extra care pulling into and out of the roadside parking lot. The park protects a majestic stand of 200- to 800-year-old Douglas firs that rise a neck-straining 70 meters (230 feet) from the forest floor and have a circumference of up to nine meters (30 feet). The trees have been a popular stop along the road to Port Alberni for almost 100 years and were officially afforded protection when one of the island's major logging companies donated the land to the government. Short trails lead from the parking lot on both the north and south sides of the highway, with the Old Growth Trail, on the south side, leading to Cameron Lake.

PORT ALBERNI AND VICINITY

If you hit Port Alberni, 84 kilometers (52 miles) west of Nanaimo, on a cloudy day, you won't know what you're missing until the sky lifts. Then beautiful tree-mantled mountains suddenly appear, and Alberni Inlet and the Somass River turn a stunning deep blue. Situated at the head of the island's longest inlet, Port Alberni is a busy town of 18,000 centered around the forestry industry. The town's three mills—lumber, specialty lumber, and pulp and paper—are its main sources of income. The town is also a port for pulp and lumber freighters, deep-sea vessels, and commercial fishing boats.

Despite all the industry, Port Alberni has much to offer, including interesting museums, nearby provincial parks, and a modern marina filled with both charter fishing boats and tour boats.

Sights

Follow the signs from Highway 4 to brightly decorated **Alberni Harbour Quay** at the end of Argyle Street. For a great view of the quay, harbor, marina, inlet, and surrounding mountains, climb the clock tower. Off Argyle Street is Industrial Road, which leads to the **Maritime Discovery Centre** (2750 Harbour

Rd., 250/723-6164, 10am-4pm Mon.-Fri., 9:30am-4:30pm Sat.-Sun. June-early Sept., donation), ensconced in a red-and-white lighthouse. Children will love the hands-on displays that explore the importance of the ocean to the town's history.

Alberni Harbour Quay is also the starting point for the **Alberni Pacific Railway** (250/723-2118, adults $35, students $25, children free), which departs at 11am Thursday to Sunday from Port Alberni Railway Station (3100 Kingsway) out to **McLean Mill National Historic Site** (5633 Smith Rd., 250/723-1376, 10am-4pm daily July-Aug., adults $10, students $5). The site has Canada's only steam-powered sawmill, and it still works, so you can watch workers milling lumber through the clunky contraption. Admission to the site is included in the train fare. To get to the mill under your own steam, take Highway 4 west through town and turn north on Beaver Creek Road.

Find out more about the origins of the famous West Coast Trail, see a collection of Nuu-chah-nulth artwork, or tinker with a variety of operating motorized machines from the forestry industry at the **Alberni Valley Museum** (4255 Wallace St., 250/723-2181, 10am-5pm Tues.-Sat., donation).

MV *Frances Barkley*

The *Frances Barkley* (250/723-8313 or 800/663-7192, www.ladyrosemarine.com), a vintage Norwegian ferry, serves the remote communities of Alberni Inlet and Barkley Sound, but because of the spectacular scenery along the route, the day cruise is also one of the island's biggest tourist attractions. Depending on the time of year, orcas and gray whales, seals, sea lions, porpoises, river otters, bald eagles, and all sorts of seabirds join you on your trip through magnificent Barkley Sound. The vessel is also a great way to reach the remote fishing village of Bamfield and the only way to reach the Broken Group Islands by scheduled transportation.

Year-round, the MV *Frances Barkley* departs Alberni Harbour Quay at 8am Tuesday, Thursday, and Saturday, reaching Kildonan at 10am and Bamfield at 12:30pm, then departs Bamfield at 1:30pm and docks back in Port Alberni at 5pm. In summer, sailings are also made to Bamfield on Sunday, with a special stop for kayakers in the Broken Group Islands. If you want to stay longer in Bamfield, accommodations are available. June-September, an extra route is added to the schedule, with the vessel departing at 8am Monday, Wednesday, and Friday for the Broken Group Islands, arriving at Ucluelet at 1pm for a 90-minute layover before returning to Port Alberni around 7pm. One-way fares from Port Alberni are Kildonan $31, Bamfield $40, Broken Group Islands (Sechart) $40, Ucluelet $42. Children under age 16 travel for half price. In summer the *Frances Barkley* does a roaring business—book as far ahead as possible.

FISHING

To get the rundown on fishing charters, head down to the full-service **Harbour Quay Marina** (5104 River Rd., 250/723-8022, dawn-dusk daily summer, 9am-5pm daily winter). The owners, local fishing guides, have put together all kinds of printed information on local fishing. They know all of the best spots and how to catch the lunkers. Expect to pay $350 for two people, $400 for three for a six-hour guided morning charter, or $220 for two people, $250 for three for a four-hour guided afternoon charter. The marina also rents boats (from $22 per hour, $120 per day, plus gas) and fishing rods ($12 per day), sells bait and tackle, and provides information about sportfishing and accommodations packages in the region.

The annual **Port Alberni Salmon Festival** (www.salmonfestival.ca) fishing derby each Labour Day weekend (1st weekend in Sept.) draws up to 3,000 anglers chasing a $15,000 prize for the largest salmon. Crowds of fishing enthusiasts gather to watch thousands of pounds of salmon being weighed in, and multitudes of salmon-eaters throng to a three-day salmon barbecue.

FOOD

At any time of day, one of the best places to find something to eat is down at Alberni Harbour Quay, where there are several small cafés and lots of outdoor seating and grassed areas running down to the waterfront. At the very end of the quay, at **Starboard Grill** (5440 Argyle St., 778/421-2826, 11am-10pm daily, $14-26), you'll find a large outdoor patio with uninterrupted views across the harbor.

At the entrance to the quay is **Blue Door Cafe** (5415 Argyle St., 250/723-8811, 8am-3pm daily, lunch $8-11), a small old-style place that's a real locals' hangout. Breakfasts are huge; an omelet with all the trimmings goes for $7-9, and bottomless self-serve coffee is an extra $1. The clam chowder ($6) is also good.

For seafood in a casual setting, the **Clam Bucket** (4479 Victoria Quay, 250/723-1315, 11am-9pm daily, $13-32) is one of the most popular places in town. Although many seafood dishes are deep-fried, there are plenty of other choices, and portions are generous and well-priced. It's located north of downtown, near where Highway 4 jogs west at the riverfront.

In a converted church on Highway 4 through town is **Bare Bones Fish & Chips** (4824 Johnston Rd., 250/720-0900, 11:30am-8pm daily, $10-18), a smallish space with a funky decor that includes lots of fish-bone artwork. Local fish such as halibut and salmon are cooked to order any way you like (grilled, battered, etc.) and come with your choice of sides.

ACCOMMODATIONS AND CAMPING

Whether you're in search of a tent site with water views, a cozy bed-and-breakfast, or a regular motel room, Port Alberni has something to suit you, although Port Alberni motels are generally more expensive than those on other parts of the island.

Right downtown, each of the large guest rooms at the **Hospitality Inn** (3835 Redford St., 250/723-8111 or 877/723-8111, www. hospitalityinnportalberni.com, $130 s, $135 d) is air-conditioned and features a comfortable bed and a writing desk. Amenities include a covered, heated saltwater pool, a fitness room, a pub, and a restaurant.

The best camping is out of town, at **China Creek Campground** (250/723-9812, www. campchinacreek.com, $25-43) right on Alberni Inlet. Choose between open and wooded full-facility sites in a relatively remote setting with sweeping views of the inlet from a sandy log-strewn beach. To get here, take 3rd Avenue south to Ship Creek Road and follow it for 14 kilometers (9 miles).

The campground within **Stamp River Provincial Park** (May-mid-Oct., $18), northwest of Port Alberni, enjoys a beautiful location on the river of the same name. A park highlight occurs each fall, when thousands of migrating salmon swim up river and over artificial fish ladders around Stamp Falls. From the campground, it's a short walk down to the river, or lace up your hiking boots for the more serious 7.5-kilometer (4.7-mile) Stamp Long River Trail that leads upstream past a succession of rapids. To get to the park, follow Highway 4 through town and immediately after crossing Kitsuksus Creek, take Beaver Creek Road north for 14 kilometers (9 miles).

INFORMATION

On the rise above town to the east is **Port Alberni Visitor Centre** (2533 Port Alberni Hwy., 250/724-6535 or 866/576-3662, www. albernichamber.ca, 9am-6pm daily summer, 9am-5pm Mon.-Fri. fall-spring). This excellent facility is a great source of local information, as well as details for Pacific Rim National Park, transportation options to Bamfield, and all west coast attractions.

BAMFIELD

One of the island's remotest communities, this tiny fishing village lies along both sides of a narrow inlet on Barkley Sound. Most people arrive here aboard the MV *Frances Barkley* from Port Alberni, but the town is also linked

The Broken Group Islands

These 100 or so forested islands in the mouth of Barkley Sound, south of Ucluelet, once held First Nations villages and some of the first trading posts on the coast. Now they're inhabited only by wildlife and visited primarily by campers paddling through the archipelago in canoes and kayaks. The islands offer few beaches, so paddlers come ashore in the many sheltered bays.

Marinelife abounds in the cool and clear waters: Seals, porpoises, and gray whales are present year-round. Birdlife is also prolific: Bald eagles, blue herons, and cormorants are permanent residents, and large numbers of loons and Canada geese stop by on their spring and fall migration routes.

The archipelago extends almost 15 kilometers (9 miles) out to sea from Sechart, the starting point for **kayakers.** The protected islands of **Hand, Gibraltar, Dodo,** and **Willis** all hold campsites and are good destinations for novice paddlers. Farther out, the varying sea conditions make a higher level of skill necessary. Predictably, a westerly wind blows up early each afternoon through summer, making paddling more difficult.

The best way to reach the Broken Group Islands is aboard the MV *Frances Barkley* (250/723-8313 or 800/663-7192, www.ladyrosemarine.com) from Port Alberni or Ucluelet. Based in Port Alberni, this sturdy vessel departs Alberni Harbour Quay (8am Mon., Wed., and Fri. June-Sept.), dropping kayakers at **Sechart,** the site of a whaling station and now home to **Sechart Lodge** (book in conjunction with the tour boat; $190 s, $315 d, including meals; no children under age 14). Originally an office building for a local forestry company, the lodge was barged to the site and converted to basic but comfortable guest rooms and a restaurant. The *Frances Barkley* then continues to Ucluelet, departing that village at 2pm and making another stop at Sechart before returning to Port Alberni. In July and August, an additional Sunday sailing departs Port Alberni at 8am, stopping at Sechart and returning directly to Port Alberni. The one-way fare between Port Alberni and Sechart is $40; between Ucluelet and Sechart it's $31.

The company that operates the boat also rents kayaks ($45-65 per day), which are left at Sechart so you don't have to pay a transportation charge. If you bring your own kayak, the transportation charge is $20-25 one-way. The trip out on this boat is worthwhile just for the scenery, with the Ucluelet sailing passing right through the heart of the archipelago.

to Port Alberni by a rough 100-kilometer (60-mile) logging road. It's well worth the trip out to go fishing, explore the seashore, or just soak up the atmosphere of this picturesque boardwalk village. Bamfield is also the northern terminus of the **West Coast Trail.**

WEST FROM PORT ALBERNI

Highway 4 west from Port Alberni meanders through unspoiled mountain wilderness, and you won't find a gas station or store for at least a couple of hours. Ninety-one kilometers (57 miles) from Port Alberni, Highway 4 splits, leading eight kilometers (5 miles) south to Ucluelet or 34 kilometers (21 miles) north through Pacific Rim National Park to Tofino.

Sproat Lake

A short drive west from Port Alberni, Highway 4 skirts the north shore of Sproat Lake, whose clear waters draw keen anglers. Along the highway, there is camping ($23) at **Sproat Lake Provincial Park,** which also has a popular beachside day-use area. Provided they're not out squelching a fire, you can also see the world's largest water bombers—Martin Mars Flying Tankers—tied up here. Originally designed as troop carriers for World War II, only four were ever built and only two remain, both here at Sproat Lake. Used to fight wildfires, these massive flying beasts—36 meters (118 feet) long and with a wingspan of more than 60 meters (200 feet)—skim across the lake, each filling its tank with 26,000 liters (7,200 gallons) of water.

UCLUELET

A small town of 1,650 on the northern edge of Barkley Sound, Ucluelet (pronounced yoo-CLOO-let, although known locally as "Ukee") has a wonderfully scenic location between the ocean and a protected bay. You can enjoy all of the same pursuits as in Tofino—beachcombing, whale-watching, sea kayaking, and fishing—but in a more low-key manner.

The Nuu-chah-nulth people lived around the bay where Ucluelet now sits for centuries before the arrival of Europeans (in their language, the town's name means "People with a Safe Landing Place"). During the 20th century, Ucluelet was also a fur sealers' trading post and a logging and sawmill center, but fishing remains the steady mainstay, as evidenced by the town's resident fishing fleet and several fish-processing plants.

Sights and Recreation

The **Wild Pacific Trail** is an ambitious project that will eventually wander along the coastline all the way to Pacific Rim National Park. Through the hard work of local oyster farmer "Oyster Jim" two sections totaling nine kilometers (5.5 miles) of beautifully maintained coastal trail has currently been completed. One section, the 2.6-kilometer (1.6-mile) Lighthouse Loop, starts from **Hetin-kis Park,** hugging the rugged and rocky coastline to a lighthouse that is not the world's most photogenic, but it gets the job done—keeping ships from running ashore along this stretch of particularly treacherous coastline. The second section of the Wild Pacific Trail starts from Marine Drive south of downtown and follows the coast for six kilometers (3.7 miles) before jogging inland through a forest of ancient cedars.

Many visitors who choose to stay in Ucluelet do so for the fishing, particularly for chinook salmon (Feb.-Sept.) and halibut (May-July). The fall runs of chinook can yield fish up to 20 kilograms (44 pounds), and the town's busy charter fleet offers deep-sea fishing excursions as well as whale-watching trips.

Food

Get your morning caffeine fix along with cakes and pastries made from scratch at **Zoe's Bakery and Cafe** (250 Main St., 250/726-2253, 8am-5pm Mon.-Fri., lunch $7-10). The selection of baked goods is extensive, and includes delicious cupcakes. Or plan on the daily soup and sandwich special for under $10. At **Huckleberry's** (329 Forbes Rd., 250/726-4448, 8am-5pm Mon.-Fri.), uphill

along the Wild Pacific Trail

to the south off Peninsula Road, just before you reach the main commercial strip, coffee is roasted in-house.

Seafood is a local specialty, and available at most local restaurants. One of the best choices for truly local fish is ★ **Jiggers Fish & Chips** (1685 Peninsula Rd., 250/726-5400, noon-8pm Fri.-Tues., $12-27), a food truck along the main street with a few picnic tables out front. It's not particularly cheap, but the fish is as fresh and delicious as anywhere on Vancouver Island. When halibut is in season, I encourage you the pay the couple of extra dollars for this delicious treat.

Another casual dining option is **Ukee Dogs Eatery** (1571 Imperial Lane, 250/726-2103, 9am-8pm daily, $7-12), down by the harbor. Here in a renovated garage, choose between a wide variety of hot dogs, meat pies, and daily soups. Along the main street, but with water views from outside tables, **Blue Room Bistro** (1627 Peninsula Rd., 250/726-4464, 7am-4pm daily, lunch $8-14) has a good selection of simple seafood dishes, including a wild salmon burger, a halibut burger, lemon-peppered calamari, and a BLT that features smoked salmon instead of bacon.

For its creative presentation of local specialties and an inviting ambience, ★ **Norwoods** (1714 Peninsula Rd., 250/726-7001, 6pm-11pm daily, $32-48) is one of my favorite island restaurants. The offerings are very seasonal, with seafood purchased daily from local fishing boats—and the chef only getting word of the day's catch when the boats dock. Herbs and mushrooms are grown in the adjacent garden and most of the produce is sourced from Vancouver Island.

Accommodations

Accommodations and campsites in Ucluelet are somewhat limited, especially if you're looking to stay somewhere inexpensive, so plan ahead by making reservations.

$50-100

If you're looking at sharing inexpensive accommodations with an younger, outdoorsy crowd, reserve a bed at **C&N Backpackers** (2081 Peninsula Rd., 250/726-7416, www.cnn-backpackers.com, mid-Apr.-late Oct., dorms $25, $65 s or d), a rambling three story house with a large backyard that extends all the way down to the water just before reaching town. The lower floor is set aside for a large communal kitchen, while the middle floor has a lounge area and couple of private rooms, while the top floor is divided into male and female dorms.

★ **Surfs Inn** (1874 Peninsula Rd., 250/726-4426, www.surfsinn.ca, dorms $28, $75-129 s or d) is also contained within a restored home along the main road. Communal facilities include a lounge with a wood-burning fireplace, a modern kitchen, and plenty of space to store bikes and surfboards. Room configurations include dorm beds, one double bed, en suites with water views, and modern cottages.

$100-150

Terrace Beach Resort (1002 Peninsula Rd., 250/726-2901 or 866/726-2901, www.terracebeachresort.ca, $109-349 s or d) was the first Tofino-style lodging in Ucluelet. The weathered "eco-industrial" exterior is a little deceiving, as the guest rooms feature west coast contemporary styling throughout livable units that range from one-bedroom motel rooms to multistory oceanfront cabins, linked by elevated boardwalks and all enclosed in an old-growth forest. Don't be surprised to see actor Jason Priestly wandering through the forest—he and his family own the lodge.

Island West Resort (160 Hemlock St., 250/726-7515, www.islandwestresort.com, $129-149 s or d) has its own marina right on the inlet and serves as the base of operations for a wide range of charter boats. The resort also has a good restaurant and pub. In the height of summer, rooms—each with full kitchen—run from a reasonable $129 s or d.

$250-300

The road leading into the lobby of the **Black Rock Oceanfront Resort** (596 Marine Dr.,

Pacific Rim National Park (Long Beach Unit)

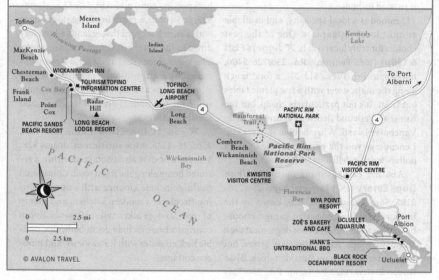

© AVALON TRAVEL

250/726-4800 or 877/762-5011, www.black-rockresort.com, $269-429 s or d) doesn't even hint at the sweeping oceanfront views enjoyed by guests at the contemporary lodging set on a rocky headland just south of town. Public areas are dominated by striking steel, rock, and wood architecture, while the 133 rooms take full advantage of the setting with floor-to-ceiling windows. For a splurge, reserve one of the Premium Suites.

CAMPING

Campers should backtrack from downtown to **Ucluelet Campground** (260 Seaplane Base Rd., 250/726-4355, www.uclueletcamp-ground.com, Mar.-Sept., $46-51), which is set around a forested cove at the west end of Ucluelet Harbour. You can also camp (RVs only) at the downtown waterfront **Island West Resort** (160 Hemlock St., 250/726-7515, www.islandwestresort.com, $43-46 s or d).

GETTING THERE

Tofino Bus (250/725-2871 or 866/986-3466, www.tofinobus.com) stops at Ucluelet on its daily run between Victoria and Tofino, with stops made at both Nanaimo ferry terminals. The fare to Ucluelet from Victoria is $65 and from Nanaimo $46. The fare between Tofino and Ucluelet is $18 one-way.

The most interesting way to reach Ucluelet is aboard the **Frances Barkley** (250/723-8313 or 800/663-7192, www.ladyrosemarine.com, $42 one-way), which sails between Port Alberni and Ucluelet daily through summer.

★ PACIFIC RIM NATIONAL PARK

Named for its location on the edge of the Pacific Ocean, this park encompasses a long, narrow strip of coast that has been battered by the sea for eons. The park comprises three units, each different in nature and accessed in different ways. The section at the end of Highway 4 is the **Long Beach Unit**, named for an 11-kilometer (7-mile) stretch of beach that dominates the landscape. Accessible by vehicle, this is the most popular part of the park and is particularly busy in July and August. To the south, in Barkley Sound, the **Broken Group Islands Unit** encompasses an archipelago of 100 islands, accessible by the MV *Frances Barkley* from Port Alberni. Farther south still is the **West Coast Trail Unit,** named for the famous long-distance hiking trail between Port Renfrew and Bamfield.

You're not charged a fee just to travel straight through the park to Tofino, but if you stop anywhere en route, a strictly enforced charge applies. A one-day permit is adults $7.80, seniors $6.80, children $3.90. Most visitors stock up on supplies in either Port Alberni or Tofino beach heading out into the park, as the only facilities are a campground and day-use areas.

PLANTS AND ANIMALS

Like the entire west coast of Vancouver Island, Pacific Rim National Park is dominated by littoral (coastal) rainforest. Closest to the ocean, clinging to the rocky shore, a narrow windswept strip of Sitka spruce is covered by salty water year-round. These forests of spruce are compact and low-growing, forming a natural windbreak for the old-growth forests of western hemlock and western red cedar farther inland. The old-growth forests are strewn with fallen trees and lushly carpeted with mosses, shrubs, and ferns.

The ocean off western Canada reputedly holds more species of marinelife than any other temperate coast. Gray whales migrate up the coast each spring, seals and porpoises inhabit the park's waters year-round, sea lions overwinter on rocky offshore outcrops, and salmon spawn in the larger creeks through late fall. The tidal zone is the best place to search out smaller sea creatures such as anemones, shellfish, and starfish—all colorful residents of the rocky shoreline.

The park's largest land mammal is the black bear, some of which occasionally wander down to the beach in search of food. Also present are black-tailed deer, raccoons, otters, and mink. Bald eagles are year-round residents. The migratory birds arrive in the largest numbers—in spring and fall, thousands of Canada geese, pintails, mallards, and black brants converge on the vast tidal mudflats of **Grice Bay,** in the north of the park beyond the golf course.

LONG BEACH

Ensconced between rocky headlands is more than 11 kilometers (7 miles) of hard-packed white sand, covered in twisted driftwood, shells, and the occasional Japanese glass fishing float. Dense rainforest and the high snowcapped peaks of the Mackenzie Range

Long Beach

form a beautiful backdrop, while offshore lie craggy surf-battered isles home to extensive marinelife.

Through summer Long Beach attracts hordes of visitors. Most just wander along the beach soaking up the smells and sounds of the sea, but some brave the cool waters for swimming or surfing. The waves here are reputed to be Canada's best; rent boards and wetsuits in Ucluelet and Tofino. In winter, hikers dress for the harsh elements and walk the surf-pounded beach in search of treasures, admiring the ocean's fury during the many ferocious storms.

You can access the beach at many places, but first stop at the renovated **Kwisitis Visitor Centre** (Wickaninnish Rd., 250/726-4212, 10am-5pm daily May-mid-Oct., 10am-5pm Fri.-Sun. mid-Oct.-Apr., free), which overlooks Long Beach from a protected southern cove near the south end of the park. This is the place to learn about the natural and human history of both the park and the ocean through exhibits and spectacular hand-painted murals.

Accommodations and Camping

My favorite lodging at **Wya Point Resort** (off Willowbrae Rd., 250/726-2625, www.wyapoint.com, campsites $35-60, yurts $150-175 s or d, lodge rooms $289-409 s or d) are the yurts, on wooden platforms overlooking the ocean—perfect for a camping experience without needing the equipment. The yurts share baths, but each is very spacious and has a large deck with barbecue, comfortable beds, kitchen equipment, and a lounge chairs. The resort also has lodge rooms in a variety of

configurations, but all are airy and spacious, with lots of exposed woodwork and large windows. They also have full kitchens. The least expensive campsites are set among towering trees of the coastal rainforest, while the more expensive ones overlook the ocean and a short stretch of sandy beach, which often has good waves for surfing. To get here, head south from the Port Alberni-Tofino highway junction and look for Willowbrae Road to the right.

Wya Point Surf Shop (2201 Pacific Rim Hwy. 250/726-2992, $25-30), north of the junction, has sites that are popular with the surfing fraternity, as well as a surf shop, board and wetsuit rentals, and café (9am-5pm daily summer).

The park's one official campground fills up very fast every day through summer, because it's in a marvelous location behind **Long Beach** (also known as Green Point Campground). Facilities include drive-in sites, restrooms, picnic tables, an evening interpretive program, and plenty of firewood, but no showers or hookups. Mid-March to mid-October, walk-in sites are $17.60, and all other sites are $23.50. Some sites can be reserved through the **Parks Canada Campground Reservation Service** (877/737-3783, www.pccamping.ca) for a small additional fee.

Information and Services

The **Pacific Rim Visitor Centre** (2791 Pacific Rim Hwy., 250/726-4600, www.pacificrimvisitor.ca, 10am-5pm daily May-mid-Oct.) sits where Highway 4 meets the road from Port Alberni. There are no stores or gas stations in the park, but supplies and gas are available in Ucluelet and Tofino.

Tofino

The bustling tourist town of Tofino sits at the end of a long narrow peninsula, with the only road access to the outside world being winding Highway 4. Originally the site of a First Nations Clayoquot village, Tofino was one of the first points in Canada to be visited by Captain Cook. It was named in 1792 for Don de Vincent Tofino, a hydrographer with a Spanish expedition. Aside from contact with fur traders and whalers, the entire district remained basically unchanged for almost 100 years.

Fishing has always been the mainstay of the local economy, but Tofino is also a supply center for the several hundred hermits living along the secluded shores of the sound and for the hordes of visitors who come in summer to visit Pacific Rim National Park, just to the south. In winter it's a quiet, friendly community with a population of fewer than 2,000. In summer the population swells to several times

that size and the village springs to life: Fishing boats pick up supplies and deposit salmon, cod, prawns, crabs, halibut, and other delicacies of the sea, and cruising, whale-watching, and fishing boats, along with seaplanes, do a roaring business introducing visitors to the natural wonders of the west coast.

The town lies on the southern edge of sheltered **Clayoquot Sound,** known worldwide for an ongoing fight by environmentalists to save the world's largest remaining coastal temperate forest. Around 200,000 hectares (494,000 acres) of this old-growth forest remain; several parks, including **Clayoquot Arm Provincial Park, Clayoquot Plateau Provincial Park, Hesquiat Peninsula Provincial Park, Flores Island Provincial Park,** and **Maquinna Marine Provincial Park** have resulted from the Clayoquot Sound Land Use Decision.

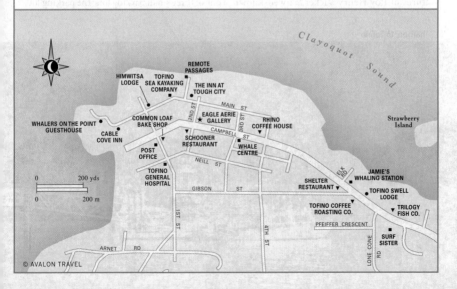

SIGHTS
Tofino Botanical Gardens

Tofino is best known for whale-watching, kayaking, and the long sandy beaches south of town, but a couple of interesting diversions are well worth a stop. The first is **Tofino Botanical Gardens** (1084 Pacific Rim Hwy., 250/725-1220, 9am-dusk daily, adults $12, students $8, under age 13 free), just before town. Developed by knowledgeable locals, it showcases local flora with the emphasis on a fun, educational experience. One garden is devoted to native species you would find in the adjacent national park and another to plants you can eat (but aren't allowed to). This is the only botanical garden I've visited where a colorfully painted camper van from the 1970s is incorporated into a display. Another botanical point of interest is the massive cedar tree on the right-hand side of the road as you enter town. Estimated to be more than 800 years old, the tree is kept from toppling over by wire stays.

Eagle Aerie Gallery

The **Eagle Aerie Gallery** (350 Campbell St., 250/725-3235, 10am-5pm daily, free) features the eye-catching paintings, prints, and sculptures of Roy Henry Vickers, a well-known and highly respected Tsimshian artist. You can watch a video about the artist and then browse among the artworks, primarily First Nations designs and outdoor scenes with clean lines and brilliant colors. If you fall for one of the most popular paintings but can't afford it, you can buy it in card or poster form. The gallery is built on the theme of a west coast First Nations longhouse, with a carved and painted exterior and interior totem poles.

RECREATION
Surfing at Tofino

If you fancy a long walk along a fabulous shell-strewn stretch of white sand, like to sit on craggy rocks watching the waves disintegrate into white spray, or just want a piece of sun all your own to lie in and work on your tan, head for **Chesterman Beach,** just south of Tofino. From that beach, at low tide you can walk all the way out to **Frank Island** to watch the surf pound the exposed side while the tide creeps in and cuts you off from civilization for a few hours. The turnoff (not marked) to Chesterman Beach is Lynn Road, on the right just past the Dolphin Motel as you leave Tofino. Follow the road and park at one of three small parking lots; the parking lot

harbour in Tofino

at the corner of Lynn and Chesterman Beach Roads is closest to Frank Island.

Surfers wanting to hit the water should head south of town to **Live to Surf** (Outside Break, 1180 Pacific Rim Hwy., 250/725-4464, www.livetosurf.com). The shop rents surfboards for $30 per day and wetsuits for $25, and offers lessons for $75 pp, including rentals. The staff will also tell you where the best surf can be found, and if there's no surf, they'll tell you how good it was last week. The shop is within Outside Break, a group of like-minded local businesses on the road leading into town. It's the perfect place to shop for surf apparel and local arts, or to just relax over a coffee. Check the website for west coast surf reports. Back in town, **Surf Sister** (625 Campbell St., 250/725-4456 or 877/724-7873, www.surfsister.com) is Canada's only all-women surf school.

Kayaking

Aside from surfing, exploring the waters around Tofino by sea kayak is the most popular recreation activity in Tofino. **Tofino Sea Kayaking Company** (320 Main St., 250/725-4222, www.tofinoseakayaking.com) has designed tours to meet the demand and suit all levels of experience. Excursions range from a 2.5-hour harbor paddle ($64 pp) to a six-hour ocean paddle to Vargas Island ($130 pp). The company's experienced staff will also help adventurous, independent paddlers plan an itinerary—many camping areas lie within a one-day paddle of Tofino. Single kayak rentals are $60 for one day or $45 per day for two or more days. Double kayaks are $95 and $80. Rental prices include all accessories. The company base, right on the harbor, has a shop selling provisions, accessories such as marine charts, and a wide range of local literature; a coffee shop; a bookstore; and a few rooms ($89 s, $99 d).

Whale-Watching

Each spring around 20,000 Pacific gray whales migrate between Baja and Alaska, passing through the waters off Tofino between March and May. Most of them continue north, but some stay in local waters through summer. Their feeding grounds are north of Tofino within **Maquinna Marine Park.** During the spring migration and some feeding periods, gray whales are also frequently sighted in the calm inland waters around **Meares Island,** just off Tofino.

Whale-watching is one of the most popular activities in town, and companies search out whales to watch them cruise up the coast, diving, surfacing, and spouting. On the whale-watching trips, you'll likely spy other marinelife as well; look for sea lions and puffins sunning themselves on offshore rocks, dolphins and harbor seals frolicking in the bays and inlets, and majestic bald eagles gracefully swooping around in the sky or perching in the treetops. Trips depart mid-March to early November and generally last two to three hours. Expect to pay $90-110 pp.

Cruises and Charters

The streets of downtown Tofino hold a profusion of charter operators offering a wide variety of trips. All of those listed go whale-watching and head out to Hotsprings Cove. Other options include a tour of Meares Island and fishing charters. For details, head to any of the following: **Jamie's** (606 Campbell St., 250/725-3919 or 800/667-9913, www.ja-mies.com), **Remote Passages** (51 Wharf St., 250/725-3330 or 800/666-9833, www.re-motepassages.com), or the **Whale Centre** (411 Campbell St., 250/725-2132 or 888/474-2288, www.tofinowhalecentre.com), where a gray whale skeleton is on display. Even with all these operators, business is brisk, so book ahead if possible.

Hot Springs

Pamper yourself and take a boat or floatplane to **Hotsprings Cove,** Vancouver Island's only hot spring. Water bubbles out of the ground at a temperature of 87°C (189°F), tumbles over a cliff, and then drops down through a series of pools—each large enough for two or three people—and into the sea. Lobsterize yourself silly in the first pool, or go for the ultimate in hot-cold torture by immersing yourself in the last pool, where at high tide you'll be slapped by breathtakingly refreshing ocean waves.

Several companies offer excursions out to the hot springs, and although prices vary slightly, expect to pay around $110-130 for a six- to seven-hour trip departing around 10am, with about three hours ashore at the hot springs and the chance to see whales en route. **Tofino Air** (250/725-4454, www.tofinoair.ca), based at the 1st Street dock, offers a scenic 20-minute flight to the hot springs by floatplane (minimum 3 people, $200 pp round-trip).

EVENTS

Tofino and Ucluelet join together each spring to put on the annual **Pacific Rim Whale Festival** (www.pacificrimwhalefestival.com), which features educational shows and special events in the adjacent national park, a First Nations song and dance festival, a parade, crab races, plays at the local theater, dances, concerts, a golf tournament, and a multitude of events and activities in celebration of the gray whale spring migration. The festival takes place the last two weeks of March.

FOOD
Cafés and Cheap Eats

For basic groceries, Tofino has a midsize **Co-op Food Store** (140 1st St., 250/725-3226, 8:30am-7pm daily) at the far end of the main street into town. For the very freshest seafood, stop by **Trilogy Fish Co.** (630 Campbell St., 250/725-2233, noon-5pm daily), which processes and smokes fish in their own facility. Everything is seasonal, with summer highlights including crab, halibut, and prawns.

Common Loaf Bake Shop (180 1st St., 250/725-3915, 7am-7pm daily) is a longtime favorite with locals (delicious cinnamon rolls for $3.50); sit outside or upstairs, where you'll have a magnificent view down Tofino's main street and across the sound. Also an established part of the café scene is **Rhino Coffee** (430 Campbell St., 250/725-2558, 7:30am-7pm

daily summer, 8:30am-4pm daily fall-spring, lunch $8-10), which has a chilled surfer vibe, along with excellent coffee. Food offerings include generously filled breakfast wraps, sandwiches, and salads. Thin crust pizza for $15-20 makes yup the bulk of the evening menu (try Viva Tofino, a pizza topped with smoked salmon, goat cheese, caramelized onions, and capers). On the road into town, the emphasis at **Tofino Coffee Roasting Co.** (605 Gibson St., 250/726-6016, 7am-5pm daily summer, 7am-2pm Mon.-Fri. fall-spring) is on high quality coffee, roasted in-house daily.

Perfectly reflecting the Tofino lifestyle is **Outside Break** (1180 Pacific Rim Hwy.), a collection of locally operated eateries, boutiques, and the coast's original surf shop, surrounded by coastal rainforest on the road into town between Lynn Road and Hellesen Drive. At the front of the complex is the **Tofitian** (250/725-2631, 7am-4pm daily summer, 7:30am-2:30pm daily fall-spring) which, once you get past the rather dark exterior, is a welcoming café with an amazing array of coffee drinks and a wide range of loose-leaf teas. The orange van at the back of Outside Break is ★ **Tacofino** (250/725-8228, 11am-8pm daily, $7-12), a brightly painted food truck that possibly has the best fish tacos on Vancouver Island. They are freshly, filled with local fish, and reasonably priced. After being served with a smile, enjoy your feast at one of the surrounding picnic tables.

Even if staying at the upscale Wickaninnish Inn is outside your budget, the resort's **Driftwood Cafe** (Wickaninnish Inn, Osprey Lane, Chesterman Beach, 250/725-3100, 7am-11pm daily, lunch $12-26) is a wonderful spot for guests and non-guests alike, especially after a morning walk along Chesterman Beach. The café itself has sweeping ocean views and is anchored by an impressive bar made from a large piece of driftwood. The menu includes a wide range of coffee drinks, fruit smoothies, and a continental breakfast buffet. Lunch is highlighted by clam chowder, salads, and a cheese platter.

Restaurants

Schooner Restaurant (331 Campbell St., 250/725-3444, 9am-9pm Tues.-Sun., $22-41) has been dishing up well-priced seafood for over 60 years. Over time the menu has gotten more creative (soy-marinated salmon baked on a cedar plank), but old favorites (grilled halibut) still appear. Expect to pay $9-21 for starters and $22-41 for a main. Also of note is the service, which is remarkably good for a tourist town.

In an unassuming building near the entrance to town, **Shelter Restaurant** (601 Campbell St., 250/725-3353, 11:30am-midnight daily, $26-37) brings some big-city pizzazz to tiny Tofino. Inside you'll find an open dining room with imaginative treats such as crab fritters and yellow Thai curry filled with local shrimp.

South of Tofino, the ★ **Pointe Restaurant** (Wickaninnish Inn, Osprey Lane, Chesterman Beach, 250/725-3100, 8am-9pm daily, $29-48) is simply superb in every respect. Built on a rocky headland, the circular dining room provides sweeping ocean views as good as those at any restaurant in Canada (ask for a window table when reserving). At breakfast, mimosas encourage holiday spirit, or get serious by ordering eggs benedict with smoked salmon. The lunch and dinner menus highlight seafood and island produce. Lunch includes seafood chowder and a wild salmon BLT. A good way to start dinner is with potato-crusted oysters or endive and berry salad before moving on to the seared wild salmon or butter-baked halibut. The impeccable service and a wine list that's dominated by Pacific Northwest bottles round out a world-class dining experience.

ACCOMMODATIONS

Tofino boasts plenty of accommodations, both in town and south along the beach-fringed coastline, but getting a room or campsite in summer can be difficult if you just turn up, so book as far ahead as possible. As elsewhere in the province, high-season rates apply late June-early September. In May and October you'll enjoy big discounts when the weather is still warm enough to take advantage of Tofino's outdoor attractions. Winter in Tofino is known as the storm-watching season, when rates are reduced up to 50 percent, although no one can guarantee the big storms.

Under $50

Tofino's least expensive lodging is **Whalers on the Point Guesthouse** (81 West St., 250/725-3443, www.tofinohostel.com, dorms $45, $129-159 s or d). Affiliated with Hostelling International, it is a world away from hostels of old, appealing to all travelers. The building is a stylish log structure, with a stunning waterfront location, of which the communal lounge area takes full advantage. Other facilities include a modern kitchen, a laundry room, a large deck with a barbecue, free wireless Internet, a game room, and bike rentals.

$100-150

Of Tofino's regular motels, least expensive is the **Dolphin Motel** (1190 Pacific Rim Hwy., 250/725-3377, www.dolphinmotel.ca, $125-170 s or d), on the road into town. The 14 rooms each have a fridge and Wi-Fi, while out front is a barbecue area.

$150-200

As you continue into town beyond the Dolphin Motel, **Tofino Swell Lodge** (341 Olsen Rd., 250/725-3274, www.tofinoswell. com, $175 s or d) is above a busy marina. This seven-room motel offers older but well-decorated rooms, shared use of a fully equipped kitchen and living room (complete with a stereo, a TV, and a telescope), a barbecue area, hot tub, and pleasant gardens with incredible views of Tofino Inlet, tree-covered Meares Island, and distant snowcapped mountains.

Out of town to the south are several oceanfront resorts. Of these, ★ **Middle Beach Lodge** (Mackenzie Beach Rd., 250/725-2900 or 866/725-2900, www.middlebeach.com, $165-480 s or d) does the best job of combining a unique west coast experience with reasonable prices. It comprises two distinct complexes: At the Beach, more intimate, with its own private beach; and the other, At the Headlands, with luxurious self-contained chalets built along the top of a rugged headland. A short trail links the two, and guests are welcome to wander between them. Rates for At the Beach start at a very reasonable $165, ocean views and a balcony from $210, and all rates include a gourmet continental breakfast served in a magnificent common room. Rates for At the Headlands start at $195, rising to over $450 for a freestanding cabin. This part of the complex has a restaurant with a table d'hôte menu offered nightly.

Overlooking the water right downtown is the **Inn at Tough City** (350 Main St., 250/725-2021 or 877/250-2021, http://tough-city.com, $169-249 s or d), a newer lodging constructed with materials sourced from throughout the region. The bricks, all 30,000 of them, were salvaged from a 100-year-old building in Vancouver's historical Gastown, while stained-glass windows, hardwood used in the flooring, and many of the furnishings are of historical value. The rooms are decorated in a stylish heritage color scheme, and beds are covered in plush down duvets.

In the best location in town, right beside the main dock, is **Himwitsa Lodge** (300 Main St., 250/725-3319 or 800/899-1947, www.himwitsa.com, $190-250 s or d). No expense has been spared in the four contemporary upstairs suites, each with a hot tub, a comfortable lounge and a TV, a fully equipped kitchen, and a private balcony with spectacular ocean views.

$250-300

Cable Cove Inn (201 Main St., 250/725-4236 or 800/663-6449, www.cablecoveinn.ca, $275-325 s or d) has a Main Street address, but you'd never know it, sitting on the private deck of your ocean-facing room. It's tucked away in a quiet location overlooking a small cove, yet it's only a two-minute walk from the center of town. Well-furnished in a casual yet

elegant style, each of the six rooms features a private deck and a gas fireplace.

Over $300

You'll find cheaper places to stay in Tofino, but you won't find a lodge like ★ **Pacific Sands Beach Resort** (Cox Bay, 250/725-3322 or 800/565-2322, www.pacificsands.com, from $400-859 s or d), which is perfect for families and outdoorsy types who want to kick back for a few days. Set right on a popular surfing beach eight kilometers (5 miles) south of town, guest units come in a variety of configurations, starting with one-bedroom, kitchen-equipped suites. Some of these hold a prime beachfront location—ask when booking. The best units are the newest: two-level timber-frame villas equipped with everything from surfboard racks to stainless steel kitchen appliances. The heated floors and gas fireplaces are a plus during the winter storm-watching season. Pacific Sands is a family-run operation, which translates to friendly service and repeat guests who have been visiting since childhood (and still bring their surfboards).

If you subscribe to one of those glossy travel mags, you've probably read about the ★ **Wickaninnish Inn** (Osprey Lane, Chesterman Beach, 250/725-3100, www.wick-inn.com, from $480 s or d), which is regarded as one of the world's great resorts—and regularly features at the top of Top Ten lists. Just for good measure, the in-house Pointe Restaurant is similarly lauded. Everything you've read is true: If you want to surrender to the lap of luxury in a wilderness setting, this is the place to do it. Designed to complement the rainforest setting, the exterior post-and-beam construction is big and bold, while the interior oozes west coast elegance. Public areas such as the restaurant, an upscale lounge, a relaxing library, and a downstairs TV room make the resort feel like a world unto itself, but the guest rooms will really wow you. Spread throughout two wings, the 76 rooms overflow with amenities, including fireplaces, oversize soaker tubs, super-comfortable beds, and furniture made from recycled old-growth woods, but the ocean views through floor-to-ceiling windows will captivate you most. The menu of spa treatments is phenomenal—think hot stone massage for two in a hut overlooking the ocean, a full-body exfoliation, or a sacred sea hydrotherapy treatment. The Wickaninnish is a five-minute drive south of Tofino.

Camping

All of Tofino's campgrounds are on the beaches south of town, but enjoying the great outdoors comes at a price in this part of the world, with some campsites costing more than $50 per night. The best of the bunch is **Bella Pacifica Campground** (250/725-3400, www.bellapacifica.com, Mar.-Oct., $46-56), right on MacKenzie Beach and offering over 100 protected tent sites and full hookups, as well as coin-operated showers and a laundry room.

Along the same stretch of sand, **Crystal Cove Beach Resort** (250/725-4213, www.crystalcovebeachresort.com, $70, cabins $310-525) is one of the province's finest campgrounds. Facilities are modern, with personal touches such as complimentary coffee each morning and a book exchange. Many of the sites are in a private, heavily wooded area.

INFORMATION AND SERVICES

Tofino Visitor Centre (250/725-3414, www.tourismtofino.com, 9am-7pm daily summer, 10am-4pm daily fall-spring) is along the Pacific Rim Highway, eight kilometers (5 miles) before town.

Within the waterfront Tofino Sea Kayaking Company base, the **Company Store** (320 Main St., 250/725-4222, 8:30am-8pm daily summer) stocks an excellent selection of local literature and has a small café with ocean views.

The **post office,** a **laundromat,** and **Tofino General Hospital** (250/725-3212) are all on Campbell Street.

Getting There

The closest town of any size to Tofino is Port Alberni, 130 kilometers (80 miles) to the east (allow at least 2.5 hours along a very narrow and winding road); Victoria is 340 kilometers (210 miles) distant.

Tofino Bus (461 Main St., 250/725-2871 or 866/986-3466, www.tofinobus.com) runs one bus daily between Victoria and Tofino, making pickups at both Nanaimo ferry terminals. The fare from Victoria is $72. Three times daily, this company runs a bus between Tofino and Ucluelet ($18 one-way), with stops made at lodges, beaches, and hiking trails along the way.

Orca Airways (604/270-6722 or 888/359-6722, www.flyorcaair.com) flies from its base at Vancouver's South Terminal to Tofino year-round. Although it doesn't offer any scheduled flights, **Tofino Air** (250/725-4454), based at the foot of 1st Street, provides scenic floatplane flightseeing and charters.

Getting around town is easiest on foot. You can rent bikes from **TOF Cycles** (660 Sharp Rd., 250/725-2453, 9am-5pm daily) for $35 per day; blend in with the locals by adding a surfboard carrier to your bike for $20.

Oceanside

Back on the east side of the island, Highway 19 (Inland Island Hwy.) north of the Highway 4 junction to the west coast bypasses a stretch of coast that has developed as a popular holiday area, with many beaches, resorts, and waterfront campgrounds known collectively as Oceanside.

PARKSVILLE

Unspoiled sand fringes the coastline between Parksville (pop. 12,000) and Qualicum Beach. Parksville Beach claims "the warmest water in the whole of Canada." When the tide goes out along this stretch of the coast, it leaves a strip of sand up to one kilometer (0.6 miles) wide exposed to the sun. When the water returns, voilà—sand-heated water.

Sights and Recreation

Running parallel to Highway 19A (Island Hwy.) through town is the **Community Park Beach,** with lots of driftwood and protected swimming in shallow water. Behind the beach is a boardwalk, a large playground, a splash park, and exercise equipment that anyone is free to use.

Rathtrevor Beach Provincial Park, a 347-hectare (860-acre) chunk of coastline just south of the town center, features a fine two-kilometer (1.2-mile) sandy beach, a wooded area of old-growth Douglas fir, signs of homesteaders dating to the 1880s, and easy walking trails. The birdwatching highlight occurs in March and April, when thousands of Brant geese stop by on their annual migration to Alaska, swooping into the water for a herring feast.

The children will probably want to stop at **Riptide Lagoon** (1000 Resort Dr., 250/248-8290, 9:30am-9:30pm daily summer), near the park entrance. This over-the-top 36-hole mini-golf complex costs $8 per game for adults, $6 for children.

Although the beach is the focus for most people visiting Parksville, there is a small museum adjacent to the information center at **Parksville Museum** (125 East Island Hwy., 250/248-6966, 10am-5pm daily May-Sept.,

Parksville is renowned for its beaches.

adults $5, seniors $4, children $2), comprising historical buildings such as an 1888 post office, an example of a century-old holiday cottage, a one-room schoolhouse, and a church that is still used for weddings.

Also known as Beachfest, the midsummer **Canadian Open Sand Sculpting Competition** (250/951-2678, www.parksvillebeachfest.ca) takes place along the greenspace behind the Community Park Beach during the middle weekend of July. Created by artists from across Canada who are given 30 hours over four days to complete their masterpieces, the sand sculptures are nothing short of amazing. But one of the good things about the event is that the sand sculptures remain on display 9am-9pm daily until mid-August, and entry to the compound is just $3. The event also features beachside concerts every Friday and Saturday evening through mid-August.

Food

Step away from the beach scene at **Pacific Brimm** (123 Craig St., 250/248-3336, 7am-6pm Mon.-Fri., 8am-3pm Sat.-Sun., lunch $8-11), an inviting café that's halfway between relaxed and refined. In addition to all the usual coffee choices, you'll find a good selection of loose-leaf teas, delicious oversize cinnamon buns, full breakfasts, and hot lunches.

One block to the west (just off the Hwy. 4A/Alberni Hwy.) is a similar café, **Bread & Honey** (162 Harrison Ave., 250/586-1021, 8am-3pm Wed.-Sun., lunch $6-10), where the menu of house-made salads, soups, and paninis are all made of local healthy ingredients. Traditional cooked breakfasts are $12, although I recommend upgrading to the delicious eggs benedict.

Lefty's (280 Hwy. 19A, 250/954-3886, 8am-9pm daily, $13-24) is a bistro-style restaurant along the main road through Parksville (beside Thrifty Foods). In addition to standard cooked breakfasts, there are delicious oatmeal pancakes made in-house. Lunch choices include cranberry quinoa salad, while in the evening choices range from thin-crust pizza to slow-roasted back ribs.

After soaking up the elegance of the Grotto Spa at Tigh-Na-Mara Seaside Spa Resort, plan on moving upstairs to the resort's **Treetop Tapas & Grill** (1155 Resort Dr., 250/248-2072, noon-8pm daily), where you are encouraged to relax in your robe over an unlimited procession of creative tapas, although unlike their Spanish originals, the cost is high—$59 pp. The resort's other restaurant, the **Cedar Room** (7am-9:30pm daily, $23-29) offers classic Pacific Northwest cooking at reasonable prices, including a delicious cedar plank salmon.

Accommodations and Camping

Parksville's many accommodations have been developed for vacationing families—with weekly rentals of self-contained units within walking distance of the water. Overlooking Craig Bay on the southeast side of town, **Ocean Sands Resort** (1165 Resort Dr., 250/954-0662 or 877/733-5969, www.oceansandsresort.ca, $249-409 s or d) is typical. Guests swim in the warm ocean water out front or in the smallish heated pool, while children make the most of the playground. Most of the units enjoy sweeping ocean views and separate bedrooms. All have full kitchens and comfortable living areas. Rates start at $150 outside summer.

Guest rooms at **Tigh-Na-Mara Seaside Spa Resort** (1155 Resort Dr., 250/248-2072 or 800/663-7373, www.tigh-na-mara.com, $249-429) are smaller, but the resort itself has more facilities, including two adventure playgrounds, mountain bike rentals, a large swimming pool, two restaurants, and a large spa facility.

At **Rathtrevor Beach Provincial Park** (mid-Mar.-mid-Oct., $35) south of downtown off Highway 19A (take exit 46 from the south), campers choose the natural setting and a great sandy beach over modern facilities (no hookups). To be ensured of a campsite, make reservations by contacting **Discover Camping** (800/689-9025, www.discovercamping.ca).

Information

Traveling north from Nanaimo, take exit 46 from Highway 19 (Inland Island Hwy.) and follow Highway 19A (Island Hwy.) for just under one kilometer (0.6 miles) to reach **Parksville Visitor Centre** (123 East Island Hwy., 250/248-3613, www.visitparksvillequalicumbeach.com, 8am-8pm daily July-Aug., 9am-5pm Mon.-Sat. Sept.-June).

QUALICUM BEACH

This beachside community (pop. 9,000) facing the Strait of Georgia is generally quieter than Parksville, but it shares the same endless sands and attracts the same droves of beachgoers, sun worshippers, anglers, and golfers on summer vacation. You can stay on Highway 19 (Inland Island Hwy.) to bypass Parksville and take the Memorial Avenue exit to reach the heart of the town, but a more scenic option is to continue along the old coastal highway through Parksville. This route is lined with motels, resorts, and RV parks. The attractive downtown area, locally known as "the Village," is away from the beach area up Memorial Avenue.

Wide sandy **Qualicum Beach** is most definitely the main attraction here. Park anywhere along its length and join the crowd walking, running, biking, or simply relaxing in one of the many cafés along the promenade. At low tide, the beach comes alive with people searching out sand dollars.

Sights

Between Parksville and Qualicum Beach, **Milner Gardens and Woodland** (2179 Island Hwy. W., 250/752-8573, 10am-4:30pm daily late Apr.-Aug., noon-4pm Thurs.-Sun. Apr. and Sept., adults $11, students $6.50) protects a historical oceanfront estate that includes a 24-hectare (60-acre) old-growth forest and over 500 species of rhododendrons. Afternoon tea (1pm-4pm daily, $8-18) is served in the drawing room of the main house.

If you appreciate high-quality arts and

Little Qualicum Falls Provincial Park

crafts, detour off the main drag at this point and head for the **Old School House Arts Centre** (122 Fern Rd. W., 250/752-6133, noon-4:30pm Mon., 10am-4:30pm Tues.-Sat., noon-4pm Sun. summer, noon-4:30pm Mon., 10am-4:30pm Tues.-Sat. fall-spring, free). The gallery occupies a beautifully restored 1912 building, while working artist studios below allow you a chance to see wood carving, printmaking, pottery, weaving, painting, and fabric art in progress. Don't miss a stop at the gallery shop, where all kinds of original handcrafted treasures are likely to lure a couple of dollars out of your wallet.

Through town to the west, take Bayswater Road inland a short way to reach the government-operated **Big Qualicum Hatchery** (215 Fisheries Rd., 250/757-8412, dawn-dusk daily, free), where a wooded trail leads to an artificial spawning channel with a fish ladder and a holding pond. The best time of year to watch salmon ascending the channel ladder is October-December. Steelhead can be viewed February-April. The hatchery is one of many on Vancouver Island; this one produces around 25,000 cutthroat trout and 100,000 steelhead each year. To get here from Qualicum Beach, head northwest on Hwy. 19A (Island Hwy.) for 11 kilometers (6.8 miles) and turn west at Fisheries Road, just past Horne Lake Caves Road.

The hatchery is the northern trailhead for the **Big Qualicum Regional River Trail**, a 10-kilometer (6.2-mile) gravel road (walking and biking only) that ends at Horne Lake.

Food

Similar to its other location just to the south in Parksville, **Lefty's** (710 Memorial Ave., 250/752-7530, 8am-8pm Sun.-Thurs., 8am-9pm Fri.-Sat., $13-24) is a contemporary restaurant where the menu is filled with dishes made from fresh, locally sourced ingredients. At lunch, enjoy a mandarin and chicken wrap, while at dinner, mains such as mango ginger-glazed salmon are mostly under $20. Adding to the appeal is friendly service and a row of outdoor tables.

Accommodations and Camping

Looking for a place to stay like no other you've ever experienced? Then make reservations at ★ **Free Spirit Spheres** (420 Horne Lake Rd., 250/757-9445, www.freespiritspheres.com, $175-314 s, $210-314 d). Accommodations consist of three perfectly round, three-meter-wide (10-foot) wooden spheres hanging from towering old-growth trees. Each comprises a small flat area, a shortish bed, windows, and a door that opens to a walkway connected to the ground. Baths are shared and also at ground level.

Qualicum Beach Inn (2690 Island Hwy. W., 250/752-6914 or 800/661-0199, www.qualicumbeachinn.com, $269-409 s or d) is across the road from the ocean and within walking distance of Qualicum Beach Golf Club. After extensive renovations in 2013, the site of the Old Dutch Inn has been completely modernized and now features modern rooms, an indoor pool than opens to an oceanfront patio, and an excellent restaurant.

Give the central campgrounds a miss and

Free Spirit Spheres

continue 16 kilometers (10 miles) northwest from Qualicum Beach to **Qualicum Bay Resort** (5970 W. Island Hwy., 250/757-2003 or 800/663-6899, www.resortbc.com, tents $22, hookups $34-38, camping cabins $84-155, motel rooms $95-165 s or d). Separated from the water by a road, this family-oriented resort has many facilities, including an artificially constructed swimming lake, a playground, a game room, an ice cream stand, and a restaurant.

Information

For the complete rundown on this stretch of the coast, stop in at **Qualicum Beach Visitor Centre** (2711 Island Hwy. W., 250/752-9532 or 866/887-7106, www.qualicum.bc.ca, 8:30am-6:30pm daily late May-early Sept., 9am-4pm Mon.-Fri. early Sept.-late May), on the promenade as you enter town from the southeast.

HORNE LAKE CAVES

If you can drag yourself away from the beach, consider a half-day detour inland to one of Vancouver Island's most intriguing natural attractions, Horne Lake Caves, which are protected as tiny **Horne Lake Caves Provincial Park. Horne Lake Regional Park,** protecting a wide swathe of forest between the provincial park and Horne Lake itself, has a campground, picnic facilities, and a beach. To get there from Qualicum Beach, continue northwest along Highway 19A for 11 kilometers (7 miles) and turn west at Horne Lake Caves Road, following the road for 16 kilometers (10 miles) west to Horne Lake. When the road reaches Horne Lake, it follows the north shore to the cave staging area.

Two small caves (10am-4pm daily year-round) are open for exploration without a guide. There's no charge for entering these caves, but you'll need a helmet and light source, which can be rented onsite for $8.50 pp. Several different guided tours of the larger caves are offered. The one-hour Main Cave Experience (May-Sept., $27 pp) is the least expensive way to get underground with a guide. The two-hour Riverbend Explorer (May-Sept., $42 pp) includes a short walk as well as underground exploration and explanation of the major formations. For those looking for more adventure, other options include the three-hour Multi Cave Adventure ($69 pp) and the five-hour Extreme Rappel (minimum age 15, July-Aug., $169 pp). A private contractor (250/248-7829, www.hornelake.com) runs the tours using qualified guides.

Horne Lake Regional Park

In addition to the caves, a beautiful sandy beach with freshwater swimming, canoeing under the shadow of Mount Mark, and a well-manicured campground within Horne Lake Regional Park make the drive out to Horne Lake worthwhile. The **campground** (250/248-1134, May-Sept., $26-28) is beyond the main entrance to the park. Reservations can be made online (www.rlcparks.ca). Trails lead down to the Qualicum River from this point, while on the south side of the river mouth, the park is less built up and there are good opportunities for bird-watching. The campground operator rents canoes, kayaks, and SUPs; and operates an interpretive program during July and August.

OFFSHORE ISLANDS
Denman Island

Ten minutes after leaving Buckley Bay, 35 kilometers (22 miles) northwest of Qualicum Beach, you'll be driving off the ferry and onto this rural oasis, similar to the Southern Gulf Islands in appearance, sans crowds. Fishing, hiking, biking, bird-watching, and sea kayaking are prime draws here, and you'll also find good beaches, parks, and an artisanal community along narrow winding roads.

Across the island, 23-hectare (57-acre) **Fillongley Provincial Park** is a prime stretch of oceanfront that longtime island resident George Beadnell donated as parkland. Beadnell lived a surprisingly grand life on the island; remains of his home still stand, a variety of trees imported from England dot the park, and the open meadow just north of the parking lot was once a bowling green. The easy Homestead Trail leads through his former estate and into an old-growth forest, then back along the beachfront. The beach itself is a long stretch of sand and pebbles backed by driftwood.

The island's southern tip is protected by **Boyle Point Provincial Park,** where an 800-meter (0.5-mile) trail (20 minutes one-way) leads to a lofty lookout with views down to Chrome Island, where a classic red-and-white lighthouse stands. If you are visiting in winter, this vantage point is a good place to view sea lions.

For travelers looking to immerse themselves in island culture, **Denman Island Guest House** (3806 Denman Rd., 250/335-2688, www.earthclubfactory.com, camping $20 s, $30 d, dorms $24.50, $45-74 s or d) is a memorable choice for its down-to-earth owners and magical setting. In a renovated 1912 farmhouse, the four rooms are simple yet comfortable and rates include a pancake breakfast and use of bikes.

At **Fillongley Provincial Park** (off Swan Rd., $24), the 10 primitive campsites fill quickly, mostly by campers that have made reservations; for these, contact **Discover Camping** (800/689-9025, www.discover-camping.ca).

Hornby Island

Beyond Denman Island, Hornby Island has my favorite beach in all of the Gulf Islands, as well as a distinct counter-cultural vibe that encourages visitors to relax and enjoy a slower pace of living—even if it's just for the few days you spend in this small piece of paradise. The island has attracted those looking to escape mainstream life since the first draft dodgers arrived at the onset of the Vietnam War. Today, the 1,000 year-round residents are mostly self-sufficient, relying on each other

and the local cooperative to live as simple lives as possible, roasting their own coffee and growing their own fruit and vegetables; there's even a couple of small wineries. The best place to immerse yourself in the island lifestyle is **Ringside Market,** a collection of local businesses at the east end of Central Road by Tribune Bay Provincial Park. Here you'll find artisans, coffee-roasters, bike and kayak rentals, cafés, and the **Hornby Island Co-op,** which was founded by island residents in 1955 and stocks everything from locally made pâté to hardware.

A large chunk of the island is protected by **Mt. Geoffrey Escarpment Provincial Park,** including the highest peak and sea cliffs facing Denman Island, but most visitors gravitate to crescent-shaped Tribune Bay, where the longest stretch of sand is protected by 95-hectare (235-acre) **Tribune Bay Provincial Park.** The sand is as white as you'll find on the Gulf Islands, crowds minimal, and the water slightly warmer than other Vancouver Island beaches due to the protected bay.

St. Johns Point Road leads along the parks northern boundary to the entrance to **Helliwell Provincial Park.** Like Fillongley, this land was bequeathed to the people of British Columbia by an island resident. Stretching to Hornby's easternmost point, the park protects one of the few remaining old-growth forests of Douglas fir on the Gulf Islands. A five-kilometer (3-mile) trail loops through the forest to St. Johns Point and then back along high sea cliffs protecting Tribune Bay to the parking lot; allow 90 minutes to complete the circuit.

Right by the ferry dock, old-fashioned **Hornby Island Resort** (4305 Shingle Spit Rd., 250/335-0136, www.thatchpub.ca, May-Sept.) offers boat rentals, tennis courts, and a laundry room. The four motel rooms ($150) have water views but need renovating, and a limited number of RV sites ($38) are off to one side.

Comox Valley

The K'omoks people lived in the Comox Valley for thousands of years before the first Europeans arrived in the 1860s to set up farms and mine coal. Today, the three communities of **Courtenay, Cumberland,** and **Comox** are nestled between the Strait of Georgia and high mountains of the Vancouver Island Ranges to the west. The valley lies almost halfway up the island, 220 kilometers (137 miles) from Victoria. The three towns merge into one, but each has its own personality: Courtenay, the staid town with a compact downtown core and all the visitor services you need; Cumberland, away from the water but historically charming nonetheless; and Comox, a sprawl of retiree housing developments and golf courses that extends across a wide peninsula to the ocean.

COURTENAY

The valley's largest town and a commercial center for local farming, logging, fishing, and retirement communities, Courtenay (pop. 56,000) extends around the head of Comox Harbour. It's not particularly scenic but has a few interesting sights and plenty of highway accommodations.

Sights

The main attraction downtown is **Courtenay and District Museum** (207 4th St., 250/334-0686, 10am-5pm Mon.-Sat. and noon-4am Sun. June-Aug., 10am-5pm Tues.-Sat. Sept.-May, donation). The highlight is a full-size replica of an *elasmosaur*. The original—12 meters (39 feet) long and 80 million years old—was found at the nearby Puntledge River. The museum leads tours out to the site (daily July-Aug., Sat. Apr.-June and Sept.), on which you have the chance to dig for your very own fossil (adults $30, children $20).

Other museum exhibits include a series of realistic dioramas and a replica of a big house containing many First Nations artifacts and items, some formerly belonging to prominent chiefs. Finish up in the gift shop, which is well stocked with local arts and crafts.

Recreation

Vancouver Island is not usually associated with snow sports by outsiders, but locals know they don't need to leave their island home to enjoy world-class skiing and boarding at **Mount Washington Alpine Resort** (250/338-1386 or 888/231-1499, www.mountwashington.ca), 35 kilometers (22 miles) northwest of Courtenay. The scope and popularity of the resort are remarkable—it ranks fourth in British Columbia for the number of skier days and has a modern base village with more than 3,500 beds—but not surprising, considering it receives an annual snowfall of 11 meters (33 feet) and temperatures that remain relatively warm compared to the interior of British Columbia. Seven chairlifts serve 370 hectares (915 acres), with the vertical rise a respectable 500 meters (1,640 feet) and the longest run just under two kilometers (1.2 miles). Other facilities include a terrain park and a half-pipe. Lift tickets are adults $89, seniors $74, and children $49.

Between July and mid-October, the resort welcomes outdoor enthusiasts who come to hike through alpine meadows, ride the chairlift ($20 pp), mountain bike down the slopes, or go trail riding through the forest. A wealth of other activities are on offer—from mini-golf to a bungee trampoline—making it a good place to escape the beachy crowd for a day or two. Inexpensive summer packages (see the website) encourage overnight stays.

Comox Valley Kayaks and Canoes (2020 Cliffe Ave., 250/334-2628 or 888/545-5595, 10am-5pm daily) offers guided tours for around $50, three-hour sea-kayaking lessons for $90 pp, and full-day guided trips from

$115. Or rent a kayak ($35-90 for 24 hours) for some exploration by yourself, around the local waterways or out on nearby Denman and Hornby Islands. The company also rents canoes ($56 per day)—great for nearby Comox Lake. It's located along the highway just south of downtown.

Food

Branching west from Cliffe Avenue (the main thoroughfare through town), 5th Street has a number of good choices for local cuisine. At the top end of the street, **Common Ground Cafe** (596 5th St., 250/897-1111, 7am-9pm Mon.-Thurs., 7am-3pm Fri., lunch $6-9) is a friendly little place with a beautifully restored home. Lattes, cappuccinos, and loose-leaf teas highlight the drinks menu, breakfasts include a vegetarian omelet and homemade granola, and lunches include a delicious cranberry nut salad. In the evening, there are only a couple of dinner mains offered, but they change with the season, meaning you'll enjoy the best local seafood at very reasonable prices.

In the heart of downtown, the **Union Street Grill** (477 5th St., 250/897-0081, 11am-9pm daily, $15-23) dishes up well-priced global choices that include a delicious jambalaya and expertly prepared fish from local waters. Save room for a slice of delicious cheesecake. Or head down one block to **Hot Chocolates** (368 5th St., 250/338-8211, 10am-6pm Mon.-Sat., 10am-5pm Sun.), which specializes in handcrafted chocolate treats. Hot Chocolates also has an in-house coffee bar and a covered patio.

Occupying one of Courtenay's original residences, **Locals** (1760 Riverside Lane, 250/338-5406, 11am-9pm Mon.-Fri., 10am-9pm Sat.-Sun., $19-34) sits among landscaped gardens of a much more modern Old House Village Hotel. The menu is filled with tempting yet well-priced Pacific Northwest choices, with produce and game sourced from local producers where possible. You could start with wild mushroom risotto, then move on to pan-seared halibut as a main.

Accommodations and Camping

The valley's least expensive motels are strung out along Highway 19 (known as Cliffe Ave. within city limits) as you enter Courtenay from the south. The 67-room **Anco Motel** (1885 Cliffe Ave., 250/334-2451, www.ancoinn.ca, $90-120 s or d) is typical, with a small outdoor pool and some kitchenettes as a bonus.

Within easy walking distance of downtown is **Old House Village Hotel** (1730 Riverside Lane, 250/703-0202 or 888/703-0202, www.oldhousevillage.com, $179 s or d), a modern, three-story hotel with a fitness center, spa services, a restaurant, and a garden with a covered barbecue. Each of the 79 guest rooms is decorated in modern, earthy tones; bathrobes, kitchenettes, and gas fireplaces add to the charm.

Overlooking Gartley Bay south of Courtenay is **Kingfisher Oceanside Resort** (4330 Island Hwy. S., 250/338-1323 or 800/663-7929, www.kingfisherspa.com, $195-455 s or d), set around well-manicured gardens and a large heated pool right on the ocean. The resort also holds a spa facility, a yoga lounge, a bar with outdoor seating, and a restaurant renowned for its West Coast cuisine (and a great Sunday brunch buffet). Lodging choices are in regular rooms, each with a private balcony, or newer beachfront suites, each with a fireplace, hot tub, and kitchen.

Information

The **Vancouver Island Visitor Centre** (3607 Small Rd., 855/400-2882, www.discovercomoxvalley.com, 9am-7pm daily summer, 9am-4pm daily fall-spring) is an architecturally striking building on the east side of Highway 19 (Inland Island Hwy.) at Exit 117 (Cumberland Rd.). In addition to the usual information services, the center has an interesting array of interpretive displays that tell the story of the Comox Valley, as well as free wireless Internet, a playground, and a picnic area.

Getting There

Courtenay in 105 kilometers (66 miles) north of Nanaimo, 215 kilometers (134 miles) north of Victoria, and 60 kilometers (38 miles) south of Campbell River. IslandLink (2663 Kilpatrick St., 250/334-2475, www.islandlinkbus.com) runs buses three to five times daily between Victoria and Courtenay, continuing north to Campbell River and Port Hardy.

CUMBERLAND

This historic town of 3,300 lies on the west side of Highway 19 (Inland Island Hwy.) seven kilometers (4.3 miles) southwest of downtown Courtenay. Its quiet streets are lined with mining-era cottages with the main street leading past numerous brink commercial buildings.

Coal was first discovered in the Comox Valley in 1869, and by the mid-1880s extraction of the most productive seam was going ahead under the direction of coal baron Robert Dunsmuir, who brought in hundreds of Chinese and Japanese workers. Cumberland's Chinatown was once home to 3,000 people, second in size on North America's west coast only to San Francisco's Chinatown. At the outbreak of World War II, the Japanese residents of Cumberland were all sent to internment camps scattered throughout mainland British Columbia.

Sights and Recreation

Cumberland Museum (2680 Dunsmuir St., 250/336-2445, 10am-5pm Mon.-Sat., noon-5pm Sun. June-Aug., 10am-5pm Tues.-Sat., noon-5pm Sun. Sept.-May, adults $5, seniors $4) is a small but excellent facility, with interesting historical photos. On the museum grounds is a recreated mine shaft open to the public. Before leaving, pick up a heritage walking-tour brochure and ask for directions to the overgrown remains of the Chinese settlement, now protected as Coal Creek Historic Park. The park lies around 1.6 kilometers (1 mile) west of the museum along the road to Comox Lake.

The ocean beaches in this region are not as inviting as those farther south around Parksville and Qualicum Beach, so many locals head out to glacier-fed Comox Lake, three kilometers (2 miles) west of Cumberland along Comox Lake Road. The swimming area is protected from motorized watercraft by a boom of large logs and the beach has a concession and kayak and SUP rentals.

Accommodations and Camping

Instead of motels, Comox has one of Vancouver Island's best backpacker lodges, Riding Fool Hostel (2705 Dunsmuir St., 250/336-8250, www.ridingfool.com, dorm $28, $60-90 s or d). It has colorful common areas, family rooms, a female dorm, a large communal kitchen, and bike rentals.

West of town, Cumberland Lake Park Campground (Comox Lake Rd., 250/336-2144, www.cumberlandlakepark.ca, $30-35) enjoys a lakefront setting, although there is no privacy between the best sites, which are right on the beach. Reservations are a must especially for the powered sites.

Information and Services

Cumberland Visitor Centre (2680 Dunsmuir St., 250/336-2445, 9am-5pm daily July-Aug., 10am-5pm Tues.-Sat. Sept.-June) is in the museum along the main street. Along Cumberland's main street, the historic brick post office has been transformed into the Wandering Moose Café (2739 Dunsmuir Ave., 250/400-1111, 8am-4pm Thurs.-Tues., lunch $6-9), with prime street-side tables the best place to enjoy daily-made sandwiches, wraps, and soups on a sunny day.

COMOX

The population of Comox is quoted at 13,500, and there's certainly enough room for everyone, but you'd never know it, driving along forested roads that lead to golf courses, retirement communities, and a magnificent stretch of coastline. To reach Comox's small downtown area, take Comox Road eastward after crossing the Courtenay River along Highway 19.

Sights

Through downtown is a highlight of the valley, **Filberg Heritage Lodge and Park** (Comox Ave. at Filberg Rd., 250/339-2715, 8am-dusk daily, free), which was bequeathed to the people of Comox by logging magnate Robert Filberg in 1977. A high hedge hides the beautifully landscaped grounds, which stretch down to Comox Harbour, from the outside world. At the bottom of the garden is the main house (11am-3pm Wed.-Fri. summer), built in 1929 and filled with period antiques and quirky architecture.

Take Pritchard Road north from Filberg Lodge and you'll eventually reach the Canadian Forces Base, which doubles as the local airport for commercial flights. Cross Knight Road to reach **Comox Air Force Museum** (Ryan Rd., 250/339-8162, 10am-4pm Tues.-Sun., donation), at the entrance to Comox Air Force Base. The museum isn't huge, but it is chock-full of Air Force memorabilia. Once you've gone through the indoor displays, you'll want to wander down to the Air Park (10am-4pm daily May-Sept.), a five-minute walk south, where a dozen planes from various eras are parked.

On the other side of the runway is **Kye Bay,** a wide strip of sand that is perfect for families. To the east, beyond the headland, are intriguing **white cliffs.** At the end of an ancient ice age, as the sheet of ice that covered this region retreated, it stalled, leaving behind a massive mound of finely ground glacial silt. Wind and water action in the ensuing years have uncovered the silt, forming white cliffs that stand in stark contrast to the surrounding bedrock. To reach Kye Bay from the airport, head east on Knight Road (past the entrance to the main terminal) and take Kye Bay Road around the south end of the runway.

Another interesting spot is **Seal Bay Nature Park,** north of downtown along Anderton and then Waveland Roads. The park protects one of the region's few undeveloped stretches of coastline. Trails lead through a lush forest of Douglas fir and ferns to a pleasant, rocky beach where bald eagles and seals are often sighted.

Food and Accommodations

The most serene place to enjoy lunch is the landscaped gardens at Filberg Heritage Lodge, where the **Filberg Summer Kitchen** (61 Filberg Rd., 250/339-2750, 11am-4pm Thurs.-Sun. summer, lunch $8-14) offers picnic tables spread out under mature trees. A delightful setting and well-priced lunches and desserts make this a popular spot on sunny days.

Regular motel accommodations are limited in Comox, but for a resort-like atmosphere, it's hard to go past **Crown Isle Resort** (399 Clubhouse Dr., 250/703-5000 or 888/338-8439, www.crownisle.com, from $179 s or d), a sprawling resort and residential estate set on 330 hectares (800 acres) north of Comox off Ryan Road. The standard rooms and one- and two-bedroom villas are comfortable and relatively spacious; some have kitchenettes and fireplaces. The best rates are available by purchasing a golf package. Other amenities include a fitness room and two restaurants.

Campers looking for a vacation vibe should make reservations at **Cape Lazo RV & Campground** (685 Lazo Rd., Comox, 250/339-3946, www.capelazo.com, tents $25, hookups $45-55), which is within easy walking distance of a sandy beach. Facilities include modern showers, a playground, and kayak and SUP rentals. To get there from the highway, take Comox Road through downtown Comox and turn right onto Balmoral Avenue, which leads into Lazo Road.

Ferry to Powell River

BC Ferries (250/386-3431, www.bcferries.com) sails four times daily between Comox and Powell River, allowing mainlanders easy access to mid-island beaches and snow slopes and saving visitors to northern Vancouver Island from having to backtrack down to Nanaimo or Victoria. To get to the terminal, stay on Highway 19 through Courtenay, then take Ryan Road east to Anderton Road. Turn left and follow the signs down Ellenor Road.

The regular one-way fare for this 75-minute sailing is adults $15.90, children $7.95, vehicles $49.70.

NORTH TOWARD CAMPBELL RIVER

From Courtenay, it's an easy 30-minute drive north along Highway 19 (Inland Island Hwy.) to Campbell River. A more enjoyable route is the original route north, now known as Highway 19A (Island Hwy.), which provides many access points to the Strait of Georgia.

Miracle Beach Provincial Park

Miracle Beach Provincial Park, off Highway 19A (Island Hwy.) 23 kilometers (14 miles) north of Courtenay, is mostly about camping, but it has one of the nicest sandy beaches along this stretch of coastline, a few forested walking trails, and the opportunity to watch salmon spawning in Black Creek each fall. The park's Miracle Beach Nature House (10am-5pm daily summer, free) has interesting natural history displays, a shop selling gifts and books, and is the focus point for an interpretive program that includes walks and talks.

The 200-site **Miracle Beach Provincial Park Campground** ($33) is open March to October, but services such as hot showers are only available May to September. Ensure there is a campsite waiting for you by making reservations through **Discover Camping** (800/689-9025, www.discovercamping.ca).

Salmon Point

A short drive north of Miracle Beach and 18 kilometers (11 miles) south of Campbell River is **Salmon Point Resort** (2176 Salmon Point Rd., 250/923-6605 or 866/246-6605, www.salmonpoint.com, campsites $39-57, cabins $140-240 s or d), also offering great views across the Strait of Georgia to the snowcapped peaks of the Coast Mountains. Facilities are excellent: an outdoor swimming pool, a restaurant overlooking the water, a couple of recreation rooms (one for adults only), fishing guide service and tackle, boat rentals ($240 per day), a heated pool, heated baths, and a laundry room. All campsites sit among small stands of pines.

Northern Vancouver Island

The northern section of Vancouver Island is mountainous, heavily treed, dotted with lakes, riddled with rivers and waterfalls, and almost completely unsettled. Just one main highway serves the region, although hundreds of kilometers of logging roads penetrate the dense forests. The gateway to the north is **Campbell River,** another small city that proudly calls itself the "Salmon Capital of the World." From this point north, the Island Highway follows a winding route over mountains and through valleys, first hitting the coast near **Telegraph Cove,** one of Canada's most photogenic communities and the departure point for orca-watching trips to the nutrient-rich waters of Johnstone Strait and Robson Bight. The island's northernmost town is **Port Hardy,** terminus for ferries heading north to Prince Rupert and the gateway to the wild West Coast and **Cape Scott Provincial Park.**

CAMPBELL RIVER

A gateway to the wilderness of northern Vancouver Island, this city of 35,000 stretches along Discovery Passage 260 kilometers (162 miles) north of Victoria and 235 kilometers (146 miles) southeast of Port Hardy. Views from town—of tree-covered Quadra Island and the magnificent white-topped mountains of mainland British Columbia—are superb, but most visitors come for the salmon fishing. The underwater topography creates prime angling conditions; the Strait of Georgia ends just south of Campbell River,

Campbell River

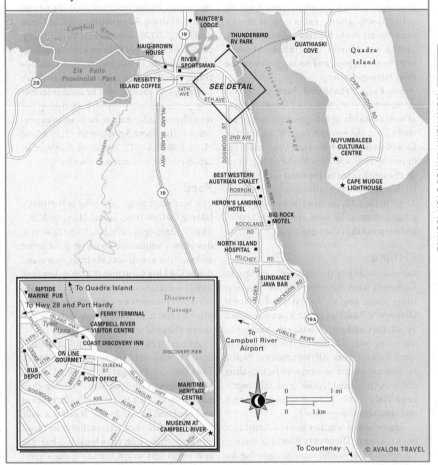

and Discovery Passage begins. The waterway suddenly narrows to a width of only two kilometers (1.2 miles) between Vancouver and Quadra Islands, causing some of the strongest tides on the coast, attracting bait fish and forcing thousands of migrating salmon to concentrate off Campbell River, much to every angler's delight.

Sights

The best place to absorb some of the local atmosphere is **Discovery Pier.** The 180-meter (590-foot) pier is fun to walk on whether you're into fishing or not. Its benches and protected shelters allow proper appreciation of the marina, strait, mainland mountains, and fishing action, even on wet and windy days.

One of the island's premier regional museums, **Museum at Campbell River** (470 Island Hwy., 250/287-3103, 10am-5pm daily mid-May-Sept., noon-5pm Tues.-Sun. Oct.-mid-May, adults $8, seniors $7, students $5) sits on four hectares (10 acres) overlooking Discovery Passage. First check out the photos and interesting written snippets that provide a look at Campbell River's early beginnings. Then feast your eyes on mystical artifacts, a huge collection of masks, exciting artwork, baskets, woven articles, carved-wood boxes, colorful button blankets, petroglyphs, and totem poles in the First Nations Gallery.

Elk Falls Provincial Park protects a salmon-rich stretch of the Campbell River as well as stands of old-growth forest. It extends from the western edge of the town of Campbell River to John Hart Lake and is cut in two by Highway 28, with the campground on the south side and the namesake Elk Falls farther west on the north side of the highway. To get to the falls, continue beyond the campground entrance for three kilometers (2 miles) and turn north at the signed road.

Fishing

Salmon fishing is the point of traveling to Campbell River for most visitors. The best thing about angling in waters of adjacent **Discovery Passage** is that it can be enjoyed by all ages and on all budgets—and without a long boat ride through rough waters to reach the best spots. All five species of Pacific salmon are caught in local waters, including chinook (July-Sept.), pink (mid-July-Sept.), coho (July-Oct.), sockeye (mid-July-Aug.), and chum (mid-Sept.-Nov.).

Regardless of whether you're a first-timer or an old-timer, **Discovery Pier** in downtown Campbell River is a fantastic place to fish for salmon. The pier sports built-in rod holders, fish-cleaning stations, glassed-in shelters for nonanglers, and colorful signs describing the fish you're likely to catch. Anglers cast for salmon, bottom fish, and the occasional steelhead, hauling them up in nets on long ropes. When the salmon are running, the pier gets extremely busy, and for a reason—chinook salmon over 14 kilograms (30 pounds) are not uncommon. Rod rentals are available on the pier ($6 per hour, $15 per half day, $25 per day). Don't forget, you also need a tidal fishing license.

The marinas along this stretch of coast are filled with charter operators, but one that comes highly recommended is **Coastal Island Fishing Adventures** (250/287-3836 or 888/225-9776, www.coastalislandfishing.com), which charges $700 for a five-hour fishing trip for up to five people. Rates include transportation in a covered boat and fish cleaning and packaging. The local information center will help out with basic fishing and boat charter information, or head to the experts at the **River Sportsman** (2115 Island Hwy., 250/286-1017, 7am-8pm daily) for licenses, tackle, and maybe a few tips.

Food

The best place to go for coffee is **Nesbitt's Island Coffee** (1995 Island Hwy., 250/287-4887, 7:30am-6pm daily, lunch $7-12), west of downtown, which also serves up good coffee and muffins, as well as sandwiches, soups, and salads. **On Line Gourmet** (970 Shoppers Row, 250/286-6521, 8am-4pm Mon.-Sat., lunch $6-10) is part Internet café but mostly an excellent place for lunch, with soup made in-house and sandwiches and wraps made to order.

Around six kilometers (3.7 miles) south of downtown along Highway 19A is **Sundance Java Bar** (80 Westgate Rd., 250/923-8827, Willow Point, 8am-5pm Mon.-Fri., 9am-5pm Sat., lunch $7-10), a friendly little place owned and operated by two locals. It offers a wide range of coffee concoctions, loose-leaf teas, and smoothies, with tasty breakfast burritos and soups and wraps rounding out a great choice for breakfast or lunch.

A short way north along the harbor-front from Tyee Plaza is **Riptide Marine Pub** (1340 S. Island Hwy., 250/830-0044, 11am-11pm daily, $16-28), a good place for a full meal, although it doesn't take full advantage of its waterfront location (unless you score a table on the glassed-in patio). The sleek interior is a little nicer than you may imagine, while the food is exactly what you'd expect: standard pub fare mixed with fresh scallops, oysters, mussels, halibut, and salmon.

Continue north through town on Highway

Tyee Club

If you're fishing between July 15 and September 15, you may want to try qualifying for Tyee Club membership. This exclusive club, famous among anglers, has been dedicated to upholding the traditional methods of sportfishing since 1925. Several rules must be followed in order to become a member: You have to preregister your intent to fish under club rules; troll from a rowboat in the eddies at the mouth of the Campbell River; use a rod between six and nine feet long, an artificial lure, and a line of 20-pound test; then catch a trophy-size tyee (a Chinook salmon weighing over 30 pounds). Most tyee fishing is done at dawn and dusk. During the tyee season, most local charter operators offer the option of traditional tyee fishing, including **Coastal Island Fishing Adventures** (250/287-3836 or 888/225-9776, www.coastalislandfishing.com, $250 for 2 people). Guests at **Painter's Lodge** (1625 MacDonald Dr., 250/286-1102 or 800/663-7090, www.painterslodge.com) are charged a similar amount.

19 and turn right on McDonald Road to reach two fishing resorts with excellent restaurants that welcome nonguests. The appetizer menu at **Legends Dining Room** (Painter's Lodge, 1625 MacDonald Dr., 250/286-1102, 7am-11am and 5pm-9pm daily, $23-35) is dominated by seafood choices, and while mains include steak and lamb, it's hard to go past the halibut, cooked two different ways. Legends also offers a breakfast buffet.

Just north of Painters is **Anglers Dining Room** (Dolphins Resort, 4125 Discovery Dr., 250/287-3066, 7am-11am and from 5pm daily, $19-40), a more rustic but equally inviting setting with a few outdoor tables. Local seafood is on the menu—oysters, ling cod, mussels, and salmon—but does not dominate.

Accommodations

Because Campbell River is a fish-centric resort town, every kind of lodging you could possibly want is here, from upscale fishing lodges to rustic campgrounds.

$50-100

Along Highway 19A (known as the South Island Highway through Campbell River) south of town, only the road separates several motels from Discovery Passage. If you want to save your money for a fishing charter, no worries—book a room at the 22-room **Big Rock Motel** (1020 S. Island Hwy., 250/923-4211 or 877/923-4211, www.bigrockmotel.com, $90 s or d, $120 with kitchen), your average two-story, cinder-block motel.

$100-150

Bed-and-breakfast accommodations are provided at **Haig-Brown House** (2250 Campbell River Rd., 250/286-6646, www.haig-brown.bc.ca, May-Oct., $110 s, $120 d), the modest 1923 riverside home of famed angler and author Roderick Haig-Brown. The old antique-filled house has changed little over time, and the grounds are a delightful place to relax. The three guest rooms share a bath. It's on the north side of Highway 28, just west of where Highway 19 spurs north to Port Hardy.

$150-200

Closer to town but along the same ocean-hugging highway as the Big Rock Motel recommended above is **Best Western Austrian Chalet** (462 S. Island Hwy., 250/923-4231 or 800/667-7207, www.bwcampbellriver.com, from $155 s or d), with a wide range of facilities including an indoor pool, a sauna, a courtyard with a barbecue for guest use, mini golf, and an adjacent restaurant and pub.

Along the same strip of accommodations overlooking the water is **Heron's Landing Hotel** (492 S. Island Hwy., 250/923-2848 or 888/923-2849, www.heronslandinghotel.com, $159-199 s or d), an older property that has undergone extensive renovations to create some of the nicest guest rooms in Campbell River. Standard rooms have one king bed or two twins, while the one-bedroom suites have kitchens. Rates include a cooked breakfast.

In the heart of downtown and across the road from a marina, 88-room **Coast Discovery Inn** (975 Shopper's Row, 250/287-7155 or 800/716-6199, www.coasthotels.com, from $175 s or d) is a full-service hotel with a fitness room, free wireless Internet, and free local calls. A hot buffet breakfast is also included in the rates.

$200-250

Follow Highway 19 beyond the town Campbell River, crossing the river of the same name, to reach **Painter's Lodge** (1625 MacDonald Dr., 250/286-1102 or 800/663-7090, www.painterslodge.com, $200-290), an impressive oceanfront fishing lodge offering all the amenities needed by keen anglers, including a marina, guided fishing trips, and fish-cleaning services. Families and nonanglers are also well-catered for, with facilities including a swimming pool, a hot tub, tennis courts, a fitness room, a water shuttle to spa services on Quadra Island, and a waterfront restaurant. The modern guest rooms are offered in a number of different configurations, including standard Garden View Rooms, two-story, family-friendly lofts, and private cabins. Many packages are offered that include a variety of fishing options, such as two night's lodging and two guided fishing trips ($480 pp).

CAMPING

A few commercial campgrounds dot the coastline around Campbell River, but although they're close to the water, the surroundings are generally nothing special. One of the closest to downtown is **Thunderbird RV Park** (2660 Spit Rd., 250/286-3344, www.thunderbirdrvpark.com, hookups $38-40, cottages $248), a 10-minute walk north of downtown. Amenities include full hookups, heated restrooms, and fish-cleaning stations.

A less commercial option, but with limited facilities, is **Elk Falls Provincial Park** (May-mid-Oct., $22), three kilometers (2 miles) west of town on Highway 28. The 122

unserviced sites are south of the highway, with many right alongside the Quinsam River. The campground has flush toilets, drinking water, and a playground. Campsites can be reserved through **Discover Camping** (800/689-9025, www.discovercamping.ca). Farther out and in a more rustic setting is **Loveland Bay Provincial Park** (mid-May-Sept., $22), on a northern arm of Campbell Lake 20 kilometers (12 miles) west of town. The 31 sites are close to the water and shaded by a second-growth forest. To get there, follow Snowden Camp Road beyond the Elk Falls day-use turnoff and turn west (left) onto Brewster Lake Road; the campground is around 12 kilometers (7.5 miles) from Elk Falls.

INFORMATION AND SERVICES

Park in the large parking lot of **Tyee Plaza**, along the waterfront in downtown Campbell River, and you're within easy walking distance of the information center and all services. At the front of the parking lot is **Campbell River Visitor Centre** (1235 Shopper's Row, 250/830-0411, 8:30am-5pm summer, 9am-5pm Mon.-Fri. fall-spring). Aside from providing tons of brochures and information on both the city and northern Vancouver Island, the knowledgeable staff can answer just about any question on the area you could think up. For other information, contact **Campbell River Tourism** (250/286-1616, www.campbellrivertourism.com).

Other plaza tenants include banks, a big-box grocery store, a laundromat, and various family-style eateries. Across from the plaza is the **post office** (1251 Shoppers Row) and **On Line Gourmet** (970 Shoppers Row, 250/286-6521, 8am-4pm Mon.-Sat.), where you can check your email for a small charge. **North Island Hospital** (375 2nd Ave., 250/287-7111) is south of downtown.

GETTING THERE AND AROUND

Although Campbell River is only 260 kilometers (162 miles) north of Victoria, you should allow over three hours for the trip by road, and at least another three hours to reach Port Hardy, 235 kilometers (146 miles) farther north, as the roads this far north are very windy and the going is often slow when stuck behind logging trucks.

Campbell River Airport (YBL), off Erickson Road 20 kilometers (12 miles) south of downtown, is served by **Pacific Coastal** (800/663-2872) and **Central Mountain Air** (888/865-8585) from Vancouver. **Campbell River Airport Shuttle** (250/914-1010) meets all scheduled flights and charges $15 pp for door-to-door drop-off in town.

From Victoria, **Islandlink Bus** (509 13th Ave., 250/287-7151) operates four or five buses daily to Campbell River; in summer, at least one daily continues north to Port Hardy timed to link with the ferry departing for Prince Rupert. Get around town by **Campbell River Transit System** (250/287-7433, $2 per sector, $4.50 day pass), which departs from Tyee Plaza via Shopper's Row along eight routes. Rental car agencies in Campbell River include **Budget** (250/923-4283) and **National** (250/923-1234), both with airport desks (but make reservations in advance).

QUADRA ISLAND

A 10-minute ferry ride across Discovery Passage from downtown Campbell River takes you to Quadra Island (pop. 2,500), which blends beautiful scenery, First Nations culture, and upscale fishing lodges to create a unique and worthwhile detour from your up-island travels. The ferry docks in the south of the island, where most of the population resides. This narrow peninsula widens in the north to an unpopulated area where provincial and marine parks protect a wealth of wildlife. Marinelife around the entire shoreline is widespread; orcas cruise Discovery Passage, and seals and sea lions are commonly spied in surrounding waters.

Captain Vancouver may have been the first European to step onto the island when he made landfall at **Cape Mudge** in 1792, but the island had been inhabited by the Kwakwaka'wakw people for many centuries before.

Sights and Recreation

Take Green Road south from the ferry dock to reach **Nuyumbalees Cultural Centre** (34 Weway Rd., 250/285-3733, 10am-4pm daily May-Sept., adults $10, senior and children $5), a waterfront complex dedicated to the Kwakwaka'wakw people. Many artifacts on display have been returned to the island by museums from around the world after being taken by early European explorers. Highlights include the Sacred Potlatch Collection and an outdoor workshop where First Nations artists can be seen at work during summer. Ask for directions to petroglyphs (rock carvings) scattered around the grounds and beyond.

Continuing south, at the island's southwestern tip, **Cape Mudge Lighthouse** was built in 1916 to prevent shipwrecks in the wild surging waters around the point that marks the southern entrance to the treacherous Discovery Passage. You can drive right up to the lighthouse.

Around nine kilometers (5.5 miles) north along Heriot Bay Road from the ferry dock on the island's east coast is **Rebecca Spit Marine Provincial Park,** which protects a two-kilometer-long (1.2-mile) beach-lined peninsula. A road leads around halfway up the peninsula, from where a two-kilometer hiking trail loops up and around the end of the spit (allow 40 minutes round-trip), but there are many access points to the beach, and it's just as enjoyable walking along the sand as the trail, especially on the east side, which is piled high with driftwood. The park's only facilities are restrooms and picnic areas.

Food

Right at the main ferry dock at Quathiaski Cove, **Q-Beans Coffee** (Quathiaski Cove Rd., 250/285-2407, 6am-5pm daily summer, cash only) pours coffee as good as any on the main island and offers a variety of slightly overpriced baked goods to tide you over waiting for the ferry. It's a takeout window with a couple of outdoor tables, so don't plan on dining here when the weather is bad. Across the island at Heriot Bay, **Aroma Café** (685 Heriot Bay Rd., 250/285-2404, 7:30am-5pm daily, lunch $6.50-10) is a full-service café with tables inside and out. It's the headquarters for a small roasting operation that distributes to stores and cafés around the island. It has healthy yet delicious cooked breakfasts, lunches made daily, and free wireless Internet access.

Herons Restaurant (Heriot Bay Inn, off Heriot Bay Rd., 250/285-3322, breakfast, lunch, and dinner daily, $15-39) has as many tables outside on the harbor-front deck as it does inside. The dinner menu includes lots of island produce and seafood, including butter-poached halibut.

At the resort of the same name in the south of the island, **Tsa-Kwa-Luten Restaurant** (1 Lighthouse Rd., 250/285-2042 or 800/665-7745, 7:30am-8:30pm daily, $24-30) has sweeping ocean views from tables inside and out. Over the years, the emphasis on traditional foods has lessened, although the salmon soup garnished with seaweed and served with a side of bannock bread is a delight. For mains, there's the usual steak, pork, and chicken choices, or stay with the local theme and order grilled salmon.

Accommodations and Camping

For over 100 years, **Heriot Bay Inn** (off Heriot Bay Rd., 250/285-3322 or 888/605-4545, www.heriotbayinn.com, rooms $109-129 s or d, cabins $259-289 s or d) has been the social hub of the island's largest community. Separated from the water by own a wide swath of landscaped garden, the lodge has 10 small but comfortable guest rooms (some with water views) and three kitchen-equipped wooden cabins.

Near Cape Mudge Lighthouse is ★ **Tsa-Kwa-Luten** (1 Lighthouse Rd., 250/285-2042 or 800/665-7745, www.capemudgeresort. bc.ca, $165-355 s or d), built by the local Kwagiulth people. The centerpiece of this

magnificent waterfront lodge is the foyer, built in the style of a big house (a traditional meeting place) using locally milled woods. Each of the 35 spacious rooms is decorated in a Pacific Northwest theme, and each has a private balcony with water views. Rates start at a reasonable $165 s or d, with meal packages available. The more expensive units are two-bedroom cottages. The lodge coordinates fishing charters and cultural activities, and its restaurant specializes in First Nations foods.

For campers, the best option is the charming **We Wai Kai Campsite** (250/285-3111, www.wewaikai.com, mid-May-early Oct., $35-45), set along a pleasant sandy beach at the head of Heriot Bay and close to Rebecca Spit Marine Provincial Park. Amenities include basic hookups, showers, and a laundromat.

Getting There

BC Ferries (250/286-1412, www.bcferries. com) offers services from Campbell River to the island, every hour on the hour 6am-11pm daily; round-trip fare is adults $10.50, children $5.25, vehicles $24.35. If you don't bring a vehicle across and need transportation, call **Quadra Taxi** (250/285-3598).

CORTES ISLAND

Accessible by ferry from Quadra Island, Cortes Island (pronounced cor-TEZ—it was named by a Spanish explorer in 1792 for Hernán Cortés, a Spanish conquistador) is a relatively remote place at the top of the Strait of Georgia, closer to the mainland of British Columbia than to Vancouver Island. Few visitors venture out here, but those who do are rarely disappointed. The island's year-round population is just 1,000 people, many of whom live in three small communities.

The island has no official visitors center. You can get an idea of island life by checking out the online version of the local newspaper (www.cortesisland.com), which has everything you'll need to know for a visit.

South of the ferry dock, **Manson's**

Landing Provincial Park is a beautiful little spot sandwiched between a large tidal lagoon and the forested shoreline of **Hague Lake.** The park is named for the Manson brothers, who emigrated from Scotland in 1887 and became the island's first European settlers. Learn about their history at **Cortes Island Museum** (957 Beasley Rd., 250/935-6340, noon-4pm Fri.-Sat., donation), which is housed in a former general store and surrounded by a garden planted with the same species of vegetables and herbs used by early settlers. South of Manson's Landing, **Smelt Bay Provincial Park** is a quiet spot for beachcombing and taking in the unique island environment.

Accommodations and Camping

Accommodations on the island are limited, so unless you plan to camp, make reservations before coming over. Close to the ferry dock on a protected waterway, ★ **Gorge Harbour Marina Resort** (Hunt Rd., Gorge Harbour, 250/935-6433, www.gorgeharbour.com, tent sites $26-31, hookups $40-48, motel rooms $165 s or d) is set across a sprawling acreage sloping down to the water. Amenities include an oceanfront outdoor swimming pool, kayak and boat rentals, fishing charters, a waterfront restaurant (breakfast, lunch, and dinner daily summer) with fantastic fish-and-chips, and a general store. **Smelt Bay Provincial Park,** 15 kilometers (9 miles) from the ferry terminal, offers a few campsites (no services, mid-May-Sept., $20).

Getting There

The ferry trip between Heriot Bay on Quadra Island and Whaletown on Cortes Island takes 40 minutes. **BC Ferries** (250/286-1412, www.bcferries.com) operates scheduled service between the two islands six times daily, with the first departing Quadra Island at 9am and the last departing Cortes Island at 5:50pm. Peak round-trip fare is adults $12.35, children $6.20, vehicles $28.40.

HIGHWAY 28

Running from the east coast to the west coast through the northern section of magnificent **Strathcona Provincial Park,** Highway 28 is another island road worth traveling for the scenery alone. Beyond Elk Falls Provincial Park, the highway parallels Upper Campbell Lake for 20 kilometers (12 miles) before splitting, with the main highway continuing west to Gold River and a side road following the east shore of Buttle Lake into Strathcona Provincial Park.

Strathcona Provincial Park

British Columbia's oldest and Vancouver Island's largest park, Strathcona preserves a vast 250,000-hectare (617,800-acre) wilderness in the northern center of Vancouver Island. Vancouver Island's highest peak, 2,220-meter (7,280-foot) **Golden Hinde,** is within the park. The peak was named for Sir Francis Drake's ship, in which he circumnavigated the world in the 1570s (some believe he would have sighted the peak from his ship). The park's other superlative natural features include 440-meter (1,440-foot) **Della Falls,** one of North America's highest waterfalls, and a 1,000-year-old, 93-meter-tall (300-foot) Douglas fir, British Columbia's tallest known tree. Douglas fir and western red cedar carpet the valley, and wildflowers—lupine, Indian paintbrush, moss campion, and kinnikinnick—cover the high slopes. Resident mammals include black bears, wolves, cougars, marmots, deer, and most of the island's 3,000 elk. Cutthroat trout, rainbow trout, and Dolly Varden fill the park's lakes, and all kinds of birds soar the skies here, including the provincial bird, the Steller's jay.

You'll get a taste of Strathcona's beauty along Highway 28, but to get into the park proper, turn south off Highway 28 halfway between Campbell River and Gold River. This access road hugs the eastern shore of **Buttle Lake,** passing many well-marked nature walks and hiking trails. One of the first is the short walk (10 minutes one-way) to **Lupin**

Falls, which are more impressive than the small creek across from the parking lot would suggest. Continuing south along the lakeshore past driftwood-strewn beaches, you'll come to the two-kilometer (1.2-mile) loop **Karst Creek Trail** (allow 40 minutes), which passes through a karst landscape of sinkholes and disappearing streams. At the lake's southern end, where the road crosses Thelwood Creek, a six-kilometer (4-mile) trail (2.5 hours one-way) climbs a steep valley to **Bedwell Lake** and surrounding alpine meadows.

As the road continues around the lakeshore, look for **Myra Falls** across the water. After passing through the Boliden-Westmin Resources mining operation, the road ends on the edge of an old-growth forest. From this point, explore on foot by taking the three-kilometer (2-mile) **Upper Myra Falls Trail** (1 hour one-way) to a lookout point above the aforementioned falls.

Apart from numerous day-use areas along the shore of Buttle Lake, the only facilities within the park are two campgrounds. **Buttle Lake Campground** (Apr.-Oct., $20) is on the west side of Buttle Lake, just west of the junction of Highway 28 and the park access road. **Ralph River Campground** (May-Sept., $20) is 35 kilometers (22 miles) farther south, on the shore of Buttle Lake. Both have pit toilets, picnic tables, and fire rings, but no hookups.

Gold River

Those looking for a glimpse of Vancouver Island away from the touristy east coast will find the 90-kilometer (56-mile) drive west from Campbell River to Gold River (pop. 1,200) along Highway 28 both enjoyable and interesting.

The big draw for visitors to this part of the island is cruising Nootka Sound from Muchalat Inlet, 14 kilometers (9 miles) south of town (see below), but the town is also a base for anglers and a jumping-off point for travel along the maze of logging roads to the west. Meanwhile, golfers rave about the forest-lined fairways of **Gold River Golf Course** (250/283-7266) simply because it's there.

Rooms at the **Ridgeview Motor Inn** (395 Donner Court, 250/283-2277 or 800/989-3393, www.ridgeview-inn.com, $125-165 s or d) were slightly nicer than expected, and each comes with a fridge, a TV, and a phone. A light breakfast is included in the rates. The adjacent pub-restaurant serves decent food and has an outdoor eating area with fantastic valley views. One of the island's premier sporting lodges, ★ **The Lodge at Gold River**

Myra Falls in Strathcona Provincial Park

(100 Muchalat Dr., 250/283-2900, www.the-lodgeatgoldriver.ca, $615 s, $1,050 d) is across the river to the south side of town on the road out to Muchalat Inlet. Although set up with anglers in mind, everyone is welcome to soak up the wilderness setting of this striking riverside log structure. Added bonuses include a fully equipped tack room, a pond to practice fly-casting, a small fitness room, and spa services. Rates include transportation from Campbell River, lodging, and three memorable meals per day.

Gold River Municipal Campground (Muchalat Dr., 250/283-2202, $12), five kilometers (3 miles) south of town, is beside the Gold River along the road out to Muchalat Inlet. Facilities include fire pits, picnic tables, and restrooms, but no hookups.

At the entrance to town, stop at the **Gold River Visitor Centre** (Muchalat Dr., 250/283-2418, www.goldriver.ca, 10am-6pm daily July-Aug.).

Upana Caves
The natural highlight of Gold River is **Upana Caves,** but unless you're a spelunker, chances are you've never heard of them. The cave system, accessed 16 kilometers (10 miles) west of town along Head Bay Road (this road

eventually leads to Tahsis), has at least 15 entrances and over 500 meters (1,500 feet) of passages to explore, including a river that flows underground for 150 meters (500 feet) through eroded limestone bedrock. Unlike Horne Lake Caves near Qualicum Beach, there are no guides or services at Upana. That said, a well-traveled trail leads through the forest to the main cave. You'll need warm and waterproof clothing, hiking boots, and a reliable light source.

Cruising Nootka Sound
The best reason to travel west from Campbell River is to take a cruise along the spectacular Muchalat Inlet to Nootka Sound, passing uninhabited islands, abundant marinelife, and remote First Nations villages. **Get West Adventure Cruises** (250/283-2515, www.getwest.ca) operates the MV *Uchuck III,* a converted World War II minesweeper, which departs from the dock at the end of Highway 28, which is 14 kilometers (9 miles) south from Gold River. The vessel's primary purpose is dropping supplies at remote west coast communities, logging camps, and fishing lodges, but interested visitors are welcome and are made to feel comfortable by the hardworking crew. Amenities include a lounge,

The MV *Uchuck III* cruises out to Nootka Sound.

a small coffee shop, restrooms, and a viewing deck.

At 9am every Tuesday, the MV *Uchuck III* sets out on its run around Nootka Sound and as far west as Yuquot (adults $80, seniors $74, children $42), returning to port at 6pm. At 10am on Wednesday and Saturday in summer, it's off to Yuquot (also known as Friendly Cove) for a six-hour round-trip (adults $90, seniors $84, children $48). Now a small village of just 25 First Nations people, Yuquot was visited by Captain James Cook but is best known as the site of the only Spanish settlement established in Canada. It was this settlement that led to the Nootka Sound Conventions, a series of negotiations between Great Britain and Spain that were attended by George Vancouver and Juan Francisco de la Bodega y Quadra at this remote outpost in 1792. The longest sailing departs at 7am every Thursday March-October, heading out to the open ocean and up the coast to the remote First Nations village of **Kyuquot** ($441 s, $615 d, children $225). This is also an overnight trip, with meals and accommodations at local lodgings included in the fare.

CAMPBELL RIVER TO PORT MCNEILL

Highway 19, covering the 235 kilometers (146 miles) between Campbell River and Port Hardy, is a good road with plenty of straight stretches and not much traffic. Passing through relatively untouched wilderness (with only logged hillsides to remind you of the ugliness humanity can produce with such ease), it's almost as though you've entered another world, or at least another island. Stop at all of the frequent lookouts for the best views of endless forest, deep blue mountains, white peaks, sparkling rivers and lakes, and cascading waterfalls.

PORT MCNEILL

After taking a convoluted inland route for 130 kilometers (81 miles), Highway 19 returns to the coastline at **Port McNeill**

(population 2,600), a logging town that dates to the 1930s. Port McNeill is a good base for visiting Malcolm Island and Alert Bay, and is also home of the world's largest burl (and the world's second largest).

Head beyond the main street and you'll find the **world's largest burl,** which was cut from a 350-year-old Sitka spruce in 2005. A burl is a rounded outgrowth-a kind of deformation-found in some tree trunks. Mopst burls are plate-size, but this one is estimated to weigh 30 tons and is around 18 meters in circumference. The world's second largest burl (it held title of world's biggest until 2005) is back up on the main highway, two kilometers (1.2 miles) north of town at the entrance to a logging company office; this one weighs an estimated 20 tons.

Campbell Way leads down off the highway to the waterfront, and along this road you'll find services such as grocery stores and gas stations. Opposite Cedar Street, **Black Bear Resort Hotel** (1812 Campbell Way., 250/956-4900 or 866/956-4900, www.port-mcneill-accommodation.com, from $152 s, $162 d) has 40 modern motel rooms and a row of compact kitchen-equipped cabins, a barbecue area, an indoor pool and hot tub, a fitness room, and a laundry. Rates include a light breakfast.

Port McNeill Visitor Centre (1594 Beach Dr., 250/956-3131, www.portmcneill.net, 9am-4pm daily summer, 9am-4pm Mon.-Fri. fall-spring) is along the waterfront near the ferry terminal.

MALCOLM ISLAND

This largish island, immediately offshore from Port McNeill, is home to around 600 people, most of whom live in the village of **Sointula** on Rough Bay. The first European settlers were of Finnish descent who had been toiling in the coal mines of Nanaimo. Led by Finnish philosopher Matti Kurikka, who had written a book on creating a Finnish utopia, they arrived in 1901, having reached an agreement with the British Columbia government to take possession of Malcolm Island. Meaning "harmony" in Finnish, Sointula evolved as a utopian community in which everyone shared everything and everyone was equal.

In town, wander along the residential streets and admire the trim homes and well-tended gardens, then visit **Sointula Museum** (280 1st St., noon-4pm daily summer, donation), in a renovated school building three blocks north of the ferry dock. Then walk the three-kilometer (2-mile) Mateoja Heritage Trail from the north end of 3rd Street to a popular swimming and bird-watching spot, **Big Lake,** passing the remains of an original Finnish homestead along the way. The best ocean access is at **Bere Point Regional Park,** on the north side of the island overlooking Queen Charlotte Strait. The beach in front of the park comprises rounded pebbles, and occasionally in summer orca whales will come close to shore to rub their bellies on the smooth rocks (a purpose-built whale-watching platform is a short walk west from the day use area). **Beautiful Bay Trail** heads out east from the park for five kilometers (3 miles) to Malcolm Point.

Food and Accommodations

On the downtown waterfront one block from the ferry dock, the **Oceanfront Hotel** (210 1st St., 250/230-6722, www.theoceanfronthotel.ca, $100-200 s or d) is a rambling old hotel with 20 simple guest rooms. All have TVs and Internet access, and many have ocean views (the more expensive ones have private decks). **Orca Lodge** (500 1st St., 250/230-6722, www.malcolmislandinn.ca, $225 s or d) comprises two self-contained suites in a renovated 1915 boathouse. Both units have ocean-facing decks, full kitchens, barbecues, and laundry facilities.

One of the many upscale fishing lodges scattered throughout this part of the world is ★ **Sund's Lodge** (250/973-6381, www.sundslodge.com, mid-June-early Sept., US$3,650 for 3 nights with meals and boat transportation from Port McNeill), located on a beautiful waterfront property east of Sointula. Inside the spacious guest cabins you'll find super-comfortable beds, log furniture, top-notch baths, and original art. Guests stay as part of all-inclusive packages, which include memorable meals and as much guided fishing as you can handle.

Drive across the island three kilometers (2 miles) to **Bere Point Regional Park Campsite** (250/956-3301, May-Sept., $16-20), where 22 campsites overlook Queen Charlotte Strait, but there are no hookups or drinking water.

Stop by the **Sointula Cooperative Store** (175 1st St., 250/973-6912, 9:30am-5:30pm Tues.-Sat.) for groceries, gas, liquor, and the island's only ATM. At Funky **Coho Joe's** (145 1st St., 250/230-2233, 7am-3pm Tues.-Sat., 9am-2pm Sun., shorter hours fall-spring, lunch $6-12), across from the downtown waterfront, soups, sandwiches, and fish tacos are made daily, and there is a good choice of coffee drinks. One block north, everything at **Upper Crust Bakery** (180 1st St., 250/973-6333, 9:30am-4:30pm Mon.-Sat.) is made daily from scratch.

Getting There

The easiest way to reach Malcolm Island is with **BC Ferries** (250/956-4533), which makes the short run across Broughton Strait from Port McNeill to Sointula around eight times daily. The round-trip fare is adults $12.35, children $6.20, vehicles $28.40.

★ ALERT BAY

This fascinating village is the only settlement on crescent-shaped **Cormorant Island,** which lies in Broughton Strait 45 minutes by ferry east from Port McNeill. The island's population of 1,000 is evenly split between First Nations and those of European descent.

Alert Bay holds plenty of history. Captain Vancouver landed there in the early 1790s, and it's been a supply stop for fur traders and gold miners on their way to Alaska, a place for ships to stock up on water, and home base to an entire fishing fleet. Today the village is one of the region's major fishing and marine service centers, and it holds two fish-processing and packing plants. Half the island is owned by the Kwakiutl people, whose powerful art draws visitors to Alert Bay.

Sights

All of the island's numerous attractions can be reached on foot or by bicycle. Start by wandering through the village to appreciate the early-1900s waterfront buildings and the colorful totems decorating **Nimpkish Burial Ground.**

For an outstanding introduction to the fascinating culture and heritage of the Kwakiutl, don't miss the **U'Mista Cultural Centre** (1 Front St., 250/974-5403, 9am-5pm daily summer, 9am-5pm Tues.-Sat. fall-spring, adults $12, seniors $10, students $5). Built to house a ceremonial potlatch collection confiscated by the federal government after a 1921 ban on potlatches, the center contains masks and other Kwakiutl art and artifacts. Take a guided tour through the center, and then wander at your leisure past the photos and colorful displays to watch two award-winning films produced by the center—one explains the origin and meaning of the potlatch. The center also teaches local children First Nations languages, culture, song, and dance. It's a 10-minute walk north along the waterfront from the ferry dock.

Along the road to the cultural center, you pass the century-old **Anglican Church.** Also on the north end of the island you'll find the **Indian Big House,** with one of the world's tallest totem poles out front (it's 53 meters/174 feet high; the tallest is in Victoria). To get here, walk uphill from the cultural center; the towering totem pole soon comes into view.

Away from the waterfront, grab an island map to find your way to **Alert Bay Ecological Park** (allow around 40 minutes from downtown). Surrounded by moss-draped forests, the park protects an open area of ghostly black-water spring-fed swamps, home to ravens, bald eagles, and other birds.

Food and Accommodations

Along the waterfront and within easy walking distance of the ferry dock, **Alert Bay Lodge** (549 Fir St., 250/974-2410 or 800/255-5057, www.alertbaylodge.com, $130-140 s or d) has three simple rooms where rates include wireless Internet access and a cooked breakfast. **Pass N Thyme** (4 Maple St., 250/974-2670, 11am-9pm Tues.-Sat., $14-22) is the bright red building across from the waterfront. Inside, you'll find a friendly, casual ambience, and a menu of pizza, pasta, and salads.

Information

Turn right after leaving the ferry dock to reach **Alert Bay Visitor Centre** (118 Fir St., 250/974-5024, www.alertbay.ca, 9am-5pm daily summer, 9am-5pm Mon.-Fri. fall-spring).

Getting There

BC Ferries (250/956-4533) runs to the island from Port McNeill a few times daily. The round-trip fare is adults $12.35, children $6.20. A vehicle is $28.40 round-trip, but there's no real point taking one over because everything on the island is reachable on foot. If you would like to combine a visit to Alert Bay with a trip to Malcolm Island, check the ferry schedule in advance, as some sailings make a direct link between the two islands.

★ TELEGRAPH COVE

Most visitors come to Telegraph Cove to go whale-watching on Johnstone Strait, but the village is well worth the eight-kilometer (5-mile) detour from the highway just east of Port McNeill. Built around a deep sheltered harbor, it's one of the last existing "boardwalk" communities on Vancouver Island. Many of the buildings stand on stilts and pilings over the water, linked by a boardwalk.

Fewer than 20 people live here year-round, but the population swells enormously during late spring and summer when whale-watching, diving, and fishing charters do a roaring trade; canoeists and kayakers arrive to paddle along Broughton and Johnstone Straits; and the campground opens for the season.

Whales are occasionally spotted from the cove, but to enjoy the full whale-watching experience, you'll need to join a boat tour. In the village itself, it's easy to spend at least an hour exploring the colorful boardwalk. Here you'll find the **Whale Interpretive Centre** (250/928-3129, 9:30am-5:30pm May-Sept., adults $5, children $3), a historic fishing shed that has been given a modern makeover and is now filled with interpretive panels and lots of whale bones. Also on the boardwalk is an art gallery, a couple of cafés, the Old Saltery Pub, and a store selling groceries and fishing tackle. Beside the boat ramp, **North Island Kayak** (250/928-3114, www.kayakbc.ca, 8am-5pm daily) has two-hour guided sea kayaking tours for $63.

Whale-Watching

More than 50 whale-watching operations have sprung up around Vancouver Island in the last three decades, but the opportunity to view orcas (killer whales) close up in Johnstone Strait is unparalleled. These magnificent, intelligent mammals spend the summer in the protected waters around northern Vancouver Island, but are most concentrated in **Robson Bight,** 20 kilometers (12 miles) east of Telegraph Cove, where they rub on the gravel beaches near the mouth of the Tsitka River, an area that has been established as a sanctuary for the whales.

Stubbs Island Whale-Watching (250/928-3185 or 800/665-3066, www.stubbs-island.com) was the province's first whale-watching company and continues to lead the way in responsible whale-watching. The company's two boats, *Lukwa* and *Kuluta,* depart two to five times daily from Telegraph Cove on 3- to 3.5-hour cruises from mid-May to September. The experienced crew takes you along the coastline to view the whales in their natural habitat and to hear their mysterious and beautiful sounds through a hydrophone (underwater microphone). Both boats are comfortable, with covered areas and baths.

The cost of the most popular whale-watching cruise, which departs up to three times daily, is adults $106, seniors $96, children $92. Reservations are required, and you should call ahead as far as possible to ensure a spot. Dress warmly and don't forget your camera for this experience of a lifetime.

Kayaking is a popular way for experienced wilderness-lovers to enjoy the whales of Johnstone Strait. **Telegraph Cove Sea Kayaking** (250/756-0094, www.tckayaks.com) makes planning a trip easy, with sea kayak rentals ($60-95 per day for single and double kayaks), GPS and VHF radio rentals, and a water taxi service to popular wilderness campsites along the strait.

Food and Accommodations

Head to ★ **Seahorse Café** (1642 Telegraph Cove Rd., 250/527-1001, 7am-8pm mid-May-Sept., $9-18) for choices such as bison burgers with fries cut and cooked to order, which can be enjoyed on the sprawling oceanfront patio. Breakfasts are mostly under $10, including delicious breakfast burritos.

At the end of the boardwalk, the **Killer Whale Café** (250/928-3155, lunch and dinner mid-May-mid-Oct., $16-27) is in yet another restored building, this one a saltery, where fish were once salted before being transported to market. Although extensively renovated, the building retains many historic elements, including exposed beams, copper tables, and stained-glass windows. The food is a little pricey, but portions are huge and the watery locale can't be beaten.

Many of the buildings on the boardwalk and around the bay have been converted to guest accommodations and can be rented by the night (reserve well in advance) May through mid-October. For reservations at any of the following options, contact **Telegraph Cove Resorts** (250/928-3131 or 800/200-4665, www.telegraphcoveresort.com, May-Sept.). The units range from extremely basic cabins ($155 s or d) spread along the boardwalk to three-bedroom self-contained homes ($330) overlooking the cove. About the only thing they have in common is the incredible setting. One of the best choices is **Wastell Manor,** with the four well-furnished guest rooms ($185-220 s or d).

Built over the water beside the main boardwalk, the self-contained suites at **Dockside 29** (250/928-3131 or 800/200-4665, www.telegraphcoveresort.com, May-Oct., $165-225 s or d) are not particularly spacious, nor do they have balconies, but each is filled with modern conveniences, including a full kitchen with full-size fridge.

A short walk from the village is the **Forest Campground** (250/928-3131 or 800/200-4665, www.telegraphcoveresort.com, May-Sept., $33-37), with 120 campsites spread through towering stands of old-growth forest. Amenities include showers, a laundromat, and an abundance of firewood.

PORT HARDY

Port Hardy (pop. 4,100) lies along sheltered Hardy Bay, 235 kilometers (146 miles) north of Campbell River and 495 kilometers (308 miles) north of Victoria. It's the largest community north of Campbell River and the terminus for ferries sailing the Inside Passage to and from Prince Rupert. The ferry is the main reason most people drive this far north, but Port Hardy is also a good base from which to explore the wild and untamed northern tip of the island or fish for salmon in the sheltered waters of "King Coho Country."

Sights and Recreation

As you enter the Port Hardy area, take the scenic route to town via Hardy Bay Road. You'll pass several original chainsaw wood carvings and skirt the edge of peaceful Hardy Bay before entering downtown via Market Street. Stroll along the promenade to reach **Tsulquate Park,** where you can appreciate First Nations carvings and do some beachcombing if the tide is out. Many bald eagles reside around the bay, and if you're lucky you'll see them swooping about in the neighborhood. Another interesting place to spend a little time is the small **Port Hardy Museum** (7110 Market St., 250/949-8143, noon-4:30pm Tues.-Sat., donation), which holds a predictable collection of pioneer artifacts.

At the **Quatse Salmon Stewardship Centre** (8400 Byng Rd., 250/949-9022, 10am-5pm daily mid-May-late Sept., adults $6, seniors and students $4), on the scenic Quatse River south of town, you can observe incubation and rearing facilities for pink, chum, and coho salmon, as well as steelhead. Good fishing on the river attracts droves of anglers year-round, but most of the fishing action takes place in the offshore tidal waters, with chinook and coho salmon, halibut, lingcod, snapper, and tuna all caught through the summer season. A well-respected company offering charters is **Tides & Tales** (250/949-0641, www.tidesandtales.com), which charges around $1,000 for an eight-hour fishing trip for up to three anglers.

Food

Port Hardy doesn't offer a large variety of dining options. Wander around town and you'll soon see what there is. **Café Guido** (7135 Market St., 250/949-9808, 7am-6pm Mon.-Fri., 8am-6pm Sat., 8am-5pm Sun., lunch $6.50-9.50) pours the best coffee this far north, with the exotically filled toasted sandwiches the best option for food. Downstairs is a bookstore. South one block is **Market Street Café** (7030 Market St., 250/949-8110, 5am-3pm Mon.-Fri., 8am-3pm Sat., $6.50-9), where the emphasis is on freshly baked breads and pastries (the cinnamon buns are delicious), as well as soups and sandwich lunchtime specials.

At **Captain Hardy's** (7145 Market St., 250/949-9008, 6:30am-8pm Tues.-Sat., 7am-2pm Sun., $9-18), the advertised breakfast specials are small but cost only about $7. The rest of the day, this place offers excellent seafood chowder and fish-and-chips, including halibut in season.

Dine at the **Quarterdeck Pub** (Quarterdeck Inn, 6555 Hardy Bay Rd., 250/902-0455, 7am-10pm daily, $14-24), south of downtown in the lodging of the same name, for the opportunity to see bald eagles feeding right outside the window. The menu is fairly standard but well priced, with many seafood choices, including fish tacos and crab linguini.

Port Hardy

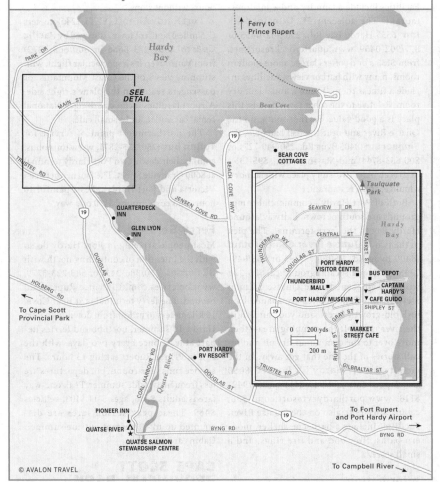

Accommodations

Lodgings in Port Hardy are limited and often fill up, especially on the night prior to ferry departures.

In a town of boring overpriced motel rooms, ★ **Bear Cove Cottages** (6715 Bear Cove Hwy., 250/949-7939 or 877/949-7939, www.bearcovecottages.ca, $195 s or d) stands out, but because there are only eight cottages, you'll need to reserve well in advance. Located right near the ferry terminal, 10 kilometers (6

miles) out of town, they sit in a neat row high above the ocean with stunning water views. Each modern unit comes with a compact but well-designed kitchen, fireplace, a bath with jetted tub, and private deck. While summer rates are $150 s or d, fall-spring the price drops to as low as $100.

Around one kilometer (0.6 miles) south of downtown, two hotels overlook Port Hardy's busy harbor from the marina. **Glen Lyon Inn** (6435 Hardy Bay Rd., 250/949-7115 or 877/949-7115, www.glenlyoninn.com, $135-195 s or d) has 44 rooms in two wings. Facilities include a laundry and a small restaurant. The adjacent ★ **Quarterdeck Inn** (6555 Hardy Bay Rd., 250/902-0455 or 877/902-0459, www.quarterdeckresort.net, from $155 s or d) offers larger, more modern rooms, many with harbor views. Facilities include a fitness room, a sauna, and a laundry room. Relative to the other town motels, this place is a good value. Farther south, on the Quatse River and near the fish hatchery, the **Pioneer Inn** (8405 Byng Rd., 250/949-7271 or 800/663-8744, mid-May-mid-Oct., $95-135 s or d) is an older two-story place with laundry, a lounge, and a restaurant.

Both of Port Hardy's commercial campgrounds are south of town, halfway around Hardy Bay to the ferry terminal. The pick of the two is **Quatse River Campground** (8400 Byng Rd., 250/949-2395 or 866/949-2395, www.quatsecampground.ca, $26-37), which is adjacent to the Quatse Salmon Stewardship Centre. Sites are shaded by a lush old-growth forest, and you can fish in the river right off the camping area—then move over to the communal fire pit and recall stories of the one that got away. In the vicinity is **Port Hardy RV Resort** (8080 Goodspeed Rd., 250/949-8111 or 855/949-8118, www.porthardyrvresort.com, $38, cabins $169-199), also on the Quatse River. Facilities include a barbecue shelter, modern baths, firewood and fire rings, and a small store.

Information

The staff at the downtown **Port Hardy Visitor Centre** (7250 Market St., 250/949-7622, www.visitporthardy.com, 9am-7pm daily May-Sept., 9am-4pm Mon.-Fri. Oct.-Apr.) will fill you in on everything there is to see and do in Port Hardy and beyond.

GETTING THERE

Most visitors who drive to Port Hardy do so to catch a ferry to points farther north. From Campbell River, 235 kilometers (146 miles) to the south, allow 2.5 to 3 hours. From Victoria, 495 kilometers (308 miles) south, allow 6 hours without stops.

Port Hardy Airport (YZT), 12 kilometers (7.5 miles) south of town, is served by **Pacific Coastal** (604/273-8666 or 800/663-2872) from Vancouver. It's a spectacular flight, with stunning views of the Coast Mountains for passengers seated on the plane's right side. Airport facilities include parking, a National rental car outlet, and a small café.

The northernmost point of service for **Tofino Bus** (250/725-2871, www.tofinobus.com) is their downtown Port Hardy terminal at 8600 Granville Street. The journey between Victoria and Port Hardy takes a painful 10 hours and costs around $150 one-way.

Ferry Service

Most people arriving in Port Hardy do so with the intention of continuing north with **BC Ferries** (250/386-3431 or 888/223-3779, www.bcferries.com) to Prince Rupert and beyond. The ferry terminal is at Bear Cove, 10 kilometers (6 miles) from downtown Port Hardy. In summer, northbound ferries depart at least once every two days, with the run to Prince Rupert taking 13 hours. The service runs year-round, but departures are less frequent outside summer. Peak one-way fare is adults $206, ages 5-11 $103, vehicles $469. These peak-season fares are discounted up to 40 percent outside summer. Cabins are available.

CAPE SCOTT PROVINCIAL PARK

Cape Scott Provincial Park encompasses 22,566 hectares (55,760 acres) of rugged coastal wilderness at the northernmost tip of Vancouver Island. It's the place to go if you really want to get away from everything and everyone. Rugged trails, suitable for experienced hikers and outdoorspeople, lead through dense forests of western red cedar, hemlock, and Sitka spruce to 23 kilometers (14 miles) of beautiful sandy beaches and rocky promontories and headlands. Wildlife, including black bears, cougars, raccoons, black-tailed deer, and otters, is prolific.

Hiking

To get to the park boundary, you have to follow 67 kilometers (42 miles) of logging roads (remember that logging trucks always have the right-of-way) leading west from Port Hardy through the logging town of Holberg, and then hike in. The classic park hike to Cape Scott Lighthouse (23 kilometers/14 miles; about eight or nine hours one-way) is relatively level, but you'll need stout footwear. A cove east of the cape was once the site of an ill-fated Danish settlement. Around 100 Danes moved to the area in 1896, cutting themselves off from the rest of the world and forcing themselves to be totally self-sufficient. By 1930, the settlement was deserted, with many of the residents relocating to nearby Holberg.

A shorter alternative to the long trek out to the cape is the trail to beautiful San Josef Bay at the southern boundary of the park (2.5 kilometers/1.6 miles; 45 minutes one-way), which has a sandy stretch of beach.

Practicalities

Needless to say, services and facilities within the park are extremely limited. Near the end of the road leading to the park entrance is road-accessible San Josef River Recreation Site (primitive campsite $8). You can also camp on one of the pads at Eric Lake, a short distance along the trail to Cape Scott, or on any park beach ($10 pp).

Before setting off for the park, go by the Port Hardy Visitor Centre (7250 Market St., 250/949-7622, www.visitporthardy.com, 9am-7pm daily May-Sept., 9am-4pm Mon.-Fri. Oct.-Apr.) and pick detailed logging-road maps for the area.

Southwestern British Columbia

O nce you've reluctantly decided to drag yourself away from Vancouver, you'll be confronted by a variety of things to see and do within a day's drive of the city.

Although British Columbia is best known for its mountains, a stretch of coastline northwest of Vancouver is a watery playground perfect for swimming, sunbathing on sandy beaches, canoeing and kayaking, beachcombing, scuba diving, boating, and fishing. Known as the Sunshine Coast, the region is reached by taking a ferry from Horseshoe Bay (west of North Vancouver) then continuing up Highway 101. The highway winds along the Strait of Georgia, passing seaside villages, provincial parks, and marine parks, and ending near Powell River, a large tourist town and service center. Powell River is the gateway to the paddler's paradise at Desolation Sound and on the Powell Forest Canoe Route.

Spectacular Highway 99, the aptly named Sea to Sky Highway, leads you northeast out of Vancouver along the edge of island-dotted Howe Sound. You pass numerous provincial parks before coming to the resort town of Whistler. This year-round outdoor-sports mecca offers outstanding opportunities for hiking, biking, golfing, fishing, and other warm-weather pursuits. But it's best known for its alpine resort: Whistler Blackcomb, boasting North America's highest lift-served vertical rise.

From Vancouver, two routes head east: You can zip along the Trans-Canada Highway on the south side of the wide Fraser River, or meander along slower Highway 7 on the north side of the river. Both highways take you through the lush, fertile, and obviously agricultural Fraser Valley, converging at Hope. After exploring Hope's spectacular canyon formations, you have another choice of routes: north along the Fraser River Canyon, northeast to Kamloops along the Coquihalla Highway, or east along Highway 3 to the picturesque lakes and alpine meadows of Manning Provincial Park.

PLANNING YOUR TIME

After exploring Vancouver, you're faced with a decision: Where to next? This chapter covers three of the options, while a fourth, Vancouver Island, is covered in the previous

Previous: Whistler Mountain; Squamish. **Above:** Wood carvings are a highlight of downtown Hope.

Look for ★ to find recommended
sights, activities, dining, and lodging.

Highlights

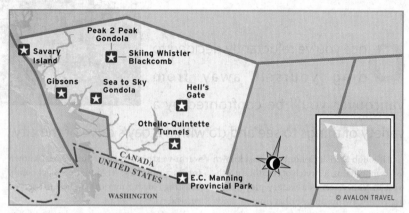

★ **Gibsons:** The Sunshine Coast is dotted with picturesque villages, none more scenic than Gibsons, where cafés and interesting shops line the rocky foreshore (page 205).

★ **Savary Island:** The only sandy island in the Strait of Georgia, Savary Island stands out among the hundreds of Gulf Islands for its great beaches (page 213).

★ **Sea to Sky Gondola:** Rising high above Howe Sound, this gondola ride ends at a lofty lookout with sweeping water and mountain views (page 216).

★ **Skiing Whistler Blackcomb:** With North America's highest vertical rise, the twin mountains of Whistler and Blackcomb come alive in winter (page 222).

★ **Peak 2 Peak Gondola:** It's worth riding this gondola regardless of the season, but for winter skiing and snowboarding, it's most spectacular (page 223).

★ **Othello-Quintette Tunnels:** At a glance, Hope doesn't have much to offer the visitor, but tucked in the mountains behind town are the Othello-Quintette Tunnels, which wind through a rugged canyon (page 236).

★ **Hell's Gate:** Even if you don't ride the tramway, Hell's Gate is an interesting and scenic stop along the Fraser River Canyon (page 238).

★ **E. C. Manning Provincial Park:** This ruggedly spectacular park in the Cascade Mountains stretches down to the Canada-U.S. border and has abundant wildlife, including black bears, moose, elk, coyotes, and beavers (page 240).

Southwestern British Columbia

Vancouver Island

To Victoria

Nanaimo

Strait of Georgia

Lund

Powell River

Saltery Bay

Texada Island

Madaleina Strait

Egmont

Sechelt

GIBSONS

Howe Sound

VANCOUVER

Horseshoe Bay

Tsawwassen

UNITED STATES

CANADA

FORT LANGLEY NATIONAL HISTORIC SITE

Squamish

THE CHIEF

SEA TO SKY GONDOLA

Brackendale

Pitt Lake

Garden Ears Provincial Park

Stave Lake

Mission

Abbotsford

CLAYBURN VILLAGE

KILBY HISTORIC SITE

Chilliwack

Hope

OTHELLO-QUINTETTE TUNNELS

E.C. MANNING PROVINCIAL PARK

Brandywine Falls Provincial Park

Garibaldi Provincial Park

Whistler

Nairn Falls Provincial Park

SKIING WHISTLER BLACKCOMB

PEAK 2 PEAK GONDOLA

Pemberton

Mount Currie

D'Arcy

Gold Bridge

Lillooet

Harrison Hot Springs

Harrison Lake

Yale

Fraser River

Boston Bar

HELL'S GATE

Lytton

Thompson River

Ashcroft

Cache Creek

COQUIHALLA HWY

Merritt

Coalmont

Princeton

Quilchena

To Keremeos and Okanagan Valley

To Kamloops

© AVALON TRAVEL

0 15 km

0 15 mi

chapter. Your choice of direction depends on the time of year and your interests. The first option is to jump aboard a ferry for the Sunshine Coast. Rather than backtracking, plan on catching a ferry from Powell River across to Vancouver Island (make the detour to delightful Lund before you do). Of course, you can make this loop by traveling in the opposite direction—from Vancouver Island to Powell River and down to Vancouver via charming seaside towns like **Gibsons**. One important thing to remember is that travel along this strip of coastline takes a lot longer than you may imagine from looking at a map, mostly due to two unavoidable ferry rides.

Regardless of the season, include Squamish and Whistler in your British Columbia travels. Stop at Squamish to ride the **Sea to Sky Gondola,** then continue to Whistler, which is close enough to Vancouver for a day trip. It's easy to spend at least a full day exploring the mountains on the **Peak 2 Peak Gondola,** which means if you want to bike, hike, or golf,

you'll need at least two days. Winter is high season in Whistler; in return for **skiing at Whistler Blackcomb** you'll be paying big bucks for accommodations. The vast majority of Whistler visitors return to Vancouver, but the Gold Nugget Route continues north through Lillooet to central British Columbia, eliminating the need to backtrack.

Most travelers heading east from Vancouver do so on their way to the Okanagan Valley, Kamloops, or beyond. But there are many reasons to stop, including Harrison Hot Springs, so plan your time accordingly. Once at Hope, the highway divides, and you're faced with three more options. Heading north is the zippy Coquihalla Highway or the more scenic Highway 1 through the Fraser River Canyon, which passes natural highlights such as **Hell's Gate.** Also from Hope, Highway 3 veers east along the U.S. border to mountainous **Manning Provincial Park** and a string of delightful towns such as Keremeos, where a historic grist mill continues to grind wheat for delicious breads.

The Sunshine Coast

The 150-kilometer-long (93-mile-long) Sunshine Coast lies along the northeast shore of the Strait of Georgia between Howe Sound in the south and Desolation Sound in the north. This rare bit of sun-drenched Canadian coastline is bordered by countless bays and inlets, broad sandy beaches, quiet lagoons, rugged headlands, provincial parks, and lush fir forests backed by the snowcapped Coast Mountains.

The route from Vancouver is punctuated by two ferry rides and offers delightful glimpses of wilderness islands in the Strait of Georgia. Settlement began here in the late 19th century, and as you work your way up this stretch of the coastline, note the odd assortment of place-names left by Coast Salish people and Spanish and British explorers.

Today the area is a recreational paradise.

Boasting Canada's mildest climate, the Sunshine Coast enjoys moderately warm summers and mild winters, with only 940 millimeters (37 inches) of rain annually and 2,400 hours of sunlight—a few more hours than Victoria, the so-called provincial hot spot. Boaters and kayakers can cruise into beautiful marine parks providing sheltered anchorage and campsites amid some of the most magnificent scenery along the west coast, or anchor at sheltered fishing villages with marinas and all the modern conveniences.

Traveling Along the Coast

Although the Sunshine Coast is part of the mainland, a trip north entails two trips with **BC Ferries** (604/669-1211 or 888/223-3779, www.bcferries.com). From **Horseshoe**

Bay, at the west end of Vancouver's North Shore, ferries regularly cross Howe Sound to Langdale, the gateway to the Sunshine Coast. From there, Highway 101 runs up the coast 81 kilometers (50 miles) to Earls Cove, where another ferry crosses Jervis Inlet to Saltery Bay. These trips take 40 and 50 minutes, respectively, and run approximately every two hours 6:30am-11:30pm daily. The ferry fare (adults $16.50, children $8.10, vehicles $54) includes one-way travel on both ferries or round-trip travel on just one ferry.

From the terminal at Saltery Bay, Highway 101 continues 35 kilometers (22 miles) to Powell River. From here you can return along the same route or loop back on Vancouver Island via the Powell River-Comox ferry (adults $15.85, children $7.95, vehicles $52.60).

★ GIBSONS

A delightful hillside community of 4,600 at the mouth of Howe Sound, Gibsons offers recreation galore. The town has two sections: the original 100-year-old fishing village around the harbor, and a commercial corridor along the highway. Around the harbor, Gower Point Road is a charming strip of seafaring businesses, antiques dealers, arty shops, and cafés (this was the setting for the popular 1970s TV series *The Beachcombers*). Down on the harbor itself is a marina and the pleasant Gibsons Seawalk, a 10-minute scenic meander that's lighted at night.

Sunshine Coast Museum (716 Winn Rd., 604/886-8232, 10:30am-4:30pm Tues.-Sat., donation) features intriguing pioneer and Coast Salish displays and holds what must be one of the largest seashell collections on the planet (some 25,000). In summer, locals participate in a couple of salmon derbies and revel at the late-July Sea Cavalcade (www.seacavalcade.ca), which features a pancake breakfast, a kids' fishing derby, a canoe and SUP race, a parade, a salmon barbecue, and fireworks.

On the main road, Cedars Inn (895 Gibsons Way, 604/886-3008 or 888/774-7044, www.thecedarsinn.com, $145 s, $155

d) features a heated outdoor pool, a sauna, a small exercise room, and spa services.

Gibsons has a surprisingly good selection of cafés and restaurants, most in the original part of town on a high point of land directly above the marina. For top-notch coffee, I recommend heading straight to Black Bean Roasting (467 Marine Dr., 604/886-1716, 7:30am-5pm Mon.-Fri., 8am-5pm Sat.-Sun., lunch $7-12), where beans are roasted in-house and food such as the turkey, brie, and cranberry panini is a cut above other places in town. For home-style cooking at reasonable prices, head to Molly's Reach (647 School Rd., 604/886-9710, 9am-9pm daily, $12-20), which was a major part of the *Beachcombers* TV show. Today, it's a bright and beachy café where cooked breakfasts average $12. Lunch and dinner mains include fish tacos, chili, and halibut and chips. The food offered at the Waterfront Restaurant (442 Marine Dr., 604/886-2831, 8am-8pm daily, $16-24), an inviting dining room with large windows that overlook the marina just up from Molly's Reach, is fairly standard, but prices are reasonable and the menu offers something for everyone.

Along the waterfront, the Gibsons Visitor Centre (417 Marine Dr., 604/886-2374 or 866/222-3806, www.gibsonschamber.com, 9am-5pm daily summer, 10am-4pm Mon.-Fri. fall-spring) is a good first stop for Sunshine Coast information.

ROBERTS CREEK

About nine kilometers (6 miles) northwest of Gibsons is the small artistic community of Roberts Creek (take the lower road off Highway 101), where arts-and-crafts appreciators can often snatch up a bargain. In an old-growth forest, Roberts Creek Provincial Park (mid-June-mid-Sept., $20), 14 kilometers (9 miles) northwest of Gibsons, has a small campground separated from the oceanfront by a 20-minute walking trail. A smaller section of the park is down on the ocean protecting a pebbly beach.

The relaxed atmosphere at ★ Up the Creek Backpacker's B&B (1261 Roberts

The Sunshine Coast

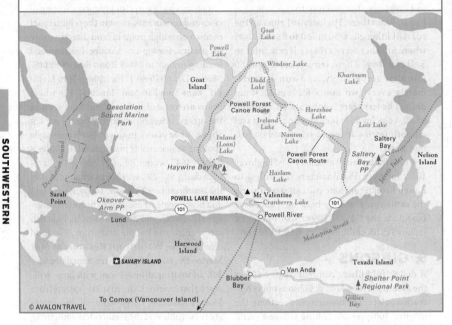

Goat Lake
Powell Lake
Windsor Lake
Khartoum Lake
Goat Island
Dodd Lake
Powell Forest Canoe Route
Horeshoe Lake
Ireland Lake
Desolation Sound Marine Park
Lois Lake
Inland (Loon) Lake
Nanton Lake
Saltery Bay
Powell Forest Canoe Route
Saltery Bay PP
Nelson Island
Haywire Bay RP
Haslam Lake
Sarah Point
Okeover Arm PP
POWELL LAKE MARINA
Mt Valentine
Cranberry Lake
Lund
Powell River
Harwood Island
Malaspina Strait
SAVARY ISLAND
Texada Island
Van Anda
Shelter Point Regional Park
Blubber Bay
To Comox (Vancouver Island)
Gillies Bay
© AVALON TRAVEL

Creek Rd., 604/885-0384 or 877/885-8100, www.upthecreek.ca, camping $14 pp, dorm $28, $84 s or d) is reason enough to rest your head here overnight. Throw in well-priced beds, modern amenities such as a full kitchen and wireless Internet access, and friendly owners, and you'll want to stay longer. Accommodations are in bright dorms, private rooms that sleep two to five, and a cozy cabin.

SECHELT AND VICINITY

Meaning "land between the waters" in the language of the Salish people, Sechelt (pop. 9,500) perches on the isthmus of the Sechelt Peninsula between the head of Sechelt Inlet and the Strait of Georgia. Logging, fishing, and summer tourism support the town.

Sights and Recreation

One of the area's nicest spots is **Porpoise Bay Provincial Park,** four kilometers (2.5 miles) north of Sechelt via East Porpoise Bay Road.

The park offers open grassy areas among forests of fir and cedar, along with a broad, sheltered sandy beach along the eastern shore of Sechelt Inlet. Hiking trails connect the beach with a day-use area and campground, and a woodland trail meanders along the bank of Angus Creek, where chum and coho salmon spawn in November and December. The park is a handy base for kayakers and canoeists exploring Sechelt Inlets Provincial Marine Recreation Area. Porpoise Bay and the nearby rivers are also noted for good sportfishing, and oysters and clams are found along the inlet northwest of the park.

Continue through the park two kilometers (1.2 miles) to reach **Hidden Groves,** a pocket of old-growth forest that has seen a lot of work by local outdoors enthusiasts in recent years to create a trail system. Trails are well-signposted and lead to a high viewpoint with views across the Strait of Georgia to Vancouver Island.

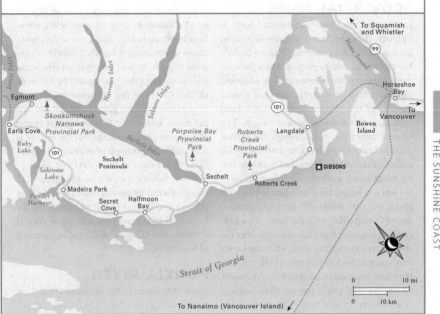

Practicalities

Out of town to the west, **Rockwater Secret Cove Resort** (5356 Ole's Cove Rd., 604/885-7038 or 877/296-4593, www.rockwatersecret-coveresort.com, $259-539 s or d) is an upscale waterfront complex overlooking Halfmoon Bay. It has a wide range of lodging options, from contemporary guest rooms to luxurious tent-house suites, which are separated from the main resort by a boardwalk and feature a waterfront setting best enjoyed from the private decks. The resort restaurant (breakfast, lunch, and dinner daily, $24-34) welcomes nonguests. It offers a refined setting with ocean views and a menu of locally sourced produce and ingredients, including delicious grilled scallops with warm potato salad.

The campground at **Porpoise Bay Provincial Park** (year-round, $29), four kilometers (2.5 miles) north of Sechelt, is one of the best on the Sunshine Coast. It has 84 forested sites and hot showers. Over half

the sites are reservable mid-April to mid-September through **Discover Camping** (519/826-6850 or 800/689-9025, www.discovercamping.ca).

Sechelt Visitor Centre (5790 Teredo St., 604/885-1036, www.secheltvisitorcentre.com, 9am-5pm daily summer, Mon.-Fri. 10am-4pm and Sat. 10am-2pm fall-spring) is well signposted along Highway 101 through downtown.

PENDER HARBOUR

Along the shores of Pender Harbour lie the villages of Madeira Park, Garden Bay, and Irvines Landing. Boating and ocean fishing are popular activities on this stretch of coast, and Ruby and Sakinaw Lakes—between Madeira Park and Earls Cove—are an angler's delight in season. Canoeists head for the chain of eight lakes between Garden Bay and Egmont, where those casting a line will find good fishing for cutthroat trout.

SKOOKUMCHUCK NARROWS PROVINCIAL PARK

Just before Earls Cove, take the road north to Egmont, then the four-kilometer (2.5-mile) hiking trail (1 hour one-way) along Sechelt Inlet to a tidal oddity protected as a park. Its name meaning "turbulent water" in Chinook, Skookumchuck protects Narrows and Roland Points and the 400-meter-wide (1,300-foot) rock-strewn waterway between them. The tides of three inlets roar through this narrow passage four times a day. The resulting rapids and eddies boisterously boil and bubble to create fierce-looking whirlpools—fascinating to see when your feet are firmly planted on terra firma, but very dangerous for inexperienced boaters unfamiliar with the tides. It's a particularly amazing spectacle one hour after the ebb of extra-low spring tides, when the rapids may reach as high as five meters (16 feet) and the water whooshes past at 20 km/h (12 mph). At any low tide, you'll also see abundant marine creatures in tidal pools—it's a fascinating spot. Take a picnic lunch, pull up a rock, and enjoy the view.

EARLS COVE

Earls Cove marks the end of this section of Highway 101. From here, BC Ferries offers regular service across Jervis Inlet to Saltery Bay. The 16-kilometer (10-mile) crossing takes 50 minutes.

SALTERY BAY AND VICINITY

Less than two kilometers (1.2 miles) from the Saltery Bay ferry terminal is 140-hectare (346-acre) **Saltery Bay Provincial Park,** one of the Sunshine Coast's diving hot spots. All the best dive spots are accessible as shore dives, including a bronze mermaid. The park is broken into two sections. The southernmost is where the diving takes place, and it also holds a campground (519/826-6850 or 800/689-9025, www.discovercamping.ca, mid-Apr.-mid-Sept., $20). Less than one kilometer (0.6 miles) farther west is the park's day-use area,

with picnic tables and a grassed area fronting the rocky foreshore.

Bookended by the park's two sections is **Kent's Beach Resort** (604/487-9386, www.kentsbeach.com, Mar.-Oct.), one of the coast's many old-fashioned family-friendly oceanfront resorts. In July and August, the eight self-contained cabins are rented by the week ($775-1,050). The rest of the season, you can snag your waterfront getaway for just $90-120 per night. Either way, furnishings are sparse (bring your own bedding), but the setting is unbeatable. The more expensive camping sites ($25-38) are right on the waterfront.

From Saltery Bay, it's 30 kilometers (19 miles) of winding road to Powell River. Along the way you'll cross Lois River, the outlet for large Lois Lake, and pass a string of coastal communities clinging to the rocky shoreline of Malaspina Strait.

POWELL RIVER

Situated between Jervis Inlet and Desolation Sound along the edge of Malaspina Strait, Powell River (pop. 13,000) is almost surrounded by water. The town is actually a municipality made up of four communities. **Townsite,** the original "Powell River," is dominated by what was once the world's largest pulp mill, which started operation in 1910. A few kilometers south is **Westview,** Powell River's main service center, home to the ferry terminal and information center as well as most accommodations and restaurants. The other two official communities are **Wildwood,** north of Townsite, and **Cranberry,** east of Townsite.

Sights

Start your exploration by visiting the excellent **Powell River Historical Museum** (4798 Marine Ave., 604/485-2222, 10am-4pm daily summer, Tues.-Sat. only fall-spring, donation), across the road from Willingdon Beach, which is like wandering back in time. Peruse the vast collection of photographs (the province's third-largest archives) and other displays to find out about this seashore

Powell River

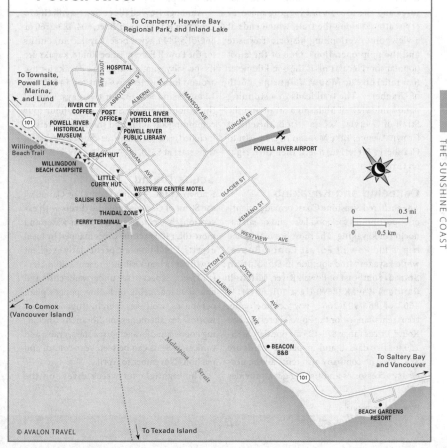

To Cranberry, Haywire Bay
Regional Park, and Inland Lake

To Townsite,
Powell Lake
Marina,
and Lund

JOYCE AVE
HOSPITAL
ABBOTSFORD ST
ALBERNI ST
MANSON AVE
DUNCAN ST

RIVER CITY
COFFEE
POST
OFFICE
POWELL RIVER
VISITOR CENTRE
POWELL RIVER
HISTORICAL
MUSEUM
POWELL RIVER
PUBLIC LIBRARY
MICHIGAN AVE

POWELL RIVER AIRPORT

Willingdon
Beach Trail
BEACH HUT
WILLINGDON
BEACH CAMPSITE

LITTLE
CURRY HUT
WESTVIEW CENTRE MOTEL
GLACIER ST

SALISH SEA DIVE
KEMANO ST

THAIDAL ZONE
FERRY TERMINAL
WESTVIEW AVE

0   0.5 mi
0   0.5 km

LYTTON ST
JOYCE AVE
MARINE AVE

To Comox
(Vancouver Island)

Malaspina Strait

BEACON
B&B

To Saltery Bay
and Vancouver

101

BEACH GARDENS
RESORT

© AVALON TRAVEL
To Texada Island

community and to see what the area was like before the town was established. Also see well-preserved artifacts, First Nations carvings and baskets, the shanty home of a hermit who once lived along Powell Lake, and even a collection of sand from around the world.

North through the main built-up area is the original town site, built around a bay that still holds a working pulp and paper mill complex operated by **Catalyst Paper,** which produces 400,000 tons of newsprint paper annually. The *Heritage Walk* brochure (available at the information center) will guide you around the interesting array of buildings

that date from 1910 to the 1930s, such as the grand Hotel Rodmay, which has reopened after being boarded up for decades. Drive along Sycamore Street and you'll see many Craftsman-style homes in varying states of disrepair.

Hiking

While most visitors to Powell River spend their time enjoying water-oriented sports, the hiking around town is also good—and chances are you'll have the trails to yourself.

From Powell River's municipal campground, the 1.2-kilometer (0.7-mile)

Willingdon Beach Trail runs north past interpretive boards describing natural features and the uses of old logging machinery scattered along the trail, which ends at a viewpoint overlooking historic Townsite and the pulp operations. One of the most popular short local trails is the one-kilometer (0.6-mile) hike up **Mount Valentine,** north of Cranberry. The trail leads to a stunning panoramic view of Malaspina Strait and the Strait of Georgia. Access it from the end of Crown Avenue: Take Manson Avenue east to Cranberry Street, turn left, then turn right on Crown.

Canoeing and Kayaking

The sheltered Sunshine Coast provides plenty of opportunities for good lake and ocean canoeing or kayaking. The most popular canoe trip is the **Powell Forest Canoe Route,** while kayakers find solitude in **Desolation Sound.** Southeast of Powell River, **Mitchell Canoe & Kayak** (8690 Hwy. 101, 604/414-4607 or 866/902-2663, www.canoeingbc.com) rents canoes for the Powell Forest Canoe Route. Prices range $75-125 for one day, $185-260 for five days. Stand-up paddleboards are $75-205. The company also rents all the necessary accessories and fishing gear, provides

free parking, and runs a shuttle service to and from the put-in ($75).

Although **Powell River Sea Kayak** (10676 Crowther Rd., Okeover Inlet, 604/483-2160 or 866/617-4444, www.bcseakayak.com) outfits for the Powell Forest Canoe Route, kayaks are its specialty. Single and double kayaks for use around local waterways rent for $44-70 for 12 hours and $84-135 for two days. Guided three-hour tours are $69, a seven-hour tour combining kayaking and snorkeling (wetsuit included) is $139, and three-day sea-kayaking trips start at $550.

Scuba Diving

Known as the "Diving Capital of Canada," the Strait of Georgia provides divers with exceptionally clear, relatively warm water and more than 100 exciting dives mapped by local experts. Conditions are particularly excellent in winter, when visibility reaches 30 meters (100 feet). Expect to see underwater cliffs and abundant marinelife, including sponges, giant octopuses, wolf eels, perch, lingcod, tubeworms, sea anemones, nudibranchs (including hooded nudibranchs), sea stars, crabs, and tunicates. Seals can be seen year-round, and sea lions November to April.

The highlight for wreck divers on the

Powell River marina

Powell Forest Canoe Route

This four- to eight-day backcountry canoe route is a great way to get away from it all, surrounding yourself with tree-covered lowlands and rugged mountain peaks while slipping through fjord-like lakes. Take side trips and you can extend the water distance from 67 kilometers (42 miles) to more than 150 kilometers (93 miles), or just do one or two sections of the trail—all the major lakes can be reached by road.

To reach the put-in at **Lois Lake,** take Highway 101 east of Powell River 20 kilometers (12 miles) to a logging road that branches north off the highway. Follow that road for one kilometer (0.6 miles), then turn right on the Branch 41 logging road and follow it seven kilometers (4 miles) to a primitive lakeside campground. The route includes paddling along part of Lois Lake, then the lengths of **Horseshoe, Dodd, Windsor,** and **Goat Lakes** to **Powell Lake.** Powell Lake Marina is the most popular pull-out point. In total, the route requires 57 kilometers (35 miles) of paddling and 10 kilometers (6 miles) of portaging. The longest single paddle is 29 kilometers (18 miles), and the longest portage is 2.5 kilometers (1.6 miles). Carry a tent, a stove, and supplies, and stay at one of the 20 Forest Service recreation sites and camping areas along the route. Don't forget your fishing rod and tackle: All the lakes are stocked with cutthroat trout, and some hold rainbow trout and kokanee.

The route's major outfitter is **Mitchell Canoe & Kayak** (8690 Hwy. 101, Powell River, 604/414-4607 or 866/902-2663, www.canoeingbc.com). Canoe rentals range $75-125 for one day, $185-260 for five days. The company provides all accessories and free parking, and shuttles paddlers to and from the route.

For a map and brochure describing the route in detail and to find out current water levels and campfire regulations, contact the **Powell River Visitor Centre** (4760 Joyce Ave., 604/485-4701, www.powellriver.info, 9am-5pm daily summer, 9am-5pm Mon.-Fri. fall-spring).

Sunshine Coast is the HMCS *Chaudière*, sunk in 1993 to form an artificial reef. The hull provides a home for colorful marinelife, and giant holes have been cut through it to enable adventurous divers to do some inside exploration.

Diving gear and a list of charter operators are available at **Salish Sea Dive** (4572 Willingdon Ave., www.salishseadive.com, 604/344-0595, 9am-5pm daily summer, shorter hours fall-spring), one block north of the ferry terminal.

Food

My recommendation for breakfast is **Edie Rae's Cafe** (6243 Walnut St., Townsite, 604/483-3343, 7am-11pm Mon.-Fri., 7am-1pm Sat.-Sun., breakfast $9-19.50), within the restored Old Courthouse Inn, a government building dating to 1939. Given its history, the space is surprisingly warm, with a cheery ambience and a menu that takes full advantage of healthy choices, using free-range eggs, real maple syrup, and home-made preserves.

Another place well worth searching out away from the main road along the water is **River City Coffee** (4871 Joyce Ave., 604/485-0011, 6:30am-5pm Mon.-Fri., 7am-5pm Sat., lunch $9-13), in the Crossroads Village Mall, where the coffee roasted is in-house, delicious bread is baked daily, soups are homemade, and the baking is gluten-free.

Back down along the oceanfront, at the road entrance to Willingdon Beach, the **Beach Hut** (4835 Marine Dr., 604/485-0224, 7am-7pm daily summer, $12-15) is busy throughout summer serving takeout battered fish-and-chips, hamburgers, and the Sunshine Coast's most popular ice cream.

Right downtown are a couple of excellent dining options that are big step up from the usual small-town Asian restaurant. **Little Hut Curry** (4623 Marine Dr., 604/485-2601, 4:30pm-8:30pm Tues.-Sat., $17) is a real find, with made-from-scratch Indian food served in a funky little space with a few out-door tables for warmer evenings. The Thai food at **Thaidal Zone** (4454 Willingdon Ave., 604/485-5171, 11:30pm-9pm Mon.-Sat., 4pm-9pm Sun., $13-19), a small, simple din-ing room opposite the ferry terminal, is also excellent and well-priced.

At the marina overlooking Powell Lake, north of town, the **Shinglemill** (6233 Powell Place, 604/483-2001, 11am-9pm daily, $21-30) is part pub, part restaurant, with the former spilling out onto a wide deck over the water. The menu is wide-ranging; a good choice is the seafood chowder served in a sourdough bread bowl as a starter and salmon baked on a cedar plank and smothered in a tomato-but-ter sauce for a main. In addition to the usual draught beers, you'll be pleasantly surprised by the well-priced wine list.

Accommodations and Camping

Powell River doesn't have a great number of motel rooms, so try to reserve in advance, plan to camp, or head north to Lund, where you'll also need reservations. A solid cheapie is **Westview Centre Motel** (4534 Marine Ave., 604/485-4023, www.powellrivermotel.com, $95-135 s or d), with wireless Internet ac-cess included and a few rooms with kitchens.

After being boarded up for decades, the **Old Courthouse Inn** (6243 Walnut St., Townsite, 604/483-4000 or 877/483-4777, www.oldcourthouseinn.ca, $129-159 s or d) has been extensively renovated and now holds eight antique-filled guest rooms and a res-taurant open daily for breakfast and lunch. Rates include a cooked breakfast, wireless Internet, and in-room DVD players with mov-ies supplied.

The ordinary rooms at **Beach Gardens Resort** (5 kilometers/3 miles south of the ferry terminal, 7074 Westminster Ave., 604/485-6267 or 800/663-7070, www.beach-gardens.com, $189-269 s or d) are more than made up for by water views and amenities like an indoor swimming pool, a sauna, tennis courts, a fitness room, and a marina with boat rentals. The resort's restaurant offers reason-ably priced food (dinner mains $14-27) and sweeping water views.

Willingdon Beach Campsite (4845 Marine Ave., 604/485-2242, $25-35) enjoys a great waterfront location one kilometer (0.6 miles) north of the ferry terminal. You'll find sheltered and very popular campsites along the beach, as well as laundry and restrooms with included hot showers.

Information and Services

Powell River Visitor Centre (4760 Joyce Ave., 604/485-4701, www.powellriver.info, 9am-5pm daily summer, 9am-5pm Mon.-Fri. fall-spring) is along the main strip of shops. Coming off the ferry from Vancouver Island, drive up the hill to Joyce Avenue and turn left. In the vicinity, **Powell River Public Library** (6975 Alberni St., 604/485-4796, 10am-6pm Mon.-Fri., 10am-5pm Sat., 1pm-5pm Sun.) has free wireless Internet access.

Getting There and Around

Powell River Municipal Airport is east of town, off Duncan Street. **Pacific Coastal** (604/483-2107 or 800/663-2872, www.paci-ficcoastal.com) flies at least three times daily between Powell River and its hub at the South Terminal of Vancouver International Airport.

The ferry terminal in Powell River is at the foot of Duncan Street, right downtown. **BC Ferries** (604/485-2943, www.bcferries.com) has regular sailings between Powell River and the town of Comox on Vancouver Island. One-way fares for the 75-minute sailing are adults $15.90, children $7.95, vehicles $49.70. You can't make reservations—just roll up and join the queue.

Sunshine Coast Transit Regional System (604/885-3234) operates local bus service between Sunshine Coast communi-ties (Mon.-Sat., $2 per sector).

TEXADA ISLAND

A 35-minute ferry trip from the Powell River ferry terminal, Texada is one of the largest of the Gulf Islands—50 kilometers (31 miles) from north to south and up to 10 kilometers (6 miles) wide—but the permanent population is only 1,200 and services are limited. Originally home to a whaling station, the island has also housed a couple of mining operations and a distillery that supplied illegal liquor to the United States during Prohibition.

From the ferry terminal at Blubber Bay, the island's main road winds south for eight kilometers (5 miles) to **Van Anda,** a historic village that once boasted saloons, an opera house, and a hospital. Take a walk along Van Anda's Erickson Beach to appreciate the island's natural beauty. Continuing south, the road leads to Gillies Bay and beyond to **Shelter Point Regional Park,** which has some short but enjoyable hiking trails and a sandy spit that leads to a private high-tide island. At low tide, look for colorful starfish along the shoreline, or maybe try your hand digging for clams. Campsites overlooking the water are $23, showers are $2, and a wagonload of firewood is $6.

Getting There

The short hop over to the island from Powell River with **BC Ferries** (604/485-2943, www.bcferries.com) costs adults $11.45, children $5.75, vehicles $27 round-trip. Ferries depart about every two hours 8am-11pm daily; reservations are not possible.

LUND AND VICINITY

Twenty-eight kilometers (17 miles) north of Powell River, Highway 101 dead-ends on the old wooden wharf of Lund, a tiny fishing village founded in 1889 and named after the Swedish hometown of the first settlers. Lund lies on a secluded harbor backed by the magnificent peaks of the Coast Mountains. Although best known as the gateway to Desolation Sound, it's worth the trip out just for the relaxed atmosphere and surrounding beauty. Wander around the bustling marina, cruise over to the white-sand beaches of Savary Island, or relax with a cold drink on the deck of the Lund Hotel. At the back of the Lund Hotel, **Powell River Sea Kayak** (604/483-2160, www.bcseakayak.com) rents kayaks for $55-100 per day; transport the kayaks to Okeover Arm and you're on your way.

★ Savary Island

A geological quirk created Savary Island, the only sandy island in the Strait of Georgia. While the hundreds of other Gulf Islands are rocky in origin, Savary is composed of glacial till that was left behind after the last ice age.

SOUTHWESTERN
THE SUNSHINE COAST

Lund waterfront

Over time, the island has become forested, but it is still ringed by telltale sandy beaches. A few hundred lucky people have summer homes on Savary, but most visitors arrive just for the day, traveling by **Lund Water Taxi** (604/483-9749, www.lundwatertaxi.com, adults $11, children $5.50 one-way), which departs four to eight times daily. Once on the island, this same company provides transfers across the island by vehicle ($12-28). By the island dock is a café and bike rental outlet. For information on island services, including accommodations, visit www.savary.ca.

Desolation Sound

Desolation Sound was named by Captain Vancouver after his visit in 1792—he was obviously unimpressed, as the name implies. Today, 8,256 hectares (20,400 acres) of the sound are protected as **Desolation Sound Marine Park,** the largest of British Columbia's 50 marine parks. The park also preserves over 60 kilometers (37 miles) of shoreline, a number of offshore islands, the Gifford Peninsula, and a section of mainland that includes Unwin Lake. A wilderness-seeker's paradise, the park is totally undeveloped and without road access. The sound is a popular yachtie hangout and a haven for sea kayakers, who need to be totally self-sufficient here.

The shallow, sheltered waters of **Okeover Arm**—a southern arm of Desolation Sound but outside the park—provide the perfect environment for all kinds of prolific marinelife; try to time your visit with the receding tide. Access is via Malaspina Road, off Highway 101 south of Lund. Forested four-hectare (10-acre) **Okeover Arm Provincial Park** lies on the water; it's a small, rustic park with just a few undeveloped campsites ($18), a pit toilet, and a kayak- and boat-launching ramp, but it's a great spot to camp if you're into canoeing or kayaking.

Food

In addition to a fine choice of accommodations, Lund and area is home to a couple of the Sunshine Coast's premier restaurants. The food at **Historic Lund Hotel** (604/414-0474, 7am-8pm daily, $13-20) is overshadowed by the views, especially if you talk your way to an outside table. Coconut curried mussels are a good starter, followed by fried oysters and chips as a main and a slab of mud cake for dessert. Choose this combo and you'll pay around $40—about the same as a main dish in Vancouver.

The upscale ★ **Laughing Oyster** (10052 Malaspina Rd., 604/483-9775, noon-8:30pm daily, $20-31) is a hidden gem. In this restaurant overlooking the water from an elevated setting, diners are seated outside on a deck or inside on tiers that allow everyone to enjoy the view. Starters include oysters prepared in a variety of ways (you can see the restaurant's oyster farm from the deck) and a healthy pecan and blue cheese salad. Mains include a perfectly presented Cajun-influenced bouillabaisse filled with local seafood. Even if you're full, try a slice of melt-in-your-mouth bourbon pecan pie for desert. The Laughing Oyster is a well-signposted five-minute drive from Lund.

Accommodations

The only lodging right in town is the **Historic Lund Hotel** (604/414-0474 or 877/569-3999, www.lundhotel.com, $140-205 s or d), right on the harbor. The historic charm of the original guest rooms has been replaced by contemporary styling and hand-painted murals. The hotel complex holds a pub, restaurant, kayak rental shop, laundry, post office, art gallery, and grocery store.

If you're looking for something a little different, choose to stay at ★ **The Dome** (off Baggi Rd., 604/483-9160, www.magicaldome.com, 3-night minimum, $150 s or d), a five-minute drive from Lund. It's one of the few places in Canada where you can stay in a geodesic dome—a quirky architectural style that employs dozens of triangular panels to form a rigid spherical structure that creates the most space with the least amount of materials. Inside is a bedroom, a loft with second bed, a well-equipped kitchen, a lounge area, and a wood-burning fireplace. Adjacent is a modern bathhouse, complete with a sauna, as well as an additional bunkhouse that sleeps five.

Set on three hectares (7 acres) overlooking Okeover Arm, ★ **Desolation Resort** (2694 Dawson Rd., 604/483-3592 or 800/399-3592, www.desolationresort.com, $169-349 s or d) offers a wonderful escape at reasonable prices. Accommodations are in freestanding wood chalets set high above the water edge on stilts. All feature rich-colored wood furnishings, and even the smallest (the bottom half of one unit) has a king bed, a large deck, a kitchen, separate living and dining areas, and a barbecue. Fishing, canoeing, and kayaking are practically right out your door at the private marina.

Sea to Sky Highway

The spectacular, aptly named Sea to Sky Highway (Hwy. 99) runs 105 kilometers (65 miles) between Horseshoe Bay and Whistler. With the almost-vertical tree-covered **Coast Mountains** to the east and island-dotted **Howe Sound** to the west, this newly upgraded, cliff-hugging highway winds precariously through a dramatic glacier-carved landscape.

HORSESHOE BAY TOWARD SQUAMISH
Porteau Cove Provincial Park
On the east shore of Howe Sound, Porteau Cove is best known among the diving fraternity for its artificial reef of four sunken wrecks, but it also offers good swimming and fishing. In addition, the area's strong winds and lack of waves make for perfect windsurfing conditions. The park holds boat-launching and scuba-diving facilities, an ecology information center, picnic tables, and a waterfront campground for tents and RVs. Walk-in tent sites are $20, vehicle-access sites $35. Between mid-April and mid-September, sites can be reserved through **Discover Camping** (519/826-6850 or 800/689-9025, www.discovercamping.ca).

Britannia Beach
Small Britannia Beach is worth a stop to visit the **Britannia Mine Museum** (604/896-2233, 9am-5:30pm daily mid-May-early Oct., 9am-5:30pm Mon.-Fri. Oct.-mid-May, adults $30, seniors and students $27, children $19), overlooking Howe Sound. In the early 1930s, the Britannia Beach Mine was the British Empire's largest producer of copper, producing more than 600,000 tons. Today it's not a working mine but a working museum. Ever wondered what it's like to slave away underground? Here's your chance to don a hard hat and raincoat, hop on an electric train, and travel under a mountain, without even getting your hands dirty. See fully functional mining equipment, along with demonstrations and displays on the techniques of mining. Then take a step into the past in the museum, where hundreds of photos and artifacts tell the story of the mine.

Continuing North
Straddling the highway, tiny **Murrin Provincial Park** provides good boating, fishing, swimming, and walking trails, as well as steep cliffs that attract novice and intermediate rock climbers. The park has picnic tables but no campsites. Farther up the highway, stop at **Shannon Falls Provincial Park** to view the spectacular 335-meter-high (1,100-foot-high) namesake falls from a platform at the base. You can picnic here or hike a few trails. No campsites are available, but just across the road is **Klahanie Campground and RV Park** (604/892-3435, www.klahaniecampground.com, $35-48), with wireless Internet, a general store, and a restaurant.

SQUAMISH

Squamish (pop. 19,500), 67 kilometers (42 miles) north of Vancouver and 53 kilometers (33 miles) south of Whistler, is surrounded by snowcapped mountains and enjoys a stunning location at the head of Howe Sound. The name is a Coast Salish word meaning "mother of the wind"—the town gets stiff breezes year-round, delighting today's sailors and windsurfers. Lumber is still the lifeblood of the area: The town holds a number of sawmills, and along **Mamquam Blind Channel** on the east side of town, you can see logs being boomed in preparation for towing to other mills.

★ Sea to Sky Gondola

The best way to appreciate the spectacular setting of Squamish is to ride the **Sea to Sky Gondola** (36800 Hwy. 99, 604/892-2550, 10am-6pm Sun.-Thurs., 10am-8pm Fri.-Sat. summer, 10am-5pm daily fall-spring, adults $42, seniors $40, youths $26, children $16) which begins at sea level south of town and rises to an elevation of 885 meters (2,900 feet) at the Summit Lodge. From this point, short trails lead to a variety of spectacular viewpoints high above Howe Sound, including across a 100-meter-long (330-foot) suspension bridge and a 1.6-kilometer (1-mile) trail leading to a lookout point across from the Stawamus Chief. The lodge itself is the perfect place for lunch, with the Summit Eatery offering healthy food choices in a cafeteria setting.

West Coast Railway Heritage Park

See around 65 vintage rail cars and engines in a mock working rail yard (the oldest dates to 1890), complete with a station garden, a replica worker's home, and a restored station at the **West Coast Railway Heritage Park** (39645 Government Rd., 1 kilometer from Hwy. 99, 604/898-9336, 10am-5pm daily summer, 10am-4pm daily fall-spring, adults $25, seniors $20, children $15), which houses one of Canada's largest collections of rolling stock. The museum is also home to the restored *Royal Hudson,* which operates on special occasions; see www.wcra.org for the schedule.

Recreation

Although Squamish has a reputation as an industrial town, it is also the center of a growing

the view from the Sea to Sky Gondola

The Eagles of Brackendale

Squamish itself doesn't have a ton of sights, but if you're in the area during winter, Brackendale, just north along Highway 99, is definitely worth a stop. Through the colder months of the year, the river flats behind this sleepy little town are home to a larger concentration of bald eagles than anywhere else on the face of the earth. Over 3,000 of these magnificent creatures descend on a stretch of the Squamish River between the Cheakamus and Mamquam tributaries to feed on spawned-out salmon that litter the banks. The dead fish are the result of a late-fall run of an estimated 100,000 chum salmon. The birds begin arriving in late October, but numbers reach their peak around late December, and by early February the birds are gone. The best viewing spot is from the dike that runs along the back of Brackendale.

The best place to learn more about these creatures is the **Brackendale Art Gallery** (604/898-3333, www.brackendaleartgallery.com, noon-5pm daily Jan., noon-5pm Sat.-Sun. Feb.-Dec.), which has an adjacent bird-watching tower that rises some 11 meters (36 feet) above the surrounding trees. Through January, the gallery is Eagle Count Headquarters, with slide presentations, talks, and other eagle-related activities. To get to the gallery, follow the main Brackendale access road over the railway tracks, take the first right, and look for the gallery nestled in the trees on the right.

recreation-based economy. Leading the way is rock climbing on the 762-meter-high (2,500-foot) **Stawamus Chief,** clearly visible across the highway from downtown. The "Chief," as it's best known, is one of the world's largest granite monoliths. It formed around 100 million years ago as massive forces deep inside the earth forced molten magma through the crust—as it cooled, it hardened and fractured, creating a perfect environment for today's climbers. The face offers a great variety of free and aided climbing on almost 1,000 routes, which take in dikes, cracks, slabs, chasms, and ridges. Climbers camp at the base for $10 per night (cash only) but head into town to the **Brennan Park Recreation Centre** (1009 Centennial Way, 604/898-3604) to shower and soak in a hot tub ($5.50). If you've never climbed or are inexperienced, consider using the services of **Squamish Rock Guides** (604/892-7816, www.squamishrockguides.com) for a variety of courses with equipment supplied; expect to pay around $135 pp for a one-day beginner's climbing course. **Climb On** (38165 2nd Ave., 604/892-2243, 10am-7pm daily) offers a full range of climbing equipment and sells local climbing guidebooks.

At first it may be difficult to see past the industrial scars along Squamish's waterways, but on the west side of downtown, a large section of the delta where the Squamish River flows into Howe Sound has escaped development. It comprises tidal flats, forested areas, marshes, and open meadows—and over 200 species of birds call the area home. Hiking trails lace the area, and there are three main access points: Industrial Road, the end of Winnipeg Street, and the end of Vancouver Street, all of which branch off Cleveland Avenue.

Squamish celebrates two very different lifestyles at its major annual events. The second week of July is the **Arc'teryx Climbing Academy** (http://squamish.arcteryxacademy.com), a social gathering of adventure-loving folk who come for climbing clinics, film screenings, photographic displays, and seminars. Then, the first weekend of August, Squamish is mobbed by loggers from around the world who congregate for the annual **Squamish Days Logger Sports Festival** (www.squamishdays.ca). Don't be surprised to see people competing at climbing trees, rolling logs, and throwing axes. The show also includes an RV rally, truck loggers' rodeo, dances, pageants, and parades.

Food

The obvious place to stop for a coffee is **Caffe Garibaldi** (38551 Loggers Lane, 604/815-4994 or 866/333-2010, www.tourismsquamish.com, 8am-5pm daily mid-May-mid-Sept., 8:30am-4:30pm daily mid-Sept.-mid-May) in the stunning log Squamish Adventure Centre, which also holds the local visitors center. The coffee is excellent and well-presented, and the tables have fantastic mountain views through the massive windows.

For a casual healthy lunch, it's hard to go past the bright yellow **Sunflower Bakery Café** (38086 Cleveland Ave., 604/892-2231, 9am-4:30pm Tues.-Sat., lunch $6-9), with a large blackboard filled with choices that change daily but always include soups, salads, sausages rolls, and smokies sandwiched between slices of sourdough bread.

Howe Sound Brewery (37801 Cleveland Ave., 604/892-2603, 11am-midnight daily, $13-22) has a modern pub-style restaurant with lots of choices perfect for sharing (calamari, fish tacos, poutine), as well as more substantial choices like jambalaya and thin-crust pizzas, all at very reasonable prices.

Summit Eatery (Sea to Sky Gondola, 36800 Hwy. 99, 604/892-2550, 10am-6pm Sun.-Thurs., 10am-8pm Fri.-Sat. summer, 10am-5pm daily fall-spring, lunch $12-20) is at the top of the Sea to Sky Gondola, 885 meters (2,900 feet) above town and Howe Sound. It's a self-serve cafeteria, but the food is excellent, including premade sandwiches, salads, and wraps. But this place is all about the view, with floor-to-ceiling windows and lots of outdoor seating. Also at the top of the gondola is a café with coffee and snacks to go.

Accommodations and Camping

★ **Squamish Adventure Inn** (38220 Hwy. 99, 604/892-9240, www.squamishhostel.com, dorms $33, $89-119 s or d) is the perfect place to rest your head in Squamish. It is designed to appeal to adventure-minded travelers, with reasonable rates, a choice of accommodations, common areas inside and out, and modern facilities, including a communal kitchen. Room configurations include three- to six-bed dorms (each bed has a light and locker), private rooms with shared baths, and en suite rooms.

Downtown, and affiliated with the local craft brewery, **Howe Sound Inn** (37801 Cleveland Ave., 604/892-2603 or 800/919-2537, www.howesound.com, $129 s or d) is a stylish place with 20 modern rooms. Underground parking and a light breakfast are included in the rates.

The best place to camp around Squamish is ★ **MTN Fun Basecamp** (1796 Depot Rd., 604/390-4200 or 866/987-6512, www.mtnfunbasecamp.com, $110 s or d, camping $40-55), six kilometers (4 miles) north of town at Depot Road. It's on six hectares (14 acres) of landscaped parkland with Garibaldi Provincial Park as a backdrop. Each of the six suite-style studios has a cedar ceiling, large skylights, wireless Internet, and fully equipped kitchen with handcrafted cabinets. The resort's campground offers a choice of forested or creek-side sites.

Information

For detailed information on Squamish, local provincial parks, and Whistler, follow the signs from the highway downtown to **Squamish Visitor Centre** (38551 Loggers Lane, 604/815-4994 or 866/333-2010, www.tourismsquamish.com, 8am-5pm daily mid-May-mid-Sept., 8:30am-4:30pm daily mid-Sept.-mid-May). It's part of the Squamish Adventure Centre, home to a theater, an activity booking desk, and a café.

NORTH TOWARD WHISTLER

Garibaldi Provincial Park

This beautiful park encompasses 195,000 hectares (481,850 acres) of pristine alpine wilderness east of Highway 99. Dominated by the snowcapped and glaciated Coast Mountains, the park reaches a high point at

Brandywine Falls

Lake, Cheakamus Lake, Singing Pass, and Wedgemount Lake. Aside from these five areas, the rest of the park is untouched wilderness, explored only by mountaineers and experienced cross-country skiers. All major trails have backcountry tent sites.

Alice Lake Provincial Park

Alice Lake, surrounded by a 400-hectare (1,000-acre) park of open grassy areas, dense forests, and impressive snowcapped peaks, is particularly good for canoeing, swimming, and fishing for small rainbow and cutthroat trout. A 1.4-kilometer (0.9-mile) trail encircles the lake, while others lead to three smaller bodies of water; allow 20 minutes for the loop. A campground (519/826-6850 or 800/689-9025, www.discovercamping.ca, year-round, walk-in tent sites $23, vehicle-accessible $35) has showers and picnic tables. The park entrance is 13 kilometers (8 miles) north of Squamish, and the lake just under two kilometers (1.2 miles) from the highway.

2,678-meter (8,790-foot) Mount Garibaldi, named in 1860 after Italian soldier and statesman Giuseppe Garibaldi. Other park features include 2,315-meter (7,600-foot) Black Tusk, the Gargoyles (eroded rock formations reached by a trail from the park's southern entrance), and a 1.6-kilometer-long (1-mile) lava flow above the west side of Garibaldi Lake.

Garibaldi is a true wilderness park, with road access only up to the park boundary. From late July through early September, the hiking is fabulous—through forests of fir, red cedar, hemlock, and balsam, across high meadows crowded with spectacular wildflowers, and past bright blue lakes, huge glaciers, and jagged volcanic peaks and lava flows.

Between Squamish and Pemberton, five clearly marked entrance roads lead off Highway 99 to trailheads providing access into the five most popular areas of the park: Diamond Head, Black Tusk/Garibaldi

Brandywine Falls Provincial Park

If you like waterfalls, stop at this small park 45 kilometers (28 miles) north of Squamish and follow the 300-meter (0.2-mile) five-minute trail from the parking lot. It's the kind of trail that excites all your senses: magnificent frosty peaks high above, dense lush forest on either side, a fast deep river roaring along on one side, and the pungent aroma and cushiness of crushed pine needles beneath your feet. The trail takes you to a viewing platform to see 66-meter-high (220-foot) Brandywine Falls, where the waters plummet down a vertical lava cliff into a massive swirling plunge pool, then roar down a forest-edged river into a lake. It's most magnificent early in summer. The falls were named in the early part of the 20th century by two railroad surveyors who made a wager on guessing the falls' height—the winner to receive bottles of, you guessed it, brandywine.

Whistler

Magnificent snowcapped peaks, dense green forests, transparent lakes, sparkling rivers, and an upmarket cosmopolitan village right in the middle of it all: Welcome to Whistler (pop. 12,000), one of the world's great resort towns, just 120 kilometers (75 miles) north of Vancouver along Highway 99. The Whistler Valley has seen incredible development in recent years and is now British Columbia's third most popular tourist destination after Vancouver and Victoria, attracting around two million visitors annually, although this number went even higher in 2010 when the resort town cohosted the Winter Olympic Games. The crowds and the costs might not be for everyone, but there *are* many things to do in Whistler, and the village takes full advantage of its magnificent natural surroundings, making a trip north from Vancouver worthwhile any time of year.

Best known among skiers and boarders, the town is built around the base of one of North America's finest resorts, **Whistler Blackcomb** (www.whistlerblackcomb.com), which comprises 3,000 hectares (7,400 acres) on two mountains accessed by an ultramodern lift system. A season stretching from November to early June doesn't leave much time for summer recreation, but in recent years, the off-season has become almost equally busy. Among the abundant summertime recreation opportunities are lift-served hiking and glacier skiing and boarding; biking through the valley and mountains; water activities on five lakes; horseback riding; golfing on some of the world's best resort courses; and fishing, rafting, and jet-boating on the rivers. The more sedentary summer visitor can simply stay in bustling Whistler Village and enjoy a plethora of outdoor cafés and restaurants.

Museums

The best place to learn about Whistler's short but colorful history is the **Whistler Museum** (4333 Main St., 604/932-2019, 11am-5pm daily, donation). Displays tell the story of skiing pioneers, the creation of Whistler Blackcomb, and the impact of the 2010 Winter Olympic Games.

Whistler Village in winter

Whistler

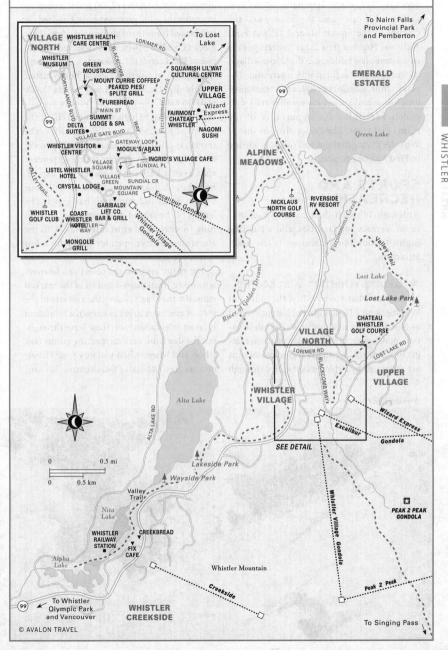

© AVALON TRAVEL

The **Squamish Lil'wat Cultural Centre** (4584 Blackcomb Way, Upper Village, 866/441-7522, 10am-4pm daily, adults $18, children $5) celebrates the history and the culture of the Squamish and Lil'wat First Nations. Housed in a large contemporary wood-and-glass building in the Upper Village, the main gallery is filled with interesting displays, while outside is a replica of a traditional long house and a short interpretive trail with panels explaining the importance of the plants and trees. The center also has one of Whistler's best gift shops and café specializing in First Nations cuisine.

SPORTS AND RECREATION

Although Whistler does have a small museum, various spa facilities, and a bustling nightlife, outdoor recreation is the main attraction.

★ Skiing Whistler Blackcomb

No matter what your ability, the skiing at Whistler and Blackcomb, consistently rated as North America's number-one ski destination, makes for a winter holiday you won't forget in a hurry. The two lift-served mountains are separated by a steep-sided valley through which Fitzsimmons Creek flows, with lifts converging at Whistler Village. Skiing is over almost 3,000 hectares (7,400 acres), comprising more than 200 groomed runs, hundreds of unmarked trails through forested areas, three glaciers, and 12 bowls. The lift-served vertical rise of Blackcomb is 1,609 meters (5,280 feet), the highest in North America, but Whistler is only slightly lower at 1,530 meters (5,020 feet). In total, the resort has 34 lifts, including 3 gondolas, 12 high-speed quad chairlifts, 5 triples, 1 double, and 12 surface lifts. The terrain is rated intermediate over 55 percent of the resort, with the remaining 45 percent split evenly between beginner and expert. Snowboarders are well catered to with four terrain parks and numerous half-pipes. The length of the season is also impressive, running from November to early May, with the Horstman Glacier open for skiing for a few weeks of summer.

For many visitors, the resort can be overwhelming. Trail maps detail all of the marked runs, but they can't convey the vast size of the area. A great way to get to know the mountain is on an orientation tour; these leave throughout the day from various meeting points (ask when and where when you buy your ticket) and are free. **Whistler Blackcomb Ski and**

Whistler Blackbomb

Snowboard School (604/932-3434, www.wbsss.com) is the country's largest ski school and offers various lesson packages and programs, such as the Esprit, a three-day women-only "camp" that provides instruction in a variety of disciplines.

Lift tickets are adults $118, seniors and youths $96, children $64; those under age seven ski for free. The resort's **website** (www.whistlerblackcomb.com) contains everything you need to know about the resort and booking winter lodging packages, or call the general **information desk** (604/967-8950 or 866/218-9690).

Cross-Country Skiing

Many kilometers of trails wind through snow-covered terrain in the valley, but the main destination for cross-country skiers is **Whistler Olympic Park** (5 Callaghan Valley Rd., 604/964-0060, adults $25, children $15), which was developed for the 2010 Winter Olympic Games. It's open throughout winter, with an extensive network of groomed trails for all levels. Rentals are available.

Back in the main village and running in a long loop past Lost Lake and Green Lake is the **Valley Trail,** a paved walking and bike path in summer that becomes a popular cross-country ski trail in winter. The biggest concentration of trails lies near Lost Lake and on the adjacent Chateau Whistler Golf Course. Most trails are groomed, while some are track-set, and a five-kilometer (3-mile) stretch is illuminated for night skiing. The trail system is operated by the **Whistler Nordics** (www.whistlernordics.com), which collects a $20 fee for a day pass from a ticket booth near Lost Lake, where you'll also find a cozy warming hut.

Heli-Skiing

Heli-skiing is offered by **Whistler Heli-skiing** (Carleton Lodge, 4280 Mountain Square, 604/905-3337, www.whistlerheliskiing.com), which takes strong intermediates and expert adventurers high into the Coast Mountains to ski fields of untracked powder. Rates ($1,120) include three runs, transportation to and from the heliport north of Whistler Village, a gourmet lunch, and a guide.

★ Peak 2 Peak Gondola

During the few months that they aren't covered in snow, the slopes of the **Whistler Blackcomb** ski resort come alive with people enjoying hiking, guided naturalist walks,

the Peak 2 Peak Gondola

mountain biking, horseback riding, or just marveling at the mountain-scape from the comfort of the lifts. Die-hard skiers will even find glacier skiing here early in the summer. More than 50 kilometers (30 miles) of hiking trails wind around the mountains, including trails through the high alpine to destinations such as beautiful Harmony Lake (Whistler Mountain, 2.5 kilometers/1.6 miles from the top of the gondola) or to the toe of a small glacier (Whistler Mountain, 2.5 kilometers/1.6 miles from the top of the gondola). It's also possible to rent snowshoes for $6 per hour to walk across areas of year-round snowpack. Or for an adrenaline rush, take the gondola up (604/967-8950) and then bicycle down the mountain with **Backroads Whistler** (604/932-3111, www.backroadswhistler.com).

The main lifts on both mountains operate mid-June through mid-October, with the classic **Peak 2 Peak** circuit allowing a 4.4-kilometer (2.8-mile) loop incorporating the mountains. A day pass for unlimited lift use is adults $60, seniors $52, children $30. Summer lift hours are 10am-5pm daily, and 11am-4pm daily during the first couple of weekends of June and October. These dates vary between the mountains and depend on snow cover or the lack of it. Dining facilities are available on both mountains, or grab a picnic lunch from any of the delis down in the village.

Even if it's a beautiful day down in the valley, expect the unexpected and take a warm wind- or waterproof coat in anticipation of a change in the weather. Also, some of the hiking trails can be rough, so wear good hiking boots if you plan to explore away from the main trails.

Hiking

The easiest way to access the area's most spectacular hiking country is to take a sightseeing lift up Whistler or Blackcomb Mountain, but many other options exist. Walking around Whistler Valley you'll notice sign-posted trails all over the place. **Valley Trail** is a paved walkway and bikeway in summer and a cross-country ski trail in winter. It makes an almost

---

Summer Skiing and Boarding

Just because the calendar, thermometer, and sun's angle say it's summer doesn't mean winter sports are months away. Whistler Blackcomb is one of just two North American resorts offering lift-served summer skiing. Between mid-June and mid-July (weather depending), a T-bar on Blackcomb Mountain's **Horstman Glacier** opens up a small 45-hectare (110-acre) area with a vertical rise of 209 meters (520 feet). The lift (noon-3pm daily, adults $67, children $35) includes transportation from the valley floor. The slopes can get crowded, with local and national ski teams in training and with visitors enjoying the novelty of summer skiing. If it's too hectic, you can always go back to the valley floor for golf or water sports.

---

complete tour of the valley, from Whistler Village to **Lost Lake** and **Green Lake,** along the **River of Golden Dreams,** past three golf courses to **Alta Lake, Nita Lake,** and **Alpha Lake,** and finally to Highway 99 in the Whistler Creekside area. If you'd rather do a short walk, head for Lost Lake via the two-kilometer (1.2-mile) trail from Parking Lot East at the back of Whistler Village, or via the transit bus from the middle of the village. Once at the beautiful lake, you can saunter along the shore, picnic, swim, or, in winter, cross-country ski.

Between Whistler and Blackcomb Mountains, a gravel road leads five kilometers (3 miles) to the trailhead for the **Singing Pass Trail.** From the parking lot, this trail follows the Fitzsimmons Creek watershed for 7.5 kilometers (4.7 miles) to Singing Pass, gaining 600 meters (2,000 feet) in elevation; allow 2.5 hours one-way. From the pass, it's another two kilometers (1.2 miles) to beautiful **Russet Lake,** where you'll find a backcountry campground.

On the opposite side of the valley, an eight-kilometer (5-mile) trail (3 hours one-way) leads from Alta Lake Road just north of the Whistler hostel up 21-Mile Creek to **Rainbow Lake.** The elevation gain is a strenuous 850 meters (2,800 feet).

Mountain Biking

The Whistler Valley is a perfect place to take a mountain bike—you'd need months to ride all of the trails here. Many of the locals have abandoned their cars for bikes, which in some cases are worth much more than cars. You can see them scooting along **Valley Trail,** a paved walking and bike path that links the entire valley and is the resident bicyclists' freeway. Another popular place for mountain bikers is beautiful **Lost Lake,** two kilometers (1.2 miles) northeast of Whistler Village.

On the mountain slopes, **Whistler Mountain Bike Park** (http://bike.whistler-blackcomb.com, mid-May–early Oct., $71 per day) is perfect for adventurous riders to strut their stuff. Using the lifts to access a vertical drop of 1,200 meters (3,900 feet), it features three "Skill Centres," filled with obstacles for varying levels of skill; a Bikercross Course; and a variety of trails to the valley floor.

If you didn't bring a bike, not to worry—they're available to rent from $22 per hour, $60-155 per day. Or perhaps a guided bicycle tour of the local area sounds appealing—it's not a bad idea to have a guide at first. Local rental companies include: **Garbanzo Bike & Bean** (4282 Mountain Square, Carleton Lodge, base of the Whistler Mountain Bike Park, 604/905-2076), **Spicy Sports** (4557 Blackcomb Way, 604/938-1111), **Whistler Village Sports** (4254 Village Stroll, 604/932-5495), and **Whistler Bike Co.** (4205 Village Square, 604/938-9511).

Water Sports

Sunbathers head for the public beaches along the shores of **Alta Lake**—watching all the windsurfers whipping across the water or beginners repeatedly taking a plunge is a good source of summer entertainment. Wayside Park at the south end of the lake has a beach, a canoe launch, an offshore pontoon, a grassy area with picnic tables, and hiking-biking trails. At Alta Lake, **Backroads Whistler** (3375 Lakeside Rd., 604/932-3111, 9am-5pm daily summer, 9am-5pm Sat.-Sun. spring and fall) rents canoes and kayaks for $35 per hour or stand-up paddle boards for $30 per hour. You can also travel by canoe along the smooth, flowing River of Golden Dreams ($79 pp), which includes canoe rental return transportation by road.

stand-up paddleboarding on Alta Lake

For a little white-water excitement, try river-rafting with **Wedge Rafting** (604/932-7171 or 888/932-5899, www.wedgerafting.com), which provides guided scenic and white-water tours between the end of May and early September. Outings range from an easy float down the Green River for $109 pp to the white-water thrills of a full-day trip on the Squamish River for $169.

Golf

Whistler boasts four world-class championship golf courses, each with its own character and charm. The entire valley has gained a reputation as a golfing destination, with many accommodations offering package deals that include greens fees. Still, golfing at Whistler is as expensive as anywhere in the country. All of the following courses offer a golf shop with club rentals ($50-65) and golfing apparel, and a clubhouse with dining facilities. The golfing season runs mid-May to October, so in late spring you can ski in the morning and golf in the afternoon. My favorite is the Jack Nicklaus-designed **Nicklaus North Course** (just north of Whistler Village, 604/938-9898) is an open layout holding numerous water hazards. It boasts 360-degree mountain vistas, and although it only plays to 6,900 yards from the back markers, it is very challenging. Weekend greens fees are $185, discounted to $155 midweek afternoons.

Other options include the Arnold Palmer-designed **Whistler Golf Club** (between Whistler Village and Alta Lake, 604/932-3280 or 800/376-1777, greens fees $149), offering large greens and narrow wooded fairways; **Fairmont Chateau Whistler Golf Club** (Blackcomb Way, 604/938-2092 or 888/938-2092, greens fees $185), which takes advantage of the rugged terrain of Blackcomb Mountain's lower slopes through holes that rise and fall with the lay of the land; and, farther up the valley, **Big Sky Golf and Country Club** (604/894-6106 or 800/668-7900, greens fees $165), a picturesque par-72 course of over 7,000 yards.

Flightseeing

Nothing beats the spectacular sight of the Coast Mountains' majestic peaks, glaciers, icy-blue lakes, and lush mountain meadows from an unforgettable vantage point high in the sky. **Harbour Air** (604/274-1277) will take you aloft in a floatplane from Green Lake, three kilometers (2 miles) north of Whistler Village. A 20-minute flight over the glaciers of Garibaldi Provincial Park costs $125; a 40-minute flight over the Pemberton Ice Cap goes for $180; and a two-hour flight landing on a high alpine lake runs $365. You can also charter the whole plane (minimum 4 people) for a remote backcountry adventure.

ENTERTAINMENT AND EVENTS
Nightlife

Throughout the year, you can usually find live evening entertainment in Whistler Village. In the heart of the action at the base of the mountain, **Garibaldi Lift Co. Bar & Grill** (Springs Lane, 604/905-2220, 11am-1am daily) features live entertainment most nights—often blues and jazz—and good food at reasonable prices. At **Buffalo Bill's** (4122 Village Green, 604/932-6613, 7pm-2am Mon.-Sat., 7pm-1am Sun.), expect anything from reggae to rock. For over two decades, **Tommy Africa's** (4216 Gateway Dr., 604/932-6090, 9pm-2am Mon.-Sat.) has been one of the village's hottest nightspots. Pumping out high-volume reggae across the valley's most crowded dance floor, it's popular with the younger crowd. Head to **Garfinkels** (4308 Main St. 604/932-2323, 7pm-2am daily) for dance, house, and alternative music.

Black's Pub (Sundial Boutique Hotel, 4270 Mountain Square, 604/932-6945, 11am-1am daily) offers more than 90 international beers and a quiet atmosphere in a small upstairs English-style bar and tables spilling out to a patio with mountain views. A more refined watering hole is the **Crystal Lounge** (Crystal Lodge, 4154 Village Green, 604/932-2221, noon-1am daily). Also in the Crystal Lodge is Basalt (4154 Village Green, 604/962-9011, noon-1am daily), an upscale wine bar.

Festivals Events

The winter season is packed with ski and snowboard races, but the biggest is the World Ski & Snowboard Festival (604/938-3399, www.wssf.com), through mid-April. This innovative event brings together the very best winter athletes for the World Skiing Invitational and the World Snowboarding Championship. These are only the flagships of this 10-day extravaganza, which also includes demo days, exhibitions, and a film festival.

Each weekend in May and June and daily through summer, the streets of Whistler come alive with street entertainment from musicians, jugglers, and comedians. Canada Day, July 1, is celebrated with a parade through Whistler Village.

FOOD

Like the town itself, the dining scene in Whistler is hip, ever-changing, and not particularly cheap. Many small cafés dot the cobbled walkways of Whistler Village, while most bars have reasonably priced pub-fare menus.

Coffee and Cheap Eats

For a caffeine fix, Moguls Coffee House (4208 Village Square, 604/932-4845, 6:30am-10pm Sun.-Thurs., 6:30am-midnight Fri.-Sat.) is as good as any place—it's popular with both locals and visitors, and the outdoor seating catches the morning sun. Also getting rave reviews for its coffee is ★ Mount Currie Coffee (4369 Main St., 604/962-2288, 7am-5pm daily, lunch $9-12), right in the heart of the village. In addition to a caffeine fix, the tea poured is loose-leaf and prepared locally, while food choices include breakfast burritos, grilled paninis, and soup. In the vicinity, Purebread (4338 Main St., 604/962-1182, 8am-6pm daily) has a great choice of gourmet breads, cakes, and pastries. They also have an outlet south of town (1040 Millar Creek Rd., Function Junction, 604/938-3013, 8:30am-5pm daily).

In Whistler Creekside, south of the main village, Fix Cafe (Nita Lake Lodge, 2131 Lake Placid Rd., 604/966-5700, 6:30am-4:30pm daily, lunch $10-15) is an appealing space within a beautiful lodge, but everyone one is welcome to stop by for coffee, healthy breakfasts, and lunchtime choices ranging from vegan wraps to hot meat sandwiches.

Aussies living in and visiting Whistler are drawn to Peaked Pies (4369 Main St., 604/962-4115, 8am-9pm daily), where you pay from $7 for traditional Australian meat pies or a little extra for offerings such as chunky pepper steak or butter chicken. In keeping with the Down Under theme, you can get a "flat white" (a type of latte) with your pie.

Continuing around Main Street, the food at Green Moustache (4340 Lorimer Rd., 604/962-3727, 8am-6pm daily, lunch $8-11) could not be more different than Peaked Pies. The emphasis at this vegetarian café is making healthy choices—think smoothies, cold-pressed juices, gluten-free soup, and *pad thai*.

Ingrid's Village Cafe (4305 Skiers Approach, 604/932-7000, 7am-6pm daily, lunch $8-11) is in the very heart of Whistler Village but manages to keep prices reasonable. Breakfasts are all under $10, including a scrambled egg, spinach, and avocado wrap. Lunch is similarly good value, with sandwiches and burgers made to order. Ingrid's is a smallish space, so expect a wait during the peak summer and winter seasons.

Well worth searching out within the Squamish Lil'wat Cultural Centre, Thunderbird Cafe (4584 Blackcomb Way, Upper Village, 866/441-7522, 10am-4pm daily, lunch $9-12) specializes in First Nations cooking. For Whistler, the food is remarkably inexpensive. For something different, it's hard to look past the bannock tacos (traditional bread topped with venison chili, cheese, spinach, salsa, and sour cream), although you could also try the salmon salad or bison pie.

If you're staying in or around Function Junction, south of Whistler Village, there are a couple of cafés of note. Firstly, Purebread

(1040 Millar Creek Rd., Function Junction, 604/938-3013, 8:30am-5pm daily) sells delicious ranges of breads and pastries, as well as sandwiches and paninis. Very different from most other Whistler cafés is **Camp Lifestyle & Coffee** (1066 Millar Creek Rd., Function Junction, 604/932-0123, 7am-6pm daily), a retailer of trendy Canadiana outdoor equipment and clothing that has an in-house espresso bar and an appealing patio with a small waterfall and a fire pit.

Casual

Ask any local where to go for the best burger in town and they will invariably point you in the direction of **Splitz Grill** (4369 Main St., 604/938-9300, 11:30am-7:30pm Mon. and Wed.-Thurs., 11:30am-8pm Fri.-Sat., $9-12), which has been serving up creative burgers for over 20 years. Bison, lamb, wild salmon, spicy lentil and just a few of over a dozen different choices. Burgers come stacked with extras, and you can dine inside or out on the small patio.

The rustic decor and great Canadian food at **Garibaldi Lift Co. Bar & Grill** (604/905-2220, 11am-1am daily, $18-33), at the base of the Whistler Village gondola, have been a big hit since it opened in 1995. The bar and sundeck are popular après-ski hangouts, and by around 8pm everyone's back for dinner. For Western-style atmosphere with mountain views, head to the **Longhorn Saloon and Grill** (Carleton Lodge, 4284 Mountain Square, 604/932-5999, 9am-1am daily, $21-38) and share a platter of finger food or order your own cut of prime Alberta beef, complete with trimmings.

Looking for creative pizza choices, made from scratch using local and organic ingredients? Then head to **Creekbread** (Whistler Creek Lodge, 2021 Karen Cres., 604/905-6666, 4pm-8:30pm Sun.-Thurs., 4pm-9pm Fri.-Sat., $14-20), a casual and inviting restaurant south of the main village. Toppings are all good, but I suggest trying the maple-fennel sausage, which is made in-house. Reservations are not taken, but call 20 minutes ahead and you'll be added to the wait list for the evening.

Nagomi Sushi (Le Chamios Hotel, 4557 Blackcomb Way, 604/962-0404, 5:30pm-10pm daily, $19-34) serves a mix of modern and traditional Japanese dishes in a casual setting. Within the Whistler Visitor Centre, **Sushi To Go** (4230 Gateway Dr., 604/905-1241, 8am-10pm daily) is even more casual, but is best known as a good place for an inexpensive meal.

Other Restaurants

Reasonably priced Mongolian fare is on the menu at **Mongolie Grill** (4295 Whistler Way, Whistler Village, 604/938-9416, 11:30am-10pm daily; $22-32). This is one of the better places to take children. They'll love choosing their own ingredients—meats and vegetables—with matching sauces, and then watching the speedy chefs fry up the personalized dish in front of them.

For steaks, seafood, a salad bar, fresh hot bread, and plenty of options for everyone, the **Whistler Keg** (Whistler Village Inn & Suites, 4429 Sundial Place, 604/932-5151, 5pm-10pm daily, $27-48) is a sure thing. The atmosphere is casual, yet the service at this Canadian chain is slick and refreshingly attentive.

At **Hy's** (Delta Hotels by Marriott Whistler Village Suites, 4308 Main St., 604/905-5555, 4pm-10pm daily, $36-58), you don't need to ask if the steak is good—everything on offer is top-notch AAA Alberta beef, including a signature not-for-the-faint-hearted 22-ounce porterhouse. The scene is upmarket, with elegant tables set within rich-colored wood walls.

★ **Araxi** (4222 Village Square, Whistler Village, 604/932-4540, 3pm-midnight daily, $28-45) consistently wins awards for its creative menu, which takes advantage of produce from along the Pacific Coast, yet also manages to offer traditional sushi and European dishes. It also boasts a seafood bar and an extensive wine list.

ACCOMMODATIONS AND CAMPING

Whistler's accommodations range from a hostel with inexpensive dorm beds to luxury resort hotels. It's just a matter of selecting one to suit your budget and location preference. Winter visitors may want to be right in Whistler Village or by the gondola base in Whistler Creekside so they can stroll out their door and jump on a lift. (The term *slopeside* describes accommodations within a five-minute walk of the lifts.)

Accommodations pricing in Whistler is complex. The best advice is to shop around using sites like www.booking.com or Expedia, and then contact the lodgings and booking agencies listed here to get a comparison. Winter is most definitely high season, with the week after Christmas and all of February and March a high season within a high season, especially for lodgings within walking distance of the lifts or that are self-contained and capable of sleeping more than two people. These are also the accommodations that discount most heavily outside winter. For example, at the Delta Hotels by Marriott Whistler Village Suites website (www.marriott.com), type in a February date and then a July date under reservations—a bargain in July and over-the-top in winter. Although winter is peak season, rates quoted here are for summertime.

Reservation Services

If you plan on skiing or golfing, a package deal is the way to go. These can be booked directly through many accommodations, but two agencies offer a wider scope of choices: **Tourism Whistler** (604/932-0606 or 800/944-7853, www.whistler.com) and **Allura Direct** (604/707-6700 or 866/425-5872, www.alluradirect.com/whistler).

Under $50

HI-Whistler (1035 Legacy Way, Cheakamus Crossing, 604/962-0025, www.hihostels.ca) is eight kilometers (5 miles) southwest of town at a site that was developed as the Athlete's Village for the 2010 Winter Olympic Games. It's a large, modern lodging with facilities such as a large communal kitchen, a dining area, free wireless Internet, an elevator, a barbecue area, and a café with lots of outdoor seating.

It's understandably popular year-round; members pay $44 per night, nonmembers $48 for a dorm bed. Upgrade to a private room for $135 (nonmembers $145).

$50-100 and $100-150

There's not too much on offer in Whistler in these price brackets—it's either a dorm bed or an expensive hotel room here.

$150-200

★ **Crystal Lodge** (4154 Village Green, 604/932-2221 or 800/667-3363, www.crystal-lodge.com, $169-239 s or d) stands out as an excellent value in the heart of the action of Whistler Village. Rooms in the original wing are spacious and have a homey feel. The North Wing holds larger suites that have balconies. All guests have the use of an outdoor hot tub and heated pool.

$200-250

The log cabins at the ★ **Riverside Resort** (8018 Mons Rd., 604/905-5533 or 877/905-5533, www.parkbridge.com, $230 s or d) aren't spacious, but you're in Whistler, so you'll be spending most of your time hiking, biking, and generally being outdoors anyway. They ooze mountain charm and come complete with a small kitchen and TV-DVD combo. An on-site grocery store and café open daily for breakfast and lunch save heading into town for food.

On the edge of the village and adjacent to one of the valley's best golf courses is **Coast Blackcomb Suites at Whistler** (4005 Whistler Way, 604/932-2522 or 800/663-5644, www.coasthotels.com, $225 s or d). Each of the 194 rooms is simply but stylishly decorated in pastel colors. Facilities include a heated outdoor pool, an exercise room, a hot tub, a restaurant, and a bar. While summer rates start at a reasonable $225 (from $145 in spring and fall), the winter rate of $335 s or d is a little steep considering you're away from the ski lifts.

Centrally located **Delta Hotels by Marriott Whistler Village Suites** (4308

Main St., 604/905-3987 or 888/890-3222, www.marriott.com, $240 s or d) combines the conveniences of a full-service hotel with more than 200 kitchen-equipped units—the only such property in Whistler.

In the heart of the action, the ★ **Listel Hotel** (4121 Village Green, 604/932-1133 or 800/663-5472, www.listelhotel.com, $249 s or d) is a self-contained resort complete with a year-round outdoor pool, outdoor hot tub, and laundry. The in-house Bearfoot Bistro means you don't need to leave for dinner. The contemporary-style rooms are $249 s or d through much of the year, rising to $329 in winter.

$250-300

Summit Lodge & Spa (4359 Main St., 604/932-2778 or 888/913-8811, www.summitlodge.com, $285 s or d) is a luxurious European Alps-style boutique hotel. Each of the 81 units features comfortable furnishings, a slate floor, a fireplace, a balcony, and a small kitchen. There's also an outdoor heated pool, a day spa, and a sushi restaurant.

Over $300

Fairmont Chateau Whistler (4599 Chateau Blvd., 604/938-8000 or 800/606-8244, www.fairmont.com, $450 s or d), at the base of Blackcomb Mountain in Upper Village, is Whistler's most luxurious lodging, with its own championship golf course, the Vida Wellness Spa, a health club with the best equipment money can buy, tennis courts, and all of the facilities expected at one of the world's best accommodations. The massive lobby is decorated in the style of a rustic lodge, but the rooms couldn't be more different. Each is elegantly furnished and offers great mountain views. The hotel has five in-house dining options, ranging from a casual café with lots of outdoor seating to a fine-dining restaurant specializing in steak and seafood.

Camping

Enjoying a pleasant location 16 kilometers (10 miles) south of Whistler Village is **Whistler RV Park** (55 Hwy. 99, 604/905-2523, www.whistlerrvpark.com, $30-55). The best serviced sites have sweeping views across the Callaghan Valley, while tent sites are in a protected forest. Hiking trails lead off from the campground, and you are within walking distance of Brandywine Falls.

Just over two kilometers (1.2 miles) north of the village, **Riverside Resort** (8018 Mons Rd., 604/905-5533 or 877/905-5533, www.parkbridge.com, tents $42, hookups $62) is within town boundaries and has a hot tub, laundry, a small general store, and a café (from 7am daily), but has little privacy between sites.

INFORMATION AND SERVICES
Information

Whistler Visitor Centre (4230 Gateway Dr., 604/935-3357, 8am-10pm daily) is centrally located. Good sources of pre-trip planning information are **Tourism Whistler** (www.whistler.com) and the **Whistler Chamber of Commerce** (www.whistlerchamber.com). The two weekly newspapers are good sources of local information: the *Question* (www.whistlerquestion.com) and *Pique* (www.piquenewsmagazine.com).

Services

In Whistler Village you'll find a post office, banks, a currency exchange, a laundromat, a supermarket, and a liquor store. For medical needs, go to **Whistler Health Care Centre** (4380 Lorimer Rd., 604/932-4911, 8:30am-10pm daily). **Whistler Public Library** (4329 Main St., 604/935-8433, 10am-7pm Mon.-Thurs., 10am-6pm Fri., 11am-5pm Sat.-Sun.) has an international selection of newspapers and magazines, as well as free public Internet access. As a bonus for winter visitors, there is underground parking.

TRANSPORTATION
Getting There

The vast majority of visitors drive up to Whistler along Highway 99 from Vancouver. The 120-kilometer (75-mile) trip takes around

90 minutes when traffic conditions allow, but can take over two hours at peak times during the winter season. If you are driving west along the Trans-Canada Highway, instead of traveling through Vancouver to reach Whistler, it's possible to head west from Kamloops on Highway 97, passing through Cache Creek and Pemberton to approach the resort town from the north. Allow at least 3.5 hours for travel between Kamloops and Whistler.

Vancouver International Airport, 130 kilometers (80 miles) to the south, is the main gateway to Whistler. **Perimeter** (604/717-6600 or 888/717-6606, www.perimeterbus.com) provides bus service between the airport and Whistler hotels (adults $85, children $45 one-way) and between downtown Vancouver and Whistler (adults $55, children $35). These services run up to 11 times daily.

Whistler has no airport, but you can fly in with **Harbour Air** (604/932-6615 or 800/665-0212, www.harbourair.com), which operates scheduled floatplane flights between downtown Vancouver and Green Lake (just north of Whistler Village) for $199 one-way. The baggage limit is 10-50 pounds, depending on the fare purchased.

Getting Around

Once you're in Whistler, getting around is pretty easy—if you're staying in Whistler Village, everything you need is within easy walking distance. **Whistler Transit System** (604/932-4020) operates extensive bus routes (6am-midnight daily) throughout the valley. The seven routes radiate from the Gondola Transit Exchange in Whistler Village south to Whistler Creekside and as far north as Emerald Estates on the shore of Green Lake. Fare is $2.50, seniors and children $2, exact change only. A 10-ride card is adults $22.50, seniors and children $18.

For a cab, call **Whistler Taxi** (604/938-4430). Most visitors traveling to Whistler by rental car pick their vehicle up in Vancouver, but **Avis** (604/932-1236) does have an outlet in town.

Gold Nugget Route

The route north between Whistler and Lillooet is best traveled in good weather—the scenery is so spectacular, you don't want to miss *anything*. See white-topped peaks all around you and big glacier-colored rivers. If you have the time, stop at provincial parks along the way for always good scenery and outdoor activities.

Make your first stop north of Whistler at **Nairn Falls Provincial Park,** on the banks of Green River, where a wooded trail leads to a waterfall. Stay overnight at the campground (mid-May.-Sept., $22), where around half the sites can be reserved through **Discover Camping** (519/826-6850 or 800/689-9025, www.discovercamping.ca).

The small mountain community of **Pemberton** (population 2,400) is growing rapidly as a cheaper housing alternative for Whistler workers, who commute the 32 kilometers (20 miles) south. Surrounded by mountains, trees, lakes, and rivers, Pemberton sits in a fertile valley known for its potatoes. It's only a short distance south of the Lillooet River, a main transportation route to the Cariboo during the 1860s gold rush days. Today's visitors leave their gold pans at home, coming mainly to fish or to hike in the beautiful valleys around Pemberton. The summer-only **Pemberton Visitor Centre** (604/894-6175, www.tourismpembertonbc.com, 9am-5pm daily mid-May-late Sept.) is back out of town on Highway 99.

From Pemberton you can take one of three routes to **Lillooet.** Whichever route you decide on, it's important to note that the weather can change rapidly, and even in summer you might find yourself traveling through a sudden snowstorm at higher elevations. However, the scenery makes the effort worthwhile. You'll see beautiful lakes, fast rivers, summer wildflowers, deep-blue mountains, steep ravines, never-ending forests, and vistas in every shade of green imaginable. Campgrounds and picnic areas mark all the best locations.

The most direct way—the route once taken by fortune seekers heading toward the Cariboo goldfields—is paved Highway 99. A few minutes' drive out of Mount Currie, the highway begins switchbacking as it climbs abruptly into the Coast Mountains and crests at a 1,300-meter-high (4,260-foot) pass. Just before the pass is 1,460-hectare (3,600-acre) **Joffre Lakes Provincial Park,** where a short trail (about 20 minutes round-trip) leads to Lower Joffre Lake. The trail continues beyond the first lake, making an elevation gain of 400 meters (1,300 feet) before reaching the main body of water, 10 kilometers (6 miles) from the highway.

From the pass, Highway 99 loses over 1,000 meters (3,300 feet) of elevation in its descent to Lillooet. Along the way is narrow **Duffey Lake** (the highway itself is referred to locally as the "Duffey Lake Road"), backed by the steep-sided Cayoosh Range.

The second, summer-only route spurs north through Mount Currie following the Birkenhead River, passing the turnoff to 9,755-hectare (24,100-acre) **Birkenhead Lake Provincial Park,** then descending to **D'Arcy.** Beyond this point, the road can get extremely rough, so check conditions in town before setting out. The third, northernmost, and longest route, over 200 kilometers (124 miles) of mostly unpaved road, also open in summer only, climbs north along the Lillooet River through Pemberton Meadows, over Hurley Pass, and to the historic mining communities of **Gold Bridge** and **Bralorne** before closely following the shore of Carpenter Lake in an easterly direction back to Lillooet.

East from Vancouver

FRASER VALLEY

When you leave Vancouver and head due east, you travel through the most built-up and heavily populated area of British Columbia, skirting modern cities, residential suburbs, and zones of heavy industry. However, it's not an unattractive area—the main roads follow the mighty Fraser River through a fertile valley of rolling farmland dotted with historic villages, and beautiful mountains line the horizon in just about any direction.

You have a choice of two major routes. The Trans-Canada Highway, on the south side of the Fraser River, speeds you out of southeast Vancouver through Abbotsford and scenic Chilliwack to Hope. Slower, more picturesque Highway 7 meanders along the north side of the Fraser River through **Mission,** named after a Roman Catholic mission school built in 1861. The town is now known for its

Benedictine monastery, which offers a retreat center open to the public. The highway then passes the access road to **Harrison Hot Springs** and crosses over the Fraser River to Hope. In summer you can pick and choose from an endless number of roadside stands selling fresh fruit at bargain prices—the raspberries in July are delectable.

Golden Ears Provincial Park

Encompassing 62,540 hectares (154,540 acres) of the Coast Mountains, this park extends from the Alouette River, near the suburb of Maple Ridge, north to Garibaldi Provincial Park. To get to the main facility areas, follow Highway 7 east out of the city for 40 kilometers (25 miles) to Maple Ridge, then follow signs north. Much of the park was logged for railway ties in the 1920s, but today the second-growth montane forest—dominated by western hemlock—has almost erased the earlier human devastation. The park access road follows the Alouette River into the park, ending at Alouette Lake. The river and lake provide fair fishing, but the park's most popular activity is hiking. **Lower Falls Trail** begins at the end of the road and leads 2.7 kilometers (1.7 miles) along Gold Creek to a 10-meter (33-foot) waterfall; allow one hour one-way. Across Gold Creek, **West Canyon Trail** climbs 200 vertical meters (660 feet) over 1.5 kilometers (0.9 miles) to a viewpoint of Alouette Lake.

Within the park are two **campgrounds** (reservations 519/826-6850 or 800/689-9025, www.discovercamping.ca, mid-June-Aug., $35) linked by hiking trails and with lake access.

Fort Langley National Historic Site

In 1827, the Hudson's Bay Company established a settlement 48 kilometers (30 miles) upstream from the mouth of the Fraser River as part of a network of trading posts, provision depots, and administrative centers that stretched across western Canada. The original site was abandoned in 1838 in favor of another, farther upstream, where today the riverside trading post has been recreated. When British Columbia became a crown colony on November 19, 1858, Fort Langley was declared capital, but one year later, the entire colonial government moved to the more central New Westminster.

Today, the **Fort Langley National Historic Site** (23433 Mavis St., Fort Langley, 604/513-4777, 10am-5pm daily, adults $8, seniors $7, children $4), springs to life as park interpreters in period costumes animate the fort's history. The park is within walking distance of Fort Langley village, where many businesses are built in a heritage style, and you'll find dozens of antiques shops, boutiques, restaurants, and cafés along its main tree-lined street. To get there, follow Highway 1 for 50 kilometers (31 miles) east from downtown and head north toward the Fraser River from Highway 1's exit 66 onto 232nd Street and then Glover Road. From the highway, it's five kilometers (3 miles) to downtown Fort Langley; the fort lies a few blocks east of the main street. It's well posted from Highway 1.

East Toward Hope

If you've visited Fort Langley, backtrack south to continue east along the valley. Instead of continuing along Highway 1, cross the transcontinental highway on Glover Road to Langley city center, then head east on Old Yale Road and into an area laced with lazy country roads. If you decide to cross from Highway 1 to Highway 7 at Abbotsford, make the detour to delightful **Clayburn Village,** originally a company town for a local brickworks. As you'd expect, most of the neat houses are built of brick, providing a local atmosphere a world away from the surrounding modern subdivisions. Along the main street, **Clayburn Village Store** (Wright St., 10am-5pm Tues.-Sat.) is a general store that has changed little in appearance since opening in 1912. The highlight is the delicious Devonshire tea, although children will say it's the candy sold from big glass jars. Reach the store by taking exit 92 north from Highway 1, follow Highway 11 north for six kilometers (4 miles), and then head east along Clayburn Road.

It is possible to continue east through Clayburn to **Sumas Mountain Provincial Park** (ask directions at the local general store), or take exit 95 from Highway 1 to Sumas Mountain Road, then take Batts Road, which climbs steadily up the mountain's southern slopes. From the end of this service road, it's a short climb to the 900-meter (2,950-foot) summit of Sumas Mountain, from which views extend north across the Fraser River and south across a patchwork of farmland to Washington's snowcapped Mount Baker. From the pullout one kilometer (0.6 miles) from the end of the road, a hiking trail descends for 1.6 kilometers (1 mile) to forest-encircled Chadsey Lake and a lakeside picnic area.

Kilby Historic Site

Off the beaten track and often missed by those unfamiliar with the area, the **Kilby Historic Site** (215 Kilby Rd., Harrison Mills, 604/796-9576, 11am-4pm Thurs.-Mon. mid-May-June, 11am-4pm daily July-Aug., 11am-4pm Sat.-Sun. Sept.-Oct., adults $10, seniors $9, youths $8) lies on the north side of the Fraser River, near the turnoff to Harrison Hot Springs, 40 kilometers (25 miles) east of Mission and six kilometers (4 miles) west of Agassiz (look for the inconspicuous sign close to Harrison Mills). The fascinating museum and country store, which operated until the early 1970s, is fully stocked with all of the old brands and types of goods that were commonplace in the 1920s and 1930s. On the two-hectare (5-acre) riverside grounds are farm equipment, farm animals, a gift shop, and a café serving delicious home-style cooking.

Harrison Hot Springs

Of British Columbia's 60 natural hot springs, the closest to Vancouver is Harrison Hot Springs, on the north side of the Fraser Valley, 125 kilometers (78 miles) east of downtown. Known as the Spa of Canada, the springs lie on the sandy southern shores of the Lower Mainland's largest body of water,

Harrison Lake. Since the opening of the province's first resort in 1886, the springs have spurred much surrounding development. Coast Salish were the first to take advantage of the soothing water. Then, in the late 1850s, gold miners stumbled upon the springs. Because of a historical agreement, only the Harrison Hot Springs Resort has water rights, but the hotel operates **Harrison Natural Hot Springs Pool** (Harrison Hot Springs Rd. and Esplanade Ave., 604/796-2244, 8am-9pm daily summer, 9am-9pm daily fall-spring, adults $10, senior and children $7.75). Scalding 74°C (165°F) mineral water is pumped from its source, cooled to a soothing 38°C (100°F), and then pumped into the pool. The lake provides many recreation opportunities, with good swimming, sailing, canoeing, and fishing for rainbow trout.

Lakeside **Harrison Hot Springs Resort** (100 Esplanade, 604/796-2244 or 800/663-2266, www.harrisonresort.com, $205-345 s or d) is the town's most elegant lodging, and it offers guests use of a large indoor and outdoor complex of mineral pools, complete with grassed areas, lots of outdoor furniture, and a café. Other facilities include boat and canoe rentals, sailing lessons, and a restaurant and lounge bar. Most of the 337 rooms have private

the lakefront at Harrison Hot Springs

Hope and Vicinity

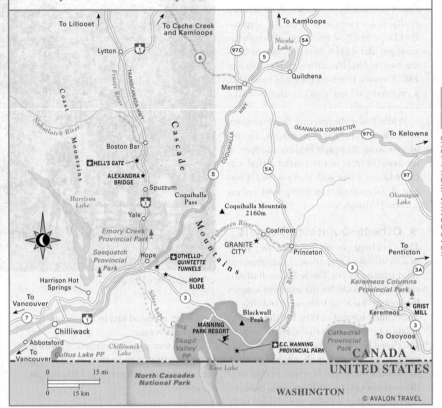

balconies, many with spectacular views across the lake.

Within walking distance of the public hot pool and lake is **Glencoe Motel** (259 Hot Springs Rd., 604/796-2574, www.glencoemotel.com, $139-159 s or d). The least expensive overnight option is to camp at one of three campgrounds along the road into town or through town in lakeside **Sasquatch Provincial Park** (Apr.-mid-Oct., $23).

HOPE AND VICINITY

Locals say "all roads lead to Hope"—and they're right. On a finger of land at the confluence of the Fraser and Coquihalla Rivers, 158 kilometers (98 miles) east of Vancouver, Hope

(pop. 6,400) really is a hub. The Trans-Canada Highway and Highway 7 from Vancouver, the Coquihalla Highway to Kamloops, and Highway 3 from the Okanagan all meet at Hope. Downtown is very walkable, but the surrounding area is the main draw, with magnificent mountains and rivers, a couple of wilderness areas only a short drive away, and an abundance of recreational opportunities.

To find out more about the history of Hope, visit **Hope Museum** (919 Water Ave., 604/869-7322, 9am-5pm daily May-June, 8am-8pm daily July-Aug., donation), in the same building as the information center. The museum's comprehensive collection of pioneer artifacts is displayed in several recreated settings, including a kitchen, a bedroom, a parlor, a schoolroom, and a blacksmith shop. Other exhibits focus on local First Nations crafts and on artifacts from the original Fort Hope and gold rush days, although the most popular display tells the story of filming *Rambo: First Blood* through downtown in 1981. Outside, climb on the Hope Gold Mill, a restored gold-ore concentrator from the Coquihalla area.

While you're discovering the downtown area, check out the tree-stump art, created by Pete Ryan. The eagle holding a salmon in its claws (in front of the district office) was carved from a tree with root rot, and it was one of the original tree-stump works of art scattered through town.

★ Othello-Quintette Tunnels

These five huge tunnels through a steep gorge of **Coquihalla Canyon** were carved out of solid granite by the Kettle Valley Railway, completing a route for the company's steam locomotives between Vancouver and Nelson. The tunnels opened in 1916, but the line was plagued by snow, rock slides, and washouts, and closed for repairs more often than it was open. It was eventually abandoned in 1959. By 1962 the tracks and four steel bridges over the awesome Coquihalla River gorge had been removed. Today a short, tree-shaded walk takes you from the **Coquihalla Canyon Provincial Park** parking lot to the massive dark **Othello-Quintette Tunnels** (May-Oct.), now a popular attraction.

Stroll through them and over the sturdy wooden bridges to admire the gorge and the power and the roar of the Coquihalla River below. If you'd visited the tunnels back in 1981, you would have seen Sylvester Stallone swinging through the canyons during the filming of *Rambo: First Blood*. To get to the tunnels from downtown, take Wallace Street to 6th Avenue and turn right. Turn left on Kawkawa Lake Road, crossing the Coquihalla River Bridge and railway tracks. At the first intersection take the right branch, Othello Road, and continue until you see a sign to the

Othello-Quintette Tunnels

right (over a rise and easy to miss) pointing to the recreation area.

On the way up to the tunnels, **Kawkawa Lake** is a pleasant body of water with a high concentration of kokanee and a lakeside picnic area.

Skagit Valley Provincial Park

This remote wilderness of 32,577 hectares (80,500 acres) southeast of Hope is bordered to the east by Manning Provincial Park and to the south by the U.S.-Canada border. Access is along the Silver-Skagit Road, which branches south off Flood Hope Road four kilometers (2.5 miles) southwest of Hope. This rough gravel road climbs steadily for 39 kilometers (24 miles) to the park entrance, then continues 22 kilometers (14 miles) farther to the international border and road's end at **Ross Lake Reservoir.**

Through the park, the road follows the Skagit River, which flows northward from Ross Lake Reservoir through a magnificent valley cloaked in spruce, pine, aspen, and maple. Black bears, cougars, wolves, coyotes, deer, beavers, and over 200 species of birds are all present within the park.

Outdoors enthusiasts can hike trails suited mainly to overnight excursions. **Skagit River Trail** begins just east of where the park access road crosses the river, following the river downstream for 15 kilometers (9 miles) to a day-use area beside Highway 3. Fishing in the Skagit River is good for Dolly Varden and rainbow trout. The access road is dotted with day-use areas, including Shawatum, six kilometers (4 miles) from the park entrance, which was once the site of a bustling town with saloons, restaurants, a sawmill, and a daily newspaper—until it was discovered that the only gold found in the area had been planted.

Hope Slide

On Highway 3, about 18 kilometers (11 miles) southeast of Hope, the effects of one of nature's amazing forces can be seen. On January 9, 1965, a minor earthquake caused a huge section of mountain to come crashing down, filling the bottom of the Nicolum Creek Valley, destroying about three kilometers (2 miles) of the Hope-Princeton Highway and killing four motorists. The highway, viewpoint, and parking area are built over the Hope Slide, but you can still see the slide's treeless boundaries along the south side of the valley.

Food

The best place in Hope for coffee is **Blue Moose** (322 Wallace St., 604/869-0729, 7am-7pm daily, lunch $6-9), with a slick polished-wood and sparkling blue interior and free Wi-Fi. Paninis, wraps, sandwiches, and soups are all under $10. For something a little more substantial, wander down Wallace Street to the corner of 3rd Avenue, where **293 Wallace** (293 Wallace St., 604/860-0822, noon-3pm and 5pm-9pm Wed.-Mon., $18-34) serves up creative cooking in a contemporary space. Lunches such as apple pecan salad cost $13-17, with the patio providing the perfect place to dine on a summer's day. Out on the highway, **Home Restaurant** (665 Old Hope-Princeton

Way, 604/869-5558, 6am-10pm daily, $8-15) has been dishing up simple, inexpensive meals for weary travelers for over 60 years.

Accommodations and Camping

Hope doesn't offer much hope if you're looking for upscale lodging. Instead you'll find a motley collection of roadside motels in town and across the Trans-Canada Highway on Old Hope-Princeton Way. On the latter, **Royal Lodge Motel** (580 Old Hope-Princeton Way, 604/869-5358 or 877/500-6620, www.royal-lodgemotel.ca, $85 s, $90-105 d) has clean rooms, some with kitchens. The newer, single-story **Alpine Motel** (505 Old Hope-Princeton Way, 604/869-9931 or 877/869-9931, $95 s, $105 d) offers large, comfortably furnished rooms, a pool, and a pleasant setting.

In a scenic setting four kilometers (2.5 miles) north of Hope, **Beautiful Lake of the Woods Resort** (22805 Trans-Canada Hwy., 604/869-9211 or 888/508-2211, www.lakewoods-resort-motel.com, motel $75 s, $85 d, cabins $85-115 d) sits on a lake with views of the surrounding mountain-scape. The property is a resort in name only, but facilities include a restaurant and canoe rentals ($10 per hour).

Along the road up to the Othello-Quintette Tunnels, **Othello Tunnels Campground** (67851 Othello Rd., 604/869-9448 or 877/869-0543, www.othellotunnels.com, $34-37) is pleasant place, with trees surrounding many sites. Facilities include a trout pond, hot showers, a barbecue area, laundry, free Wi-Fi, and a game room.

Information and Services

Right downtown, the friendly staff at **Hope Visitor Centre** (919 Water Ave., 604/869-2021, 8am-8pm daily summer, 9am-5pm daily fall-spring) can help you decide which of the routes to take out of Hope, but might also convince you to stay in town a little longer.

FRASER RIVER CANYON

From Hope, the old Trans-Canada Highway runs north along the west bank of the fast-flowing Fraser River. Although the Coquihalla Highway is a much shorter option for those heading for Kamloops and beyond, the old highway offers many interesting stops and is by far the preferred route for those not in a hurry. Head north through downtown Hope, cross the Fraser River, take the first right, and you're on your way.

The first worthwhile stop is tiny **Emory Creek Provincial Park,** 15 kilometers (9 miles) from Hope. Stopping at this quiet riverside park, it's hard to believe that 130 years ago it was the site of Emory City, complete with saloons, a brewery, a large sawmill, and all the other businesses of a bustling frontier gold town. The city had virtually disappeared by the 1890s, and today no hint of its short-lived presence remains. Wander along riverside trails, try some fishing, or stay at one of the wooded campsites ($21).

Yale

This small town of 200 has quite a history. It started off as one of the many Hudson's Bay Company posts, then became a transportation center at the head of the navigable lower section of the Fraser River. Enormous Lady Franklin Rock blocked the upriver section to steamer traffic, so all goods heading for the interior had to be carried from this point by wagon train along the **Cariboo Wagon Road.** By 1858, Yale was a flourishing gold rush town of 20,000, filled with tents, shacks, bars, gambling joints, and shops. But when the gold ran out in the 1890s, so did most of the population, and Yale dwindled to the small forestry and service center it has been ever since. To find out more about Yale's past, visit the **Historic Yale Site** (31187 Douglas St., 604/863-2324, 10am-5pm daily May-Sept., adults $9.50, seniors and students $7.50), which comprises a small museum, a tea house, gold-panning, the 1863 **St. John's Church,** and the local visitors center.

If you're looking for a place to spend the night, choose between the downtown 12-room **Fort Yale Motel** (31265 Trans-Canada Hwy., 604/863-2216, $79-99 s or d), which is very

basic and close to a busy rail line, or head back down the highway 12 kilometers (7.5 miles) to the campground at **Emory Creek Provincial Park** ($21).

Alexandra Bridge

The treacherous Fraser Canyon posed a major transportation obstacle during the 1850s gold rush. In 1863, Alexandra Bridge, 22 kilometers (14 miles) north of Yale, was completed. However, with the successful completion of the Canadian Pacific Railway line through the canyon, the bridge and the Cariboo Wagon Road fell into disrepair. The popularity of the automobile forced engineers to construct a new suspension bridge in 1926. The new bridge used the original abutments and lasted right up to 1962, when it was replaced by today's bridge on Highway 1. **Alexandra Bridge Provincial Park** now protects a section of the old Cariboo Wagon Road, including the old bridge. The trail down to the bridge makes a good place to get out and stretch your legs.

★ Hell's Gate

At well-known Hell's Gate, the Fraser River powers its way through a narrow, glacially carved, 34-meter-deep (112-foot) gorge. When Simon Fraser saw this section of the gorge in 1808, he wrote, "we had to travel where no human being should venture—for surely we have encountered the gates of hell," and the name stuck. In 1914, a massive rockslide rocketed down into the gorge, blocking it even further and resulting in the almost total obliteration of the sockeye salmon population that spawned farther upstream. In 1944, giant concrete fishways were built to slow the waters and allow the spawning salmon to jump upstream, and the river soon swarmed with salmon once again. Today you can cross the canyon aboard the 25-passenger **Hell's Gate Airtram** (43111 Trans-Canada Hwy., 604/867-9277, 10am-4pm daily mid-Apr.-mid-Oct., 10am-5pm July and Aug., adults $22, seniors $20, children $16). Once across the river you can browse through landscaped gardens, learn more about the fishway and salmon, or even try your hand at gold panning.

North Toward Cache Creek

Another small town with a gold rush history, **Boston Bar** is today a popular white-water rafting destination for those brave enough to float the Fraser River's roaring rapids. A bridge crossing at Boston Bar accesses the **Nahatlatch River,** renowned for white-water kayaking. Along quieter stretches of this river are some great fishing spots, three lakes, and numerous primitive campgrounds. **REO Rafting Resort** (16 kilometers/10 miles west of Boston Bar, 604/461-7238 or 800/736-7238, www.reorafting.com, May-Sept.) offers relatively inexpensive all-inclusive adventures. For example, camping for one night, three meals, and a rafting trip is $199 pp, with an upgrade to a tent cabin an extra $70 pp. Fishing, rock climbing, and guided hiking are also offered.

Continuing up the canyon, the narrow highway winds northward for 34 kilometers (21 miles) to **Lytton,** a historic village at the confluence of the Fraser and Thompson Rivers, before spurring eastward and following the Thompson River. This route eventually reaches Cache Creek, the gateway to Cariboo Country, and continues on to the major interior city of Kamloops.

COQUIHALLA HIGHWAY

Opened in 1986, the Coquihalla Highway is the most direct link between Hope and the interior of British Columbia. It saves at least 90 minutes by cutting 72 kilometers (45 miles) from the trip between Hope and Kamloops and bypassing the Trans-Canada Highway's narrow, winding stretch along the Fraser River Canyon.

The highway ascends and descends through magnificent mountain and river scenery to dry semiarid grasslands. You'll cruise through the valleys of the Lower Coquihalla River and Boston Bar Creek, climb to the 1,240-meter (4,070-foot) summit of Coquihalla Pass near Coquihalla Lake, descend along the Coldwater River, then climb the Coldwater's eastern valley slope to Merritt. From Merritt the highway climbs the valleys of the Nicola River and Clapperton Creek to join the Trans-Canada Highway eight kilometers (5 miles) west of Kamloops.

Merritt

This town of 7,000 in the Nicola Valley, 115 kilometers (71 miles) north of Hope,

Hell's Gate Airtram

provides the only services along the Coquihalla Highway. It's also the exit point for those heading east to the Okanagan on the Okanagan Connector. Make your first stop the **Merritt Visitor Centre** (Hwy. 5 and Hwy. 97C, 250/315-1342, www.tourismmerritt.ca, 10am-6pm daily May-Sept.), out on the main highway.

Since the Coquihalla Highway opened, many motels have been built around Merritt, but by far the best choice is one of the originals, the ★ **Quilchena Hotel** (250/378-2611, www.douglaslake.com, $139-199 s or d), on Nicola Lake, 20 kilometers (12 miles) east of town on Highway 5A (take exit 290). Built in 1908 and now part of Douglas Lake Ranch, Canada's largest working cattle ranch, the property is a destination in itself, especially for avid anglers. There is also golfing (9 holes $22, 18 holes $32), swimming, biking, and canoeing. The hotel is a stately old building surrounded by well-tended gardens and oozing Victorian charm. A grand staircase leads up to guest rooms decorated with period antiques, lace curtains, and solid wooden beds. Rates for rooms with shared baths are $139 s or d, while en suite rooms start at $169. Downstairs are a saloon (complete with bullet holes in the bar) and a restaurant serving up beef raised on the hotel ranch. A number of campsites are spread across the property, each beside a lake. The campgrounds ($25-50) offer minimal services and are very private (one has just two sites), but the fishing is excellent.

★ E. C. MANNING PROVINCIAL PARK

This rugged 70,844-hectare (175,100-acre) park in the Cascade Mountains, 64 kilometers (40 miles) east of Hope along Highway 3, stretches down to the Canada-U.S. border. Highway 3 makes a U through the park—from the northwest to south to northeast sections. But to really appreciate the park, you need to get off the highway—take in the beautiful bodies of water, drive up to a wonderful stretch of high alpine meadows, or hike on the numerous trails.

Hiking

A highlight of the park is the paved road immediately across Highway 3 from Manning Park Resort; it climbs northward steadily to **Cascade Lookout,** a viewpoint offering a magnificent 180-degree panoramic view. Beyond the lookout, the road turns to gravel and continues climbing for nine kilometers (6 miles), ending at a parking lot beneath 2,063-meter (6,700-foot) Blackwall Peak. From this area of flower-filled alpine meadows, views extend over the park's remote northern boundary. Take time to soak up the color by taking one of the short trails originating from the parking lot. Or hike **Heather Trail** (10 kilometers/6 miles one-way; allow 3 hours) to Three Brothers Mountain. If you're there between late July and mid-August, you won't believe what you're seeing: a rich yellow, orange, and white carpet of wildflowers as far as you can see.

Along Highway 3 are some short self-guided nature trails, including a 700-meter (0.4-mile) walk (20 minutes) through a stand of ancient western red cedars. The trailhead is Sumallo Grove day-use area, 10 kilometers (6 miles) east of where Highway 3 enters the park from the west. Just east of the Visitor Information Centre, on the south side of the road, is the 500-meter (0.3-mile) **Beaver Pond Trail.** If you notice people arriving on foot in this parking lot with worn soles, bent backs, and great big smiles on their faces, give them a pat on the back—they may have just completed one of the world's greatest long-distance hikes. The **Pacific Crest Trail** runs 3,860 kilometers (2,400 miles) from the U.S.-Mexico border to this small and undistinguished trailhead.

Skiing and Snowboarding

The park gets plenty of dry snow for skiing and boarding. At **Manning Park Resort** (250/840-8822 or 800/330-3321, www.manningpark.com), 11 kilometers (7 miles) west of Highway 3 along Gibson Pass Road, downhill enthusiasts can take advantage of a 437-meter (1,430-foot) vertical rise served

kayaks at E.C. Manning Provincial Park

604/668-5922 or 800/330-3321, www.manningpark.com, $169-349 s or d) is a full-service lodging providing comfortable hotel rooms, cabins, and triplexes, as well as a restaurant (breakfast, lunch, and dinner daily), an alpine-themed pub, and a small grocery store. Other facilities include saunas, an indoor pool, a TV room, a fitness center, tennis courts, a coin-operated laundry, and a gift shop. Through summer, rooms in the main lodge start at $169 on weekends, and are discounted to $119 midweek; cabins with kitchens start at $249 on weekends and $209 midweek.

The park's four vehicle-accessible campgrounds hold over 350 sites; in summer, get in early to be assured of snagging one. Each campground provides drinking water and toilets. Firewood is available for a fee. The most popular campground is **Lightning Lakes** ($25), which has showers, two kilometers (1.2 miles) west of Manning Park Resort on Gibson Pass Road. Others include **Coldspring Campground,** on Highway 3 two kilometers (1.2 miles) west of the resort; **Hampton Campground,** on Highway 3 four kilometers (2.5 miles) east of the resort; and **Mule Deer Campground,** four kilometers (2.5 miles) farther east; all three charge $23. Around half the campsites are reservable May to September through **Discover Camping** (519/826-6850 or 800/689-9025, www.discovercamping.ca) and a few are open (with no services) year-round.

by two chairlifts, a T-bar, and a rope tow. Most runs are for intermediate skiers, but novices and experts will also find suitable terrain. Lift tickets are adults $57, seniors and children $37.

The resort is geared toward families, with other activities including a skating rink, terrain park, and tubing park, keeping all ages happy. On-hill facilities include a cafeteria, a ski school, and ski rentals (from $35 full-day). A free shuttle bus transfers guests to the ski area from Manning Park Resort, which offers winter packages from $200 pp for two nights' midweek high-season accommodations and two days' skiing.

Along with 190 kilometers (118 miles) of wilderness trails, cross-country skiers can enjoy 30 kilometers (19 miles) of groomed trails, with a daily pass costing adults $20, seniors and children $12.

Practicalities

In the heart of the park on Highway 3, **Manning Park Resort** (7500 Hwy. 3,

CONTINUING TOWARD THE OKANAGAN VALLEY

From the eastern boundary of E. C. Manning Provincial Park, Highway 3 follows the Similkameen River north to Princeton, then turns sharply southeast to Osoyoos, at the southern end of the Okanagan Valley, a total distance of 158 kilometers (98 miles).

Princeton

At the confluence of the Similkameen and Tulameen Rivers, surrounded by low tree-covered hills, lies the small friendly ranching town of Princeton (pop. 3,000). **Princeton and District Pioneer Museum** (167 Vermilion Ave., 250/295-7588, noon-4pm Mon.-Fri., donation) features pioneer artifacts from Granite City, Chinese and Interior Salish artifacts, and an extensive fossil display.

On the northeast side of Princeton, the stone and concrete ruins of a 1910 cement plant have been incorporated in a unique resort complex, ★ **Princeton Castle Resort** (375 Rainbow Lake Rd., 250/295-7988 or 888/228-8881, www.castleresort.com). The cement works was built at a cost of $1 million, yet operated for only one year. In the ensuing decades, the buildings have been reclaimed by nature. Around, through, and over the crumbling ruins grow trees, wild roses, lilacs, and lupines. Take a look at the concrete paths and steps leading down from the back of the administrative building to the ruins—the concrete is loaded with fossilized shells.

Surrounding the ruins are cabins and chalets of varying configurations, with the larger chalets taking pride of place along a ridge overlooking a sparkling creek. Rooms in the main lodge are $99-149 s or d, and chalets complete with baths, kitchens, and TV cost from $155. Beyond the ruins, a road leads up to the resort campground (May-Oct.), where sites are $30 and cabins with shared baths (no linens) are $85. Aside from admiring the ruins, children will love the large playground, while all ages can enjoy horseback riding or canoeing on the small lake. To get there from Princeton, cross the bridge at the north end of Bridge Street, turn right on Old Hedley Road, cross Highway 5, turn left on Five Mile Road, then continue until the sign to the park leads you right.

Just a short stroll from downtown, **Riverside Cabins** (307 Thomas Ave., at the north end of Bridge St., 250/295-6232, $50-70 s or d) was built in 1934 as a hunting and fishing lodge. The aptly named lodging is right beside the river, and in the height of summer the water level drops to expose a small beach and shallow swimming hole. (Ask the owners to show you a photo of the place taken in

Granite City

After the discovery of a gold nugget in Granite Creek back in 1885, a 13-saloon gold rush city sprang to life on this spot. Soon it was the third-largest city in the province, supporting a population of over 2,000. But the boom was short-lived, and the town was quickly abandoned. What remains of Granite City lies two kilometers (1.2 miles) from Coalmont. To get there, head straight through Coalmont to Granite Creek, turn left on Hope Street, right over the creek, and then follow the road to a fork. Straight ahead is the site of the boomtown, marked by a riverside cairn and the broken-down remains of a few log buildings among wild lilac bushes—it's really up to your imagination to recreate the good ol' days. On the bluff to the north of Granite City (take the right fork and then the first right) is a small graveyard with headstones showing dates from the boom years.

1937—the cabins still look exactly the same.) Each basic cabin has a toilet, a shower, and a kitchen with a fridge, a stove, cooking utensils, crockery, and cutlery. If you're just looking for somewhere to rest your head, reserve a standard motel room at **Canadas Best Value Princeton Inn & Suites** (169 Hwy. 3, 250/295-3537, www.redlion.com/princeton, $95-125 s or d), where a light breakfast and use of an outdoor pool is included in the rates.

The best coffee in town is poured at **Cowboy Coffee** (255 Vermilion Ave., 250/295-3431, 4:30am-4pm Sun.-Mon., 4:30am-6pm Tues.-Sat., lunch $7-11), in a renovated residence just off the main highway. Seating is in cozy rooms, out front facing the street, or on a more private patio out back. In addition to good coffee, you'll find a wide array of inexpensive breakfasts and lunches, including toasted sandwiches, soup, salads, and a daily special. Continuing into downtown, **Thomasina's** (279 Bridge St., 250/295-3810, 8am-4pm Mon.-Sat., 10am-3pm Sun., lunch $6-10) is an appealing small-town bakery, where the breads and pastries are delicious. Light lunches are also made from scratch daily, including soups and sandwiches. Also on the main street is my favorite dinner stop in Princeton, **Little Creek Grill** (117 Bridge St., 250/295-6644, 4pm-9:30pm Tues., 11am-9:30pm Wed.-Sun., $19-29), where a local family serves up traditional Greek dishes in a contemporary setting.

At the east entrance to town is **Princeton Visitor Centre** (Hwy. 3, 250/295-3103, www. princeton.ca, 9am-5pm daily summer, 9am-5pm Mon.-Fri. fall-spring).

Coalmont and Beyond

If you want to see some impressive canyon scenery off the main tourist drag, cross the river at the north end of Princeton's Bridge Street and turn left, heading west toward Coalmont for 18 kilometers (11 miles). Coalmont came to the forefront when gold rush activity moved from Granite City to this village in 1911. Today, you can't help but notice that the town's residents have a sense of humor. The welcoming sign states that Coalmont has no industry but plenty of activity, in the form of sleeping and daydreaming. It also claims Coalmont has a hot, cold, wet, and dry climate, warns traveling salespeople to stay away, and advises single women that their safety is not guaranteed due to the predominance of bachelors. The currently abandoned 1912 three-story **Coalmont Hotel** dominates the main street, while quite a number of homes—some with backyards crammed with eclectic collections of rusting mine machinery—line the streets.

The main road through Coalmont winds its way north to Merritt, providing a handy shortcut, if that's the direction you're heading. The only town en route is the hamlet of **Tulameen** (pop. 250). Along the main street, the museum in a one-room log schoolhouse may or may not be open, while at the north end of town, you'll probably have the beach at **Otter Lake Provincial Park** to yourself. The park's **campground** (519/826-6850 or 800/689-9025, www.discovercamping.ca,

mid-May-Sept., $23) is farther along the lake to the north.

Hedley and Vicinity

From Princeton, Highway 3 takes you on a scenic route through the beautiful **Similkameen River Valley,** which holds lots of places to camp in either provincial parks or private campgrounds. Between Princeton and Keremeos the road follows the Dewdney Trail, a 468-kilometer (290-mile) track used in the 1860s to connect Hope with the Wildhorse Creek goldfields. This stretch itself has also been a major mining area, supplying a fortune in gold, silver, nickel, and copper over the years.

The landscape east of Princeton is different from that to the west, but the change is most pronounced east of Hedley—going from ragged tree-covered mountains, through rolling hills covered in sagebrush and lush irrigated orchards around Keremeos, to desert (complete with lizards, cactus, and rattlesnakes) around Osoyoos on the Canada-U.S. border.

Cathedral Provincial Park

Wilderness hikers and mountaineers should not miss the turnoff to this spectacular 33,272-hectare (82,200-acre) park just west of Keremeos. Access along the 21-kilometer (13-mile) road leading into the park is restricted to guests of ★ **Cathedral Lakes Lodge** (250/226-7560 or 888/255-4453, www. cathedrallakes.ca, June-Oct.) or those willing to walk. For this reason, most park visitors stay at the lodge, which provides basic accommodations, meals, use of canoes, a recreation room and hot tub, and transportation to and from the base camp. The minimum stay is a two-day package: original cabins and bungalow rooms start at $530 pp, while rooms in the main lodge are $570. Rates include all meals and the shuttle ride. The lodge also offers the option of a day trip (adults $120, children $60), which covers the cost of the 8am shuttle up the lodge from the highway.

About 60 kilometers (37 miles) of

wilderness trails lead from the resort to a variety of striking and enticingly named rock formations, including Stone City, Giant Cleft, Devil's Woodpile, Macabre Tower, Grimface Mountain, Denture Ridge, and Smokey the Bear. Wander through meadows waving with dainty alpine flowers, climb peaks for tremendous views, fish for trout in sparkling turquoise lakes, and capture images of immense glacier-topped mountains.

KEREMEOS

As you approach mountain-surrounded Keremeos from the west, the road is lined with lush, irrigated orchards and fruit stands, one after another, which is probably what inspired the town's claim to fame as the "Fruit Stand Capital of Canada." Keremeos has one of the longest growing seasons in the province. Try a taste bud-tingling fruit-juice shake in summer; recommended is the second-to-last stand as you head east out of town. Harvest dates are mid-June to mid-July for cherries, mid-July to early August for apricots, mid-July to early September for peaches, mid-August to mid-September for pears, early August to mid-October for apples, early to mid-September for plums, and early September to early October for grapes.

Old Grist Mill and Gardens

The town's main historic attraction is the **Old Grist Mill and Gardens** (2691 Upper Bench Rd., 250/499-2888, of 9am-5pm daily June-Aug., 10am-4pm daily May and Sept.-mid-Oct., adults $7, children $5), a restored water-powered mill built in 1877. This is where pioneer Similkameen Valley settlers used to grind locally produced wheat into flour. Costumed interpreters lead tours of the property, then invite you to try your hand at the many informative and entertaining hands-on displays in the museum and visitors center. A pleasant café overlooks garden plots carefully planted to reflect various eras (the $12 lunch is delicious) and also on the property is a **campground** ($20-30). To get there, go through town on the main highway, turn north on Highway 3A toward Penticton, then right at the Historic Site sign on Upper Bench Road.

Keremeos Columns

Another local highlight, although it takes some effort to reach, is **Keremeos Columns Provincial Park.** The park is named for a 90-meter (300-foot) cliff of remarkable hexagonal basalt columns rising from a lava base just outside the park boundary (the columns were supposed to be in the park, but because of a surveying accident actually stand on private land). Access the viewpoint by taking a steep eight-kilometer (5-mile) logging road off Highway 3 about four kilometers (2.5 miles) north of town (turn right at the Keremeos cemetery), then take another steep six-kilometer (3.7-mile) hike (allow at least two hours one-way) across private property; ask for permission from the Clifton family at the house at the end of the paved road.

Okanagan Valley

Highlights

★ **Nk'Mip Desert Cultural Centre:** Native history combined with walking trails through a very un-Canadian desert define this unique attraction (page 249).

★ **Covert Farms:** All ages will love this friendly family-operated farm, where you can pick your own fruits, taste organic wine, and shop in a country-style market (page 253).

★ **Naramata Wineries:** Not only do you get to enjoy fine wines at the vineyards near Naramata, the lake and mountain views are unparalleled (page 253).

★ **Summerland:** On a map of the Okanagan, Summerland is just a small dot with an enticing name. But this lakeside hamlet is home to one of the valley's finest wineries (Sumac Ridge) and the departure point for train rides along the Kettle Valley Steam Railway (page 259).

★ **Kalamalka Lake:** Choosing a favorite Okanagan lake is difficult, but my nod goes to Kalamalka Lake, between Kelowna and Vernon, for its beautiful hue, sandy beaches, and warm clear water (page 272).

★ **Silver Star Mountain Resort:** This resort has more than just great skiing and boarding; its gold rush-style buildings and a packed activity program make it a worthwhile destination at any time of year (page 274).

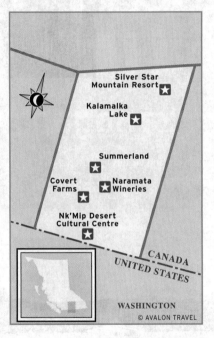

This warm, sunny valley 400 kilometers (250 miles) east of Vancouver extends 180 kilometers (112 miles) between the U.S.-Canada border in the south and the Trans-Canada Highway in the north.

Lush orchards and vineyards, fertile irrigated croplands, low rolling hills, and a string of beautiful lakes line the valley floor, where you'll also find 40 golf courses, dozens of commercial attractions, and lots and lots of people—especially in summer.

The Okanagan Valley's three main cities—Penticton, Kelowna, and Vernon—are spread around long, narrow Okanagan Lake. Numerous smaller communities also line the valley floor, doubling or tripling in size in July and August, when hordes of vacationers turn the valley into one big resort. Most of these summer pilgrims are Canadians from cooler climes, who come in search of guaranteed sunshine, lazy days on the beach, and a take-away tan. In winter, the valley draws pilgrims of another sort: skiers and snowboarders on their way to the world-class slopes flanking the valley.

All the credit for developing the Okanagan into Canada's fruit basket goes to the original planter, Charles Pandosy, a French oblate priest who established a mission in the Kelowna area in 1859. Within a couple of years he had successfully introduced apple trees to the district. The trees positively thrived under his care, thanks to the valley's long five-and-a-half-month growing season, over 2,000 hours of sunshine a year, relatively mild winters, and the ready availability of water. Soon fruit orchards of all types were springing up everywhere, and today the Okanagan Valley region produces 30 percent of Canada's apples, 60 percent of its cherries, 20 percent of its peaches, half of its pears and plums, and all the apricots in the country.

PLANNING YOUR TIME

Regardless of your approach to the Okanagan Valley, you'll spend time driving Highway 97, which is the main north-south thoroughfare. This highway passes through the four largest towns—from south to north Osoyoos,

Okanagan Valley

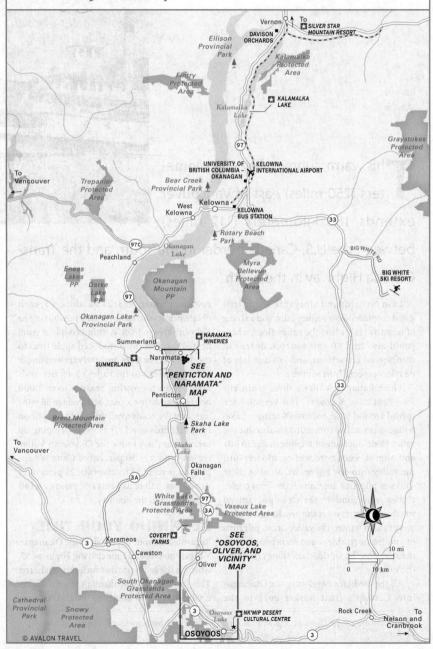

© AVALON TRAVEL

Penticton, Kelowna, and Vernon—closely parallels Okanagan Lake, and is rarely out of sight of an orchard or vineyard. It's a truly spectacular drive, but don't plan on doing it in one day. You could spend at least one day in and around each population center, mixing traditional sights such as the **Nk'Mip Desert Cultural Centre** at Osoyoos with winery tours (the **Naramata wineries** are a personal favorite), golf, and time out on the beaches. Younger children will revel in the many outdoor activities: exploring family-operated **Covert Farms,** relaxing at **Kalamalka Lake,** or getting back to nature in one of the many provincial parks.

If you have a beach-loving family in tow on your British Columbia vacation, the Okanagan Valley is the place to plan a break from the rigors of sightseeing. Use my accommodations recommendations in this chapter to choose a lodging that suits your needs and budget, and make reservations as far in advance as possible. Even if you haven't set your itinerary for the rest of your travels, having a few days' downtime to look forward to will make your vacation more enjoyable.

As in the rest of British Columbia, July-August is by far the busiest time of year in the Okanagan. This is when temperatures are at their highest and the waterways at their busiest. If you're planning on camping, reserve a spot as far in advance as possible, especially at commercial lakeside campgrounds. As a general rule, the summer weather will be hot and windy along the valley floor, with temperatures cooling off as you climb into the surrounding mountains. Take this into consideration if you don't like the heat, and plan on staying somewhere like **Beaver Lake Resort,** in the hills east of Kelowna, or **Silver Star Mountain Resort,** near Vernon.

Osoyoos and Vicinity

This town of 5,000 is nestled on the west shore of **Osoyoos Lake,** Canada's warmest freshwater lake (up to 24°C, 75°F in summer). The town itself also boasts Canada's highest year-round average temperature, so locals and visitors alike flock to the lakefront and **Gyro Community Park,** where a floating swimming pool provides the perfect spot for cooling off.

The town is in a desertlike setting, which is a feature of the two attractions detailed below, or you can take to the sagebrush-lined fairways of **Osoyoos Golf and Country Club** (Golf Course Rd., 250/495-3355, greens fees $63) for a very un-Canadian-like golfing experience.

SIGHTS
★ Nk'Mip Desert Cultural Centre

The Okanagan Indian Band, whose land spreads along the east side of the lake, is one of the most progressive in North America. They own and operate a number of very successful enterprises; among those most visible to visitors will be the winery, golf course, resort, and campground. Their culture is showcased at the **Nk'Mip Desert Cultural Centre** (1000 Rancher Creek Rd., 250/495-7901, 9:30am-4:30pm daily, adults $12, seniors $11, children $8), pronounced "in-KA-meep." Integrated with the surrounding desert, the main building is filled with displays telling the story of the First Nations people and their close relationship with the land. The documentary *Coyote Spirit,* shown regularly in a larger theater, is particularly endearing. There's also a display of desert critters. Outside, interpreters present various programs, including a rattlesnake show-and-talk. Walking trails lead through the desert to viewpoints and past various native structures, all with interpretive panels.

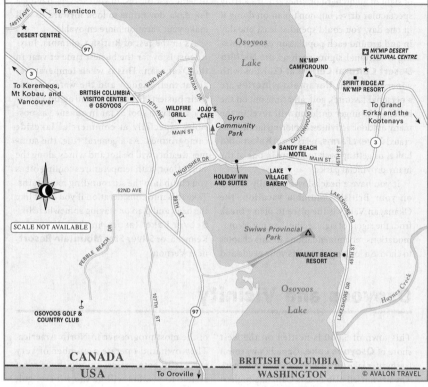

Osoyoos

To Penticton

146TH AVE

DESERT CENTRE

97

3

To Keremeos, Mt Kobau, and Vancouver

BRITISH COLUMBIA VISITOR CENTRE ■ @ OSOYOOS

92ND AVE

SPARTAN DR

76TH AVE

Osoyoos Lake

NK'MIP CAMPGROUND

★ **NK'MIP DESERT CULTURAL CENTRE**

■ **SPIRIT RIDGE AT NK'MIP RESORT**

COTTONWOOD DR

To Grand Forks and the Kootenays

3

WILDFIRE GRILL

JOJO'S CAFE

MAIN ST

Gyro Community Park

KINGFISHER DR

SANDY BEACH MOTEL

MAIN ST

45TH ST

HOLIDAY INN AND SUITES

LAKE VILLAGE BAKERY

62ND AVE

89TH ST

PEBBLE BEACH DR

SCALE NOT AVAILABLE

LAKESHORE DR

Swiws Provincial Park

WALNUT BEACH RESORT

45TH ST

Osoyoos Lake

LAKESHORE DR

Haynes Creek

107TH ST

97

OSOYOOS GOLF & COUNTRY CLUB

CANADA
USA
To Oroville ↓

BRITISH COLUMBIA
WASHINGTON
© AVALON TRAVEL

Desert Centre

Across the lake from Nk'Mip, a 100-hectare (250-acre) "pocket desert" has the distinction of being Canada's driest spot, receiving less than 300 millimeters (11 inches) of precipitation annually. It is a desert in the truest sense, complete with sand, cacti, prickly pears, sagebrush, lizards, scorpions, rattlesnakes, and other desert dwellers, including 23 invertebrates found nowhere else in the world. Learn more about this unique landscape at the **Desert Centre** (14580 146th Ave., 250/495-2470 or 877/899-0897, 10am-2pm daily late Apr.-June and Sept.-early Oct., 10am-4pm daily July-Aug., adults $7, seniors and children $6), a research and interpretive facility where a boardwalk leads through this very un-Canadian environment. To get there, follow Highway 97 north from Osoyoos and take 146th Avenue west.

Mount Kobau and Vicinity

For a bird's-eye view of the lake, take Highway 3 west from town 12 kilometers (7.5 miles), then follow a 20-kilometer (12-mile) gravel road to the 1,874-meter (6,150-foot) summit of **Mount Kobau.** Short trails there lead to viewpoints of the Similkameen and Okanagan Valleys. Along the section of Highway 3 before the turnoff, watch for **Spotted Lake,** a bizarre natural phenomenon on the south side of the road. As summer progresses and the lake's water evaporates, high concentrations of magnesium, calcium, and sodium crystallize, forming colorful circles.

FOOD

Walk down Main Street and take your pick from various cafés and the usual smattering of Italian and Chinese restaurants. At the bottom end of the main street, **Jojo's Cafe** (8316 Main St., 250/495-6652, 7am-4pm daily, lunch $6-10) features a good range of coffee concoctions in a modern setting, delicious breakfast sandwiches on English muffins, as well a daily lunch special ($6). On the east side of the lake, **Lake Village Bakery** (6511 Main St., 250/495-3364, 9am-4pm Wed.-Fri., 9am-3pm Sat.) bakes an amazing array of breads, as well as sweet treats like carrot cake and a seasonal pumpkin chai loaf.

Along the main street through downtown, the **Wildfire Grill** (8526 Main St., 250/495-2215, 11am-2pm and 5pm-9pm Mon.-Thurs., 11am-9pm Fri., 5pm-9pm Sat., $16-27) gives a contemporary take on traditional dishes and has a quiet patio out back. Across the lake, **Mica** is the signature restaurant at Spirit Ridge at Nk'Mip Resort (1200 Rancher Creek Rd., 250/495-5445, 9am-9pm daily, $15-33). Talk your way to an outdoor table overlooking the vineyard and lake to enjoy modern dishes prepared with local game and produce, such as free-range chicken breast slow-roasted in apple cider. In the adjacent building, the **Patio Restaurant** at Nk'Mip Cellars (11:30am-4pm daily late Apr.-mid-Oct., lunch $16-24) offers Pacific Northwest-inspired dishes and the same memorable views from tables that extend outdoors to a grassy embankment.

ACCOMMODATIONS

In summer, Osoyoos Lake attracts hordes of water lovers and sun worshippers, so getting accommodations can be difficult—especially along the prime stretch of lakefront east of downtown along Highway 3. You'll need to book well in advance to get a room during summer at the **Sandy Beach Motel** (6706 Ponderosa Dr., 250/495-6931 or 866/495-6931, www.sandybeachmotel.com, $169-299 s or d), but you'll be glad you did. Set on a private stretch of sandy beach, the 25 kitchen-equipped units (most with two bedrooms) face a grassy courtyard, landscaped with crushed gravel pathways and cacti. Along the same stretch, but larger and less personal, is **Holiday Inn & Suites** (7906 Main St., 250/495-7223 or 877/786-7773, www.ihg.com, $189 s or d), with many of the 85 rooms overlooking the resort's sandy beach. The resort also has an indoor pool, a fitness center, and two restaurants.

★ **Spirit Ridge at Nk'Mip Resort** (1200 Rancher Creek Rd., 250/495-5445 or

Osoyoos Golf and Country Club

844/755-4622, www.spiritridge.ca, from $275 s or d) is part of the Nk'Mip development, overlooking Osoyoos Lake across the water from town. This self-contained resort includes the Nk'Mip cultural center, a golf course, a winery, two outdoor heated pool complexes, a day spa, multiple restaurants, and a small section of private beach easily reached on foot through the vineyard. The spacious guest rooms have modern kitchens, wireless Internet, and TV-DVD combos, and most have separate bedrooms. It's worth paying extra for a lake view. Nearby, **Walnut Beach Resort** (4200 Lakeshore Dr., 250/495-5400 or 877/936-5400, www.walnutbeachresort.com, $269-509 s or d) is a similar but smaller complex, with studio, one-, and two-bedroom self-contained units set around a lakefront pool area. Having stayed at both places, I'd recommend the former for a romantic getaway and the latter for a family vacation.

Enjoy fresh berries at Covert Farms.

Camping

Formerly known as Haynes Point, **Swiws Provincial Park** (off 32nd Ave., Apr.-early Oct., $32) protects an extremely narrow low-lying spit that juts into Osoyoos Lake south of downtown. At the far end of the spit is a beautiful campground, with many sites enjoying lakefront settings. But with just 41 sites, you'll need reservations, which are taken mid-May to August through **Discover Camping** (519/826-6850 or 800/689-9025, www.discovercamping.ca). Like most other provincial parks, Haynes Point has no showers or hookups, so if you need more amenities, consider **Nk'Mip Campground** (8000 45th St., 250/495-7279, www.campingosoyoos.com, $48-60). This campground, almost directly opposite downtown Osoyoos, has some sites set along the lake and offers its own private beach and a lakeside café.

INFORMATION

In a parking lot at the corner of Highways 3 and 97 is the **British Columbia Visitor Centre@Osoyoos** (9912 Hwy. 3, 250/495-7142 or 888/676-9667, www. destinationosoyoos.com, 9am-6pm daily summer, Mon.-Fri. fall-spring), set up for travelers arriving in the province from the nearby U.S. border crossing, but with loads of local and Okanagan information.

Getting There

Osoyoos is at the southern end of the Okanagan Valley at the junction of Highway 97, which leads north to Penticton (63 kilometers/39 miles), and Highway 3, which leads west to Vancouver (400 kilometers /250 miles, allow 5 hours) and east to Nelson (260 kilometers /163 miles, allow 3 hours).

NORTH TOWARD PENTICTON

It's an easy hour's drive north from Osoyoos to Penticton, but there are a number of food-and-wine-related stops along the way. The main town of note is **Oliver,** with a main street lined by interesting shops and a spring-fed lake that attracts hordes of sun-loving locals through summer.

★ Covert Farms

Tucked out of sight from travelers zooming along Highway 97 is **Covert Farms** (300 Covert Place, off Seacrest Rd., 250/498-9463, 9am-3pm Tues.-Sat. June, 9am-5pm daily July-Aug., 9am-4pm Wed.-Sun. Sept.), which has been owned and operated by the Covert family since the early 1960s. The focus for most visitors (and the many locals who swear by the Coverts' quality and prices) is the on-site market and wine lounge, which is filled with produce, ranging from corn to melons, all picked fresh daily and farmed organically. A section of the farm is set aside for U-pick customers, trails lead out into and around the farm, and a picnic area encourages visitors to linger a little longer. Or take a 1.5-hour farm tour in a classic 1952 Mercury one-ton truck (adults $59, children $20), which includes a private wine tasting. Look for the Covert Farms sign at the base of Seacrest Road, eight kilometers (5 miles) north of Oliver.

Wineries

Over 20 wineries around Oliver are open for tours and tastings. Overlooking the north end of Osoyoos Lake is **LaStella** (8123 148th Ave., 250/495-8180, 11am-5pm daily mid-Mar.-Oct.), where quality trumps quantity and the ambience is very Italian. On the east side of the Okanagan River between Osoyoos and Oliver is the Black Sage Bench region, renowned for its premium Bordeaux-style grapes. Of many wineries off Black Sage Road, two stand out for very different approaches to winemaking. **Stoneboat Vineyards** (356 Orchard Grove Lane, 250/498-2226, 10am-5:30pm daily May-mid-Oct.) is a welcoming family-run operation that opened in 2007. Operated by the Martiniuks and their three sons, it has a small tasting room where the pinot noir gets rave reviews (and usually sells out by the end of the summer season). To the south, **Burrowing Owl Estate Winery** (500 Burrowing Owl Place, 250/498-0620, 10am-5pm daily early Mar.-early Dec.) is a much larger operation, with a large tasting room, guided tours, a restaurant, and accommodations. Visitors can climb the bell tower for sweeping valley views.

Penticton

One of the Okanagan's three major population centers, Penticton (pop. 34,000) lies between the north end of Skaha Lake and the south end of Okanagan Lake. Approaching from the south, you'll see a roadside plaque honoring pioneer Thomas Ellis, who arrived in the valley in 1886, built a great cattle empire, and planted the area's first orchard. Today fruit orchards are everywhere, and Penticton's nickname is Peach City.

★ NARAMATA WINERIES

Like many other rural routes through the Okanagan, Naramata Road, running northeast from Penticton for 14 kilometers (9 miles), passes row after row of grape vines grown by over 20 well-respected wineries. The bonus to visiting this concentration of vineyards are the stunning views across Okanagan Lake to the mountains beyond, making tours, tastings, and outdoor lunches extra enjoyable.

The first of many well-respected wineries along the way is the **Red Rooster Winery** (891 Naramata Rd., 250/492-2424, 10am-6pm daily May-mid-Oct., lunches $15-28), easily recognized by the mission-style tasting room beside the highway. Enjoy a tasting session of the winery's award-winning pinot gris and chardonnay wines, then soak up the lake views over a cheese platter or grilled beef on the veranda of the winery's **Pecking Room Patio Grill** (noon-5pm Fri.-Sun. May-mid-Oct.).

Also notable for the scenic setting is the aptly named **Hillside Estate** (1350 Naramata Rd., 250/493-6274, 11am-6pm daily), with an

Penticton

Okanagan
Lake

Riverside
Park

To ✚NARAMATA
WINERIES, and
Naramata

SS SICAMOUS
PENTICTON
LAKESIDE RESORT

PENTICTON
ART GALLERY

PRAGUE
CAFÉ

SALTY'S BEACH
HOUSE

LAKESHORE DR

PENTICTON
FARMERS
MARKET

VANCOUVER

ROSE
GARDEN

SPANISH VILLA
RESORT

POST OFFICE

▼DREAM
CAFÉ

RIVERSIDE
MOTEL

WESTMINSTER AVE

HI-PENTICTON

BRUNSWICK ST

BUS DEPOT

COYOTE
CRUISES

GOVERNMENT ST

RAMADA INN &
SUITES

To
Kelowna

ECKHARDT AVE

WINE COUNTRY
VISITOR CENTRE

MARTIN ST

WINNIPEG ST

THEO'S
RESTAURANT

Okanagan River
River Channel

RAILWAY AVE

★ PENTICTON
MUSEUM

MAIN ST

To
Apex
Mountain Resort

WALLA ARTISAN
BAKERY & CAFÉ
▼

FAIRVIEW RD

INDUSTRIAL AVE

GREEN MOUNTAIN RD

KINNEY AVE

CHANNEL PKWY

SKAHA LAKE RD

SCALE NOT AVAILABLE

PENTICTON
AIRPORT
✕

To
Osoyoos
and Vancouver

97

WRIGHT'S BEACH
CAMP RV RESORT

Skaha
Park

MARINA

Skaha
Lake

© AVALON TRAVEL

impressive three-story wooden building holding the main winery. Hillside is known for its pinot noir, but it also produces an unusually dry but fruity riesling. The winery bistro is open for lunch and dinner Wednesday to Sunday, with lots of outdoor seating and sweeping vineyard and lake views.

SIGHTS

The emphasis in Penticton is on sun and sand, but there's also a little history to explore at **Penticton Museum** (785 Main St., 250/490-2454, 10am-5pm Tues.-Sat., donation), where eight display areas highlight the region's past, starting with a geology lesson and ending with how the city sees its future.

Wander along the tree-shaded shores of Lake Okanagan to see the **SS *Sicamous*** (1099 Lakeshore Dr. W., 250/492-0403, 7am-7pm daily summer, noon-4pm Thurs.-Sun. fall-spring, adults $6, seniors $5, children $3). This Canadian Pacific Railway stern-wheeler operated on Lake Okanagan from 1914 to 1936. Now it rests on the lakeshore, and it's easy to spend an hour wandering through the ship, peeking into the purser's office, admiring the furnishings in the grand dining room, and clambering up to the observation deck.

At the opposite end of Lakeshore Drive (to the east) is **Penticton Art Gallery** (199 Marina Way, 250/493-2928, 10am-5pm Tues.-Fri., 11am-4pm Sat.-Sun., adults $2, free Sat.-Sun.). The craft shop is a good place to pick up creative treasures and handmade souvenirs. Continue east from the gallery to the local **marina**—another enjoyable spot for a lakeside stroll.

RECREATION

Sandwiched between two lakes, Penticton has two distinct beaches—one at each end of town. **Okanagan Lake Beach** stretches along Lakeshore Drive, bookended by the SS *Sicamous* to the west and Penticton Lake Resort in the east. It boasts floating slides and pontoons, while behind the beach are a number of cafés with lots of outdoor seating. At the south end of town is **Skaha**

Okanagan Wines

Okanagan wines receive acclaim worldwide, although this success is only recent. In fact, it was doubted that quality grapes could be grown north of the 49th parallel until the late 1980s, when the Canada-United States Free Trade Agreement (now NAFTA) forced local vintners to revisit their quality control. As a result, most of the original hybrid vines were ripped out and replaced with classic European varietals.

The valley's climate—long summer days and cool nights—produces small grapes with a higher-than-usual sugar content, creating intensely flavored and aromatic wines. A wide variety of red and white wine grapes are planted, with the reds thriving in the warmer south end of the valley, where merlot, cabernet franc, and pinot noir grapes produce the best local wines. The entire wine-making process in the Okanagan has been one of experimentation, and along the way more unusual varietals such as ehrenfelser and auxerrois have been grown with success, which makes tasting local wines all the more interesting.

The best introduction to the valley's vino offerings is the **Wine Country Visitor Centre** (553 Vees Dr., Penticton, 250/276-2170, 9am-5pm daily). As much a wine shop as anything else, it offers plenty of information along with wine tour maps and knowledgeable staff to set you off in the right direction.

Lake, where the beach is wider and less protected from the wind, but with water that is slightly warmer. The two beaches are linked by the seven-kilometer-long (4-mile) **River Channel.** On a hot summer day, the channel attracts thousands of people, who float its length from a launch point near Okanagan Lake, taking one to two hours to reach the main pullout point at Green Mountain Road. At the launch point is **Coyote Cruises** (215 Riverside Dr., 250/492-1115, www.coyote-cruises.ca, 10am-5pm daily summer), which rents inner tubes ($6), supplies air ($2), and offers bus transfers back from the south end of the channel ($6).

Apex Mountain Resort (250/292-8222 or 877/777-2739, www.apexresort.com, adults $80, seniors $66, children $50), 31 kilometers (19 miles) west of Penticton, provides 605 vertical meters (1,990 feet) and 56 runs over 450

Okanagan Lake Beach

hectares (1,100 acres). The slopes are served by a T-bar and two chairlifts, one of which—the Quickdraw Express—zips skiers and boarders to the summit of Beaconsfield Mountain and opens up most of the expert terrain. Boarders are catered to with a terrain park and half-pipe, or you can slide downhill on an inflatable tube in the tube park.

Events

Penticton seems to have festivals, parades, events, or competitions going on throughout the year. The biggest event is the **Penticton Peach Festival** (250/487-9709, www.peachfest.com), best known as Peachfest, held on the first full weekend of August; it's a tradition going back to 1947. Events include a parade along Lakeshore Drive, the crowning of Miss Penticton, Kiddies Day (the Sunday), a sandcastle contest, a beachfront midway, and nightly entertainment in Gyro Park.

Other annual happenings include the **Spring Okanagan Wine Festival** (250/861-6654, www.thewinefestivals.com), hosted by many local wineries in late April; and the **Pentastic Jazz Festival** (www.pentastic-jazz.com), the second weekend of September, at venues through town, including aboard the SS *Sicamous*.

FOOD

Penticton has a wide variety of restaurants spread along the beach and through downtown. If you're in town on Saturday, head to the northern end of Main Street to the **Penticton Farmers Market** (8:30am-1pm Sat. Apr.-Oct.) for lots of local produce and baking.

★ **Bench Market** (368 Vancouver Ave., 250/492-2222, 7am-5pm Mon.-Fri. 8am-5pm Sat.-Sun., lunch $6-9) is a great place to enjoy healthy breakfasts such as granola made in-house and topped with Okanagan honey. Soups, paninis, and salads are all made fresh daily, and there are a few picnic tables out front for warmer weather. The café is part grocery store, with lots of Okanagan produce to purchase.

In the vicinity of Bench Market, and overlooking the lake, the **Prague Cafe** (250 Marina Way, 778/476-0440, 8am-4pm daily, lunch $6-8) is a small space, but many diners enjoy their meal in the green space out front. The menu is limited to a few simple breakfast choices, European-style breads and pastries, and lunches such as a beef baguette, but everything is tasty and well-priced.

Well worth searching out for innovative and healthy food is **Walla Artisan Bakery &**

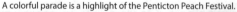

A colorful parade is a highlight of the Penticton Peach Festival.

Cafe (1475 Fairview Rd., 250/770-2001, 8am-3pm Wed.-Fri., lunch $12-25), part bakery, part Middle Eastern café, but the combination works well in this nondescript location. Ordering breakfast is easy—go for the french toast, which is drizzled with real maple syrup. Lunch can be as simple as soup made in-house from scratch or as filling as osso buco. You can also pick up delicious Mediterranean-style breads and filled focaccia sandwiches to go.

One of my favorite casual dining spots in Penticton is **Dream Café** (67 Front St., 250/490-9012, www.thedreamcafe.ca, 10am-2pm Sat., from 6pm on event nights, $13-20), away from the water but with a dreamy ambience (think eclectic furniture, colorful kites hanging from the ceiling, and soothing background music), friendly staff, and innovative cuisine. It's only open on Saturday and for live evening musical performances. Both the Saturday brunch menu and the evening menu take inspiration from throughout Asia and steers clear of red meat: poached lime chicken salad, salmon spinach pie, rice noodle wraps, Alaskan crab cakes, and tandoori chicken. Check the website for an entertainment schedule.

Across the road from the beach along the busy downtown tourist strip is **Salty's Beach House** (1000 Lakeshore Dr., 250/493-5001, 11am-10pm daily, $14-30), with tables inside and out. The menu blends conventional pub fare with Thai and Caribbean cuisine, such as pistachio-crusted mahimahi and a tandoori pizza topped with mango chutney and cilantro. The fruity drink menu befits the location.

On Main Street between Okanagan and Skaha Lakes are several decent eateries. At **Theo's Restaurant** (687 Main St., 250/492-4019, 11am-9pm Mon.-Sat., 4pm-9pm Sun., $17-33) you can tuck into European favorites such as lamb moussaka or wine-marinated calamari in an older open-plan eatery.

ACCOMMODATIONS AND CAMPING

In July and August, you'll need to make reservations far in advance to snag a room at any of Penticton's beachfront motels. A good summer alternative is Apex Mountain Resort, 31 kilometers (19 miles) west of Penticton, where on-hill lodgings provide steeply discounted rooms for visitors looking to escape the busy valley floor. Check the resort's website (www.apexresort.com) for packages.

Under $50

As you'd expect in a resort town, the only lodging under $50 is in a dormitory. **HI-Penticton** (464 Ellis St., 250/492-3992, www.hihostels.ca, dorm $34, $78 s or d) occupies a 1908 stucco residence close to the heart of downtown. Facilities include a kitchen, laundry, bike rentals, Internet access, and an outdoor barbecue area. Check-in is 8am-noon and 5pm-10pm.

$100-150

Village Motel (244 Robinson Dr., Naramata, 250/496-5535, www.villagemotel.com, $138-158 s or d) will bring back memories of a bygone era. Located in the village of Naramata, 14 kilometers (9 miles) north of Penticton, the nine older guest rooms are nicely decorated and open to landscaped gardens and a communal barbecue area. Some have basic kitchens.

The **Riverside Motel** (110 Riverside Dr., 250/492-2615, www.riversidemotel.ca, $135-185 s or d) is a two-minute walk from the sandy beaches of Okanagan Lake, but a large outdoor pool surrounded by lounge chairs keeps many guests close to home. The rooms are older, but spacious and comfortable, with most having kitchenettes. Other amenities include barbecues and laundry.

$150-200

Best value of several lodgings on Lakeshore Drive, across from Okanagan Lake Beach, is the **Spanish Villa Resort** (890 Lakeshore Dr., 250/492-2922 or 800/552-9199, www.spanishvillaresort.ca, $165-225). Some units have a kitchen and separate bedrooms, and there are communal barbecues and an indoor pool.

A few blocks back from the beach, **Ramada Inn & Suites** (1050 Eckhardt Ave. W., 250/492-8926 or 800/665-4966, www. pentictonramada.com, from $189 s or d) is a family-friendly self-contained resort adjacent to an 18-hole golf course. Amenities include an outdoor pool, a sprawling courtyard, a playground, a fitness center, a restaurant with poolside service, and a stylish pub. The rooms are decorated in smart color schemes and are air-conditioned.

$200-250

For the atmosphere of an old-fashioned resort, it's difficult to surpass the ★ **Naramata Heritage Inn & Spa** (3625 1st St., Naramata, 250/496-6808 or 866/617-1188, www.naramatainn.com, mid-Apr.-Oct., $198-448 s, $218-448 d), north of Penticton along the east side of the lake. Dating to 1908, the hotel has been completely renovated, yet none of its historic appeal has been lost. The guest rooms have mission-style beds covered with plush duvets, baths with heated floors and claw-foot tubs, and either a balcony or a patio. Other amenities include spa services and a wine bar-restaurant with occasional live blues or jazz.

Camping

South of downtown, **Wright's Beach Camp RV Park** (4200 Skaha Lake Rd., 250/492-7120, www.wrightsbeachcamp.com, mid-Mar.-mid-Oct., $49-68) is right on the lake and has a huge playground and an outdoor pool.

If being by the lake isn't important, choose to stay at **Twin Lakes Golf & RV Resort** (79 Twin Lakes Rd., 250/497-8379, www.twin-lakesgolfresort.com, Apr.-Sept., $40-46), 19 kilometers (12 miles) southwest of Penticton. The campground is in the middle of a full-length golf course (greens fees $45-65, for campers $40-60), which is surrounded by barren cliffs. Amenities include modern restrooms, free firewood, a restaurant, and a lounge. A five-minute drive west of the campground, you can fish from the banks of Yellow Lake for brook trout and perch. To get to Twin Lakes, head south from Penticton and turn west off Highway 97 at Kaleden. If you're traveling east from Princeton, turn off Highway 3 at Keremeos.

INFORMATION AND SERVICES

Wine Country Visitor Centre (553 Railway Ave., 250/493-4055 or 800/663-5052, www. tourismpenticton.com, 9am-5pm daily) is well worth searching out. Inside the adobe-style structure are free Internet access, a wine information center, and lots of local literature. **Penticton Regional Hospital** is on Carmi Avenue (250/492-4000). The post office is on the corner of Winnipeg Street and Nanaimo Avenue.

GETTING THERE

On Highway 97, Penticton is 63 kilometers (39 miles) north of Osoyoos and 64 kilometers (40 miles) south of Kelowna. The most direct route to Penticton from Vancouver is to head east on Highway 3 and then take Highway 3A north from Keremeos. Total distance is just over 400 kilometers (250 miles), but you should allow around five hours as the going is slow through mountain passes.

Although Penticton has the small **Penticton Airport,** most visitors flying into the Okanagan area use Kelowna Airport, to the north, where they pick up rental cars. The **Greyhound Bus Depot** (307 Ellis St., 250/493-4101) is busy with services heading south to Osoyoos and north through the Okanagan Valley to Salmon Arm on the Trans-Canada Highway.

NORTH OF PENTICTON

Highway 97 links Penticton and Kelowna, running along the west side of Okanagan Lake for the entire 64 kilometers (40 miles). The first worthwhile stop is tiny **Sun-Oka Beach Provincial Park,** a sun-drenched, south-facing park with a sandy beach, paddleboat rentals, and a concession (but no camping).

★ Summerland

As you enter picturesque Summerland (population 11,000), nestled between Giants Head Mountain and the lake 16 kilometers (10 miles) north of Penticton, it's hard not to be charmed by the beach, the vineyards, and the rows of trim homes.

Turn west (away from the lake) at either of the stoplights and follow the signs to Prairie Valley Station, the departure point for **Kettle Valley Steam Railway** (250/494-8422 or 877/494-8424, www.kettlevalleyrail.org, adults $22, seniors $20, children $13). This steam train, dating to the early 1900s, runs along a historic 10-kilometer (6-mile) stretch of track through orchards and vineyards and over a 75-meter-high (246-foot) trestle bridge. Departures are at 10:30am and 1:30pm Saturday-Monday late May-mid-October, with additional trips Thursday-Friday in July-August.

Two stops in town are worthwhile for foodies. **Summerland Sweets** (6206 Canyon View Rd., 250/494-0377, 9:30am-6pm Mon.-Fri., 10am-6pm Sat.-Sun.), on the south side of town, produce their own syrups, jams, and candy from local fruits and sells them on-site at their factory. To get there, take Arkell Road west from Highway 97 and follow the signs. In the heart of downtown, **True Grain** (10108 Main St., 250/494-4244, 8am-5pm Tues.-Sat.) bakes organic handcrafted breads and pastries, but also pours expertly blended coffee.

Through Summerland to the north, **Sumac Ridge Estate** (17403 Hwy. 97N, 250/494-0451, 10am-6pm daily July-Aug., 10am-5pm daily Sept.-June) was British Columbia's first estate winery. Today, this well-recognized name appears on a wide variety of red and white wines, including an award-winning cabernet franc and one of the Okanagan's few sparkling wines. Tours and tastings are offered three times daily May-mid-October, and a bistro is open for lunch (daily year-round) and dinner (daily summer).

Continuing Toward Kelowna

On the way to Kelowna, you pass two entrances to grassy, beach-fringed **Okanagan Lake Provincial Park,** popular for boating and swimming. Ponderosa pines line the shore, while exotic trees such as maple and oak shade dozens of picnic tables. The park has two **campgrounds** (519/826-6850 or 800/689-9025, www.discovercamping.ca, late Mar.-mid-Oct., $35) with showers.

Farther along is the community of **Peachland.** Crammed between a rocky bluff and Okanagan Lake, Peachland was founded in 1908 by Manitoba entrepreneur and newspaperman John Robinson, who came to the Okanagan in search of mining prospects but turned his talents to developing the delicious locally grown dessert peaches. The drive through downtown is a pleasant diversion from Highway 97. On one side are the lake and a long pebbly beach dotted with grassed areas of parkland and supervised swimming areas. On the other is a collection of shops and cafés.

Kelowna

British Columbia's largest city outside the Lower Mainland and Victoria, Kelowna (pronounced kuh-LOW-nah, pop. 130,000) lies on the shores of 170-kilometer-long (106-mile) Okanagan Lake, approximately halfway between Penticton in the south and Vernon in the north. The city combines a scenic location among semiarid mountains with an unbeatable climate of long sunny summers and short mild winters. The low rolling hills around the city hold lush terraced orchards, and the numerous local vineyards produce some excellent wines. Visitors flock here in summer to enjoy the area's warm water, sandy beaches, numerous provincial parks, and golfing; in winter they come for great skiing and boarding at nearby Big White Ski Resort.

For thousands of years before the arrival of the first Europeans, the nomadic Salish people inhabited the Okanagan Valley, hunting (*kelowna* is a Salish word for grizzly bear), gathering, and fishing. The first European to settle in the valley was an oblate missionary, Father Pandosy, who established a mission in 1859. Since the first apple trees were planted at the mission, Kelowna has thrived as the center of the Okanagan fruit, vegetable, and vineyard industry (the valley is Canada's largest fruit-growing region).

SIGHTS

Along the waterfront, **City Park** is the largest of Kelowna's many parks. Its 14 hectares (35 acres) hold lots of flowers and large shady trees, expansive lawns, and a long sandy beach. You can rent a boat, houseboat, and fishing equipment at one of several marinas. Near the entrance to the park is the large and sparkling-white attention-grabbing Dow Reid sculpture *Sails,* as well as a replica of the famed lake-dwelling serpent, Ogopogo.

A promenade leads north from the Ogopogo statue past a large marina and a prime waterfront site undergoing redevelopment. Beyond the construction is the **Delta Hotels by Marriott Grand Okanagan Resort,** one of the Okanagan's most luxurious accommodations. Even if you can't afford a lakefront suite, the resort holds a bar and restaurant with water views and full spa

The marina is a good starting point for a walking tour of Kelowna.

Benvoulin Heritage Park

services. Beyond the resort, the promenade crosses a small lock, which allows boaters to travel between the higher water level of an artificial lagoon and the lake itself.

Okanagan Heritage Museum (470 Queensway Ave., 250/763-2417, 10am-5pm Mon.-Sat., donation) is opposite the post office. The museum holds a mishmash of fascinating displays, including horse-drawn carriages; fossils found in the Princeton area; indigenous arts, crafts, clothing, jewelry, beads, and furs; children's books and games; radio equipment; pioneer artifacts; re-creations of an 1861 Kelowna trading post and a Chinese store; and a display of the interior of a Salish winter dwelling. Behind the museum are the **Kasugai Gardens.** Built with the cooperation of Kelowna's Japanese sister city, Kasugai, the gardens are a quiet retreat from the downtown business district; admission is free, and the gates are locked at dusk.

In an old downtown packing house that saw renovations completed in 2016, complete with exposed redbrick walls and hand-hewn wooden beams, the **Okanagan Wine and Orchard Museum** (1304 Ellis St., 250/763-0433, 10am-5pm Tues.-Sat., 11am-4pm Sun., donation) tells the story of the local orchard and wine industries through rare photographs, displays, and a hands-on discovery corner.

Benvoulin Heritage Park (east of downtown at 2279 Benvoulin Rd., dawn-dusk daily) surrounds the Gothic-revival Benvoulin Church, which dates to 1892. The church and a historic residence also within the grounds are closed to the public, but the xeriscape garden, designed to take advantage of the local climate and environment, holds the most interest. In this case, plants grown here require little moisture, reflecting problems encountered by professional and amateur gardeners along the entire valley.

Farther south along Benvoulin Road is the **Father Pandosy Mission** (3685 Benvoulin Rd., 8am-dusk daily, donation), the site of the mission established by oblate priest Father Pandosy in 1859. He operated a church, a school, and a farm here, ministering to First Nations people and settlers until his death in 1891. His mission claimed a lot of firsts: the first nonindigenous settlement in the Okanagan Valley, the first school in the valley, the first fruit and vine crops in the valley, and the first Roman Catholic mission in the BC interior. Not much has changed within the broken-down wooden fences that hold the mission—four of the eight buildings onsite date to Pandosy's era, including a chapel and barn.

WINERIES

Viticulture has been a mainstay of the Okanagan's economy for almost a century, but it has really taken off in the last two decades, with local wines exported and winning awards worldwide. Most of the local wineries welcome visitors with tours and free tastings year-round (but call ahead outside summer to check hours). Because of the popularity of visiting the wineries, most charge a small fee for tasting. **Okanagan Wine Country Tours**

Kelowna

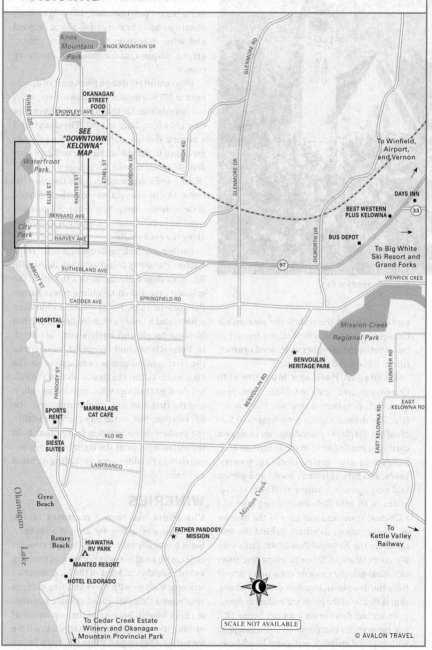

Knox
Mountain
Park

KNOX MOUNTAIN DR

SUNSET DR

CROWLEY AVE

OKANAGAN
STREET
FOOD

SEE
"DOWNTOWN
KELOWNA"
MAP

Waterfront
Park

ELLIS ST

RICHTER ST

ETHEL ST

GORDON DR

HIGH RD

GLENMORE RD

GLENMORE DR

DILWORTH DR

To Winfield,
Airport,
and Vernon

DAYS INN

BEST WESTERN
PLUS KELOWNA

33

BUS DEPOT

To Big White
Ski Resort and
Grand Forks

WENRICK CRES

BERNARD AVE

City
Park

HARVEY AVE

SUTHERLAND AVE

97

ABBOTT ST

CADDER AVE

SPRINGFIELD RD

HOSPITAL

Mission Creek
Regional Park

DUNSTER RD

BENVOULIN RD

BENVOULIN
HERITAGE PARK

PANDOSY ST

EAST
KELOWNA RD

SPORTS
RENT

MARMALADE
CAT CAFE

KLO RD

EAST KELOWNA RD

SIESTA
SUITES

LANFRANCO

Okanagan Lake

Gyro
Beach

Mission Creek

Rotary
Beach

HIAWATHA
RV PARK

FATHER PANDOSY
MISSION

To
Kettle Valley
Railway

MANTEO RESORT

HOTEL ELDORADO

To Cedar Creek Estate
Winery and Okanagan
Mountain Provincial Park

SCALE NOT AVAILABLE

© AVALON TRAVEL

Downtown Kelowna

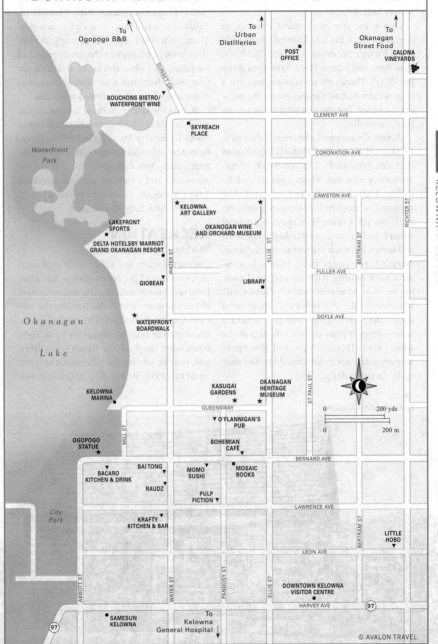

To
Ogopogo B&B

To
Urban
Distilleries

To
Okanagan
Street Food

SUNSET DR

POST
OFFICE

CALONA
VINEYARDS

BOUCHONS BISTRO/
WATERFRONT WINE

CLEMENT AVE

SKYREACH
PLACE

CORONATION AVE

RICHTER ST

Waterfront
Park

CAWSTON AVE

KELOWNA
ART GALLERY

OKANOGAN WINE
AND ORCHARD MUSEUM

ELLIS ST

BERTRAM ST

LAKEFRONT
SPORTS

DELTA HOTELSBY MARRIOT
GRAND OKANAGAN RESORT

FULLER AVE

WATER ST

GIOBEAN

LIBRARY

WATERFRONT
BOARDWALK

DOYLE AVE

Okanagan

Lake

ST PAUL ST

KELOWNA
MARINA

KASUGAI
GARDENS

OKANAGAN
HERITAGE
MUSEUM

QUEENSWAY

0   200 yds

0   200 m

OGOPOGO
STATUE

O'FLANNIGAN'S
PUB

BOHEMIAN
CAFÉ

MILL ST

BERNARD AVE

BACARO
KITCHEN & DRINK

BAI TONG

RAUDZ

MOMO
SUSHI

PULP
FICTION

MOSAIC
BOOKS

LAWRENCE AVE

City
Park

KRAFTY
KITCHEN & BAR

BERTRAM ST

LITTLE
HOBO

LEON AVE

ABBOTT ST

WATER ST

PANDOSY ST

ELLIS ST

DOWNTOWN KELOWNA
VISITOR CENTRE

97

HARVEY AVE

97

SAMESUN
KELOWNA

To
Kelowna
General Hospital

© AVALON TRAVEL

OKANAGAN VALLEY

KELOWNA

(250/868-9463, www.okwinetours.com) has a variety of tours, including a four-hour, four-winery tour ($99 pp).

One of the province's oldest wineries, in operation since 1932, is **Calona Vineyards** (1125 Richter St., downtown, 250/762-9144, 9am-6pm daily June-Dec., 9am-4pm daily Jan.-May). There's no actual vineyard, just a large winery that uses grapes grown throughout the valley. Tastings and sales are in a room set up as a cellar.

Across Okanagan Lake from Kelowna is **Mission Hill Family Estate** (1730 Mission Hill Rd., Westbank, 250/768-6448, 10am-6pm daily summer, 11pm-6pm daily fall-spring), high atop a ridge and surrounded by vineyards with stunning lake views. Mission Hill, British Columbia's most successful winery, includes a 45-meter-high (148-foot) bell tower, open for visitors to climb. Tours depart three times daily through summer, each ending with an informal tasting session. At nearby **Quail's Gate** (3303 Boucherie Rd., 250/769-4451, 10am-6pm daily), the reserve pinot noir is a signature wine—enjoy a glass or two alfresco at the winery bistro (11am-2:30pm and 5pm-9pm). Winery tours are conducted May-October up to six times daily.

Back on the main highway and farther south is **Hainle Vineyards Estate Winery** (5355 Trepanier Bench Rd., Peachland, 250/212-5944, 11am-5pm daily summer, 11am-5pm Mon.-Fri. fall-spring). Walter Hainle was a pioneer in the development of ice wines, and while this is the style that the vineyard is best known for, limited quantities of red and white wines are also produced.

Across the lake from these wineries is the much-heralded **Cedar Creek Estate Winery** (5445 Lakeshore Dr., 250/764-8866, 11am-6pm daily May-June, 10am-7pm daily July-Sept., 11am-5pm daily Oct.-Apr.), where the vineyards and extensive gardens overlook Lake Okanagan. Tours are offered at 11am, 1pm, and 3pm daily May-August.

RECREATION
Water Sports

During the warm and sunny months of summer, Okanagan Lake comes alive with a colorful array of watercraft, anglers, and swimmers out on the water, and sunbathers dot the surrounding sandy beaches. The busiest spot is the stretch of sand fronting City Park, right downtown. Beyond the beach's northern end, you can rent watercraft from **Lakefront Sports** (1310 Water St., 250/862-2469,

Father Pandosy Mission

The Okanagan Lake Monster

Ogopogo is the friendly Loch Ness-style sea serpent that allegedly lives on the bottom of "bottomless" Okanagan Lake. Local indigenous people told the first European settlers who came to live in the Okanagan Valley that a fast-swimming monster called N'ha-a-tik, meaning "devil of the lake," lived in a deep part of the lake near present-day Kelowna. Whenever they had to canoe near that particular point, they unceremoniously threw an animal overboard as a sacrifice.

Since 1942, when the mysterious monster became known as Ogopogo, there have been thousands of alleged sightings, and the creature has been the subject of feature stories on the television shows *Unsolved Mysteries* and *Inside Edition*. Consensus is that Ogopogo is a snakelike creature with small humps, green skin, and a nice big smile—the latter feature confirmed by enterprising locals who print his image on T-shirts, posters, and postcards.

Although many times a prize has been put up for anyone providing definitive proof of Ogopogo's existence—the most recent is $2 million—no one has yet claimed the reward. But keep your eyes open and your camera at hand; you just never know, you may be one of the few (sober) ones to spot him.

10am-6pm daily May-Oct.), in front of the Delta Hotels by Marriott Grand Okanagan Resort, including canoes and kayaks ($25-35 per hour), stand-up paddleboards ($45 for 2 hours), Jet Skis ($138 per hour), and small motorboats ($259 for 2 hours).

Gyro Beach and adjacent **Rotary Beach** are beautiful stretches of sand south of downtown along Lakeshore Drive. Less crowded are the beaches in **Okanagan Mountain Provincial Park,** farther south.

Sports Rent (2936 Pandosy St., 250/861-5699, 8am-8pm daily summer, 10am-6pm daily fall-spring) rents kayaks, wetsuits, bikes, and winter sports equipment.

Hiking and Biking

The **Kettle Valley Railway** bed, which winds around the back of Kelowna, may be protected as a national historic site, but unfortunately nothing could protect its 18 trestle bridges from the wildfires in 2003. Plans are in place to have them rebuilt, but until then, opportunities for extended trips along the rail bed are somewhat limited. It's still an interesting spot, well worth the effort to reach. To get here, take K.L.O. Road to McCulloch Road, turn south (right) and then south (right) again, following Myra Forest Service Road for 8.5 kilometers (5.3 miles). From the parking lot at this point,

it's under one kilometer (0.6 miles) to the first of the burned trestles.

The cacti-covered top of **Knox Mountain** offers great lake and city views. A hiking trail and a paved road popular with bicyclists both lead to the summit. To get here, head north out of town along the lakeshore, passing pretty lakeside Sutherland Park, then take Knox Mountain Drive up to Knox Mountain Park, stopping at Crown Viewpoint on the way to the top. Trails lead off the summit in all directions. Vehicle access is possible 9:30am-9pm Monday-Saturday and noon-9pm Sunday; in the morning and evening, hikers and bikers have the road to themselves.

Skiing and Snowboarding

Big White Ski Resort (250/765-3101 or 800/663-2772, www.bigwhite.com), 57 kilometers (35 miles) east of Kelowna on Highway 33, is one of the Okanagan's three major winter resorts and British Columbia's second largest. Its network of modern lifts, including a gondola and four high-speed quads, opens up over 850 hectares (2,100 acres) of terrain. Lifts operate 8:30am-3:30pm daily December-mid-April, and for night skiing and boarding 5pm-9pm Tuesday-Saturday. Lift tickets are adults $105, seniors $89, children $62, and under age five free. Adjacent to the main lift-served area is Happy Valley Adventure Centre, a tube park with its own lift. Big White is also home to a terrain park, a half-pipe, cross-country ski trails, and an ice-skating rink. On-mountain facilities in the 9,000-bed base village include rental shops, a ski and snowboard school, accommodations, restaurants and cafés, and a large mall.

ENTERTAINMENT AND EVENTS
Nightlife

Enjoy a drink overlooking Okanagan Lake in the stylish lounge at the **Hotel Eldorado** (500 Cook Rd., 250/763-7500, 11am-2am daily), where tables spread along the waterfront boardwalk. Downtown, close to the lakefront, **Bacaro Kitchen & Drink** (231 Bernard Ave., 778/484-6994, 5pm-10pm Tues.-Thurs., 5pm-midnight Fri.-Sat.) is contemporary wine bar with a tapas-style menu. In addition to a wine list dominated by local bottles, there's an impressive range of cocktails and spirits. Also downtown, but very different from Bacaro's hip ambience, **O'Flannigan's Pub** (319 Queensway Ave., 250/763-2292, 11:30am-1am Mon.-Sat.) has a more traditional pub atmosphere, with occasional live music, comedy nights, drink specials, and decent pub food.

At **Lake City Casino** (Delta Hotels by Marriott Grand Okanagan Resort, 1310 Water St., 250/860-9467, 9am-2am daily), don't expect the ritz and glitz of Las Vegas—this is gambling Canadian-style, with the action restricted to slot machines, blackjack, roulette, Caribbean stud poker, and mini baccarat, and everyone's ushered out the front door at 2am.

Festivals and Events

The **Spring Okanagan Wine Festival** (250/861-6654, www.thewinefestivals.com) is somewhat less pretentious than the fall equivalent, with many wineries not normally open to the public offering tours and tasting sessions through the first week of May. The **Knox Mountain Hill Climb** (www.knox-mtnhillclimb.ca), North America's longest paved motor-vehicle hill climb, has been

contested using street-legal vehicles annually since 1957; it's on in late May. The valley's biggest event is the **Fall Okanagan Wine Festival** (250/861-6654, www.thewinefestivals.com), held annually over 10 days ending on the Canadian Thanksgiving long weekend (2nd Mon. in Oct.) to celebrate the end of the grape harvest. Thousands of visitors participate in tastings of food and wine, releases of new wines, cooking classes, and art displays, with all sections of the industry participating.

FOOD

Although most hotels and resorts have in-house restaurants, it's worth venturing downtown to try one of the recommendations below, unless you're staying at the Hotel Eldorado, where outdoor dining at the lakefront **Boardwalk** (500 Cook Rd., 250/763-7500, l11am-10am daily May-Sept., $16-31) is a great option for dinner on a warm night.

Cafés

Many locals will tell you **Giobean** (Delta Hotels by Marriott Grand Okanagan Resort, 1320 Water St., 250/868-2992, 7:30am-4pm Tues.-Sun., lunch $7-10) is their favorite coffee hangout—and it is good, with a distinctive European flavor to the ambience and serving styles. The location is perfect if you are strolling along the waterfront—it's just back from the foreshore and has a few street-side tables.

Bohemian Café (524 Bernard Ave., 250/862-3517, 7:30am-2:30pm Wed.-Fri., 8:30am-2pm Sat., 8:30am-2pm Sun., lunch $5.50-9) has a loyal local following for gourmet coffee, bagels baked in-house, and inexpensive cooked breakfasts. With a similar ambience, and just around the corner, **Pulp Fiction Coffee House** (1598 Pandosy St., 778/484-7444, 7am-8pm Mon.-Fri., 8am-7pm Sun., lunch $6) combines great coffee with an eclectic collection of art, antiques, and rare books. Drinks such as the espresso milk shake are exceptional, with food options range from pastries to paninis.

In 2016, after being at the same location since the 1970s, ★ **Little Hobo** (596 Leo

Ave., 778/478-0411, 8am-2:30pm Mon.-Fri., lunch $7-10) moved into a bigger space. Why? Because Little Hobo serves up exactly what local diners are looking for—inexpensive, no-frills breakfast and lunch choices, most made daily from scratch. The soups, sandwiches, and pierogi are especially good. Adding to the charm are friendly owners who seem to really love serving their customers.

Head north of downtown to **Okanagan Street Food** (812 Crowley Ave., 778/478-0807, 8am-3pm Tues.-Sat., lunch $9-13) for the most creative and well-priced lunches in Kelowna. Highlights include candied salmon risotto fritters, fish tacos topped with fruity salsa, and hand-cut fries with blackberry ketchup.

Canadian

If you are looking for farm-to-table concept cooking using local produce, Kelowna has three restaurants to recommend. The longest-running of these is **RauDZ** (1560 Water St., 250/868-8805, 5pm-10pm daily, $17-30), a Kelowna favorite for years. In the surroundings of a heritage commercial building are exposed redbrick walls adorned with photos of local suppliers and their produce, a glassed-in kitchen, a long wooden bar, and comfortable seating. The menu features an abundance of regional produce and game, all sourced directly from local farms. Signature dishes include a crab cappuccino soup to start and lamb sirloin as a main. Adding to the charm is a well-priced list of regional wines.

One block south, ★ **Krafty Kitchen + Bar** (281 Lawrence Ave., 250/868-7228, noon-3pm and 5pm-10pm Mon.-Fri., 10:30am-3pm and 5pm-10pm Sat.-Sun., $22-32) is a large, bustling industrial-chic space where the emphasis is also on modern preparations of local produce and game. Krafty Kitchen also has an impressive wine and cocktail list.

Competing with the above two places for the best place to enjoy innovative cooking is ★ **Waterfront Wines** (1180 Sunset Dr., 250/762-3336, 5pm-10pm daily, $26-32), a slick dining room where the emphasis is on local seasonal produce. Anything you order—pork, chicken, or beef—you can be assured is from a local high-quality supplier.

For vineyard dining, make reservations at **Old Vines Restaurant** (Quail's Gate, 3303 Boucherie Rd., 250/769-2500, 11am-9pm daily, $25-48), where you can dine in a welcoming room with a stone floor and an abundance of wood, or outside on a patio with views extending across Okanagan Lake. The menu includes lots of lighter choices, including soups and salads, but also substantial mains such as a vegetarian squash pasta and grill bison.

Asian

Bai Tong (upstairs at 1530 Water St., 250/763-8638, 11:30am-2:30pm Mon.-Fri. and 4:30pm-9:30pm daily, $13-16) is a step above your average small-town Thai restaurant. Feast on chicken cooked in a black bean sauce and wrapped in lettuce leaves, or stir-fry combos of vegetables and noodles with your choice of meat. Prices are reasonable, including the wine list, with a glass of house wine under $5.

You'll find Kelowna's best Japanese food at **Momo Sushi** (377 Bernard Ave., 250/763-1030, 11am-3pm and 5pm-9pm Mon.-Sat., 4:30pm-8:30pm Sun., $13-22), a long, narrow space with an open kitchen and modern furnishings. **Everest Indian Restaurant** (2430 Main St., Westbank, 250/768-8700, 11:30am-2pm and 4pm-10pm Mon.-Fri., noon-10pm Sat.-Sun., $11-16) is across the lake from downtown Kelowna, but worth searching out for my favorite Indian food in the Okanagan Valley.

French

Bouchons Bistro (1180 Sunset Dr., 250/763-6595, 5:30pm-10:30pm daily, $26-36) is a little slice of France in the heart of downtown Kelowna. The setting is elegant yet welcoming, with an extensive collection of Okanagan and French wines stored in a stone cellar in the middle of the main dining room. You could start with a classic baked French onion soup, then move on to veal tenderloin topped with shrimp and lobster coulis or a roasted rack of lamb with olive-infused au jus.

ACCOMMODATIONS AND CAMPING
Under $50

Samesun Kelowna (245 Harvey St., 250/763-9814 or 877/972-6378, www.samesun.com, dorms $35-40, $80-110 s or d, includes light breakfast) is a centrally located, purpose-built backpacker lodge. Inside the distinctive three-story building are 120 beds, many in private rooms (some with en suites), with communal kitchens, baths, a large lounge area, and included Wi-Fi. Out back is a pleasant grassy barbecue area.

$50-100

High in the highlands northeast of Kelowna, **Beaver Lake Mountain Resort** (6350 Beaver Lake Rd., 250/762-2225, www.beaverlakeresort.com, May-Oct., camping $35, camping cabins $55 s or d, self-contained cabins $135-155 s or d) is very different from the beachy resort complexes down on the valley floor. Set in a forest on the edge of a lake famed for rainbow trout fishing, the resort comprises a restaurant, a small petting zoo, and a fishing shop. Boat rentals are well priced at $75 per 24 hours, including gas. Canoes, kayaks, and belly boats are $65 per day. Cabins range from tiny "camping cabins" that share baths to peeled log chalets with full kitchens. Cabin 9 is typical: It's rustic but enjoys an absolute lakefront setting, with a private floating dock, a big deck, a full kitchen, a log fireplace, one bedroom, and a loft. Make cabin reservations well in advance—locals know a bargain when they see one and book their favorite cabin up to a year in advance. To get here, head north to Winfield, then 16 kilometers (10 miles) east on Beaver Lake Road.

$100-150

South of downtown, ★ **Siesta Suites** (3152 Lakeshore Rd., 250/763-5013 or 800/663-4347, www.siestasuiteskelowna.com, $149-189 s or d) is a well-priced family-run motel that doesn't need to be affiliated with the big chains to sell out each night through summer. Siesta offers a beachside atmosphere one block from the water. Spacious rooms open onto a wide balcony overlooking a courtyard and outdoor pool; other facilities include an indoor pool, barbecue area, and free wireless Internet. Many units have kitchens and separate bedrooms.

$150-200

Highway 97 (also known as Harvey Ave.) east of downtown holds many motels tucked between shopping malls, gas stations, and fast-food restaurants. Along this strip is **Days Inn Kelowna** (2469 Hwy. 97 N., 250/868-3297 or 800/337-7177, www.daysinnkelowna.com, $159-189 s or d), with large modern rooms decorated in Santa Fe style, as well as an outdoor pool and hot tub, a courtyard, and a fitness room; the smallest rooms cost $159 s or d, but it's worth an extra $30 for a much larger suite. As at all Days Inns, rates include a light breakfast and wireless Internet access.

$200-250

In the vicinity of the Days Inn, **Best Western Plus Kelowna** (2402 Hwy. 97 N., 250/860-1212 or 888/860-1212, www.bestwesternkelownahotel.com, $249-299 s or d) is a good choice for those who want the amenities of a full resort but don't want to pay for a waterfront location. Many of the 176 guest rooms are set around a grass courtyard. Other facilities include an indoor pool, outdoor hot tubs, a fitness room, and a restaurant and pub (both open for lunch and dinner daily). The rooms are spacious and modern and come filled with niceties such as air-conditioning, bathrobes, blow-dryers, and free local calls.

Over $300

As throughout this book, rates quoted for the three recommendations below are midsummer rack rates. Advertised rates are often lower, and you can get rooms for well under $200 at all three in the off season.

Built in 1926 and moved to its present

location in 1989, the ★ **Hotel Eldorado** (500 Cook Rd., 250/763-7500 or 866/608-7500, www.eldoradokelowna.com, $359-524 s or d), south of downtown along Pandosy Street, is a delightful lakeside place offering 55 rooms in two distinct styles. In the original hotel are 19 Heritage rooms furnished with antiques, and many offering a lake view and private balcony. Rooms in the Arms wing (starting at $269 s or d) are larger, have high ceilings, and offer a distinct contemporary feel. Other facilities include a small indoor pool, spa services, valet parking, and included Wi-Fi. The Boardwalk is a bustling outdoor restaurant set right on the lake, while in the original hotel building the Lakeside Dining Room and a lounge provide different dining options. Also out front is a marina with boat rentals.

Overlooking the same stretch of lake as the Hotel Eldorado is the colorful and modern **Manteo Resort** (3762 Lakeshore Rd., 250/860-1031 or 800/445-5255, www.manteo.com, $329-449 s or d). This self-contained complex includes a 78-room hotel and guest and resident facilities such as a private beach, a marina with boat rentals, a pool complex with a waterslide, tennis courts, a small movie theater, a lounge with billiard table, and a barbecue area.

The grandest of Kelowna's accommodations is the **Delta Hotels by Marriott Grand Okanagan Resort** (1310 Water St., 250/763-4500 or 800/465-4651, www.marriott.com, $399-599 s or d), a sprawling lakeside development right downtown and integrated with parkland and walking paths. Along the lake side of the resort are restaurants with lots of outdoor seating and a lagoon with its own private lock and watercraft rentals. Inside, once past the cavernous lobby, you'll find a fitness center, spa services, restaurants, a lounge bar, and 390 luxuriously appointed rooms.

Camping

The closest campground to downtown is **Hiawatha RV Park** (3787 Lakeshore Rd., 250/861-4837 or 888/784-7275, www.hiawatharvpark.com, Mar.-Oct., tent sites $54, hookups $62-75). It has an outdoor pool, a tenting area, showers, laundry, a game room, and a playground.

Two provincial parks in the vicinity of Kelowna offer camping with hot showers, but to ensure a site you should make reservations through **Discover Camping** (519/826-6850 or 800/689-9025, www.discovercamping.ca). The closest is **Bear Creek Provincial Park** (late Mar.-mid-Oct., $35) across the bridge from downtown and then nine kilometers (6 miles) north on Westside Road. The campground holds 122 sites nestled under cottonwood trees. Campers also enjoy a short beach and trails that cross back over Westside Road and into desertlike terrain above the lake. **Fintry Provincial Park** (Apr.-mid-Oct., $35) lies a 23 kilometers (14 miles) farther north along Westside Road in the same beachside setting as Bear Creek, although the campground is less developed. A trail leads from the campground to a deep canyon along Shorts Creek.

INFORMATION AND SERVICES

Kelowna Visitor Centre (544 Harvey Ave., 250/861-1515 or 800/663-4345, www.tourismkelowna.com, 9am-5pm daily summer, 9am-5pm Mon.-Fri., 10am-3pm Sat.-Sun. fall-spring) is beside Highway 97 as it passes through the center of the city—watch for the signs. Coming into town from the south on Highway 97, turn left on Richter Street at the traffic lights and go back one block. A good map for immediate orientation is posted outside the center; it also incorporates a legend of motels and attractions.

Mosaic Books (411 Bernard Ave., 250/763-4418, 9am-6pm Mon.-Tues., 9am-9pm Wed.-Fri., 9am-7pm Sat., 10am-5pm Sun.) is an independent bookseller that has been serving the valley since 1968. The eye-catching, semicircular building on Ellis Street is **Kelowna Library** (1380 Ellis St., 250/762-2800, 10am-8pm Mon.-Thurs., 10am-5pm Fri.-Sat.). The **post office** (530 Gaston Ave., 250/763-4095, 9:30am-5pm Mon.-Fri.) is on the north side of downtown. **Kelowna General Hospital** (Strathcona Ave. and Pandosy St., 250/862-4000), is open 24 hours daily.

GETTING THERE AND AROUND

Kelowna is in the heart of the Okanagan Valley, 64 kilometers (40 miles) north of Penticton and 50 kilometers (31 miles) south of Vernon. Highway 97 along the valley floor links all three cities, while southwest of Kelowna Highway 93C provides the most direct access from Vancouver, which is around four hours and 390 kilometers (244 miles) to the west.

Modern **Kelowna Airport,** the province's third busiest, is 15 kilometers (9 miles) north of downtown along Highway 97. It's served by **Air Canada** (250/542-3302) and **WestJet** (800/538-5696), both of which offer daily flights to and from Vancouver, Calgary, and Edmonton. At the airport are car-rental outlets, a lounge bar, and a café. **Greyhound** (2366 Leckie Rd., 250/860-3036 or 800/661-8747) provides bus service throughout the Okanagan and beyond.

Getting Around

Local buses are run by **Kelowna Regional Transit System.** Get schedule and route information from the downtown terminal (Bernard Ave. and Ellis St., 250/860-8121). For a taxi, call **Kelowna Cabs** (250/762-2222) or **Checkmate Cabs** (250/861-1111). Another taxi service is offered by **Let's Go! Transportation** (778/821-0101 or 844/877-0101, www.letsgotransportation.ca), which schedules personalized drop-offs at local wineries, golf courses, ski resorts, and the airport.

Rental car agencies include **Avis** (250/491-9500), **Budget** (250/491-7368), **Enterprise** (250/491-9611), **Hertz** (250/491-8939), and **National** (250/765-2800). All these companies have vehicles out at the airport, but call in advance to ensure availability, especially in midsummer and during the ski season.

Vernon and Vicinity

The city of Vernon (pop. 41,000) lies between Okanagan, Kalamalka, and Swan Lakes, at the north end of the Okanagan Valley 50 kilometers (31 miles) from Kelowna. Downtown itself holds little of interest insofar as attractions go; the surrounding area boasts the main attractions. Among the area highlights: sandy beaches; provincial parks; Silver Star Mountain Resort, a year-round recreation paradise east of the city; and fishing in more than 100 lakes within an hour's drive.

SIGHTS AND RECREATION

Greater Vernon Museum and Archives (3009 32nd Ave., 250/542-3142, 10am-4:30pm Tues.-Sat., donation) holds photos from the early 1900s and a large collection of pioneer and First Nations artifacts. Displays cover natural history, recreation, period clothing, and steamships. In the same vicinity is **Vernon Public Art Gallery** (3228 31st Ave., 250/545-3173, 10am-5pm Mon.-Fri., 11am-4pm Sat., free), featuring works by local artists as well as touring exhibitions.

Polson Park (off Hwy. 97 at 25th Ave.) has a Chinese teahouse, a small Japanese garden, and paths along a willow-lined creek, but most people go to stare at the floral clock: nine meters (30 feet) wide, made up of more than 3,500 plants, and the only one of its kind in western Canada.

Historic O'Keefe Ranch

Established in 1867, the **O'Keefe Ranch** (9380 Hwy. 97, 250/542-7868, 10am-5pm daily May-June and Sept., 10am-6pm daily July-Aug., adults $13.50, seniors $12, children $8.50), 13 kilometers (8 miles) north

Vernon and Vicinity

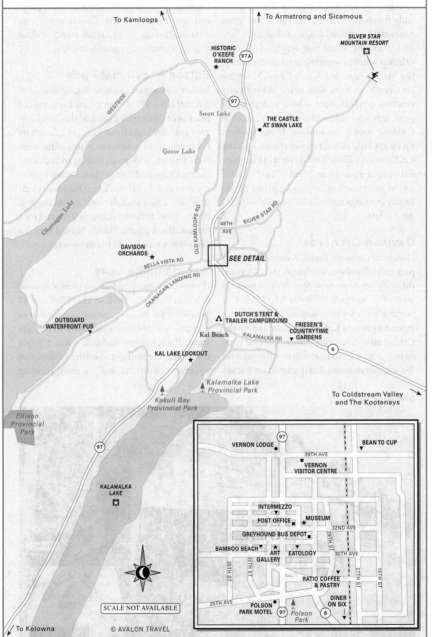

To Kamloops

To Armstrong and Sicamous

SILVER STAR MOUNTAIN RESORT ★

HISTORIC O'KEEFE RANCH ★

97A

97

Swan Lake

THE CASTLE AT SWAN LAKE ●

Goose Lake

WESTSIDE

Okanagan Lake

48TH AVE

SILVER STAR RD

OLD KAMLOOPS RD

SEE DETAIL

DAVISON ORCHARDS ★

BELLA VISTA RD

OKANAGAN LANDING RD

OUTBOARD WATERFRONT PUB ▼

DUTCH'S TENT & TRAILER CAMPGROUND

FRIESEN'S COUNTRYTIME GARDENS ▼

Kal Beach

KALAMALKA RD

6

KAL LAKE LOOKOUT ★

Kalamalka Lake Provincial Park

Kekuli Bay Provincial Park

To Coldstream Valley and The Kootenays

Ellison Provincial Park

97

KALAMALKA LAKE ✪

SCALE NOT AVAILABLE

To Kelowna

© AVALON TRAVEL

Detail

VERNON LODGE ●

97

BEAN TO CUP ▼

39TH AVE

VERNON VISITOR CENTRE ■

INTERMEZZO ▼

POST OFFICE

MUSEUM ★

GREYHOUND BUS DEPOT ■

32ND AVE

BAMBOO BEACH ▼

ART GALLERY ★

EATOLOGY ▼

30TH AVE

35TH ST

35TH ST

29TH ST

RATIO COFFEE & PASTRY ▼

DINER ON SIX ▼

27TH ST

15TH ST

25TH AVE

POLSON PARK MOTEL ●

97

Polson Park

6

of Vernon toward Kamloops on Highway 97, was one of the Okanagan's first cattle ranches. Today you can tour the opulent, fully furnished O'Keefe Mansion and other noteworthy outbuildings, including a furnished old log house that was the O'Keefes' original home; a working blacksmith's shop; the still-in-use St. Ann's Church, where services have been held since 1889; a fully stocked general store where you can buy postcards and old-fashioned candy; and the Chinese cook's bunkhouse. If you worked up an appetite in your explorations, visit the **Cattlemen's Club Restaurant** (11am-3pm daily, 5pm-9pm Thurs.-Sun., $16-39), with lots of meaty dishes, including prime rib on Friday evenings and Sunday brunch and dinner buffets.

Davison Orchards

Dozens of farms surround Vernon, but one in particular, **Davison Orchards** (3111 Davison Rd., 250/549-3266, 8am-6pm daily May-Oct.), west of downtown off Bella Vista Road, is worth a visit. Set on a sloping hill with views extending across Kalamalka Lake and up the Coldstream Valley, this family-operated business is a hive of tourist activity throughout the warmer months. A self-guided walk leads

through a garden where everything from cucumbers to cantaloupe is grown, a wagon tour traverses the entire 20-hectare (50-acre) property, and there's a Critter Corral, a café with outside dining, an ice cream stand, and, of course, a fruit and vegetable market.

Ellison Provincial Park

Follow Okanagan Landing Road (from 25th Ave. off Hwy. 97) west to access the northern reaches of Okanagan Lake and this 200-hectare (494-acre) lakefront park, 16 kilometers (10 miles) from downtown. Most of the park is on a bench, with trails leading to and along the rocky shore. Ellison is best known by divers as British Columbia's first freshwater marine park. Enjoy shallow-water snorkeling and diving, weed beds full of life, underwater rock formations, a plastic bubble "Dive Dome," a deep-water wreck, and beach showers.

★ Kalamalka Lake

If you've driven up to Vernon from Kelowna, this was the beautiful lake that Highway 97 paralleled for much of the way. It's known as a "marl" lake because as summer warms the water, the limestone bedrock forms crystals that reflect the sunlight, creating a distinctive aquamarine color that is all the more stunning

Davison Orchards

with surrounding parched hills as a backdrop. The continuously changing emerald and turquoise water and surrounding mountain panorama is best appreciated from **Kal Lake Lookout,** five kilometers (3 miles) back toward Kelowna along Highway 97. Just south of the information center, a steep road winds down to the lakeshore and fine **Kal Beach,** fringed by trees. Parking is across the railway line from the beach (access is under the rail bridge). Also on the beach is a concession and, at the east end, a pub with a huge deck overlooking the water.

Continue beyond the beach for eight kilometers (5 miles) to **Kalamalka Lake Provincial Park,** on the east side of the lake. Within this 978-hectare (2,420-acre) park, a 1.5-kilometer (0.9-mile) trail winds down through bunchgrass and ponderosa pines to Turtle Head Point, while other trails lead to a low-lying wetland and a lofty viewpoint.

FOOD

The dining choices in Vernon have improved vastly in recent years, as has the coffee scene. One of two recommended coffee joints is **Ratio Coffee & Pastry** (3101 29th St., 250/545-9800, 7am-6pm Mon.-Fri., 8am-6pm Sat., $8-13), in Vernon's original redbrick railway station, with soups, paninis, and sandwiches, as well as delicious pastries (doughnuts are the main draw on Friday). A few blocks north and across the rail line, **Bean to Cup** (3903 27th St., 250/503-2222, 6am-8pm Mon.-Fri., 6:30am-8pm Sat., 7am-8pm Sun., lunch $6.50-9) is in a converted residential house with wireless Internet. It offers a wide range of hot drinks and light meals, best enjoyed on the heated patio.

Eatology (3100 30th St., 236/426-4400, 6:30am-3pm daily, lunch $9-14) is a popular breakfast hangout in the heart of downtown. Casual and brightly lit, the menu features healthy, creative cooking and reasonable prices. The many versions of eggs benedict highlight the breakfast menu while large salads bring in the lunchtime crowd. Keep it simple at **Diner on Six** (2511 Hwy. 6,

778/475-5979, 6am-2pm Tues.-Sat., 7am-2pm Sun., lunch $9-12.50), with an old-fashioned diner atmosphere, but with modern presentations of breakfast and lunch.

Bamboo Beach (3313 30th Ave., 250/542-7701, 11am-2pm and 5pm-8:30pm Tues.-Sat., $12-18) is your typical small-town Asian restaurant, but the setting is a notch more inviting than you may expect, and the Japanese, Thai, and Korean choices please most tastes. **Intermezzo** (3206 34th Ave., 250/542-3853, 5pm-10pm Mon.-Fri., 4pm-10pm Sat.-Sun., $17-34) has a casual yet somewhat romantic setting and is a local favorite for its wide choice of southern European specialties, including inexpensive pastas and more creative choices such as a rack of lamb baked in Moroccan spices. At the Vernon Lodge, **BX Creek Bar & Grill** (3914 32nd St., 250/545-3385, 6:30am-10pm daily, $14-32) is hotel dining, but the restaurant is set in a tropical atrium with a natural stream flowing through the middle. The wide-ranging menu features lots of BC game and produce.

Two out-of-town choices are worth searching out. Originating as a fruit stand, **Friesens Countrytyme Gardens** (9172 Kalamalka Rd., 250/549-3587, 7am-5pm daily, lunch $7-12) has grown into a destination for those searching out a hearty meal (eggs and bacon for breakfast, Mennonite sausage for lunch) in an orchard setting. Sunday brunch is very busy. **Outboard Waterfront Pub** (7673 Okanagan Landing Rd., 250/475-5981, 11am-9pm daily, $14-20) is a few kilometers west of downtown, but well worth the drive for the setting more than anything else. It sits right on Okanagan Lake, and a large deck right on the water is the most popular of the pub's dining areas. The menu is fairly standard, with lots of dishes to share, but as it's off the tourist path, prices are reasonable.

ACCOMMODATIONS

Downtown and around the outskirts of Vernon is the usual collection of hotels and motels of greatly varying standards. These are handy for a simple overnight stay, but to make the most of your time in the area, book a room at Silver Star Mountain Resort.

Polson Park Motel (3201 24th Ave., 250/549-2231 or 800/480-2231, www.polsonparkmotel.ca, $85 s, $95 d) is the least expensive of Vernon's 20-odd motels. Across from Polson Park, the three-story motel has an outdoor pool and basic rooms. Moving up in price and quality is **Vernon Lodge** (3914 32nd St., 250/545-3385 or 800/663-9400, www.vernonlodge.com, $170-300 s or d), where stylishly decorated rooms overlook an enclosed three-story tropical atrium and indoor pool.

If you don't need to be close to downtown, **The Castle at Swan Lake** (7905 Greenhow Rd., 778/475-4232 or 844/854-0490, www.swanlakecastle.com, $195-245 s or d), to the north, is an excellent choice if you are looking for large, modern, self-contained suites, complete with full kitchens and separate bedrooms. Other amenities include an outdoor pool. Rates include a cooked breakfast at the adjacent restaurant.

Camping
Dutch's Tent and Trailer Campground (15408 Kalamalka Rd., 250/545-1023, $40-48), three kilometers (2 miles) south of downtown, is a five-minute walk from Kal Beach, but doesn't have much else going for it, as sites are close together and there's lots of highway noise.

Two provincial parks within a 15-minute drive of downtown provide campsites. Sixteen kilometers (10 miles) southwest of town on Okanagan Landing Road is **Ellison Provincial Park** (519/826-6850 or 800/689-9025, www.discovercamping.ca, Apr.-Oct., $32), on the east shore of Okanagan Lake, while south along Highway 97 toward Kelowna, **Kekuli Bay Provincial Park** (519/826-6850 or 800/689-9025, www.discovercamping.ca, Apr.-Oct., $32) slopes down to a boat launch and pebbly beach on Kalamalka Lake. Although open to the elements, it has showers and electric hookups.

INFORMATION AND SERVICES
Vernon Visitor Centre (3004 39th Ave., 250/542-1415 or 800/665-0795, www.vernontourism.com, 8:30am-6pm daily summer, 8:30am-4:30pm Tues.-Sat. fall-spring) is on the north side of downtown.

GETTING THERE AND AROUND
Vernon is near the top of the Okanagan Valley, 64 kilometers (40 miles) north of Kelowna. From Vancouver, take Highway 97C and drive through Kelowna to reach Vernon in under five hours. From Kamloops, in Central British Columbia, take Highway 97 off the Trans-Canada Highway to reach Vernon in around 90 minutes.

The **Greyhound** bus depot (250/545-0527) is on the corner of 30th Street and 31st Avenue. For local bus information and schedules, contact **Vernon Regional Transit System** (250/545-7221).

★ SILVER STAR MOUNTAIN RESORT
For summer or winter recreation, head up to **Silver Star Mountain Resort** (250/542-0224 or 800/663-4431, www.skisilverstar.com), a colorful gold rush-style fully self-contained resort town 22 kilometers (13.6 miles) northeast of Vernon (take 48th Ave. off Hwy. 97). The views of Vernon as you climb the mountain are worth the fairly long, steep drive, and the resort at the top offers great skiing and snowboarding, plus summer recreation to suit all ages.

Skiing and Snowboarding
November to April, skiers and boarders mob Silver Star, coming for great terrain and the facilities of an outstanding on-hill village. The two main faces—Vance Creek, good for beginners, and Putnam Creek, for intermediates and experts—are served by six chairlifts and a couple of T-bars. The resort's 80 runs cover 1,240 hectares (3,065 acres) with

a vertical rise of 760 meters (2,500 feet). Lift tickets are adults $96, seniors $79, children $60; those under age 6 ski free. For snow reports, call 250/542-1745.

Silver Star Cross-Country Centre features 35 kilometers (22 miles) of groomed and set tracks, while beyond these are 50 kilometers (30 miles) of backcountry trails. A day pass is adults $18, seniors $15, children $10; rentals are available for an additional $30.

Summer Recreation

Silver Star offers the biggest range of summer recreation of any alpine resort in the interior. Starting at the end of June, a chairlift runs from the village to the top of 1,915-meter (6,280-foot) Silver Star Mountain for terrific views of Vernon and surrounding lakes. Much of the alpine area around the summit is protected by 8,714-hectare (21,500-acre) **Silver Star Provincial Park;** pick up a hiking guide in the village. The summer lift operates 10am-4pm daily June-September and costs adults $16, seniors $14, children $10. Mountain bike rentals are $25 for one hour, $40 for two hours, and $65 for a full day.

Accommodations

The base village contains numerous types of lodging; book year-round through central reservations (800/663-4431, www.skisilver-star.com) or contact each directly. The rates quoted here are for summer, which is low season. Throughout the winter, expect to pay double.

Pinnacles Suite Hotel (9885 Pinnacles Rd., 250/542-4548 or 800/551-7466, www.pinnacles.com, from $165 s or d with kitchen) has standard motel rooms as well as multi-room suites in the heart of the village. The **Lord Aberdeen Hotel** (250/542-0224 or 800/663-4431, www.skisilverstar.com) also offers self-contained suites and is similarly priced. The most luxurious on-mountain lodging is **Vance Creek Hotel** (250/549-5191 or 800/610-0805, www.vancecreekhotel.com, $175-255 s or d), which offers standard hotel rooms and self-contained suites spread through three buildings. Guests enjoy use of fitness facilities at the nearby National Altitude Training Centre.

OKANAGAN VALLEY
VERNON AND VICINITY

Silver Star Mountain Resort is a short drive from Vernon.

The Kootenays

The wild and rugged Kootenays region of British Columbia lies east of the Okanagan Valley and south of the Trans-Canada Highway.

It is bordered by the United States to the south and Alberta to the east. Three north-to-south-trending mountain ranges—the Monashees, Selkirks, and Purcells—run parallel to each other across the region, separated by lush green valleys and narrow lakes up to 150 kilometers (90 miles) long. The snowcapped mountains and forested valleys abound with wildlife, including large populations of deer, elk, moose, black bears, and grizzly bears.

Europeans first entered the Kootenays in the late 1800s, searching for precious metals such as gold, silver, lead, and zinc, all of which were found in large quantities. While many of the boomtowns from this era have slipped into oblivion, others live on: Sandon is a ghost town, Fort Steele survives as a heritage theme park, and the grand old city of Nelson is today a heritage masterpiece, its streets lined with restored buildings.

Recreational opportunities abound throughout the Kootenays in all seasons. In summer, anglers flock to the lakes and rivers for trout, kokanee, and bass. Other visitors enjoy canoeing, swimming, or sunbathing on the beaches, or take to the mountains for hiking and wildlife viewing. Much of the region's higher elevations are protected in rugged and remote parks, including the spectacular Valhalla, Kokanee Glacier, Top of the World, and Purcell Wilderness Conservancy Provincial Parks. While these natural preserves offer plenty of opportunities for day-trippers, it takes extended backcountry trips to fully experience their beauty.

PLANNING YOUR TIME

The most important thing to remember when planning a driving tour through the Kootenays is that the region is very mountainous. Roads are generally narrow and winding, with mountain passes and ferry crossings slowing down travel time considerably. The main east-west thoroughfare is Highway 3, which runs through the southern extent of the region, traversing no less than five mountain passes between Osoyoos in the west and Cranbrook in the east. Even without

---

Previous: Windermere Lake; Island Lake. **Above:** Canadian Museum of Rail Travel.

Highlights

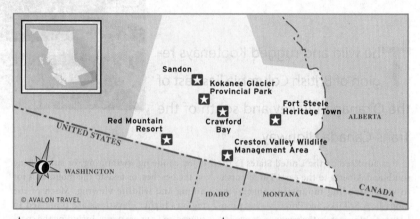

★ **Red Mountain Resort:** Rossland is a beautiful town to visit at any time of year, but in wintertime, the steep slopes of nearby Red Mountain draw experienced skiers and boarders from across the land (page 281).

★ **Sandon:** In the late 1800s, Sandon was home to over 5,000 miners. Today, you could fit the entire population in the back of a pickup truck—not that they'd want to leave western Canada's most authentic ghost town (page 286).

★ **Kokanee Glacier Provincial Park:** This remote park takes some effort to reach, but the rewards are many, including alpine lakes, ancient glaciers, and abundant wildlife (page 292).

★ **Crawford Bay:** Even if the crafty shops don't appeal to you, the price of visiting will: The village is accessed by the world's longest free ferry ride (page 294).

★ **Creston Valley Wildlife Management Area:** Protecting vital resting grounds along the Pacific Flyway, this site provides a haven for more than 250 species of birds, including ospreys, the rare Forester's tern, and a nesting colony of western grebes (page 295).

★ **Fort Steele Heritage Town:** The gold rush era comes to life through costumed interpreters and musical theater. You can even try your hand at panning for gold (page 302).

The Kootenays

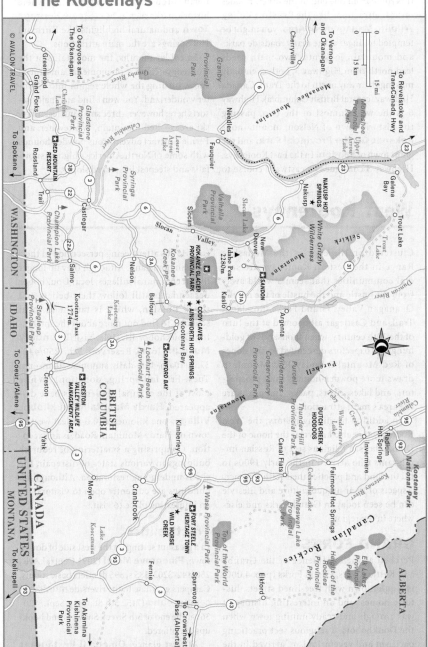

© AVALON TRAVEL

To Vernon and Okanagan

To Revelstoke and TransCanada Hwy

0   15 km
0   15 mi

To Osoyoos and The Okanagan

Greenwood
Grand Forks

Christina Lake

WASHINGTON

To Spokane

Cherryville

Granby Provincial Park

Granby River

Needles

Monashee Provincial Park

Monashee Mountains

6

Gladstone Provincial Park

Columbia River

RED MOUNTAIN RESORT
3B
Rossland

Lower Arrow Lake

Fauquier

22
Trail

Champion Lake Provincial Park
22A
Salmo

Stagleap Provincial Park

Kootenay Pass 1774m

3

To Coeur d'Alene

IDAHO

Castlegar

Syringa Provincial Park

Slocan

Valhalla Provincial Park

Upper Arrow Lake

23

23

Galena Bay

Trout Lake

Trout Lake

31

NAKUSP HOT SPRINGS
Nakusp

White Grizzly Wilderness

Selkirk Mountains

6

Slocan Valley

New Denver

SANDON

Idaho Peak 2260m

Nelson

3A

Balfour

Kootenay Lake

Duncan River

Kaslo

31A

Argenta

Purcell Wilderness Conservancy Provincial Park

KOKANEE GLACIER PROVINCIAL PARK

Kokanee Creek PP.

CODY CAVES
AINSWORTH HOT SPRINGS

Kootenay Bay

CRAWFORD BAY

Lockhart Beach Provincial Park

BRITISH COLUMBIA

Creston

CRESTON VALLEY WILDLIFE MANAGEMENT AREA

Yahk

3

Moyie

Kimberley

95

Cranbrook

Lake Kootenay

CANADA
UNITED STATES

To Kalispell

MONTANA

93

Fernie

3

Wild Horse Creek

FORT STEELE HERITAGE TOWN

Wasa Provincial Park

Sparwood

To Crowsnest Pass (Alberta)

43

Elkford

Top of the World Provincial Park

Whiteswan Lake Provincial Park

Premier Lake Provincial Park

Canal Flats

95

93

Columbia Lake

Fairmont Hot Springs

Invermere

Windermere Lake

Toby Creek

Thunder Hill

DUTCH CREEK HOODOOS

Dutch Creek

Radium Hot Springs

93

95

Kootenay National Park

Kootenay River

Columbia River

Canadian Rockies

Height of the Rockies Provincial Park

Elk Lakes Provincial Park

ALBERTA

To Akamina Kishinena Provincial Park

Purcell Mountains

Canadian Rockies

detours north, allow a couple of days to travel this route from one end to the other. Besides official attractions like the **Creston Valley Wildlife Management Area,** you might be tempted to linger at the many roadside parks and mountain lookouts. Two main roads lead north from Highway 3, both eventually making their way north to the Trans-Canada Highway (central British Columbia). Highway 6 is the westernmost of the two, passing the historic town of Nelson, mountainous **Kokanee Glacier Provincial Park,** and the ghost town of **Sandon.** In the East Kootenays, Highway 3 continues its eastward course to southern Alberta, while Highway 93/95 jogs north through the Columbia Valley, where historic parks such as **Fort Steele Heritage Town** and natural highlights like Fairmont Hot Springs are the main attractions.

In colder months, the mountains of the Kootenays catch a phenomenal amount of snow, turning the whole region into a winter wonderland. You won't find any major resorts here; however, three small but legendary ski areas—Red Mountain, Whitewater, and Fernie—attract adventurous powder-hounds with some of North America's highest snowfalls and steepest lift-served slopes.

West Kootenays

Clustered on the edge of the Monashee Range in the western Kootenays are several communities that seem a world away from the hustle and the bustle of the nearby Okanagan Valley. Grand Forks, Rossland, Trail, and Castlegar all boomed at the turn of the 20th century, when thousands of gold-hungry prospectors descended on the slopes of Red Mountain. Today Red Mountain draws more powder-hounds than prospectors, and lakes, rivers, parks, and peaks are the area's main attractions.

In addition to mining history, the West Kootenays are also known as the home of the Doukhobors, a religious sect of Russian immigrants who arrived in the early 1900s to till the land and practice their faith in peace. Aspects of their unique culture and lifestyle can be seen today in Grand Forks and elsewhere in the region.

GRAND FORKS

Perched at the confluence of the Granby and Kettle Rivers, Grand Forks (pop. 4,000) is a quiet town with tree-lined streets, historic homes, and an interesting history. It was a rough-and-ready mining town when the Doukhobors, a religious sect practicing pacifism and vegetarianism, arrived in the early 1900s after fleeing persecution in their Russian homeland. Although they no longer live in communal villages, local Doukhobor descendants still follow their beliefs and speak Russian, which is taught in local schools. To find out more about the intriguing Doukhobor lifestyle, visit **Boundary Museum** (6145 Reservoir Rd., 250/442-3737, 10am-4pm daily summer, 10am-4pm Tues.-Fri. fall-spring, donation). While most of the original settlements have disappeared, **Hardy Mountain Doukhobor Village,** one kilometer (0.6 miles) west of town on Hardy Mountain Road, is an exception. Comprising a smattering of redbrick buildings in various states of disrepair, the site is undergoing restoration. Although no buildings are currently open to visitors, it's an interesting place to visit.

Practicalities

In a pleasant setting on the west side of downtown, **Pinegrove Motel** (2091 Central Ave., 250/442-8203, $85 s, $95 d) offers basic rooms. Campers gravitate to the riverside **municipal campground** (7152 5th St., May-Sept., $20-36) at the end of 5th Street. Showers and hookups are offered.

At first glance, **Omega II Restaurant**

(7400 Hwy. 3, 250/442-3124, 7:30am-9pm daily, $14-25), on the east side of town, looks no different from any other small-town restaurant, but on closer inspection you'll see the roots of Grand Forks show themselves with Russian dishes such as borscht and *galooptsi* (meat-filled cabbage rolls). Try a little of everything by ordering a platter of Russian specialties.

CHRISTINA LAKE

This 19-kilometer-long (12-mile) lake, 25 kilometers (16 miles) east of Grand Forks along Highway 3, is a summer favorite for folks from throughout the West Kootenays, who come for the warm waters and fishing for rainbow trout, bass, and kokanee.

The town of Christina Lake is spread around the southern end of the lake, where the best beach is protected from development by a small day-use area. The best-value lodging is the **New Horizon Motel** (2037 Hwy. 3, 250/447-9312 or 888/859-0159, www.newhorizonmotel.com, $125-195 s or d), along the highway at the eastern edge of town. Rooms are spacious and comfortable, and a light breakfast is included in the rates. New Horizon also has extensive grounds with outdoor seating and a barbecue area. Signposted at the north end of the lake is **Gladstone Provincial Park,** where you need reservations to ensure a site at **Texas Creek Campground** (519/826-6850 or 800/689-9025, www.discovercamping.ca, May-mid-Sept., $27).

ROSSLAND

Clinging to the slopes of an extinct volcanic crater deep in the tree-covered Monashee Mountains, Rossland (pop. 4,000) was once a gold rush boomtown known as "The Golden City." The precious yellow metal was discovered on 1,580-meter (5,180-foot) Red Mountain by Joe Moris in 1890. Moris, like thousands of other prospectors unaware of the nearby wealth, had been traveling eastward on the Dewdney Trail to goldfields farther away. He nevertheless staked five claims

on Red Mountain, the richest of which, Le Roi, later sold for $3 million. When word got out, thousands of diggers rushed in, and the township of Rossland was born. The town's population peaked at 7,000 in 1897. At that time, the city boasted four newspapers, 40 saloons, and daily rail service south to Spokane. By 1929, the mountain had yielded six million tons of ore worth $165 million. Today, tourism supplies the bulk of Rossland's gold; the town serves as a hidden haven for mountain bike enthusiasts and adventurous skiers and boarders.

Sights

Downtown Rossland is a picturesque place full of historic buildings and old-fashioned street lamps. On the west side of downtown is the **Rossland Museum** (Hwy. 3B and Columbia Ave., 250/362-7722, 10am-5pm Tues.-Sun. mid-May-June, 10am-6pm daily July-Aug., noon-5pm Wed.-Sat. Sept.-mid-May, adults $10, seniors $8, children $3). At the entrance of the Le Roi mine, the museum catalogs the area's lustrous geological and human history. The museum also holds the Western Canada Ski Hall of Fame, which honors such luminaries as Olaus Jeldness—instigator of the local ski craze—and champion skier Nancy Greene, a local heroine who won a gold medal in the 1968 Olympics.

Mountain Biking

As snow as the snow melts each spring, Rossland comes alive with pedal power as mountain bike enthusiasts take advantage of the maze of old logging and mining trails surrounding the city. Now known as the "Mountain Bike Capital of Canada," Rossland has hosted both the Canadian and North American championships. Rent bikes from **The Powderhound** (2040 Columbia Ave., 250/362-5311, 10am-5:30pm daily).

★ Red Mountain Resort

The site of what was once one of the world's richest gold mines is now part of an alpine resort offering some of North America's most

Olaus Jeldness: Canada's First Ski Champion

In the late 1890s, after the first frantic summer of gold mining on Red Mountain, a group of prospectors put on a winter carnival, including a ski race down the slopes of Red Mountain. The organizer was Olaus Jeldness, a legendary Norwegian who had prospected all over the western United States before moving north of the border. Jeldness admitted that the mountain was "far too steep and the snow conditions too extreme" for a proper race. But it went ahead nevertheless. First the competitors hiked all the way to the summit. Then Jeldness gave the signal to go before strapping on his own skis and schussing off after the rest of the field. Despite their head start, Jeldness easily passed the other racers to become Canada's first national champion. His wooden skis and trophies are housed in the Western Canada Ski Hall of Fame in the Rossland Museum.

Jeldness was the first of many heroes to have skied the legendary slopes of "Red"—the mountain has been a breeding ground for more members of the Canadian National Ski Team than any other resort. Not bad, considering the adjacent town has just 3,200 residents.

challenging lift-served runs. Facilities on the mountain have certainly improved since the days of Olaus Jeldness, but **Red Mountain** (250/362-7384 or 877/969-7669, www.redresort.com, adults $92, seniors $64, ages 7-12 $46, under age 7 free) is no megaresort. Nevertheless, the skiing and boarding are still world-class. While three mountains provide opportunities for all ability levels, the resort holds most appeal for experts—and as any local will tell you, the advertised 1,080 hectares (2,700 acres) of terrain doesn't do justice to the opportunities for skiing in the backcountry. The heart-stopping face of Red Mountain is the star of the show. But adjacent Granite and Grey Mountains offers a vertical rise of over 900 meters (3,000 feet) each and almost unlimited intermediate, expert, and extreme skiing and boarding, mostly on unmarked trails through powder-filled glades. Beginners are catered to with a magic carpet while shredders will gravitate to the terrain park.

Food

Across from the distinctive redbrick post office, **Alpine Grind** (2104 Columbia Ave., 250/362-2280, 7am-5pm Mon.-Fri., 8am-4pm Sat.-Sun., lunch $7-11) is a modern air-conditioned café with a few outdoor tables along the sidewalk. The coffee is roasted in nearby Nelson and ground in-house to create a wide variety of caffeine drinks. All the breads and pastries are baked in the Alpine Grind kitchen, including pizzas (lunch Fri. only).

For dinner, my pick is **Idgie's** (1999 2nd Ave., 250/362-0078, 5pm-9:30pm daily, $21-32), a casual cozy dining room a short walk uphill from the main street. The small menu features modern Canadian food, with a surprisingly good selection of seasonal seafood sourced from west coast suppliers.

On the road up to Red Mountain, **Rock Cut Pub** (3052 Hwy. 3B, 250/362-5814, 11am-1am daily, $17-28) is busiest in winter but opens year-round for lunch and dinner. It offers typical pub fare, smartly presented and well-priced. Enjoy the mountain surroundings by eating on the heated deck.

Accommodations

The ★ **Ram's Head Inn** (4465 Red Mountain Rd., 250/362-9577, www.ramsheadinn.ca, $110-250 s or d), one of Canada's premier small lodges, lies in the woods at the base of Red Mountain. Primarily designed for wintertime, the inn offers 14 ultracomfy guest rooms that ooze mountain magnetism. Factor in a congenial dining room (breakfast only in summer), a game room, a sauna, an outdoor hot tub, and a spacious communal lounge with luxurious chairs and a large fireplace, and you have the perfect place to spend a couple of nights. Winter packages ($150-200 pp) include lift tickets.

Information

Rossland Visitor Centre (250/362-7722 or 888/448-7444, www.rossland.com, 10am-5pm Tues.-Sun. mid-May-June, 10am-6pm daily July-Aug., noon-5pm Wed.-Sat. Sept.-mid-May) is in the museum complex south of downtown, at the corner of Highway 3B and Columbia Avenue.

TRAIL AND VICINITY

Sprawling along both sides of the mighty Columbia River, Trail (pop. 7,500) lies 10 kilometers (6 miles) and 600 vertical meters (2,000 feet) below Rossland. On the edge of downtown, the world's largest lead and zinc smelter is the foundation of Teck Resources, one of the world's largest mining companies. Head to the **Teck Interpretive Centre** (1199 Bay Ave., 250/368-3144, 9am-5pm daily, free) to learn about the smelting process. Free tours of the **Teck Trail Operations** show you the area where ores are melted and separated and tell you about the byproducts, such as fertilizers, converted from the waste. The tours (10am Mon.-Fri.) depart from the interpretive center.

Champion Lakes Provincial Park

Escape the smokestacks in this 1,426-hectare (3,520-acre) park, 23 kilometers (14 miles) east along Highway 3B toward Nelson, then a few kilometers farther along the access road. The park encompasses a chain of three small lakes nestled in the Bonnington Range. Hiking trails connect the lakes; First Lake, accessed from a trail at road's end, is the least busy. The park **campground** (519/826-6850 or 800/689-9025, www.discovercamping.ca, June-mid-Sept., $25), between Second and Third lakes, has 95 sites, of which 30 can be reserved in advance.

Salmo Toward Creston

East of Trail on Highway 3, the small village of Salmo (pop. 1,100) features old-fashioned wooden buildings, a small museum (1pm-5pm daily summer), and streets decorated in summer with huge hanging flower baskets bursting with brilliant color. The promise of quick fortune brought prospectors to gold diggings in the Salmo River watershed through the 1860s, but as in so many other boomtowns in the Kootenays, the riches were short-lived.

About 35 kilometers (22 miles) east of Salmo, at 1,133-hectare (2,800-acre) **Stagleap Provincial Park,** travelers can pause to picnic by Bridal Lake or go for a short hike. Continuing east, you'll crest 1,774-meter (5,820-foot) **Kootenay Pass,** where a beautiful alpine lake makes a pleasant stop. The parking lots at either end of the lake are linked by a short trail showcasing the stunted trees of this high alpine environment. From the pass, Highway 3 descends to Creston.

CASTLEGAR

Though endowed with the rich history of the Doukhobors, Castlegar (pop. 7,800) is not a particularly attractive place. Spread out along the barren Columbia River Valley, it's a real crossroads town. Here the Kootenay River drains into the much larger Columbia River, Highway 3 passes through east to west, Highway 3A leads north to Nelson, and Highway 22 leads south to Rossland and Trail. The town is also the major air gateway for the Kootenays.

The area's first European residents, the Doukhobors arrived in 1908. These pacifist Russian immigrants planted orchards, built sawmills, and even operated a jam factory while living in segregated villages along the valley floor. Many of their descendants still live in the area.

Sights

Castlegar's major attraction is the **Doukhobor Discovery Centre** (112 Heritage Way, 250/365-5327, 10am-5pm Mon.-Sat., noon-5pm Sun. May-Sept., adults $10, seniors $8, students $5), on the east side of the Columbia River along Highway

Castlegar

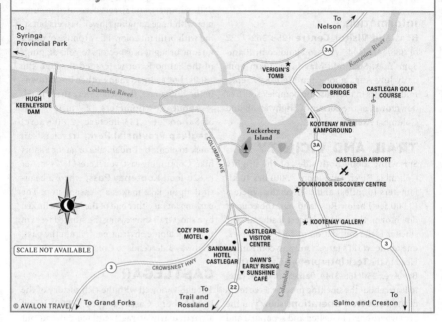

To
Syringa
Provincial Park

To
Nelson

Kootenay River

VERIGIN'S
TOMB

DOUKHOBOR
BRIDGE

CASTLEGAR GOLF
COURSE

HUGH
KEENLEYSIDE
DAM

Columbia River

KOOTENAY RIVER
KAMPGROUND

Zuckerberg
Island

COLUMBIA AVE.

CASTLEGAR AIRPORT

DOUKHOBOR DISCOVERY CENTRE

KOOTENAY GALLERY

COZY PINES
MOTEL

CASTLEGAR
VISITOR
CENTRE

SCALE NOT AVAILABLE

SANDMAN
HOTEL
CASTLEGAR

CROWSNEST HWY

DAWN'S
EARLY RISING
SUNSHINE
CAFÉ

Columbia River

© AVALON TRAVEL   To Grand Forks

To
Trail and
Rossland

To
Salmo and Creston

3A. The village allows a glimpse of the traditional lifestyle of these intriguing Russian immigrants. Admission includes a guided tour, led by Doukhobor descendants, through the main building and the simply furnished brick dwellings and outbuildings. Along the way you'll see some of the sect's artifacts, including handwoven clothing, crocheted bedspreads and shawls, a barn full of antique farming implements, and carved wooden spoons and ladles.

Zuckerberg Island, at the confluence of the Kootenay and Columbia Rivers, was the home of Russian immigrant Alexander Zuckerberg, who came to Castlegar to teach Doukhobor children in 1931. Connected to the mainland by a 150-meter (492-foot) suspension bridge, the tree-covered two-hectare (5-acre) island is interesting to explore. A one-kilometer (0.6-mile) trail passes a full-scale model of a *ckukuli* (First Nations winter pit house), as well as a Russian Orthodox chapel house, a cemetery, a log house, and many

other Zuckerberg creations. To get there, turn off Highway 22 at 9th Street, turn left on 7th Avenue, then immediately turn right.

While you're in a Russian frame of mind, visit the old **Doukhobor Bridge,** which crosses the Kootenay River along Highway 3A. It was built by the Doukhobors in the 1910s as a link from their community to Nelson; none of them had any bridge-building experience, but the 100-meter-long (328-foot) hand-poured concrete suspension bridge was used until 1968, and the remains can still be seen today.

Practicalities

The comfortable and reasonably priced **Cozy Pines Motel** (2118 Crestview Cres., 250/365-5613, www.cozypines.com, $80 s, $90 d) offers spotless rooms with kitchenettes and Wi-Fi. Immediately south of the Highway 3 and Highway 22 intersection is the **Sandman Hotel Castlegar** (1944 Columbia Ave., 250/365-8444 or 800/726-3626,

Valhalla Wilderness Society

Originally founded in the 1970s to lobby for the establishment of Valhalla Provincial Park, the Valhalla Wilderness Society was instrumental in convincing the BC government to designate the Khutzeymateen Valley, north of Prince Rupert, as Canada's first grizzly bear sanctuary. Closer to home, the organization also successfully campaigned for the creation of the White Grizzly Wilderness. Its latest successful crusade was for protection for the habitat of the Kermode bear in the north of the province, while ongoing wilderness protection issues include saving the world's boreal forests. For more information on their latest crusade, contact the **Valhalla Wilderness Society** (250/358-2333, www.vws.org).

www.sandmanhotels.ca, $135 s, $145 d), with an indoor pool, a fitness room, a business center, and a light breakfast included in the rates. Campers looking for hookups should head to **Kootenay River Kampground** (651 Rosedale Rd., 250/365-5604 or 877/318-0008, www.kootenayriverrv.com, tents $25, RVs $32-36), beside the Kootenay River just north of the airport. The setting at **Syringa Provincial Park** (519/826-6850 or 800/689-9025, www.discovercamping.ca, May-Sept., $26), on the banks of Lower Arrow Lake north out of town toward Nelson, then west off Highway 3A, has a beautiful white-sand beach, but facilities are limited.

For a mix of Canadian and Russian-influenced cooking, plan on breakfast or lunch at **Dawn's Early Rising Sunshine Café** (2305 Columbia Ave., 250/365-4916, 8am-2pm Tues.-Sat., lunch $8-12). In addition to the recognizable choices, you can feast on chili chowder borscht in a friendly, small-town café atmosphere. Head north of town, and across the river, to **Lion's Head Smoke & Brew Pub** (2629 Broadwater Rd., 250/365-2739, 11:30am-9pm Mon.-Sat., 10am-9pm Sun., $13-21), which is mostly the haunt of locals in the know. The menu combines traditional pub favorites and meats cooked in the pub's smoker, with a range of craft beers on tap to wash your meal down.

Castlegar Visitor Centre (1995 6th Ave., 250/365-6313, www.castlegar.com, 9am-5pm daily July-Aug., 9am-5pm Mon.-Fri. Sept.-June) is just south of Highway 3 as it passes through downtown.

THE SLOCAN VALLEY

The historically rich Slocan Valley, or "Silvery Slocan," nestles snugly between the Slocan and Valhalla Ranges of the Selkirk Mountains. In the 1890s, the valley sprang into the limelight when silver was discovered at Sandon. It's much quieter today, offering many picturesque towns and an abundance of outdoor-recreation opportunities.

New Denver

Named after Denver, Colorado, this picturesque town of 500 on Slocan Lake reached its mining peak in the 1890s. Today the short main street is lined with funky false-front stores and pioneer-style buildings left over from the prosperous silver days.

Down on the lake within easy walking distance of the main street, **Sweet Dreams Guesthouse** (702 Eldorado St., 250/358-2415, www.newdenverbc.com, $95 s or d) offers three large guest rooms and a cooked breakfast. Out of New Denver to the south, ★ **Silverton Resort** (250/358-7157, www.silvertonresort.com, $210-330 s or d) takes advantage of its watery location with self-contained cottages that are as close to the water as any I've seen in British Columbia. Campers can head to **Centennial Campground** (3rd Ave., 250/358-2867, May-Sept., $25-30), just off Highway 6 on the south side of the town and with full hookups, or beside Wilson Creek to **Rosebery Provincial Park** (no reservations, early May-mid-Sept., $20), six kilometers (4 miles) north of town.

Valhalla Provincial Park

This 49,893-hectare (123,290-acre) park

preserves the high peaks, deep valleys, and magnificent alpine lakes between the Valhalla Range of the Selkirk Mountains to the west and the west shores of Slocan Lake to the east. The most imposing peaks are in the south of the park, where spectacular spires rise above alpine meadows to a height of 2,800 meters (9,190 feet). With no roads, the most popular access is by boat from New Denver or Slocan, across the lake. An eight-kilometer (5-mile) lakeshore trail also connects Slocan with the west shore. There, hiking trails lead into the heart of the park. The most rewarding and popular is the **Beatrice Lake Trail,** 12.5 kilometers (7.8 miles) one-way. As with all trails starting from the lake, elevation gain is steady; you'll climb just under 1,000 vertical meters (3,280 feet) as you pass Little Cahill and Cahill Lakes and enter the massive cirque in which Beatrice Lake lies.

★ Sandon

The original Slocan Valley boomtown, Sandon was once a thriving town of 5,000 people. After the discovery of silver on the slopes of Idaho Peak, Sandon grew quickly, and at one time boasted 24 hotels, 23 saloons, banks, general stores, mining brokers' offices, and a newspaper. Sandon was destroyed by fire in 1902 but quickly rebuilt and incorporated as a city in 1908. The town remained the "soul of the Silvery Slocan" until the spring of 1955. That year the creek running through town flooded, sweeping away most of the city and leaving a ghost town. Today you can count the population on two hands.

The best place to start a visit to Sandon is the 1900 city hall, where the "Sandon Walking Tour Guide" is sold. The brochure details all the original structures—only a fraction of which remain—with a map that makes exploring on foot more enjoyable. Up the creek from city hall is **Sandon Museum** (250/358-7920, 10am-5pm daily June-mid-Oct., adults $5.50, seniors and children $3.50), where exhibits bring the old town back to life. Also on this side of the creek is the road to 2,280-meter (7,480-foot) **Idaho**

an interesting building in Sandon

Peak. The road is very rough, passable only in July and August. From the end of the 12-kilometer (7.5-mile) road, a steep one-kilometer (0.6-mile) trail leads to the summit and spectacular 360-degree views of the Kootenays.

NAKUSP

Forty-eight kilometers (30 miles) northwest of New Denver, Nakusp (pop. 1,600) was established during the mining-boom years. Today the small town is best known for its hot springs and its stunning location on Upper Arrow Lake at the foot of the Selkirk Mountains.

To get to **Nakusp Hot Springs** (250/265-4528, 9am-9pm daily), take Highway 23 north out of town for one kilometer (0.6 miles), then follow the signposted road along Kuskanax Creek for 12 kilometers (7.5 miles). Single entry is adults $10, seniors and children $9, or soak all day for adults $15 and seniors and children $12. To see the source of the springs, take the sandy 500-meter (0.3-mile) trail that starts behind the pools. You'll cross the river and clamber through damp rainforest crammed with ferns and mosses, then come to an impressive waterfall, where you can smell the sulfur from the springs.

Practicalities

A nearby resort with its own private hot springs is ★ **Halcyon Hot Springs Village & Spa** (32 kilometers/20 miles north of Nakusp, 250/265-3554 or 888/689-4699, www.halcyon-hotsprings.com, $229-449 s or d). Accommodations are in cabins, cottages (my favorite), chalets, or a luxury family-oriented Lodge Suite. On a terrace beside the main resort buildings is a campground ($70-85); the rates include access to the hot springs (day pass $22 pp). **Nakusp Municipal Campground** (314 8th Ave., www.nakusp-campground.com, mid-May-mid-Oct., $19-27), within walking distance of the beach and the main street, has large shaded sites, 10 powered and 30 unpowered sites, coin-operated showers, and firewood.

Nakusp Visitor Centre (92 6th Ave., 250/265-4234 or 800/909-8819) is open 9am-5pm daily in summer and 10am-4pm Monday-Friday in spring and fall.

Nelson

The elegant city of Nelson (pop. 10,500) lies in a picturesque setting on the West Arm of Kootenay Lake, 660 kilometers (410 miles) east of Vancouver. Its relaxed pace, hilly tree-lined streets, and late-19th-century architectural treasures have helped attract a mix of jaded big-city types, artists, and counterculture seekers. For visitors there is much to see and do around town, many good places to eat, and an eclectic atmosphere unlike anywhere else in the province. But while the city itself is uniquely charming, the surrounding wilderness of the Selkirk Mountains is Nelson's biggest draw.

SIGHTS

Nelson has 350 designated heritage buildings, more per capita than any other city in British Columbia except Victoria. Most can be viewed by walking around the downtown core between Baker and Vernon Streets. Pick up the detailed "Heritage Walking Tour" or "Heritage Motoring Tour" brochures from the information center. The walking-tour brochure details 26 downtown buildings, including the 1909 courthouse on Ward Street and the impressive stone-and-brick 1902 city hall on the corner of Ward and Vernon Streets.

Touchstones Nelson

Named for an instrument used to test for the purity of precious minerals, **Touchstones Nelson: Museum of Art & History** (502 Vernon St., 250/352-9813, 10am-5pm Mon.-Sat., 10am-4pm Sun. summer, 11am-4pm Tues., 10am-5pm Wed.-Sat., 11am-4pm Sun. fall-spring, adults $8, seniors $6, children $4) is in the historic stone post office building. The focus is on local history, with bright modern displays covering First Nations, explorers, miners, traders, early transportation, Nelson's contribution to World War I, and the Doukhobors.

Nelson Artwalk

Organized by the local arts council, Nelson's annual **Artwalk** (250/352-2402, www.ndac.ca) highlights the work of up to 100 local artists. For six weeks from early July, works are displayed citywide at various venues such as restaurants, hotels, the theater building, art galleries, and even the local pool hall. On one Friday of every month, receptions are held at each of the venues. The receptions feature live entertainment, refreshments, and the artists themselves, who are on hand to discuss their work. A brochure available at the information center and motels and galleries around town

Nelson

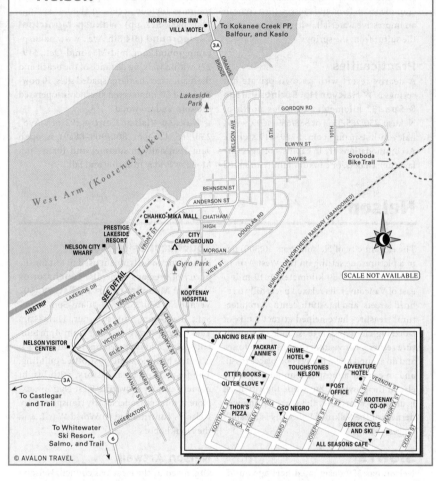

NORTH SHORE INN
VILLA MOTEL

To Kokanee Creek PP,
Balfour, and Kaslo

3A

ORANGE BRIDGE

Lakeside Park

GORDON RD

NELSON AVE

5TH

10TH

ELWYN ST

DAVIES

Svoboda Bike Trail

BEHNSEN ST

ANDERSON ST

West Arm (Kootenay Lake)

CHATHAM

CHAHKO-MIKA MALL

FRONT ST

HIGH

DOUGLAS RD

BURLINGTON NORTHERN RAILWAY (ABANDONED)

PRESTIGE LAKESIDE RESORT

NELSON CITY WHARF

CITY CAMPGROUND

MORGAN

Gyro Park

VIEW ST

SCALE NOT AVAILABLE

AIRSTRIP

LAKESIDE DR

SEE DETAIL

KOOTENAY HOSPITAL

VERNON ST

BAKER ST

CEDAR ST

HENDRYX ST

NELSON VISITOR CENTER

VICTORIA

SILICA

3A

STANLEY ST

WARD ST

JOSEPHINE ST

HALL ST

To Castlegar and Trail

OBSERVATORY

To Whitewater Ski Resort, Salmo, and Trail

6

© AVALON TRAVEL

DANCING BEAR INN

PACKRAT ANNIE'S

HUME HOTEL

TOUCHSTONES NELSON

ADVENTURE HOTEL

OTTER BOOKS

OUTER CLOVE

POST OFFICE

VERNON ST

VICTORIA

BAKER ST

HALL ST

KOOTENAY CO-OP

HENDRYX ST

KOOTENAY ST

THOR'S PIZZA

STANLEY ST

OSO NEGRO

WARD ST

SILICA

JOSEPHINE ST

GERICK CYCLE AND SKI

CEDAR ST

ALL SEASONS CAFE

contains biographies of each featured artist, tells where his or her work is displayed, and provides a map showing you the easiest way to get from one venue to the next.

RECREATION

In summer, the focus is on **Lakeside Park,** by the Orange Bridge (known locally as BOB, an acronym for Big Orange Bridge). It has a sandy beach, tennis courts, and a picnic area. Another pleasant spot to escape suburbia is **Cottonwood Falls,** which tumble from below a highway overpass off Baker Street. The surrounding area has been nicely landscaped and is well worth a visit, especially when spring runoff creates a massive flow of water.

The best nearby hiking is in **Kokanee Glacier Provincial Park,** but the bed of the Burlington Northern Railway, built in 1893, provides an interesting 9-kilometer (5.5-mile) trek right on Nelson's back doorstep. Access the railway from the top end of South Cherry Street. The many old logging

Nelson City Hall

ENTERTAINMENT

The **Hume Hotel** (422 Vernon St., 250/352-5331) is the center of Nelson's after-dark scene. This old hotel contains **Mike's Place** (11am-1am Mon.-Thurs., 11:30am-1:30am Fri.-Sat., 11:30am-midnight Sun.), an English-style pub that comes alive on weekends; **Spiritbar** (from 8pm daily), a live music venue; and the elegant **Library Lounge** (11am-11pm Mon.-Thurs., 11am-midnight Fri.-Sat., 11am-10pm Sun.), with tapestried chairs by a fireplace, books to read, and an elaborate draped ceiling—the perfect place to head to for a quiet drink or listen to live jazz. Down on the water, the bistro in the **Prestige Lakeside Resort** (701 Lakeside Dr., 250/352-7222, from 11am daily) has an expansive riverfront deck that catches the afternoon sun.

FOOD

Nelson's reputation as a center of good eating has come ahead in leaps and bounds during the past two decades, but a few old Chinese places hang on along Baker Street and remain open later than all the other restaurants listed.

Cafés

The independent spirit of Nelson is evident at the **Kootenay Co-op** (777 Baker St., 250/354-4077, 7:30am-9pm daily), where you can pick up goat's milk ice cream, organic apple juice, hemp toaster waffles, west coast salmon caught by the Nisga'a First Nations, eco-sweet chocolate, and preservative-free bread. If you're looking for lunch on the run, pick up healthy snacks, such as sweet curry rolls and vegan carrot cake, from the Hot Bar or Salad Bar.

Over the last two decades, ★ **Vienna Café** (411 Kootenay St., 250/354-4646, 8am-2:30pm Mon.-Sat., 10am-2:30pm Sun., lunch $6.50-10), in Packrat Annie's bookstore, has lost its counterculture vibe, but the food has gotten better. You can't go wrong with eggs benedict or an omelet—with free-range eggs, of course. At lunch, a chicken burger loaded with feta cheese and green pepper costs just $8. A generous serving of vegetarian five-bean

and mining roads surrounding the city are great for mountain biking; one favorite is the **Svoboda Bike Trail,** accessed along Elwyn Street beyond the college. For bike rentals and a trail map, head to **Gerick Cycle and Ski** (702 Baker St., 250/354-4622, 9am-5:30pm Mon.-Thurs., 9am-7pm Fri., 9am-5:30pm Sat., 11am-5pm Sun.).

Legendary powder and an off-the-beaten-path location make **Whitewater Ski Resort** (250/354-4944 or 800/666-9420, www.ski-whitewater.com, adults $84, seniors $67, children $42) a hidden gem. The small resort 20 kilometers (12 miles) south of Nelson sits beneath a string of 2,400-meter (7,900-foot) peaks that catch an amazing amount of snow. Three double chairlifts access 18 marked trails (the Summit Chair opens up the best powder-packed slopes). The area's abundant snowfall makes for a long season, but conditions are best in February and March. Whitewater has no on-mountain accommodations—just the lifts and a day lodge with a cafeteria, a rental shop, and a ski and snowboard school.

chili will also set you back just $8, or order a bowl of butternut squash soup livened up by a dash of maple syrup for $9.

With a more refined atmosphere, but also recommended for good breakfasts, is **General Store Restaurant** (Hume Hotel, 422 Vernon St., 250/352-5331, 6:30am-9pm daily). Breakfast is included for hotel guests, but even if you're not staying at the Hume, stop by for huge portions of traditional cooked breakfasts, including specializes such as crab eggs benedict with wasabi hollandaise ($15).

While the coffee is good at each of the above cafés, it's the specialty at **Empire Coffee** (616 Vernon St., 250/352-7211, 6am-6pm daily), at street level of the Adventure Hotel and my favorite place in town for a caffeine fix, and up the hill at **Oso Negro** (604 Ward St., 250/352-7661, 7am-6pm Mon.-Sat., 8am-4pm Sun.), which has an in-house roaster.

Casual Dining

Outer Clove (536 Stanley St., 250/354-1667, 11:30am-2:30pm and 4:30pm-8:30pm Mon.-Sat., $15-26) is typical of Nelson's better restaurants, appealing to modern tastes but in a relaxed, low-key environment. As the name suggests, the emphasis is on garlic (it's even an ingredient in a couple of the desserts), including starters such as Inner & Outer Cloves (heads of roasted garlic served with a wedge of brie and French bread).

The best and healthiest pizza in town comes straight from the oven at **Thor's** (303 Victoria St., 250/352-1212, 11am-10pm Mon.-Thurs., 11am-midnight Fri.-Sat., 4pm-9pm Sun., pizzas from $15.50). Everything is made from scratch, including the dough and sauces, and there's a flavor for everyone.

Tucked into a back alley behind the main street is ★ **All Seasons Café** (620 Herridge Lane, 250/352-0101, from 5pm daily, $22-36), a small yet stylish place with a delightful tree-shaded patio. Dishes such as pan-seared lamb sirloin will have you raving, while desserts like bourbon pecan pie will have you wishing you had more room. As a bonus, All Seasons has a well-thought-out selection of wines dominated by regional British Columbia selections, many available by the glass.

ACCOMMODATIONS
Under $50

Right downtown, ★ **Dancing Bear Inn** (171 Baker St., 250/352-7573 or 877/352-7573, www.dancingbearinn.com, dorms $26.50, $58-74 s or d) offers clean and comfortable accommodations at a very reasonable price. It features a cozy lounge area with a TV, reading material, information on local attractions and restaurants, and a cupboard full of board games. Other amenities include wireless Internet, a kitchen and laundry, and lockers. The dorm-style rooms are spacious, with a maximum of six beds in each. A few doubles and a single room are also available. Members of Hostelling International enjoy a $4 discount on the rates quoted above.

$50-100

Similar to the Dancing Bear in concept, but on a larger scale, the **Adventure Hotel** (616 Vernon St., 250/352-7211 or 888/722-2258, www.adventurehotel.ca, $88-144 s or d) provides clean, comfortable lodging at reasonable prices in the heart of downtown. Within the walls of what was once the New Grand Hotel are modern dorms and private rooms with clean lines and mood lighting. Options range from Budget rooms with a double-twin bunk combo and shared bath to Deluxe rooms with private baths and river views. Amenities include a rooftop sauna and downstairs café and pub.

$100-150

Villa Motel (250/352-5515 or 888/352-5515, www.thevillamotel.com, $125-189 s or d) and **North Shore Inn** (250/352-6606 or 800/593-6636, www.nshoreinn.com, $104-149 s or d) are directly across the Orange Bridge from downtown. Both offer regular motel rooms of a respectable standard, while the former has a small saltwater indoor pool and Chinese restaurant.

$150-200

Dating to 1898, the four-story **Hume Hotel** (422 Vernon St., 250/352-5331 or 877/568-0888, www.humehotel.com, $180-340 s, $119-159 d) is a city landmark and has a reputation as one of Nelson's finest accommodations. It provides attractive, heritage-themed rooms last renovated in 2016. Some have lake views while others have king beds and soaker tubs. Rates include hot breakfast in the downstairs restaurant.

Prestige Lakeside Resort (701 Lakeside Dr., 250/352-7222, www.prestigehotelsandresorts.com, $189-249 s or d) is the bright spot along Nelson's rather barren waterfront. This resort features a spa facility, a fitness center, a swimming pool, a private marina, and a restaurant.

Campgrounds

The best place to camp near Nelson is **Kokanee Creek Provincial Park** (reservations 519/826-6850 or 800/689-9025, www.discovercamping.ca, May-Sept., $28-32), 20 kilometers (12 miles) northeast of Nelson, but if you haven't made reservations well in advance, plan on staying at the **City Campground** (90 High St., 250/352-7618, May-mid-Oct., $26-45), on the northeast side of downtown. Amenities are limited, but it does have a kitchen shelter with basic cooking facilities.

INFORMATION AND SERVICES

All the information you'll need on Nelson and the Kootenays is available at **Nelson Visitor Centre** (91 Baker St., 250/352-3433 or 877/663-5706, www.discovernelson.com, 8:30am-5pm daily summer, 8:30am-4:30pm Mon.-Fri. fall-spring), in a restored railway station at the west end of town.

Otter Books (398 Baker St., 250/352-3434, 9:30am-5:30 Mon.-Sat., 11am-4pm Sun.) has an excellent selection of books about the Kootenays ranging from ghost town guides to the history of the Kettle River Railway. Cavernous **Packrat Annie's** (411 Kootenay St., 250/354-4722, 9am-5:30pm Mon.-Fri., 9am-5pm Sat., 10am-3pm Sun.) sells used books and CDs, and offers good people-watching opportunities. **Kootenay Hospital** is east of downtown (3 View St., 250/352-3111). The **post office** is at 514 Vernon Street.

GETTING THERE AND AROUND

Although roads radiate out from Nelson in all directions, it's a long way to other major centers. Closest is Spokane, in Washington State, which is 237 kilometers (148 miles) south. Driving in from the Okanagan Valley takes around four hours from Kelowna (338 kilometers/211 miles) and at least seven or eight hours from Vancouver (660 kilometers/410 miles). Continuing eastward, allow three hours for the 221-kilometer (138-mile) mountain drive to Cranbrook.

Long-distance bus transportation is provided by **Greyhound.** The depot (1128 Lakeside Dr., 250/352-3939) is at the Chahko-Mika Mall. From Vancouver, buses come into Nelson via Castlegar, then continue east to Cranbrook. For details on local bus transportation, call the **Nelson Transit System** (250/352-8201).

Kootenay Lake and Creston

Heading first north, then east from Nelson, Highway 3A follows a narrow arm of Kootenay Lake before coming to the main 100-kilometer-long (60-mile) body of water at Balfour. From there, you have a choice of routes. You can cross Kootenay Lake by ferry and follow the east shore of the lake down to Creston, or you can continue north up the west shore of the lake, passing through Ainsworth Hot Springs and Kaslo before arcing back west to Slocan Valley and Arrow Lake.

NELSON TO KASLO

It's 70 kilometers (44 miles) north from Nelson to Kaslo. A number of parks and small communities dot the route, with Kootenay Lake nearly always in view.

Kokanee Creek Provincial Park

This 257-hectare (630-acre) lakefront park 20 kilometers (12 miles) northeast of Nelson features a great sandy beach and one of the Kootenays' most popular campgrounds. Short walking trails crisscross the park, and kokanee (freshwater salmon) can be viewed in Kokanee Creek at the end of summer (access is from the visitors center). Instead of migrating in from the ocean like their anadromous cousins, kokanee spend their lives in the larger lakes of British Columbia's interior, spawning each summer in the rivers and streams draining into the lakes. The very popular day-use area runs the length of a one-kilometer (0.6-mile) sandy beach.

The large campground's sites (May-Sept., $28-32) have showers and a few have electrical hookups; regardless, they all fill fast through summer, so make reservations through **Discover Camping** (519/826-6850 or 800/689-9025, www.discovercamping.ca) well in advance.

★ Kokanee Glacier Provincial Park

Straddling the highest peaks of the Selkirk Mountains, this 32,035-hectare (79,160-acre) mountain wilderness park can be seen from downtown Nelson. This is one of British Columbia's premier provincial parks, filled with magnificent scenery and abundant wildlife and providing some unrivaled opportunities for backcountry travel. The park is named for a massive glacier that, along with two other glaciers and 30 lakes, feeds dozens of creeks and rivers flowing west to Slocan Lake and east to Kootenay Lake. Almost entirely above 1,800 meters (5,900 feet) elevation, the park's environment is very different from the valley floor—dominated by barren peaks and, for a few short weeks in the middle of summer, meadows of lush subalpine wildflowers.

The heart of the park is too steep and rugged to be penetrated by roads, so all the best features must be reached on foot. The main access is via an unsealed road that turns off Highway 3A about 20 kilometers (12 miles) from Nelson and follows Kokanee Creek 16 kilometers (10 miles) to **Gibson Lake.** A 2.5-kilometer (1.6-mile) trail circles the lake, but the best hiking is farther afield. From Gibson Lake, it's four kilometers (2.5 miles) uphill to beautiful **Kokanee Lake.** There the trail flattens out, continuing three kilometers (2 miles) to Kaslo Lake and another two kilometers (1.2 miles) to **Slocan Chief Cabin,** a century-old structure that sleeps 12 ($25 pp).

Because of the park's remote location, it's vital to pick up information on road and hiking-trail conditions at the visitors center in Nelson. In years of high snowfall, some hiking trails are impassable until late July.

World's Longest Free Ferry Ride

Back in the 1890s, stern-wheelers plied Kootenay Lake, dropping off prospectors and supplies at isolated mining camps and settlements along its shores. But completion of the railway in the early 1900s quickly put most of the stern-wheelers out of action. Today one public ferry remains, and it's now the "world's longest free ferry ride." The 45-minute trip across Kootenay Lake from Balfour to Kootenay Bay offers majestic lake and mountain scenery and makes a good route to Creston and points east. It departs every 60 to 90 minutes 6:30am-9:30pm daily.

Ainsworth Hot Springs

Overlooking Kootenay Lake from a hillside 17 kilometers north of Balfour, the **Ainsworth Hot Springs** (Hwy. 31, 250/229-4212, 10am-9pm daily, adults $12.50, seniors $11, children $9) were discovered in the early 1800s by First Nations people who found that the hot, odorless water helped heal their wounds and ease their aches and pains. Today the springs have been commercialized and include a main outdoor pool, a hot tub, a steam bath, and a cold plunge pool.

If you want a bit more pampering, stay at **Ainsworth Hot Springs Resort** (250/229-4212 or 800/668-1171, www.ainsworth-hotsprings.com, $179-329 s or d), which features exercise and massage rooms, wireless Internet, a lounge, and a restaurant overlooking the main pool and beautiful Kootenay Lake. Although room rates start at $179, you pay from $219 for a lake view.

KASLO

Tree-lined streets graced by elegant late-19th-century architecture, lake and mountain views from almost every street, and the world's oldest passenger stern-wheeler tied up at the wharf make Kaslo (pop. 1,000), 70 kilometers (44 miles) north of Nelson, a worthwhile stop.

Another of the Kootenays' great boomtowns, Kaslo began as a sawmill community in 1889. But nearby silver strikes in 1893 quickly turned the town into a bustling city of 3,000 and an important commercial hub; a railway brought silver down from Sandon to Kaslo, where it was loaded onto steamers and shipped out to Creston and the outside world. The town's 1898 city hall is one of only two wooden buildings in the country that are still the seats of local government.

SS *Moyie*

Dry-docked by the lakefront stands the 50-meter-long (164-foot) **SS *Moyie*** (324 Front St., 250/353-2525, 10am-5pm daily

the SS *Moyie*

mid-May-early Oct., adults $12, seniors $10, children $5), the last Canadian Pacific Railway stern-wheeler to splash up Kootenay Lake. Built in 1897 and launched the following year at Nelson, the grand old red-and-white vessel was used for transportation of passengers, freight, and mail right up until its retirement in 1957. Today, protected as a National Historic Site, the ship serves as a museum containing a fine collection of photos, antiques, and artifacts of the region.

Practicalities

Right downtown, the **Kaslo Motel** (330 D Ave., 250/353-2431 or 877/353-2431, www.kaslomotel.ca, $78-88 s or d) has 18 clean and convenient but basic motel rooms and cabins, some with small kitchens and air-conditioning. North of town, **Lakewood Inn** (Kohle Rd., 250/353-2395, www.lakewood-inn.com) has been taking in guests since the 1920s. Lakefront cabins are $120-140 s or d, while campers pay $30-50 for one of just seven sites.

Front Street is lined with small-town businesses, many with historic facades. If you're hungry, the ones to look for are **Landmark Bakery** (416 Front St., 250/353-1917, 8:30am-5pm daily summer, 10am-4pm Mon.-Sat. Sept.-June, lunch $6.50-10), with good coffee, a wide range of sweet treats, and wireless Internet access; **Sunnyside Naturals** (404 Front St., 250/353-9667, 9am-6pm Mon.-Sat., 11am-5pm Sun., lunch $6-9), for freshly squeezed juices and organic foods; and, at the top end, **Rosewood Café** (213 5th St., 250/353-7673, 11:30am-8pm Wed.-Sun., $14-22) for more substantial meals.

In a restored railway station that also serves as the entrance to the SS *Moyie* is **Kaslo Visitor Centre** (324 Front St., 250/353-2525, 9am-5pm daily mid-May-mid-Oct.).

ACROSS KOOTENAY LAKE

From Balfour, the world's longest free ferry ride takes you across Kootenay Lake to Kootenay Bay. The *Osprey* offers lots of outside spots at which to sit and soak up the surrounding mountain panorama.

★ Crawford Bay

From the ferry dock, Highway 3A traverses a low ridge before dropping into Crawford Bay, a small community sandwiched between the Purcell Mountains and the water. Artisans' outlets have put this village of 200 on the map. On the left as you descend the hill is **North Woven Broom** (16126 Hwy. 3A, 250/227-9245, 9:30am-5pm daily early Apr.-mid-Oct.), western Canada's only traditional broom manufacturer. The raw materials (collected by hand in Arizona by the owners) are handcrafted into brooms using 19th-century methods. Stop in anytime and you're likely to find craftspeople hard at work and eager to share their knowledge of this lost art. The workshop is crammed with brooms of all shapes and sizes, ranging in price $30-220. A little farther along is **Kootenay Forge** (16095 Hwy. 3A, 250/227-9467, 10am-5pm daily May-mid-Oct.), a traditional blacksmith shop where you can watch artisans practicing this ancient trade.

Also at Crawford Bay is **Kokanee Springs Resort** (250/227-9226 or 800/979-7999, www.kokaneesprings.com, $159-199 s or d), where the 64 rooms and suites are decorated in a stylish deep-blue color, offset by the natural colors of wooden trim and furniture. The resort is also home to one of the province's most picturesque golf courses (greens fees $82), which is the major draw.

The pick of local accommodations is ★ **Wedgwood Retreat** (16002 Crawford Creek Rd., 250/227-9233 or 888/960-6017, www.wedgwoodretreat.ca, Apr.-Oct., $150-168 s or d). Set on 20 beautiful hectares (50 acres) adjacent to the golf course and within walking distance of a beach, this 1910 home offers six heritage-style rooms and two cabins, each with a private bath and wireless Internet.

South Along Kootenay Lake

From Crawford Bay, it's 80 kilometers (50 miles) of lake-hugging road to Creston. Along the way you'll pass small clusters of houses and **Lockhart Beach Provincial Park,** which has a small campground (no reservations, mid-May-Sept., $23).

CRESTON

In a wide, fertile valley at the extreme southern end of Kootenay Lake lies Creston, a thriving agricultural center of 5,200. Although the town is south of the Kootenays' most spectacular mountains, the scenery is still impressive; the Selkirk Mountains flank the valley to the west, while the Purcell Mountains do the same to the east. Fruit stands lining Highway 3 on the east side of Creston from the west are a sign of the district's most obvious industry. Stop for locally grown asparagus (May-early June), strawberries (July), cherries (mid-July-mid-Aug.), peaches (late July-Sept.), and apples (Aug.-Oct.).

Sights

Creston Museum (219 Devon St., 403/428-9262, 9am-4pm Tues.-Sat. summer, call for off-season hours, adults $4, children $3), on the west side of town and south across the railway tracks, is home to a canoe built by the Kutenai people that's unlike any other in North America but similar to the style used by the Gilyaki people in Russia, leading ethnologists to speculate about possible links.

Creston is home to the **Columbia Brewery** (1220 Erickson St., 250/428-1238), producer of British Columbia's popular Kokanee beer. Tours (5 times daily Mon.-Fri., 4 times daily Sat.-Sun. summer, $5 pp) are offered. At the brewery entrance is the Kokanee Beer Gear Store (9am-4:30pm Mon.-Fri. Apr.-Oct.).

★ Creston Valley Wildlife Management Area

The 7,000-hectare (17,300-acre) **Creston Valley Wildlife Management Area** (1874 Wildlife Rd., 250/402-6908, 9am-4pm Tues.-Sat. mid-May-June, 9am-4pm daily July-Aug., 9am-4pm Wed.-Fri. Sept., free) lies 10 kilometers (6 miles) west of Creston. It extends from Kootenay Lake to the Canada-U.S. border. Protecting vital resting grounds along the Pacific Flyway, the site provides a haven for more than 250 species of birds, including a large population of ospreys, a flock of the rare Forester's tern, and a nesting colony of western grebes. Start a visit at the park's wildlife center, where displays focus on the abundant birdlife, as well as on mammals and reptiles present in the reserve. From the

Wood ducks are one of the many birds you may see at the Creston Valley Wildlife Management Area.

center, hiking trails lead along dikes separating wetlands and ponds. Even along the boardwalk leading into the center you may spy some local residents: turtles that sun themselves on half-submerged logs. Special events through the year coincide with various natural cycles, such as the spring **Morning Chorus** (Sat. in June) guided walk in search of songbirds.

Food and Accommodations

The busiest place in town each morning is **Creston Valley Bakery** (113 10th Ave., 250/428-2661, 6:30am-5:30pm Mon.-Sat., lunch $8-12), where you'll find plenty of tables and a large selection of freshly baked cakes and pastries, as well as a soup-and-sandwich menu of lunches.

Nothing stands out here; you could stay right downtown at the aptly named **Downtowner Motor Inn** (1218 Canyon St., 250/428-2238 or 800/665-9904, www.downtownercreston.com, $90-130 s or d). Rooms are air-conditioned and come with wireless Internet. **Scottie's RV Park** (1409 Erickson Rd., 250/428-4256 or 800/982-4256, www.scottiesrv.com, $28-39) enjoys a pleasant treed setting across the road from the Columbia Brewery.

Information

Creston Visitor Centre is along the main highway through town (121 Northwest Blvd., 250/428-4342, www.crestonvalleybc.com, 9am-5pm daily summer, 9am-5pm Mon.-Fri. fall-spring).

East Kootenays

In the southeastern corner of the province, the East Kootenays encompass the Purcell Mountains and the upper reaches of the Columbia River, with the Rocky Mountains rising abruptly from the Columbia Valley to the Continental Divide and the British Columbia-Alberta border to the west. The crossroads of the region is the service center of Cranbrook, from where Highway 3 heads west to Fernie and the neighboring province of Alberta, and Highway 93/95 parallels the Columbia River northward through a region dotted with golf courses, hot springs, and many provincial parks.

EAST FROM CRESTON

From Creston, the Crowsnest Highway (Hwy. 3) crosses the **Purcell Mountains** and descends to Cranbrook, the region's largest town. The distance between the two towns is a little over 100 kilometers (62 miles).

Yahk

Yahk grew into a thriving lumber town in the 1920s but was abandoned by the 1930s. Today,

empty houses and a still-operating hotel are all that remain along the main street. Tiny **Yahk Provincial Park** lies beside the rushing Moyie River east of town. The campground (mid-May-Sept., $21) has only 26 sites and reservations are not taken, so arrive in early afternoon to be assured of a spot. South of Yahk is the U.S.-Canada border and the **Kingsgate port of entry,** open daily 24 hours.

Moyie

North from Yahk, Highway 3/95 parallels the Moyie River to its source at **Moyie Lake,** a deep-blue body of water backed by cliffs. Halfway along the lake, Moyie, once boasting a population of 1,500, today holds nothing more than a few historic buildings, a pub, and a gas station; the 1904 church on Tavistock Street and the 1907 fire hall beside the highway are among the original survivors. Miners working the nearby St. Eugene Mine for lead and silver were the first settlers. The old mine is visible on the hill by wandering down to the lakeshore.

Around 13 kilometers (8 miles) north of

town is 91-hectare (220-acre) **Moyie Lake Provincial Park,** which has a sandy swimming beach, a rocky dog beach, short interpretive trails, and the chance to view kokanee spawning on gravel river beds in late summer. The large campground (519/826-6850 or 800/689-9025, www.discovercamping.ca, early May-Sept., $33) has semiprivate sites scattered through an open forest, hot showers, and easy access to the beach.

CRANBROOK

Crossroads of the eastern Kootenays, Cranbrook (pop. 19,500) nestles at the base of the Purcell Mountains 106 kilometers (66 miles) east of Creston and provides spectacular views eastward to the Canadian Rockies. The main touristy reason to stop is the rail museum, but with the surrounding wilderness, nearby Fort Steele Heritage Town, and well-priced motels, it's a good base for further exploration.

Canadian Museum of Rail Travel

Cranbrook's main attraction, the **Canadian Museum of Rail Travel** (57 Van Horne St., 250/489-3918, 10am-5pm daily mid-May.-mid-Oct., 10am-5pm Tues.-Sat.

mid-Oct.-mid-May, Grand Tour adults $21.30, seniors $18, children $5.50) is on a siding of the main Canadian Pacific Railway line directly opposite downtown. Most of the displays are outdoors, spread along three sets of track, including the only surviving set of railcars from the *Trans-Canada Limited,* a luxury train (also called "The Millionaires' Train") built for the Canadian Pacific Railway in 1929. The dining, sleeping, and solarium lounge cars sport inlaid mahogany and walnut paneling, plush upholstery, and brass fixtures. Restoration displays, a viewing corridor, a model railway display, a slide show, and guided tours of the car interiors are included in the price of the two-hour Grand Tour, or you can choose abbreviated tours (from adults $6, seniors $5, children $2.50), but you'll miss the best of the museum.

Heritage Walking and Driving Tour

The locals are proud of their downtown heritage buildings, which you can view on a self-guided walking tour by picking up the handy *Cranbrook Heritage Tour* brochure from the visitors center or the railway museum (stop number 1 on the tour). You can still

Moyie Lake

Cranbrook

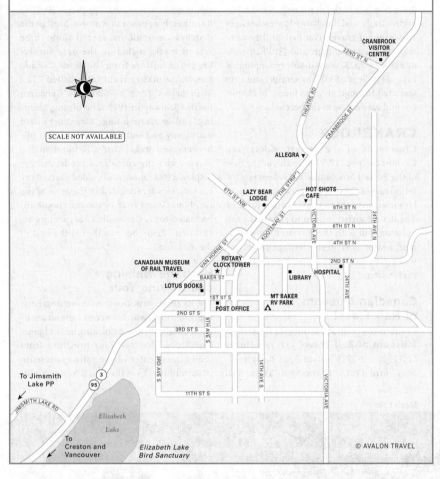

SCALE NOT AVAILABLE

CRANBROOK VISITOR CENTRE

22ND ST N

THEATRE RD

CRANBROOK ST

ALLEGRA

6TH ST NW

LAZY BEAR LODGE

"THE STRIP"

KOOTENAY ST

HOT SHOTS CAFE

8TH ST N

VICTORIA AVE

6TH ST N

24TH AVE N

4TH ST N

VAN HORNE ST

CANADIAN MUSEUM OF RAIL TRAVEL

ROTARY CLOCK TOWER

BAKER ST

LOTUS BOOKS

1ST ST S

POST OFFICE

2ND ST N

LIBRARY

HOSPITAL

MT BAKER RV PARK

24TH AVE

2ND ST S

9TH AVE S

3RD ST S

3RD AVE S

14TH AVE S

VICTORIA AVE

To Jimsmith Lake PP

JIMSMITH LAKE RD

3 95

11TH ST S

Elizabeth Lake

To Creston and Vancouver

Elizabeth Lake Bird Sanctuary

© AVALON TRAVEL

see the home of Colonel Baker—the original Cranbrook developer for whom downtown's main street is named—in Baker Park, off 1st Street South.

If you're still in a heritage mood and heading for Kimberley, take Old Airport Road (a continuation of Theatre Rd.) north to **St. Eugene's Mission Church,** between Cranbrook and Kimberley. Built in 1897, this is the finest Gothic-style mission church in the province; it features beautiful hand-painted Italian stained-glass windows. The adjacent mission has been extensively renovated and is now a hotel, itself well worth walking through for its historic value.

Elizabeth Lake Bird Sanctuary

Beside the highway at the southern city limits (park at the information center), this large area of wetlands is a haven for many species of waterfowl, including Canada geese, teal, and ringneck, scaup, redhead, bufflehead, goldeneye, and ruddy ducks. You can also see coots, grebes, black terns, and songbirds. Mammals present include muskrats, white-tailed deer, and occasionally moose.

Food

A local favorite for an inexpensive meal is **Hot Shots Café** (1924 8th St., 250/489-2010, 7:30am-9:30pm Mon.-Sat., 9am-5:30pm Sun., lunch $10-15). Breakfast choices include homemade granola; a Mediterranean breakfast pita; and a prosciutto, egg, and blue cheese panini. Asian-inspired menu choices at lunch include lemongrass and curried prawn salad, grilled satays, and a Thai coconut noodle bowl.

Allegra (1225 Cranbrook St. N, 250/426-8812, 5pm-9pm Wed.-Sun., $16-33) is an intimate restaurant with a menu dominated by southern European specialties: think air-dried beef carpaccio for a starter and duck breast simmered in a rosemary and huckleberry sauce as a main, or save a few bucks with one of the deliciously creative pastas. The wine list has lots of Canadian choices sold by the glass or bottle, including from the nearby Skimmerhorn Winery.

Accommodations and Camping

Most motels are along Highway 3 through town. The highway is known as Van Horne Street south of 4th Street North and Cranbrook Street to the north. On average, motel prices here are among the lowest in the province, making it a good spot to rest overnight.

In the heart of the commercial strip, **Lazy Bear Lodge** (621 Cranbrook St., 250/426-6086 or 888/808-6086, www.lazybear-lodge. ca, $75 s, $80-85 d) is an old roadside motel snazzed up with log trim, beds of bright flowers, and a colorful coat of paint. The rooms remain basic, but each has a coffeemaker and some have a fridge and microwave. Out front is a small swimming pool for guest use.

North of town, the Ktunaxa nation have transformed an abandoned mission building into the sprawling **St. Eugene Golf Resort & Casino** (7777 Mission Rd., 250/420-2000 or 866/292-2020, www.steugene.ca, $160-215 s or d). Surrounded by rolling farmland and with distant views to the Canadian Rockies, it's a beautiful property, complete with a golf course, an outdoor swimming pool, a casino, and a restaurant and bar. Check the website for packages offered year-round.

One of the area's most attractive campgrounds is in **Jimsmith Lake Provincial Park,** four kilometers (2.5 miles) off the main highway at the southern outskirts of the city. The park has a sandy beach on a small lake (swimming, fishing) and 35 **campsites** (no reservations, mid-May-early Oct., $23). Downtown, **Mt. Baker RV Park** (1501 1st St. S., 250/489-0056, www.mountbakerrvpark. com, Apr.-Oct., $26-39) provides grassy tent sites, full hookups, wireless Internet, and clean restrooms with showers.

Information and Services

The main **Cranbrook Visitor Centre** (2279 Cranbrook St. N., 250/426-5914 or 800/222-6174, www.cranbrookchamber. com, 9am-5pm daily summer, 9am-5pm Mon.-Fri. fall-spring) is at the northern entrance near the beginning of the strip. **Lotus Books** (33 10th Ave. S., 250/426-3415, 9am-5:30pm Mon.-Sat.) is loaded with local reading material, including some interesting books on the region's gold rush history. **Cranbrook Regional Hospital** is off 2nd Street on 24th Avenue North (250/426-5281). The **post office** is downtown (10th Ave. and 1st St. S.).

Getting There

Although Cranbrook does have a small airport with scheduled flights from Vancouver with **Air Canada,** most visitors arrive by road. Cranbrook is in the far southeast corner of the province, closer to Calgary (390 kilometers/244 miles) via Highway 3 and Highway 2 than Vancouver (840 kilometers/522 miles); allow at least nine hours from Vancouver as Highway 3 is a winding mountain road for much of the route across the bottom of the province.

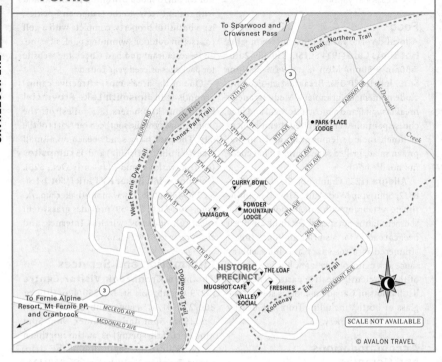

Fernie

To Sparwood and
Crowsnest Pass

Great Northern Trail

SCALE NOT AVAILABLE

© AVALON TRAVEL

FERNIE AND VICINITY

Fernie (pop. 5,200) nestles in the Elk Valley 100 kilometers (60 miles) east of Cranbrook on Highway 3. Town center is a couple of blocks south of the highway, holding the usual array of historic buildings and small-town shops. The main attraction is winter, when one of British Columbia's great little alpine resorts comes alive nearby.

About five kilometers (3 miles) south of town is 259-hectare (850-acre) **Mount Fernie Provincial Park,** where hiking trails lead along a picturesque creek and to a waterfall.

Fernie Alpine Resort

Fernie Alpine Resort (7 kilometers/4.5 miles south of Fernie, 250/423-4655, www.skifernie. com) is another of British Columbia's legendary winter resorts, boasting massive annual snowfalls, challenging skiing and riding, and

uncrowded slopes. The 1,000-hectare (2,500-acre) lift-serviced area lies under a massive ridge that catches an incredible nine meters (30 feet) of snow each year, filling a wide, open bowl with enough of the white fluffy stuff to please all powder-hounds. Lift tickets cost adults $105, seniors $84, youths $79, children $42, under age six free.

In July and August, one chairlift operates, opening up hiking and mountain biking terrain. Sightseers pay adults $26, seniors $22, children $13 to ride the chairlift. Use the lift to take the hard work out of mountain biking for $53 for a full day. Bikes can be rented at the base village for $50-80 per day.

Food

You will find a good selection of cafés and restaurants scattered through the historic downtown core. Best exemplifying Fernie's laid-back vibe is ★ **Valley Social** (562 2nd Ave., 778/519-5272, 7am-5pm Mon.-Thurs., 7am-10pm Fri., 8am-10pm Sat., 9am-5pm Sun., lunch $8-18), in the heart of the historic precinct. The rustic-hip design, the bustle of locals getting coffee to go, the expertise of the baristas, and the use of local vendors for everything from the coffee beans to the beer make the Valley Social a great place to spend some time. Food choices range from pastries to cheeseboards to share.

Two other downtown cafés are well-worth investigation. Don't be put off by the nondescript facade of **Freshies Cafe** (592 3nd Ave., 250/423-3833, 5am-5pm Mon.-Fri., 6am-5pm Sat.-Sun., lunch $5.50-11); inside you'll find a warm and welcoming small-town café with good coffee and inexpensive food, including delicious crepes. **Mugshots Cafe** (592 3nd Ave., 250/423-8018, 7am-5pm Mon.-Fri., 8am-4pm Sat., lunch $6-11) is a low-key place one block back from the historic main street. Its draw is simple healthy cooking, prepared from scratch in-house. Soups and sandwiches are mostly under $10, and the tables out front are shaded.

The Loaf (641 2nd Ave., 250/423-7702, 10am-10pm daily, $12-18) has morphed from a bakery into a full restaurant, without losing its friendly small-town vibe. You can still preorder their delicious bread, but its fresh, healthy cooking that draws the locals in now. The menu is dominated by simple pastas from $12. Pizza, made from scratch, is $11-18, but 3pm-5pm daily all pizzas are just $10 and beer is $5.

Opposite Powder Mountain Lodge in a converted residence, the ★ **Curry Bowl** (931 7th Ave., 250/423-2695, 4pm-10pm daily, $15-24) won't win any design awards, but with delicious dishes like mango shrimp curry and a Vietnamese chicken stir-fry, it really doesn't matter. Along the same strip, **Yamagoya** (741 7th Ave., 250/430-0090, 5pm-10pm daily, $8-14) is a stylish dining room that offers top-notch Japanese cuisine at equally reasonable prices.

Accommodations and Camping

Best of the bunch for budget-conscious travelers is ★ **Powder Mountain Lodge** (892 Hwy. 3, 250/423-4492, www.powdermountainlodge.com, $89-155 s or d). This renovated motel has loads of parking, an indoor hot tub, an outdoor pool, and a barbecue area. **Park Place Lodge** (742 Hwy. 3, 250/423-6871 or 888/381-7275, www.parkplacelodge.com, $129 s, $139 d) is a modern three-story hotel along the main road. Amenities include spacious and elegant rooms opening to an atrium-enclosed pool, a family-friendly restaurant, and a pub.

Up at the alpine resort, **Griz Inn** (250/423-9221 or 800/661-0118, www.grizinn.com, $104-154 s or d) offers a mix of hotel rooms and kitchen-equipped suites, an smallish indoor pool, an oversize outdoor hot tub, and a restaurant (11am-8pm Thurs.-Sun. summer, 11am-8pm daily winter).

The best bet for campers is **Mount Fernie Provincial Park** (519/826-6850 or 800/689-9025, www.discovercamping.ca, mid-May-Sept., $30), five kilometers (3 miles) south of town and four kilometers (2.5 miles) north of the Akamina-Kishinena Provincial Park access road. Facilities are basic, but it's a pleasant setting in an old-growth forest, and a short trail leads along Lizard Creek. This park is extremely popular, so book as far in advance as possible.

Information

Beside the highway, through town to the north, is **Fernie Visitor Centre** (250/423-6868, www.ferniechamber.com, 9am-6pm daily July-Aug., 9am-5pm Mon.-Fri. Sept.-June).

Akamina-Kishinena Provincial Park

Bordering Glacier National Park in Montana and Waterton Lakes National Park in Alberta, this remote tract of 10,920 hectares (27,000 acres) protects the extreme southeastern corner of British Columbia. The park is named for its two main waterways, which flow southward into Montana. The landscape has changed little in thousands of years, since the Kootenay people rested in the open meadows beside Kishinena Creek before crossing the Continental Divide to hunt bison on the prairies.

The only access is on foot from one of two trailheads. The longer option is from the end of an unsealed road that leaves Highway 3 about 16 kilometers (10 miles) south of Fernie. The road leads 110 kilometers (68 miles) into the Flathead River Valley, where trails climb along Kishinena and then Akamina Creek into the park. The most popular and easiest access to the park is by hiking trail from the Akamina Parkway in Waterton Lakes National Park in Alberta.

Sparwood

Thirty kilometers (19 miles) northeast of Fernie, Sparwood (pop. 4,200) is a small coal-mining community (the coal seams and part of the mining operations can be seen on the ridge high above town), but a more eye-catching element of the local industry is the **world's largest truck,** which sits beside Highway 3 in the center of town. Beside the truck is **Sparwood Visitor Centre** (141 Aspen Dr., 250/425-2423 or 877/485-8185, www.sparwood.ca, 9am-6pm daily summer, 9am-5pm Mon.-Fri. fall-spring), where you can arrange a tour of the mines (1pm Tues.-Thurs. July-Aug., free). Those looking for a roof over their head should plan on staying down the road in Fernie, while campers will enjoy full services and the forested setting at **Mountain Shadows Campground** (606 Sparwood Dr., 250/425-7815, www.mountainshadows.ca, May-Oct., $25-35) signposted from Highway 93 south of town.

Elkford and Vicinity

Surrounded by towering peaks, this coal-mining community of 2,500 lies 35 kilometers (22 miles) north of Sparwood on Highway 43. Abundant recreation opportunities in the area include fishing, wildlife viewing,

and exploring the wilderness of Elk Lakes. There's a small **municipal campground** ($20) within walking distance of downtown. On the north side of town, **Elkford Visitor Centre** (750 Fording Dr., 250/865-4015 or 877/355-9453, www.elkford.ca, 9am-5pm daily mid-May-Aug., 9am-5pm Mon.-Fri. Sept.-mid-May) is in the community center, well worth visiting in itself for its impressive architecture.

Elk Lakes Provincial Park encompasses more than 17,000 hectares (42,000 acres) of rugged wilderness 67 kilometers (42 miles) north of Elkford. From the end of the road, it's an easy one-kilometer (0.6-mile) walk to **Lower Elk Lake,** and then one kilometer (0.6 miles) beyond the end of the lake to **Upper Elk Lake.** At the lower lake, a narrow trail climbs to a lookout. Aside from the long drive in, the ratio of effort to reward in reaching these lakes is unmatched in the Kootenays.

NORTH FROM CRANBROOK

At the north end of Cranbrook, the highway heading north divides, with the western option passing through Kimberley and a more direct route following the Kootenay River through an area that was flooded with miners after gold was discovered on Wild Horse Creek in 1865.

★ Fort Steele Heritage Town

At **Fort Steele Heritage Town** (9851 Hwy. 93/95, 250/417-6000, 9:30am-5pm daily May-mid-June, 9:30am-6pm daily mid-June-Aug., 9:30am-5pm daily Sept.-mid-Oct., adults $17, seniors $15, children $10), 16 kilometers (10 miles) north of Cranbrook, you'll see over 60 restored and reconstructed buildings, including log barracks, hotels, a courthouse, a jail, a dentist's office, a ferry office, a printing office, and a general store all crammed to the rafters with intriguing historical artifacts. Park staff bring Fort Steele back to life with appropriately costumed working blacksmiths, carpenters, quilters, weavers, bakers, ice-cream makers, and many others. Hop on

Fort Steele Heritage Town

Kootenays and once home to over 5,000 miners—was established at the diggings in 1864 but was relocated upstream when it was discovered that the richest seam of gold was right below the main street. About five kilometers (3 miles) from the highway is Wild Horse Graveyard. From this point you can hike a section of Wild Horse Creek to see a number of historic sites, including the Chinese burial ground, the site of the Wild Horse post office, the remains of Fisherville, and the diggings. It takes about two hours to do the trail, allowing for stops at all the plaques along the way.

Wasa Provincial Park

Unlike the several backcountry parks in the area, 144-hectare (360-acre) **Wasa Provincial Park,** 30 kilometers (19 miles) north of Cranbrook, is easily accessible along Highway 93/95 north of Fort Steele. The lake is warm, making for good summer swimming. The park is divided into a number of different sections scattered around the lake, but all are linked by an eight-kilometer (5-mile) trail that encircles the lake. The main campground (519/826-6850 or 800/689-9025, www.discovercamping.ca, May-Sept., $30) is across the road from a small stretch of park beach and has hot showers.

KIMBERLEY

Kimberley (pop. 7,000), 31 kilometers (19 miles) north of Cranbrook on Highway 95A, is a charming little town with no commercial strip or fast-food outlets, just streets of old stucco mining cottages and a downtown that was "Bavarianized" in the 1970s to attract more visitors. A few downtown shops and businesses have been decorated Bavarian-style with dark wood finish and flowery trim, steep triangular roofs, fancy balconies, brightly painted window shutters, and flower-filled window boxes.

Although named for a famous South African diamond mine, Kimberley boomed as a result of the silver and lead deposits unearthed on nearby North Star Mountain. The deposits were discovered in 1892, and

a steam train (adults $12, children $7), heckle a street politician, witness a crime and testify at a trial, pan for gold, watch a silent movie, and view operatic performances in the Opera House. One of the highlights is Fort Steele Follies, a professional 1880s-style live-theater company performing a musical comedy (2pm daily summer, adults $15, seniors $10, children $5) at the Wild Horse Theatre.

Across the road from the park entrance is **Fort Steele Resort & RV Park** (250/489-4268, www.fortsteele.com, $29-44), which offers a solar-heated outdoor pool, showers, laundry, and a barbecue and cooking facility. It also has a log cabin with shared bath ($119 s or d.).

Wild Horse Creek

To get to the original Wild Horse Creek diggings, continue north from Fort Steele and take the logging road to Bull River and Kootenay Trout Hatchery, then the first road on the left (before the creek crossing). Fisherville—the first township in the East

Kimberley

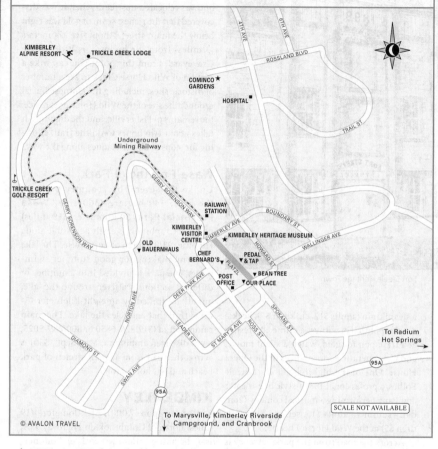

KIMBERLEY
ALPINE RESORT

TRICKLE CREEK LODGE

4TH AVE

6TH AVE

ROSSLAND BLVD

COMINCO ★
GARDENS

HOSPITAL

TRAIL ST

Underground
Mining Railway

GERRY SORENSON WAY

TRICKLE CREEK
GOLF RESORT

GERRY SORENSON WAY

RAILWAY
STATION

BOUNDARY ST

KIMBERLEY
VISITOR
CENTRE

KIMBERLEY AVE

KIMBERLEY HERITAGE MUSEUM

WALLINGER AVE

OLD
BAUERNHAUS

CHEF
BERNARD'S

HOWARD ST

PEDAL
& TAP

PLATZL

BEAN TREE

POST
OFFICE

OUR PLACE

DEER PARK AVE

NORTON AVE

SPOKANE ST

To Radium
Hot Springs

DIAMOND ST

LEADER ST

ST MARY'S AVE

ROSS ST

95A

SWAN AVE

95A

To Marysville, Kimberley Riverside
Campground, and Cranbrook

© AVALON TRAVEL

SCALE NOT AVAILABLE

by 1899 over 200 claims had been staked. As was so often the case, only operations run by larger companies proved profitable. The last of these, and one of the world's largest lead and zinc mines, Cominco's **Sullivan Mine,** closed in late 2001 as reserves became exhausted.

Sights

Strolling the **Bavarian Platzl,** you'll feel as though you've just driven into a village high in the Swiss Alps, with only bell-wearing cows and brightly dressed milkmaids missing.

This is the focus of downtown: a redbrick pedestrian plaza complete with babbling brook, ornamental bridges, and the "World's Largest Cuckoo Clock." At the far end of the Platzl, **Kimberley Heritage Museum** (105 Spokane St., 250/427-7510, 9am-4:30pm Tues.-Sat. July-Aug., 1pm-4pm Mon.-Fri. Sept.-June, donation) houses mining-history exhibits, a taxidermied grizzly bear, and displays relating to local recreation. **Cominco Gardens** (290 Rossland Blvd., 250/427-2293, free) enjoys a hilltop location. Originally planted in 1927 to promote a fertilizer developed by Cominco,

the Bavarian Platzl in Kimberley

greens fee $95-120) along the lower slopes of North Star Mountain. The layout features huge elevation changes (such as the 11th hole, a par 3, which drops over 20 meters/66 feet from tee to green) and rolling mountain scenery.

From early December to early April, **Kimberley Alpine Resort** (250/427-4881 or 800/258-7669, www.skikimberley.com, adults $80, seniors $58, children $30) provides great skiing and snowboarding on a wide variety of slopes four kilometers (2.5 miles) west of downtown. Additional facilities at the resort include a mid-mountain terrain park, a cross-country ski area, accommodations, and restaurants.

Food

For the most reliable breakfast in town, head to **Our Place** (290 Spokane St., 250/427-3739, 8am-2pm daily, lunch $8-11), which is always busy with locals. Simple full-cooked breakfasts are around $12 and lunches such as salads and sandwiches are mostly under $10. Directly across the Platzl, **Bean Tree** (295 Spokane St., 250/427-7889, 8am-5pm Mon.-Sat., 9am-4pm Sun., lunch $7-10) has the usual selection of light lunches, good coffee, and friendly service. Tables are inside a room adorned by local art or out on the Platzl.

At the north end of the Platz, **Snowdrift Cafe** (110 Spokane St., 250/427-0001, 9am-4pm daily, lunch $8-14) is a cozy, small-town café with coffee as good as it gets in town, freshly made lunches such as vegetarian lasagna, and oversize cinnamon buns. Find a table in the back room, or snag a spot out front on the Platzl.

Kimberley has two Bavarian-themed restaurants. **Chef Bernard's Platzl Restaurant** (170 Spokane St., 250/427-4820, 11:30am-2:30pm and 5pm-9pm daily, $12-21) in the Platzl features German specialties such as bratwurst and wiener schnitzel, but the interior has seen few revamps over the last couple of decades. Away from the Platzl, **Old Bauernhaus** (280 Norton Ave., 250/427-5133,

the five-hectare (12-acre) gardens now hold over 40,000 flowers each summer.

Departing up to six times daily in summer, Saturday and Sunday only in spring and fall, the **Underground Mining Railway** (111 Gerry Sorenson Way, 250/427-0022, June-early Sept., adults $25, youths $15, children $10) was constructed from materials salvaged from mining towns around the province. From just northwest of the Platzl, the seven-kilometer (4-mile) track climbs a steep-sided valley, crosses a trestle bridge, passes through a tunnel, and stops at particularly impressive mountain viewpoints and the original town site before arriving at Kimberley Alpine Resort.

Recreation

The Columbia Valley is one of British Columbia's premier golfing destinations, and while most of the best courses are farther north, Kimberley is home to **Trickle Creek Golf Resort** (250/427-5171 or 877/282-1200,

5pm-9pm Thurs.-Mon., $22.50-32) features Bavarian specialties and plenty of atmosphere. It's in a post-and-beam building originally constructed about 350 years ago in southern Bavaria. The building was taken apart, shipped to Canada, and painstakingly rebuilt.

If you're looking for something lighter and healthier than Bavarian food, wander along the Platzl to ★ **Pedal and Tap** (215 Spokane St., 250/427-3325, 3pm-10pm daily July-Aug., 4pm-9pm daily Sept.-June., $13-28), distinctive for its patio surrounded by old bikes. The menu features lots of fresh healthy cooking, balanced by twists on classics, such as bison meatloaf and meat and "spaghettiballs" (fried balls of spaghetti on Bolognese sauce). They also have a standalone gluten-free menu and a wine list dominated by handpicked BC bottles.

Accommodations and Camping

Trickle Creek Lodge (500 Stemwinder Dr., 250/427-5175 or 877/282-1200, www.tricklecreeklodge.com, $159-229 s or d) is at the base of Kimberley Alpine Resort. This contemporary log and stone structure holds 80 spacious rooms, each with a kitchen, a balcony, and a fireplace. Guest facilities include a fitness center and a year-round slope-side outdoor heated pool and hot tub complex.

Kimberley Riverside Campground (250/427-2929, www.kimberleycampground.com, May-Sept., $29-45) is seven kilometers (4 miles) south of downtown on Highway 95A and then three kilometers (2 miles) west along St. Mary's River Road. It's a large facility with an outdoor pool, a convenience store, a playground, and treed sites within walking distance of the river.

Information

For information on Kimberley and the surrounding area, drop by **Kimberley Visitor Centre** (270 Kimberley Ave., 778/481-1891, www.tourismkimberley.com, 10am-5pm daily July-Aug., 10am-5pm Mon.-Sat. Sept.-June), at the north end of the Platzl.

NORTH TOWARD INVERMERE

This stretch of highway passes through a wide valley filled with farms, golf courses, and small towns. The low elevation makes for relatively mild winters and an early start to the summer season. And with the Purcell Mountains on one side and the Rockies on the other, the valley certainly doesn't lack for scenery.

Whiteswan Lake Provincial Park

Continuing north, the Canadian Rockies close in and the scenery becomes more dramatic. Twenty-eight kilometers (17 miles) north of Skookumchuck and five kilometers (3 miles) south of Canal Flats, an unsealed logging road takes off east into the mountains, leading to 1,994-hectare (4,930-acre) Whiteswan Lake Provincial Park. The road climbs steadily from the highway, entering Lussier Gorge after 11 kilometers (7 miles). Within the gorge, a steep walking trail descends to **Lussier Hot Springs.** Two small pools have been constructed to contain the odorless hot (43°C/110°F) water as it bubbles out of the ground and flows into the Lussier River. Within the park, the road closely follows the southern shorelines of first **Alces Lake** and then the larger **Whiteswan Lake.** The two lakes attract abundant birdlife; loons, grebes, and herons are all common. They also attract anglers, who come for great rainbow trout fishing. Both lakes are stocked and have a daily quota of two fish pp. The road through the park passes five popular campgrounds (no reservations, May-Sept., $23) with basic services but no hookups.

Top of the World Provincial Park

If you thought the scenery around Whiteswan Lake was wild and remote, wait till you see this 8,790-hectare (21,720-acre) wilderness, a rough 52 kilometers (32 miles) from Highway 95 (turn off the Whiteswan Lake access road at Alces Lake). You can't drive into the park, but it's a fairly easy six-kilometer (3.7-mile) hike from the end of the road to picturesque **Fish Lake,** the park's largest body of water, which is surrounded by peaks up to 2,500 meters (8,200 feet) high.

Canal Flats and Vicinity

The small lumber-mill town of Canal Flats lies between the Kootenay River and **Columbia Lake.** In 1889 the two waterways were connected by a canal with a single lock, but the passage was so narrow and dangerous that only two steamboats ever got through.

North of Canal Flats, the highway passes tiny **Thunder Hill Provincial Park,** which overlooks turquoise-and-blue Columbia Lake. The highway then approaches and passes the weirdly shaped **Dutch Creek Hoodoos,** a set of photogenic rock formations carved over time by ice, water, and wind.

Fairmont Hot Springs

The Kootenay people used these springs as a healing source for ages prior to the arrival of Europeans, but they wouldn't recognize the place today. Surrounding the site is **Fairmont Hot Springs Resort** (250/345-6311 or 800/663-4979, www.fairmontresort.com), comprising a sprawling residential and resort complex, three golf courses, a small ski resort, a strip of shops and restaurants, and an airstrip. Despite all the commercialism, the **hot springs** (5225 Fairmont Resort Rd., 8am-10pm daily, adults $18, seniors $16, children $12) are still the main attraction. Their appeal is simple: Unlike most other springs, the hot water bubbling up from underground here contains calcium, not sulfur with its attendant smell. The pools are a magical experience, especially in the evening. Lazily swim or float around in the large warm pool, dive into the cool pool, or soak away your cares in the hottest pool.

A lodge and a campground within walking distance of the hot springs provide accommodations for all budgets. Lodge rooms are $179-325 s or d, which includes pool admission, with the more expensive having a kitchen. Campers have a choice of over 240 sites ($35-65), all just a few minute's stroll from the hot pools. The campground has full hookups and showers, but no fire pits, and the sites are not

Fairmont Hot Springs Resort

particularly private. Just south of the resort is **Spruce Grove Resort** (Hwy. 3, 250/345-6561 or 888/629-4004, www.sprucegroveresort.com, Apr.-early Oct., $33-52), where campsites are spread through a tree-shaded area and along a quiet eddy in the Columbia River. Amenities for children include an outdoor pool and playground.

INVERMERE AND VICINITY

The next area to lure travelers off Highway 93/95 is large and busy **Windermere Lake.** Overlooking the lake's north end, **Invermere** (pop. 4,200) is the commercial center of the Columbia Valley. The area was the site of an 1807 trading post set up by David Thompson to trade with the Kootenay people (a small plaque along the road to Wilmer marks the exact spot), the first such post along the Columbia River. The original lakefront town site is now a popular recreation spot, where a pleasant grassy area dotted with picnic tables runs right down to a sandy beach and the shallow waters of the lake. It's on the left as you travel along the Invermere access road. As you approach the town itself, consider a stop at **Windermere Valley Museum** (222 6th Ave., 250/342-9769, 10am-4pm daily June-Aug., donation), where the history of the valley is contained in seven separate buildings. The main street itself (7th Ave.) is lined with restored heritage buildings and streetlights bedecked with hanging baskets overflowing with colorful flowers.

Practicalities

The Invermere Bakery (250/342-9913, 7:30am-6pm Mon.-Sat., lunch $7.50-10) has been a local favorite since the 1950s. Today, the menu features huge range of ultrahealthy sandwiches and not-so-healthy cakes and pastries. The town's most upscale dining room is **Strand's** (818 12th St., 250/342-6344, 5pm-10pm daily, $24-38), up the hill from the main street. It's contained in a restored 1912 heritage house set on landscaped gardens, with diners seated in small, intimate rooms. The immaculately presented seasonal menu often includes delicacies such as trout, salmon, and venison that are served with a wide selection of vegetables.

Along the highway, just south of the Invermere turnoff, is the **Invermere Visitor Centre** (651 Hwy. 93/95, 250/342-2844, www.cvchamber.ca, 9am-5pm daily July-Aug., 9am-5pm Mon.-Fri. fall-spring).

Panorama Mountain Village

In the Purcell Mountains immediately west of Invermere, **Panorama** (250/342-6941 or 800/663-2929, www.panoramaresort.com) is an ambitious year-round resort and residential development highlighted by a ski resort and challenging **Greywolf Golf Course** (250/341-4100, greens fees $129), where the signature sixth hole, "the Cliffhanger," requires an accurate tee shot across a narrow canyon to a green backed by towering cliffs. During the warmer months, there are also chairlift rides, white-water rafting and inflatable kayak trips down Toby Creek, and horseback riding. In the village itself you'll find tennis, a climbing wall, and a network of connected hot pools.

Skiing first put Panorama on the map, mainly because the resort boasts one of North America's highest vertical drops (1,200 meters/3,940 feet). Lift tickets are adults $99, seniors $86, children $46. The village is also home to **R. K. Heli-Ski** (250/342-3889 or 800/661-6060, www.rkheliski.com), one of the few heli-skiing operations that specialize in day trips (from $800 for 3 runs).

Accommodations in Panorama Mountain Village are all relatively new and well-priced; book through the resort. Outside the resort's marketing department, summer is still thought of as the off-season, and there are some great summer deals to be had, such as two nights' lodging and unlimited use of the chairlift for $150 pp.

Canadian Rockies

Look for ★ to find recommended
sights, activities, dining, and lodging.

Highlights

★ **Radium Hot Springs:** After a long day hiking, the best recipe for soothing aching muscles is a soak in hot springs (page 323).

★ **Paint Pots:** The Paint Pots are a unique natural wonder that make for a colorful stop along Highway 93 (page 323).

★ **Stanley Glacier Trail:** Although it takes around 90 minutes to reach the end of the trail, the stunning views make it worth every step (page 325).

★ **Emerald Lake:** At Emerald Lake, you can hike, canoe, fish, or simply soak up the mountain scenery (page 330).

★ **Lake O'Hara:** Quite simply, this is a magical lake. Access is limited by a quota system, so take heed of the reservation information and be prepared for a day of hiking you will always remember (page 332).

★ **Kicking Horse Mountain Resort:** I've ridden each of the four gondolas in the Canadian Rockies, and my favorite for unbeatable top-of-the-world views is at Kicking Horse Mountain Resort, near Golden (page 338).

The highest peaks of the Canadian Rockies form British Columbia's eastern boundary, separating the province from neighboring Alberta.

On the British Columbia side of the Canadian Rockies (often called the British Columbia or BC Rockies) are Kootenay and Yoho National Parks and their gateway towns of Radium Hot Springs and Golden. The two national parks may lack the bustling resort towns of their famous Alberta neighbors, Banff and Jasper, but they boast the same magnificent mountain vistas, glacially fed streams and rivers, unlimited hiking opportunities, and abundant wildlife.

Many factors combine to make the Canadian Rockies so beautiful. The peaks themselves exhibit drastically altered sedimentary layers visible from miles away, especially when accentuated by a particular angle of sunlight or a dusting of snow. Between the peaks lie numerous cirques, or basins gouged into the mountains by glaciers. These cirques fill with glacial meltwater each spring, creating lakes that shimmer a trademark translucent green. And thanks to a climate that keeps the tree line low and the vegetation relatively sparse, fantastic views of the wide sweeping valleys are assured.

Encompassing close to 20,000 square kilometers (7,700 square miles) of Mother Nature's finest offerings, Kootenay and Yoho, along with neighboring Banff and Jasper National Parks (both in Alberta), have been declared a World Heritage Site by UNESCO. For detailed coverage of the entire mountain range north of the 49th parallel, get a copy of *Moon Canadian Rockies*.

PLANNING YOUR TIME

Lay out a map of British Columbia, and you'll see that visiting both Kootenay and Yoho National Parks as part of a loop through the Canadian Rockies is an obvious extension to a trip to the Kootenay region. What the map won't tell you is that nowhere in British Columbia is the scenery-to-distance-traveled ratio as good as it is in this part of the province. For the traveler, this means you should schedule a little longer than you may think to see everything.

Previous: Iceline Trail in Yoho National Park; Emerald Lake. **Above:** Highway 93 parallels the Vermilion River.

British Columbia Rockies

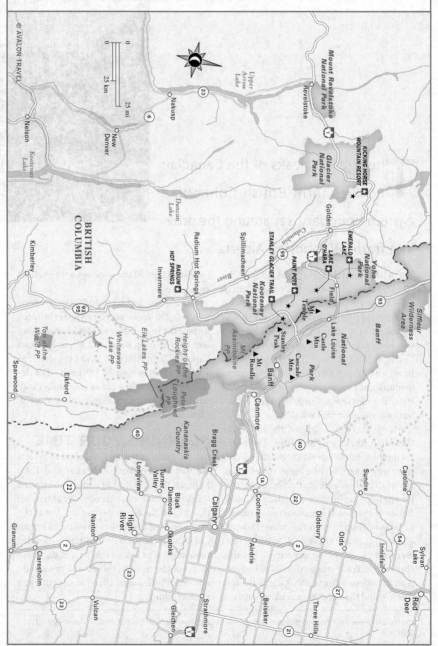

© AVALON TRAVEL

0 — 25 km
0 — 25 mi

Nelson

Kootenay Lake

New Denver

Nakusp

Upper Arrow Lake

Revelstoke

Mount Revelstoke National Park

Glacier National Park

KICKING HORSE MOUNTAIN RESORT

Golden

BRITISH COLUMBIA

Kimberley

Duncan Lake

Radium Hot Springs

Spillimacheen

Columbia

RADIUM HOT SPRINGS

Invermere

STANLEY GLACIER TRAIL

Kootenay National Park

PAINT POTS

EMERALD LAKE

LAKE O'HARA

Yoho National Park

Field

Mt. Temple

Castle Mtn

Lake Louise

Cascade Mtn

Stanley Peak

Siffleur Wilderness Area

Banff National Park

River

Sparwood

Top of the World PP

Whiteswan Lake PP

Elkford

Elk Lakes PP

Height of the Rockies PP

Mt. Assiniboine PP

Peter Lougheed PP

Mt. Rundle

Banff

Canmore

Kananaskis Country

Bragg Creek

Cochrane

Sundre

Caroline

Granum

Nanton

Longview

High River

Black Diamond

Turner Valley

Okotoks

Calgary

Airdrie

Didsbury

Olds

Three Hills

Innisfail

Sylvan Lake

Red Deer

Claresholm

Vulcan

Gleichen

Strathmore

Beiseker

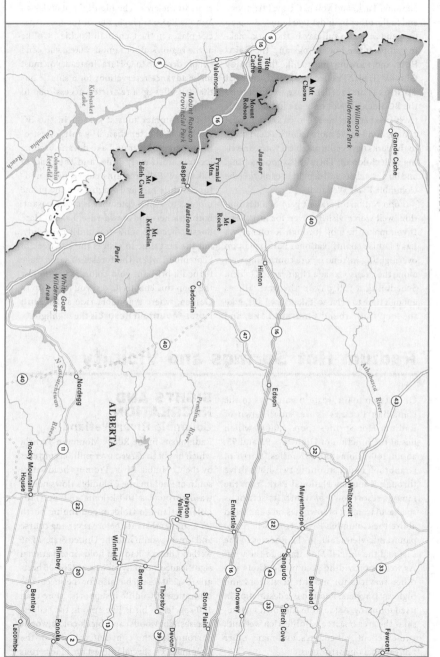

Just one road passes through Kootenay National Park, and you can travel from one end to the other in under two hours. But plan to spend at least a full day in the park, making stops at the hot springs and the **Paint Pots,** and allowing time to hike the **Stanley Glacier Trail.** The town of **Radium Hot Springs** is an excellent base for exploring the BC Rockies. Not only are lodgings relatively inexpensive, but the town's commercial campgrounds have more facilities than those in the parks (especially notable if you're traveling with children). There's also good golfing, and bird-watchers will delight in exploring the Columbia River Wetlands.

Yoho National Park is a gem of a destination, well worth visiting even for just a day. If you make the loop through Kootenay via Lake Louise (Banff National Park), plan on overnighting in Yoho before continuing west along the Trans-Canada Highway to Golden. Scheduling a full day in the park allows enough time to drive to Takakkaw Falls, hike the loop trail around **Emerald Lake,** and

enjoy lunch in between at one of the restaurants in the area. The highlight of a visit to Yoho is **Lake O'Hara,** one of the most special places in the Canadian Rockies. Unlike at the region's other famous lakes, you can't simply drive up to O'Hara. Instead, you must make advance reservations for a shuttle bus that trundles up a restricted-access road to the lake.

The summer tourist season in the BC Rockies is shorter than it is in the rest of the province. Emerald Lake doesn't become ice-free until early June, and the road to Takakkaw Falls remains closed until mid-June. While July and August are the prime months to visit, September is also pleasant, both weather- and crowd-wise. Lake O'Hara doesn't become snow-free until early July, but the best time to visit is the last week of September, when the forests of larch have turned a brilliant gold color. If you follow the loop this chapter takes, you'll end up in Golden, where a gondola ride at **Kicking Horse Mountain Resort** is the highlight.

Radium Hot Springs and Vicinity

One of two main western gateways to the Canadian Rockies is the small town of Radium Hot Springs (pop. 1,000), which lies at the junction of Highways 93 and 95, about 140 kilometers (87 miles) north of Cranbrook and a stunning two-hour drive through Kootenay National Park from the famous resort town of Banff. Its setting is spectacular; most of town lies on benchland above the Columbia River, from where the panoramic views take in the Rockies to the east and the Purcell Mountains to the west. As well as providing accommodations and other services for mountain visitors and highway travelers, Radium is a destination in itself for many. Aside from the town's namesake, the area boasts a wildlife-rich wetland, two excellent golf courses, and many other recreational opportunities.

SIGHTS AND RECREATION
Columbia River Wetland

Radium sits in the Rocky Mountain Trench, which has been carved over millions of years by the Columbia River. From its headwaters south of Radium, the Columbia flows northward through a 180-kilometer-long (110-mile) wetland to Golden, continuing north for a similar distance before reversing course and flowing south into the United States. The wetland nearby Radium holds international significance, not only for its size (26,000 hectares/64,250 acres), but also for the sheer concentration of wildlife it supports. More than 100 species of birds live among the sedges, grasses, dogwoods, and black cottonwoods surrounding the convoluted banks of the Columbia. Of special interest are blue herons

Radium Hot Springs

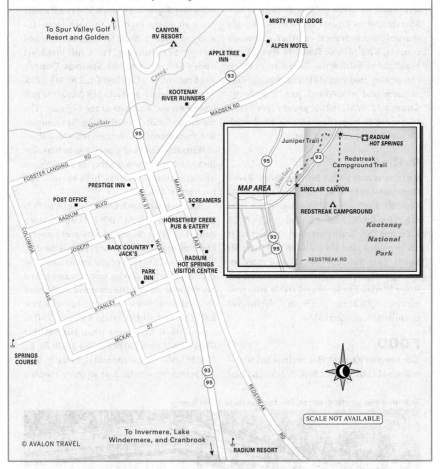

To Spur Valley Golf Resort and Golden

MISTY RIVER LODGE

CANYON RV RESORT

ALPEN MOTEL

APPLE TREE INN

93

KOOTENAY RIVER RUNNERS

MADSEN RD

Creek

Sinclair

95

FORSTER LANDING RD

PRESTIGE INN

POST OFFICE

RADIUM BLVD

JOSEPH ST

COLUMBIA

MAIN ST

SCREAMERS

HORSETHIEF CREEK PUB & EATERY

BACK COUNTRY JACK'S

WEST ST

EAST ST

PARK INN

RADIUM HOT SPRINGS VISITOR CENTRE

AVE

STANLEY ST

MCKAY ST

SPRINGS COURSE

93
95

© AVALON TRAVEL

To Invermere, Lake Windermere, and Cranbrook

REDSTREAK RD

RADIUM RESORT

SCALE NOT AVAILABLE

Inset map:

Juniper Trail

RADIUM HOT SPRINGS

95

93

Redstreak Campground Trail

MAP AREA

Sinclair Creek

SINCLAIR CANYON

REDSTREAK CAMPGROUND

93
95

REDSTREAK RD

Kootenay

National

Park

---

in large numbers and ospreys in one of the world's highest concentrations.

The wetland also lies along the Pacific Flyway, so particularly large numbers of ducks, Canada geese, and other migratory birds gather here in spring and autumn. The northbound spring migration is celebrated with the **Wings over the Rockies Bird Festival** (888/342-9464, www.wingsovertherockies.org), which is held in the second week of May in conjunction with International Migratory Bird Day. The festival features ornithologist speakers, field trips on foot and by boat, workshops, and events tailored especially for children, all of which take place in Radium and throughout the valley. At any time of year, use the festival website to source the valley's best birding spots.

Golf

The Columbia River Valley supports many golf courses and is marketed around western Canada as a golfing destination. Aside from the excellent resort-style courses and stunning Canadian Rockies scenery, golfers here enjoy the area's mild climate. Warm temperatures allow golfing as early as late March and as late as October—a longer season than is typical at other mountain courses. The 36-hole **Radium Resort** is a highlight of golfing the Canadian Rockies, comprising two very different courses. One of them, the 6,767-yard, par-72 **Springs Course** (250/347-6200, greens fees $118), is generally regarded as one of British Columbia's top 10 resort courses.

Rafting

Radium is also a base for **Kootenay River Runners** (4983 Hwy. 93, 250/347-9210 or 800/599-4399), who offer white-water rafting trips for $90 for a half-day trip, $135 for a full day. Transportation and wet suits are provided, and the full-day trip includes lunch. This company also offers a more relaxing evening float through the Columbia River Wetland in large and stable voyageur canoes, which depart at 5:30pm daily; the cost is adults $55, children $38.

FOOD

The town of Radium Hot Springs holds several good choices for a food break. The best coffee in town is poured at **Meet on Higher Ground** (7527 Main St. W., 250/347-6567, 6:30am-4:30pm daily, lunch $8-11), a friendly place along the highway through town. It's also the place to come for light lunches and free wireless Internet. For a full breakfast under $15, head to the **Springs Course Restaurant** (4714 Springs Dr., 250/347-6200, 7am-9pm daily Apr.-Oct., $18-26), at the golf course on the west side of the highway. The view from the deck, overlooking the Columbia River and Purcell Mountains, is nothing short of stunning. The food is good and remarkably inexpensive; in the morning, for example, an omelet with three fillings, hash browns, and toast is just $14.

Back in town, **Back Country Jack's** (7555 Main St. W., 250/347-0097, 11:30am-11pm daily, $13-21) is decorated with real antiques and real hard-bench seats in private booths. There's a wide variety of platters to share, including Cowboy Caviar (nachos and baked beans) and a surprisingly good barbecued chicken soup. For a main, the half-chicken, half-ribs and all the extras for two ($34) is a good deal. Across the road, **Horsethief Creek Pub and Eatery** (7358 Main St. E., 250/347-6400, 11:30am-midnight daily, $14-24) serves up similar fare in more modern

Bighorn sheep are often seen on the streets of Radium Hot Springs.

surroundings. Both places have a few outdoor tables.

As always, **Husky House Restaurant** (4918 Hwy. 93, 250/347-9811, 7am-10pm daily, $10-17.50), at the junction of Highways 93 and 95, serves a solid menu of no-frills North American fare at reasonable prices. Just around the corner is **Screamer's** (7518 Main St. E, 250/347-9335, noon-10pm daily summer), the place to hang out with an ice cream on a hot summer afternoon. The ice cream here has been researched many times, most often when returning from camping trips in the Columbia Valley. Also along this strip is **Mountainside Market** (7546 Main St. E., 250/347-9600, 8am-10pm daily), with an excellent choice of groceries and an in-house deli and butcher.

ACCOMMODATIONS AND CAMPING

Radium, with a population of just 1,000, has more than a dozen motels, an indication of its importance as a highway stop for overnight travelers. Those that lie along the access road to Kootenay National Park come alive with color through summer as each tries to outdo the others with floral landscaping. When booking any of these accommodations, ask about free passes to the hot pools.

Under $50

At the top end of the motel strip, closest to the national park, **Misty River Lodge** (5036 Hwy. 93, 250/347-9912, www.radiumhostel. bc.ca, dorm $30, $75-105 s or d) provides an excellent base for travelers on a budget. Also known as Radium Hot Springs International Hostel, this converted motel sleeps 28 in dormitories and private rooms, and it includes a room that combines valley views with a full kitchen. Amenities include a communal kitchen, a lounge, and a big deck with even bigger views to the distant Purcell Mountains.

$50-100

Kootenay Motel (5000 Hwy. 93, 250/347-9490 or 877/908-2020, $75 s, $80 d) is up the hill from the junction of Highway 95. The rooms are nothing special (but have air-conditioning), and a kitchenette is $10 extra. Also on-site is a barbecue area and gazebo. Up the hill a little and across the road is **Apple Tree Inn** (Hwy. 93, 250/347-0011, www.appletreeinnbc.com, Apr.-Oct., $80-140 s or d), with a pleasant outdoor barbecue area. Continuing toward the national park entrance, the **Gables Motel** (5058 Hwy. 93, 250/347-9866 or 877/387-7007, www.gablesmotel.ca, $85-135 s or d) has 17 smallish rooms with mountain views; it is well furnished.

In the quiet residential streets west of Highways 93/95 is the **Radium Park Inn** (4873 Stanley St., 250/347-9582 or 800/858-1155, www.parkinn.bc.ca, $95-125 s or d), with rates that remain reasonable even though the motel undergoes regular revamps. It features a small indoor pool and a covered barbecue area. Some units have kitchenettes and separate bedrooms.

$100-150

While the rustic ambience of **Addison's Bungalows** (250/346-6888 or 800/794-5024, www.addisonsbungalows.com, mid-Mar.-mid-Oct., $110-200 s or d) hasn't changed for generations, the surrounding scenery has. Originally located opposite the town's hot springs, the cabins were moved in 2001 to improve habitat for resident bighorn sheep. Today you'll find them just south of Brisco, 27 kilometers (17 miles) north of town along Highway 95. Each of the eight cabins has a small kitchen, a bath, a stone fireplace, a deck, a TV, and wireless Internet.

In the middle of the motel strip is the **Alpen Motel** (Hwy. 93, 250/347-9823 or 888/788-3891, www.alpenmotel.com, $119-139 s or d), which arguably has the best and brightest flowers out front. The air-conditioned rooms are the best along the strip, which is reflected in the price (but hot springs passes are included).

$150-200

On the west side of town, **Bighorn Meadows**

Resort (10 Bighorn Blvd., 250/347-2323 or 877/344-2323, www.bighornmeadows.com, $165-345 s or d) overlooks the Springs Course, one of the province's best golf courses. The units range from studios to two bedrooms and each is spacious, modern, and fully equipped with a large kitchen. All rooms have balconies with outdoor furniture.

Part of the Best Western chain, Prestige Inn Radium Hot Springs (7493 Main St. W., 250/347-2300 or 877/737-8443, www.prestige-hotels andresorts.com, $195-255 s or d) sits at the town's main intersection. Facilities include a fitness room, an indoor pool, a gift shop, spa services, an Italian restaurant, and a lounge bar.

Campgrounds

Within Kootenay National Park, but accessed from in town off Highways 93/95, is Redstreak Campground (mid-May-mid-Oct., unserviced sites $28, hookups $32-39, fire permits $8.80), which has 144 sites, showers, and kitchen shelters. Sites can be reserved through the Parks Canada Campground Reservation Service (877/737-3783, www.pccamping.ca). The closest commercial camping is at Canyon RV Resort (5012 Sinclair Creek Rd., 250/347-9564, www.canyonrv.com, Apr.-Oct., $39-65), nestled in its own private valley immediately north of the Highway 93/95 junction. Treed sites are spread along both sides of a pleasant creek, and all facilities are provided, including a playground and laundry.

Perfectly described by its name, Dry Gulch Provincial Park (250/422-3003, May-mid-Oct., $21) offers 26 sites four kilometers (2.5 miles) south of town. Typical of provincial park camping, each site has a picnic table and fire pit but no hookups. Reservations are not taken.

INFORMATION

On the east side of the highway, just south of the Highway 93/95 junction, is the Radium Hot Springs Visitor Centre (7556 Main St., 250/347-9331 or 800/347-9704, www.

radiumhotsprings.com, 9am-5pm daily mid-May-mid-Oct.). This building is also home to the national park information center and a small retail store.

Getting There

Radium is at the junction of Highways 95 and 93, about 140 kilometers (87 miles) north of Cranbrook and 105 kilometers (65 miles) south of Golden.

NORTH ALONG HIGHWAY 95

From Radium, most travelers head into Kootenay National Park, but another option is to continue north for 105 kilometers (65 miles) to Golden, from where the Trans-Canada Highway heads east, through Yoho National Park and across the Continental Divide to Banff National Park, which is in the neighboring province of Alberta. From this point it is possible to continue south and link up with Highway 93, making a 350-kilometer loop through the three parks.

Past Radium and Golden, several small historic towns are worthy of a stop. Named for a member of the 1859 Palliser expedition, Brisco was founded on the mining industry and later grew as a regional center for surrounding farmland. Brisco General Store is a throwback to those earlier times, selling just about everything. Nearby Spillimacheen, meaning "white water" in the language of the area's earliest inhabitants, sits at the confluence of the Spillimacheen River and Bugaboo Creek.

Bugaboo Glacier Provincial Park

Inaccessible to all but the most experienced hikers and climbers, this vast tract of wilderness in the Purcell Mountains northwest of Radium Hot Springs is reached along a 45-kilometer (28-mile) gravel road west from Brisco. At road's end, a trail climbs steeply to a glaciated area that rivals the Canadian Rockies in beauty. Aside from the ice fields covering half the park, the most dominant features here are spectacular granite spires rising to elevations above 3,000 meters (9,840 feet). While the Purcell Mountains are an ancient range 1.5 billion years old, the spires formed as intrusions thrust skyward only about 70 million years ago. Since then, erosion has shaped them into today's granite needles towering over the surrounding ice fields.

The Conrad Kain Hut, a base for hikers and climbers wanting to explore the park, is a five-kilometer (3-mile) hike from the end of the road, up a valley carved by the retreating Bugaboo Glacier. The trail gains around 700 meters (2,300 feet) in elevation; allow at least two hours. Camping is also possible near the hut. No set trails lead from the hut to the spires or ice fields, and you'll need climbing and glacier-travel experience to continue deeper into the park.

The Bugaboos were the birthplace of heli-skiing: in the mid-1960s that Hans Gmoser used a helicopter to transport skiers into normally inaccessible areas. Canadian Mountain Holidays (403/762-7100 or 800/661-0252, www.canadianmountainholidays.com), the company Gmoser founded, now has a lodge deep in the Bugaboos.

MOUNT ASSINIBOINE PROVINCIAL PARK

Named for one of the Canadian Rockies' most spectacular peaks, this 39,050-hectare (96,500-acre), roughly triangular park lies northeast of Radium Hot Springs, sandwiched between Kootenay National Park to the west and Banff National Park to the east. It's inaccessible by road; access is on foot or by helicopter. A haven for experienced hikers, the park offers alpine meadows, lakes, glaciers, and many peaks higher than 3,050 meters (10,000 feet) to explore. The park's highest peak, 3,618-meter (11,870-foot) Mount Assiniboine (seventh-highest in the Canadian Rockies), is known as the Matterhorn of the Rockies for its resemblance to that famous Swiss landmark. The striking peak can be seen from many points well outside the boundaries of the park, including Buller Pond in Kananaskis Country and Sunshine Village winter resort in Banff National Park.

Lake Magog is the destination of most park visitors. Here you'll find the park's only facilities and the trailheads for several interesting and varied day hikes. One of the most popular walks is along the Sunburst Valley-Nub Ridge Trail. From Lake Magog, small Sunburst Lake is reached in about 20 minutes, then the trail continues northwest a short distance to Cerulean Lake. From this lake's outlet, the trail descends slowly along the Mitchell River to a junction four kilometers (2.5 miles) from Lake Magog. Take the right fork, which climbs through a dense subalpine forest to Elizabeth Lake, nestled in the southern shadow of Nub Peak. From this point, instead of descending back to Cerulean Lake, take the Nub Ridge Trail, which climbs steadily for one kilometer (0.6 miles) to a magnificent viewpoint high above Lake Magog. From the viewpoint, it's just less than four kilometers (2.5 miles), downhill all the way, to the valley floor. The total length of this outing is 11 kilometers (6.8 miles), and elevation gained is only just over 400 meters (1,310 feet); the trail can comfortably be completed in four hours.

Accommodations

Getting to and staying at ★ Mount Assiniboine Lodge isn't cheap, but the number of repeat guests is testament to an experience that you will never forget. The mountain scenery may take most of the kudos, but the lodge's congenial atmosphere makes the stay equally memorable. Built in 1928 by the CPR, the delightfully rustic lodge is set in a lakeside meadow below its distinctive namesake peak. The main building holds six double rooms that share bath facilities and a dining area where hearty meals (included in the rates) are served up communal-style. Scattered in the surrounding trees are six one-room cabins that sleep two to five people. Each has running water and uses propane to heat and light the space. Outhouses and showers are shared. The rate for lodge rooms is $325 pp, while cabin accommodations range $325-400. Children 12 and under are $165.

You can reach the lodge on foot or fly in with Alpine Helicopters from a heliport in Spray Valley Provincial Park. The departure days are the same as for campers (Wed., Fri., and Sun.); the only difference is that helicopter departures begin at 11:30am for lodge guests. Lodge guests flying in may bring 18 kilograms (40 pounds) of gear, plus one pair of skis. If you decide to hike in or out, the charge for luggage transfers is $5 per kilogram ($2.25 per pound).

The operating season is late June to the first weekend of October, and then mid-February to late March, for cross-country skiing. There is a minimum stay of two nights. The lodge has no landline phone; for reservations or information call 403/678-2883 (8:30am-2:30pm Mon.-Fri.) or check the website (www.assiniboinelodge.com).

Campground and Huts

Lake Magog is the park's main facility area, such as it is. A designated camping area ($10 pp) on a low ridge above the lake's west shore provides a source of drinking water, bearproof food caches, and pit toilets. Open fires are prohibited. No reservations are taken, but even those who visit frequently have told me they've never seen it full. Also at the lake are the **Naiset Huts,** where bunk beds cost $25 pp (book through Mount Assiniboine Lodge, 403/678-2883, 8:30am-2:30pm Mon.-Fri., www.assiniboinelodge.com). The cabins contain nothing more than bunk beds with mattresses, so you'll need a stove, cooking utensils, food, a sleeping bag, and your own source of non-gas-powered light.

Information

In addition to the government agency responsible for the park (the provincial Ministry of Environment, www.env.gov.bc.ca/bcparks), park information centers in Radium Hot Springs, Lake Louise, and Banff provide information and up-to-date trail conditions.

Getting There
APPROACHING THE PARK ON FOOT

Three trails provide access to **Lake Magog,** the park's largest body of water. The most popular comes in from the northeast, starting at the Sunshine Village winter resort in Banff National Park and leading 29 kilometers (18 miles) via Citadel Pass to the lake. Not only is this trail spectacular, but the high elevation of the trailhead (2,100 meters/6,890 feet) makes for a relatively easy approach. Another approach is from the east, in Spray Valley Provincial Park (Kananaskis Country). The trailhead is at the southern end of Spray Lake; take the Mount Shark staging area turnoff 40 kilometers (25 miles) south of Canmore. By the time the trail has climbed the Bryant Creek drainage to 2,165-meter (7,100-foot) Assiniboine Pass, all elevation gain (450 meters/1,480 feet) has been made. At 27 kilometers (17 miles), this is the shortest approach, but its elevation gain is greater than the other two trails. The longest and least-used access is from Highway 93 at Simpson River in Kootenay National Park. This trail climbs the Simpson River and Surprise Creek drainages and crosses 2,270-meter (7,450-foot) Ferro Pass to the lake for a total length of 32 kilometers (20 miles).

THE EASY WAY IN

If these long approaches put visiting the park out of your reach, there's one more option: You can fly in by helicopter from the Mount Shark Heliport, at the southern end of Spray Valley Provincial Park, 40 kilometers (25 miles) southwest of Canmore. Flights depart at 12:30pm Wednesday, Friday, and Sunday and cost $175 pp one-way, including an 18-kilogram (40-pound) per-person baggage limit. Although **Alpine Helicopters** (403/678-4802, www.alpinehelicopter.com) operates the flights, all bookings must be made through **Mount Assiniboine Lodge** (403/678-2883, www.assiniboinelodge.com, 8:30am-2:30pm Mon.-Fri.).

If you're planning on hiking into the park, Alpine Helicopters will fly your gear in for $6.50 per kilogram ($3 per pound). This same company, which also operates from a base in Canmore, charges $300 pp for a 30-minute flightseeing trip over the park. For more information, contact Alpine Helicopters.

Kootenay National Park

Shaped like a lightning bolt, this narrow 140,600-hectare (347,400-acre) park lies northeast of Radium Hot Springs, bordered to the east by Banff National Park and Mount Assiniboine Provincial Park and to the north by Yoho National Park. Highway 93, extending for 94 kilometers (58 miles) through the park, provides spectacular mountain vistas. Along the route you'll find many short and easy interpretive hikes, scenic viewpoints, hot springs, picnic areas, and roadside interpretive exhibits. The park isn't particularly noted for its day-hiking opportunities, but backpacker destinations such as Kaufmann Lake and the Rockwall rival almost any other area in the Canadian Rockies.

Even if you never leave the highway, the hillsides scarred by wildfires that swept through the park in 2001 and 2003 will be obvious. The fires jumped the highway in places, burned bridges and information booths, and forced the closure of some trails because of the danger of falling trees; check at local information centers for the latest updates.

Day-use areas, a gas station and lodge, and three campgrounds are the only roadside services inside the park; Radium Hot Springs, at the junction of Highways 93 and 95, is the park's main service center. The park is open year-round, although you should check road conditions in winter, when avalanche-control work and snowstorms can close Highway 93 for short periods of time.

DRIVING HIGHWAY 93

Climbing eastward from the town of Radium Hot Springs, Highway 93, still known locally as the Banff-Windermere Highway, enters the boundary of Kootenay National Park at narrow **Sinclair Canyon,** a natural gateway to

Vermilion River

Kootenay National Park

Moraine Lake

Mt Little

To Lake Louise

Quadra Mtn

Taylor Lake

Boom Lake

Bow

1A

Castle Mtn

CASTLE JUNCTION

ALBERTA

Mt Ishbel

1

BOW VALLEY PARKWAY

Tokumm Creek

Mt Whymper

Vermilion Pass

Storm Mtn

Mt Goodsir

Sharp Mtn

MARBLE CANYON

PAINT POTS

STANLEY GLACIER TRAIL

Twin Lakes

Redearth Ct

Pilot Mtn

River

Yoho National Park

MARBLE CANYON

Stanley Glacier

Stanley Peak

Banff National Park

Buttress Peak

Mt Drysdale

The Rockwall

93

Shadow Lake

Bourgeau Lake

To Banff

Mt Mollison

Numa Falls

Isabelle Peak

Scaral Lake

GONDOLA

Beaverfoot

River

Vermilion

River

Verdant

Sunshine Meadows

SUNSHINE VILLAGE

Quartz Hill

Vermilion Range

Foster Peak

Eloe Lake

Creek

Citadel Peak

BRITISH COLUMBIA

River

Mt Verendrye

VERMILION CROSSING

Mt Shanks

To Golden

Kootenay

Mt Wardle

Simpson

River

Surprise

Creek

Spillimacheen

Kootenay National Park

Mount Assiniboine Provincial Park

KOOTENAY CROSSING

Mt Selkirk

Creek

Mitchell

Brisco

95

Dart

Creek

Columbia

Mt Crook

Mt Harkin

Dog Lake

River

Mt Docking

Frances Creek

MCLEOD MEADOWS

Kootenay

Mt Kindersley

Kindersley Pass

Edgewater

VIEWPOINT

SETTLER'S RD

Sinclair Pass

93

River

Creek

Radium Hot Springs

RADIUM HOT SPRINGS

Olive Lake

Forster Creek

0   5 mi

0   5 km

93

95

To Invermere

© AVALON TRAVEL

Radium Hot Springs

the wonders beyond. After squeezing through the canyon, the highway emerges at the actual springs that give the town of Radium Hot Springs its name.

★ Radium Hot Springs

The soothing **Radium Hot Springs** (250/347-9485, 9am-11pm daily summer, noon-9pm daily fall-spring) lies inside the park but just three kilometers (2 miles) northeast of the town of the same name, which is outside the park boundary. It was discovered many centuries ago by the Kootenay people, who, like today's visitors, came to enjoy the odorless mineral water that gushes out of the Redwall Fault at 44°C (111°F).

Steep cliffs tower directly above the hot pool, whose waters are colored a milky blue by dissolved salts, which include calcium bicarbonate and sulfates of calcium, magnesium, and sodium. The hot pool (39°C/97°F) is particularly stimulating in winter, when it's edged by snow and covered in steam—your head is almost cold in the chill air, but your submerged body melts into oblivion. Admission is adults $7 (or swim all day for $10), seniors and children $5.75 (day pass $9.55). Towel and locker rentals are available, as are spa services. If you're camping at the park's Redstreak Campground, you can reach the complex on foot along a forested trail.

To Kootenay Valley

Leaving the hot springs, the road parallels Sinclair Creek, crests 1,486-meter (4,870-foot) Sinclair Pass, and passes small Olive Lake, which is ringed with bright yellow wildflowers in summer. At **Kootenay River Viewpoint** a splendid view overlooks the wild Kootenay River Valley below and the snowcapped mountains along the Continental Divide.

The highway then descends to the valley floor, passes two riverside picnic areas, and crosses the pretty Kootenay River at **Kootenay Crossing.** The official ribbon-cutting ceremony opening the Banff-Windermere Road took place here in 1923. Today you'll find a roadside historical exhibit, hiking trails, and a warden's station. As you cross the river and pass small green Kootenay Pond, your eyes will revel in views of milky-green rivers, lush grassy meadows, tree-covered hills, and craggy snowcapped peaks; keep your eyes peeled for mountain goats.

The highway then climbs over a low saddle and descends to the Vermilion River. On the descent, you'll pass a particularly nice picnic spot at Wardle Creek. The mountainsides along this stretch of highway are scarred black—across the river, the result of wildfires that devastated over 4,000 hectares (9,900 acres) of forest in 2001 and 2003, and on the highway side of the river, 2017 wildfires that extended all the way to the Continental Divide.

★ Paint Pots

A scenic one-kilometer (0.6-mile) trail (20 minutes one-way) leads over the Vermilion River to this unique natural wonder: three circular ponds stained red, orange, and mustard yellow by oxide-bearing springs. The

First Nations people, who believed that animal spirits resided in these springs, collected ocher from around the pools and mixed it with animal fat or fish oil and then used it in ceremonial body and rock painting. The ocher had a spiritual association and was used in important rituals. Europeans, seeing an opportunity to "add to the growing economy of the nation," mined the ocher in the early 1900s and shipped it to paint manufacturers in Calgary.

Marble Canyon

Be sure to stop and take the enjoyable self-guided trail, one kilometer (0.6 miles) one-way, that leads along this ice-carved, marble-streaked canyon. The walk takes only about 30 minutes or so, yet as one of several interpretive plaques says, it takes you back more than 500 million years.

From the parking lot, the trail follows a fault in the limestone and marble bedrock through Marble Canyon, which has been eroded to depths of 37 meters (130 feet) by fast-flowing Tokumm Creek. As the canyon narrows, water roars down through it in a series of falls. The trail ends at a splendid viewpoint where a natural rock arch spans a gorge. Marble Canyon is also the trailhead for the Kaufmann Lake Trail.

East to the Continental Divide

Well before the Paint Pots, you'll see entire hillsides burned by a devastating fire in 2003. As the highway climbs, the burned areas become more apparent. Started by lightning, the blaze combined numerous fires to cross the highway, burn entire watersheds, and extend high up surrounding mountains to the tree line.

Continuing eastward from Marble Canyon, Highway 93 climbs steadily to the **Vermilion Pass Burn.** Lightning started the fire that roared through this area in 1968, destroying thousands of hectares of trees. Lodgepole pine, which requires the heat of a fire to release its seeds, and fireweed were the first plant species to sprout up through the charred ground. The 0.8-kilometer (0.5-mile) **Fireweed Trail** leads through the area, although the transition to regenerated forest is almost complete, as the interpretive boards describe.

At the Continental Divide, which the highway crosses at an elevation of 1,640 meters (5,380 feet), a sign marks the border between Kootenay National Park to the west and Banff National Park in Alberta to the east. From the divide, it's 11 kilometers (7 miles) to Highway 1, from which point the Town of Banff lies 29 kilometers (18 miles) southeast

Paint Pots

National Park Passes

Permits are required for entry into all national parks of the Canadian Rockies. A **National Parks Day Pass** is adults $10, seniors $8, children $5, to a maximum of $20 per vehicle. It is interchangeable between parks and is valid until 4pm the day following its purchase.

An annual **Discovery Pass**, good for entry into national parks and national historic sites across Canada, is adults $68, seniors $58, to a maximum of $136 per vehicle. Both types of pass are available at the entrance to Kootenay, at all park visitors centers, and at campground fee stations. For more information or to purchase passes in advance, visit the Parks Canada website (www.pc.gc.ca).

and Lake Louise lies 27 kilometers (17 miles) northwest.

HIKING

Some 200 kilometers (125 miles) of trails lace Kootenay National Park. Hiking opportunities range from short interpretive walks to challenging treks through remote backcountry. All trails start from Highway 93 on the valley floor, so you'll be facing a strenuous climb to reach the park's high alpine areas, especially those in the south. For this reason, many hikes require an overnight stay in the backcountry. The following hikes are listed from west to east. The best source of detailed hiking information is the *Canadian Rockies Trail Guide*, available for sale at both park information centers.

★ Stanley Glacier Trail

The Stanley Glacier Trail starts along Highway 93 seven kilometers (4.5 miles) west of the Continental Divide. Although this glacier is no more spectacular than those alongside the Icefields Parkway, the sense of achievement from traveling on foot makes this trail well worth the effort.

From Highway 93, the trail crosses the upper reaches of the Vermilion River, then begins a steady climb through an area burned by devastating fires in 1968. After two kilometers (1.2 miles), the trail levels off and begins winding through a massive U-shaped glacial valley, crossing Stanley Creek at the 2.4-kilometer (1.5-mile) mark. In open areas, fireweed, harebells, and yellow columbine carpet the ground. To the west, the sheer face of Mount Stanley rises 500 meters (1,640 feet) above the forest. The trail officially ends atop the crest of a moraine after 4.2 kilometers (2.6 miles), with distant views to Stanley Glacier. Allow 90 minutes to reach this point. It's possible (and worthwhile, for improved glacier views) to continue 1.3 kilometers (0.8 miles) to the tree-topped plateau visible higher up the valley. Surprisingly, once on the plateau, you'll find a gurgling stream, a healthy population of marmots, and incredible views west to Stanley Glacier and north back down the valley. Be especially careful on the return trip—it's extremely easy to lose your footing on the loose rock.

Day Hikes

The most popular short walks are to Paint Pots and through Marble Canyon. Just west of the Radium Hot Springs park gate is the **Juniper Trail**, an easy 3.2-kilometer (2-mile) loop. Named for the abundance of juniper along one section, this trail traverses a variety of terrain in a relatively short distance. You'll pass Sinclair Creek, an avalanche slope, and a lookout offering views of Windermere Valley and the Purcell Mountains. Beginning on the north side of the road just inside the park boundary, this trail rejoins the highway 1.5 kilometers (0.9 miles) farther into the park. There you can retrace your steps back to the start or return along the highway via Sinclair Canyon. Allow one hour.

For fit hikers only, sweeping mountain views from **Kindersley Summit** make up for the pain endured along the way. Starting from Highway 93 two kilometers (1.2 miles) west of Sinclair Pass, the trail gains 1,050 meters

(3,445 feet) in 10 kilometers (6.2 miles); allow four hours one-way.

Backcountry Hikes

Overnight backcountry trips are somewhat limited, but the **Rockwall** is a classic. The 54-kilometer (34-mile), three-day trek focuses on a 30-kilometer-long (19-mile) escarpment that rises more than 1,000 meters (3,280 feet) from an alpine environment. Four different routes provide access to the spectacular feature; each begins along Highway 93 and traverses a steep valley to the Rockwall's base. Hikers will need to make arrangements for shuttle transportation between the beginning and end of this route—about 13 kilometers (8 miles) apart—or allow extra time to hike back. As with elsewhere in the park, all hikers spending the night in the backcountry must register and pick up a permit ($8 pp per night) at either of the park information centers.

ACCOMMODATIONS AND CAMPING

Accommodations within the park are limited, but the recommendations below are good ones. If you feel the need to be in town, the town of Radium Hot Springs offers a dozen or so inexpensive motels.

$150-200

The only lodging in the heart of the park is **Kootenay Park Lodge** (250/434-9648, www. kootenayparklodge.com, mid-May-late Sept., $150-225 s or d, including continental breakfast), a cabin complex at Vermilion Crossing, 65 kilometers (40 miles) from Radium Hot Springs. Although no railway passes through the park, the 1923 lodge was one of many built by the CPR throughout the Canadian Rockies. It consists of a main lodge with restaurant, 12 cabins, and a general store stocked with souvenirs and light snacks. The most basic cabins each have a bath, a small fridge, and a coffeemaker, with rates rising to a reasonable $225 for the newer Vermilion Cabins with a separate bedroom and a fireplace.

$200-250

★ **Nipika Mountain Resort** (250/342-6516 or 877/647-4525, www.nipika.com, $210 s, $308 d) offers the same wilderness experience as the Cross River cabins and is in the same vicinity—along Settler's Road, which branches off Highway 93 about 114 kilometers (71 miles) from Banff and 32 kilometers (20 miles) from Radium Hot Springs. Sleeping up to eight people, the seven cabins are larger than those at Cross River and have full en suite baths and kitchens with wood-burning stoves. The cabins are modern but were constructed in a very traditional manner—the logs were milled on-site, and construction is dovetail notching. Guests bring their own food and spend their days hiking, fishing, and wildlife-watching. In winter, an extensive system of trails is groomed for cross-country skiing.

$250-300

The well-kept ★ **Cross River Wilderness Centre** (403/271-3296 or 877/659-7665, www. crossriver.ca, $250 s or d plus $90 pp for meals) has a real sense of privacy and of being well away from the well-worn tourist path of Highway 93. That's because it is—the complex is tucked in a riverside setting 15 kilometers (9 miles) down Settler's Road, which branches off the highway 114 kilometers (71 miles) from Banff and 32 kilometers (20 miles) from Radium Hot Springs. The smart, spacious cabins are equipped with wood-burning fireplaces, log beds draped in down duvets, toilets, and sinks. Showers are located in the main building, along with the main lounge, cooking facilities, a dining area, and a deck. As you can imagine, the atmosphere is convivial, with the cabins attracting outdoorsy types who want to enjoy the Canadian Rockies in their natural state—without room service and fine dining.

Campgrounds

The park's largest camping area is **Redstreak Campground** (reservations 877/737-3783, www.pccamping.ca, mid-May-mid-Oct., unserviced sites $28, hookups $32-39, oTEN-Tiks $120 s or d, fire permits $8.80) on a narrow plateau in the extreme southwest of the park (vehicle access from Highway 93/95 on the south side of Radium Hot Springs township at the visitors center). The campground holds 144 sites, showers, and kitchen shelters. In summer, free slide shows and talks are presented by park naturalists five nights a week and typically feature topics such as wolves, bears, the park's human history, or the effects of fire. Trails lead from the campground to the hot springs, town, and a couple of lookouts.

The park's two other campgrounds lie to the north of Radium Hot Springs along Highway 93. Neither have hookups or showers. The larger of the two is **McLeod Meadows Campground,** beside the Kootenay River 27 kilometers (17 miles) from Radium Hot Springs. Facilities include flush toilets, kitchen shelters, and a fire pit and picnic table at each of the 98 sites. **Marble Canyon,** across the highway from the natural attraction of the same name, offers 61 sites and similar facilities. Both are open late June-early September, and all sites cost $23. No reservations are taken at these two campgrounds.

Hikers planning overnight trips in the backcountry must register at either of the park information centers and pick up a backcountry camping pass ($10 pp per night, $70 season pass).

INFORMATION

Kootenay Park Visitor Centre (7556 Main St., 250/347-9331 or 800/347-9704, www.radiumhotsprings.com, 9am-5pm daily mid-May-mid-Oct.) is outside the park in the town of Radium Hot Springs, at the base of the access road to Redstreak Campground. Here you can collect a free map with hiking trail descriptions, find out about trail closures and campsite availability, and get the weather forecast.

GETTING THERE AND AROUND

Kootenay National Park is not served by public transportation, nor do any tour companies include the park on their itineraries. The vast majority of visitors arrive by vehicle. Visitors can either base themselves in the village of Radium Hot Springs, 132 kilometers (82 miles) southwest of the town of Banff, or make the journey from Banff itself.

Yoho National Park

Yoho, a Cree word for amazement, is a fitting name for this 131,300-hectare (324,450-acre) national park on the western slopes of the Canadian Rockies. East of Golden, the Trans-Canada Highway bisects the park. Kootenay National Park lies immediately to the south, while Banff National Park in Alberta borders Yoho to the east. The park's only watershed is that of the **Kicking Horse River,** which is fed by the Wapta and Waputik Icefields. The Kicking Horse, wide and braided for much of its course through the park, flows westward, joining the mighty Columbia River at Golden.

Yoho is the smallest of the four contiguous Canadian Rockies national parks, but its

wild and rugged landscape holds spectacular waterfalls, extensive ice fields, a lake to rival those in Banff, and one of the world's most intriguing fossil beds. In addition, you'll find some of the finest hiking in all of Canada on the park's 300-kilometer (186-mile) trail system.

Within the park are four lodges, four campgrounds, and the small railway town of **Field,** offering basic services. The park is open year-round, although road conditions in winter can be treacherous, and occasional closures occur on Kicking Horse Pass. The road out to Takakkaw Falls is closed through winter, and it often doesn't reopen until mid-June.

Yoho National Park

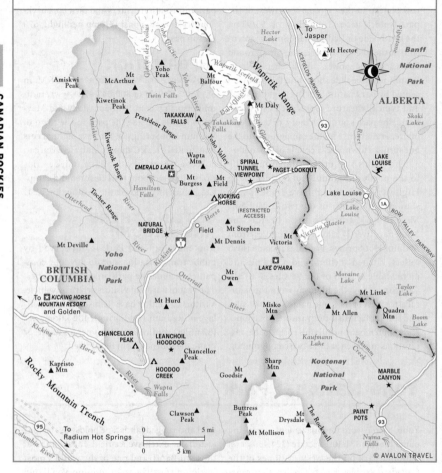

ROADSIDE SIGHTS

As with all other parks of the Canadian Rockies, you don't need to travel deep into the backcountry to view the most spectacular features—many are visible from the roadside. The following sights are listed from east to west, starting at the park boundary (the Continental Divide).

Spiral Tunnel Viewpoint

The joy that Canadian Pacific Railway president William Van Horne felt upon completion of his transcontinental rail line in 1886 was tempered by massive problems along a stretch of line west of Kicking Horse Pass. Big Hill was less than five kilometers (3 miles) long, but its gradient was so steep that runaway trains, crashes, and other disasters were common. A trail from Kicking Horse Campground takes you past the remains of one of those doomed trains. Nearly 25 years after the line opened, railway engineers and builders finally solved the problem. By building two spiral tunnels down through two kilometers (1.2 miles) of solid rock to the valley floor, they lessened the grade dramatically and the terrors came to an end. Today, a viewpoint along the way includes interpretive displays telling the fascinating story of Big Hill.

Yoho Valley

Fed by the Wapta Icefield in the far north of the park, the **Yoho River** flows through this spectacularly narrow valley, dropping more than 200 meters (660 feet) in the last kilometer before its confluence with the Kicking Horse River. The road leading up the valley passes the park's main campground, climbs a *very* tight series of switchbacks (watch for buses reversing through the middle section), and emerges at **Upper Spiral Tunnel Viewpoint,** which offers a different perspective on the aforementioned tunnel. Another 400 meters (0.25 miles) along the road is a pullout for viewing the confluence of the Yoho and Kicking Horse Rivers—a particularly impressive sight, as the former is glacier-fed and therefore silty, while the latter is lake-fed and clear.

Yoho Valley Road ends 14 kilometers (9 miles) from the main highway at **Takakkaw Falls,** the most impressive waterfall in the Canadian Rockies. The falls are fed by the Daly and Des Poilus Glaciers of the Waputik Icefield, which straddles the Continental Divide. Its name meaning "wonderful" in the Cree language, Takakkaw tumbles 254 meters (830 feet) over a sheer rock wall at the lip of the Yoho Valley, creating a spray bedecked by rainbows. It can be seen from the parking lot, but it's well worth the easy 10-minute stroll over the Yoho River to appreciate the sight in all its glory.

HIKING

Yoho Valley provides many fine opportunities for serious day hikers to get off the beaten track. The following day hikes begin from different trailheads near the end of the road up Yoho Valley. In each case, leave your vehicle in the Takakkaw Falls parking lot.

One of the most spectacular day hikes in the Canadian Rockies is the **Iceline Trail.** Gaining 690 meters (2,260 feet) of elevation over 6.4 kilometers (4 miles), it's a relatively strenuous hike, one that you should dedicate a full day to. The length given is from the hostel (across from the Takakkaw parking lot) to the highest point along the trail, 2,250 meters (7,380 feet). From the hostel, the trail begins a steep and steady one-kilometer (0.6-mile)

the confluence of the Yoho and Kicking Horse Rivers

Burgess Shale

High on the rocky slopes above Mount Field is a layer of sedimentary rock known as the Burgess Shale, which contains what are considered to be the world's finest fossils from the Cambrian Period. The site is famous worldwide because it has unraveled the mysteries of a major stage of evolution.

In 1909, Smithsonian Institute paleontologist Charles Walcott was leading a pack train along the west slope of Mount Field, on the opposite side of the valley from the newly completed Spiral Tunnel, when he stumbled across these fossil beds. Encased in the shale, the fossils here are of marine invertebrates about 510 million years old. Generally, fossils are the remains of vertebrates, but at this site some freak event—probably a mudslide—suddenly buried thousands of soft-bodied animals (invertebrates), preserving them by keeping out the oxygen that would have decayed their delicate bodies. Walcott excavated an estimated 65,000 specimens from the site. Today paleontologists continue to uncover perfectly preserved fossils—albeit in far fewer numbers than in Walcott's day. They've also uncovered additional fossil beds, similar in makeup and age, across the valley on the north face of Mount Stephen.

Protected as a UNESCO World Heritage Site, the two research areas are open only to those accompanied by a licensed guide. The **Burgess Shale Geoscience Foundation** (250/343-6006 or 800/343-3006, www.burgess-shale.bc.ca, 10am-3:30pm Mon.-Fri.) guides trips to both sites between July and mid-September. The access to **Burgess Shale (Walcott Quarry)** is along a strenuous 10-kilometer (6-mile) trail that gains 760 meters (2,500 feet) in elevation. Trips (adults $120, under age 12 $25) leave at 8am Friday-Monday from the Yoho Trading Post at the Field intersection, returning around 6:30pm. Trips to the **Mount Stephen Fossil Beds** (adults $90, children $25) depart at 8:30am Saturday-Sunday from the Yoho Trading Post, returning at around 4:30pm. The trail to the Mount Stephen beds also gains 780 meters (2,560 feet) of elevation in three kilometers (2 miles). Trails to both sites are unrelenting in their elevation gain—you must be fit to hike them. Reservations are a must.

climb to a point where two options present themselves: the Iceline Trail is to the right, Yoho Pass is straight ahead. After a short climb, the Iceline Trail option now enters its highlight: a four-kilometer (2.5-mile) traverse of a moraine below Emerald Glacier. Views across the valley improve as the trail climbs. Many day hikers return from this section of trail, although officially it continues into Little Yoho River Valley. The trail to **Yoho Pass** can be combined with the Iceline. It leads 3.7 kilometers (2.3 miles) to spruce-encircled Yoho Lake, then continues another easy one kilometer (0.6 miles) to the pass. The pass is below the tree line, so views are limited, but from this point it's 5.5 kilometers (3.4 miles) and an elevation loss of 530 meters (1,740 feet) down to Emerald Lake, or 2.4 kilometers (1.5 miles) north, with little elevation gain or loss, to an intersection with the Iceline Trail.

Natural Bridge

Three kilometers (2 miles) west of Field is the turnoff to famous Emerald Lake. On your way out to the lake, you pass another intriguing sight. At Natural Bridge, two kilometers (1.2 miles) down the road, the Kicking Horse River has worn a narrow hole through a limestone wall, creating a bridge. Over time, the bridge will collapse and, well, it won't be such an intriguing sight anymore. A trail leads to several viewpoints—try to avoid the urge to join the foolish folks clambering over the top of the bridge.

★ Emerald Lake

Outfitter Tom Wilson stumbled on stunning Emerald Lake while guiding Major A. B. Rogers through the Kicking Horse River Valley in 1881. He was led to the lake by his horse, which had been purchased from First Nations people. He later surmised that the

Takakkaw Falls

Much discussion is made of which is Canada's highest waterfall. Della Falls, on Vancouver Island, also in British Columbia, is 440 meters (1,440 feet), but this drop is broken by a ledge. Takakkaw Falls is considerably lower, at 254 meters (830 feet), but the drop is unbroken, which, officially, makes it Canada's highest. There is one thing of which there is no doubt: Takakkaw Falls will leave you breathless, much as it did famous alpinist Sir James Outram:

The torrent, issuing from an icy cavern, rushes tempestuously down a deep, winding chasm till it gains the verge of the unbroken cliff, leaps forth in sudden wildness for a hundred and fifty feet, and then in a stupendous column of pure white sparkling water, broken by giant jets descending rocketlike and wreathed in volumed spray, dashes upon the rocks almost a thousand feet below, and, breaking into a milky series of cascading rushes for five hundred feet more, swirls into the swift current of the Yoho River.

Takakkaw Falls

horse had been accustomed to traveling up to the lake, meaning that the horse's former owners must have known about the lake before the Europeans arrived.

One of the jewels of the Canadian Rockies, the beautiful lake is surrounded by a forest of Engelmann spruce, as well as many peaks more than 3,000 meters (9,840 feet) high. It is covered in ice most of the year but comes alive with activity for a few short months in summer. In addition to hiking, you can paddle across the lake by renting a canoe from **Emerald Lake Canoe Rentals** (250/343-6000, 9am-8pm June-Sept., $30 per hour, $45 for 2 hours, $80 all day). **Emerald Lake Lodge** is the grandest of Yoho's accommodations, offering a restaurant, café, lounge, and recreation facilities for both guests and nonguests.

HIKING

One of the easiest yet most enjoyable walks in Yoho is the **Emerald Lake Loop,** which, as the name suggests, encircles Emerald Lake.

The best views are from the western shoreline, where a massive avalanche has cleared away the forest of Engelmann spruce. Across the lake from this point, Mount Burgess can be seen rising an impressive 2,599 meters (8,530 feet). Traveling in a clockwise direction beyond the avalanche slope, and at the 2.2-kilometer (1.4-mile) mark, a small bridge is crossed. Views from this point extend back across the Emerald Lake Lodge to the Ottertail Range. Beyond the lake's inlet, the vegetation changes dramatically. A lush forest of towering western red cedar creates a canopy, protecting moss-covered fallen trees, thimbleberry, and bunchberry extending to the water's edge. Just over one kilometer (0.6 miles) from the bridge, the trail divides: The left fork leads back to the parking lot via a small forest-encircled pond, while the path straight ahead passes through the grounds of Emerald Lake Lodge. Allow 90 minutes for the 5.2-kilometer (3.2-mile) circuit. From along the loop, a trail climbs steadily to **Emerald Basin,** which is reached in 4.5 kilometers

(2.8 miles). The most impressive sight awaiting you there is the south wall of the President Range, towering 800 vertical meters (2,630 feet) above the end of the basin. Allow three to four hours for the round-trip.

From the parking lot at Emerald Lake, it's just 800 meters (0.5 miles) to **Hamilton Falls.** It's an easy walk through a forest of Engelmann spruce and subalpine fir to a viewpoint at the base of the falls. A little farther along, the trail begins switchbacking steeply and offers even better views of the cascade. The trail continues beyond the waterfall to **Hamilton Lake,** which lies in a small glacial cirque a steep 880 vertical meters (2,890 feet) above Emerald Lake. Total distance from Emerald Lake to Hamilton Lake is 5.5 kilometers (3.4 miles) one-way; allow two to three hours one-way.

★ LAKE O'HARA

Nestled in a high bowl of lush alpine meadows, Lake O'Hara, 11 kilometers (7 miles) from the nearest public road, is surrounded by dozens of smaller alpine lakes and framed by spectacular peaks permanently mantled in snow. As if that weren't enough, the entire area is webbed by a network of hiking trails established over the last 90 years by luminaries such as Lawrence Grassi. Trails radiate from the lake in all directions; the longest is just 7.5 kilometers (4.7 miles), making Lake O'Hara an especially fine hub for day hiking. What makes this destination all the more special is that a quota system limits the number of visitors.

Getting There

It's possible to walk to Lake O'Hara, but most visitors take the shuttle bus along a road closed to the public. The departure point is a signed parking lot 15 kilometers (9 miles) east of Field and 3 kilometers (2 miles) west of the Continental Divide. Buses for day visitors depart at 8:30am and 10:30am daily mid-June-early October, returning at 2:30pm, 4:30pm, and 6:30pm. To book a seat, visit www.reservation.pc.gc.ca or call the dedicated

Lake O'Hara

reservations line (250/343-6433). Reservations are taken from mid-April for the summer season; check the website for the exact date. As numbers are limited, you will need to **reserve exactly on the day that bookings open** to be assured of a seat; even then, you should call as early in the day as possible. Reservations are only required for the inbound shuttle; outgoing buses fill on demand. If you are camping at Lake O'Hara, you do not require a separate booking for the bus. All times—bus departures and reservation center hours—are mountain time, the same time zone as Banff.

Practicalities

After the 20-minute bus trip to the lake, day hikers are dropped off at **Le Relais,** a homely log shelter where books and maps are sold, including the recommended Gem Trek *Lake Louise and Yoho* map. Hot drinks and light snacks are served—something to look forward to at the end of the day, as this is also the afternoon meeting place for the return trip (no reservations necessary).

Several overnight options are available at the lake—including a lodge, a campground, and a rustic hut—but each should be booked well in advance.

Hiking

A basic trail map is available at Le Relais, or invest in the *Canadian Rockies Trail Guide,* the premier hiking guide to the region (pick up a copy from the visitors center in Field). The most obvious trail is the **Lake O'Hara Shoreline,** a 2.8-kilometer (1.7-mile) loop that can be completed in 40 minutes. Starting from the warden's cabin across from Le Relais, most visitors use sections of this circuit to access the other trails detailed here, but it is an enjoyable walk in its own right, especially in the evening.

Three kilometers (2 miles) one-way, the trail to **Lake Oesa** gains 240 meters (790 feet) of elevation before reaching a small aqua-colored lake surrounded by talus slopes—one of the area's gems. The Continental Divide peaks of Mount Victoria (3,464 meters/11,365 feet)

hiking in the Lake O'Hara area

and Mount Lefroy (3,423 meters/11,230 feet) rise dramatically behind the lake.

One of my favorite hikes in all of the Canadian Rockies is the 5.9-kilometer (3.7-mile) **Opabin Plateau Circuit,** especially in late September, when larches have turned golden. Separated from Lake Oesa by 2,848-meter (9,344-foot) Mount Yukness, this plateau high above the tree line is dotted with small lakes. Two trails lead up to the plateau, which itself is laced with trails. The most direct route is the Opabin Plateau West Circuit, which branches right from the Shoreline Trail 300 meters (1,000 feet) beyond Lake O'Hara Lodge. It then passes Mary Lake, climbs steeply, and reaches the plateau in a little less than two kilometers (1.2 miles). Opabin Prospect is an excellent lookout along the edge of the plateau. From this point, take the right fork to continue to the head of the Cirque and Opabin Lake. This section of trail passes through a lightly forested area of larch that comes alive with color in late September.

Lake McArthur is the largest and (in my opinion) most stunning body of water in the Lake O'Hara area. Beginning from behind Le Relais, the 3.5-kilometer (2.2-mile) access trail passes Schäffer Lake after 1.6 kilometers (1 mile). At a junction beyond that lake, take the left fork, which climbs steeply for 800 meters (0.5 miles) then levels out and traverses a narrow ledge before entering the Lake McArthur Cirque. (Stay high, even if trails descending into the McArthur Valley look like they offer an easier approach.) After leveling off, the trail enters the alpine and quickly reaches its maximum elevation and the first views of Lake McArthur. Backed by Mount Biddle and the Biddle Glacier, the deep-blue lake and colorful alpine meadows are an unforgettable panorama.

FOOD

In downtown Field, ★ **Truffle Pigs Bistro** (Kicking Horse Lodge, 250/343-6303, 7am-10:30am, 11am-4:40pm, and 5pm-9pm daily, $20-35) is one of those unexpected finds that makes traveling such a joy. In the evening this place really shines, with dishes as adventurous as kale caesar to start and as simple as Alberta-raised beef served with local vegetables for a main.

Overlooking an arm of Emerald Lake, ★ **Cilantro on the Lake** (250/343-6321, noon-8pm Wed.-Mon. mid-May-mid-Sept., $20-34) is a casual café featuring magnificent views from tables inside an open-fronted, log chalet-style building or out on the lakefront deck. The menu is varied—you can sit and sip a coffee or have a full lunch or dinner. Starters—such as thick and creamy corn and potato chowder—are all less than $15, while mains such as wild boar tenderloin range to $34. The café is part of **Emerald Lake Lodge,** which also includes a more formal but historically attractive dining room where dinner dishes such as grilled caribou with raspberry black pepper sauce ($36) are served from 6pm daily. This restaurant is also open year-round for breakfast and lunch, or choose the more casual lounge bar and sink into one of the comfy couches with an abbreviated but still appealing menu.

ACCOMMODATIONS
Under $50
Marvel at the wonder of Takakkaw Falls from the deck at **HI-Yoho National Park** (Yoho Valley Rd., 403/760-7580 or 866/762-4122, www.hihostels.ca, late June-Sept., HI members $28, nonmembers $32), also known as Whiskey Jack Hostel, which offers basic dormitory lodging for up to 27 guests and includes use of a communal kitchen and showers. Check-in is 5pm-11pm.

In downtown Field, ★ **Fireweed Hostel** (313 Stephen Ave., 250/343-6999 or 877/343-6999, www.fireweedhostel.com, dorms $45, $135 d, 2-bedroom suite $200) is one of the few private backpacker lodges in the Canadian Rockies—and it's a good one. It's a modern purpose-built building with solid bunk beds topped by pillow-top mattresses, a beautiful lounge with a log fireplace and a

deck, wireless Internet, and a modern well-equipped kitchen. The two-bedroom suite has a private entrance and kitchen.

At Lake O'Hara is the **Elizabeth Parker Hut,** one of over a dozen rustic accommodations scattered throughout the Canadian Rockies owned and operated by the **Alpine Club of Canada** (403/678-3200, www.alpineclubofcanada.ca). What stands this lodging apart from the other Alpine Club properties is its accessibility—just a short walk from the shuttle bus drop-off point at Lake O'Hara. Guests bring their own bedding and food, and sleep in dorm-style beds. The rate is $40 pp, $30 for Alpine Club members. Most beds are filled via a lottery system that requires registration by late November for the following summer; see the website for details. If you are successful in the lottery for a bed at Elizabeth Parker Hut, your reservation includes a guaranteed seat on the bus.

$150-200
In the hamlet of Field is the simple yet elegant **Kicking Horse Lodge** (100 Centre St., 250/343-6303, www.trufflepigs.com, $180-280 s or d), which offers 13 modern, well-furnished rooms and the highly recommended Truffle Pigs Bistro. Outside of summer, rooms are discounted as low as $120—a great alternative to higher-priced Lake Louise for winter visitors.

$200-250
The streets of Field are lined with private homes offering reasonably priced overnight accommodations in rooms of varying privacy and standard. One of the better choices is the **Alpine Guesthouse** (313 2nd Ave., 250/343-6878, www.alpineguesthouse.ca), with a modern two-bedroom suite complete with a kitchen, cable TV, outdoor patio, and private entrance for $225 (as low as $110 in winter). Like everywhere else in Field, it's within walking distance of the general store and Truffle Pigs Bistro.

Don't be put off by the dull redbrick

exterior of the **Canadian Rockies Inn** (Stephen St., 250/343-6046, www.canadian-rockiesinn.com, from $225 s or d), housed within what was once the local police station; inside the rooms are spacious and filled with contemporary styling. Each unit has a fridge and coffeemaker.

Over $300

Comprising upscale cabins set alongside the Kicking Horse River, ★ **Cathedral Mountain Lodge** (250/343-6442 or 866/619-6442, www.cathedralmountain.com, late May-early Oct., $440-550 s or d) lies along Yoho Valley Road one kilometer (0.6 miles) from the Trans-Canada Highway. The original cabins have been replaced by fancy log chalets, with modern amenities and plenty of space to spread out. Each has a log bed topped by a down duvet, as well as a stone fireplace, a bath with a soaker tub and bathrobes, and a private deck. Rates include continental breakfast, a naturalist program, and the use of canoes at Moraine Lake. Within a magnificent timber-frame building in the center of the complex is a stylish restaurant and lounge.

★ **Emerald Lake Lodge** (250/343-6321 or 800/663-6336, www.crmr.com, from $525 s or d) is a gracious, luxury-class place along the southern shore of one of the Canadian Rockies' most magnificent lakes. The original lodge was built in 1902 in the same tradition as the Fairmont Chateau Lake Louise and Fairmont Banff Springs—as a playground for wealthy railway travelers. No original buildings remain (although the original framework is used in the main building); instead guests lap up the luxury of richly decorated duplex-style units and freestanding cabins. Each spacious unit is outfitted in a heritage theme and has a wood-burning fireplace, a private balcony, a luxurious bath, a comfortable bed topped by a plush duvet, and in-room coffee. Other lodge amenities include a hot tub and a sauna, a swimming pool, a restaurant, a lounge, and a café. Guests can also go

horseback riding, or go boating and fishing on Emerald Lake.

Spending a night at ★ **Lake O'Hara Lodge** (250/343-6418, www.lakeohara.com, mid-June-early Oct. and Feb.-Apr.) is a special experience, and one that draws familiar faces year after year. On a practical level, it allows hikers not equipped for overnight camping the opportunity to explore one of the finest hiking destinations in all the Canadian Rockies at their leisure. The 15 one-bedroom cabins, each with a private bath, are spread around the lakeshore, while within the main lodge are eight rooms, most of which are twins and share baths. Rates of $515 s, $685 d for a room in the main lodge (shared baths) and $970-975 d for a cabin include all meals, taxes, gratuities, and transportation. As the lodge is located 13 kilometers (8 miles) from Highway 1, guests arrive by a shuttle bus that departs from a parking lot three kilometers (2 miles) west of the Continental Divide and 15 kilometers (9 miles) east of Field. Between February and April, the eight rooms in the main lodge are available for cross-country skiers for $370 pp, including meals and ski tours.

Campgrounds

Unlike neighboring Banff and Jasper, no reservations are taken for camping in Yoho's vehicle-accessible campgrounds. All sites have a picnic table and fire ring, with a fire permit costing $9, which includes firewood. When all campgrounds are filled, campers are directed to overflow areas.

The park's main camping area (and my favorite for its off-highway, riverside location) is **Kicking Horse Campground** (mid-May-early Oct., $28), five kilometers (3 miles) northeast of Field along the road to Takakkaw Falls. Facilities include coin showers ($1), kitchen shelters, and flush toilets. Back toward the Trans-Canada Highway, **Monarch Campground** (mid-June-early Sept., $17.60) offers more limited facilities and some less-private walk-in tent sites; **Hoodoo Creek Campground** (mid-June-Aug., $22), along the Trans-Canada Highway 23 kilometers (14 miles) southwest of Field, provides 30 sites among the trees and facilities that include a kitchen shelter, hot water, and flush toilets.

At the end of the road up the Yoho Valley, **Takakkaw Falls Campground** (July-Sept., $18) is designed for tent campers only. Park at the end of the road and load up the supplied carts with your gear for a pleasant 400-meter (1.300-foot) walk along the valley floor. No showers are provided, and the only facilities are picnic tables and pit toilets.

Just below **Lake O'Hara,** alongside the access road, is a delightful little campground surrounded by some of the region's finest hiking. Each of 30 sites has a tent pad, a fire pit, and a picnic table, while other facilities include two small kitchen shelters with woodstoves, bear-proof food caches, and toilets. Reservations for sites are made in conjunction with the bus trip along the restricted-access road from Highway 1 to Lake O'Hara, although the process is slightly different than booking the bus for a day trip. Instead of being able to book online, to reserve a campsite call 250/343-6433 up to three months in advance of the day you would like to arrive at the campground. The procedure is simple enough, but to be assured a campsite, it's important you call three months in advance to the day: For example, to visit on September 25 (when the larches are at their colorful peak), start dialing at 8am on June 25 with a credit card ready. Be prepared to hit "redial" continuously, and if you don't get through by 10am, chances are the campground will have filled. Even though access is aboard a bus, you should treat the trip as one into the backcountry; passengers are limited to one large or two small bags, and no coolers or fold-up chairs are permitted on board the shuttle. Camping is $10 pp, the bus costs $15 pp round-trip, and the reservation fee is $12.

INFORMATION

The main source of information about the park is the **Field Visitorn Centre** on the Trans-Canada Highway at Field (250/343-6783, 9am-7pm daily June-Aug., 9am-5pm daily May and Sept.-mid-Oct.). Inside you'll find helpful staff, information boards, interpretive panels, and a Friends of Yoho bookstore. This is also the place to pick up backcountry camping permits, buy topographical maps, and find out schedules for campground interpretive programs.

For more information, check out the Parks Canada website (www.pc.gc.ca/yoho). For park road conditions, call 403/762-1450; for avalanche reports, call 403/762-1460.

GETTING THERE AND AROUND

Transportation to and around the park is limited. Most visitors arrive in their own vehicles, allowing just under one hour to travel east from Golden to Field and just over an hour to travel to Field from the town of Banff in Alberta along the Trans-Canada Highway. **Greyhound** (403/762-6767) stops in Field daily on its route between Banff and Golden, from where it continues west to Vancouver. **Brewster** (403/762-6767) offers a nine-hour Mountain Lakes and Waterfalls Tour (adults $145, children $78) of the park, departing Banff at 8:30am daily in summer. This tour takes in both the Yoho Valley and Emerald Lake, as well as Lake Louise.

Golden

From the western boundary of Yoho National Park, the Trans-Canada Highway meanders down the beautiful Kicking Horse River Valley to the town of Golden (pop. 3,700), at the confluence of the Kicking Horse and Columbia Rivers. As well as being a destination in itself, Golden makes a good central base for exploring the region or as an overnight stop on a tour through the Canadian Rockies.

SIGHTS AND RECREATION

Take Highway 95 off the Trans-Canada Highway, and you'll find yourself in the old

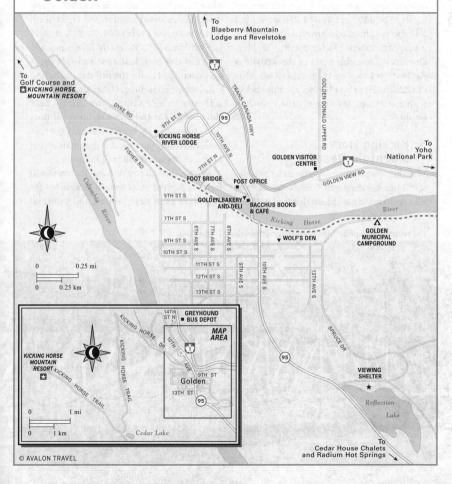

© AVALON TRAVEL

section of town, a world away from the commercial strip along the main highway. There's not really much to see in town, although you may want to check out the **Golden Museum** (1302 11th Ave. S., 250/344-5169, 9am-5pm Mon.-Fri., adults $5, seniors $3, children $2), on the south side of the river. The 8.8-kilometer (5.5-mile) **Rotary Loop** is a paved walking and biking trail that leads across the river from downtown via an impressive timber-frame pedestrian bridge, then upstream across Highway 95 (10th Ave. S.) to the campground.

The **Columbia River Wetland,** which holds international significance not only for its size (26,000 hectares/64,250 acres) but also for the sheer concentration of wildlife it supports, extends as far north as Golden. One easily accessible point of the wetland is **Reflection Lake,** on the southern outskirts of Golden. Here you'll find a small shelter with a telescope for viewing the abundant birdlife.

★ Kicking Horse Mountain Resort

Whether it's summer or winter, as you descend into Golden from Yoho National Park, it's easy to make out the ski slopes of **Kicking Horse Mountain Resort** (250/439-5400 or 866/754-5425, www.kickinghorseresort.com) across the valley.

The resort's eight-person detachable **Golden Eagle Express gondola** (10:30am-4:30pm daily late June-Sept.) transports visitors high into the alpine mid-June-September in just 18 minutes. The 360-degree panorama at the summit is equal to any other accessible point in the Canadian Rockies, with the Purcell Mountains immediately to the west and the Columbia Valley laid out below. Graded hiking trails lead from the upper terminal through a fragile, treeless environment, while mountain bikers revel in a challenging descent in excess of 1,000 meters (3,280 feet). A single gondola ride is adults $40, seniors $26, children $20. Mountain bikers pay $53 for a full-day pass, with rent-and-ride packages costing $115 for the full day, including a full-suspension bike. Other on-mountain activities include visiting the Grizzly Bear Interpretive Centre, where sightings of Boo, the resident grizzly bear, are almost guaranteed, and trying your hand at mountaineering on the *via ferrata* ($130 for 2 hours).

With a vertical rise of 1,260 meters (4,130 feet), 45 percent of its terrain designated for experts, lots of dry powder, and minimal

The timber-frame pedestrian bridge spans the Kicking Horse River.

crowds, Kicking Horse has developed a big reputation. In addition to the 3.5-kilometer-long (2.2-mile) gondola, four other lifts transport skiers and boarders to hidden bowls and to a high point of 2,450 meters (8,040 feet). Lifts operate mid-December-early April, and lift tickets are adults $94, seniors $82, children $52. Facilities in the base lodge include rentals, a cafeteria, and a ski school, while the summit restaurant is also open for lunch daily and for dinner Friday and Saturday.

To get to Kicking Horse, follow the signs from Highway 1 into town and take 7th Street North west from 10th Avenue North; cross over the Columbia River and travel 13 kilometers (8 miles) uphill from this intersection.

White-Water Rafting

Anyone looking for white-water-rafting action will want to run the Kicking Horse River. The rafting season runs mid-May-mid-September, with river levels at their highest in late June. The Lower Canyon, immediately upstream of Golden, offers the biggest thrills, including a three-kilometer (2-mile) stretch of continuous rapids. Upstream of here the river is tamer but still makes for an exciting trip, while even farther upstream, near the western boundary of Yoho National Park, it's more of a float—a good adventure for the more timid. The river is run by several companies, most of which offer the option of half-day ($70-90) or full-day ($110-160) trips. The cost varies with inclusions such as transportation from Banff and lunch.

Alpine Rafting (250/344-6778 or 888/599-5299, www.alpinerafting.com) offers trips ranging from a family-friendly float to the excitement of descending the Lower Canyon. They operate from a signposted base 25 kilometers (16 miles) east of Golden, where there is also camping (free for rafters; limited services). Other local companies include **Wet 'n' Wild Adventures** (250/344-6521 or 877/344-7238, www.wetnwild.bc.ca) and **Glacier Raft Company** (250/344-6521 or 877/344-7238, www.glacierraft.com). From Lake Louise, **Wild Water Adventures** (403/522-2211 or 888/647-6444, www.wildwater.com) leads half-day trips down the river for $93, including a narrated bus trip to their purpose-built RiverBase put-in point 27 kilometers (17 miles) east of Golden. Departures are from Lake Louise at 8:15am and 1:30pm daily. The full-day trip is broken up by a riverside lunch. **Canadian Rockies Rafting** (403/678-6535 or 877/226-7625, www.rafting.ca) operates on the river from Banff, as does the similarly Banff-based **Hydra River Guides** (403/762-4554 or 800/644-8888, www.raftbanff.com).

Other Summer Recreation

Golden Golf and Country Club (576 Golf Course Dr., 250/344-2700 or 866/727-7222, www.golfgolden.com, greens fees $85-95, twilight $65) is a challenging 18-hole course in a forested section of the valley north of town. This course is generally in excellent condition, with water coming into play on many holes—including the signature 11th and 12th holes along Holt Creek—and numerous streams and lakes to catch wayward shots.

The hills surrounding Golden are laced with mountain biking trails, many developed and maintained by local enthusiasts. A good source of information is the **Golden Cycling Club** (www.goldencyclingclub.com). Accessed from along the road up to Kicking Horse Mountain Resort are the Moonraker Bike Trails, popular for scenery and varied difficulty. Off the resort access road you'll find **Cedar Lake,** starting point for many trails and also a popular spot with locals for swimming, picnicking, and canoeing. More adventurous souls are drawn to Golden for its thermals, perfect for hang gliding and paragliding, and to the steep face of Jubilee Mountain, a renowned sport-climbing destination.

FOOD
Kicking Horse Mountain Resort

At an elevation of 2,347 meters (7,700 feet), ★ **Eagle's Eye** is the crowning glory of Kicking Horse Mountain Resort

(250/439-5400 or 866/754-5425, lunch daily, dinner Sat.-Sun., $28-42) and is Canada's highest-elevation restaurant. Access is by gondola from the resort's base village, 13 kilometers (8 miles) west of downtown Golden. As you'd expect, the views are stunning and are set off by a stylish timber-and-stonework interior, including a floor-to-ceiling fireplace and a wide wraparound deck protected from the wind by glass paneling. Dinner choices are more adventurous than lunch, but the food remains distinctly Canadian. Check out the gondola-lunch combos before purchasing your ticket, as they are a very good deal.

Downtown

Start your day with the locals at the **Golden Bakery & Deli** (419 9th Ave., 250/344-2928, 6:30am-6pm Mon.-Sat.), where the coffee is always fresh and the faces friendly. Baked goodies include breads, pastries, cakes, and meat pies, with inexpensive daily specials displayed on a blackboard in a seated section off to the side of the main counter.

Bacchus Books & Cafe (409 9th Ave., 250/344-5600, 9am-5:30pm Mon.-Sat., 10am-5:30pm Sun., lunch $7-12) has an upstairs café offering a breakfast and lunch menu filled with healthy, inexpensive meals, such as soups made daily and delicious sandwiches.

Constructed of rough-cut logs complete with bulging burls, the **Wolf's Den** (1105 9th St. S., 250/344-2330, 4pm-midnight Mon.-Thurs., noon-midnight Fri.-Sun., $18-34) is a friendly space that is part restaurant, part pub, with live music some nights. The menu features mostly steak and burgers, but also offers some creative salads and vegetarian choices.

South of Golden

A five-minute drive south of Golden off Highway 95, the **Cedar House Restaurant** (735 Hefti Rd., 250/344-4679, 5pm-10pm daily, $26-39) is a good choice for wonderfully flavored food that takes advantage of seasonal Canadian produce, including vegetables organically grown on the property. The soup of the day is a good way to get things going; then choose between mains such as prawn risotto or grilled Alberta beef tenderloin. The dining room is in a log building, but on warmer evenings you'll want to be outside on the patio.

ACCOMMODATIONS AND CAMPING

You can stay in one of the regular motels lining the highway, but don't. Instead, choose one of the unique mountain lodgings that surround the town.

Under $50

Kicking Horse River Lodge (801 9th St. N., 250/439-1112 or 877/547-5266, www.khrl. com, dorm $36, $125-240 s or d) epitomizes the new wave of lodging in the Canadian Rockies. It is a modern, riverfront log building with amenities that include wireless Internet, a living area with a large-screen TV, and a large deck with outdoor seating overlooking the Columbia River.

$100-150

Blaeberry Mountain Lodge (1680 Moberly School Rd., 250/344-5296, www.blaeberrymountainlodge.bc.ca) is on a 62-hectare (150-acre) property among total wilderness. Rooms are in the main lodge or self-contained cabins, with plenty of activities available to guests. Standard rooms with shared bath are $115 s or d, and the large cabins, which feature a separate bedroom and full kitchen, are $160. The three-bedroom cottage is $350 for up to four people. Breakfast ($15 pp) is offered. Blaeberry is nine kilometers (5.5 miles) north of Golden along Highway 1, then seven kilometers (4 miles) farther north along Moberly School Road.

$200-250

Of the accommodations at the base of Kicking Horse Mountain Resort, **Copper Horse Lodge** (1587 Cache Close, 250/344-7644 or 877/544-7644, www.copperhorselodge.com, $245-295 s or d, including breakfast) comes highly recommended. Guest rooms are huge and each is outfitted in earthy yet stylish color schemes and include bathrobes, luxurious baths, and comfortable beds. Other amenities include a restaurant, a lounge with wood-burning fireplace, and an outdoor hot tub.

$250-300

Cedar House Chalets (735 Hefti Rd., 250/290-0001, www.cedarhousechalets. com, $270-380 s or d) are spacious one- to three-bedroom cabins with full kitchens, wood-burning fireplaces, wireless Internet, barbecues, and hot tubs—with the bonus of an excellent on-site restaurant.

Campgrounds

Continue south through the old part of town over the Kicking Horse River and take 9th Street South east at the traffic lights to reach **Golden Municipal Campground** (250/344-5412, www.goldenmunicipalcampground. com, $35-42). It's a quiet place, strung out along the river and two kilometers (1.2 miles) from downtown along a riverfront walkway. Facilities include picnic shelters, coin-operated hot showers, wireless Internet, and 72 sites (32 with power hookups) with fire pits. Adjacent is a recreation center with a swimming pool and fitness facility.

Golden Eco-Adventure Ranch (872 McBeath Rd., Nicholson, 250/344-6825, www.goldenadventurepark.com, Apr.-early Oct., $35-46) is a sprawling facility on the west side of the Columbia River five kilometers south of Golden. Campsites are spread through a forest and through an open field, with access to the river via a short trail. It has the cleanest, most impressive baths I've seen at any Canadian Rockies campground, but on the downside, mosquitos are a major problem in the heat of summer.

INFORMATION AND SERVICES

While accommodations, fast-food restaurants, and gas stations line the Trans-Canada Highway, downtown Golden holds other basic services, including the **post office** (502 9th Ave.). Ninth Avenue also holds outdoor equipment shops and **Bacchus Books & Cafe** (409 9th Ave., 250/344-5600, 9am-5:30pm Mon.-Sat., 10am-5:30pm Sun.), offering a wide selection of new and used books, with plenty of local reading and detailed maps of the Columbia Valley.

The year-round **Golden Visitor Centre** (111 Golden Upper Donald Rd., 250/344-7125 or 800/622-4653, www.tourismgolden.com, 9am-8pm daily summer, 9am-4pm daily fall-spring) is ensconced in an architecturally striking building beside the highway before it descends into town from the east. Interpretive displays describe the valley and everything there is to do and see, while outside a short walking trail leads to a lookout.

GETTING THERE AND AROUND

Golden is on the Trans-Canada Highway, 134 kilometers (83 miles) west of the town of Banff and 713 kilometers (443 miles) east of Vancouver. **Greyhound** (250/344-2917, www. greyhound.ca) buses stop four times daily in Golden, utilizing the Husky gas station (1050 Trans-Canada Hwy.) as a depot. For a cab, call **Mount 7 Taxi** (250/344-5237).

Central British Columbia

Ranging from the western slopes of the Rocky Mountains to the Pacific Ocean, central British Columbia holds such varied natural features as the massive Fraser River, the lofty peaks of the Cariboo and Coast Mountains, and

the deeply indented coastal fjords around Bella Coola.

The region's history is dominated by colorful sagas of Canada's biggest gold rush, when over 100,000 miners and fortune seekers passed through the area on their way to the goldfields. However, the best-remembered man in these parts was not a miner but an explorer. In 1793, Alexander Mackenzie left the Fraser River for the final leg of his epic transcontinental journey. Fourteen days later he reached the Pacific Ocean, becoming the first person to cross the continent.

Today the most heavily traveled route through central British Columbia is the Trans-Canada Highway, which for the purposes of this book also forms the region's southern boundary. In the east of the province, the highway bisects Glacier National Park, a small but spectacular park of glaciers and towering peaks. Heading west from the park, the highway passes the heli-skiing hub of Revelstoke and the watery playground of Shuswap Lake before coming to the large population center of Kamloops.

From Kamloops, two highways lead north. Highway 5 accesses Wells Gray and Mount Robson Provincial Parks, the former a vast forested wilderness and the latter named for one of the most spectacular mountain peaks in all of Canada. The other route, Highway 97, runs through Cariboo Country, best-known for the 1860s gold rush town of Barkerville, now completely restored and one of the highlights of a trip north.

PLANNING YOUR TIME

Planning how to spend your time in central British Columbia has as much to do with integrating the region with the rest of your itinerary as it does with trying to work out how to hit all the highlights. The main route through the region is the east-west Trans-Canada Highway, which runs from Golden to Kamloops and on

Look for ★ to find recommended sights, activities, dining, and lodging.

Highlights

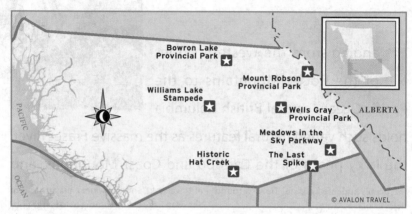

★ **Meadows in the Sky Parkway:** From the Trans-Canada Highway, this road climbs to a magnificent alpine meadow high above the tree line (page 352).

★ **The Last Spike:** Railway buffs in particular will enjoy seeing the spot where the final link was made in Canada's transcontinental railway (page 357).

★ **Wells Gray Provincial Park:** Waterfalls and wildlife combine to make this a worthwhile detour between Kamloops and Jasper (page 366).

★ **Mount Robson Provincial Park:** It's impossible not to be impressed on the drive into Mount Robson Provincial Park, unless clouds are covering the highest peak in the Canadian Rockies (page 370).

★ **Historic Hat Creek:** Over 100 years since the Cariboo Wagon Road bustled with miners heading north in search of their fortune, it's still possible to experience the frontier feeling at this historic ranch (page 374).

★ **Williams Lake Stampede:** Rodeos take place across British Columbia, but none are bigger than the Williams Lake Stampede the first weekend of July (page 377).

★ **Bowron Lake Provincial Park:** The main attraction in this park is the wilderness canoe circuit, but it's also worth visiting for its scenic locale—and hopefully you'll find time to go for a quick paddle (page 385).

to Vancouver. This can easily be traveled in one day, but with two national parks and a string of interesting towns en route, the trip calls for at least one overnight stop (Revelstoke is a good choice). Even if you're in a hurry, detour along the **Meadows in the Sky Parkway** in Mount Revelstoke National Park. The region's biggest city is Kamloops, from where highways lead in four directions. Hands down, the most scenic is Highway 5 north to **Mount Robson**

Provincial Park, from where the choices are to head northwest to Prince George (northern British Columbia) or east to Jasper National Park and then south through to Banff. If you drive far enough north along Highway 97 from Kamloops, you'll reach Prince George. A good way to kick off the long drive north is with a stop at **Historic Hat Creek Ranch,** where buildings from the Cariboo gold rush still stand.

Glacier National Park

Encompassing 135,000 hectares (333,600 acres) of the Selkirk Mountains, this park is a wonderland of jagged snowcapped peaks, extensive ice fields, thundering waterfalls, steep-sided valleys, and fast-flowing rivers. The Trans-Canada Highway bisects the park, cresting at 1,327-meter (4,350-foot) **Rogers Pass.**

Those from south of the 49th parallel probably associate the park's name with the U.S. national park in Montana. The two parks share the same name and glaciated environment, but the similarities end there. In the "other" park, buses shuttle tourists here and there and the backcountry is crowded with hikers. Here in the Canadian version, commercialism is almost totally lacking, and use of the backcountry is blissfully minimal.

The best place to start a visit to the park is the **Rogers Pass Information Centre.** Looking south from the center, you can see the **Illecillewaet, Asulkan,** and **Swiss Glaciers.** Immediately to the west of the **summit of Rogers Pass,** you'll find more stunning views and a display erected in 2010 to commemorate the 125th anniversary of the rail line reaching the pass. As far as actual "sights" go, driving through the park you'll be surrounded by one of the most awe-inspiring panoramas visible from any Canadian highway. Each roadside viewpoint seems to outdo the last. You can also get out of the car and go hiking to get a better feeling for the park, but most of the trails entail strenuous climbs.

Through-traffic excepted, permits are required for entry into Glacier National Park; they're available from the information center. A one-day permit is adults $8, seniors $7, children $4, to a maximum of $20 per vehicle.

THE LAND

Regardless of whether you approach the park from the east or west, you'll be climbing from a valley only 600 meters (1,970 feet) above sea level to 1,327-meter (4,350-foot) Rogers Pass in under 15 kilometers (9 miles). The pass is not particularly high, but it's impressive. Surrounding peaks, many topping 3,000 meters (10,000 feet), rise dramatically from the pass and draw massive amounts of precipitation from eastward-moving clouds. The resulting heavy snows feed more than 400 glaciers and permanently cloak some 14 percent of the park's landscape in snow and ice. Most of the glaciers lie in the park's southern half. Notable among them are Deville Icefield, which surrounds 3,393-meter (11,130-foot) Mount Dawson, the park's highest peak, and Illecillewaet Icefield, whose glacial arms can be viewed up close from hiking trails starting at the Illecillewaet Campground.

PLANTS AND ANIMALS

Three distinct vegetation zones can be seen within the park: montane (600-1,300 meters/1,970-4,260 feet), subalpine (1,300-1,900 meters/4,260-6,230 feet), and alpine (1,900

Central British Columbia

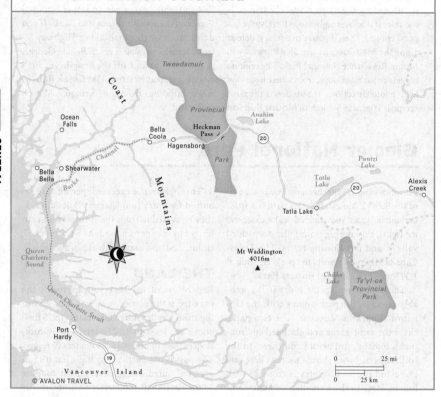

© AVALON TRAVEL

meters/6,230 feet to over 3,050 meters/10,000 feet). The montane forest supports a lush variety of tree species, including mountain hemlock, subalpine fir, Engelmann spruce, western red cedar, western hemlock, lodgepole pine, whitebark pine, western white pine, black cottonwood, Douglas fir, aspen, and white birch. Flower lovers will be impressed by the 600 species of flowering plants that have been identified within the park. The best time to see wildflowers in the high meadows and forests is early August.

The rugged terrain and long, hard winters in Glacier National Park mean that resident mammals are a tough and hardy bunch. Healthy populations of both black and grizzly bears inhabit the park. The black bears often feed along the roadside in late spring.

Grizzlies are less common and tend to remain in the backcountry, but early in the season, lingering snow can keep them at lower elevations; look for them on avalanche slopes.

HISTORY

In a scenario familiar throughout western Canada, the proclamation of Glacier National Park was influenced by the Canadian Pacific Railway's desire to see tourists use its rail line. For CPR engineers, finding a passable train route through the Columbia Mountains proved a formidable challenge. The major obstacle was the threat of avalanche—high snowfall was coupled with narrow valleys and steep approaches from both east and west, all attributes spelling danger. Through three summers, rail workers toiled with picks

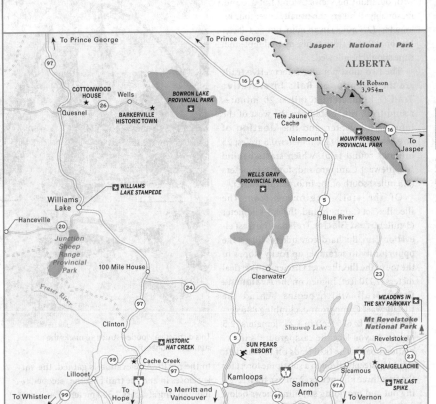

and shovels, finally completing a rail bed on November 7, 1885. A national park was proclaimed, protecting the pass and surrounding wilderness and, much to the delight of the cash-strapped CPR, bringing visitors to the area—by rail, of course. For the next three decades, the CPR operated passenger and freight services over the pass, thrilling thousands of pioneer passengers. Unfortunately, despite railway engineering ingenuity, frequent and devastating avalanches took their toll, killing over 200 workers in the first 30 years of operation. Forced to stop the carnage, the CPR rerouted the line, tunneling under the pass in 1916. The rerouted line bypassed the park's most spectacular scenery, and the number of visitors to the park dropped dramatically.

In the early 1950s, a new team of engineers tackled the same problem—this time in an effort to build a highway across the pass. The tunnel approach that had worked for the railway was deemed impractical for a highway, so a new solution to the avalanche danger was required. In 1962 a route through the national park and over the pass was completed—this time with the addition of concrete snow sheds over sections of the highway.

HIKING

The park's 21 hiking trails cover 140 kilometers (87 miles) and range from short interpretive walks to long, steep, difficult climbs. Aside from the interpretive trails, most gain a lot of elevation, rewarding the energetic hiker with outstanding views. Along flat ground, reasonably fit hikers can usually cover four kilometers (2.5 miles) in an hour, but on Glacier National Park's steep trails, up to double that time should be allowed.

The two most popular interpretive trails are the **Abandoned Rails Interpretive Trail** (1 kilometer/0.6 miles; 20 minutes round-trip), which starts to the west of the information center, and the **Meeting of the Waters Trail** (1 kilometer/0.6 miles; 25 minutes round-trip), which starts behind Illecillewaet Campground, four kilometers (2.5 miles) south of the information center.

Of the trails beginning from the Illecillewaet Campground, the 4.8-kilometer (3-mile) **Great Glacier Trail** has the least elevation gain. But hard-core hikers will get the opportunity to scramble up rocky slopes to the toe of the Illecillewaet Glacier, 340 vertical meters (1,110 feet) higher, on the **Avalanche Crest Trail,** which begins behind the Illecillewaet Campground, climbing 800 vertical meters (2,620 feet) in 4.2 kilometers (2.5 miles). As you face the campground's information board. The trail leads off to your left, climbing steeply through a subalpine forest for the first three kilometers (2 miles), then leveling out and providing stunning views below to Rogers Pass and south to the Illecillewaet and Asulkan Glaciers. While elevation gain on the **Asulkan Valley Trail** is similar to that of others in the steep-sided Illecillewaet River Valley, it is gained over a longer distance (6.5 kilometers/4 miles), meaning a less-strenuous outing. Nevertheless, a full day should be allowed round-trip. The trail follows Asulkan Brook through a valley of dense subalpine forest. Whereas other trails lead to panoramic overlooks, the highlight of this trail's final destination is a view of the immense ice field rising high above you.

From the park information center, the five-kilometer (3-mile) **Balu Pass Trail** climbs a gut-wrenching 1,020 vertical meters (3,350 feet) between Mount Cheops to the south and a ridge of 2,700-meter (8,860-foot) peaks

This distinctive wooden structure marks the summit of Rogers Pass.

to the north. As elevation is gained, the valley closes in and the trail becomes steeper, finally ending at a pass 2,300 meters (7,450 feet) above sea level.

From the west side of the highway one kilometer (0.6 miles) north of the information center, the **Hermit Trail** climbs very steeply through a subalpine forest, breaking out above the tree line and ending at a view of glaciated peaks towering 1,000 meters (3,300 feet) above. Total elevation gain is 940 meters (3,080 feet) over 2.8 kilometers (1.7 miles). This trail is for fit hikers only.

ACCOMMODATIONS AND CAMPING

Since the closure of the park's Glacier Park Lodge in 2012, the closest motel accommodations are in Golden or Revelstoke, an hour's drive to the east and west, respectively.

At **Illecillewaet Campground** (3.5

Time Zones

Glacier National Park is in two time zones. If you pass through the park westbound, turn your watch back one hour to **Pacific time.** If you're eastbound, turn it forward one hour to **mountain time.**

The resort offers showers, laundry, and a restaurant. Basic sleeping cabins with a toilet but no shower are $95, while more comfortable family suites start at $175. Those staying in a cabin enjoy free access to the hot pools, while campers and the public pay adults $18.50, seniors and children $15.50 for a day pass.

kilometers/2.2 miles south of Rogers Pass, late June-Sept., $21.50), facilities include kitchen shelters, picnic tables, firewood, flush toilets, and an evening interpretive program. Sites are not particularly private, and the surrounding peaks and towering cedar trees mean little sunshine before noon, but the campground is the perfect base for exploring, because it's the trailhead for the park's main concentration of hiking trails. When this campground fills, campers are directed to an overflow area in the nearby Sir Donald Picnic Area ($16). Smaller **Loop Brook Campground** (3 kilometers/2 miles beyond the Illecillewaet Campground toward Revelstoke, July-Sept., $21.50) holds just 20 sites.

If the above options are full or don't appeal to your budget and tastes, head 40 kilometers (25 miles) west to **Canyon Hot Springs Resort** (250/837-2420, www.canyonhotsprings.com, May-Sept., camping $35-55, cabins $135-325 s or d), a family-style complex of accommodations and activities with something for everyone. Two outdoor swimming pools (9am-9pm daily) filled with water pumped from nearby hot springs are the advertised highlight, while the short trail to historic Albert Canyon is a good way to escape the crowds. Aside from the solitude, you can explore the broken-down remains of log cabins dating to the days of railway construction.

INFORMATION AND SERVICES

Rogers Pass Discovery Centre (250/837-7500, www.pc.gc.ca, 9am-5pm daily May-mid-June, 8am-7pm daily mid-June-early Sept., 9am-5pm daily early Sept.-Nov., 7am-4pm daily Dec.-Apr.) is beside the highway 1.2 kilometers (0.7 miles) north of the actual pass and resembles the old-fashioned snow sheds that once protected the railroad from avalanches. The center's fascinating displays focus on the park's natural and human history. Videos on various aspects of the park are shown on the TV (the viewing area by the fireplace is a great spot to while away time waiting for the clouds to lift), and the center's theater screens documentaries on mountain wildlife and avalanche protection. Staff members provide information on trail conditions and closures, operate a small bookstore, and conduct interpretive programs. The center is also the only place in the park to buy park passes, necessary for those planning any hiking or camping.

GETTING THERE

Glacier National Park is bisected by the Trans-Canada Highway. From the highway summit at Rogers Pass, Golden is 80 kilometers (50 miles) east and Revelstoke is 72 kilometers (45 miles) west. From Vancouver, allow seven hours to travel the 632 kilometers (395 miles) to Rogers Pass.

Revelstoke

Revelstoke lies 72 kilometers (45 miles) west of Rogers Pass at the confluence of the Illecillewaet River and the mighty Columbia River, surrounded by mountains—the Monashees to the west and the Selkirks to the east. The setting couldn't be more spectacular.

An 1850s gold rush along the Columbia River brought the first Europeans to the area, but the town really began to grow with the coming of the railroad in the 1880s. In fact, the city is named for Lord Revelstoke, who provided funding for completion of the Canadian Pacific Railway's line through town. Finally, the Trans-Canada Highway came to town early in the 20th century, helping turn Revelstoke into today's midsize city of 7,200.

The town holds a couple of museums, but the main attractions are farther afield, including two massive dams, a national park on the back doorstep, and great skiing and snowboarding on Mount Mackenzie.

SIGHTS

The Trans-Canada Highway makes a lazy loop around the back of Revelstoke, missing downtown completely. It's well worth the detour to downtown, not just for the best dining but to enjoy the laid-back atmosphere of a small city that has done an excellent job of preserving its heritage. The rejuvenated downtown core centers around the appealing, all-brick Grizzly Plaza. Southwest from the plaza along Mackenzie Avenue are many frontier-style false-fronted buildings and the art deco-style Roxy Theatre. Pick up the *Heritage Walking & Driving* brochure at the information center for routes that take in the historic highlights.

Museums

Railway buffs shouldn't miss **Revelstoke Railway Museum** (719 Track St. W, 250/837-6060, 10am-5pm daily May-early Oct., adults $10, seniors $8, children $5), a re-creation of an early Canadian Pacific Railway station. Reflecting the importance of this mode of transportation in Revelstoke's history, the museum centers on a massive 1948 steam locomotive and Business Car No. 4, the ultimate in early rail-travel luxury.

Revelstoke's main street at dusk

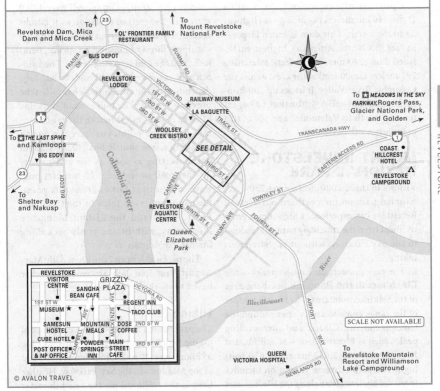

Revelstoke

Map labels:

To 23 Revelstoke Dam, Mica Dam and Mica Creek
OL' FRONTIER FAMILY RESTAURANT
To Mount Revelstoke National Park
FRASER DR
BUS DEPOT
REVELSTOKE LODGE
VICTORIA RD
1ST ST W
2ND ST W
3RD ST W
SUMMIT RD
RAILWAY MUSEUM
LA BAGUETTE
TRACK ST
WOOLSEY CREEK BISTRO
SEE DETAIL
THIRD ST E
To MEADOWS IN THE SKY PARKWAY, Rogers Pass, Glacier National Park, and Golden
TRANSCANADA HWY
To THE LAST SPIKE and Kamloops
BIG EDDY INN
23
To Shelter Bay and Nakusp
BIG EDDY RD
Columbia River
CAMPBELL AVE
NINTH ST E
REVELSTOKE AQUATIC CENTRE
Queen Elizabeth Park
RAILWAY AVE
TOWNLEY ST
FOURTH ST E
EASTERN ACCESS RD
COAST HILLCREST HOTEL
REVELSTOKE CAMPGROUND
Illecillewaet River
AIRPORT WAY
SCALE NOT AVAILABLE
QUEEN VICTORIA HOSPITAL
NEWLANDS RD
To Revelstoke Mountain Resort and Williamson Lake Campground

Detail inset:
REVELSTOKE VISITOR CENTRE
GRIZZLY PLAZA
SANGHA BEAN CAFE
VICTORIA RD
1ST ST W
MUSEUM
REGENT INN
TACO CLUB
MACKENZIE AVE
SAMESUN HOSTEL
MOUNTAIN MEALS
DOSE COFFEE
2ND ST W
CUBE HOTEL
CAMPBELL AVE
POST OFFICE & NP OFFICE
POWDER SPRINGS INN
MAIN STREET CAFE
3RD ST W

© AVALON TRAVEL

Revelstoke Museum (315 1st St., 250/837-3067, 10am-5pm Mon.-Fri., 11am-5pm Sat., adults $5, seniors and youths $4) fills two stories of a historic downtown post office building. It preserves plenty of pioneer memorabilia and a great collection of historical black-and-white photos, and offers displays on local industries, early Chinese miners, winter recreation, and avalanche science.

Dams

The 1,900-kilometer (1,180-mile) Columbia River, North America's third longest, is controlled by many dams. Four of these are in British Columbia, and two are in the vicinity of Revelstoke. The local dams provide the necessary water for two massive hydroelectric

operations. These generating stations are each capable of producing 1,800 megawatts of electricity—combined, 30 percent of the province's needs.

Revelstoke Dam, eight kilometers (5 miles) north of the city on Highway 23, was completed in 1985. It's 470 meters (1,540 feet) wide and 175 meters (590 feet) high. The massive reservoir behind the dam stretches over 130 kilometers (80 miles). Nestled in the valley downstream of the dam is the generating station. Exhibits at the two-story **Revelstoke Dam Visitor Centre** (250/814-6697, 10am-4pm daily late May-Aug., adults $6, seniors and children $5), above the generating station, explain the valley's history and the operation and impact of the dams. From the center, a high-speed elevator whisks visitors to the top of the dam for an excellent view.

Upstream of Revelstoke Dam is **Mica Dam,** 140 kilometers (87 miles) via Highway 23 to the north. This dam is much larger—in fact, it's North America's highest earth-filled dam (240 meters/790 feet), stretching 792 meters (2,600 feet) at the crest across the Columbia River Valley. It backs up 200-kilometer-long (124-mile) **Kinbasket Lake,** extending north to Valemount and south to a point just north of Golden.

MOUNT REVELSTOKE NATIONAL PARK

Visitors to this 26,000-hectare (64,250-acre) national park on the northern outskirts of Revelstoke can experience a high-alpine environment from the enticingly named Meadows in the Sky Parkway, without any strenuous hiking.

The park protects the highest peaks of the **Clachnacudiann Range,** a northern arm of the Selkirk Mountains. The forested slopes of the range come to an icy apex around the Clachnacudiann Glacier and surrounding peaks, such as **Mount Coursier** and **Mount Inverness,** both 2,637 meters (8,650 feet) high. The park's diverse vegetation includes forests of ancient cedar along the Illecillewaet River, subalpine forests of Engelmann spruce and fir on higher slopes, and finally, above the tree line, meadows of low-growing shrubs that come alive with color for a few weeks in midsummer.

As with all Canadian national parks, a permit is required for entry; in this case it applies only for travel on the Meadows in the Sky Parkway. Permits are issued at the park gate, at the lower end of the parkway. A one-day permit is adults $8, seniors $7, children $4, to a maximum of $20 per vehicle.

★ Meadows in the Sky Parkway

This 26-kilometer (16-mile) road one kilometer (0.6 miles) west of the downtown Revelstoke turnoff climbs from the Trans-Canada Highway to a magnificent alpine meadow high above the tree line. The road is very steep, gaining well over 1,000 meters (3,280 feet) of elevation as it climbs seemingly endless hairpin bends through a subalpine forest of Engelmann spruce, hemlock, and the odd towering cedar. The summit area is snowed in until mid- to late July, depending on how much snow has fallen the previous winter. The public road ends one kilometer (0.6 miles) before the true summit. From this point, you have the option of taking a free shuttle bus (10am-4:20pm daily, starting as soon as the snow melts off the road) or walking (20 minutes one-way) to **Heather Lake.** From this point, the panoramic view takes in the Columbia River Valley and the distant Monashee Mountains, with hiking trails beckoning further exploration.

The parkway is open 7am-10pm daily May-August, 9am-5pm daily September. At other times, the parkway is closed.

Hiking

The park doesn't have an extensive network of hiking trails—just 10 marked trails totaling 65 kilometers (40 miles) in length. At the end of the Meadows in the Sky Parkway, Heather Lake is the trailhead for the one-kilometer (0.6-mile) round-trip **Meadows in the Sky Trail,** which features signs explaining the flora of the fragile alpine environment. From the east side of Heather Lake, a nine-kilometer (5.5-mile) trail leads through alpine meadows to the **Jade Lakes.** Along the route, short side trails lead to **Miller** and **Eva Lakes.**

Most other trails take under an hour and are posted with interpretive panels. Two of these start beside the Trans-Canada Highway east of Revelstoke, where the Illecillewaet River forms the park's southern boundary. The 500-meter (0.3-mile) **Giant Cedars Boardwalk** (allow 10 minutes) traverses a meadow before disappearing into an ancient cedar forest and then along a sparkling creek. Farther west along the highway is the trailhead for **Skunk Cabbage Interpretive**

Trail, which leads 1.2 kilometers (0.7 miles) down to the Illecillewaet River (allow 40 minutes round-trip).

The park's most demanding trail is the 10-kilometer (6-mile) **Summit Trail,** which begins—or, more sensibly, ends—at the entrance to the Meadows in the Sky Parkway and runs to the Balsam Lake warden's cabin. The trail makes an elevation gain of 1,200 meters (3,940 feet), so allow at least 3.5 hours for this strenuous uphill slog. The eight-kilometer (5-mile) **Lindmark Trail** is equally strenuous, gaining 950 meters (3,120 feet) in elevation as it leads up to Balsam Lake from the lookout eight kilometers (5 miles) from the park gate.

Information and Services

Services within the park are limited to picnic areas. Although backcountry camping is allowed in designated areas (permit required, $10 pp), no road-accessible campgrounds lie within the park. Revelstoke is home to the park's **administration office** (300 3rd St., 250/837-7500, 8:30am-4:30pm Mon.-Fri. year-round). Other sources of information are **Rogers Pass Information Centre,** in nearby Glacier National Park, and the Parks Canada website (www.pc.gc.ca).

RECREATION

In summer, recreation revolves around the national park, the local golf course (250/837-4276), and the Columbia River. In winter, an expanding alpine resort draws the visitors. One of the most attractive things about Revelstoke in winter are the prices, with local accommodations combining with the resort to offer some of the best-priced packages to be found anywhere in Canada.

Skiing and Snowboarding

Famed for its powder snow, **Revelstoke Mountain Resort** (250/837-4675, www.revelstokemountainresort.com) is anchored by an eight-person gondola and a high-speed quad, which combine to provide a vertical rise of 1,713 meters (5,620 feet)—North America's highest. Lift tickets are a reasonable adults $80, seniors and ages 13-18 $61, ages 6-12 $28, under age 6 free.

Nestled between the Selkirk and Monashee Mountains, Revelstoke is also the center of much heli-skiing. **Selkirk Tangiers Heli-skiing** (250/837-5378 or 800/663-7080, www.selkirk-tangiers.com) operates from town, offering day trips for $900-1,000 and all-inclusive packages—including heli-skiing (over 30,000 meters/100,000 feet of vertical

Mount Revelstoke National Park

runs), accommodations (at the Coast Hillcrest Resort Hotel), and meals. Prices range from $2,955 for three days in December to $9,400 for seven days in February.

Water Sports

Looking for a rainy day activity with children? **Revelstoke Aquatic Centre** (600 Campbell Ave., 250/837-9351, 6:30am-9pm Mon.-Fri., 10am-8pm Sat., noon-8pm Sun., adults $7, seniors $5.50, children $4) is an excellent facility comprising multiple indoor saltwater pools, waterslides, a slow-moving "lazy river," and a climbing wall built over one pool.

ENTERTAINMENT

In July and August, free entertainment takes place nightly at the **Grizzly Plaza band shell,** at the bottom end of Mackenzie Avenue. Whether it be comedy or country, crowds of up to a few hundred gather, sitting in plastic chairs, snagging a table at a surrounding restaurant, or just standing in the background. For music and dancing of a more formal nature, the young crowd heads for **Big Eddy Inn** (2108 Big Eddy Rd., 250/814-0095, from 11am daily). Downtown in the Regent Inn (112 1st St., 250/837-2107), you'll find live music or a DJ Wednesday-Saturday at the **River City Pub,** and plenty of quiet corners at the more subdued **Traverse Lounge.**

FOOD

Just off the main street, **Dose Coffee** (101 2nd St., 250/837-6215, 6:30am-5pm daily) is where local coffee and tea aficionados head for a wide range of organically sourced choices. **Mountain Meals** (311 1st St., 250/837-3565, 8am-6pm Mon.-Fri., 8am-4pm Sat.-Sun., lunch $7-12) is a deli-style café stocked with lunches to go, including sausage rolls and filled rolls and wraps. They also have a café section and good coffee.

Look no farther than **Taco Club** (204 Mackenzie Ave., 250/837-5960, 7am-4pm Mon.-Thurs., 7am-9pm Fri.-Sat., 7am-4pm Sun., lunch $7-11) for healthy, inexpensive Mexican food along the main street.

Street-side tables are most sought after, but inside is cheerful and welcoming. You'll be impressed by the flavor of dishes such as tequila-citrus chicken enchiladas and enchiladas filled with coconut prawns and mango coleslaw. Wash dinner down with a local craft beer.

At the top end of Mackenzie Avenue, in a restored heritage home, the ambience at the **Main Street Grill** (317 Mackenzie Ave., 250/837-6888, 8am-3pm Tues.-Sun., $8-14) is a little more reserved than Taco Club. Cooked breakfasts are around $8 and lunches, including a tangy Thai salad, are all under $15. Tables on a covered patio surrounded by greenery are a bonus.

On the west side of downtown, **La Baguette** (607 Victoria Rd., 250/837-3755, 6:30am-9pm daily summer, 6:30am-7pm daily fall-spring, lunch $7-12) is popular for its weekly pizza and pasta specials, both of which are always creative and well-priced. A few blocks from the heart of downtown is my favorite restaurant in all of central British Columbia, the ★ **Woolsey Creek Bistro** (600 2nd St. W., 250/837-5500, 5pm-11pm daily, $18-34). It has a warm, friendly atmosphere but is always full and noisy with locals enjoying a wide range of healthy, well-prepared, and remarkably inexpensive dishes, such as baked halibut topped with apricot salsa. Still hungry? The cheesecake is made from scratch in-house.

Despite the many good choices downtown, **Ol' Frontier Family Restaurant** (Trans-Canada Hwy. at Hwy. 23 N., 250/837-5119, 7am-9pm daily, $10-17) may appeal to hurried highway travelers because of its location. It's a typical roadside diner with nothing fancy that doesn't need to be. The wood interior is decorated with red-and-white checkered curtains, cowboy boots, hats, antlers, and cattle horns; the waitresses wear jeans; and a sign outside says "Y'all come back, y'hear!"

ACCOMMODATIONS AND CAMPING
Under $50

The least expensive lodging option in

Revelstoke is the ★ **Samesun Hostel** (400 2nd St. W., 250/837-4050, www.samesun.com, dorms $28, $64 s or d), within easy walking distance of downtown. Providing a true home away from home, this heritage house has been fully restored, complete with hardwood floors. Amenities include kitchen facilities, laundry, free wireless Internet access, bike rentals, a game room, and a barbecue area. The 26 double and twin rooms share baths, but beds are comfortable and linen is supplied.

$50-100

Cube Hotel (311 Campbell Ave., 250/837-4086, www.cubehotel.ca, $72-94 s or d) combines the privacy of a regular hotel room with the feeling of a hostel. Each room has a basic restroom and TV, but showers are shared. Other communal facilities include a kitchen and lounge filled with books and board games. A light breakfast is included in the rates. The distinctive cube-spaced building and colorful square exterior panels make spotting the Cube easy.

$100-150

Inexpensive motels are spread through downtown and out on the highway. The best is the **Revelstoke Lodge** (601 1st St. W., 250/837-2181 or 888/559-1979, www.revelstokelodge.com, $109-129 s or d), with air-conditioned guest rooms, wireless Internet included in the rates, a small outdoor hot tub, and an adjacent restaurant.

Downtown, the ★ **Powder Springs Inn** (200 3rd St. W., 250/837-5151 or 800/991-4455, www.powdersprings.ca, $149 s or d) is a centrally located two-story motel providing good value year-round in 45 regularly revamped rooms. Rates include passes to the local aquatic center. A mountain-themed pub with a full menu and an outdoor hot tub are also on the premises.

$250-300

At the eastern entrance to town, five kilometers (3 miles) from downtown, the **Coast Hillcrest Hotel** (2100 Oak Dr., 250/837-3322 or 800/716-6199, www.coasthotels.com, $229-309 s or d) is a large property with spacious contemporary rooms, a fitness room, an outdoor hot tub, a restaurant that opens to an outdoor terrace with sweeping mountain views, and a lounge.

Camping

Revelstoke Campground (250/837-2085 or 800/562-3905, www.revelstokecampground.com, tents $38, hookups $45-55 basic cabins with shared baths $85 s or d, chalets $175-195) is off the Trans-Canada Highway six kilometers (4 miles) east of downtown. The well-kept campground offers grassy sites, lots of trees, a swimming pool, propane-filling facilities, a well-stocked store, free wireless Internet, hot showers, laundry facilities, and a main lodge that looks like a Swiss chalet. The fun stuff includes a heated outdoor pool, two playgrounds, rock-climbing lessons, evening campfires, and pancake breakfasts.

Quiet **Williamson Lake Campground** (7 kilometers/4.5 miles south of town on Airport Way, 250/837-5512, www.williamsonlake-campground.com, mid-Apr.-mid-Oct., $30-40) lies on the edge of a small lake perfect for mid-summer swimming. Mini golf, canoe and SUP rentals, a general store, free hot showers, and a relaxed atmosphere help make this an appealing choice.

INFORMATION AND SERVICES

Turn off the highway into town, and just before reaching downtown, **Revelstoke Visitor Centre** (301 Victoria Rd., 250/837-5345 or 800/487-1493, www.seerevelstoke.com, 8:30am-4:30pm Mon.-Fri., 9am-4pm Sat.-Sun.) is signposted to the right. **Mount Revelstoke National Park administration office** (313 3rd St., 250/837-7500, 8:30am-4:30pm Mon.-Fri. year-round) is in the post office building.

Queen Victoria Hospital (250/837-2131) is on Newlands Road (off Airport Way), on the southeast side of town. The **post office** (307 3rd St.) is a couple of blocks from downtown.

GETTING THERE

Revelstoke is on the Trans-Canada Highway, 152 kilometers (95 miles) west of Golden and 560 kilometers (350 miles) northeast of Vancouver. **Greyhound** buses come through Revelstoke four to seven times daily in both directions along the Trans-Canada Highway. The depot is by the Sandman Inn (1899 Fraser Dr., 250/837-5874).

West Toward Kamloops

Continuing west along the Trans-Canada Highway from Revelstoke, it's 62 kilometers (39 miles) to the next town, Sicamous, then 42 kilometers (26 miles) farther to the much larger center of Salmon Arm. The first stop along the way should be intriguingly black **Summit Lake,** lying in a heavily forested ravine and fed by a waterfall that plunges over a cliff face high above. A few kilometers farther west is similarly black **Victor Lake,** also fed by a waterfall. Shore-side **Victor Lake Provincial Park** makes a good spot for a picnic.

THREE VALLEY LAKE

Several attractions on the next stretch of road compete for your tourist dollar. On the shore of Three Valley Lake is the difficult-to-miss "ghost" town **Three Valley Gap** (250/837-2109, 9am-5pm daily mid-Apr.-early Oct., adults $12, seniors $10, children $5), a rebuilt pioneer community with more than 20 historic buildings moved to the site from around the province. Part of the same complex is **Three Valley Lake Chateau** (250/837-2109 or 888/667-2109, www.3valley.com, Apr.-mid-Oct., $145-300 s or d), a large motel (200 rooms) overlooking extensive gardens and the lake. Amenities include a café, a restaurant, and an indoor pool. Standard rooms start at $145, but some are designed especially for families ($195 for a room that sleeps two adults and four children) while The Cave—complete with real stone walls, roof, fireplace, and bath—is $275 s or d.

The next commercial attraction, eight kilometers (5 miles) west, is **Enchanted Forest** (250/837-9477, 9am-8pm daily July-Aug.,

Three Valley Lake Chateau

The site of the Last Spike is an important part of Canada's railway history.

9am-5pm daily early May-June and Sept.-early Oct., adults $12, seniors $11, children $9), where a trail through towering trees meanders past more than 350 handcrafted figurines to fairyland buildings and western Canada's biggest tree house. Also on the property, a walking trail leads through wetlands to a creek where you can watch salmon spawn in the fall.

★ THE LAST SPIKE

At Craigellachie, signs point off the highway to the Last Spike. It was here on November 7, 1885, that a plain iron spike joined the last two sections of Canadian Pacific's transcontinental rail line, finally connecting Canada from sea to sea. A cairn with a plaque and a piece of railway line marks the spot. Craigellachie Station (10am-5pm daily May-early Oct.) is home to a small information center and gift shop selling ice cream.

SICAMOUS

This town of 2,500 people, 62 kilometers (39 miles) west of Revelstoke, lies on the shore of Shuswap Lake and is known as the "Houseboat Capital of Canada." The lake itself is a convoluted body of water with four distinct arms, edged by secluded beaches, rocky coves, 25 marine parks, and more than 1,000 kilometers (620 miles) of shoreline. Houseboating is the number-one activity in these parts, and Sicamous is headquarters to major agencies, including Bluewater Houseboats (250/836-2255 or 800/663-4024, www.bluewaterhouseboats.ca) and Twin Anchors Houseboat Vacations (250/836-2450 or 800/663-4026, www.twinanchors.com). Rates vary widely through the May-early October season. Expect to pay around $2,400 for four days' rental in July, with the same boat going for around $1,400 in September.

Sandwiched between the two natural features referenced in its name, Hyde Mountain on Mara Lake Golf Course (250/836-4653, Apr.-Oct.) is not particularly long, but golfers enjoy fantastic lake views from elevated greens. Rates, including cart rental, are $85. To get there, head three kilometers (2 miles) south of town on Old Spallumcheen Road, which branches off the Trans-Canada Highway immediately west of the bridge. The clubhouse restaurant (from 6:30am daily, $15-25) combines good food with views to make it the best place in town to eat, even for nongolfers.

Highway 97A, south from Sicamous, is the main northern artery leading into the Okanagan Valley. Even if you're not planning on heading that far, it's worth taking this route a short way along the shoreline of Mara Lake. Aside from being particularly picturesque, the warm water tempts swimming during July and August.

SALMON ARM

Known as the "Gem of the Shuswap," Salmon Arm (pop. 17,500) lies along Shuswap Lake where the Salmon River drains into the Salmon Arm of the lake. After the railway arrived in 1885, the surrounding land was settled and many fruit farms were established.

Forestry was the biggest local employer for most of Salmon Arm's history, but since the closure of the local sawmill in 2008, summer tourism has taken over as the driving force behind the town.

Sights

From downtown, follow the Salmon Arm Wharf signs to lakeside **Marine Park,** where picnic tables dot the lawns and colorful flower boxes hang from the lampposts. The attractive **Salmon Arm Wharf,** the largest marina structure in British Columbia's interior, lures you out over the water, past a boat-launching area, a snack bar, and businesses renting motorboats and houseboats. A wide swath of lakefront on either side of the wharf is undeveloped, inviting exploration on foot. Immediately west of the wharf, you'll find a bird-watching hide tucked into the trees above a marshy area rich with specimens.

Two kilometers (1.2 miles) east of Salmon Arm on Highway 97B, **R. J. Haney Heritage Village & Museum** (751 Hwy. 97B, 250/832-5243, 10am-5pm daily June-early Sept., adults $6, children $3) holds the town's main historic attractions, including Salmon Arm Museum, which relates the town's earliest days through a slide show, photo albums, and the adjacent

Haney House, an early-20th-century farmhouse on beautiful parklike grounds. The park also holds a blacksmith's shop, an old fire hall, a church, and a teahouse (10am-4pm Wed.-Sun. mid-May-mid-Sept., lunch $9).

Food

Head to the old section of downtown, on the north side of the Trans-Canada Highway, to reach **Pink Cherry** (111 Hudson Ave., 250/832-9626, 7:45am-8pm Mon.-Fri., 8:15am-8pm Sat., 8:45am-6pm Sun., lunch $7-10). You'll find a range of quality tea and coffee (including unique tea espresso), breakfast wraps, panini, and salads, as well as a huge selection of gelato. Right on the lakefront is the Prestige Harbourfront Resort, home to **Cafe Tasse** (251 Harbourfront Dr., 250/833-5800, 8am-3pm Tues.-Sat., 8am-2pm Sun., crepes $12-16), a stylish café and patisserie specializing in espressos and sweet crepes.

Namaste (200 Trans-Canada Hwy., 778/489-5044, 11:30am-9:30pm Mon.-Sat., noon-9pm Sun., $15-22) is beside the main highway on the west side of downtown. It's a large, modern dining room where traditional Indian cuisine takes center stage, with a few combo plates allowing you to try a little of everything.

Salmon Arm Wharf

This church is one of the buildings preserved at R. J. Haney Heritage Village & Museum.

My recommendation for the best food in town is **Table 24** (1460 Trans-Canada Hwy., 250/832-5024, 7am-9pm daily, $18-36), on the eastern side of town in the Podollan Inn. The emphasis is on local ingredients prepared in-house: The pasta is made fresh daily, the meat is cut to order, and the produce is sourced directly from local farms. The end result is a wide-ranging menu of delicious dishes at reasonable prices.

Accommodations and Camping

In general, the major chains charge less for rooms in Salmon Arm than elsewhere along the Trans-Canada Highway, making the city a good base for exploring the surrounding region. Two familiar faces, both up the hill to the east of downtown offer clean, comfortable rooms at reasonable prices, often selling rooms for under $100 through major booking engines. They are the **Super 8** (2901 10th Ave. NE, 250/832-8812, $120-160) and **Comfort Inn & Suites** (1090 22nd St. NE,

250/832-7711, $129-199). Rates at both include breakfast, and the latter has an indoor pool and waterslide.

If it's a pool you're looking for, the one offered at ★ **Podollan Inn** (1460 Trans-Canada Hwy., 250/832-6025 or 888/668-4180, www.podollanhotels.com, $179-289) is British Columbia's largest freeform hotel pool, which winds its way around two wings and has two hot tubs and a large pool deck. Other pluses are stylish guest rooms, lake and mountain views, the town's finest restaurant, and excellent off-season prices. It is above the highway between downtown and the two choices detailed above.

The landscaped **Salmon Arm Camping Resort** (381 Hwy. 97B, 250/832-6489 or 866/979-1659, www.salmonarmcamping.com, May-Sept., tents $30, hookups $59, cabins $79-99 s or d) has hot showers, laundry, a pleasant outdoor pool area, a kitchen shelter, free wireless Internet, a convenience store, and a playground. The wooden cabins share baths but sleep up to six and have electricity, heaters, and covered porches. It's off Highway 97B, which branches south toward Vernon just east of town.

Information

Salmon Arm Visitor Centre (20 Hudson Ave., 250/832-2230, www.sachamber.bc.ca, 9am-5pm daily July-Aug., 9am-4:30pm Mon.-Fri. and 10am-4pm spring and fall, 10am-3pm Mon.-Fri. winter) is on the north side of the Trans-Canada Highway as it passes through downtown.

ADAMS RIVER SOCKEYE RUN

Turn off at the Squilax Bridge to get to 988-hectare (2,440-acre) **Roderick Haig-Brown Provincial Park,** named for noted British Columbian conservationist and writer Roderick Haig-Brown, but best known for protecting in its entirety the Adams River sockeye salmon run, North America's biggest. The salmon runs occur annually, but every four years (2018, 2022, etc.), a dominant run brings up to two million fish congregating in the river. These salmon are near the end of their four-year life cycle, having hatched in the same section of the Adams River four years previously. Unlike other species, after hatching, sockeye spend up to two years of their life in a "nursery" lake, which in the case of the Adams River run is Shuswap Lake. It is estimated that in conjunction with dominant runs, 15 million Adams River sockeye enter the Pacific, with about 10 million running back toward their birthplace, of which just one in five make it past fishing nets to their goal. After

an arduous 500-kilometer (310-mile) swim from the Pacific Ocean, the salmon spawn on shallow gravel bars here during the first three weeks of October (numbers generally peak in the second week). For more information, visit www.salmonsociety.com.

Forested with Douglas fir, cottonwood, birch, hemlock, and cedar, the park flanks the Adams River between Adams Lake and Shuswap Lake, protecting the spawning grounds in their entirety. When the salmon aren't filling the river, the park is still interesting, and interpretive boards describe the salmon run.

Kamloops

Kamloops (pop. 90,000) is 110 kilometers (68 miles) west of Salmon Arm and 355 kilometers (220 miles) northeast of Vancouver. It is the province's sixth-largest city and a main service center along the Trans-Canada Highway. The city holds a few interesting sights, but is certainly no scenic gem—the surrounding landscape is dominated by barren, parched rolling hills. The downtown area, however, lies along the south bank of the Thompson River and is set off by well-irrigated parkland.

Entering the city from the west, the Trans-Canada Highway descends the Aberdeen Hills, passing shopping malls, motels, and Kamloops Visitor Centre. The highway bypasses downtown; take Columbia Street West to get to the city center. From the east, the Trans-Canada Highway parallels the Thompson River through almost 20 kilometers (12 miles) of industrial and commercial sprawl.

The Secwepemc people, whose descendants are now known as Shuswap, were the first people to live in this region, basing their lifestyle on hunting and salmon fishing. They knew the area as T'kumlups, meaning "meeting of the rivers." The first European settlement occurred in 1812, when the North West

Company established a fur-trading post at the confluence of the north and south branches of the Thompson River. Prospectors began arriving in 1858, followed by entrepreneurs who began setting up permanent businesses. Kamloops grew as a transportation center, and today the economy revolves around the forest-products industry, copper mining, cattle and sheep ranching, and tourism.

SIGHTS

Excellent displays at the three-story, gold-colored **Kamloops Museum** (207 Seymour St., 250/828-3576, 9:30am-8pm Mon.-Fri., 10am-5pm Sat., 1pm-5pm Sun. summer, 9:30am-4:30pm Tues.-Sat. fall-spring, adults $3, children $1) cover local First Nations culture, the fur trade (look in the reconstructed fur trader's cabin), pioneer days, natural history (many stuffed and mounted critters), industry, and transportation. You'll see a furnished late-19th-century living area, a stable complete with tack and carriage, a blacksmith shop, paddle wheels, old wall clocks and cameras, and a 15-minute slide presentation on the city's history.

Kamloops Art Gallery (465 Victoria St., 250/377-2400, 10am-5pm Mon.-Wed. and Fri.-Sat., 10am-9pm Thurs., adults $5, seniors

Kamloops

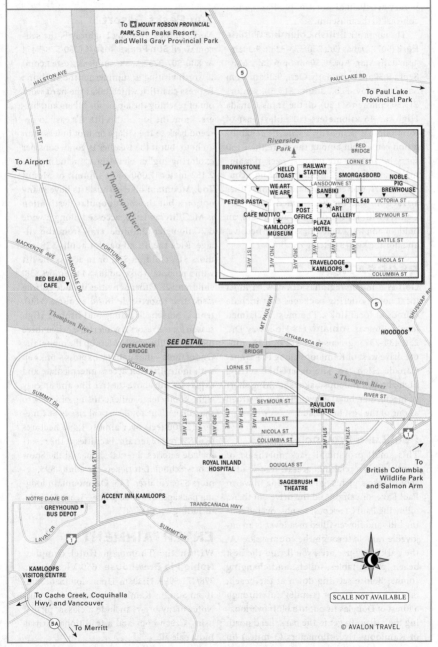

To ★ MOUNT ROBSON PROVINCIAL PARK, Sun Peaks Resort, and Wells Gray Provincial Park

HALSTON AVE

8TH ST

To Airport

N Thompson River

MACKENZIE AVE

FORTUNE DR

TRANQUILLE DR

RED BEARD CAFE

Thompson River

OVERLANDER BRIDGE

SUMMIT DR

COLUMBIA ST W

NOTRE DAME DR

GREYHOUND BUS DEPOT

ACCENT INN KAMLOOPS

LAVAL CR

KAMLOOPS VISITOR CENTRE

To Cache Creek, Coquihalla Hwy, and Vancouver

5A To Merritt

PAUL LAKE RD

To Paul Lake Provincial Park

5

MT PAUL WAY

ATHABASCA ST

SHUSWAP RD

HOODOOS ▾

5

SEE DETAIL

RED BRIDGE

VICTORIA ST

LORNE ST

S Thompson River

RIVER ST

1ST AVE 2ND AVE 3RD AVE 4TH AVE 5TH AVE 6TH AVE

SEYMOUR ST

BATTLE ST

NICOLA ST

COLUMBIA ST

PAVILION THEATRE

9TH AVE 12TH AVE

To British Columbia Wildlife Park and Salmon Arm

ROYAL INLAND HOSPITAL

DOUGLAS ST

SAGEBRUSH THEATRE

TRANSCANADA HWY

SUMMIT DR

1

Detail

Riverside Park ▲

RED BRIDGE

LORNE ST

BROWNSTONE

HELLO TOAST

RAILWAY STATION

SMORGASBORD

NOBLE PIG BREWHOUSE

WE ART WE ARE

LANSDOWNE ST

SANBIKI

PETERS PASTA

HOTEL 540

VICTORIA ST

CAFE MOTIVO ★

POST OFFICE

● ★ ART GALLERY

SEYMOUR ST

KAMLOOPS MUSEUM ★

PLAZA HOTEL

4TH AVE 5TH AVE 6TH AVE

BATTLE ST

1ST AVE 2ND AVE 3RD AVE

TRAVELODGE KAMLOOPS ●

NICOLA ST

COLUMBIA ST

SCALE NOT AVAILABLE

© AVALON TRAVEL

$3, children free) features an impressive collection of more than 1,000 works by contemporary artists in all sorts of media—quite a contrast to the museum.

The nonprofit **British Columbia Wildlife Park** (9077 Dallas Dr., 250/573-3242, 9:30am-4pm daily Mar.-Apr., 9:30am-5pm daily May-Sept., 9:30am-4pm daily Oct., 9:30am-4pm Sat.-Sun. Nov.-Feb., adults $15.50, seniors $13.50, children $11.50), off the Trans-Canada Highway 16 kilometers (10 miles) east of Kamloops, is primarily a wildlife rehabilitation center, but among the more than 150 furry inhabitants are many species of mammals from western Canada, including a couple of bears, wolves, cougars, and lynx. Other attractions are the BC-themed Discovery Centre, with reptile displays and a café, an outdoor amphitheater, a glass-walled beehive, and, for the kids, a petting zoo.

RECREATION

Golf is a major regional draw, with most local hotels offering packages that include rounds at local links. The most acclaimed local course is **Tobiano** (38 Holloway Dr., 250/434-7373, greens fees $129), a 15-minute drive west of Kamloops along the Trans-Canada Highway. The desert-like setting high above Kamloops Lake is nothing short of spectacular, but the layout is also regarded as one of the best in Canada.

Paul Lake Provincial Park

This small provincial park northeast of Kamloops is a relaxing, grassy, tree-shaded spot to take a picnic, go swimming in warm Paul Lake, or camp. And the drive out there, following Paul Creek past scrub-covered rolling hills and flower-filled meadows, is an enjoyable ramble through the countryside. At the park's day-use area you'll find the best beach, picnic tables, toilets, and changing rooms. Before settling down at the beach, take the 1.6-kilometer (1-mile) trail through a forest of Douglas fir out to a bluff overlooking the valley. To get to the park, head north of Kamloops five kilometers (3 miles) on Highway 5, then 17 kilometers (11 miles) east on Paul Lake Road.

Sun Peaks Resort

North of the city along Highway 5, the self-contained **Sun Peaks Resort** (250/578-5474 or 800/807-3257, www.sunpeaksresort.com) is worth visiting in summer for the Sunburst Express chairlift, which takes the hard work out of reaching the alpine for hikers and bikers. From the top of this lift, it's easy to descend back to the village on foot in less than an hour, but if the weather is good, consider exploring higher elevations, including the 2,152-meter (7,060-foot) summit of Mount Tod. Mountain bike enthusiasts have many options, but the most popular destination is McGillivray Lake, accessed along a wide 6.2-kilometer (3.8-mile) trail from the village. Ride the lift all day for adults $20, seniors $17, children $11, or to access the lift with a mountain bike, adults $44, seniors $38, children $27. Other activities include golfing a shortish resort-style 18-hole course ($80), tennis, horseback riding, and fishing. High season for the resort is wintertime, when three high-speed lifts whisk skiers up the mountain. One of these—the Sunburst Express—links up with more lifts that access intermediate and expert terrain above the tree line and an easy eight-kilometer (5-mile) cruising run back to the village. The total vertical rise is 882 meters (2,900 feet) over almost 1,490 hectares (3,678 acres) of terrain. Facilities at the resort include eateries, a rental shop, and the Snow Sports School. Lift tickets are adults $95, seniors $76, children $48. On-mountain lodging packages are good value—from $150 pp, including a lift ticket.

ENTERTAINMENT

Within the Thompson Hotel complex, **Noble Pig Brewhouse** (650 Victoria St., 778/471-5999, 11:30am-11pm Mon.-Sat., 3pm-10pm Sun.) is Kamloops' premier brewpub. Noteworthy brews include a classic pilsner using Czech hops and a traditional British India pale ale.

British Columbia's third-largest theater company, Kamloops-based **Western Canada Theatre** (www.wctlive.ca), presents live theatrical productions by top Canadian actors, producers, and designers. Performances take place in the **Pavilion Theatre** (1025 Lorne St., 250/372-3216) and at the **Sagebrush Theatre** (1300 9th Ave., 250/372-0966). The latter is also home to the **Kamloops Symphony Society** (www.kamloopssymphony.com).

FOOD

Kamloops has the dining scene you would expect from a midsize city: the usual chain and fast-food restaurants along the Trans-Canada Highway, numerous hotel dining choices, and a mix of cafés and restaurants in the downtown core.

Cafés and Cheap Eats

Hello Toast (428 Victoria St., 250/372-9322, 7:30am-3pm Mon.-Sat., 8am-3pm Sun., lunch $7-11) is a great downtown choice for an inexpensive breakfast in bright and cheery surroundings. Two blocks west, **The Art We Are** (246 Victoria St., 250/828-7998, 9am-9pm Mon.-Sat., $6-10) is a funky space where the exposed redbrick walls are covered in bright artworks. Lots of local produce is used to create delicious and healthy salads, wraps, and more substantial meals such as spanakopita. Across the road, **Café Motivo** (229 Victoria St., 250/372-3565, 6am-5pm Sun.-Wed., 6am-6pm Thurs.-Sat.) is a city-style café pouring European-style coffee in a slick setting.

Top choice for a caffeine fix is ★ **Red Beard Cafe** (449 Tranquille Rd., 250/376-0083, 8am-10pm Mon.-Thurs., 8am-11pm Sat., 8am-5pm Sun., $12-15), where beans are roasted in-house in small batches. Since my last trip to Kamloops, Red Beard has expanded from a coffee roaster into a full-blown café with some of the best breakfasts ($7-12) in town, creative lunch and dinner mains (think a combo duck and bison burger, under $15), and an impressive selection of craft beers.

Continuing the European theme, **Oops Café** (274 3rd Ave., 250/377-0021, 7:30am-3pm Mon.-Sat., lunch $5.50-10.50) is a simple space where crowds are drawn in by pretzel sandwiches with tasty filings. The daily soup and sandwich special is $10.50.

A reliable lunch spot slightly off the main downtown thoroughfare is the old-fashioned **Smorgasbord** (225 7th Ave., 250/377-0055, 7:30am-5pm Mon.-Sat., lunch $5-9), which is not a smorgasbord as the British know it, but a small café offering a wide range of soups, salads, and sandwiches, with a daily special offering the best value.

Restaurants

Superb sushi is the draw at **Sanbiki** (120 5th Ave., 250/377-8857, 11:30am-2pm and 5pm-9pm Mon.-Sat., $14-24), in a distinctive orange building with a sun-splashed patio out front. The chefs do a great job of sourcing the freshest of ingredients, including—most importantly—seafood. The most popular lunch combo dish is just $10, while dinner combos start at $15. Other choices include asparagus Shira-ae (salad), doused in a creamy sesame sauce; hearty rice bowls; and crumbed panko prawns.

Peter's Pasta (149 Victoria St., 250/372-8514, 5pm-pm Tues.-Sat., $12-20) is a small family-run eatery where classic Italian dishes are made from scratch daily. It also gets very busy. At the western edge of downtown, look for **Brownstone** (118 Victoria St., 250/851-9939, 5pm-9pm daily, $19-38) in a historic two-story redbrick building that was formerly a bank where famed Canadian poet Robert Service once worked. The menu is stacked with local game and produce prepared using international cooking styles, with professional service also notable. The wine list is dominated by British Columbia wines, including many available by the glass.

Noble Pig Brewhouse (650 Victoria St., 778/471-5999, 11:30am-11pm Mon.-Sat., 3pm-10pm Sun., $14-26) is a large, slick room within the confines of the Thompson Hotel. The substantial menu has the predictable choices to share, as well as bison chili, a lamb burger with roasted garlic and melted brie, and vegetarian risotto.

Hoodoos (1000 Clubhouse Dr., 250/828-9404, 7am-10pm daily summer, 11am-5pm Tues.-Sun. fall-spring, $20-29) is part of the Sun Rivers golf and residential subdivision on the north side of the city (access off Hwy. 5), and offers a menu to match, but the draw here are the unparalleled views, which extend across the city and river confluence to the barren mountains beyond.

ACCOMMODATIONS AND CAMPING

You won't find quaint or memorable here. Instead, expect reliable chain motels serving the needs of highway travelers. On the western approach to the city, many newer motels offer clean and comfortable rooms but no particular bargains. The top end of Columbia Street West has some unspectacular older motels for travelers on a budget.

$100-150

It's nothing to write home about, but the **Travelodge Kamloops** (430 Columbia St., 250/372-8202 or 800/525-4055, $109 s or d) is centrally located and offers a higher standard of rooms than the exterior may suggest, with an indoor pool.

$150-200

Kamloops has two excellent choices located right downtown in this price range. ★ **Hotel 540** (540 Victoria St., 250/372-2281 or 800/663-2837, www.hotel540.ca, $159-249 s or d) has spacious, comfortable rooms, a restaurant-lounge combo, and a rooftop patio with a pool and a hot tub. Check the website to see exactly what you're booking, but Club Rooms (from $179) include a cooked breakfast and free parking. Book at least seven days in advance for a discount.

Just off the highway near the west side access to downtown, **Accent Inn Kamloops** (1325 Columbia St. W., 250/374-8877 or 800/663-0298, www.accentinns.com, $169-189 s or d) offers modern and spacious rooms,

with guests having use of an outdoor pool, a hot tub, and a fitness room. Other pluses include a national paper delivered to your door and free wireless Internet.

Right downtown is **The Plaza Hotel** (405 Victoria St., 250/377-8075 or 877/977-5292, www.theplazahotel.ca, $169-299 s or d includes a cooked breakfast), first opened in 1928 as one the interior's finest accommodations. Its restoration and opening as a boutique hotel is more recent, and the last major revamp was completed in 2012. The 67 rooms feature rich woods, a heritage color scheme, comfortable beds covered in plush duvets, and wireless Internet included in the rates. Rack rates are usually discounted by around 30 percent online.

Camping

The region's most scenic campground is at **Paul Lake Provincial Park** (519/826-6850 or 800/689-9025, www.discovercamping.ca, mid-May-mid-Sept., $18), north of Kamloops five kilometers (3 miles) on Highway 5, then 17 kilometers (11 miles) east on Paul Lake Road. Facilities are basic (no hookups or showers), but the treed setting just a short walk to the beach makes up for it. This park is very popular with local families, so make reservations as far in advance as possible.

INFORMATION AND SERVICES

Kamloops Visitor Centre (Hillside Rd., 250/374-3377 or 800/662-1994, www.tourismkamloops.com, 9am-6pm daily late May-late Sept., 9am-5pm Mon.-Fri. Oct.-May) is beside the Trans-Canada Highway on the western outskirts of town, opposite the Aberdeen Mall. **Royal Inland Hospital** (311 Columbia St., 250/374-5111) is at the south end of 3rd Avenue. The **post office** is at 301 Seymour Street.

GETTING THERE AND AROUND

Most visitors reach Kamloops along the Trans-Canada Highway; allow around 3.5

hours from Vancouver, which is 355 kilometers (220 miles) southwest. Westbound travelers reach the city in just over an hour from Salmon Arm, which is 110 kilometers (68 miles) to the east.

Kamloops Airport (YKA) is on Airport Road, seven kilometers (4 miles) northwest of the city center; follow Tranquille Road through the North Shore until you come to Airport Road on the left. **Air Canada** (888/247-2262) has scheduled flights to Kamloops, Vancouver, and Calgary. **Central Mountain Air** (888/865-8585) flies north to Prince George. **VIA Rail** (800/561-8630) runs scheduled service three times weekly southwest to Vancouver and northeast to Jasper from the downtown railway station (north end of 3rd Ave.).

Greyhound provides daily service to most parts of the province from its Kamloops bus depot (725 Notre Dame Dr., 250/374-1212), off Columbia Street West at the west end of town. Local bus transportation (including out to the airport) is provided by **Kamloops Transit System** (250/376-1216); adult fare is $2.50, while a day pass is $6. Taxi companies include **Kami Cabs** (250/374-9999) and **Yellow Cabs** (250/374-3333). For a rental car, call **Budget** (250/374-7368) or **National** (250/376-4911), which both have desks out at the airport.

North to Mount Robson

From Kamloops, Highway 5 follows the North Thompson River to Tête Jaune Cache on Highway 16. This stretch of highway is part of the most direct route between Vancouver and Jasper National Park, and is also worthwhile for two excellent provincial parks: **Wells Gray,** a vast wilderness of rivers and mountains, and **Mount Robson,** protecting a spectacular peak that is the highest point in the Canadian Rockies.

BARRIERE

In the summer of 2003, Barriere, 66 kilometers (41 miles) north of Kamloops, was evacuated as wildfires surrounded the small town during a spell of hot weather that kept the surrounding mountains alight for six weeks. A sawmill—the town's main employer—and 70 homes were lost in the blaze. Driving through today, you will see scarred hillsides and open areas along the valley floor where burned trees and buildings have been cleared.

Along the highway through town, the **Monte Carlo Motel** (4380 Hwy. 5, 250/672-9676 or 888/660-5050, www.montecarlomotelbarrierebc.com, from $85 s, $95 d) is good value. The 25 medium-size rooms are older but air-conditioned, and if it's a hot day, take a dip in the small outdoor pool or take advantage of the barbecue area.

CLEARWATER

The small town of Clearwater (pop. 2,300), 125 kilometers (78 miles) north of Kamloops, is the gateway to Wells Gray Provincial Park. A few motels, restaurants, gas stations, services, and an information center are on the highway; the rest of the community is off the highway to the south.

Accommodations

A couple of good overnight options lie along the park access road, or stay beside a pleasant lake in Clearwater at **Dutch Lake Resort & RV Park** (361 Ridge Rd., 250/674-3351 or 888/884-4424, www.dutchlake.com, Apr.-Oct., camping $38-44, cabins $172-325 s or d). The largest of the cabins has two bedrooms and a full kitchen. Resort activities revolve around families and the water; the on-site restaurant (8am-9pm daily Apr.-Oct., $18-29) has a wide patio overlooking the water.

Information

At the turnoff to Wells Gray Provincial Park is **Clearwater Visitor Centre** (250/674-3334,

9am-5pm daily May-mid-Oct.). Look for the moose sculpture out front. It's a popular spot for tour buses, so it can be crowded.

★ WELLS GRAY PROVINCIAL PARK

Snow-clad peaks, extinct volcanoes, and ancient lava flows. Amazing waterfalls—so many the park is often referred to as the "Waterfall Park." Icy mineral springs, subalpine forest, and flower-filled meadows. Prolific wildlife (I counted four bears, six deer, and one moose on my last visit). An abundance of lakes and rivers where anglers can fish to their heart's content for rainbow trout and Dolly Varden: This is Wells Gray Provincial Park.

The main road into the 540,000-hectare (1.3-million-acre) park leads north from Clearwater for 37 kilometers (23 miles) to the park boundary. From there it continues 11 kilometers (7 miles) to one of the park's highlights, Helmcken Falls, where it turns to gravel and continues another 18 kilometers (11 miles) to its end at Clearwater Lake. Although this access road barely penetrates the park, driving its length is enough to get a taste of the rugged northern reaches. If it's not, you can take a canoe trip or boat tour from the end of the road.

Sights and Recreation

Make your first stop 10 kilometers (6 miles) from Clearwater, where a short trail leads through an old-growth forest of cedar and hemlock to a colorful lava canyon where 60-meter-high (200-foot) **Spahats Creek Falls** plummets over multicolored bedrock into the Clearwater River.

Continuing through the park, take a signposted gravel road to the west to **Green Viewing Tower** atop Green Mountain. The viewpoint provides panoramic views of a volcanic cone and many spectacular rugged peaks, including snow-covered Garnet Peak, highest in the park.

Wells Gray is best known for its waterfalls, the two most spectacular of which are accessible by road. Southernmost is **Dawson Falls,** four kilometers (2.5 miles) into the park, where the **Murtle River** cascades over a 90-meter-wide (295-foot) ledge. A little farther along the main road is the **Mush Bowl** (or Devil's Punchbowl), where the river has carved huge holes in the riverbed. But save some film for incredible **Helmcken Falls,** British Columbia's fourth-highest falls, where the Murtle River cascades off the edge of Murtle Plateau in a sparkling 137-meter-high (449-foot) torrent to join the Clearwater River.

Murtle River in Wells Gray Provincial Park

In winter, the frozen falls create an enormous ice cone as tall as a 20-story building.

For an enjoyable short walk from the road (20 minutes one-way), hike the one-kilometer (0.6-mile) trail out to **Ray Farm,** former home of one of the area's first settlers. The picturesque abandoned farm buildings sit among rolling meadows full of wildflowers.

Farther north up the road, a 500-meter (0.3-mile) trail (10 minutes one-way) winds through a stand of towering cedar trees to **Bailey's Chute,** a narrow rapids-filled passage. In fall, large numbers of chinook salmon battle the torrent, trying in vain to leap up the chute. After a number of valiant attempts, they're washed back downstream to the gravel beds, where they spawn and die.

Clearwater Lake

The road ends at a boat ramp and canoe dock beside the southern end of Clearwater Lake, 66 kilometers (41 miles) from the town of Clearwater. To make the most of the lake, you really need to take to the water. Based just before the end of the road (take the Clearwater Campground turnoff), **Clearwater Lake Tours** (250/674-2121, www.clearwaterlaketours.com) offers a couple of options. A full day motorboat cruise to Azure Lake (adults $155, children $105), including a short walk and picnic lunch, departs daily at 10:30am and 2:30pm. The company rents canoes and kayaks ($60-75 per day) for those who would rather propel themselves.

Camping

Each of the four park campgrounds (May-Sept., $23) along the access road has drinking water, toilets, and picnic tables; none have hookups or showers. Heading up the road from Clearwater, you'll pass, in order, **Spahats Creek Campground,** within walking distance of the falls; **Pyramid Campground,** just beyond Dawson Falls; **Falls Creek Campground,** with large riverside sites; and finally **Clearwater Lake Campground,** which is almost at the end of the road, right on the lake, and is the

first to fill each night. Make reservations through **Discover Camping** (519/826-6850 or 800/689-9025, www.discovercamping.ca).

Accommodations Outside the Park

Between Clearwater and the park are three lodging options. They are listed here from south to north.

Around halfway between Clearwater and Helmcken Falls, ★ **Wells Gray Guest Ranch** (250/674-2792 or 866/467-4346, www.wellsgrayranch.com, June-Sept., $60-180 s or d) is surrounded by grassy meadows full of wildflowers and grazing horses. Activities organized for guests include horseback riding (3.5-hour ride $100), canoeing, white-water rafting, fishing, and dining in a Western-style restaurant each evening. Overnight options are well-furnished kitchen-equipped duplex units within log cabins ($150-180 s or d) and dorm beds in wooden huts ($60 per room).

If you need a serviced campsite, stay at tranquil **Wells Gray Golf Resort & RV Park** (6624 Clearwater Valley Rd., 250/674-0009, www.wellsgraygolfresortandrvpark.com, May-Oct., $30-45), 35 kilometers (22 miles) north of Clearwater, which has 50 campsites set in the middle of a full-length nine-hole golf course (greens fee $25). Rates include hookups, free firewood, and use of modern shower facilities.

Overlooking the golf course, **Helmcken Falls Lodge** (6664 Clearwater Valley Rd., 250/674-3657, www.helmckenfalls.com, May-Sept., campsites $28-36, lodge rooms $200-225 s or d) has views across seemingly endless forested hills. The main lodge was constructed as a fishing camp in the 1940s but has been revamped since, with a mix of older motel-like rooms, log cabins, and an on-site restaurant cooking up simple, well-priced meals (7am-9:30am and 6pm-8:30pm daily) in a character-filled room.

Information

Park information is available at **Clearwater**

Visitor Centre (250/674-2646, 9am-5pm daily May-mid-Oct.).

BLUE RIVER

Although right on busy Highway 5, about 215 kilometers (134 miles) north of Kamloops, this onetime railway division point has remained small, holding just a few hundred residents along with services for passing travelers. Lake Eleanor, signposted on the east side of the highway, offers a small beach and swimming (on the lake's east side), but most visitors head into the surrounding wilderness—the Cariboo Mountains to the north, Wells Gray Provincial Park to the west, and the northern reaches of the North Thompson River just to the east. Access to the eastern reaches of Wells Gray Provincial Park is by a 24-kilometer (15-mile) gravel road heading west from the middle of Blue River. From the trailhead at the end of the road, it's a 2.5-kilometer (1.5-mile) walk to Murtle Lake, the park's largest freshwater lake.

Accommodations and Camping

★ Mike Wiegele Helicopter Skiing Resort (972 Harrwood Dr., 250/673-8381 or 800/661-9170, www.wiegele.com, early May-Sept., $170-335 s or d), the base for the renowned Mike Wiegele Heli-Skiing operation, is designed for the wintertime heli-skiing crowd, but it's open in summer, providing luxury accommodations in 22 log chalets at very reasonable prices. Upgrade from a standard room to a chalet room with a kitchen and fireplace for just $235. In summer, there are canoe, stand-up paddleboard, and bike rentals, as well as a number heli-hiking tours. While summer is beautiful at Blue River, winter is high season. Mike Wiegele was instrumental in the development of "fat boy" skis that helped revolutionize powder skiing by making it easier for everyone. His resort has grown from humble beginnings to a world-class facility, featured in many ski movies. Wintertime visitors enjoy helicopter access to some of the world's most famous powder skiing in the Cariboo and Monashee Mountains, then kick back each evening at the upscale resort in Blue River.

Glacier Mountain Lodge (869 Shell Rd., 250/673-2393 or 877/452-2686, www.glaciermountainlodge.com, $139-229 s or d) is another stylish Blue River lodging, this one offering 35 well-appointed guest rooms, an indoor hot tub, and a light breakfast for overnight guests.

Wells Grey Guest Ranch

Terry Fox: Legacy of Hope

Terry Fox is a name that is sure to come up at some point on your Canadian travels. In 1977, as a college-bound teenager, Fox lost his right leg to cancer. On April 12, 1980, after three years of training, with next to no sponsorship and little media coverage, he set off from Newfoundland on his **Marathon of Hope,** with the aim of raising money for cancer research. After he ran over 5,000 kilometers (3,100 miles) in 143 days, a recurrence of the cancer forced him to stop just outside Ontario's Thunder Bay. Cancer had begun spreading to his lungs, and on June 28, 1981, aged just 22, he died. As his run had progressed, the attention had grown, and, more important, the donations poured in. In total, his Marathon of Hope raised $24 million, far surpassing all goals.

The legacy of Terry Fox lives on in many ways, including 2,650-meter (8,700-foot) **Mount Terry Fox,** along the Yellowhead Highway northeast of Valemount; the **Terry Fox Run** (www.terryfox.org), an annual fall event in over 6,000 Canadian towns that has raised over $750 million dollars; and Vancouver's **Terry Fox Plaza** and a tribute in the adjacent BC Sports Hall of Fame and Museum.

The least expensive place to stay in town is **Blue River Campground** (991 West Frontage Rd., 250/673-8203, www.blueriver-campground.ca, May-mid-Oct., camping $26-40, cabins $50-60), which has a log cooking shelter and canoe and stand-up paddleboard rentals. The campground is within walking distance of Lake Eleanor.

VALEMOUNT AND BEYOND

North of Blue River, Highway 5 follows the North Thompson River through the Cariboo Mountains to Valemount, 20 kilometers (12 miles) south of the Yellowhead Highway. This small town boasts two scenic golf courses, overnight horseback trips with **Headwaters Outfitting** (250/566-4718, www.davehenry. com), lots of fishing holes (ask for a brochure at the information center), and mountain scenery all around. If you're passing through between mid-August and late September, be sure to visit **Swift Creek,** below the information center, where chinook salmon spawn after a 1,200-kilometer (745-mile) journey from the Pacific Ocean. At the south end of town is the spring-fed **Cranberry Marsh,** where you can expect to see Canada geese, teal, ducks, and red-winged blackbirds. Park at the Best Western Plus Valemount Inn (1950 Hwy. 5 S.) and follow the marked trail 500

meters (0.3 miles) to a bird tower for the best viewing opportunities.

Food

Cariboo Grill (1002 5th Ave., 250/566-8244, 4:30pm-10pm daily Dec.-mid-Oct., $15-34) is in an oversize log building beyond the downtown core along 5th Avenue. It's a good place for enjoying simple, hearty food, such as pastas, prime rib, steak, seafood, and a few Canadian specialties, such as salmon baked in a creamy tarragon sauce and elk grilled with sun-dried cranberries.

Accommodations

★ **Mica Mountain Lodge** (15658 Old Tete Jaune Rd., 250/566-9816 or 888/440-6422, www.micamountainlodge.bc.ca, $165-175 s or d, children $25 extra) is in a wilderness setting on the northwest side of town. During summer, guests ride horses, canoe, fish, and mountain bike. Come winter, it's cross-country skiing, dog sledding, and snowmobiling that are the major draws. The cabins are charming and practical, with full kitchens, three-piece en suite baths, decks, TVs, and pine log beds. **Irvin's Park and Campground** (1 kilometer/0.6 miles north of town, 250/566-4781, www.irvinsrvpark.com, $27-42) has a few tent sites along one side, but it's best suited for RVs and trailers.

Information

Mount Robson Provincial Park

Valemount Visitor Centre (785 Cranberry Lake Rd., 250/566-9893, www.visitvalemount. ca, 9am-8:30pm daily July-Aug., 10am-4pm daily May-June and Sept.-early Oct.) is along Highway 5, across from the turnoff to downtown.

Valemount to Mount Robson

From the Yellowhead Highway junction 20 kilometers (12 miles) north of Valemount, Prince George is 270 kilometers (168 miles) to the west, and the BC-Alberta border is 76 kilometers (47 miles) east. Although most of the distance to the border is through Mount Robson Provincial Park, two worthwhile stops lie between the highway junction and the park. The first of these is **Rearguard Falls,** a one-kilometer (0.6-mile) hike (20 minutes one-way) from the highway. Eight kilometers (5 miles) downstream from the falls—some 1,200 kilometers (745 miles) up the Fraser River from the Pacific Ocean—is a spawning ground for Pacific salmon; many of the hardy fish make it all the way to the falls. Farther east along the highway is a viewpoint for **Mount Terry Fox.**

★ MOUNT ROBSON PROVINCIAL PARK

Spectacular Mount Robson Provincial Park was created in 1913 to protect 224,866 hectares (555,650 acres) of steep canyons and wide forested valleys; icy lakes, rivers, and streams; and rugged mountain peaks permanently blanketed in snow and ice. Towering over the park's western entrance is magnificent 3,954-meter (12,970-foot) Mount Robson, the highest peak in the Canadian Rockies. The park lies along the Continental Divide, adjacent to Jasper National Park. The main watershed is the Fraser River, one of British Columbia's most important waterways. Highway 16, from where many roadside sights present themselves, splits the park in two, but for experienced backpackers it is the super-scenic Berg Lake Trail that attracts.

Roadside Sights

If you're approaching the park from the west along Highway 16, you'll see **Mount Robson** long before you reach the park boundary (provided the weather is cooperating). It's impossible to confuse this distinctive peak with those that surround it—no wonder it's known as the "Monarch of the Canadian Rockies." Once inside the park boundary, the highway climbs gradually to the main facility area, where you'll find a visitors center, campgrounds, a gas station, and a restaurant. From this point, the sheer west face of Mount Robson slices skyward just seven kilometers (4 miles) away across a flower-filled meadow. This is as close as you can get to the peak in your vehicle.

From the visitors center, the highway climbs steeply, then parallels photogenic **Moose Lake.** Waterfalls on the far side of the lake create a scenic backdrop. The Moose River drains into the Fraser River at **Moose Marsh,** a good spot for wildlife-watching at

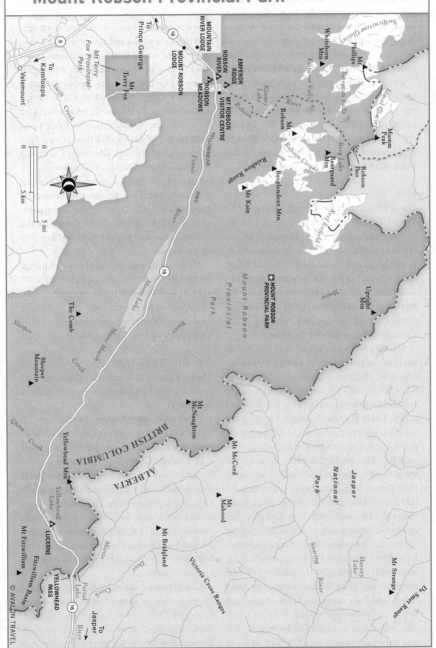

Mount Robson Provincial Park

To Prince George

MOUNTAIN RIVER LODGE

MOUNT ROBSON LODGE

ROBSON RIVER

EMPEROR RIDGE

ROBSON MEADOWS

MT ROBSON VISITOR CENTRE

To Kamloops

Mt Terry Fox Provincial Park

Mt Terry Fox

Valemount

Swift Creek

Yellowhead Hwy

Fraser River

Kinney Lake

Emperor Falls

Robson River

Whitehorn Mtn

Mt Phillips

Swiftcurrent Glacier

Toboggan Falls

Berg Lake

Mt Robson

Robson Cirque

Rearguard Mtn

Robson Pass

Munn Peak

Kinal Glacier

Rainbow Range

Resplendent Mtn

Mt Kain

Red Icefield

0
5 km
0
5 mi

The Comb

Sleeper Mountain

Sleeper Creek

Moose Lake

Moose Marsh

16

Ghita Creek

Mount Robson Provincial Park

MOUNT ROBSON PROVINCIAL PARK

Moose River

Upright Mtn

Yellowhead Mtn

Mt McNaughton

Mt McCord

BRITISH COLUMBIA

ALBERTA

Yellowhead Lake

LUCERNE

Mt Fitzwilliam

Fitzwilliam Basin

YELLOWHEAD PASS

Miette River

Deer Creek

Portal Lake

Mt Bridgland

Mt Mahood

Victoria Cross Ranges

Jasper National Park

Snaring River

Harvey Lake

Mt Strange

De Smet Range

To Jasper

© AVALON TRAVEL

5

16

the southeast end of the lake. Moose often feed here at dawn and dusk, and waterfowl are present throughout the day. Continuing westward, the highway crosses the upper reaches of the Fraser River before passing long and narrow Yellowhead Lake at the foot of 2,458-meter (8,060-foot) **Yellowhead Mountain.**

Finally, Highway 16 exits the park at the 1,066-meter (3,500-foot) **Yellowhead Pass,** on the BC-Alberta border 60 kilometers (37 miles) east of the visitors center. It's the lowest highway pass over the Continental Divide. Right before the pass is picturesque **Portal Lake,** with a small lakeside picnic area.

Hiking

The 19.5-kilometer (12-mile) **Berg Lake Trail** is the most popular overnight hike in the Canadian Rockies, but don't let the crowds put you off—the hike is well worth it. Beautiful aqua-colored Berg Lake lies below the north face of Mount Robson, which rises 2,400 meters (7,880 feet) directly behind the lake. Glaciers on the mountain's shoulder regularly calve off into the lake, resulting in the icebergs that give the lake its name.

Starting from two kilometers (1.2 miles) north of the visitors center along a narrow access road, the trail follows the Robson River 4.5 kilometers (2.8 miles) through dense subalpine forest to glacially fed **Kinney Lake.** There the trail narrows, crossing the fast-flowing river at the eight-kilometer (5-mile) mark and climbing alongside it. The next four kilometers (2.5 miles), through the steep-sided Valley of a Thousand Falls, are the most demanding, but views of four spectacular waterfalls ease the pain of the 500-verticalmeter (1,640-foot) climb. The first glimpses of Mount Robson come soon after reaching the head of the valley, from where it's another kilometer to the outlet of Berg Lake, 17.5 kilometers (11 miles) from the trailhead. While the panorama from the lake is stunning, most hikers who have come this far want to spend some time exploring the area. From the north end of the lake, trails lead to Toboggan Falls and more mountain views, to the head of

Robson Glacier, and to Robson Pass, which opens up the remote northern reaches of Jasper National Park.

It's possible to traverse the trail's first section to Kinney Lake and return the same day; to get all the way to Berg Lake and back, you'll need to stay in the backcountry overnight. Along the route seven primitive campgrounds hold 75 campsites, including three campgrounds along the lakeshore. Reservations for these sites can be made from October 1 onward for the following mid-June to mid-September season through **Discover Camping** (519/826-6850 or 800/689-9025, www.discovercamping.ca); the booking fee is $6 per night to a maximum of $18. Book early, because the quota fills quickly. Upon arrival in the park, all overnight hikers must then check in at the visitors center and pay the camping fees ($10 pp per night).

If the uphill walk in seems too ambitious, contact **Robson Helimagic** (250/566-4700 or 877/454-4700, www.robsonhelimagic.com), which makes helicopter drop-offs at Robson Pass from Valemount (minimum 4 people, $275 pp) every Monday and Friday.

Accommodations

The park has no indoor accommodations, but two lodges lie just outside the park's western boundary.

Mountain River Lodge (4 kilometers/2.5 miles west of the visitors center, 250/566-9899, www.mtrobson.com, $135-229 s or d) is in a delightful setting right alongside the Fraser River. The main lodge holds four guest rooms, each with a different character, a balcony, and a private bath. The smallest of the rooms (with twin beds and a private bath down the hall) is $135 s or d; rates include a cooked breakfast. Self-contained cabins cost from $199 s or d, with breakfast available at an extra charge.

One kilometer (0.6 miles) west of Mountain River Lodge is **Mount Robson Lodge** (250/566-4821, www.mountrobsonlodge. com, May-Oct., $129-179 s or d), with 18 freestanding cabins; the more expensive ones have kitchens, or guests can eat at the lodge's small café.

Campgrounds

Within the park are four auto-accessible campgrounds, with another just outside the park boundary. Three of these are park operated. Closest to the visitors center (and my favorite) is **Robson River Campground** (250/566-4811, mid-May-early Sept., $28), where numerous trails lead down to the river for the classic upstream view of Mount Robson. It's also only a short walk to the visitors center and a café. Across the highway is the larger **Robson Meadows Campground** (250/566-4811, mid-May-Sept., $28), with 125 sites on a spiral road system that centers on an outdoor theater that hosts evening interpretive programs throughout the summer. Both campgrounds have showers and flush toilets but no hookups. A small number of sites at both campgrounds can be reserved through **Discover Camping** (519/826-6850 or 800/689-9025, www.discovercamping.ca), but most are first-come, first-served.

Beside the east end of Yellowhead Lake, where swimming is for the brave, 50 kilometers (30 miles) from the visitors center, is the more rustic **Lucerne Campground** (250/566-4811, mid-May-mid-Sept., $22).

Facilities include drinking water, picnic tables, and pit toilets.

Emperor Ridge Campground (250/566-8438, mid-May-late Sept., $30) is a small commercial facility right behind the visitors center that offers hot showers but no hookups. **Robson Shadows Campground,** part of Mount Robson Lodge (250/566-4821, www.mountrobsonlodge.com, May-Oct., $28), five kilometers (3 miles) west of the visitors center, has unobstructed views of the distinctive peak, with a riverside location as a bonus. It also has showers but no hookups at the 25 campsites.

Information

At the park's western entrance, **Mount Robson Visitor Centre** (250/566-9174, www.env.gov.bc.ca/bcparks, 8am-7pm daily mid-June-early Sept., 8am-5pm daily mid-May-mid-June and early Sept.-mid-Oct.) features informative natural-history slide shows and trail reports updated daily.

Getting There

No public transportation serves Mount Robson Provincial Park. By road, Prince George is 280 kilometers (175 miles) west along Highway 16, and Kamloops is 345 kilometers (215 miles) southwest along Highway 5.

Cariboo Country

The wild, sparsely populated Cariboo region extends from Kamloops north to Prince George and west to the Pacific Ocean. Its most dramatic natural features are the mountain ranges rising like bookends on either side. In the west, the **Coast Mountains** run parallel to the coast and rise to a height of 4,016 meters (13,200 feet) at **Mount Waddington.** In the east, the **Cariboo Mountains** harbor numerous alpine lakes, high peaks, and several provincial parks. Between the two ranges flows the **Fraser River,** which is flanked to the west by expansive plateaus home to British

Columbia's biggest ranches. One of the most obvious natural features is black scarring from wildfires that swept through the region in the summer of 2017, burning millions of hectares from Ashcroft in the north to Williams Lake in the north, including one fire on the Chilcotin Plateau alone that burned 520,000 hectares (1.2 million acres), the largest wildfire ever recorded in British Columbia.

This is cowboy country, where horseback holidays and the Williams Lake Stampede are the main visitor draws. This was once gold rush country—most of the region's towns began as stopping places along the Gold Rush Trail. Those such as **100 Mile House** owe their names to the trail but have remained small, while others, such as **Williams Lake** and **Quesnel,** have continued to grow and are service centers for the ranching and forestry industries. The only coastal access in Cariboo Country is via Highway 20, which runs through **Tweedsmuir Provincial Park** to **Bella Coola,** at the head of a long fjord.

CACHE CREEK

A town born with the fur trade at a spot where traders cached furs and food supplies, Cache Creek was once the largest town between Vancouver, 337 kilometers (200 miles) to the south, and Kamloops, 80 kilometers (50 miles) to the east. But since the Coquihalla Highway opened in the 1980s, the town is but a shadow of its former self. The surrounding desertlike climate is intriguing: Sagebrush and cacti grow on the relatively barren volcanic landscape, tumbleweeds blow through town, and scarring from 2017 wildfires that reached the edge of town dominates the scene. Due to the town's former highway prominence, the main drag is lined with older motels, roadside diners, and gas stations.

★ Historic Hat Creek

Between 1885 and 1905, the Cariboo Wagon Road bustled with stagecoaches and freight wagons. One of the few sections of the original road still open to the public is at **Historic Hat Creek** (250/457-9722 or 800/782-0922, www.historichatcreek.com, 9am-5pm daily May-June and Sept., 9am-6pm daily July-Aug., adults $13.50, seniors $12, children $8, includes a tour and stagecoach ride), 11 kilometers north of Cache Creek on Highway 97. Many of the original buildings—some dating as far back as 1861—still stand, and visitors can watch the blacksmith at the forge, appreciate a collection of antique farm machinery, enjoy a picnic lunch in the orchard, or take a guided tour of the ranch house.

For those looking for accommodations, a lack of creature comforts is a trade-off for experiencing the western atmosphere of this historic property. Cabins with private baths ($100 s or d) sleep up to six. Other overnight options include unserviced campsites ($20), powered sites ($25), canvas miners' tents ($40), tepees ($45), a covered wagon ($65), and wooden cabins ($80). Other amenities include modern baths, First Nations sweat lodges (similar to a sauna), and a café beside the main reception area.

Historic Hat Creek

Food

At the junction of the Trans-Canada Highway and Highway 97, the food at **Chum's Restaurant** (1108 Trans-Canada Hwy., 250/457-6735, 7am-2pm Sun.-Tues., 7am-10pm Thurs.-Sat., $13-20) is a step above what you may expect from a roadside diner in small-town British Columbia.

Two dining options are north of Cache Creek. **Horsting's Farm Market** (2540 Hwy. 97, 250/457-6546, 8am-6pm daily Mar.-Dec., $6-8) is part of a working farm two kilometers (1.2 miles) north of town. In additional to seasonal fruit and vegetables and bread baked daily, the market is part café with combos such as a cinnamon bun and coffee for $5.50. They also offer sandwiches made to order and soup made from scratch. The best place to enjoy this farm-fresh food is the outdoor tables overlooking the orchard.

The restaurant at **Historic Hat Creek Ranch** (Hwy. 97, 250/457-9722, 9am-5pm daily May-Sept., lunch $10-14), 11 kilometers north of Cache Creek, has a casual setting with tables inside and out on the patio of a historic homestead. Most choices are suitably Western, including bison chili and beef dip, although modern styles kick in for dishes such as grilled salmon salad.

Accommodations and Camping

The **Sage Hills Motel** (1390 Hwy. 97, 250/457-6451, $75 s or d, $85 with kitchen) is one of many local motels that would have filled every night before the highway was re-routed. Today, it has seen better days, but the owners try their best, keeping the place clean and planting a colorful bed of flowers out front each spring.

Summer temperatures around Cache Creek can get very high, so the outdoor pool at **Brookside Campsite** (Trans-Canada Hwy., east of town, 250/457-6633, Apr.-Oct., www.brooksidecampsite.com, $24-40) is a good enough reason to choose this commercial campground with all facilities, including an outdoor pool, a playground, and free wireless Internet.

LILLOOET

This historic town of 2,300 was founded as Mile Zero of the 1858 Cariboo Wagon Road—also known as the Gold Rush Trail—which led north to the Barkerville and Wells goldfields. Several towns along the Gold Rush Trail—70 Mile House, 100 Mile House, and 150 Mile House among them—were named for their distance up the wagon road from Lillooet. With thousands of prospectors passing through in the mid-1800s, Lillooet was the scene of its own gold rush. By this time the city held some 16,000 residents, making it the second-largest population center north of San Francisco and west of Chicago. But as with most other boomtowns, the population explosion was short-lived.

Sights and Recreation

A row of rusty farming relics out front marks **Lillooet Museum** (790 Main St., 250/256-4308, 10am-4pm Tues.-Sat. May-Oct., 9am-5pm daily July-Aug., donation). Inside are ore samples and details about the onetime boomtown's mining history and growth. Within the museum is the local visitor info center. After visiting here, saunter along wide Main Street and pretend you're back in the gold rush era—it won't be hard if you happen to be here during the **Apricot Tsaqwem Festival.** During this mid-July celebration, the town fills with visitors who enjoy activities ranging from walking tours of traditional pit houses to a sturgeon fishing derby.

The town is also home to the unique nine-hole **Lillooet Sheep Pasture Golf Course** (5000 Texas Creek Rd., 250/256-0550, Apr.-Oct., $20), eight kilometers (5 miles) southwest of town, best known for a herd of sheep that keep the grass fairways in good condition.

Accommodations and Camping

One block up the hill from the museum, **4 Pines Motel** (108 8th Ave., 250/256-4247

Echo Valley Ranch & Spa

You can choose between several guest ranches in Cariboo Country, but none comes close to the luxury offered at **Echo Valley Ranch & Spa** (northwest of Clinton, 250/459-2386 or 800/253-8831, www.evranch.com, mid-Mar.-Oct.). Deep in the heart of ranching country, the resort provides the opportunity to immerse yourself in Western culture while indulging in the amenities of an upscale lodge. The emphasis is on horseback riding, with lessons and guided rides scheduled each day, but there are plenty of other things to do, such as taking a four-wheel-drive excursion into the nearby Fraser River Canyon, watching a falcon trainer at work, and learning about First Nations culture. The centerpiece of the sprawling property is an impressive main lodge built entirely of glistening spruce logs. Inside is a comfortable lounge area, the communal dining room overlooking an open kitchen, and a downstairs billiards and TV room. Adjacent is an impressive Baan Thai structure, with full spa services, an indoor pool, and the Pavilion, for quiet contemplation.

Rooms in the main lodge are beautifully furnished, and each has a private balcony, while the Honeymoon Cabin sits high above a deep ravine and has a wraparound deck complete with hot tub. Dining is ranch-style, at a couple of long tables with plenty of interaction between guests. But the food is anything but chili and beans.

As you'd expect, staying at Echo Valley isn't cheap (high season $470-920 d, including meals), but it's a very special place that my wife and I hold dear memories of from our own honeymoon.

or 800/753-2576, www.4pinesmotel.com) has older rooms ($90 s or d) and a newer wing ($110 s or d), all of which are air-conditioned. **Cayoosh Creek Campground** (no reservations, mid-May-Sept., $20-30) is a treed spot near the south end of town, where Cayoosh Creek drains into the much larger Fraser River. Facilities include hot showers and full hookups.

CLINTON TO 100 MILE HOUSE
Clinton

The old-fashioned town of Clinton lies 40 kilometers (25 miles) north of Cache Creek on Highway 97. **Clinton Museum** (1419 Hwy. 97, 250/459-2442, 10am-6pm Wed.-Sun. summer, donation) occupies an old schoolhouse made of handmade bricks fired locally in the 1890s. The museum contains pioneer belongings, guns, historical photos, First Nations and Chinese artifacts, freight wagons, and all sorts of items from the gold rush days. A nearby natural attraction worth seeing is Painted Chasm, in **Chasm Provincial Park,** 16 kilometers (10 miles) north of town, then four kilometers (2.5 miles) east. During the last ice age, glacial meltwater carved a

300-meter-deep (984-foot) box canyon here out of mineral-laden volcanic bedrock. It's quite a spectacle when the sunlight brings out the sparkling reds, yellows, and purples of the minerals. An old road leads along the top of the canyon, which provides the best vantage points.

North to 100 Mile House

Back on the main highway, between 70 Mile House and 100 Mile House, are several turn-offs leading to hundreds of lakes, big and small. All information centers in Cariboo Country stock the invaluable *Cariboo-Chilcotin Fishing Guide*. Updated annually, the booklet features essential fishing information (where, when, and with what) for many of the lakes, plus maps, camping spots, and even recipes for the ones that didn't get away.

The most accessible provincial park between Clinton and 100 Mile House is at **Green Lake,** 14 kilometers (9 miles) east of Highway 97; turn off Highway 97 16 kilometers (10 miles) northeast of 70 Mile House. This 16-kilometer-long (10-mile) emerald-colored lake lies along an old Hudson's Bay Company fur-brigade trail; you can see traces of the trail along the lake's shoreline. The park protects 11 different parcels of land around the lake, with Sunset View, on the south shore, the main focus for campers and picnickers. Here you'll find a sandy beach, a shaded lakeside picnic area, a playground, horseshoe pits, relatively warm water for swimming, and a campground (mid-May-Sept., $18).

100 Mile House

Named during the 1862 gold rush, when a roadhouse was constructed 100 miles north of Lillooet, 100 Mile House (population 2,000) is a forestry and ranching center that promotes itself as "Log Home Building Capital of North America." True to its word, as you pass through town you'll see many log home construction businesses lining the highway (the log homes are put together in town, then deconstructed and rebuilt at their final destination).

Passing through 100 Mile House, it's difficult to miss the log construction **South Cariboo Visitor Centre** (250/395-5353 or 877/511-5353, www.southcaribootourism. ca, 8:30am-4:30pm daily summer, 8:30am-4:30pm Mon.-Fri. fall-spring)—just look for the world's largest cross-country skis out front. An area of wetland lies directly behind the information center, with signage depicting the many bird species that are often present.

Toward Williams Lake

Three kilometers (2 miles) north of 100 Mile House, a road heads east off the highway, leading 30 kilometers (19 miles) to **Ruth Lake,** which is stocked with rainbow trout; 44 kilometers (27 miles) to **Canim Beach Provincial Park,** with campsites ($16); and 70 kilometers (43 miles) to **Canim River Falls,** between Canim and Mahood Lakes.

Back out on the highway and continuing north, you'll come to 19-kilometer-long (12-mile) **Lac La Hache,** one of the most picturesque bodies of water in Cariboo Country, known by boat anglers for its hungry kokanee and lake trout. At the lake's south end is the small community of Lac La Hache, with a small museum and information center on

the east side of the highway. At the lake's north end, a provincial park offers campsites ($17).

The next main turnoff, at **150 Mile House,** takes you on a 65-kilometer (40-mile) scenic drive (the last 10 kilometers/6 miles are unpaved) northeast to **Horsefly Lake Provincial Park** (519/826-6850 or 800/689-9025, www.discovercamping.ca, mid-May-mid-Sept., $23), protecting a forest of old-growth western red cedar and Douglas fir. You can swim, rent a canoe, or just relax on the pebbly beach.

WILLIAMS LAKE

Originally bypassed by the builders of the Cariboo Wagon Road because of protests from a stubborn landowner, Williams Lake (pop. 11,000), 95 kilometers (59 miles) north of 100 Mile House, has ironically become the Cariboo region's largest city. Today the ranching and forestry center is best known for the Williams Lake Stampede, one of Canada's biggest rodeos.

★ Williams Lake Stampede

On the last weekend of June, the town comes alive as North America's best cowboys and cowgirls compete in the **Williams Lake Stampede** (250/392-6585 or 800/717-6336, www.williamslakestampede.com). The whole town dresses up for the occasion; the locals put on Western garb, and the shop fronts are decorated accordingly. The highlight of each day's action is the rodeo, and events include bareback riding, saddle-bronc riding, calf-roping, steer-wrestling, barrel racing, chuck wagon racing, and the crowd favorite, bull riding. Scheduled around these traditional rodeo events are cow-milking contests, tractor pulls, cattle penning, chariot races, raft races, a parade, barn dances, all-you-can-eat breakfasts and steak-outs, and a host of other decidedly Western-flavored activities.

Sights and Recreation

The highlight of the **Museum of the Cariboo Chilcotin** (1660 Broadway, 250/392-5025, 8am-8pm daily summer, 9am-5pm

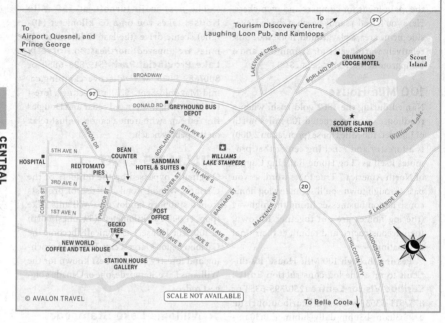

Williams Lake

To
Airport, Quesnel, and
Prince George

To
Tourism Discovery Centre,
Laughing Loon Pub, and Kamloops

97

DRUMMOND
LODGE MOTEL

Scout
Island

BROADWAY

LAKEVIEW CRES

BORLAND DR

97

DONALD RD   GREYHOUND BUS
DEPOT

★
SCOUT ISLAND
NATURE CENTRE

Williams Lake

CARSON DR

8TH AVE N

BORLAND ST

5TH AVE N

BEAN
COUNTER

☆
WILLIAMS
LAKE STAMPEDE

HOSPITAL

RED TOMATO
PIES

SANDMAN
HOTEL & SUITES

OLIVER ST

7TH AVE S

20

3RD AVE N

PROCTOR ST

5TH AVE S

BARNARD ST

MACKENZIE AVE

S LAKESIDE DR

1ST AVE N

COMER ST

POST
OFFICE

GECKO
TREE

2ND AVE S

3RD
AVE S

4TH AVE S

CHILCOTIN HWY

HODGSON RD

NEW WORLD
COFFEE AND TEA HOUSE

STATION HOUSE
GALLERY

© AVALON TRAVEL

SCALE NOT AVAILABLE

To Bella Coola ↓

Mon.-Fri. fall-spring, donation), located south of town in Tourism Discovery Centre, is the BC Cowboy Hall of Fame and associated rodeo, ranching, and Stampede displays. Other exhibits include historical photos, remains of the Chinese settlement at Quesnel Forks, and all kinds of picks, pans, and axes from gold-mining days. Downtown, **Station House Gallery** (1 Mackenzie Ave. N., 250/392-6113, 10am-5pm Mon.-Sat., free), in the original railway station, displays an excellent collection of western-themed art.

On the eastern outskirts of the city, **Scout Island Nature Centre** (1305 Borland Rd., 250/398-8532, 9am-4pm daily May-Aug., 9am-4pm Sat.-Sun. Aug., free) is surrounded by wetlands that serve as a staging area for migratory waterfowl. Colorful displays inside the center catalog the surrounding ecosystem, but the idea is to get out into the wetlands. Wander along one of the short hiking trails or climb the observation tower for a bird's-eye view of the watery landscape.

The region's diverse waterways provide plenty of opportunities for boating. Numerous gently flowing streams and serene lakes make perfect spots for canoe and kayak discovery trips, while the Fraser River provides opportunities for exciting rafting trips down steep-walled canyons, through semiarid hill country, and past abandoned boom towns.

Food

Give the chains along the highway a miss and head downtown to ★ **New World Coffee and Tea House** (72 Oliver St., 778/412-5282, 8am-5pm Mon.-Fri., 9:30am-5pm Sat., lunch $8-15) for the best range of coffee and loose-leaf teas in town, as well as Italian sodas and smoothies made with real fruit. Either breakfast crepes or the Salsa Scramble are a good way to start the morning, while the rest of the day salads, pierogi, sandwiches, wraps, and worldly dishes such tandoori chicken.

Down the hill and around the corner from New World, **Gecko Tree** (54 Mackenzie Ave.,

250/398-8983, 7:30am-4pm Tues.-Fri., 9am-3pm Sat., lunch $7-11) is a bustling little café where as many ingredients as possible are sourced locally. In addition to the usual salads and wraps, quesadillas add an exotic element to the menu.

Although it's a little out of the way between the highway and downtown, **Bean Counter Bistro** (180 3rd Ave., 250/305-2326, 7:30am-5:30pm Mon.-Fri., 8:30am-5:30pm Sat., lunch $6-9) is also worth investigating for excellent coffee and gluten-free and dairy-free baked treats that can be enjoyed in a bright, family-friendly setting. They also serve lunches such as quinoa salad and chicken with wild rice soup.

On the southeastern edge of town overlooking Williams Lake, **The Laughing Loon** (1730 S. Broadway, 778/412-6655, 11:30am-midnight daily, $14-30) is a large neighborhood pub-style venue with a welcoming, heritage-style atmosphere. The extensive menu includes something for everyone, including top notch grilled steaks, vegetarian and gluten-free options, and a kid's menu.

Accommodations

If you're after somewhere to simply rest your head, stay on the east side of town at the **Drummond Lodge Motel** (1405 Hwy. 97, 250/392-5334 or 800/667-4555, www.drummondlodge.com, $105-115 s or d, including light breakfast), set on extensive grounds overlooking the lake, one kilometer (0.6 miles) east of downtown.

The best rooms in town are at the **Sandman Hotel & Suites** (664 Oliver St., 250/392-6557, www.sandmanhotels.ca, $139-169 s or d). They are air-conditioned and come with wireless Internet. Hotel facilities include an indoor pool, a fitness room, a business center, and a 24-hour chain restaurant.

Information

Beside the highway on the southeast side of town is impressive log and timber-frame **Tourism Discovery Centre** (1660 Broadway, 250/392-5025, www.williamslake. ca, 8am-8pm daily summer, 9am-5pm Mon.-Fri. fall-spring). Inside is the local visitors center, a museum, a café, a gift shop, and displays on local natural and human history.

Getting There

Williams Lake is 288 kilometers (180 miles) north of Kamloops on Highway 97 and 550 kilometers (344 miles) north of Vancouver. Continuing north, it's just over an hour's driving north to Quesnel (118 kilometers/76 miles) and a similar distance beyond Quesnel to Prince George.

HIGHWAY 20

Highway 20 west of Williams Lake leads 485 kilometers (300 miles) to Bella Coola, the only road-accessible town along the 500 kilometers (310 miles) of coastline between Powell River and Prince Rupert. The highway is paved for less than half its length; the rest of the way it's mostly all-weather grave, and can be slow going in spots. But experiencing the vast and varied wilderness of the **Chilcotin Coast** is worthy of as much time as you can afford. And with a ferry at the end of the road providing a link to Port Hardy on Vancouver Island, you'll only need to make the trip one-way.

Services along Highway 20 are spaced at regular intervals, but don't take the trip too lightly; make sure your vehicle is in good condition, and carry tools and spare tires to alleviate the necessity of an expensive tow-truck ride.

West from Williams Lake

The road west from Williams Lake meanders through the Fraser River Valley before crossing the river and beginning a steady climb to the **Chilcotin Plateau,** the heart of British Columbia's ranching country.

The first worthwhile detour is **Junction Sheep Range Provincial Park,** at the end of a 20-kilometer (12-mile) unpaved road that branches south off Highway 20 at Riske Creek, 47 kilometers (29 miles) west of Williams Lake. The triangular park protects 4,573 hectares (11,300 acres) of mostly semiarid grasslands between the Fraser and Chilcotin Rivers, home to around 600 bighorn sheep. The confluence of these two major rivers forms the southern tip of the park and can be reached on foot in well under one hour from the end of the access road.

Back on Highway 20, the scarring from a 2017 wildfire, the largest recorded in British Columbia, is evident all around. Its epicenter was the Bald Mountain area to the south, but it crossed the highway in many places, including the historic Lee's Corner settlement that was burned to the ground. That leaves the first community with services as **Alexis Creek,** 114 kilometers (71 miles) west of Williams Lake. Beside the Chilcotin River, 10 kilometers (6 miles) west of Alexis Creek, is **Bull Canyon Provincial Park** (no reservations, May-early Sept., $18), at a bend in the Chilcotin River.

Continuing west, the highway follows the Chilcotin River for 60 kilometers (37 miles) to Chilanko Forks; here a spur road leads 10 kilometers (6 miles) north to **Puntzi Lake.** This picturesque body of water is home to a number of low-key fishing resorts, including **Kokanee Bay Fishing Resort** (250/481-1130, www.kokaneebayfishingresort.ca, camping $25, cabins $80-150 s or d), with everything an angler needs. The largest of the seven lakefront cabins come with basic cooking facilities. If you plan on rising early to fish for kokanee, make arrangements to rent a motorboat the night before.

Chilko Lake

Continuing toward the coast, Highway 20 continues westward to Tatla Lake, which is also the turnoff to remote **Ts'yl-os Provincial Park.** Pronounced SIGH-loss, Ts'yl-os is the Chilcotin name for the park's highest peak, 3,066-meter (10,060-foot) Mount Tatlow, but its most magnificent feature is 84-kilometer-long (52-mile) glacially fed Chilko Lake, which is ringed by the highest peaks of the Coast Mountains. The park is home to a wide variety of wildlife, including grizzly and black bears, bighorn sheep, and,

at higher elevations, mountain goats. Fishing in the lake is legendary for rainbow trout up to 2.5 kilograms (6 pounds).

Toward the Coast

From Tatla Lake, Highway 20 veers northward, climbing steadily to **Nimpo** and **Anahim Lakes,** where more self-contained resorts put the emphasis on fishing. Anglers will be tempted to linger at **Anahim Lake Resort** (250/742-3242 or 800/667-7212, www. anahimlakeresort.com, May-Oct., camping $32-35, cabins $100-160 s or d), where rainbow trout fishing is consistently good throughout summer. All but one of the eight cabins share a communal bath facility, but they all have a woodstove, a fridge, running water, and a screened-in veranda.

From Anahim Lake, the road narrows, the pavement ends, and it's a steady 30-kilometer (19-mile) climb to 1,524-meter (5,000-foot) **Heckman Pass** over the Coast Mountains. West across the pass, you face **The Hill.** This infamous descent from Heckman Pass to the Bella Coola Valley drops nearly the full 1,524 meters (5,000 feet) in less than 10 kilometers (6 miles). Be prepared for numerous switchbacks and a gradient as steep as 18 percent.

Tweedsmuir Provincial Park

At nearly a million hectares (2.5 million acres), this is British Columbia's largest provincial park. Roughly triangular, the park is bounded by Ootsa Lake on the north, the high peaks of the Coast Mountains on the west, and the Rainbow Range—so named for its colorful volcanic formations—on the east. Within these boundaries lies an untouched landscape, wild and remote, holding numerous river systems, forested valleys, alpine meadows, waterfalls, and glaciers. Most of those park highlights are accessible only on foot. Black and grizzly bears, mountain goats, caribou, wolves, and moose are all present, but they tend to remain well away from the highway. In fall, grizzlies descend from higher elevations to feed on spawned-out salmon along the Atnarko River. The best viewing spot is **Belarko Wildlife Viewing Platform** (7am-7pm daily Sept.1-21, 7am-6pm daily Sept. 22-30, free), which is surrounded by a subtle electric fence, allowing clear views of the bears. The platform is signposted along Highway 20 near the park's west end.

Campgrounds ($20) are on the north bank of the Atnarko River (at the base of The Hill) and 30 kilometers (19 miles) west at Fisheries Pool. Facilities at both include drinking water, picnic tables, and pit toilets.

BELLA COOLA

The urge to see what's at the end of the road brings many travelers over The Hill and down to Bella Coola, 485 kilometers (300 miles) west of Williams Lake. Here the Bella Coola River drains into North Bentinck Arm, a gateway to the Inside Passage and the Pacific Ocean. The town of less than 200 lies in a coastal valley that was originally the home of the Nuxalk people, with another 1,600 residents spread along the floor of the Bella Coola Valley.

Sights and Recreation

Housed in a historic 1890s log schoolhouse, the **Bella Coola Valley Museum** (269 Hwy. 20, 250/799-5767, 9am-5pm Wed.-Mon. mid-June-early Sept., adults $3, children $1) features artifacts of early Norwegian settlers and the Hudson's Bay Company, which established a post here in 1869. Over in Hagensborg, 15 kilometers (9 miles) inland, the many hand-hewn timber buildings still standing are testament to the construction skills of the Norwegian settlers, who first arrived in the valley in 1894.

There's plenty of outdoor recreation to keep visitors busy. Unfortunately, most of the action is out on the water and requires the services of a boat charter company (not cheap). Fishing is the most popular activity; expect to pay from $180 per hour for four people. Those with a sense of history will want to visit **Mackenzie Rock,** in the Dean Channel and accessible only by boat, where Alexander Mackenzie, in his own words, "mixed up some vermillion and melted grease and inscribed

in large characters on the face of the rock on which we slept last night, this brief memorial: Alexander Mackenzie, from Canada, by Land, the Twenty Second of July, One Thousand Seven Hundred and Ninety Three." In doing so, he became the first person to cross continental North America. For boat charter information, contact **Bella Coola Harbour Tours** (250/982-2348, www.bccentralcoast.com), which charges $85 for a harbor tour and $450 for a five-hour trip out to Mackenzie Rock.

Accommodations and Camping

Right on the river is **Bella Coola Motel** (1224 Clayton St., 250/799-5323, $115 s, $125 d), with clean and comfortable old-style motel rooms each with a full kitchen. On the east side of Hagensborg, at **Bella Coola Cabins and Lodge** (2752 Hwy. 20, 250/982-2348, $125 s or d) you have the choice of two comfortable cabins beside the Nusatsum River or bed-and-breakfast rooms in the main residence. Between Bella Coola and Hagensborg, the friendly hosts at **Eagle Lodge** (1103 Hwy. 20, 250/799-5587 or 866/799-5587, www.eaglelodgebc.com, $99-155 s, $135-155 d) will make you feel welcome the moment you step through the front door. Each of seven guest rooms is configured differently, with the smallest having a twin bed and the largest having two queens and a double. Continental breakfast is included, and guests have use of wireless Internet and an outdoor hot tub positioned to take full advantage of the rural setting.

Gnome's Home Campground and RV Park (Hagensborg, 250/982-2504, www.gnomeshome.ca, Apr.-Oct., $15-18) has showers, a cook shelter, and laundry, and is the starting point for a short trail leading through the temperate rainforest.

DISCOVERY COAST PASSAGE

BC Ferries (250/386-3431 or 888/223-3779, www.bcferries.com) sailings between Port Hardy and Bella Coola aboard the *Northern Sea Wolf* open a remote section of the British

Columbia coastline that would otherwise be inaccessible. The direct summer-only sailing (adults $200, ages 5-11 $100, vehicles $396 one-way) takes 10 hours. Study the timetable on the BC Ferries website to see other options, as there is also a connector service linking Bella Coola to other Discovery Passage villages and the option to make a stop on the Port Hardy-Prince Rupert sailing. When the ferry does make a stop, it's only for around two hours each time, so if you want to get off, plan on overnighting until another ferry comes by.

The most accessible and interesting stop along the Discovery Coast Passage is **Shearwater,** on Denny Island. Shearwater is an old cannery village that has also been a logging camp, a base for flying boats patrolling the coast during World War II, and a stop for major shipping lines. The community was sold off to a private enterprise and today operates as **Shearwater Resort & Marina** (250/957-2666 or 800/663-2370, www.shearwater.ca), complete with two lodges ($125-200 s or d) and an RV park (tents $20, RVs $40). The resort has a large marina with boat and kayak rentals, a well-stocked general store, and the waterfront Fisherman's Bar & Grill. Resort guests come either for the salmon and halibut fishing or wildlife viewing (or both). Tours leave the resort in search of whales and bears, including one tailored specifically to search out the mythical spirit bears of the Great Bear Rainforest. The resort has its own airstrip, and some arrive on their own boats, but most guests fly into nearby Bella Bella with **Pacific Coastal** (604/483-2107 or 800/663-2872, www.pacificcoastal.com) from the South Terminal of Vancouver International Airport and then jump aboard the short boat shuttle to Shearwater ($5 pp one-way). **BC Ferries** (250/386-3431 or 888/223-3779, www.bcferries.com) makes a stop at Bella Bella on its run up the coast between Port Hardy and Prince Rupert, or use the BC Ferries connector service (adults $43, ages 5-11 $21.50, vehicles $85) from the western

end of Highway 20 at Bella Coola to get to the resort.

QUESNEL

Back inland, Highway 97 north from Williams Lake takes you to Quesnel (pop. 10,000). The town began during the Barkerville gold rush of the 1860s. Today the town's economy continues to thrive, with an asphalt plant, ranching, mining, and, especially, forestry industries (Two Mile Flat, east of downtown, is North America's most concentrated wood-products manufacturing area).

Sights

At **Heritage Corner** (Carson Ave. and Front St.), you can see the Old Fraser Bridge, the remains of a boiler from the steamer *Enterprise*, a restored Cornish waterwheel used by gold miners, and the original Hudson's Bay Store. To learn all about Alexander Mackenzie or the gold rush days, head to **Quesnel and District Museum** (705 Carson Ave., 250/992-9580, 9:30am-5pm daily June-Aug., 9:30am-4pm Wed.-Sat. May and Sept., adults $5, seniors $4, children $2), which holds almost 30,000 artifacts. The scenic four-kilometer (2.5-mile) **Riverfront Walking Trail** loops around the downtown core, with plaques honoring early residents; start at any point along the river (allow 75 minutes).

Eight kilometers (5 miles) west of Quesnel on Baker Drive are the geologically intriguing, glacially eroded hoodoos at **Pinnacles Provincial Park.** The viewpoint is one kilometer (0.6 miles) from the day-use area; allow 40 minutes for the round-trip. Another local provincial park is **Ten Mile Lake,** 11 kilometers (7 miles) north of town. Fishing is regarded as good for rainbow trout, and there's a large beaver dam near the day-use area.

Events

The main event in Quesnel is **Billy Barker Days** (250/992-1234, www.billybarkerdays. ca), named for the prospector who made the first gold strike in the Cariboo. Over the third weekend of July, downtown streets are

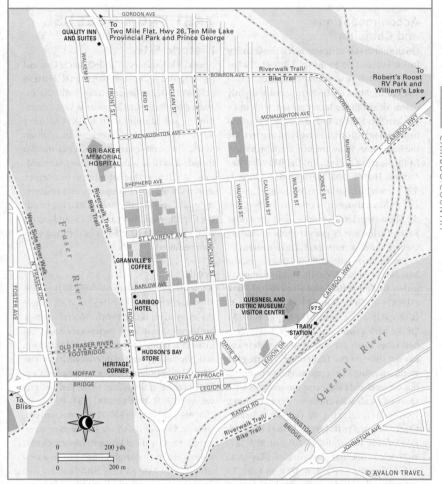

Quesnel

CENTRAL
CARIBOO COUNTRY

closed to traffic in favor of an outdoor crafts fair, parade, and dancing. Residents casually stroll around town in period costumes from the gold-mining days—men in cowboy hats, women in slinky long dresses with brightly feathered hats. The **Quesnel Rodeo** is one of some 150 events staged during the festival.

Food

Downtown, **Granville's Coffee** (383 Reid St., 250/992-3667, 7am-9pm Mon.-Sat., 8am-5pm Sun., $6-10) is one of the few nonchain places in town selling coffee. It also has the usual array of lunch choices and a few roadside tables out beside the sidewalk.

In an unassuming strip mall on the west side of the Fraser River, **Bliss** (462 Anderson Dr., 250/992-7066, 9am-7pm Mon.-Fri., 10am-7pm Sat., $10-14) is part Canadian (think poutine—fries topped with gravy and cheese curds), part Indian (delicious butter chicken) and everything in between (butter chicken pizza!), but the food is all very tasty and inexpensive.

Accommodations and Camping

On the north side of downtown is the **Quality Inn & Suites** (753 Front St., 250/992-7247 or 800/663-8090, www.choicehotels.ca, $114-154 s or d). Most of the 85 rooms are slightly dated, although the larger rooms, with more modern furnishings and particularly spacious baths, along with microwaves and toasters, are the best value. Rates include a hot breakfast. In the heart of downtown, the **Billy Barker Casino Hotel** (308 Maclean St., 250/992-5533, www.billybarkercasino.com, $125-175 s or d) has a distinctive exterior modeled on the stern-wheelers that once plied the Fraser River. Inside are 39 guest rooms, including themed suites, a restaurant, and a casino.

For campers who don't need services, the best bet is to head north 11 kilometers (7 miles) to **Ten Mile Lake Provincial Park** (519/826-6850 or 800/689-9025, www.discovercamping.ca, mid-May-Sept., $20-25). Of the park's two campgrounds, Lakeside is best (sites 4 to 9 are closest to the water) and has hot showers and flush toilets. During the week, snagging a spot isn't usually a problem, but on weekends the campground fills with Quesnel locals who come for the swimming, fishing, and relaxing on the sandy beach. Closer to town is **Robert's Roost RV Park** (3121 Gook Rd., 250/747-2015 or 888/227-8877, www.robertsroostrvpark.ca, May-Oct., $30-40), on the west side of Dragon Lake. To get here, take Highway 97 south, turn east on Gook Road, and go to the end. Amenities include coin showers, laundry, free wireless Internet, a playground, boat and rentals, a restaurant (4pm-8pm Tues.-Sat.), and a narrow stretch of sand with swimming.

Information

Quesnel Visitor Centre (703 Carson Ave., 250/992-8716 or 800/992-4922, www.tourismquesnel.com, 9am-6pm daily June-Aug., 9am-4pm Tues.-Sat. Sept.-May) is beside Lebourdais Park.

EAST FROM QUESNEL
Cottonwood House Historic Site

About 28 kilometers (17 miles) east of Quesnel on Highway 26, **Cottonwood House** (250/992-2071, www.cottonwoodhouse.ca, 10am-5pm daily late May-early Sept., donation) is a roadhouse built in 1864 to serve Barkerville-bound gold seekers. In addition to the old guesthouse, structures at the site include a barn, a stable, and other outbuildings. You'll also find an interpretive center, displays of old farming equipment, a country-style café, and a candy store. Camping beside the Cottonwood River is $15-25, and cabins with shared baths are $35 s or d (bring your own bedding).

Wells

A few kilometers before reaching Barkerville, Highway 26 passes the village of Wells, where the main street is lined with colorful heritage buildings. Most local businesses hand out historic walking tour brochures of the town, which includes points of interest such as a one-time illegal gambling hall below a barbershop. In the center of the village is the distinctively yellow 1933 ★ **Wells Hotel** (2341 Pooley St., 250/994-3427 or 800/860-2299, www.wellshotel.com, $95 s or d), which has been wonderfully restored without losing its historic charm. Rooms are in the original hotel or in a new wing, but all have en suite baths and are well furnished. Lounging in front of the log fireplace, surrounded by historic photos and with polished hardwood floors underfoot, is the perfect way to end a day of sightseeing. Or head down to the pub and relax over a meal and watch the world of Wells go by.

Barkerville Historic Town

In 1862 Billy Barker struck gold on Williams Creek, in a narrow forested valley 88 kilometers (55 miles) east of Quesnel. One of

Bowron Lake Provincial Park

baked goods in the province; stagecoach rides ($8-10); the chance to try your hand at gold-panning ($8.50); and the musical comedy performances ($15-20) at the Theatre Royal, presented two or three times daily.

You can spend the night in one of two historic buildings within the town. Inside and out, **Kelly House** (250/994-3328 or 866/994-0004, www.kellyhouse.ca, $100 s or d shared bath, $120 en suite) fits the heritage theme of Barkerville. Rates include a cooked breakfast that may include delightful apple pancakes topped with real cream. More upscale, the 1898 **St. George Hotel** (250/994-0008 or 888/246-7690, www.stgeorgehotel.bc.ca, $130-150 s or d, including breakfast) has been fully restored and offers seven guest rooms, some of which share baths; all are tastefully furnished with comfortable beds and authentic antiques.

The pick of three Barkerville campgrounds (250/994-3297, www.barkerville-campgrounds.ca, mid-June-Sept., $25-30) is **Lowhee Campground,** with showers and a playground. **Forest Rose** also has shower facilities. **Government Hill Campground** is closest to the historic site, but as all three campgrounds are within walking distance, this is of little consequence. It's also the most rustic, with no showers and pit toilets.

Canada's major gold rushes followed, as thousands of prospectors streamed in to what soon became known as Barkerville. The area turned out to be the richest of the Cariboo mining districts, yielding over $40 million in gold. By the mid-1860s, Barkerville's population had peaked at over 10,000. But fortunes began to fade after the turn of the 20th century. In 1916, Barkerville was destroyed by fire. Although the town was quickly rebuilt, the gold ran out soon thereafter, and many of the miners lost interest and moved on. Today, **Barkerville** (250/994-3332 or 888/994-3332, www.barkerville.ca, 8am-8pm daily mid-May-Sept., 2-day pass adults $15, seniors $14, children $10) comprises over 160 restored and replica buildings and claims the title of North America's largest heritage site. Historic reenactments take place throughout summer, when the town's shops, stores, and restaurants all operate in a century-old time warp. Highlights include the town bakery, which sells some of the most mouthwatering

★ BOWRON LAKE PROVINCIAL PARK

Best known for the **Bowron Lake Canoe Circuit,** Bowron Lake Provincial Park encompasses 149,207 hectares (386,700 acres) of magnificent forests, lakes, and rivers in the Cariboo Mountains. To get here, take Highway 26 east of Quesnel toward Barkerville, but just past Wells take a signed gravel road north.

The park boundary follows a chain of six major lakes—Indianpoint, Isaac, Lanezi, Sandy, Spectacle, and Bowron—and some smaller lakes and waterways that, roughly, form a diamond-shaped circuit. Campsites, cabins, and cooking shelters are strategically spaced along the way. To circumnavigate the entire 116-kilometer (72-mile) route takes 6 to 10 days of paddling and requires seven portages, the most difficult being a 2.5-kilometer (1.5-mile) uphill hike at the very start. As well as being proficient in the use of canoes, those attempting the route should be well prepared for backcountry travel and wet weather. July and August are the most popular months; try to avoid departing on a weekend if you like solitude. September is one of the most colorful months, with lakeside trees in their fall colors.

Bear River Mercantile (7090 Bowron Lake Rd., 604/424-4330, www.bowronlake.com, late May-late Sept.) and **Becker's Lodge** (250/992-8864 or 800/808-4761, www.beckerslodge.ca, May-early Oct.) rent canoes and camping equipment (from $200 for an 8-day canoe rental), with the latter also offering canoe circuit packages inclusive of lodging upon completion of your trip.

Before setting out on the circuit, paddlers must obtain a permit ($60 pp) from the **BC Parks Registration Centre** (7am-8pm daily May 15-Sept. 30) at the end of the park access road. Because a limited number of people are permitted on the circuit at any given time, you should reserve a spot as far in advance as possible (lines open October 1 for the following season) by calling 519/826-6850 or 800/689-9025 or visiting www.discovercamping.com. The reservation fee is $18 per canoe. A few spots are set aside each day for drop-ins, but the sensible course of action is to reserve as far ahead as possible. More information is online at www.env.gov.bc.ca/bcparks.

Accommodations and Camping

Bear River Mercantile (7090 Bowron Lake Rd., 604/424-4330, www.bowronlake.com, late May-late Sept., camping $25, cabins $65-75 s, $75-85 d) has rustic cabins overlooking Bowron Lake with wood heat and indoor plumbing, but you need to bring your own bedding or sleeping bag. It also has a lakeside campground with a kitchen shelter but no hookups. Friendly owners offer outfitting services for paddlers and supply breakfast and dinner with advance notice. They also have basic groceries and a small room of Bowron Lake memorabilia. You can pay in advance online, but at the resort it's cash only. Bear River is through the village of Bowron Lake toward the BC Parks Registration Centre.

Becker's Lodge (4480 Bowron Lake Rd., 250/992-8864 or 800/808-4761, www.beckerslodge.ca, May-Sept.) has a choice of cabins ($80-260 s or d). The Trapper Cabins with shared baths are the most basic, and the best is the family-friendly Betty Wendle Cabin, with an upstairs loft that has water views, a full kitchen, a practical bath, separate bedrooms, and solid wooden furnishings throughout. Camping is $12 pp for tents and $30-40 s or d for RVs. If you are using Becker's as an outfitter for the Bowron Lake Canoe Circuit, you take off from right in front of the property.

Taking in guests since the 1930s, **Bowron Lake Lodge** (Bowron Lake Rd., 250/255-2396, www.bowronlakelodge.com) was looking rundown when I visited in 2017, and the old cabins were not being rented, but the new owners will hopefully breathe life into a resort with a prime lakefront setting. At press time, lakefront campsites were $35, with no hookups, but check the website for other options in the future. Canoe, kayak, and paddleboard rentals are $20 per hour or $60 per day.

At the very end of the access road is a small provincial park campground (519/826-6850 or 800/689-9025, www.discovercamping.ca, mid-May-Sept., $18) with 25 sites but no hookups. The campground is between the BC Parks Registration Centre and the lake.

Northern British Columbia

Highlights

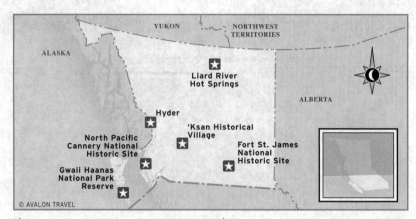

★ **Fort St. James National Historic Site:** It's a little out of the way, but the detour to Canada's largest collection of buildings from the fur-trade era is well worthwhile (page 398).

★ **'Ksan Historical Village:** Learn about First Nations culture at this village, where totem poles, longhouses, and Gitxsan arts and crafts are on display (page 404).

★ **North Pacific Cannery National Historic Site:** Step back in time to experience the sights and sounds of the west coast's oldest cannery village (page 411).

★ **Gwaii Haanas National Park Reserve:** Traveling to Haida Gwaii is an adventure in itself, but to *really* get off the beaten track, schedule a trip to the Gwaii Haanas National Park Reserve (page 425).

★ **Hyder:** Defining the tiny hamlet of Hyder is difficult. It's scenic, it's eccentric, and it's unforgettable—especially in late summer, when bears are as common as visitors along the main street (page 429).

★ **Liard River Hot Springs:** This is more of a must-soak than a must-see (page 441).

Wild, remote northern British Columbia extends from the Yellowhead Highway (Hwy. 16) north to the 60th parallel.

Its mostly forested landscape is broken by two major mountain ranges—the Rockies and the Coast Mountains—and literally thousands of lakes, rivers, and streams. Wildlife is abundant here; the land is home to moose, deer, black and grizzly bears, elk, Dall's sheep, and mountain goats.

The region's largest city is Prince George, a forestry and service center 780 kilometers (485 miles) north of Vancouver in the heart of a recreational paradise. From Prince George, the Yellowhead Highway runs west to the towns of Vanderhoof, Burns Lake, Smithers, and Terrace, all jumping-off points for fishing and boating adventures on surrounding lakes and rivers.

The western terminus of the Yellowhead Highway is Prince Rupert, a busy coastal city at the north end of the BC Ferries network and a stop on the Alaska Marine Highway. It's northern British Columbia's sole coastal city; north of here the coastline is part of Alaska.

Off the coast from "Rupert" is Haida Gwaii (formerly the Queen Charlotte Islands), part of British Columbia yet entirely unique. The islands beckon adventure, with legendary fishing, great beachcombing, ancient Haida villages, and a typical laid-back island atmosphere.

Two routes head north off the Yellowhead Highway. The Stewart-Cassiar Highway begins west of Prince George and parallels the Coast Mountains, passing the turnoff to the twin towns of Stewart and Hyder and some remote provincial parks. It ends at its junction with the other route north—the famous Alaska Highway. Mile Zero of the Alaska Highway is at Dawson Creek, northeast of Prince George. From there the highway winds through kilometer after kilometer of boreal forest, past lakes and mountains to the great northland of the Yukon and Alaska.

PLANNING YOUR TIME

The most important thing to remember when planning your time in northern British Columbia is that this part of the province is vast. It is as big as all the other regions

Previous: Moose are common along the Alaska Highway; lake along the Alaska Highway.
Above: Salmon Glacier.

Northern British Columbia

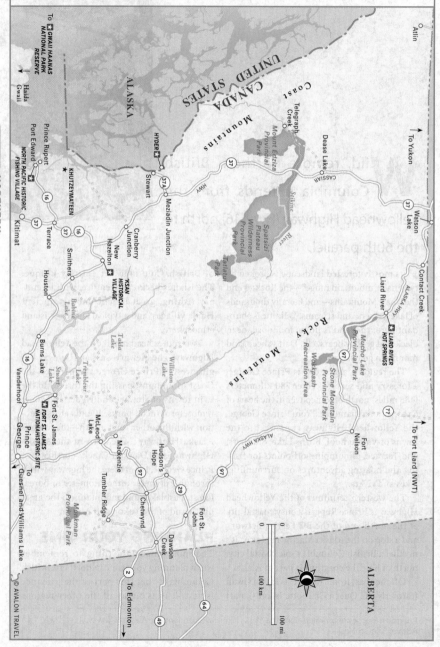

combined, so plan accordingly. Though you can loop up through Williams Lake to Prince George and then head south again, you'll be missing all the highlights. If you want to see the best of the region, schedule at least three days to drive the length of Highway 16 west to Prince Rupert. To drive the Alaska-Cassiar Highway loop will take at least another four days, including a stop at **Liard River Hot Springs** and detours to **Hyder** and **Atlin.** Add another three days in Haida Gwaii for good measure. One good way to visit northern British Columbia without retracing your steps is to take the ferry between Prince Rupert and Vancouver Island in one direction. If you do make ferry connections in Prince Rupert, allow at least one full day in town, and be sure to visit the **North Pacific Cannery National Historic Site.**

The summer season in northern British Columbia is shorter than elsewhere in the province. For general-interest travel, plan a trip during the peak July-August period. June and September are also good for traveling— it's still warm enough to camp, and as a bonus, you'll miss the worst of the high-summer bug season. Those keen to see grizzly bears in their natural habitat will want to schedule a visit to the Khutzeymateen in June or to Hyder in August or September.

Prince George

British Columbia's seventh-largest city, Prince George (pop. 73,000) lies roughly at the geographical center of the province, at the confluence of the historically important Fraser and Nechako Rivers. Early trappers and explorers used the rivers as transportation routes into the northern reaches of the province. When they discovered the region's wealth of wolves, foxes, lynx, mink, wolverines, otters, and muskrat, they quickly established forts and trading posts by rivers and lakes so that furs could be sent out and supplies could be brought in. In 1807, Simon Fraser of the North West Company began construction of Fort George. The railroad reached the area in 1908, and in 1915 the Grand Trunk Pacific Railway platted the town site of Prince George a few kilometers south of the original Fort George. The new town went on to become a major logging, sawmill, and pulp-mill town, the center of the white spruce industry in British Columbia's central interior. Hundreds of sawmills started cutting local timber, and Prince George became the self-proclaimed "Spruce Capital of the World." The city has continued from strength to strength and has grown to become northern British Columbia's economic, social, and cultural center.

SIGHTS

The best place to start a Prince George sightseeing trip is at the top of **Connaught Hill,** which affords a panoramic view of the city. To get there from downtown, take Queensway Street south, turn right on Connaught Drive, then right again on Caine Drive. At the summit are grassy tree-shaded lawns, picnic spots, and several well-kept gardens bursting with color in summer.

Exploration Place

At **Exploration Place** (333 Becott Place, 250/562-1612, 9am-5pm daily, adults $11, seniors $9, children $8), you'll discover the fascinating natural and human history of Prince George and the lifestyle and culture of the indigenous Carrier people. The facility is filled with modern exhibits that go beyond the meaning of a museum in the usual sense. You'll find a technological dinosaur display, a small IMAX-style theater, high-speed Internet terminals, and many hands-on exhibits. Among the items on display in the History Hall are many taxidermied and mounted specimens of wild animals and birds native to British Columbia—including two towering grizzly bears in the foyer—fine crafts of

Prince George

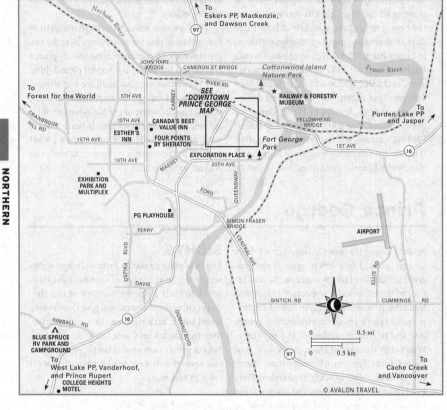

the local Carrier people, an impressive sternwheeler anchor, snowshoes, guns, horrific animal traps and other relics of the fur trade, artifacts from early sawmilling days, an old buggy, mock-ups of early business establishments, and a hands-on Science Centre.

Exploration Place is within **Fort George Park,** a 36-hectare (90-acre) riverside site where Simon Fraser established Fort George in 1807. Walking trails lead through the park along the Fraser River and to the Indian Burial Grounds, or jump aboard the Little Prince Steam Engine (adults $3.50, seniors $2, children $1), which runs from noon to 8pm daily through summer.

Two Rivers Gallery

The architecturally stunning, wood and glass, **Two Rivers Gallery** (725 Canada Games Way, 250/614-7800, 10am-5pm Mon.-Sat., noon-5pm Sun., adults $7.50, seniors $6, children $3) is Prince George's major cultural attraction. The permanent collection is the main drawing card, but temporary shows that change every four or five weeks are included in the admission fee. It's also a good place to buy high-quality local artwork at a reasonable price. Look for paintings, sculpture, pottery, beadwork, woven and painted silk items, and jewelry. On Thursday, admission is free, and the gallery stays open until 9pm.

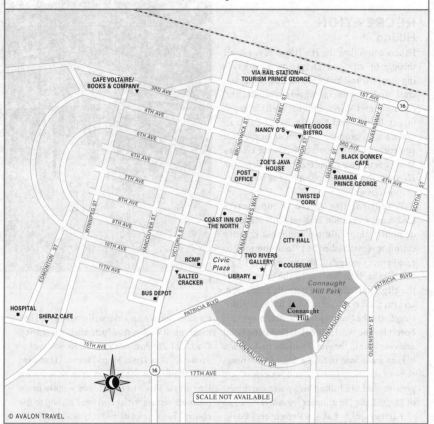

Downtown Prince George

Prince George Railway and Forestry Museum

North of Downtown, **Prince George Railway and Forestry Museum** (850 River Rd., 250/563-7351, 10am-5pm daily summer, 11am-4pm Wed.-Sun. fall-spring, adults $8, seniors $7, children $5) catalogs the region's industrial history. Take a self-guided tour through some of the antiquated railway cars and buildings, clamber on retired railway equipment, and chug back in time via the black-and-white photo displays and assorted memorabilia. To get here from downtown, take Highway 16 east to the River Road exit (just before the Yellowhead Bridge over the Fraser River) and continue north down River Road one kilometer (0.6 miles) to the museum.

Surrounding the railroad museum is **Cottonwood Island Nature Park**—one of Prince George's 16 city parks and a beautiful spot for a quiet stroll or picnic. The park lies beside the Nechako River, which overflows each spring; over time, sediment from the overflow has built up an island. The park's dominant feature is an extensive forest of northern black cottonwood trees. In spring, sticky buds cover the cottonwoods, and in summer the air is thick and the ground white with seed-bearing tufts of fluff.

RECREATION
Hiking

Hikers can follow the **Heritage River Trail** through the city, past interpretive signs detailing local natural history. The clearly marked trail, open to hikers, joggers, cyclists, and cross-country skiers, runs between Cameron Street Bridge and Carney Park. You can make an 11-kilometer (6.8-mile) loop of it if you complete the circuit by following Carney Street north back to the trailhead. Ask for the *Heritage River Trails* pamphlet at the information center.

Forest for the World, a 106-hectare (262-acre) recreation area set aside for forest demonstrations, hiking, and cross-country skiing, was established in 1986 to commemorate Prince George's 75th anniversary. To get there, take 15th Avenue to the west end of the city, continue onto Foothills Boulevard, and turn left on Cranbrook Hill Road, which steeply climbs Cranbrook Hill. At the signs for Forest for the World, turn left on Kueng Road and continue to the end. From the parking lot, hiking trails lead to Shane Lake (10 minutes one-way), where beavers and waterfowl are present, and to a hilltop viewpoint northwest of Shane Lake (15 minutes one-way).

Farther out is **Eskers Provincial Park,** 40 kilometers (25 miles) northwest of Prince George (access is off Hwy. 97 along Pine Marsh Rd.). Named for the park's main features, the eskers, or long gravel ridges, were deposited by a receding glacier at the end of the last ice age. Fifteen kilometers (9 miles) of hiking trails lead around Circle Lake to two viewing platforms and through forests of aspen, lodgepole pine, and Douglas fir.

ENTERTAINMENT
Nightlife

Of the city's many pubs and nightclubs, one of the most popular is **Steamers** (2595 Queensway St., 250/562-6654, 11am-midnight Mon.-Thurs., 11am-1am Fri.-Sat.), a country

Fort George Park

music venue with good Southern food and live music most weekends. Much smaller is **Nancy O's** (1261 3rd Ave., 250/562-8066, www.nancyos.ca, 11am-11pm Mon.-Thurs., 11am-1am Fri., 10am-1am Sat., 10am-3pm Sun.), with live music three to four times weekly in an intimate setting with good food adding to the charm. For a quiet drink in typical hotel surroundings, head for **Cornerstone Lounge** (Ramada Prince George, 444 George St., 250/563-0055, 11am-11pm daily), which has a variety of seating including couches.

The Arts

Studio 2880 (2820 15th Ave., 250/562-4526, 11am-5pm Tues.-Fri.) is the local arts center, operated by the local Community Arts Council. It hosts many cultural activities, acts as a ticket office for events, and organizes workshops, art classes, concerts, ballets, special events, and two major craft markets each year. **Theatre North West** (556 N. Nechako Rd., 250/563-6969, www.theatrenorthwest.com) offers a five-play season running late

September-May. **Prince George Symphony Orchestra** (250/562-0800, www.pgso.com) combines professional and amateur musicians to produce a September-May performance season at various venues through the city.

FOOD

Venture beyond the fast food chains lining the highway and head downtown to enjoy freshly roasted coffee, healthy breakfasts and lunches, and a selection of recommended restaurants.

Cafés

In the heart of downtown, **Black Donkey Cafe** (1085 3rd Ave., 250/596-7276, 8am-midnight Mon.-Thurs., 8am-5am Fri.-Sat., 11am-5pm Sun., lunch $6-12) is a friendly place open long hours, with lingering locals playing board games and listening to occasional live music. The drink menu is extensive, including well-priced smoothies. Close by, **Zoe's Java House** (1259 4th Ave., 250/563-4369, 7:30am-5:30pm Mon.-Fri., 9am-5pm Sat., lunch $7-11) is a midsize café filled with an eclectic collection of furnishings. The emphasis is on top-notch coffee and loose-leaf teas, which are accompanied by a choice of soups and sandwiches listed on an ever-changing blackboard menu.

Located within the city's premier bookstore, Books & Company, **Cafe Voltaire** (1685 3rd Ave., 250/563-6637, 7am-7pm Mon.-Wed., 7am-9pm Thurs., 7am-10pm Fri., 7am-6pm Sat., 9am-5pm Sun., lunch $6-8.50) is an artsy-themed café with an excellent selection of coffee and teas, as well breakfast wraps, light lunches, and baked goods.

Salted Cracker (1485 10th Ave., 250/562-1110, 10am-6pm Mon.-Sat., 11am-5pm Sun., lunch $6-10) is a takeout place just off the main road leading south out of downtown. The soups are made from scratch daily and sandwiches are made to order and stacked high with quality ingredients. The café has a couple of tables, but most customers order takeout, with nearby Fort George Park the preferred picnic spot.

Restaurants

With its thoughtful menu and casually elegant heritage-themed setting, ★ **Twisted Cork** (1157 5th Ave., 250/561-5550, 11am-9pm Mon.-Sat., 5pm-9pm Sun., $24-40) stands out as the restaurant of choice for a nice night out in Prince George. The setting is a big old stone-and-brick building, with lots of exposed beams and polished wood throughout. Lunches (mostly under $15) provide good value, but it is the main menu that is most notable, with dinner entrées such as halibut baked on a cedar plank making this restaurant a standout. I'm not usually a fan of brownies, but the Twisted Cork version, covered with warm vanilla ice cream and caramel sauce, was delectable.

Nancy O's (1261 3rd Ave., 250/562-8066, 11am-11pm Mon.-Thurs., 11am-1am Fri., 10am-1am Sat., 10am-3pm Sun., $17-24) attracts a generally younger crowd to a rustic room decorated with historic photos of the city. The menu covers all bases—from a Madras curry to fried chicken with a Belgian waffle—but the food is well-priced and the accompanying drinks menu extensive.

Right by Twisted Cork and similar in style, although slightly more romantic, **White Goose Bistro** (1205 3rd Ave., 250/561-1002, 11am-2pm and 5pm-9pm Mon.-Sat., 5pm-8pm Sun., $18-36) is as close to fine dining as you'll find this far north. The menu is creative (think ostrich steak grilled with a pesto rub), the setting stylish, and the presentation excellent.

Don't be put off by the strip-mall setting southwest of downtown: bright and cheery **Shiraz Café** (Parkwood Mall, 1600 15th Ave., 250/596-7397, 11:30am-3pm and 4pm-9pm Mon.-Sat., noon-3pm and 4:30pm-8pm Sun., $15-20) is a local's favorite for Persian dishes such as *fesenjoon,* a slow-cooked chicken stew that uses a pomegranate paste as a base and is served on a bed of rice and topped with crushed walnuts.

A good choice for a reliable, inexpensive meal in an interesting setting is **Umma Restaurant** (Super 8 Prince George,

1151 Commercial Cres., 250/562-4131, 6am-10am, 11am-2pm, and 5pm-9pm daily, $16-22), where diners choose from three different seating areas within a massive tropical atrium: under a thatched roof, around the pool, or in the bar. A buffet breakfast draws mostly in-house guests. Lunch and dinner are à la carte, with a mix of Korean and Western choices at reasonable prices.

ACCOMMODATIONS AND CAMPING
$50-100
Many Prince George accommodations fall into the $50-100 range, and they are spread throughout the city. The most concentrated area of these is along the Highway 97 bypass west of downtown. After checking out each property, I am confident that **Canadas Best Value Inn** (1630 Central St., 250/563-3671, www.redlion.com, $89-129 s or d) is indeed best value, with clean rooms, comfortable beds, and an adjacent family-style restaurant.

$100-150
The least expensive rooms at **Super 8 Prince George** (1151 Commercial Cres., 250/562-4131 or 800/663-6844, www.esthersinn.com, $109-139 s or d) are on the small side. Instead, request a renovated third-floor room, with Internet access and a king bed. Unlike most other properties in the chain, this Super 8 is a tropical-themed hotel, with rooms surrounding a lush tropical atrium packed with palms and philodendrons, waterfalls, Polynesian artifacts, swimming pools, a water slide, and a thatched-roof restaurant.

$150-200
The ★ **Four Points by Sheraton** (1790 Hwy. 93 S., 250/564-7100, www.starwoodhotels.com, $160-240 s or d) is a standout in Prince George—not because it's a fantastic place to stay, but because the other choices are all a little tired. It features 74 large rooms with LCD TVs. Amenities include a restaurant (breakfast, lunch, and dinner daily), a fitness room, and a business center.

Two major downtown hotels are more convenient for business travelers but come with regularly revamped rooms, in-house dining, and indoor pools. They are **Ramada Prince George** (444 George St., 250/563-0055 or 800/830-8833, www.ramadaprincegeorge.com, $160 s or d) and **Coast Inn of the North** (770 Brunswick St., 250/563-0121 or 800/716-6199, www.coasthotels.com, from $175 s or d).

Camping
Privately operated **Blue Cedars RV Park** (4433 Kimball Rd., 250/964-7272 or 888/964-7271, www.bluecedarsrvpark.com, $25-39) is five kilometers (3 miles) south on Highway 97 from downtown. Like most RV parks around the city, it fills up each night during the busy summer months. Each site has a picnic table and a barbecue grate, and the facilities include spotlessly clean heated baths, an outdoor pool, and wireless Internet.

The closest provincial park to Prince George is at **Purden Lake** (519/826-6850 or 800/689-9025, www.discovercamping.ca, mid-May-late Sept., $22), 55 kilometers (34 miles) east of the city on Highway 16. The picturesque lake has a small stretch of sandy beach and offers fishing for rainbow trout and burbot.

INFORMATION AND SERVICES
Tourism Prince George operates an excellent information center (1300 1st Ave., 250/562-3700 or 800/668-7646, www.tourismpg.com, 8am-7pm daily summer, 8:30am-4:30pm Mon.-Fri. fall-spring) with wireless Internet access, free computer Internet access, a gift shop, and bikes that visitors can use for free.

Prince George Public Library (88 Canada Games Way, 250/563-9251, 10am-9pm Mon.-Thurs., 10am-5:30pm Fri.-Sat., 1pm-5pm Sun.) has newspapers and magazines from across North America, as well as a good display of First Nations art and artifacts. **Books & Company** (1685 3rd Ave.,

250/563-6637, 7am-7pm Mon.-Wed., 7am-9pm Thurs., 7am-10pm Fri., 7am-6pm Sat., 9am-5pm Sun.) features a great selection of local and northern BC literature, plus major Canadian newspapers.

The main **post office** is on the corner of 5th Avenue and Quebec Street. **University Hospital of Northern British Columbia** (250/565-2000 for routine calls or 250/565-2444 for emergencies) is at 1475 Edmonton Street. A private health clinic deals with walk-in problems; turn off 15th Avenue on Edmonton Street by the hospital. The **Royal Canadian Mounted Police** (250/562-3371) is on the corner of Brunswick Street and 10th Avenue, behind the library.

GETTING THERE AND AROUND

Prince George is roughly in the center of British Columbia. To drive from Vancouver, which is 780 kilometers (484 miles) south via Highway 1 and Highway 97, takes around nine hours.

Prince George Airport (YXS) is 18 kilometers (11 miles) east of town. It is linked to Vancouver by **Air Canada** (888/247-2262) and **WestJet** (800/538-5696) and to many British Columbian regional centers by

Central Mountain Air (888/865-8585). The **Airporter Shuttle Service** (250/563-2220, www.pgairportsuttle.ca) provides shuttle service between the airport and downtown and meets all arriving flights. **VIA Rail** (250/564-5233, www.viarail.ca) operates transcontinental service from Prince George west to Prince Rupert and east through Jasper and Edmonton to Toronto and beyond. The VIA Rail station is at 1300 1st Avenue at the north end of Quebec Street. **Greyhound** (1566 12th Ave., 250/564-5454) runs regularly scheduled services from Prince George south to Kamloops and Vancouver (via Williams Lake and Quesnel); west along the Yellowhead Highway to Terrace and Prince Rupert; north to Dawson Creek via Chetwynd; and east along the Yellowhead Highway to Jasper and Edmonton.

The **Prince George Transit System** operates buses throughout the city daily except Sunday. Pick up a current *Prince George Rider's Guide* from the information center or call 250/563-0011 for an automated timetable. For a cab, call **Prince George Taxi** (250/564-4444). Car-rental agencies with desks out at the airport are **Hertz** (250/963-0300) and **National** (250/963-7473).

West from Prince George

VANDERHOOF

The first town west of Prince George, at 65 kilometers (40 miles), is Vanderhoof (pop. 4,400), a service center for the Nechako Valley and British Columbia's geographical center (the exact spot is marked by a cairn 5 kilometers/3 miles east of town). Vanderhoof grew as a stop on the Grand Trunk Pacific Railway. Today it's a prosperous farming and logging town.

Sights

The 1914 building at the corner of Highway 16 and Pine Avenue houses **Vanderhoof Community Museum** (478 1st St.,

250/567-2991, 10am-5pm daily late May-Sept., free). The museum displays mounted specimens of birds and animals, pioneer equipment, blacksmithing tools, a rock collection, and plenty of local history from gold rush and pioneer days. Surrounding the main building are 11 restored heritage buildings, among them a jail, a 1922 schoolhouse, and a gambling room. Also here is the **OK Café** (250/567-5262, 10am-6pm daily late May-Sept., lunch $7.50-11), where you can tuck in to hearty homemade soup and rolls, salads, and tasty pie and ice cream. It's inside a heritage building that was Vanderhoof's first restaurant.

Vanderhoof's town symbol is the Canada

goose. You can see these beautiful birds and other waterfowl in spring and fall at their transient home, **Nechako Bird Sanctuary,** along the banks of the Nechako River. Access it via the wooden bridge at the north end of Burrard Avenue, the town's main street.

Food

For decent food at reasonable prices, head to the comfortable **North Country Inn Restaurant** (2625 Burrard Ave., 250/567-3048, 6am-10pm daily, $15-30), where the restaurant is in an imposing alpine-style log building. Breakfasts are hearty and cost from $7; lunch is mostly burgers and sandwiches. In the evening, try the delicious chicken lasagna ($20).

Accommodations and Camping

Inexpensive accommodations are available at the **Hillview Motel** (1533 Hwy. 16, 250/567-4468, www.hillviewmotel.com, $85-105 s or d), on the east side of town and with an on-site restaurant. Similarly priced, but right downtown and home to Vanderhoof's best restaurant, is the 37-room **North Country Inn** (2625 Burrard Ave., 250/567-3047, www.northcountryinnmotel.com, $90-110 s or d).

Riverside Park Campground (3100 Burrard Ave., 250/567-4710, mid-June-mid-Sept., $24-32) enjoys a pleasant setting beside the Nechako River. Turn north off Highway 16 onto Burrard Avenue and continue through town; the campground is to the west side of Burrard Avenue. Showers and firewood are supplied.

Information

Incorporated into the Vanderhoof Community Museum is the **Vanderhoof Visitor Centre** (478 1st St., 250/567-2124, 10am-5pm daily late May-Sept. 10am-5pm Mon.-Fri. Oct.-May).

FORT ST. JAMES

A sealed road leads 60 kilometers (37 miles) north from Vanderhoof to Fort St. James

(pop. 2,000), the earliest European settlement in northern British Columbia. While it's worth a detour to check out Fort St. James Historic Site, you can also see other historic buildings, including the lakefront Our Lady of Good Hope Catholic Church, built in 1873. The town fronts 90-kilometer-long (56-mile) **Stuart Lake,** the province's seventh-largest body of water. North of Fort St. James, Germanson Landing North Road (well-maintained but unpaved) leads to the **Takla-Nation Lakes** region—a favorite with campers in search of untouched wilderness and with anglers wanting to pull grayling, char, rainbow trout, and Dolly Varden from the region's dozens of fish-filled lakes.

★ Fort St. James National Historic Site

In the early 1800s, **Fort St. James** (250/996-7191, 9am-5pm daily June-late Sept., adults $8, seniors $7, children $4) was the chief fur-trading post and capital of the large and prosperous district of New Caledonia—the name originally given to central British Columbia by Simon Fraser, who was instrumental in expanding the fur trade west of the Rockies. It continued to operate until the early 1900s, and today the restored fort forms the centerpiece of a historic site holding Canada's largest collection of original fur-trade buildings. Enter the fort through the Visitor Reception Centre, which holds displays on pioneer explorers, fur traders, and the indigenous Carrier people. In July and August, characters dressed in pioneer garb lurk in the log-constructed general store, the fish cache, the single men's bunkhouse, the main house, and the veggie garden. You're actively encouraged to get into the spirit of things and play along. Tell them you've just arrived by canoe, want to stay the night in the men's house, and need a good horse and some provisions . . . then see what happens!

Accommodations and Camping

The best place to stay in the area is **Stuart Lodge** (5540 Stones Bay Rd., 250/996-7917, www.stuartlodge.ca, $90-115 s, $80-100 d), overlooking Stuart Lake five kilometers (3 miles) west of Fort St. James. The complex's five cabins come with cooking facilities, decks, and TVs. **Paarens Beach Provincial Park** and **Sowchea Bay Provincial Park,** west of Fort St. James, both offer **camping** (519/826-6850 or 800/689-9025, www.discovercamping.ca, mid-May-early Sept., $22), swimming, and fishing; Paarens Beach is better suited for RVs, although neither has hookups.

FORT JAMES TO FRASER LAKE

Heading west from Vanderhoof, the Yellowhead Highway passes through low rolling terrain before crossing the wide **Nechako River** and passing **Beaumont Provincial Park.** At the end of the park access road is a large day-use area and a stretch of sandy beach. Behind this area is a nature trail dotted with interpretive panels. To be assured of a site in the campground (mid-May-mid-Sept., $22), make reservations through Discover Camping (519/826-6850 or 800/689-9025, www.discovercamping.ca). The park also marks the eastern edge of an area known as the **Lakes District,** comprising more than 300 fish-filled lakes. Traveling this stretch of the highway in summer, you'll notice all the vehicles hauling canoes, kayaks, or small fishing boats.

The town of Fraser Lake (pop. 1,200), 60 kilometers (37 miles) west of Vanderhoof, lies on a chunk of land sloping gently down to its namesake lake. In winter, trumpeter swans settle in at each end of the lake. In summer, a salmon run on the **Stellako River**—a short stretch of water between Fraser and Francois Lakes—draws scores of eager anglers. Overlooking Fraser Lake, **Piper's Glen RV Park** (14108 Hwy. 16, 250/690-7565, www.pipersglenresort.com, May-Sept., camping $22-30, cabins $40-90) has a grassy lakeshore camping area with full hookups, showers, wireless Internet, and peddle-boat rentals.

Just west of Fraser Lake, a turnoff leads south to **Francois Lake,** another popular fishing hole. **Glenannan Tourist Area,** at the lake's east end, boasts a handful of fishing resorts providing everything an angler could possibly desire. Right on the lake and excellent value, **Noralee Resort** (49400 Colleymount Rd., 250/695-6399, www.noraleeresort.com, camping $20-25, cabins $85-100 s or d) is well suited for anglers (tackle shop and motorboat rentals for a reasonable $80 per day), but everyone is welcome.

BURNS LAKE AND VICINITY

The first thing you see when you enter Burns Lake (pop. 2,100) is an enormous chainsaw-carved trout with the inscription "Three Thousand Miles of Fishing!" That pretty much sums up what attracts visitors to the town and surrounding Lakes District.

Sights and Recreation

Continue west along the highway through downtown for about one kilometer (0.6 miles) until you come to the green and white **Lakes District Museum** (540 Hwy. 16, 250/692-3773, 9am-5pm daily July-Aug., adults $3), comprising a museum and the local information center. The museum is housed in a 1919 home whose furnished rooms contain an odd assortment of articles, including memorabilia from an old ship (viewed through a porthole). For a wonderful view of the area, follow 5th Avenue up the hill out of town, then take the turnoff to **Boer Mountain Forestry Lookout.** Rockhounds will prefer to head 6.5 kilometers (4 miles) south of town to **Eagle Creek Opal Beds,** one of Canada's few opal deposits. From the parking lot, a two-kilometer (1.2-mile) trail (40 minutes one-way) leads to the creek-side deposit and an intriguing outcrop of hoodoos.

Accommodations

On the east side of town before Highway 16 descends to the main street, the low-slung **Wanakena Motel** (250/692-3151 or 888/413-3151, www.blwana.com, $89-99 d) is an older place, but rooms are cheery and clean, and wireless Internet is included.

Information

Burns Lake Visitor Centre (540 Hwy. 16, 250/692-3773, www.visitburnslake.ca, 9am-5pm daily July-Aug.) is along Highway 16 west of downtown in the museum complex.

TWEEDSMUIR PROVINCIAL PARK

The town of Burns Lake is not only near British Columbia's smallest provincial park (Deadman's Island in Burns Lake), it's also the northern gateway to the largest: 981,000-hectare (2.4-million-acre) Tweedsmuir Provincial Park. The park extends over 200 kilometers (124 miles) from north to south. Its northern boundary, formed by **Ootsa** and **Whitesail Lakes,** is accessed along a network of logging roads south from Burns Lake. The only road within the park is Highway 20. Most of the park's northern section is made up of the **Quanchus Mountain Range,** holding many peaks topping 1,900 meters (6,230 feet), and the **Nechako Plateau,** which is riddled with lakes and streams. The lakes are filled with fish, including rainbow trout, kokanee, mountain whitefish, and burbot. Aside from fishing, the most popular activity in the park's northern reaches is boating, canoeing, or kayaking the circular route through Ootsa, Whitesail, Eutsuk, Tetachuck, and Natalkuz Lakes, with some portaging required.

Practicalities

Wilderness campsites ($5 pp) sprinkle some of the lakes within the park. To get to Ootsa Lake, follow Highway 35 for 16 kilometers (10 miles) south from Burns Lake to Francois Lake, take the free vehicle ferry (summer only) across Francois Lake, then continue south another 44 kilometers (27 miles) to the settlement of Ootsa Lake. To get into the park itself, you'll need a canoe, kayak, motorboat, or chartered floatplane. **Lakes District Air Services** (250/692-3229 or 866/235-2155, www.ldair.ca) flies charters from a base along Francois Lake Road. See their website for package details that include lodging in remote cabins.

TOPLEY TO TELKWA
Babine Lake

At Topley, 51 kilometers (32 miles) west of Burns Lake, a side road leads north to 177-kilometer-long (110-mile) Babine Lake, the province's largest natural lake and yet another spot known for producing trophy-size rainbow trout, Dolly Varden, kokanee, coho salmon, and whitefish.

Topley Landing, 30 kilometers (19 miles) from the Yellowhead Highway, is a former trapping and trading center dating back to the 1700s. Beyond the landing, over the Fulton River, is **Red Bluff Provincial Park,** named for iron-impregnated cliffs that descend into the water. The park's small **campground** (519/826-6850 or 800/689-9025, www.discovercamping.ca, May-Aug., $20) enjoys a picturesque lakefront location, but facilities are limited.

Houston

Like Burns Lake, Houston's welcoming sign also proudly bears a carved fish—this time a steelhead. Houston calls itself "Steelhead Country," for the only species of trout that migrates to the ocean. The forestry town of 3,200 lies in the stunning Bulkley Valley, with the Telkwa and Babine Ranges for a backdrop. As in the rest of this region, the local fishing is superb. At the information center, pick up a copy of the local forestry district recreation map, showing the area's rivers, lakes, logging roads, and campgrounds. The best steelhead fishing is in the Morice River, on the northeast side of town, during late fall.

Houston Visitor Centre (Hwy. 16 at Benson Ave., 250/845-7640, www.houston-chamber.ca, 9am-5pm daily July-Aug., 9am-5pm Mon.-Fri. Sept.-June) is easy to spot—out front is the world's largest fly-fishing rod.

Telkwa

As you continue west from Houston, the

Smithers

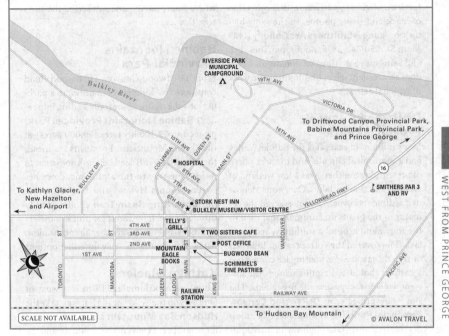

Riverside Park Municipal Campground

19TH AVE

Bulkley River

VICTORIA DR

To Driftwood Canyon Provincial Park, Babine Mountains Provincial Park, and Prince George

16TH AVE

16

10TH AVE

QUEEN ST

COLUMBIA

HOSPITAL

MAIN ST

8TH AVE

7TH AVE

BULKLEY DR

To Kathlyn Glacier, New Hazelton and Airport

6TH AVE

STORK NEST INN
BULKLEY MUSEUM/VISITOR CENTRE

SMITHERS PAR 3 AND RV

YELLOWHEAD HWY

VANCOUVER

4TH AVE
3RD AVE

TELLY'S GRILL

TWO SISTERS CAFE

ST

ST

2ND AVE

MOUNTAIN EAGLE BOOKS

POST OFFICE
BUGWOOD BEAN
SCHIMMEL'S FINE PASTRIES

PACIFIC AVE

1ST AVE

MANITOBA

TORONTO

QUEEN ST

ALDOUS

MAIN ST

KING ST

RAILWAY STATION

RAILWAY AVE

SCALE NOT AVAILABLE

To Hudson Bay Mountain

© AVALON TRAVEL

scenery gets more dramatic. You'll pass open fields and rolling, densely forested hills, all the while surrounded by mountain peaks. The neat little village of Telkwa lies at the confluence of the Bulkley and Telkwa Rivers, almost exactly halfway between Prince George and Prince Rupert. Several species of anadromous fish make spawning runs up the rivers here at various times of year—spring chinook salmon in late June, coho salmon in August, and steelhead between fall and freeze-up. The area also appeals to canoeists, offering stretches of water to suit novices through intermediates. Many of the buildings in the village date to between 1908 and 1924.

On the east side of town, **Tyhee Lake Provincial Park** has a good swimming beach, a 2.5-kilometer (1.5-mile) loop trail, picnic facilities, a playground, and a **campground** (519/826-6850 or 800/689-9025, www.discovercamping.ca, mid-May-mid-Sept., $27).

SMITHERS AND VICINITY

The Coast Mountains surround the town of Smithers (pop. 5,400), while the splendid 2,560-meter (8,400-foot) Hudson Bay Mountain towers directly above. It's a vibrant community with some excellent accommodations, fine restaurants, and interesting arts-and-crafts shops. Hiking trails close to town lead to a magnificent glacier, intriguing fossil beds, and a remote recreation area.

Town Sights

With a backdrop of magnificent mountains, it's no surprise that Main Street is done up in a Bavarian theme. Visitors shop here for First Nations crafts and tourist paraphernalia. The grand old 1925 courthouse, at the junction of the Yellowhead Highway and Main Street, is home to **Bulkley Valley Museum** (1425 Main St., 250/847-5322, 9am-5pm Mon.-Fri., plus 9am-4pm Sat. summer, donation), which houses a predictable collection of historic artifacts, highlighted by an interesting collection of black-and-white photos. In the same historic building is **Smithers Art Gallery** (1425 Main St., 250/847-3898, noon-5pm Tues.-Fri. and 9am-4pm Sat. summer, donation), which does an excellent job of highlighting the work of regional artists.

Driftwood Canyon Provincial Park

Many millions of years ago, the Bulkley Valley had a subtropical climate, and the area north of present-day Smithers was a low wetland of swamps and shallow lakes. Over eons, deposited sediments covered and preserved the remains of the plants and animals that died in the water, and around a million years ago, a lava flow covered the entire region. But then during the last ice age, melting ice carved out a canyon that sliced right through the ancient wetlands, exposing the fossil beds. The site is now protected as **Driftwood Canyon Provincial Park.** It is 17 kilometers (11 miles) northeast of town; take Highway 16 three kilometers (2 miles) southeast, head north on Old Babine Lake Road, turn left on Telkwa High Road, then right on Driftwood Road. A short

walk from the road leads to a viewing platform over the east bank of Driftwood Creek, where interpretive panels describe the site's significance.

Babine Mountains Provincial Park

From Driftwood Canyon, Driftwood Road continues five kilometers (3 miles) to a parking lot—the trailhead for trails leading into remote **Babine Mountains Provincial Park,** protecting 32,400 hectares (80,000 acres) of the Skeena Mountains. From this trailhead, the **McCabe Trail** leads eight kilometers (5 miles) one-way to the alpine meadows between Mounts Hyland and Harvey, while the **Silver King Basin Trail** climbs steadily through a subalpine forest for nine kilometers (5.5 miles) one-way to another alpine meadow. Allow three hours one-way for either option.

Kathlyn Glacier

About eight kilometers (5 miles) west of Smithers on the Yellowhead Highway, take the **Hudson Bay Mountain Lookout** turnout for magnificent views of the mountain and the quickly receding Kathlyn Glacier on its north face. In the same vicinity, turn south off the highway at Lake Kathlyn Road to the trailhead

Fishing draws many visitors to Babine Lake.

for **Glacier Gulch,** a strenuous 1,000 vertical meters (3,280 feet) above the parking lot. The trail is only six kilometers (3.7 miles) one-way, but allow at least three hours to reach the toe of Kathlyn Glacier. Just 500 meters (0.3 miles) along the trail is dramatic **Twin Falls,** a worthy destination in itself. Beyond the Glacier Gulch trailhead, Lake Kathlyn Road ends, appropriately enough, at **Lake Kathlyn,** a photogenic body of water at the base of Hudson Bay Mountain.

Skiing and Snowboarding

The smallish winter resort on **Hudson Bay Mountain** (250/847-2058, www.hudsonbaymountain.com, adults $65, seniors $45, children $33) is mostly geared to beginners and intermediates, but a few of the 19 designated runs challenge more experienced skiers and boarders. Four lifts serve a vertical rise of 553 meters (1,750 feet) and 120 hectares (300 acres) of mostly intermediate terrain. Facilities include two day lodges, a rental shop, and a ski and snowboard school. To get to the resort, take either Main Street or King Street south onto Railway Avenue and turn left; the base area is 23 kilometers (14 miles) from downtown Smithers.

Food

Easy to spot on Smither's main downtown street, **Bugwood Bean** (1206 Main St., 250/877-3505, 7:30am-4:30pm daily) is a beautiful timber-frame building with a couple of tables under a covered porch and the rest scattered around the building. It has a delightful small-town ambience with excellent coffee.

Two Sisters Cafe (3763 4th Ave., 250/877-7708, 8am-4:30pm Mon.-Fri., 9am-4:30pm Sat., lunch $10-14) is a funky little space with a stylish yet uncomplicated decor. The lunch menu changes almost daily, using mostly seasonal, locally sourced produce. Daily offerings may include quesadillas or a beef stew—all made from scratch by the hands-on sister-owners.

Simple and classy, **Telly's Grill** (3843 4th Ave., 250/847-0017, 3pm-10pm Tues.-Sat.,

$18-30) is the best place in Smithers for dinner. The menu has many Mediterranean influences, including tasty and filling lasagna, but if salmon is in season, it's hard to go past this local delicacy.

Accommodations and Camping

Because skiers and snowboarders flock to the slopes of Hudson Bay Mountain when the snow falls, the local lodgings are apt to be as busy in winter as in summer. The 23-room **Stork Nest Inn** (1485 Main St., 250/847-3831 or 877/647-3831, www.storknestinn.com, $105 s, $120 d) is styled on a Bavarian lodge. It features 23 comfortable rooms with air-conditioning and small fridges, and rates that include a cooked breakfast. The premier lodging in this region is the ★ **Logpile Lodge** (3105 McCabe Rd., 250/847-5152, www.logpilelodge.com, $119-169 s, $139-169 d), north of town (call for directions) and surrounded by a magnificent mountain panorama. Guest rooms on the upper floor have vaulted ceilings, while exposed log walls dominate those on the lower floor. All seven guest rooms have solid log beds and private balconies. A big breakfast, cooked to order, will set you up for an activity-filled day.

Riverside Park Municipal Campground (3843 19th Ave., mid-May-mid-Oct., $20-33) is beside the Bulkley River, north of town. It provides shaded sites, a few electrical hookups, showers, and a cooking shelter. **Smithers Par 3 and RV** (Hwy. 16 east of town, 250/847-3229, www.smitherspar3andrv.com, mid-Apr.-mid-Oct., $27-30) has better facilities (including wireless Internet) and is within the bounds of a golf course.

Information

In the museum complex is **Smithers Visitor Centre** (1411 Court St., 250/847-5072 or 800/542-6673, www.tourismsmithers.com, 9am-5pm Mon.-Fri., 9am-4pm Sat. June-Aug., 9am-5pm Mon.-Fri. Sept.-May). A good source of northern literature is **Mountain Eagle Books** (3775 3rd Ave., 250/847-5245,

8am-6pm Mon.-Sat.), which mixes used books with fresh coffee.

CONTINUING WEST FROM SMITHERS

The next place to stop and stretch your legs is the viewpoint at **Moricetown Canyon,** where the 500-meter-wide (1,640-foot) Bulkley River funnels and roars its way down through a 15-meter-wide (49-foot) canyon. Salmon desperately hurl themselves up these spectacular rapids in autumn. Below the canyon the river pours into a large pool, creating one of the best fishing spots in the area. The canyon is part of **Moricetown Indian Reserve,** which recognizes an area that has been a Carrier village site for more than 5,000 years. Villagers still fish the canyon using traditional spears and nets; look for locals congregated around the canyon in summer.

Continuing west, the scenery changes dramatically; suddenly pine trees line the Bulkley River and cover the hills and mountains. About 50 kilometers (30 miles) from Smithers, a four-kilometer (2.5-mile) unpaved road to the north leads to 307-hectare (760-acre) **Ross Lake Provincial Park,** named for a lake with crystal-clear waters full of trout and Dolly Varden. The backdrop is one of forested hills and spectacular snowcapped peaks. In the early mornings you can hear loons; in the evenings beavers slide into the water, slapping their tails.

NEW HAZELTON AND VICINITY

It's easy to be confused by the three Hazeltons—Hazelton, New Hazelton, and South Hazelton—situated at the most northerly point on the Yellowhead Highway. As usual, the arrival of the Grand Trunk Pacific Railway caused the confusion. The original Hazelton (called Old Town) was established 50 years before the railway came. The other two Hazeltons were founded because each of their respective promoters thought he owned a better spot for a new railway town. Today, the largest of the three small communities is New Hazelton (pop. 700), a service center watched over by spectacular Rocher DeBoule (French for "mountain of the rolling rock").

From New Hazelton, Highway 62 leads about eight kilometers (5 miles) northwest to Hazelton. Along the way it crosses **Hagwilget Suspension Bridge,** 79 meters (260 feet) above the turbulent Bulkley River. Stop and read the plaque about the original footbridge—made from poles and cedar rope—that once spanned the gorge here; you'll be glad you live in modern times. At the junction of the Bulkley and Skeena Rivers, Hazelton has retained its unique 1890s-style architecture and pioneer settlement atmosphere.

★ 'Ksan Historical Village

'Ksan Historical Village (250/842-5544, 10am-5pm daily Apr.-Sept., 10am-4:30pm Mon.-Fri. Oct.-Mar., adults $12, seniors and students $9) is an authentically reconstructed Gitxsan village on the outskirts of Hazelton. *'Ksan* means "between the banks." In the main building, a museum features cedar boxes and cedar-bark mats, woven and button blankets, masks, coppers (the most valuable single object a chief possessed), and an art gallery with changing exhibitions. In the adjacent gift shop are the works of on-site artists. Beyond the museum is the village, which can be visited only as part of a fascinating guided tour (included in admission). Tours leave every hour on the hour, visiting the burial house, food cache, smokehouse, community houses, and 'Ksan artists' carving shop and studio. You'll see traditional Northwest Coast carved interiors, paintings and painted screens, totem poles, and fine examples of First Nations artifacts, arts and crafts, and personal possessions.

The Seven Sisters

These impressive peaks lie west of New Hazelton, immediately south of the junction of the Yellowhead Highway and Highway 37. From the highway you'll get only occasional glimpses of the range; for the best panorama take Highway 37 north across the Skeena

Heritage Park Museum

Prince George and 146 kilometers (91 miles) east of Prince Rupert. The city is built on a series of terraces along the beautiful Skeena River, the province's second-largest river system, and is completely surrounded by the spectacular Hazelton and Coast Mountains. The town offers basic tourist services and little else. But the surrounding area makes up for it with a mix of intriguing sights, beautiful parks, and outstanding recreation opportunities.

Heritage Park Museum

At the outdoor-indoor **Heritage Park Museum** (4702 Kerby Ave., 250/635-4546, 10am-6pm daily June-Aug., donation), you can wander the grounds or join a one-hour guided tour taking you through an old, beautifully furnished log hotel, a dance hall, a barn, and six authentic log cabins dating from between 1910 and 1955. Some of the cabins are furnished; others contain historical artifacts or collections of antique farming and mining equipment. To get there from downtown, head north up Skeenaview Street to Kerby Avenue.

Nisga'a Memorial Lava Bed Provincial Park

Protecting Canada's youngest lava flow, the fascinating landscape of this 17,683-hectare (43,700-acre) park is unique within the province. The flow is about 18 kilometers (11 miles) long and three kilometers (2 miles) wide; experts think the molten rock spewed through the earth's crust between 1650 and 1750, killing an estimated 200 First Nations people. You can see all different types of lava, as well as crevasses, spiky pinnacles, sinkholes, craters, and bright blue pools where underground rivers have risen to the surface. Explore the lava with caution—in some parts the surface may be unstable, and it's very hard on footwear. The only facilities are a day-use area and a couple of short hiking trails.

To get to the park, take Highway 16 west out of town for three kilometers (2 miles), then head north around the back of the sawmill on Kalum Lake Drive. The park is 78

River, turn west (left) toward Cedarvale, and stop after about 10 kilometers (6 miles) at the picnic area by Sedan Creek. Several walking trails also lead to good views of the peaks. The one-kilometer (0.6-mile) **Gull Creek Trail** climbs about 200 vertical meters (660 feet) from the trailhead at Gull Creek, which is signposted along Highway 16.

Practicalities

Along the highway through New Hazelton is the **28 Inn** (250/842-6006 or 877/842-2828, www.28inn.com, $75 s, $85-95 d), with slightly nicer rooms than the rates may suggest and wireless Internet access included. In a small log building at the intersection of Highways 16 and 62, **Hazelton Visitor Centre** (4070 9th Ave., 250/842-6071, 9am-5pm daily June-mid-Sept.) has all the usual literature and holds a display detailing local history.

TERRACE AND VICINITY

Terrace (pop. 12,000) lies on the Yellowhead Highway, 580 kilometers (360 miles) west of

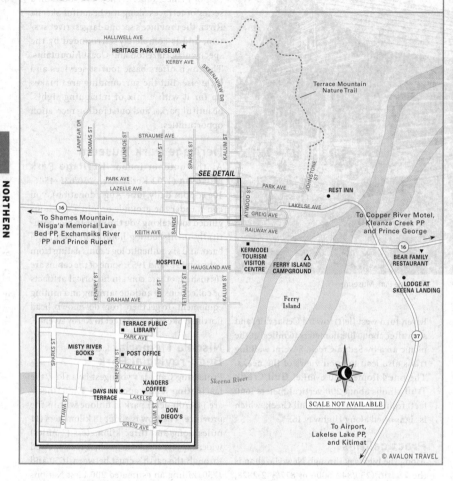

Terrace

© AVALON TRAVEL

kilometers (49 miles) along this road; watch for logging trucks.

Recreation

Many trails in the area tempt hikers. For an easy stroll, take the three-kilometer (2-mile) path (50 minutes or less) around **Ferry Island,** in the middle of the Skeena River east of downtown (reached via Highway 16). More demanding is **Terrace Mountain Nature Trail,** a five-kilometer (3-mile) trail providing great views of the city and the surrounding area. It takes about two hours round-trip, since much of it is uphill. Start at the intersection of Halliwell Avenue and Anderson Street (by the Heritage Park Museum), climbing the lower slopes of Terrace Mountain to a clearing where views are best, then descending to town at the end of Johnstone Street. Farther afield, consider scenic **Clearwater Lakes Trail,** which begins from Highway 37 about 27 kilometers (17 miles) south of Terrace. The trail leads 1.8 kilometers (1.1 miles) to Little Clearwater Lake, then another 700 meters (0.4

The Spirit Bear

Little known outside British Columbia, the **Kermode** (pronounced kerr-MO-dee) is an elusive subspecies of black bear *(Ursus americanus kermodei)*. The Tsimshian called the Kermode "Spirit Bear" and often rendered it in human form in their artwork. The bear inhabits only the vast tract of wilderness north of Terrace as well as uninhabited Princess Royal Island south of Kitimat, where it is protected by the Spirit Bear Conservancy.

First studied by Francis Kermode, director of the British Columbia Museum, at the turn of the 20th century, the bear was originally thought to be a distinct species. It's slightly larger than other black bears, has a different jaw structure, and, although its color varies, some individuals are pure white. These white bears are not albinos, but instead contain a recessive gene that results in the light coloring. Once close to extinction, the Kermode is now fully protected and is the mammal emblem of British Columbia.

miles) to Big Clearwater Lake. The two lakes are linked by a shallow creek, along the banks of which are many good picnic spots and berries to pick in season.

When locals want to cool down on a hot summer's day, they head south along Highway 37 for 26 kilometers (16 miles) to 354-hectare (874-acre) **Lakelse Lake Provincial Park,** at the north end of beautiful Lakelse Lake. It offers good swimming beaches backed by shaded picnic areas, and a hiking trail through an old-growth forest of towering spruce.

Food

Xanders Coffee (Days Inn Terrace, 4620 4th Ave., 250/635-2800, 7am-6:30pm Mon.-Sat., 8am-6pm Sun., lunch $7-11) is an appealing downtown spot for breakfast or lunch, with a blackboard menu that really does change daily. The food is both healthy and hearty, ranging from salads to chili.

One of the most popular places to go for traditional cooked breakfasts is the **Bear Family Restaurant** (Northern Motor Inn, 3086 Hwy. 16, 250/635-6375, 6am-11pm daily, $10-25), near the Chevron gas station on Highway 16 just east of Terrace. For breakfast, large omelets, hash browns, toast, and coffee run $9-11.

For delicious Mexican food, head downtown to **Don Diego's** (3212 Kalum St., 250/635-2307, 11am-9pm Mon.-Sat., 10am-2pm and 5pm-9pm Sun., $13-23), where a few outdoor tables catch the evening sun. It's a small, bright restaurant with lots of plants and Mexican wall hangings. It's always busy, so you may have to wait for a table.

Accommodations

The less expensive motels are strung out along Highway 16 on the eastern and western outskirts of the city, but I recommend spending a few dollars extra and staying on the east side of downtown at **Rest Inn** (4326 Lakelse Ave., 250/635-7216, www.restinnterrace.com, $99-129 s or d), a newer motel not affiliated with the major chains. Rooms have one queen or two double beds, and each is air-conditioned and has a small fridge. Continental breakfast is included in the rates. On the other side of town is **Copper River Motel,** three kilometers (2 miles) east (4113 Hwy. 16, 250/635-6124 or 888/652-7222, www.copperrivermotel.com, $95 s or d), set up for anglers, with fishing supplies and guides, and free ice. Rooms are clean and have coffee- and tea-making appliances. On the down side are the paper-thin walls. Right downtown is **Days Inn Terrace** (4620 Lakelse Ave., 250/638-8141, www.daysinn.ca, $105-135 s or d), where each of the 50 air-conditioned rooms is decorated in stylish pastel colors. Downstairs is Xanders Coffee, with the best coffee in town.

The nicest rooms in town are within the **Lodge at Skeena Landing** (4055 Motz Rd., 250/638-0444, www.skeenalanding.com,

$149-209 s or d), a modern commercial and residential complex just off Highway 16 along the road to Kitimat. The rooms provide a relaxing stay for those just passing through or spending a few days in the area, with the more expensive ones having full kitchens.

Camping

On Ferry Island in the Skeena River, just over three kilometers (2 miles) east of downtown, **Ferry Island Campground** (4301 Hwy. 16, 250/615-9657, mid-Apr.-early Oct., $22-28) offers 100 sheltered sites among birch and cottonwood trees, berry bushes, and wildflowers. A few sites have excellent views of the river and mountains, and a hiking trail runs through the woods and around the island. Facilities include picnic tables and shelters, fire grates, firewood, and pit toilets; a few sites have electrical hookups, but no showers.

Two local provincial parks have campgrounds. **Kleanza Creek Provincial Park** (519/826-6850 or 800/689-9025, www.discovercamping.ca, mid-May-mid-Sept., $20), site of a short-lived gold rush, is 20 kilometers (12 miles) east of Terrace on Highway 16. The campground has only 34 sites, but the riverside location is scenic, and a short trail leads into a box canyon. But my pick of the two is **Lakelse Lake Provincial Park** (519/826-6850 or 800/689-9025, www.discovercamping.ca, mid-May-mid-Sept., $28), 16 kilometers (10 miles) south of Terrace along Highway 37. The most developed of the three parks, it offers a sandy beach, lake swimming, hot showers, and flush toilets. The campground is very popular, so make reservations well in advance.

Information and Services

Kermodei Tourism Visitor Centre (4511 Keith Ave., 250/635-4944, www.visitterrace.com, 9am-5pm daily July-Aug., 9am-5pm Mon.-Fri. Sept.-June) is beside Highway 16 on the east side of town. In addition to a solid collection of northern literature, **Terrace Public Library** (4610 Park Ave., 250/638-8177, 1pm-9pm Mon., 10am-9pm Tues.-Fri., 10am-5pm Sat., 1pm-5pm Sun.) holds a community art gallery offering exhibitions that change monthly. For local reading and a good selection of Canadiana, head to **Misty River Books** (4710 Lazelle Ave., 250/635-4428, 9am-6pm Mon.-Thurs., 9am-8pm Fri., 9am-6pm Sat., 11am-4pm Sun.).

KITIMAT

The planned industrial community of Kitimat (pop. 8,300), at the northern end of Douglas Channel 62 kilometers (39 miles) south of Terrace, was founded by the aluminum giant Alcan (Aluminum Company of Canada) in the 1950s. Described at the time by *National Geographic* as "the most expensive project ever attempted by private industry," the project included one of the world's largest aluminum smelters, a company town to house the workers, and a massive hydroelectric scheme 75 kilometers (47 miles) south of Kitimat.

Sights

In **Radley Park,** along the Kitimat River on the southwest side of downtown, stands the province's largest living tree, a 50-meter-high (164-foot) 500-year-old Sitka spruce. It's behind the Riverlodge Recreation Centre. Also in Radley Park, but on the other side of the Kitimat River, is **Kitimat River Hatchery** (283 Haisla Blvd. 250/639-9888, 8am-4pm Mon.-Fri., free), which releases 11 million steelhead and salmon fingerlings annually.

Kitimat Museum (293 City Centre, 250/632-8950, 10am-4pm Mon.-Fri. June-Aug., 10am-4pm Mon.-Fri., noon-4pm Sat. Sept.-May, donation) tells the story of the planned town and displays historic and First Nations artifacts; a gallery features locally produced artwork.

Practicalities

Kitimat's premier lodging is **Minette Bay Lodge** (2255 Kitimat Village Rd., 250/632-2907, www.minettebaylodge.com, $250 s, $300 d, or $350 pp with meals), a grand estate that looks like it has been transported from the English countryside to the Kitimat waterfront. Guests enjoy activities such as heli-hiking, jet boat tours, and fishing charters through the day, then kick back in the lap of luxury. The guest rooms are spacious and feature a pinky pastel color scheme; most have water views. **Radley Park Campground** (signed from Haisla Blvd., mid-May-mid-Sept., $24-28) has a riverside setting, coin-operated showers, 24 sites with electrical hookups, and a kitchen shelter.

Kitimat Visitor Centre (2109 Forest Ave., 250/632-6294 or 800/664-6554, www.tourismkitimat.ca, 8:30am-4:30pm daily June-Aug., 8:30am-4:30pm Mon.-Fri. Sept.-May) is at the entrance to town.

WEST TOWARD PRINCE RUPERT

The 147-kilometer (91-mile) stretch of the Yellowhead Highway between Terrace and Prince Rupert rivals any stretch of road in the province for beauty. For almost the entire distance, the highway hugs the north bank of the beautiful Skeena River (Skeena is a Gitxsan word for "river of mist"). On a fine day, views from the road are stunning—forested mountains, ponds covered in yellow water lilies, and waterfalls like narrow ribbons of silver, snaking down vertical cliffs from the snow high above. In some sections the highway shrinks to two extremely narrow lanes neatly sandwiched between the railway tracks and the river—drive defensively.

Exchamsiks River Provincial Park, on the north side of the highway 50 kilometers (30 miles) west of Terrace, protects an area where the deep green Exchamsiks River drains into the much larger Skeena River. As the highway continues westward, the Skeena widens, eventually becoming a tidal estuary. Sandbars and marshes, exposed at low tide, are a mass of colorful mosses, and wading birds feed in shallow pools. Keep an eye out for bald eagles on the sandbars or perched in the trees above the highway.

Prince Rupert

Prince Rupert (pop. 12,500), on hilly Kaien Island 726 kilometers (451 miles) west of Prince George, is busy with travelers throughout the summer. The city itself holds an odd but intriguing mixture of cultural icons—totem poles, old English coats of arms and street names, high-rise hotels and civic buildings—all crammed together on the edge of the Pacific Ocean. Wildlife is varied and prolific. Prince Rupert is gateway to the Khutzeymateen Grizzly Bear Sanctuary, but around town, you're likely to spot bald eagles, seals, and even black bears.

SIGHTS

You can easily spend several hours at the fascinating **Museum of Northern British Columbia** (100 1st Ave. W., 250/624-3207, 9am-5pm daily June-Sept., 9am-5pm Tues.-Sat. Oct.-May, adults $6, children $2), which occupies an imposing post-and-beam building overlooking the harbor. Exhibits trace the history of Prince Rupert from 5,000-year-old Tsimshian settlements through fur-trading days to the founding of the city in 1914 as the western terminus of the Grand Trunk Pacific Railway. Many of the most fascinating displays spotlight the Coast Tsimshian people—their history, culture, traditions, trade networks, and potlatches. Among the Tsimshian artifacts on display: totem poles, pots, masks, beautiful wooden boxes, blankets, baskets, shiny black argillite carvings, weapons, and petroglyphs. The Monumental Gallery—filled with contemporary art—is worth visiting for the sweeping harbor views alone.

Right by the Museum of Northern British Columbia is **Pacific Mariner's Memorial Park,** a grassed area with benches strategically placed for the best ocean views. A statue of a mariner staring out to sea is surrounded by plaques remembering those lost at sea. Also

Prince Rupert

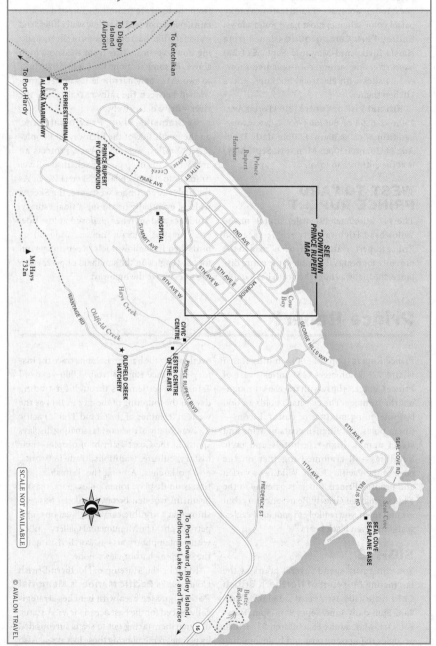

To Digby
Island
(Airport)

To Ketchikan

To Port Hardy

ALASKA MARINE HWY

BC FERRIES TERMINAL

PRINCE RUPERT
RV CAMPGROUND

Morse Creek

PARK AVE

11TH ST

Prince
Rupert
Harbour

SEE
"DOWNTOWN
PRINCE RUPERT"
MAP

HOSPITAL

SUMMIT AVE

2ND AVE

5TH AVE W

6TH AVE W

9TH AVE W

MORROW

Cow
Bay

▲ Mt Hays
732m

Hays Creek

Oldfield Creek

WANTAGE RD

CIVIC
CENTRE

LESTER CENTRE
OF THE ARTS

★ OLDFIELD CREEK
HATCHERY

PRINCE RUPERT BLVD

GEORGE HILLS WAY

6TH AVE E

11TH AVE E

FREDERICK ST

To Port Edward, Ridley Island,
Prudhomme Lake PP, and Terrace

SEAL COVE RD

BELLIS RD

Seal Cove

SEAL COVE
SEAPLANE BASE

Butze
Rapids

16

SCALE NOT AVAILABLE

© AVALON TRAVEL

in the park is the *Kazu Maru,* a small fishing boat that drifted across the Pacific from Japan after its owner was lost. It washed up on Haida Gwaii in 1987, two years after it was reported missing. On the other side of the museum to the memorial park and beside the fire hall is the **Prince Rupert Fire Museum** (200 1st Ave. W., 250/624-2211, 9am-noon and 1pm-5pm Tues.-Sun. July-Aug., donation), which features a 1925 REO Speedwagon along with various other firefighting memorabilia. From this museum, continue south along 1st Avenue, then head to the foot of 2nd Street, which ends harborside. Here you'll find the **Kwinitsa Railway Station Museum** (250/624-3207, 9am-noon and 1pm-5pm daily June-Aug., donation), housed in a small railway station—one of only four such remaining buildings that were once part of a chain of 400 identical stations along the Grand Trunk Railway. Displays tell the story of the railway and its implications for Prince Rupert.

★ North Pacific Cannery National Historic Site

South of Prince Rupert in Port Edward, the **North Pacific Cannery** (1889 Skeena Dr., Port Edward, 250/628-3538, 9:30am-5pm daily May-Sept., adults $12, seniors $10,

children $8) is the oldest remaining cannery village from over 1,000 similar facilities that were once operating along the west coast of North America. Dating to 1889 and now classified as a national historic site, this living museum is one of the highlights of a visit to Prince Rupert. You can find out everything you've ever wanted to know about fish, the fishing industry, canning—even which fish tastes the best (locals say it's red snapper every time). You're free to stroll at your own pace along the boardwalk through the riverside settlement with its many original buildings, including a church, schoolroom, general store, and living quarters. When you're done with the sightseeing, take lunch at the **Mess House** (10:30am-3:30pm daily July-Aug., $7-10), ordering seafood such as salmon chowder, of course. To get to the village, head out of Prince Rupert on the Yellowhead Highway and take the first road to the right after leaving Kaien Island.

ENTERTAINMENT AND EVENTS

Nightlife

The most popular spot in town for a beer is **Breakers Pub** (117 George Hills Way, Cow Bay, 250/624-5990, 11:30am-midnight

Prince Rupert waterfront

Downtown Prince Rupert

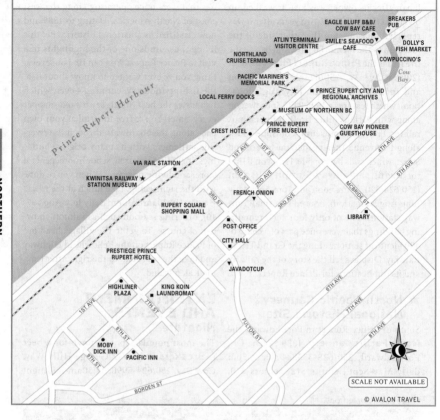

EAGLE BLUFF B&B/ COW BAY CAFE
BREAKERS PUB
ATLIN TERMINAL/ VISITOR CENTRE
SMILE'S SEAFOOD CAFE
DOLLY'S FISH MARKET
NORTHLAND CRUISE TERMINAL
COWPUCCINO'S
Cow Bay
PACIFIC MARINER'S MEMORIAL PARK
LOCAL FERRY DOCKS
PRINCE RUPERT CITY AND REGIONAL ARCHIVES
Prince Rupert Harbour
MUSEUM OF NORTHERN BC
PRINCE RUPERT FIRE MUSEUM
COW BAY PIONEER GUESTHOUSE
CREST HOTEL
4TH AVE
1ST AVE
1ST ST
5TH AVE
VIA RAIL STATION
2ND ST
2ND AVE
MCBRIDE ST
KWINITSA RAILWAY STATION MUSEUM
FRENCH ONION
3RD ST
3RD AVE
RUPERT SQUARE SHOPPING MALL
LIBRARY
POST OFFICE
CITY HALL
PRESTIEGE PRINCE RUPERT HOTEL
JAVADOTCUP
6TH AVE
HIGHLINER PLAZA
KING KOIN LAUNDROMAT
7TH ST
7TH AVE
1ST AVE
8TH ST
FULTON ST
8TH AVE
9TH ST
MOBY DICK INN
PACIFIC INN
BORDEN ST
SCALE NOT AVAILABLE
© AVALON TRAVEL

Mon.-Sat., noon-11pm Sun.). This waterfront drinking hole boasts plenty of atmosphere, an outdoor deck with harbor views, and a bistro-style restaurant. Downtown and also with great water views, **Charley's Lounge** (Crest Hotel, 222 1st Ave. W., 250/624-6771, 11:30am-midnight Mon.-Sat., noon-11pm Sun.) is more subdued than Breakers.

The Arts

At the **Lester Centre of the Arts** (1100 McBride St., 250/627-8888, www.lestercentre. ca), just about anything could be happening. Symphony concerts, plays, lectures, and operas are among the events scheduled.

Festivals and Events

The major annual celebration is **Seafest** (250/624-9118, www.prspecialevents.com), on the second weekend of June. All sorts of wacky events involving the sea are scheduled—a canoe-dunking contest (the water is icy, so no one wants to lose), bathtub races, and fish-filleting competitions. There's also a more serious side to the weekend: a memorial barbecue for those lost at sea, followed by a ceremony to dedicate new bricks at the mariner's statue. Another event held June 21st is **National Aboriginal Day,** featuring a salmon feast and plenty of authentic First Nations dancing and singing.

Grizzly Bear Sanctuary

Officially protected as a provincial park, the **Khutzeymateen** is a rugged and remote 44,300-hectare (109,500-acre) tract of wilderness 50 kilometers (30 miles) northeast of Prince Rupert that is Canada's only grizzly bear sanctuary. To the Tsimshian people, the area was known as the K'tzim-a-Deen, which translates to "the long inlet surrounded by a steep valley." To Canadian conservationists, the name Khutzeymateen is synonymous with one of their earliest victories: a 1984 decision to set aside an area where grizzly bears would be safe from hunters. In 1994, further protection was given with the proclamation of a provincial park where grizzly numbers were highest within the no-hunting zone. The park extends from the upper reaches of Khutzeymateen Inlet to the high peaks of the Kitimat Range, protecting the tidal zone at the head of the inlet where approximately 50 grizzly bears, fresh out of hibernation in May and June, come down to the water's edge to feed on sedges and grasses. Through summer, the bears remain in the area, feeding in the salmon-rich Khutzeymateen and Kateen Rivers.

Given the inaccessibility of the region, most visitors arrive on a guided trip. For adults $205, children $165, **Prince Rupert Adventure Tours** (250/627-9166 or 800/201-8377, www. adventuretours.net, mid-May-July) runs visitors into the area by boat from Prince Rupert, but most of the six-hour trip is spent traveling. Overnight tours are run by **SunChaser Charters** (250/624-5472, www.sunchasercharters.ca, from $2,200 for 4 days), which offers trips on a live-aboard motor cruiser. Departing from Prince Rupert and taking half a day to reach the sanctuary, the trips emphasize bear viewing, but time is also spent exploring other aspects of the area's natural and human history.

FOOD
Downtown

Most of Rupert's larger motels have restaurants, but the place to head for substantial and inexpensive breakfasts is the **Moby Dick Inn** (935 2nd Ave. W., 250/624-6961, 6:30am-9:30pm daily, dinner mains $12-21). You can order anything from a bowl of fruit and a muffin to eggs, bacon, and toast or steak and eggs. It's always crowded, and service can be slow.

At street level of a historical downtown bank building is **Javadotcup** (516 3rd Ave. W, 250/622-2822, 7:30am-6pm Mon.-Fri., 9am-5pm Sat., lunch $7-11), whose name dates to the mid-1990s, when it was an Internet café. Today, it offers excellent coffee and tea drinks, and a tasty selection of inexpensive Asian-inspired dishes, such as a Thai chicken burger for just $6.

Another tasty downtown option is **The Fresh Onion** (309 2nd Ave. W., 250/624-9231, 8am-4pm Mon.-Fri., lunch $7-14), in the Ocean Centre Mall. In addition to the usual array of salads and sandwiches, there are East Indian and vegetarian choices, as well as a daily special that really does change every day.

Combining water views, good food, and pleasant surroundings, the **Waterfront Restaurant** (Crest Hotel, 222 1st Ave. W., 250/624-6771, 6:30am-9pm Mon.-Fri., 7am-9pm Sat.-Sun., $26-48) is as upscale as it gets in Prince Rupert. You could start with alder-smoked steelhead and then move on to oven-roasted rack of lamb with a balsamic red grape reduction. Or enjoy the same watery views for under $15 at breakfast.

Cow Bay

East of downtown is Cow Bay, originally a fishy-smelling, rough-and-tumble part of town home to a large fishing fleet. The boats are still here, moored in a marina, and a few old buildings still stand. But for the most part, the bay is a changed place. Rowdy dives have been replaced by trendy art and crafts shops and an excellent choice of cafés and seafood restaurants.

Cowpuccino's (25 Cow Bay Rd., 250/627-1395, 7am-9pm Mon.-Fri., 7am-6pm Sat.-Sun., lunch $8-12) is a busy little café with the best coffee in town, magnificent muffins, delicious desserts, newspapers and magazines to read, and a laid-back atmosphere.

Across the way from Cowpuccino's and right on the harbor is **Cow Bay Cafe** (205 Cow Bay Rd., 250/627-1212, 11:30am-2pm and 5pm-9pm Tues.-Fri., noon-3pm and 5pm-9pm Sat., 1pm-8pm Sun., $16-22), where you can sit at an outside table and take in the smells of the ocean, or stay inside and enjoy the classy setting while viewing the harbor. Good home-cooked meals dominated by well-priced pizza and pasta make this a popular place regardless of the weather.

It's all about the very freshest seafood at ★ **Dolly's Fish Market** (7 Cow Bay Rd., 250/624-6090, 10am-9pm daily, $12-26), which is a small dining room that's part of a fish market. The choices are all delicious—halibut and chips, halibut nuggets and sweet-potato fries, Dungeness crab cakes, Caesar salad topped with smoked sockeye salmon, and creamy seafood chowder. You can also buy fresh seafood to go as well as smoked and canned seafood.

Ask a local where to go for seafood and the answer is invariably **Smile's Seafood Cafe** (113 Cow Bay Rd., 250/624-3072, 9am-9pm daily June-Sept., 11:30am-8pm daily Oct.-May, $14-30), although judging from my last couple of visits, its glory days are behind it. This diner-style café, decorated with black-and-white fishing photos and colored-glass floats, has been serving seafood since 1934. Most of the seafood is deep-fried, but that doesn't seem to deter the throngs of local fisherfolk, residents, and visitors no matter what time of day.

ACCOMMODATIONS AND CAMPING

Prince Rupert's 700 motel rooms fill fast every night in summer (late June-early Sept.) with travelers waiting for ferries—so book well

Eagle Bluff Bed and Breakfast

in advance (if you're traveling onward from Prince Rupert, you should have already made ferry reservations, so you know which nights you'll be in town). Accommodations choices are wide-ranging, and although no one property stands out as being good value, all are moderately priced. On the other hand, Prince Rupert has a great campground within easy walking distance of the ferry terminals.

$50-100

Affiliated with Hostelling International, the distinctive blue and white **Cow Bay Pioneer Guesthouse** (167 3rd Ave. E., 250/624-2334, dorms $30-35, $65-85 s, $70-90 d) is mostly full of "steadies" in winter, but in summer daily accommodations are offered. Facilities include cheery dorm rooms with shared baths, a couple of private doubles, an outside yard with a barbecue, a living room with a TV, and a small but well-equipped kitchen.

One of many reasonably priced motels is the **Moby Dick Inn** (935 2nd Ave.

King Pacific Lodge

Part of the Rosewood Hotels & Resorts group, **King Pacific Lodge** (604/987-5452 or 855/825-9378, www.kingpacificlodge.com, mid-May-mid-Sept., from $4,800 pp for 3 nights) provides an unforgettable wilderness experience, far removed from what the casual highway traveler might encounter. The floating lodge is on remote Princess Royal Island, best known for its population of Kermode, the albino-like "Spirit Bear." Its three-story timber structure is built over the waters of a protected cove, the perfect base for searching out abundant marine mammals, kayaking, wildlife viewing, and fishing. It is this last activity that attracts most guests, with chinooks (kings) biting best May-July and peak season for other salmon August-September.

The minimum stay is three nights, with all packages including floatplane transportation from Prince Rupert, all meals and drinks, and all activities. The lodge itself holds 17 spacious guest rooms, each with ample amenities and luxurious furnishings. The Great Room is a sea-level lounge centered on a huge stone fireplace; a wraparound veranda faces the ocean out front. Gourmet meals are served in an elegant setting overlooking the water, with fresh seafood the order of the day.

W., 250/624-6961 or 800/663-0822, www.mobydickinn.com, $79-99 s, $85-129 d), which is home to a restaurant with the best-priced breakfast restaurant in town.

$100-150

In the same part of town as the Moby Dick Inn is the **Pacific Inn** (909 3rd Ave. W., 250/627-1711 or 888/663-1999, www.pacificinn.bc.ca, $109-219 s or d), with larger rooms, each with stylish decor, and an in-house Greek restaurant.

My favorite Rupert lodging is ★ **Eagle Bluff Bed and Breakfast** (201 Cow Bay Rd., 250/627-4955 or 800/833-1550, www.eaglebluff.ca, $100-115 s, $135-155 d), with seven guest rooms, each with a different configuration. The house is built out over the water, overlooking the marina and harbor, and lies within easy walking distance of cafés and restaurants. The smallest two rooms share a bath while the largest is a suite sleeping five. A cooked breakfast—complete with freshly baked muffins—is included.

The massive building right downtown is the 15-story **Highliner Plaza** (815 1st Ave. W., 250/624-9060 or 800/668-3115, www.highlinerplaza.com, $139-169 s or d). Rooms are no nicer than at the aforementioned

Pacific Inn, but the location is central and all 94 rooms have balconies (the hotel website makes clear which rooms have harbor views when booking online).

In a prime harborside location, the full-service **Crest Hotel** (222 1st Ave. W., 250/624-6771 or 800/663-8150, www.cresthotel.bc.ca, from $165-325 s or d) holds a glass-enclosed waterfront café, a dining room, and a lounge with water views. Upgrade to Crest Class (from $185 s or d) and enjoy water views.

Camping

Like the rest of Rupert's accommodations, **Prince Rupert RV Campground** (1750 Park Ave., 250/627-1000, www.princerupertrv.com, $21-48) fills and empties on a daily basis with the arrival and departure of the ferries. If you know when you're arriving in the city, phone ahead to avoid any hassles. The campground is a one-kilometer (0.6-mile) hike from both the city center and ferry terminals. Facilities include hot showers, cooking shelters, raised tent pads, a mail drop, and visitor information. The other alternative is **Prudhomme Lake Provincial Park** ($20), along the Yellowhead Highway 16 kilometers (10 miles) east of downtown, where there are limited facilities and reservations are not taken.

INFORMATION AND SERVICES

Information

Prince Rupert Visitor Centre (215 Cow Bay Rd., 250/624-5637 or 800/667-1994, www.visitprincerupert.com, 9am-6pm daily late May-Sept., 9am-5pm Tues.-Sat. Oct.-late May) is in the Atlin Terminal in Cow Bay.

Books

Just off McBride Avenue, the **library** (101 6th Ave., 250/627-1345, 9 10am-9pm Tues.-Thurs., 10am-5pm Fri.) has free Wi-Fi and a good selection of local literature. If you're looking for books, especially on BC First Nations art or history, spend some time at the gift shop at the **Museum of Northern British Columbia** (100 1st Ave. W., 250/624-3207, 9am-5pm daily June-Sept., 9am-5pm Tues.-Sat. Oct.-May).

Services

Prince Rupert Regional Hospital (1305 Summit Ave., 250/624-2171) is south of downtown. The **post office** (417 2nd Ave. W., 250/624-2353) is open 9am-5pm Monday to Friday. **King Koin Laundromat** (745 2nd Ave. W., 250/624-2667) is open 8am to 8pm daily.

GETTING THERE AND AROUND

The easiest way to reach Prince Rupert is by ferry from Port Hardy on Vancouver Island. If you're planning on driving to Prince Rupert, fill your gas tank: it's 726 kilometers (451 miles) west of Prince George via Highway 16. From Vancouver, allow around 17 hours for the 1,506-kilometer (935-mile) road trip.

Air

Prince Rupert Airport (YPR) is served by **Air Canada** (888/247-2262, www.aircanada.com), with scheduled flights from Vancouver a few times daily. The airport is west of town on Digby Island. It is linked to downtown by a city-operated ferry that takes buses and foot passengers only—no vehicles. The fare is included in your airline ticket. The downtown pickup and drop-off point for passengers is the Prestige Prince Rupert Hotel (118 6th St. W.). Go to www.ypr.ca for a schedule.

Rail and Bus

Prince Rupert is the western terminus of Canada's transcontinental rail system, which runs east from here to Prince George and Edmonton, across the prairies to Toronto, and on to the Atlantic provinces. The route through British Columbia is the highlight of the trip, especially the couple of hundred kilometers just outside Prince Rupert, where the line follows the Skeena River. To get to the **VIA Rail** station (250/627-7589), take 2nd Street north over the rail line. Trains arrive in Prince Rupert at 8pm on Monday, Thursday, and Saturday and depart at 8am on Wednesday, Friday, and Sunday.

From the local **Greyhound bus depot** (815 1st Ave. W, 250/624-5090), buses travel east along the Yellowhead Highway to Terrace and Prince George, then either north to the Alaska Highway, east to Edmonton, or south to Kamloops and Vancouver.

Ferry

Prince Rupert is the northern terminus of the **BC Ferries network** (250/386-3431 or 888/223-3779, www.bcferries.com), which offers regular services south to Port Hardy on Vancouver Island and west to Haida Gwaii. The terminal is two kilometers (1.2 miles) from downtown, right alongside the Alaska Marine Highway terminal. Ferries serving Prince Rupert have both day rooms and sleeping cabins, shower facilities, food service, and plenty of room to sit back and relax. During the busy summer months, it's imperative that you book well in advance, especially if you plan to transport a vehicle.

The 15-hour, 440-kilometer (273-mile) ferry trip between Prince Rupert and Port Hardy is a beautiful ride, with ferries departing through summer every second day, less frequently fall-spring. The summer one-way fares are adults $206, ages 5-11 $103, vehicles $469. Discounts of up to 40% are offered between October and April. Cabins ($90-250) and reserved seating ($35) are also available.

The **Alaska Marine Highway** (907/465-3941 or 800/642-0066, www.dot.state.ak.us/amhs) operates an extensive network of ferries through southeastern Alaska and down to Prince Rupert. The first stop north from Prince Rupert is Ketchikan, six hours away. Walk-on passengers need not make reservations, but if you require a cabin or have a vehicle, make reservations as far in advance as possible (up to one year), especially for sailings in July and August. Check-in time is three hours ahead of sailing time—it takes up to two hours to go through customs and one hour to load up. Foot passengers must be there one hour ahead of sailing.

Getting Around

Local bus service along four routes is provided by **Prince Rupert Transit System** (2nd Ave. W., 250/624-3343). Adult fares start at $2. All-day passes cost $4 and are available from the driver. Have exact fare ready—drivers don't carry change. If you're looking to rent a vehicle, reserve ahead with **National** (250/624-5318), which based at the Prestige Prince Rupert Hotel (118 6th St. W.), the drop-off point for the airport shuttle. For a cab, call **Skeena Taxi** (250/624-2185).

Haida Gwaii

Wild. Quiet. Mysterious. Primordial. Inhabited by the proud and ferocious Haida people for over 10,000 years, Haida Gwaii (formerly known as the Queen Charlotte Islands) spread like a large upside-down triangle approximately 100 kilometers (60 miles) off the northwest coast of mainland British Columbia, linked to the mainland by scheduled ferry and air services. Visitors have the opportunity to immerse themselves in First Nations culture, view the abundant wildlife, explore the rugged coastline, and share a laid-back island camaraderie with the 4,700 permanent residents.

Of the chain's 150 mountainous and densely forested islands and islets, the main ones are **Graham Island** to the north and **Moresby Island** to the south, separated by narrow **Skidegate Channel.** The islands stretch 290 kilometers (180 miles) from north to south and up to 85 kilometers (53 miles) across. Running down the west side of the islands are the Queen Charlotte and San Christoval ranges, which effectively protect the east side from Pacific battering. Nevertheless, the east coast, where most of the population lives, still receives over 1,000 millimeters (39 inches) of rain annually.

Life on the islands is very different from elsewhere in the province. Visitors can expect a friendly reception and adequate services. Motel-style accommodations are available in each town, but bed-and-breakfasts provide a better glimpse of the island lifestyle. Other services are similar to any small town, though choices of fresh fruit and vegetables can be limited. Gasoline is only slightly more expensive than on the mainland, and raging nightlife is nonexistent.

The Haida

The Haida people have lived on this remote archipelago since time immemorial. Fearless warriors, expert hunters and fishers, and skilled woodcarvers, they owned slaves and threw lavish potlatches. They had no written language, but they carved records of their history, legends, and important events on totem poles rising up to 104 meters (340 feet) high. Living in villages scattered throughout the islands, they hunted sea otters for their luxuriant furs, fished for halibut and Pacific salmon, and collected chitons, clams, and seaweed from tide pools.

The first contact the Haida had with Europeans occurred in 1774, when Spanish

Haida Gwaii

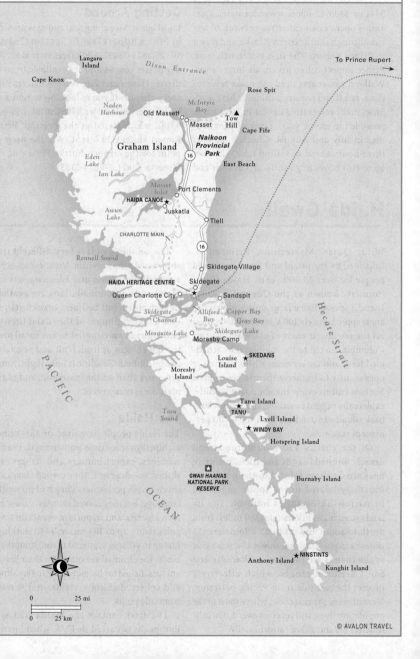

Langara Island

Cape Knox

Dixon Entrance

To Prince Rupert

Naden Harbour

Old Massett

McIntyre Bay

Rose Spit

Masset

Tow Hill

Cape Fife

Naikoon Provincial Park

Graham Island

16

Eden Lake

Ian Lake

East Beach

Masset Inlet

Port Clements

HAIDA CANOE

Awun Lake

Juskatla

Tlell

CHARLOTTE MAIN

16

Rennell Sound

Skidegate Village

HAIDA HERITAGE CENTRE

Skidegate

Queen Charlotte City

Sandspit

Skidegate Channel

Alliford Bay

Copper Bay

Gray Bay

Mosquito Lake

Skidegate Lake

Moresby Camp

PACIFIC

Louise Island

★ **SKEDANS**

Moresby Island

Tanu Island

Tasu Sound

★ **TANU**

Lyell Island

★ **WINDY BAY**

Hotspring Island

Hecate Strait

GWAII HAANAS NATIONAL PARK RESERVE

Burnaby Island

OCEAN

Anthony Island

★ **NINSTINTS**

Kunghit Island

0   25 mi

0   25 km

© AVALON TRAVEL

Beachcombing

Beachcombing on Haida Gwaii is popular year-round, but it's especially good after heavy winter storms. You may find fishing floats from countries around the Pacific (glass balls from Japan are especially prized), bottles, rope, driftwood, shells, whale bones, semiprecious agate, or just about anything that floats. When I first visited the islands in the early 1990s, a container of Nike running shoes had broken apart somewhere in the Pacific; they were being found scattered on beaches throughout the Charlottes and as far south as the Oregon coast. Before that, an abandoned fishing boat from Japan washed ashore and caused excitement; it's now on display in Prince Rupert.

GETTING THERE

Air

The main gateway is Sandspit, where the small air terminal holds car-rental agencies (book ahead) and an information center, and across the road is the Sandspit Inn. **Air Canada** (888/247-2262) flies daily between Vancouver and Sandspit. The Airporter bus meets all Sandspit flights and transports passengers to Queen Charlotte City for $18. From Prince Rupert's Seal Cove Air Base, **Inland Air** (250/624-2577, www.inlandair.bc.ca) has scheduled flights to Masset ($240 one-way).

Ferry

In summer, **BC Ferries** (250/386-3431 or 888/223-3779, www.bcferries.com) operates the *Northern Adventure* between Prince Rupert and Skidegate five or six times a week, less frequently fall-spring. Departure times vary, but most often it's 11am from Prince Rupert, arriving at Skidegate at 5:30pm, and 11pm from Skidegate, arriving at Prince Rupert at 6am or 7:30am. Peak one-way fares are adults $48, children $24, vehicles $169. BC seniors get a discount, as do all travelers outside peak summer season. Cabins are available for $85-200. The ferry terminal is five kilometers (3 miles) east of Queen Charlotte City at Skidegate. Taxis usually wait at the terminal when the ferry arrives; expect to pay around $20 to get into town.

GETTING AROUND

A ferry connects Graham and Moresby Islands, departing hourly in each direction 7am-10pm daily; peak round-trip fare is adults $10.50, children $5.25, vehicles $24.50. Apart from that, the islands have no public transportation. If you are arriving by air, **Budget** (250/637-5688) has vehicles at Sandspit Airport. **Haida Gwaii RV** (888/244-4262, www.haidagwaiirv.com) is based in Queen Charlotte City with older camper vans for $70 per day plus $0.18 per kilometer ($0.30 per mile).

explorer Juan Perez landed on Haida Gwaii. At the turn of the 19th century, white settlers from the mainland began moving over to Haida Gwaii to live along the low-lying east coast and the protected shores of Masset Inlet. By the 1830s, the traditional lifestyle of the Haida was coming to an end. The governments on the mainland prohibited the Haida from owning slaves and throwing potlatches—an important social and economic part of their culture—and forced all Haida children to attend missionary schools. The Haida abandoned their village sites and moved onto reserves at Skidegate and Masset on Graham Island.

For many years the Haida struggled alongside the Island Protection Society to preserve their heritage. Their longtime efforts paid off in two major events: in 1981 the best-known of the abandoned Haida villages, **Ninstints,** was declared a UNESCO World Heritage Site, and in 1988 the southern section of the archipelago was proclaimed **Gwaii Haanas National Park Reserve.**

QUEEN CHARLOTTE CITY

Known to the locals simply as "Charlotte," Queen Charlotte City is spread along the shores of Bearskin Bay, five kilometers (3 miles) west of the dock for the mainland ferry. It's not really a city at all—most places that include "city" in their name aren't—but instead a laid-back fishing and tourist town of 1,000 people. Heritage buildings dating back to the early 1900s (most along the main road) are interspersed with all the services of a small town, with a colorful array of private residences sprawling east and west, overlooking the water and backed by forested wilderness. The main street is 3rd Avenue, a continuation of the road from the ferry dock.

Food

The place to go for coffee is **Queen B's** (3208 Wharf St., 250/559-4463, 8am-5pm Mon.-Fri., 9am-4pm Sat., lunch $7.50-10), with a welcoming ambience, walls decorated in local art, and a delicious selection of light lunches and sweet treats. Head for an outside table if the weather is warm. For something more substantial, head to the **Ocean View Restaurant** (upstairs at 2600 Oceanview Ave., 250/559-8008, 11am-9pm Mon.-Tues. and Thurs.-Fri., 9am-9pm Sat.-Sun., $14-23), which specializes in local seafood in a no-frills dining room. Don't be intimidated by the concept of **Dining with the Kings** (4307 Husband Rd., 250/559-4260, from 7pm Fri.-Mon., $55) as it is one of the most unique and enjoyable dining experiences you will find in northern British Columbia. Four nights a week, Jeff and Diane King open their home to 18 diners who have made advance reservations, serving up a four-course meal in their home for $55 pp. There is generally a choice of starters, followed by two separate main courses and desert.

Accommodations and Camping

Queen Charlotte City is a good base for exploring the islands and has a wide variety of accommodations. Built in 1910, the old Premier Hotel has been totally renovated and now operates as ★ **Premier Creek Lodging** (3101 Oceanview Dr., 250/559-8415 or 888/322-3388, $40-110 s or d), offering beds to suit all budgets. In the main lodge, single "sleeping rooms" with shared facilities cost $40 pp, but definitely worth the extra money are the rooms with private baths, balconies, and harbor views (from $70 s, $80 d); some have kitchens.

Many island homes are decorated with colorful buoys and driftwood.

The least expensive rooms at **Dorothy and Mike's Guest House** (3127 2nd Ave., 250/559-8439, rooms $90 s or d, suites $125, cottage $245) are simple spaces with a shared bath and shared kitchen facilities, but my favorite is the en suite Kumdis Room ($90 s or d), where a sliding door opens to a private deck with fantastic views. A modern three-bedroom cottage is perfect for families. Common areas include a kitchen, a TV room, a large deck area, and a library overflowing with island literature. A hearty cooked breakfast will get you going each morning.

The only regular motel is Queen Charlotte City is the **Sea Raven Motel** (3301 Oceanview Dr., 250/559-4423, www.seara-ven.com, $85 s, $95-145 d), which has 30 guest rooms and a restaurant. Choices include a small single, kitchenettes, family rooms, and ocean-view rooms with private balconies. **Haydn Turner Park,** through town to the west, has toilets, picnic tables, and fire rings for camping ($10), but no showers or hookups.

Information and Services

Down on the waterfront, **Queen Charlotte Visitor Centre** (3220 Wharf St., 250/559-8316, www.queencharlottevisitorcentre.com, 9am-7pm Mon.-Sat. and noon-7pm Sun. summer, noon-4pm Mon. and Fri.-Sat. fall-spring) offers natural history displays, a wide variety of brochures and information on everything that's going on around the islands, current weather forecasts, and an excellent selection of island gifts. The most comprehensive source of island information is www.gohaid-agwaii.ca.

Emergency services in Queen Charlotte City include **Haida Gwaii Hospital** (3101 Oceanview Ave., 250/559-4900) and the **Royal Canadian Mounted Police** (250/559-4421).

NORTH TO PORT CLEMENTS

From Queen Charlotte City, Graham Island's main road follows the eastern coastline past the ferry terminal and Haida Heritage Centre to the Haida community of Skidegate Village,

from where it's a pleasant 65-kilometer (40-mile) coastal drive to Port Clements.

Haida Heritage Centre at Kaay Llnagaay

While totem poles and other ancient Haida art can be seen in various places around the islands, the **Haida Heritage Centre** (2nd Beach Rd., 250/559-7885, 10am-5pm Mon.-Sat. June, 10am-6pm daily July-Aug., 10am-5pm Tues.-Sat. Sept.-May, adults $15, students $10, children $5), on the north side of the Skidegate Landing ferry terminal, gives visitors the opportunity to see a variety of such art under one roof. Inside the impressive log building are striking Haida wood and argillite carvings, pioneer artifacts, a beautiful woven blanket, jewelry, historic black-and-white photos, stunning prints by Haida artist Robert Davidson, ancient totems from Tanu and Skedans dating to 1878, the skull of a humpback whale, shells galore, and a collection of stuffed birds. Outside, be sure to visit the longhouse-style **cedar carving shed,** where the fantastic 15-meter-long (49-foot) canoe *Loo Taas* ("wave eater") is housed.

Between late April and early June, migrating **gray whales** rest and feed on the shallow gravel bars of Skidegate Inlet in front of the museum on their annual 15,000-kilometer (9,300-mile) odyssey between Mexico and Alaska. Behind the museum, a wooden deck overlooking the water is a great vantage point for watching these magnificent creatures, or continue a few hundred yards farther around the bay and search them out from the roadside.

Skidegate Village and Vicinity

Continuing north from the museum, you'll soon come to Skidegate Village, a Haida reserve of 700 residents. A weathered totem pole, over 100 years old, still stands here, as do six newer ones. Facing the beach is a traditional longhouse, home to the Skidegate Haida Band Council House, where local artisans fashion miniature totem poles, argillite ornaments, and jewelry in traditional designs.

Cross the road from the local recreation center to the trailhead of a hiking trail to **Spirit Lake.** The trail passes through an old-growth forest of hemlock, Sitka spruce, and red cedar and passes two picturesque bodies of water, one with picnic tables. The round-trip is three kilometers (2 miles)—an easy hour's walk.

From Skidegate, the road follows the shoreline of Hecate Strait, past driftwood-strewn beaches, an attractive old graveyard, and **Balance Rock,** one kilometer (0.6 miles) north of Skidegate Village. A highway sign and turnout mark the start of a short trail down to the rock. Continuing north, the scenery becomes rural, as the road skirts land cleared by early settlers for cattle-grazing; watch for black-tailed deer in this area. Near **Lawn Hill** look for tree stumps that have been carved into the shapes of animals and birds.

Naikoon Provincial Park

Just north of Tlell, 48 kilometers (30 miles) north of Queen Charlotte City, is the southern tip of Naikoon Provincial Park. While the park's main entrance is farther north out of Masset, visitors exploring the Tlell area will find interesting things to see and do here in the park's south end as well. The main attraction down here is the wreck of the *Pesuta*, a wooden log barge that ran aground in 1928. To get there, park at the picnic area on the north side of the Tlell River and follow the river to its mouth, then walk north along the beach. It's about six kilometers (3.7 miles) one-way. Keen hikers may want to attempt the **East Beach Hike,** a 94-kilometer (58-mile) trail that leads all the way north from the Tlell River to Tow Hill via Rose Spit.

Misty Meadows Campground (no reservations, June-mid-Sept., $18), immediately north of park headquarters, has around 30 sites but is usually uncrowded. Facilities include a picnic area and pit toilets.

Port Clements

Weather-beaten houses decorated with driftwood, shells, fishing floats, and other sea-washed treasures line the streets of this logging and fishing village on the shore of Masset Inlet. **Port Clements Museum** (45 Bayview Dr., 250/557-4255, 11am-4pm daily June-mid-Sept., adults $3) houses an intriguing selection of pioneer artifacts from the area, as well as black-and-white photos of logging camps and early village life.

Charlotte Main

This rough logging road links Port Clements to Queen Charlotte City via an inland route, a good alternative to returning via Tlell. To get to it, take Bayview Drive southwest out of Port Clements. Twelve kilometers (7.5 miles) from town, a short trail leads through the forest to an unfinished **Haida canoe,** estimated to have been abandoned around 100 years ago. Continuing south, the road passes through the **Juskatla** logging camp. From this point on, the logging road continues south to Queen Charlotte City. You are now driving on active logging roads, so travel is safest outside operating hours (7am-6pm Mon.-Fri.).

A signed turnoff to the west leads to **Rennell Sound,** the only point on the island's remote west coast accessible by road. At the end of the road await great beachcombing opportunities and free primitive campsites. The final descent to Rennell Sound is a hair-raising 24 percent gradient, one of the steepest public roads in North America.

MASSET AND VICINITY

Known as Graham City when founded in 1909, Masset (pop. 900) lies just south of a Haida community named Massett. Over time, Massett became known as Old Massett or Haida, and Graham City was incorporated as Masset (with one "t"). The population has decreased since downsizing began on the local Canadian Armed Forces Station, where at one time half the local population lived. Today, Masset's economy revolves around the ocean, with most workers involved in the fishing industry—either as fishers or as workers in the local fish canning and freezing plant.

Delkatla Wildlife Sanctuary

Bordering Masset to the east is Delkatla Wildlife Sanctuary, where you can observe Canada geese, sandhill cranes, trumpeter swans, great blue herons, many varieties of ducks, and other waterfowl resting during migration. Several short walking trails wind through the preserve near town; follow Hodges Avenue west onto Trumpeter Drive and continue alongside the inlet to the trailhead. For better views, drive along Tow Hill Road toward Naikoon Provincial Park, turning left at the sanctuary sign onto Masset Cemetery Road. Along this road, more signs mark trails or other points of interest. You first pass a turnout for the **Bird Walk Trail,** which winds along the edge of a marshy area. Then farther down the road, you come to **Simpson Viewing Tower,** where you may spy waterfowl, bald eagles, peregrine falcons, and other birds of prey, as well as four-legged marsh animals such as muskrats.

Back on Tow Hill Road, continue east to a parking lot and a trail to the beach. Just across from the parking lot is beautiful **Masset Cemetery,** where the graves are marked by large aboveground mounds of moss planted with flowering bulbs and surrounded by bushes and trees. It's a peaceful place to ponder the beauty of Haida Gwaii.

Old Massett

If you're in search of Haida treasures, head for the village of Old Massett, also known as Haida. It's just a five-minute drive from Masset, west down the coastal road. Go as far as the road takes you and you'll end up at the old blue schoolhouse, now **Ed Jones Haida Museum** (9am-5pm Sat.-Sun. summer, donation). Exhibits include a large collection of fascinating old photographs showing how the villages used to look, Haida art and prints, and some of the original totem poles from around Haida Gwaii. Outside, you'll find a partly completed canoe and a field sprinkled with more totems, these from a more recent era. Across from the museum is a carving shed where artists can be seen working throughout summer. Continue up behind the museum to the impressive weathered building with the two totem poles out front; this is **Sarah's Haida Arts and Jewelry** (387 Eagle Rd., 250/626-5560, 11am-5pm Mon.-Sat., noon-5pm Sun. July-Aug., 11am-5pm Mon.-Sat. Sept.-June), where you can buy custom argillite carvings, silk-screen prints, handcrafted silver and abalone jewelry, books on First Nations culture, and greeting cards.

Food

Even though Masset has a large fishing fleet, most of the catch ends up in mainland canneries. In town, **Island Sunrise Cafe** (1645 Main St., 250/626-9344, 7am-3pm daily, lunch $7-15) is a friendly little place with good coffee, simple lunches, and delicious halibut and chips in season. In the evening, the recommended choice for dinner is **Charters Restaurant** (1650 Delkatla Rd., 250/626-3377, 5pm-9pm Wed.-Sun., $18-26), a small, simply decorated dining room with a small menu that covers all bases.

In addition to these two recommendations, I also encourage you to head east from town to ★ **Moon Over Naikoon** (16750 Tow Hill Rd., 250/626-7737, 10am-6pm daily, lunch $6-8) for the quintessential island dining experience. Within a brightly painted school bus surrounded by old-growth forest, this café serves up hearty lunch specials, pours delicious coffee, and has a rush on their in-house baked cinnamon buns each morning.

Accommodations

Several B&Bs in Masset provide lodgings and local flavor. Next to the pier, rustic ★ **Copper Beech House** (1590 Delkatla Rd., 250/626-5441, www.copperbeechhouse.com, $110-150 s, $130-160 d) is a New England-style saltbox, decorated with sea treasures and with a beautiful flower garden. Rates include a delicious breakfast, and for an extra $30 pp, dinner is available.

With six contemporary guest rooms right

on the beach and backed by dense temperate rainforest of Sitka spruce, **Alaska View Lodge** (Tow Hill Rd., 250/626-3333 or 800/661-0019, www.langara.com, $155 s, $185 d), 12 kilometers (7.5 miles) east of Masset, is the choice of those looking for a piece of luxury in the wilderness. An oceanfront deck, an outdoor hot tub, and a communal lounge area add to the charm. Continuing toward Tow Hill, **Rapid Ritchie's Rustic Rentals** (250/626-5472, www.beachcabins.com, $80-160 s or d) is a much more rustic setup, with five cedar-shake cabins spread through the forest. If you can do without modern conveniences, you'll love this place—but be prepared for outhouses, no electricity, and no phones.

NAIKOON PROVINCIAL PARK

This wild coastal park encompasses some 72,640 hectares (179,500 acres) along the northeast tip of Graham Island. Tlell marks the park's southern boundary, while access to the northern reaches is via the road out to Tow Hill, 26 kilometers (16 miles) east of Masset. The park's dominant features are its beaches, 97 kilometers (60 miles) of them, bordering Hecate Strait on the east and the turbulent Dixon Entrance on the north. Most of the rest of the park is lowlands, surrounded by stunted lodgepole pine, red and yellow cedar, western hemlock, and Sitka spruce. Wildlife is abundant; black-tailed deer, black bears, marten, river otters, raccoons, red squirrels, beavers, muskrat, small herds of wild cattle, and many species of birds inhabit the park. Dolphins, orcas, porpoises, and seals swim offshore year-round, and northern fur seals and California gray whales migrate north past the park in May and June.

Sights

The drive out to the park from Masset is superb, passing through seemingly endless moss-draped trees. Along the way you pass **Tow Hill Ecological Reserve,** a beautiful spruce forest where birds tweet from the treetops, and the ground and most of the trees are completely cushioned by spongy yellow moss.

The road passes the base of Tow Hill and ends at the southern end of long, sandy **North Beach.** This strip of sand, strewn with shells, driftwood, and shiny sea-worn pebbles of every color under the sun, is a beachcomber's delight. The beach is best known for semi-precious agate, ranging from light yellow in color to almost translucent, which is found among piles of pebbles that become exposed at low tide starting about three kilometers (2 miles) along the beach. At the end of North Beach is **Rose Spit.** Known to the Haida as Naikoon, meaning "long nose," this narrow point of land separates the waters of Hecate Strait and Dixon Entrance. From the end of Tow Hill Road, it's about 10 kilometers (6.2 miles) of easy beach walking to the end of the spit; if you allow six hours for the round-trip, you'll have enough time to enjoy a picnic lunch among the driftwood along the way.

Head back toward Masset, along the beach from the end of the road, and **Tow Hill** is impossible to miss. A one-kilometer (0.6-mile) trail leads to the top of this 130-meter-high (430-foot) basalt monolith, or satisfy yourself with exploring the tidal pools at its base.

Cape Fife Trail

From near the end of the park access road, the **Cape Fife Trail** (3 hours one-way) heads in a southeasterly direction, passing bog lands and stunted pine trees on its 10-kilometer (6.2-mile) route to Fife Point, overlooking Hecate Strait. The shore above the high-tide line is blanketed by a mass of driftwood logs, crushed together during the fierce storms that regularly lash this coast. A rough shelter at the end of the trail provides some protection from the elements. Backcountry camping is permitted; hide among the trees on especially windy days. From this point you can hike north along the beach to Rose Spit, then continue back along North Beach to the parking lot at Hiellen River—a total of 34 kilometers (21 miles) and an easy two-day trip. Well-equipped adventurers can continue south from Fife Point along

East Beach to finish at Tlell, a total distance of 72 kilometers (45 miles). This has become a popular hike—take your time (allow 4-5 days) and bring adequate food and water.

Camping

Agate Beach Campground (no reservations, June-Sept., $18) is near Tow Hill, about 26 kilometers (16 miles) from Masset. The campsites lie along the back of the beach and offer outstanding views. A shelter and pit toilets are provided, but no showers. In summer you need to nab a spot early in the day—by late afternoon they're usually all taken. The campground is open year-round.

SANDSPIT AND VICINITY

Across Skidegate Channel from Queen Charlotte City, Sandspit (pop. 300) is the only community on Moresby Island. Home to the islands' main airport and linked to Graham Island by a short ferry trip, the town occupies a low-lying, windswept spit overlooking Shingle Bay. The northern half of Moresby Island is largely given over to logging, while the southern half and over 100 outlying islands fall within Gwaii Haanas National Park Reserve, which protects a high concentration of abandoned Haida villages.

Those determined to tour the forests in their own vehicle can make an enjoyable loop trip south out of Sandspit. Logging roads lace the forest, leading to beaches strewn with driftwood, streams alive with salmon and steelhead, and beautiful Skidegate and Mosquito Lakes, where you'll find good trout fishing. Free campgrounds are available at Gray Bay and Mosquito Lake.

Practicalities

Sandspit lacks the appeal of communities on Graham Island, but services are available. Friendly **Moresby Island Guest House** (385 Beach Rd., 250/637-5300, www.moresbyislandguesthouse.com, $60-95 s or d) is a popular kayakers' hangout across the road from Shingle Bay. Some of the 10 newly renovated rooms share baths, but everyone has use of a kitchen, laundry, and wide deck with water views. **Sandspit Visitor Centre** is a small desk inside the airport terminal (250/637-5362, 9am-11am and 1pm-4pm daily summer).

★ GWAII HAANAS NATIONAL PARK RESERVE

Renowned around the world for its ancient Haida villages dotted with totem poles, the **Gwaii Haanas National Park Reserve** (250/559-8818, www.pc.gc.ca) encompasses the southern half of Moresby Island as well as 137 smaller islands in the south of the archipelago—1,480 hectares (3,660 acres) of land and 1,600 kilometers (1,000 miles) of coastline. It's a remarkable place. Ancient, brooding totems and remnants of mighty Haida longhouses stand against a backdrop of lush wilderness: dense trees, thick spongy moss, and rock-strewn beaches with incredibly clear water. Colonies of nesting seabirds and an abundance of marinelife—killer and minke whales, sea lions, tufted puffins—all add to the atmosphere.

Jointly managed by Parks Canada and the Haida nation, the park was established in 1988 after a long bitter struggle between the Haida people and forestry companies. The area now protected was home to seafaring Haida for almost 10,000 years, but by the early 1900s, less than 100 years after their first contact with Europeans, their communities were abandoned, the inhabitants having been wiped out by disease or having moved to Old Massett and Skidegate.

Nan Sdins (Ninstints), on tiny SGaang Gwaii (Anthony Island) near the south end of the park, was once home to around 300 Haida people and had been occupied for thousands of years before the arrival of the Europeans. Today, weathered totem poles stretch along the shoreline, with the nearby ruins of cedar longhouses slowly being consumed by the surrounding rainforest. In 1981 Anthony Island was declared a UNESCO World Heritage Site, 97 years after the last Haida families had abandoned their remote home. Gandle K'in (Hotspring Island), the site of another abandoned village, has the bonus of oceanfront hot pools that held special healing and spiritual qualities to the Haida. Other well-known villages include Kuuna (Skedans), closest to Sandspit; T'aanuu (Tanu); and Hik'yah (Windy Bay).

Tours

Most park visitors travel as part a guided tour. Archipelago Ventures (604/652-4913 or 888/559-8317, www.tourhaidagwaii.com) combines the best of the park into a six-day tour ($2,900). The main mode of transportation is a stable 42-foot mother ship, with the focus on kayaking, hiking, and soaking up culture in the abandoned Haida villages, including Nan Sdins. Along the way, freshly caught shrimp and halibut create enticing meals. The turnaround point for these tours is Rose Harbour; travel is by boat in one direction and floatplane in the other, which allows for a relaxed pace in one direction and a spectacular ride above the park in the other. Ocean Light II Adventures (604/328-5339, www.oceanlight2.bc.ca) has been conducting sailing trips through the south end of the

archipelago since well before the proclamation of a park. Board the company's 71-foot *Ocean Light II* for eight days of sailing, visiting all the best-known abandoned Haida villages, exploring the waterways, and searching out land and sea mammals. All meals and accommodations aboard the boat are included in the rate ($4,000 pp).

Independent Travelers

If you aren't visiting the park as part of an organized tour, reserve a permit through Parks Canada (877/559-8818, www.pc.gc.ca, adults $20, seniors $18, children $9 per day) and participate in an orientation session (9am Mon.-Fri. June-early Sept., additional Sat. sessions July-Aug.)., held at the Haida Heritage Centre.

Moresby Explorers (250/637-2215 or 800/806-7633, www.moresbyexplorers.com) provides drop-offs and pickups for those heading into the park unguided. Expect to pay around $800 for two people for a week's kayak rental, use of a VHF radio, and boat transportation to and from road-accessible Moresby Camp. Inland Air (250/624-2577, www.inlandair.bc.ca) is a floatplane operation based at the wharf in Queen Charlotte City. It offers flightseeing tours to Ninstints and Skedans.

Stewart-Cassiar Highway

An alternative to the Alaska Highway, this route—often referred to simply as "the Cassiar"—spurs north off the Yellowhead Highway 45 kilometers (28 miles) west of New Hazelton and leads north to the Yukon, joining the Alaska Highway just west of Watson Lake. The highway opens up a magnificent area of northern wilderness that in many ways rivals that along the more famous Alaska Highway. The highlight of the Stewart-Cassiar Highway is definitely the side trip west to the twin coastal villages of Stewart and Hyder.

From the Yellowhead Highway it's 155 kilometers (96 miles) north to Meziadin Junction, then 65 kilometers (40 miles) west to Stewart,

official beginning of the Stewart-Cassiar Highway. The total length of the trip between the Yellowhead and Alaska Highways is 733 kilometers (455 miles), excluding the 130 kilometers (80 miles) round-trip for the jaunt to Stewart.

FROM YELLOWHEAD HIGHWAY TO MEZIADIN JUNCTION

Tree-covered hills, dense patches of snow-white daisies, banks of pink-and-white clover and purple lupine, craggy mountains and distant peaks, beautiful lakes covered in yellow water lilies, and lots of logging trucks flying along the road—these are images of the 155 kilometers (96 miles) between the Yellowhead Highway and Meziadin Junction, the turnoff to Stewart.

Kitwanga

This small village just north of the Yellowhead Highway is home to **Gitwangak Battle Hill Historic Site** (Kitwanga North Rd., year-round, free), the first national historic site commemorating First Nations culture in western Canada. The site protects 13-meter-high (43-foot-high) Battle Hill, where in the early 1800s a First Nations warrior named Nekt fought off attacks from hostile neighbors. A trail leads from the parking lot down to the flat area around the bottom of the hill, where you can read display panels describing the hill's history.

Gitanyow Totem Poles

Continuing north, you're paralleling what was commonly called the Grease Trail, the route the earliest coastal people took to the interior to trade their *oolichan* (tiny oily fish) with other communities. At the First Nations village of Gitanyow (also called Kitwancool), 23 kilometers (14 miles) from Kitwanga, is the world's greatest remaining concentration of totem poles still in their original location. The oldest, *Hole in the Ice,* is approximately 140 years old; some say it's the oldest standing totem pole in the world. It tells the story of a man preventing his people from starving by chopping a hole in the ice and doing a spot of ice fishing.

STEWART AND HYDER

At Meziadin Junction is 335-hectare (830-acre) **Meziadin Lake Provincial Park** (519/826-6850 or 800/689-9025, www.discovercamping.ca, mid-May-mid-Sept., $22), one of the most picturesque camping spots along the Cassiar, including some sites right on the lakeshore. The campground has a concession selling fishing tackle, and the operator offers guided fishing trips ($80 per hour).

From Meziadin Junction, Stewart is 65 kilometers (40 miles) west along a spectacular stretch of highway that crosses the glaciated Coast Mountains. The first 40 kilometers (25 miles) is all uphill, through thick subalpine forests and past lakes, waterfalls, and a string of glaciers sitting like thick icy slabs atop almost-vertical mountains. Suddenly, and quite unexpectedly, the highway rounds a corner and there in front of you is magnificent, intensely blue **Bear Glacier.** The glacier

Bear Glacier

Life in Stewart and Hyder

RESIDENTS OF STEWART AND HYDER . . .

- Send their kids to school in Canada.
- Are supplied power by BC Hydro.
- Use the Canadian phone system (area code 250).
- Are policed by the Royal Canadian Mounted Police.
- Never have to wait for a drink; Hyder has one bar for every 30 residents.

TIPS FOR VISITORS

- Buy your booze in Hyder; it's cheaper (but is only tax-free if you have been in town for more than 48 hours).
- Watch for bears; they often wander along the streets.
- Use Canadian currency in both towns.
- Post your mail on whichever side of the border saves the cost of international postage.
- Bring your passport; border checks are made when reentering Canada.
- Don't miss the drive to Salmon Glacier.

tumbles down into small Strohn Lake, where small icebergs float across the surface in the breeze. From Bear Glacier it's downhill all the way to Stewart. Keep an eye out for three mighty waterfalls on the north side of the highway, one after another.

The twin towns of Stewart (Canada) and Hyder (United States) are separated by an international border, but you'd hardly know it. Crossing into Hyder comes without any of the formalities or checkpoints you'd expect at a border—until the mid-1990s there were no border checks at all. Now, upon reentering Canada, an ATCO trailer serves as the port of entry, mostly in place to check for cheap U.S. booze purchased at the Hyder liquor store.

Stewart

The twin towns of Stewart, British Columbia, and Hyder, Alaska, straddle the international boundary at the headwaters of the **Portland Canal,** the world's fourth-longest fjord. Stewart (pop. 500) enjoys a stunning setting, with snowcapped peaks rising abruptly

from the surrounding fjord. After a 1910 gold strike, Stewart's population mushroomed to 10,000. But the boom was short-lived, and what's left of the local economy now revolves around the lumber industry. To get the low-down on the town's interesting past, head to **Stewart Historical Museum,** in the original Government Agent Building (703 Brightwell St., 250/636-2229, 9am-5pm Mon.-Fri., noon-4pm Sat.-Sun. May-Sept., donation). Displays include an exhibit on the town's boom-and-bust mining industry and a room filled with memorabilia from Hollywood movies filmed in town, including *Leaving Normal* and *Insomnia,* starring Robin Williams.

The premier lodging is the **Ripley Creek Inn** (306 5th Ave., 250/636-2344, www.ripley-creekinn.com, $115-155 s or d), a funky collection of guest rooms in historic buildings centrally located to downtown. One is an old hotel, another was once home to a brothel, another is above the Bitter Creek Café. All rooms have modern baths, and most are in a contemporary style. Those in the main lodge overlook the estuary and have wireless Internet. Nestled below the towering peaks of the Coast Mountains at the back of town is **Rainey Creek Campground** (8th Ave., 250/636-2537, $22-26), with coin-operated showers and firewood sales.

Along the main street is a string of good dining options, including **Temptations Bakery** (307 5th Ave., 250/636-2777, 6am-5pm June-Aug., shorter hours Sept.-May, lunch $10-14), where the bread is baked daily and which cooks up the best breakfasts in town. When Temptations is closed, head next door to **Silverado Café & Pizza** (309 5th Ave., 250/636-2737, 4pm-10pm Mon.-Sat., $15-22) for surprisingly good pizza at reasonable prices. Outside of summer, these two places combine their hours so one is always open; call ahead for hours. In an old three-story building beside Silverado, **Bitter Creek Café** (311 5th Ave., 250/636-2166, 2:30pm-11pm July-Aug., $18-28) serves creative meals through summer afternoons and evenings.

Stewart Visitor Centre (222 5th Ave., 250/636-9224, 10am-5pm daily June, 9am-5pm daily July-early Sept.) overlooks the estuary at the north end of 5th Avenue. The staff offers a wealth of local information, including directions out to Salmon Glacier, hiking-trail brochures, and history sheets.

★ Hyder

Continue through Stewart along the Portland Canal, and next thing you know you've crossed an international border and you're in Hyder, Alaska—without all the formalities and checkpoints you'd expect at an international border. The "Friendliest Little Ghost Town in Alaska" is a classic end-of-the-road town, with a population of 90 people, unpaved roads, and a motley assortment of buildings. Local residents send their kids to school in Canada and use the Canadian phone system. Everyone sets their clocks to Pacific time (except the postmaster, who's on Alaska time). Prices are quoted in Canadian dollars (except for that same postmaster, who only accepts U.S. currency). Finally, no one ever has to wait for a drink: Hyder has one bar for every 30 residents.

Soak up the historic charm of Hyder by wandering the main street and poking your nose in the few remaining businesses. Join the tradition and tack a bill to the wall of the **Glacier Inn** (Main St., 250/636-9248, 10am-10pm daily summer, shorter hours fall-spring) to ensure that you won't return broke, then toss back a shot of 190-proof, pure grain alcohol in one swallow to qualify for your "I've Been Hyderized" card. The Glacier Inn is also the best place in town to eat, with halibut and chips highly recommended.

At the end of the main drag, head left out to the wharf, where the mountain panorama extends for 360 degrees. Head right and you're on the way to **Fish Creek,** the most accessible place in all of North America to watch bears feasting on salmon (late July-Sept.).

If you want to stay the night in Hyder, choose between very, very basic rooms at the **Sealaska Inn** (250/636-9006, www.sealaskainn.com, $42-79 s, $48-89 s or d), set up your tent at the adjacent campground ($18), or pull up your rig into the parking lot up the road ($28-34). If you want to stay forever, marry a local.

The Road to Salmon Glacier

Continuing beyond Hyder, the unpaved road continues up Fish Creek, passing an abandoned mining operation and then the ruins of a covered bridge that provided access to a remote mine up the Texas Creek watershed. From this point the road narrows considerably and becomes increasingly steep (travel is not recommended for RVs), crossing back into Canada and winding through former living quarters for the abandoned gold and mineral ore Premier Mine. The road makes a loop around tailing ponds and continues climbing steeply, with **Salmon Glacier** first coming into view 25 kilometers (16 miles) from Hyder. The road parallels the glacier and climbs to a high point after another 10 kilometers (6 miles), where the best lookout point is. This glacier, fifth largest in North America but also one of the most accessible, is one of British Columbia's most awesome sights, snaking for many kilometers through the highest peaks of the Coast Mountains.

NORTH OF MEZIADIN JUNCTION
Meziadin to Dease Lake

Around 100 kilometers (62 miles) from the junction, **Bell II Lodge** (250/275-4770 or 888/499-4354, www.bell2lodge.com, camping $25-39, $175-220 s or d) comes into view. It's the winter base for Last Frontier Heli-skiing but through the rest of the year is a lot more than a spot to spend the night before heading north. Fishing is the biggest attraction, especially is summer for chinook salmon and late September-early November for steelhead. Also here is a café and restaurant (8am-8pm daily summer, $18-26) and a bar. The lodge sells all the fishing tackle you'll need and offers a variety of daily guiding services, including heli-fishing and heli-hiking.

At the 200-kilometer (124-mile) mark is 1,800-hectare (4,450-acre) **Kinaskan Lake Provincial Park** (mid-May-Sept., camping $20), known for its hungry rainbow trout. In the south of the park, a trail leads one kilometer (0.6 miles) to another reliable fishing hole, **Natadesleen Lake,** then another one kilometer (0.6 miles) along an overgrown trail to beautiful tiered **Cascade Falls.**

The small Tahltan town of **Iskut** has a post office, gas station, and **Tatogga Lake Resort** (Hwy. 37, 250/643-2575, www.tatogga.com, May-Oct., camping $20, cabins and motel rooms $50-80 s or d, restaurant 7am-midnight daily). Continuing north, the highway runs through the **Stikine River Provincial Park,** a long and narrow 217,000-hectare (536,200-acre) park straddling the Stikine River. The park also links **Spatsizi Plateau Provincial Park** and **Mount Edziza Provincial Park.** Spatsizi Plateau is British Columbia wilderness at its wildest—656,780 hectares (1.6 million acres) of broad plateaus, stunning glacier-capped peaks, roaring rivers, and fish-filled lakes. Wildlife abounds: Grizzly bears, moose, wolves, wolverines, mountain goats, woodland caribou, and more than 100 species of birds are all present, but access is by foot or floatplane only. Mount Edziza Provincial Park protects a moonlike volcanic landscape, above the tree line and dominated by 2,787-meter (9,140-foot) **Mount Edziza,** an extinct volcano whose glaciated crater is over two kilometers (1.2 miles) wide.

The small community of **Dease Lake,** on

Salmon Glacier

the shores of its namesake lake 65 kilometers (40 miles) north of Iskut, provides basic tourist services, including gas and groceries.

Telegraph Creek

From Dease Lake, an unsealed road leads 119 kilometers (74 miles) west along the Tanzilla River to Telegraph Creek (pop. 300), which lies on a terraced hill overlooking the Stikine River. The town boasts friendly people, gorgeous scenery, and heritage buildings dating to the 1860s. The only services in town are offered by **The Stikine** (250/235-3004, www.tahltan.ca), on the main street through town, comprising a general store and café (8am-7pm daily) and a few motel rooms ($125 s or d). A 20-kilometer (13-mile) road leads west from town to **Glenora,** which had 10,000 residents in its gold rush heyday. Nowadays, only one or two of the original buildings remain.

Continuing to the Alaska Highway

As you continue north from the turnoff to Telegraph Creek, the road parallels the east shore of Dease Lake. Good campsites are found by the lake, along with the occasional chunk of jade on the lakeshore—the area has been called the jade capital of the world. From Dease Lake to the Alaska Highway it's clear sailing for 235 kilometers (146 miles) along the northern slopes of the Cassiar Mountains.

The next worthwhile stop is 4,597-hectare (11,360-acre) **Boya Lake Provincial Park,** 150 kilometers (92 miles) north of Dease Lake. White, claylike beaches ring the incredibly clear lake. Walking along the shoreline is worthwhile, or take the short hiking trail that leads to an active beaver pond. The park also has a primitive campground (no reservations, mid-May-mid-Sept., $20). From Boya Lake, the highway traverses the Liard Plain across the border and into the Yukon. From the border it's another four kilometers (2.5 miles) to the junction of the Alaska Highway, then 21 kilometers (13 miles) east to Watson Lake.

Prince George to the Alaska Highway

Most travelers use the route north from Prince George to access Mile Zero of the Alaska Highway at Dawson Creek. But this direct route, a distance of 405 kilometers (252 miles), bypasses the region's highlight at **Hudson's Hope,** halfway between Chetwynd and Fort St. John. Whichever route you take, there's plenty to see and do, with interesting provincial parks and towns offering northern hospitality.

TO HUDSON'S HOPE

The first worthwhile stop along Highway 97 is 970-hectare (2,300-acre) **Crooked River Provincial Park,** 80 kilometers (50 miles) north of Prince George. The park's centerpiece is Bear Lake, which is encircled by a hiking trail that passes a sandy beach, a forested picnic area, and a spur trail to Square Lake.

At the end of the park access road, a largish campground has 65 well-spaced sites on two loops (519/826-6850 or 800/689-9025, www.discovercamping.ca, mid-May-early Sept., $22), easy access to a beach, pit toilets, drinking water, and a playground.

Carp Lake Provincial Park lies 140 kilometers (87 miles) north of Prince George, then 32 kilometers (20 miles) west (turn off at McLeod Lake) along a sometimes rough unsealed road. The park's epicenter is Carp Lake, a picturesque body renowned for its rainbow trout fishing (although you really need a canoe or motorboat to get out to the best fishing grounds). Despite its name, you won't catch carp—the lake was named by explorer Simon Fraser, who noted that the Carrier people journeyed to the lake for fish "of the carp kind." The park holds two campgrounds

Dinosaurs in the Peace River Valley

During construction of Peace Canyon Dam, fossilized remains of the plesiosaur, a marine reptile, were discovered. This wasn't the first time evidence of prehistoric life had been discovered in the Peace River Valley. As early as 1922, dinosaur footprints over 100 million years old were found in the area where Hudson's Hope now lies. The footprints belonged to several species of dinosaurs, most common among them the hadrosaur. This plant-eater was around 10 meters (33 feet) long and weighed about four tons. It was amphibious but preferred the land, walking around on its hind legs ever-alert for the ancestors of the dreaded tyrannosaurus.

Footprints are as important as skeletons in unraveling the mysteries of dinosaurs. They provide clues about the ratios of various dinosaurs in a particular area, and information on herds and how they traveled. Most of the 1,500 dinosaur footprints discovered in the valley have been excavated and transported to museums throughout Canada (a couple are on display in the Hudson's Hope Museum). Plant and shell fossils can still be found. The best time for searching them out is after heavy rain—try looking downstream from the dam (a few short trails lead from the highway into the canyon, but it's a bit of a scramble).

(519/826-6850 or 800/689-9025, www.discovercamping.ca, mid-May-early Sept., $20) with facilities limited to pit toilets, picnic tables, and fire rings. The larger of the two, right on Carp Lake, is a 15-minute walk to a sandy beach inaccessible by road.

To Powder King

The forestry town of **Mackenzie** (pop. 3,500) lies 180 kilometers (112 miles) north of Prince George on the southern arm of massive Williston Lake, North America's largest artificial reservoir. At the town's entrance is the world's largest tree crusher, used during that logging operation. Nearby **Morfee Lake** has swimming off a sandy beach. Take the logging road to the summit of Morfee Hill for lake views. Stay in a regular motel room at **Williston Lake Lodge** (305 Mackenzie Blvd., 250/997-3131, www.willistonlakelodge.com, $105-140 s or d), some with kitchenettes, or park your rig at **Mackenzie Municipal RV Park** (10 Cicada Dr., $22-26), which has showers and hookups.

Continuing east toward Chetwynd, the landscape becomes more dramatic as the highway climbs steadily up the western slopes of the Rocky Mountains. Near Pine Pass, **Powder King** (250/964-0645, www.powderking.com, Thurs.-Sun. Dec.-mid-Apr.) is a remote skiing and boarding destination legendary for its incredible snowfall—over 12 meters (40 feet) annually. One triple chair and two surface lifts serve a vertical rise of 640 meters (2,100 feet) and 600 hectares (1,500 acres). Lift tickets are adults $67, seniors $50, children $32.

Chetwynd

The touristy highlight of Chetwynd (pop. 2,600), at the junction of Highways 97 and 29, are over 150 log sculptures carved with chainsaws, many of which line the highway through town. If you happen to be visiting Chetwynd the second weekend of June, the **Chetwynd International Chainsaw Carving Championship** is well worth attending. Champion carvers from around the world have 35 hours to carve a 2.5-meter-long (8-foot) slab of cedar—and the results are incredible, ranging from bears to benches.

Beside Highway 97, **Pine Inn & Suites** (5224 53rd St., 250/788-3311 or 800/663-8082, www.pineconeinn.ca, $99-129 s, $109-129 d) has 54 largish air-conditioned rooms with comfortable beds, including a few kitchenettes. Out front of the motel is the **Riverhouse Restaurant** (5224 53rd St., 250/788-1038, 8am-10pm daily, $15-26). The menu is exactly what you expect at this latitude, but portions are good and the dining arrangements are comfortable. Around 16 kilometers (10 miles) west of town, **Caron Creek RV Park** (7537 Hwy. 97, 250/788-2522, $20-30) has pull-through sites, laundry, showers, and a picturesque setting. **Chetwynd Visitor Centre** (5217 N. Access Rd., 250/788-1943, www.gochetwynd.com, 8am-4:30pm Mon.-Fri.) is in a railway caboose beside the highway through town to the south.

HUDSON'S HOPE

This small town of 1,000 is the only settlement between Chetwynd and Fort St. John. Founded as a fur-trading post in 1805, it is a picturesque spot with two nearby dams attracting the most attention.

Sights

Across from the log building holding the **Hudson's Hope Visitor Centre** (9555 Beattie Dr., 250/783-9154, 8:30am-5pm daily May-Sept.) is **Hudson's Hope Museum** (9510 Beattie Dr., 250/783-5735, 9am-5pm daily May-Sept., 9am-4:30pm Mon.-Fri. Oct.-Apr., donation), comprising historic buildings such as a trapper's cabin and the log-walled St. Peter's Church, that were moved to the site from throughout the Peace River Valley. The site itself is of some historical significance: Simon Fraser spent the winter of 1805-1806 here.

W. A. C. Bennett Dam, seven kilometers (4 miles) west of town, is one of the world's largest earth-filled structures. The 183-meter-high (600-foot) structure backs up

Williston Lake, British Columbia's largest lake, which extends more than 300 kilometers (186 miles) along three flooded valleys. At the top of the dam's control building is **W. A. C. Bennett Dam Visitor Centre** (250/783-5048, 10am-5pm daily late mid-May-Aug.). Guided bus tours (adults $6, seniors and children $5) of the inner workings of the dam depart from the visitors center six times daily. The much smaller **Peace Canyon Dam** is downstream from Bennett Dam, nine kilometers (5.5 miles) south of Hudson's Hope on Highway 29. Although there is no public access, you can wander up to the outside observation deck.

Accommodations and Camping

Neither of the town's accommodations is outstanding, but the **Sportsman Inn** (10101 Beattie Dr., 250/783-5523, $100 s or d) has the biggest rooms and an in-house pub and restaurant. The town has three municipal campgrounds (June-Sept., $20). Closest to civilization is **King Gething Campground,** on the south end of town, which has flush toilets, coin-operated showers, and plenty of firewood. **Alwin Holland Park,** southeast of town, is more primitive (pit toilets) but is off the main highway and has some nice hiking trails. The third, **Dinosaur Lake Campground,** seven kilometers (4 miles) southeast, has pit toilets, firewood, and good fishing and swimming.

Alaska Highway

When the Japanese threatened invasion of Canada and the United States during World War II, the Alaska Highway was quickly built to link Alaska with the Lower 48. It was the longest military road ever constructed in North America—an unsurpassed road-construction feat stretching 2,288 kilometers (1,422 miles) between Dawson Creek and Delta Junction, Alaska.

Construction began March 9, 1942, and was completed, incredibly, on November 20 that same year. In less than nine months troops had bulldozed a rough trail snaking like a crooked finger through almost impenetrable muskeg and forest, making literally hundreds of detours around obstacles and constructing 133 bridges. At a cost of more than $140 million, the highway was the major

Alaska Highway

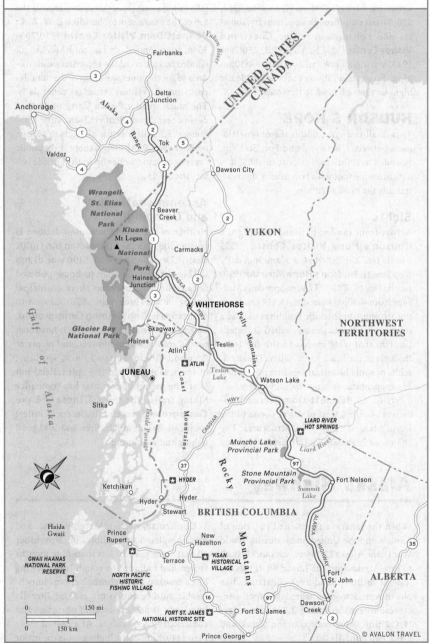

© AVALON TRAVEL

contributing factor to the growth of northern British Columbia in the 1940s. At the height of construction, the region's population boomed. Dawson Creek's population alone rose from 600 to over 10,000, and Whitehorse replaced Dawson City as a more convenient capital of the Yukon.

Driving the highway was notoriously difficult in its earliest days. Highway travelers returned with tales of endless mud holes and dust, washed-out bridges, flat tires, broken windshields and smashed headlights, wildlife in the road, mosquitoes the size of hummingbirds, and sparse facilities. But they also sported "I drove the Alaska Highway" bumper stickers as though they'd won a prize. Nowadays the route doesn't merit quite the bravado—it's paved most of the way, has roadside lodges fairly frequently, and can easily be driven in three days, or two in a pinch. What hasn't changed is the scenery. You'll still see kilometer after kilometer of unspoiled wilderness, including boreal forests of spruce and aspen, the majestic snow-dusted peaks of the northern Canadian Rockies, and gorgeous rivers and streams (and you can still buy the bumper stickers).

Although official signage along the Alaska Highway is in kilometers, many services are marked in miles, a legacy of imperial measurement. This only becomes confusing when you consider that highway improvements have shortened the original route. For example, Liard River Hot Springs is still marked as Mile 496, though it's now only 462 miles (754 kilometers) from Dawson Creek.

DAWSON CREEK

Although Dawson Creek (pop. 13,000) marks the southern end of the Alaska Highway, it's still a long way north—over 1,200 kilometers (746 miles) north of Vancouver. While the city thrives on its historic location at Mile Zero, it's also an important service center whose economy is more closely tied to neighboring Alberta, a few kilometers to the east, than to British Columbia.

Sights

Upon entering town, make **Northern Alberta Railway (NAR) Park** on the corner of Highway 2 and the Alaska Highway your first stop. Here you'll find **Dawson Creek Visitor Centre** (900 Alaska Ave., 250/782-9595, 9am-5pm daily late-May-Aug., 10am-4:30pm Mon.-Fri. Sept.-May), an art gallery, and the **Mile Zero Cairn,** the Alaska Highway's official starting point. (The original marker was mowed down by a car in the 1940s). The wooden banner above the cairn reads "You are now entering the world famous Alaska Highway." The visitors center is housed in the original 1931 Northern Alberta Railway station, and offers exhibits on a wide variety of topics, including construction of the Alaska Highway, the area's railroad history, pioneer life, and local flora and fauna. In the annex of the towering grain elevator adjacent to the museum is the **Dawson Creek Art Gallery** (816 Alaska Ave., 250/782-2601, 9am-5pm daily late-May-Aug., 10am-5pm Tues.-Fri. Sept.-May, free). The elevator itself is fascinating. It was saved from demolition and redesigned with a spiral walkway around the interior walls to make the most of the building's height.

Despite the cairn's official status, the **Mile Zero Signpost** in the center of 102nd Avenue at 10th Street is more often photographed. It notes the following distances: Fort St. John, 48 miles; Fort Nelson, 300 miles; Whitehorse, 918 miles; Delta Junction, 1,398 miles, and Fairbanks, 1,523 miles. At this intersection is **Alaska Highway House** (10201 10th St., 250/782-4714, 9am-5pm daily late-May-Aug., 10am-4:30pm Mon.-Fri. Sept.-May, free), a small but wonderful museum dedicated to the building of the highway. To put the enormity of the construction project into perspective, watch the short documentary screened on demand.

Food

The distinctive wooden facade across from the Mile Zero Signpost announces **Hug a Mug** (1012 102nd Ave., 250/782-6659, 7:30am-4pm

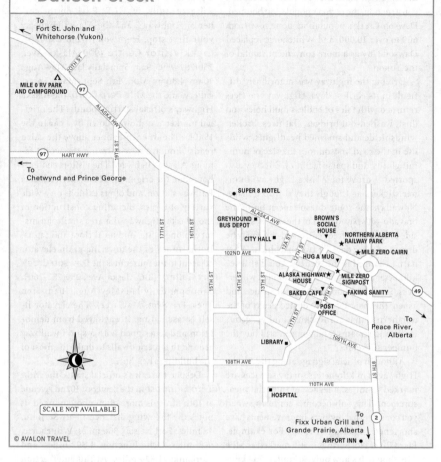

Dawson Creek

To
Fort St. John and
Whitehorse (Yukon)

20TH ST

MILE 0 RV PARK
AND CAMPGROUND

97

ALASKA HWY

19TH ST

97   HART HWY

To
Chetwynd and Prince George

SUPER 8 MOTEL

ALASKA AVE

17TH ST   16TH ST

GREYHOUND
BUS DEPOT

CITY HALL

102ND AVE

BROWN'S
SOCIAL
HOUSE

12A ST   12TH ST

NORTHERN ALBERTA
RAILWAY PARK

MILE ZERO CAIRN

HUG A MUG

15TH ST   14TH ST   13TH ST

ALASKA HIGHWAY
HOUSE

MILE ZERO
SIGNPOST

10TH ST

BAKED CAFE

FAKING SANITY

POST
OFFICE

11TH ST

To
Peace River,
Alberta

49

LIBRARY

106TH AVE

108TH AVE

8TH ST

110TH AVE

HOSPITAL

SCALE NOT AVAILABLE

To
Fixx Urban Grill and
Grande Prairie, Alberta

2

© AVALON TRAVEL

AIRPORT INN

Mon.-Fri., 9am-4pm Sat., lunch $7-11), a welcoming café where the soups are made from scratch and sandwiches and wraps made to order. One block south, **Faking Sanity** (901 103rd Ave., 250/782-8811, 11am-6pm Mon.-Wed., 11am-9pm Thurs., 11am-6pm Fri., 10am-5pm Sat., lunch $8-13) is part café, part used bookstore. Sweet treats such as the carrot cake are especially good.

For a well-priced meal in pleasant surroundings, **Brown's Social House** (1100 Alaska Ave., 250/782-2400, 11am-midnight Mon.-Fri., 10am-midnight Sat.-Sun., $16-29)

is a good option. A menu of standard pub fare is dotted with more exotic choices, such as a blackened halibut burger. With the same neighborhood pub feeling is **Fixx Urban Grill** (512 Hwy. 2, 250/782-3006, 11am-11pm daily, $15-36), on the south side of town. Menu choices range from a sweet chili salmon burger to beef tenderloin topped with Cajun-battered prawns.

Accommodations and Camping

Unfortunately, Dawson Creek's oldest and

and tent sites, an RV wash, free showers, and laundry.

Information

An almost obligatory stop for travelers heading north on the famous highway is **Dawson Creek Visitor Centre** (900 Alaska Ave., 250/782-9595, www.tourismdawsoncreek.com, 9am-5pm daily late-May-Aug., 10am-4:30pm Mon.-Fri. Sept.-Apr.), in the railway station at NAR Park.

Getting There

Reaching Dawson Creek by road is easy—it just takes a long time. To get there from Vancouver, head up Highway 1 and then Highway 97, allowing at least two days to complete the 1,200-kilometer (746-mile) run. The only major city en route is Prince George, which is 400 kilometers (250 miles) southwest of Dawson Creek.

FORT ST. JOHN

As the second-largest community along the Alaska Highway (only Whitehorse, Yukon, is larger), Fort St. John (pop. 18,500), 72 kilometers (45 miles) northwest of Dawson Creek, is an important service center for local industries, including oil, gas, and coal extraction; forestry; and agriculture. It's one of the province's oldest European settlements—the Beaver and Sekani peoples both occupied the area when European traders arrived in the 1790s—and it served as a fur-trading post until 1823. But it wasn't until construction of the Alaska Highway began that Fort St. John really boomed.

Sights

Fort St. John-North Peace Museum (9323 100th St., 250/787-0430, 8am-8pm daily summer, 9am-5pm Mon.-Sat. fall-spring, adults $6, seniors $5, students $4) is difficult to miss as you drive through town—look for the outside exhibits, including a 40-meter-tall (130-foot) oil derrick. In the museum, local history springs to life with reconstructed historical interiors. A trapper's cabin recalls the original

The Mile Zero Signpost is in the heart of downtown.

most colorful lodging, the Alaska Hotel, burned to the ground in 2012, leaving travelers looking for simple overnight accommodations no choice but to book at either an older roadside motel like the **Airport Inn** (800 120th Ave., 250/782-9404, www.airportinndawsoncreek.com, $99 s or d) or one of the chains, such as the **Super 8 Motel** (1440 Alaska Ave., 250/782-8899 or 800/800-8000, www.super8.com, $150-300 s or d).

Mile 0 Campground (1901 Alaska Ave., 250/782-2590, www.mile0park.ca, May-Sept., $30-45) isn't at Mile Zero of the famous highway—it's about one kilometer (0.6 miles) north from downtown—but it's the pick of Dawson Creek's numerous campgrounds. Sites sit around a large shaded grassy area, and each one has a picnic table. Facilities include hot showers and laundry, and there's an adjacent Pioneer Village that's free to walk around. Take Highway 97S west from town to reach **Northern Lights RV Park** (250/782-9433, www.nlrv.com, May-Oct., $28-45), which holds a tight mix of RV

Rocky Mountain fort and fur-trading days, while the pioneer days are commemorated in fully furnished rooms, including a kitchen, a bedroom, a schoolroom, a dentist's office, a post office, an outpost hospital, and a blacksmith's shop. Don't miss the fur press, the birch-bark canoe, and the grizzly bear with claws big enough to send shivers up your spine.

Peace River Canyon Lookout provides splendid panoramic views taking in the wide deep-green Peace River, its rocky canyon walls, and the lush fields along the canyon rim. From the museum, head south along 100th Street, crossing the Alaska Highway and continuing along the gravel road, which ends at the edge of the canyon.

Food

Steer off the highway to the town's original main street and you'll find spacious and stylish **Whole Wheat & Honey** (10003 100th St., 250/787-9866, 6am-4pm Mon.-Fri., 9am-4pm Sat., lunch $6-11), a real treat this far north. All the food is prepared from scratch, including daily soup specials, and the coffee is as good as it gets in town.

My favorite place to eat dinner in Fort St. John isn't in town, but 6.5 kilometers (4 miles) north at Mile 52 of the Alaska Highway. ★ **Jackfish Dundee's** (250/785-3233, 11am-10pm daily, $14-26) is in a big wooden building that has an inviting atmosphere and lake views. The food is delicious and well-priced. Start with calamari with a tangy lemon dill sauce and choose from mains such as salmon baked on a cedar plank and veal manicotti.

Accommodations and Camping

One of the least expensive motels along the highway is **Blue Belle Motel** (9705 Alaska Hwy., 250/785-2613, $85 s, $95 d), where basic rooms have microwaves and coffeemakers, while guests also have use of a barbecue and laundry facility.

The seven-story ★ **Stonebridge Hotel** (9830 100th Ave., 250/263-6881 or 888/419-4657, www.stonebridgefortstjohn.com,

$139-169 s or d) is a modern, full-service hotel with regularly revamped rooms and a restaurant. It's also centrally located one block from the Alaska Highway and a similar distance from the visitors center and Centennial Park.

Two small provincial parks with campgrounds lie along the shoreline of Charlie Lake, just over six kilometers (4 miles) north of town. **Charlie Lake Provincial Park** (519/826-6850 or 800/689-9025, www.discovercamping.ca, mid-May-Aug., $20), at the junction of the Alaska Highway and Highway 29, is mainly a campground, while 312-hectare (770-acre) **Beatton Provincial Park,** on the lake's east shoreline, features beautiful aspen-lined hiking trails, a beach, boating, fishing, and swimming, but a smaller **campground** (519/826-6850 or 800/689-9025, www.discovercamping.ca, mid-May-Aug., $20). For more facilities, check in to the **Rotary RV Park** (13016 Lakeshore Dr., Charlie Lake, 250/785-1700, www.rotaryrvparkfsj.com, tents $19, hookups $29-38). Amenities include hot showers and laundry, and it's within walking distance of a general store and Jackfish Dundee's restaurant.

Information

Fort St. John Visitor Centre (9324 96th St., 250/785-3033, www.fortstjohn.ca, 8am-7pm Mon.-Fri. and 9am-6pm Sat.-Sun. summer, 9am-5pm Mon.-Fri. Sept.-mid-May) is in the impressive Pomeroy Sport Centre, between the Alaska Highway and downtown.

TO FORT NELSON

The 374-kilometer (232-mile) stretch of the Alaska Highway between Fort St. John and Fort Nelson passes through boreal forest and a landscape that becomes more and more mountainous. It also provides one of your best chances of spotting wildlife, especially if you travel in the cool of the early morning. Species you may spy are moose, grizzly and black bears, deer, elk, and bison.

From Wonowon, the highway climbs

Digging Up the Past

Overlooking Charlie Lake is **Charlie Lake Cave,** where buffalo bones and artifacts such as stone tools, a fluted basalt spear point, and a handmade stone bead have been discovered. Hunters may have hid there while chasing buffalo. Dated at 10,500 years old, this is the oldest such site discovered on the continent, leading archaeologists to postulate that this area was one of the earliest North American sites occupied by humans.

During the period of earliest occupation, Charlie Lake was a much larger body of water, an enormous ice-dammed lake where larger mammals were common. In the ensuing centuries, silt has built up on the floor of the cave, decreasing its original size. The cave is on private property. Although access is not possible, a display in the Fort St. John-North Peace Museum tells the story of the cave dwellers and the archaeologists who excavated the site.

steadily to **Pink Mountain,** at Mile 147. Numerous services perch on the low summit, where snow can fall year-round. On the west side of the highway, **Pink Mountain Campsite** (250/772-5133) provides tent and RV sites for $28 (power hookups).

Sikanni Chief to Prophet River

The next services are 30 kilometers (19 miles) north of Pink Mountain at **Sikanni River Campground** (250/772-5400, www.sikannirivercampground.ca, tents $20, hookups $30-40, basic cabins $50-75 s or d). Twenty kilometers (13 miles) north from Sikanni Chief, you'll pass the small **Buckinghorse River Wayside Provincial Park.** The river is alive with arctic grayling, providing the perfect meal for campers (no reservations, June-Aug., $20). From here north, a newer, scenic stretch of the highway runs through **Minaker River Valley,** then parallels the **Prophet River,** passing a rustic campground (May-Sept., $16) where a short hiking trail leads down to the river.

FORT NELSON

At Mile 300 of the Alaska Highway, 454 kilometers (281 miles) north of Dawson Creek, Fort Nelson (pop. 4,000) is the largest town between Fort St. John and the Yukon. The earliest of many trading posts was built here in 1800. Over 200 years later, the town continues to be a supply center—now for the surrounding forestry, oil, and gas industries.

Sights

On the south side of the highway at the west end of town, **Fort Nelson Heritage Museum** (250/774-3536, 10am-7pm daily mid-May-Aug., adults $5, seniors and children $3) contains a great collection of Alaska Highway construction items and First Nations and pioneer artifacts. An interesting 30-minute movie, shown throughout the day, uses footage taken during the construction of the highway to effectively convey what a mammoth task the project was. The building is surrounded by machinery and vehicles used during the early days. Around back is a trapper's cabin crammed with antiques.

Practicalities

Fort Nelson has many hotels and motels spread out along the Alaska Highway. The least expensive is the **Blue Bell Inn** (4103 50th Ave., 250/774-6961 or 800/663-5267, $100-105, RV sites $32), next to the Petro-Canada gas station. The 57-room two-story lodging has air-conditioned rooms (some with kitchenettes), laundry, Internet access, and an adjacent 24-hour restaurant. Beside the museum is **Triple G Hideaway** (5651 50th Ave., 250/774-2340, Apr.-Oct., $24-34), where you can choose from tent sites in an open area or hookups surrounded by trees. Facilities include coin-operated showers, wireless Internet, laundry, a gift shop, and firewood.

Give the fast food joints a miss and plan on breakfast or lunch at **Gourmet Girl**

(5415 51st Ave., 250/774-9362, 7am-5pm Mon.-Fri., 9am-4pm Sat., lunch $8-12), where the wraps and sandwiches are huge but healthy and the coffee excellent. As you enter town from the southeast, **Dan's Neighbourhood Pub** (4204 50th Ave. N., 250/774-3929, 6am-midnight daily, $14-24) wouldn't look out of place in a big city—although it's not that family-friendly.

On the west side of town is **Fort Nelson Visitor Centre** (5500 Alaska Hwy., 250/774-6400, www.tourismnorthernrockies.ca, 7am-8pm daily mid-May-mid-Sept., 8:30am-4:30pm Mon.-Fri. mid-Sept.-mid-May).

CONTINUING TO WATSON LAKE

Awaiting the traveler on this 525-kilometer (326-mile) portion of the Alaska Highway are mountain peaks, glacial lakes, mountain streams, provincial parks with some great scenery, and the mighty Liard River.

Soon after leaving Fort Nelson, you'll come to a junction with the gravel **Liard Highway,** which runs north 175 kilometers (109 miles) to Fort Liard in the Northwest Territories. From this junction, the Alaska Highway climbs the lower slopes of **Steamboat Mountain,** which, with a certain amount of imagination, resembles an upturned boat.

Summit Lake

This intensely blue lake 140 kilometers (87 miles) west of Fort Nelson is a popular stopping point for travelers. It lies at the north end of 25,691-hectare (63,480-acre) **Stone Mountain Provincial Park,** a vast wilderness at the northern reaches of the Rocky Mountains. Named for the predominantly stony nature of mountains that have been folded and faulted by massive forces deep below the earth's surface, the park is predominantly above the tree line. For super-fit hikers, the best way to appreciate the landscape is by hiking the 2.6-kilometer (1.6-mile) **Summit Peak Trail,** which ends in a treeless alpine area a strenuous 1,000 vertical meters (3,300 feet) above the trailhead; allow at least

two hours one-way. The trailhead is on the north side of the highway, across from the campground. Much easier is the 2.5-kilometer (1.5-mile) trail to **Flower Springs Lake,** nestled in alpine peaks south of the highway. Allow one hour one-way. The trailhead is three kilometers (2 miles) along Microwave Tower Road, which turns south at the café.

The park extends to the highway at Summit Lake's eastern end, and here you'll find an exposed campground (no reservations, May-mid-Sept., $20) with pit toilets and picnic tables.

Muncho Lake Provincial Park

Lying among mountains and forested valleys at the north end of the Rocky Mountains, this 86,079-hectare (212,700-acre) park surrounds stunning **Muncho Lake,** one of the scenic highlights of the Alaska Highway. The magnificent 12-kilometer-long (8-mile) body of water is encircled by a dense spruce forest, which gives way to barren rocky slopes at higher elevations. Around three kilometers (2 miles) beyond the north end of the lake, natural mineral licks attract Stone sheep and woodland caribou to a roadside quarry. In the vicinity, a hiking trail leads to an escarpment above the Trout River; allow 20 minutes to walk the 1.5-kilometer (0.9-mile) loop.

At around Mile 463 of the Alaska Highway, the small community of Muncho Lake spreads out along the eastern banks of the lake, providing services for park visitors. Spread along the lakeshore, ★ **Northern Rockies Lodge** (250/776-3481 or 800/663-5269, www.northernrockieslodge.com, $159-209 s or d) has a variety of accommodations, while a huge common room with a stone fireplace and towering cathedral ceiling brings it all together. Choose from rustic cabins or more comfortable rooms in the main lodge, or park your rig at a lakeside campsite ($42-58).

Campers who don't need serviced sites have the option of staying at two campgrounds in the provincial park itself (no reservations, May-mid-Sept., $20), but with only 15 sites in each one, they fill up fast.

★ Liard River Hot Springs

One of the most wonderful places to stop on the whole highway is this 1,082-hectare (2,670-acre) park, 40 kilometers (25 miles) north of Muncho Lake. Most travelers understandably rush to soak their tired, dusty limbs in the hot pools (6am-11pm daily, adults $5, children $3, family $10). But the rest of the park is also worth exploring. Hot gases deep underground force heated groundwater upward through a fault in the sedimentary rock. The water fills rock pools constructed by Alaska Highway workers in the 1940s, then overflows into a wide area of marshland. Even in the middle of winter, the water doesn't freeze, creating a microclimate of aquatic plants not normally associated with the northern latitude. Also inhabiting the swamp are many species of small fish, plus mammals such as moose, woodland caribou, and black bears, as well as 100 species of birds.

A 500-meter (0.3-mile) boardwalk leads from the main parking lot over warm-water swamps to Alpha Pool, where water bubbles up into a long, shallow concrete pool. The pool area, surrounded by decking, has pit toilets and changing rooms. A rough trail leads farther to undeveloped Beta Pool, which is cooler, much deeper, and not as busy.

At the entrance to the hot springs is a campground (May-Sept., $26) providing showers and toilets. In summer, a percentage of sites can be booked through Discover Camping (519/826-6850 or 800/689-9025, www.discovercamping.ca). The other 32 sites are first-come, first-served and are usually filled by noon each day.

To the Yukon Border

Anglers will find good fishing for grayling in the Liard River below Smith River Falls, 30 kilometers (19 miles) or so northwest of the hot springs. Canyon and river views dot the highway heading north and west, and visitor services are available at Coal River and Fireside. The highway crosses the 60th parallel and enters the Yukon just before Contact Creek Lodge (all services). It then meanders back and forth across the border six times before reaching the final crossing, 58 kilometers (36 miles) farther west.

The Yukon

Wilderness and history enriched by the Klondike gold rush combine to create a unique destination in the Yukon. It's very different from the rest of Canada, but easily accessible by road from British Columbia.

Bordered by Alaska, British Columbia, the Northwest Territories, and the Arctic Ocean, the Yukon sits like a great upside-down wedge at the northwestern corner of Canada. The massive St. Elias Mountains pass through the territory's southwest corner, while the rest of the Yukon is a huge expanse of rolling hills, long narrow lakes, and boreal forests that give way to rolling tundra north of the Arctic Circle.

The territorial human population is just 34,000, almost 70 percent of them living in the capital, Whitehorse. One of the world's largest northern cities, this bustling city is filled with gold rush history, but is also a great place to soak up city luxuries before heading into the wilderness. In addition to modern hotels, Whitehorse boasts a couple of golf courses, great biking and canoeing, good food, and an unexpected surprise: simply divine coffee roasted within city limits. From the capital, the Alaska Highway draws many road warriors farther west, passing by the magnificent wilderness of Kluane National Park before jogging north to Alaska. The Klondike Highway runs 536 kilometers (333 miles) from Whitehorse to Dawson City, site of the world's most frenzied gold rush.

PLANNING YOUR TIME

Although the days of needing multiple spare tires and extra gas cans for the trip north to the Yukon are long gone, the trip north does require that you plan ahead insofar as scheduling goes—it's still a *very* long drive from everywhere. You need to allow at least two days just for the Dawson Creek to Whitehorse section of the **Alaska Highway** (1,471 kilometers/914 miles), plus the drive from your original destination to Dawson Creek, which is one day's drive from Edmonton and two day's driving from Vancouver. In addition to the four days travel time along the Alaska Highway

---

Previous: The Gold Fields; downtown Whitehorse. **Above:** Carcross Desert was an important stop on the White Pass & Yukon route.

Look for ★ to find recommended sights, activities, dining, and lodging.

Highlights

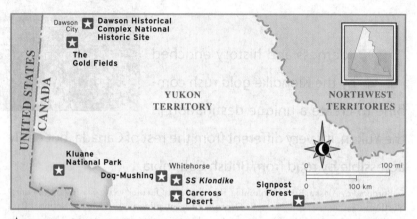

★ **Signpost Forest:** The first attraction north of the border is a little bit corny, but with an interesting history and thousands of town signs to look at, it's a good place to stretch your legs (page 446).

★ **Carcross Desert:** Listed in the *Guinness Book of World Records* as the world's smallest desert, this surprising natural feature will astound you (page 448).

★ **SS Klondike:** Step aboard one of the grandest stern-wheelers ever to ply the waters of the Yukon River (page 450).

★ **Dog-Mushing:** A summertime visit to the kennels of Frank Turner will give you a taste of what winter brings. And if you are visiting in winter, there's the opportunity to try the pastime yourself (page 455).

★ **Kluane National Park:** This park may border the Alaska Highway, but plan on hiking or canoeing to soak up this northern wilderness in all of its raw beauty (page 460).

★ **Dawson Historical Complex National Historic Site:** A walk through Dawson City leads past all of Dawson's most important and distinctive historic buildings, now protected as a National Historic Site (page 467).

★ **The Gold Fields:** Once you've seen Dawson City, get out into the actual gold fields—and even try your hand at panning for gold (page 468).

The Yukon

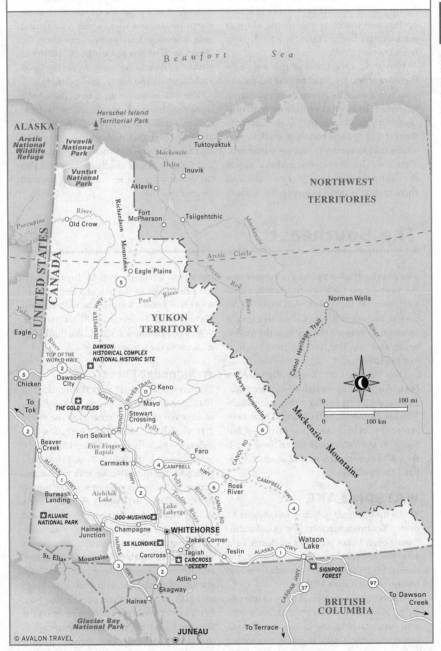

Beaufort Sea

ALASKA

Arctic National Wildlife Refuge

Herschel Island Territorial Park

Ivvavik National Park

Vuntut National Park

Tuktoyaktuk

Mackenzie Delta

Inuvik

Aklavik

NORTHWEST TERRITORIES

Porcupine

River

Old Crow

Fort McPherson

Tsiigehtchic

Richardson Mountains

Mackenzie

Arctic Circle

UNITED STATES
CANADA

Eagle Plains

Arctic Red

River

Norman Wells

5

Yukon

River

Eagle

Peel River

YUKON TERRITORY

DEMPSTER HWY

TOP OF THE WORLD HWY

DAWSON HISTORICAL COMPLEX NATIONAL HISTORIC SITE

Canol Heritage Trail

River

5

Chicken

2

Dawson City

NORTH KLONDIKE

THE GOLD FIELDS

SILVER TRAIL

11

Keno

Mayo

Selwyn Mountains

100 mi

100 km

To Tok

2

Stewart Crossing

Mackenzie Mountains

Beaver Creek

Fort Selkirk

Pelly River

6

Five Finger Rapids

Faro

CANOL RD

ALASKA HWY

Carmacks

4

CAMPBELL HWY

1

Aishihik Lake

2

6

Ross River

CAMPBELL HWY

Burwash Landing

HWY

Pelly River

KLUANE NATIONAL PARK

DOG-MUSHING

Teslin River

CANOL RD

4

Champagne

Lake Laberge

Haines Junction

WHITEHORSE

SS KLONDIKE

HAINES HWY

St. Elias Mountains

Carcross

Jakes Corner

Tagish

Teslin

Watson Lake

CARCROSS DESERT

ALASKA HWY

1

SIGNPOST FOREST

3

2

Atlin

CASSIAR HWY

37

97

To Dawson Creek

Skagway

BRITISH COLUMBIA

Haines

Glacier Bay National Park

To Terrace

JUNEAU

© AVALON TRAVEL

from Dawson Creek, add in a minimum of four days in the Yukon. For the amount of driving involved, this isn't a very practical option, and therefore you should allow at least six days in the Yukon for a 10-day trip from Dawson Creek.

Why should you travel all this way? Sure there are official "sights," but the purpose of your trip should be primarily to experience wilderness in its most pristine form, in officially designated areas such as the **Carcross Desert** and **Kluane National Park** or anywhere in the seemingly endless wilderness. That said, almost everyone makes a stop at the **Signpost Forest** in Watson Lake, and then spends a day exploring the history

of Whitehorse at attractions like the **SS Klondike.**

From Whitehorse, it's an easy day's drive north to Dawson City, where you should plan to spend at least one full day visiting the **Dawson Historical Complex National Historic Site** and exploring the nearby **Gold Fields,** where you can try gold-panning.

The Yukon is a destination in itself, with some excellent packages offered by the local airline, **Air North** (867/668-2228, www.fly-airnorth.com), that include airfares from the southern gateways of Vancouver, Edmonton, and Calgary as well as accommodations and the option of traveling one-way in a rented camper van.

The Southeast

The **Alaska Highway** (Alcan) crosses into the Yukon some 1,000 kilometers (620 miles) northwest of Dawson Creek, then ducks back in and out of British Columbia a couple more times before crossing into the Yukon again and reaching the highway town of Watson Lake.

Over the years, the Alaska Highway has been shortened by straightening some sections and cutting out big bends completely. Mileage posts in British Columbia have been replaced to reflect these new distances, but those on the Yukon side haven't—so you'll see a 40-kilometer (25-mile) discrepancy beyond the border.

WATSON LAKE

This is the first town in Yukon Territory for all drivers heading north from British Columbia. Even though it's not pretty, it's a welcome sight after the several hundred kilometers on the Cassiar Highway or the all-day ride from Fort Nelson on the Alaska Highway.

Watson Lake was created to serve one of a string of airfields constructed across northern Canada in 1940, and its existence was ensured when the Alaska Highway was routed

through to service the airfield. Today Watson Lake functions as the hub of a large area of southern Yukon, southwestern Northwest Territories, and northern British Columbia. With a population of 1,500, it's the third-largest town in the territory.

★ Signpost Forest

The famous **Signpost Forest** originated in 1942 by a GI working on the highway who, when given the task of repainting the road's directional sign, added the direction and mileage to his hometown of Danville, Illinois. Since then, more than 40,000 other signs have been added to the collection with town signs, license plates, posters, pie tins, gold-panning pans, mufflers, driftwood, even flywheels stating where the contributor is from and who he or she is. You can put up your addition personally or take it inside to the adjacent **Visitors Interpretive Centre** (Alaska Hwy. and Robert Campbell Hwy., 867/536-7469, www.watsonlake.ca, 8am-8pm mid-May-mid-Sept.) and have them put it up for you. In the center, you'll get a history lesson on the Signpost Forest, as well as the engineering feat that is the Alaska Highway through photos, displays, dioramas, and a three-projector audiovisual presentation.

Sights

Across from the information center, the **Northern Lights Centre** (867/536-7827, May-Sept.) is dedicated to the enthralling aurora borealis, also known as the northern lights. The highlight is a planetarium-type theater that shows a stunning one-hour presentation of northern lights footage shot in the Yukon. It runs up to six times 1pm-8:30pm daily. The center also has a live feed to NASA's James Webb Space Telescope and a SciDome space show.

Take 8th Street north a few blocks up from the Alaska Highway to **Wye Lake,** where a trail encircles the lake, complete with a boardwalk platform from which to view migrating shorebirds and resident grebes. If you're traveling with kids, make a stop five kilometers (3 miles) south of town at **Lucky Lake,** a day-use recreation area complete with North America's northernmost outdoor waterslide that will land them into the surprisingly warm lake.

Food and Accommodations

Nugget City (867/536-2307 or 888/536-2307, www.nuggetcity.com, May-Oct.) is a large tourist complex 20 kilometers (12 miles) west of Watson Lake (just past the Cassiar turnoff). The wooden cabins ($135-220 s or d) are spotlessly clean and come with a deck and satellite TV. Even taking into consideration the nondescript interiors, they are a good value. Fancier suites come with jetted tubs and covered decks. Tent sites are $30 and large pull-through sites come with power, water, and satellite TV hookups for $48-58. At Nugget City, **Wolf it Down Restaurant** (867/536-2307, 6:30am-9:30pm daily May-Oct., $16-28) is a touristy place with decent food, including northern specialties like bison burgers and an in-house bakery.

Coming into Watson Lake from the road, you'll be tired and hungry, guaranteed. Half a dozen motels, several campgrounds, and a handful of restaurants are there to serve. A few blocks east of the signpost forest, **A Nice Motel** (705 Frank Trail, 867/536-7222, www.anicemotel.com, $125 s or d) has 10 of the nicer guest rooms in town.

WATSON LAKE TO WHITEHORSE

It's 454 kilometers (282 miles) from Watson Lake to Whitehorse. A pullout at Kilometer 1,163 marks the **Continental Divide** between rivers that drain (via the Mackenzie River system) into the Arctic Ocean and those that empty (via the Yukon River) into the Pacific.

Teslin

Just over halfway between Watson Lake and Whitehorse, Teslin (Km 1,293) is reached after crossing the impressive Nisutlin Bay Bridge (longest on the Alaska Hwy.). Its mostly Tlingit population live a traditional lifestyle: hunting, fishing, trapping, carving, and sewing. The **George Johnston Museum** (804 Alaska Hwy., 867/390-2550, 9am-6pm daily June-Aug., adults $5, seniors $4, children $2.50) has displays on First Nations culture, Yukon frontier artifacts, and one-of-a-kind photographs taken from 1910 to 1940 by Johnston, a Tlingit hunter and trapper.

Teslin to Whitehorse

It's 183 kilometers (114 miles) between Teslin and Whitehorse, with the Alaska Highway closely paralleling Teslin Lake for the first 40 kilometers (25 miles) or so. At the lake's northern outlet is **Johnson's Crossing Lodge** (Km 1,346, 867/390-2607, www.johnsonscrossinglodge.com, May-Sept., camping $30-40), which has the usual Alaska Highway setup—campground (some sites with electricity), gas, groceries, a restaurant (delicious cinnamon buns), and showers.

At Kilometer 1,413, halfway between Jake's Corner and Whitehorse, is ★ **Inn on the Lake** (McClintock Place, Marsh Lake, 867/660-5253, www.exceptionalplaces.com, $189-259 s or d), the most upscale lodging along the entire

Alaska Highway. The main lodge is a peeled-log building with a living room, a library, a solarium, and a spiffy dining room (reservations required) with a vaulted ceiling. Each of guest rooms and cottages is decorated with stylish furnishings and has a comfortable bed, quality linens, wireless Internet, and a well-appointed bath. Rates include breakfast and the use of canoes and kayaks.

ATLIN

The small community of Atlin lies 100 kilometers (62 miles) south of Jake's Corner, back over the border in British Columbia. It is British Columbia's northernmost and westernmost settlement. Although isolated from the rest of British Columbia, it is one of the province's most picturesque communities. The glaciated peaks of the Coast Mountains form a stunning backdrop for the town, which is on a gently sloping hill overlooking beautiful 140-kilometer-long (85-mile) **Atlin Lake.**

Atlin was a boomtown with more than 8,000 people during the 1898 Klondike gold rush, when gold was discovered in nearby Pine Creek. Today they're still finding some color hereabouts, but the town's population has dwindled to about 400.

The highlight of Atlin is the surrounding scenery. Wandering along the lakeshore you'll have outrageous views of sparkling peaks, glaciers, waterfalls, and mountain streams. Tied up on the lake in front of town is the **SS** *Tarahne,* a 1916 steamer that has been restored.

Sights

Atlin Historical Museum (3rd St. and Trainor St., 250/651-7522, 9am-5:50pm daily June-early Sept., adults $4), housed in a 1902 schoolhouse, lets you relive the excitement of the gold rush. Scattered through town are many historic buildings and artifacts pretty much untouched from the gold rush era.

South of Atlin along Warm Springs Road are various lakes, camping areas, and, at the end of the road, **warm springs.** The springs bubble out of the ground at a pleasant 29°C

(84°F) into shallow pools surrounded by flower-filled meadows.

Practicalities

Holding a prime downtown lakefront location is the **Atlin Mountain Inn** (1st St., 250/651-7546, www.atlininn.com, $120-150 s or d), which comprises 18 motel rooms and a string of kitchen-equipped cottages. It also has an inviting pub with a lakefront patio (from 5pm daily). For primitive camping, the first of four spots through Atlin to the south is **Pine Creek Campground** ($10), with pit toilets and firewood but no drinking water.

CARCROSS AND VICINITY

Rather than drive straight through to Whitehorse, many travelers hang a left at Jake's Corner to Carcross (a contraction of "caribou crossing"), on Highway 2 between Skagway, Alaska, and Whitehorse. This picturesque village of 300 sits at the north end of Lake Bennett, which forms the headwaters of the Yukon River. It was an important stopping point for miners during the Klondike gold rush and today is chock-a-block with buildings from that era.

Sights

Make your first stop the **Carcross Visitor Information Centre** (7 Austin St., 867/821-4431, 8am-8pm daily May-Sept.), housed in a railway station that served passengers along the White Pass & Yukon Route. Beside the center is the **SS** *Tutshi* **Memorial and Carcross Gateway Pavilion**, an outdoor display that is centered on the remains of a historic 1917 stern-wheeler that once plied local waters. Across the road are a number of historic wooden buildings, including the century-old **Matthew Watson General Store** (1 Bennett Ave., 867/821-3501, 9am-5:30pm daily May-Sept.), which is filled with tasteful northern souvenirs and books.

★ Carcross Desert

The most remarkable natural feature in the

area is the Carcross Desert, which is considered to be the world's smallest desert. It was created 10,000 years ago, at the end of the last ice age, when a lake formed by the retreating ice cap dried up, exposing a huge expanse of glacial silt. Over the ensuing years, prevailing winds have pushed the sand into high dunes that cover 260 hectares (640 acres) extending north from Lake Bennett. This dune system has an extremely dry microclimate that receives just 280 millimeters (11 inches) of precipitation annually. It is also home to a number of rare plant and insect species, including Baikal sedge, an ancient grass that was present soon after the last ice age ended.

The main access point for the desert is two kilometers (1.2 miles) north of town. From the parking lot, there are no official trails—you simply climb up into the dune system and explore this unique environment that seems out of place this far north (but do not traipse across areas of vegetation).

Equally enjoyable, but less desertlike in its setting, is the long stretch of fine sand running along the shoreline of Bennett Lake in front of town. You can walk the length of the beach in around 40 minutes.

Food and Accommodations

The standout lodging is on Spirit Lake, a 10-minute drive north of Carcross toward Whitehorse. At **Spirit Lake Wilderness Resort** (867/821-4337 or 866/739-8566, www. spiritlakeyukon.com, May-Sept.) the lakeside cabins ($75 s or d) are my pick for the views and rustic charm, although they don't have electricity or running water, and shower facilities are shared. Other choices are cottages ($65 s or d) and motel rooms ($99 s or d) that lack the atmosphere but are more comfortable. Tent sites are $25 and hookups $30-35.

★ **Wheaton River Wilderness Retreat** (867/668-2997, www.wheatonriver.net, $60-135 s or d) is truly in the wilderness, 22 kilometers (14 miles) along Annie Lake Road, which branches off Highway 2 north of Spirit Lake. Lodging is in the main building or one of three cabins; my favorite is the River Cabin, offered for up to four people in a riverfront cabin constructed with timber milled on-site by the owners. The interior is spacious, airy, and modern, with wooden furniture carved by the owners. Breakfast is $12 pp, and other meals are also available; or you can cook up a feast yourself on the wood stove or barbecue.

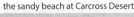
the sandy beach at Carcross Desert

Whitehorse

Whitehorse is a friendly oasis in the heart of an unforgiving land. With 25,000 residents, Whitehorse is the largest city in northern Canada and is home to almost 75 percent of the Yukon's total population. It squats on the western bank of the Yukon, hemmed in by high bluffs that create something of a wind tunnel along the river. To the east, the bare rounded hulk of Grey Mountain (1,494 meters/4,900 feet) fills the horizon. Whitehorse has its share of gold rush history and nostalgia, but is not dominated by it; as the capital of Yukon Territory for the past half-century, this small city has a brash, modern frontier energy all its own. It's easy to slip into Whitehorse's strong stream of hustle and bustle, which seems to keep pace with the powerful Yukon itself. Yet the town also has a warm, home-spun vitality to it, like huddling around the fire on a cold northern night.

The name Whitehorse was given to the treacherous rapids encountered by stampeders, who likened them to the flowing manes of Appaloosas. A few men drowned; many managed to hang onto their lives but lost their boats and grubstakes. Regulations were put in place that allowed only expert handlers to pilot the rapids. Undoubtedly, this saved countless lives and supplies in the more than 7,000 boats that passed through in the first crazy rush to the Klondike. Soon after, an eight-kilometer (5-mile) horse-drawn tramway was built around the rapids to the present site of Whitehorse, where goods were reloaded into boats to complete the journey to Dawson City. A tent city sprang up at the tramway's lower end, and Whitehorse was born.

SIGHTS

In addition to providing big-city comforts before folks head into the wilderness, Whitehorse has enough attractions to keep you busy for at least a full day. Many of these are within walking distance of downtown and most accommodations. One natural attraction that is well worth extra time is the Yukon River. The riverfront along downtown has undergone a dramatic transformation in the last decade, with **Shipyards Park,** at the north end of downtown, featuring a wide-open green space, picnic tables, a viewing platform, a playground, and a summer market.

★ SS *Klondike*

Start your visit to Whitehorse with a tour of this national historic site—the largest stern-wheeler ever to ply the waters of the Yukon, the *SS Klondike* (867/667-3910, 9:30am-5pm daily mid-May-mid-Sept., tour $6.05 pp), which is dry-docked along 2nd Avenue at the south end of town. Launched in 1929 and re-built after it sank in 1936, the *Klondike* made 15 round-trips a season, requiring 1.5 days and 40 cords of wood for the downstream trip to Dawson, and 4.5 days and 120 cords back to Whitehorse. The *Klondike* is beautifully and authentically restored, right down to the 1937 *Life* magazines and the food stains on the waiters' white coats. Bridges erected along the road to Dawson in the mid-1950s blocked the steamer's passage, and it has sat in the same spot since its last run in 1955. The best way to learn about the vessel and its colorful history is by joining a tour that runs every 30 minutes, proceeding from the boiler, freight, and engine deck, up to the dining room and first-class cabins, and finally up to the bridge. Outside of operational hours you can still view the vessel, along with the adjacent 1934 restored *Atlin* barge, but there is no on board access.

MacBride Museum of Yukon History

Three blocks north of the Yukon Visitor Information Centre is the excellent **MacBride**

Whitehorse and Vicinity

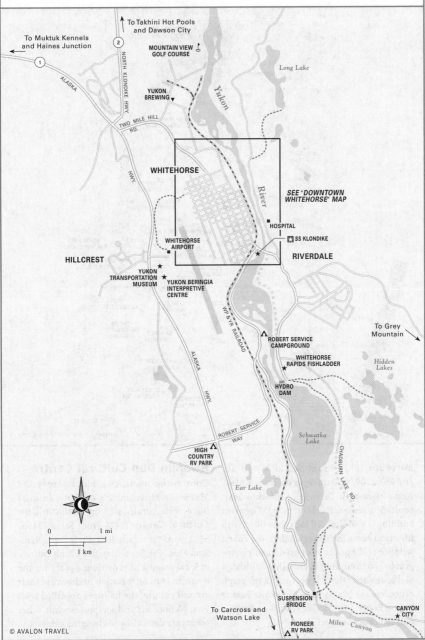

To Takhini Hot Pools
and Dawson City

To Muktuk Kennels
and Haines Junction

MOUNTAIN VIEW
GOLF COURSE

NORTH KLONDIKE HWY.

ALASKA

Long Lake

YUKON BREWING

Yukon

TWO MILE HILL RD.

HWY.

WHITEHORSE

River

SEE "DOWNTOWN
WHITEHORSE" MAP

HOSPITAL

SS KLONDIKE

WHITEHORSE
AIRPORT

HILLCREST

RIVERDALE

YUKON
TRANSPORTATION
MUSEUM

YUKON BERINGIA
INTERPRETIVE
CENTRE

WP & Y.R. RAILROAD

To Grey
Mountain

ROBERT SERVICE
CAMPGROUND

ALASKA HWY.

WHITEHORSE
RAPIDS FISHLADDER

Hidden
Lakes

HYDRO
DAM

ROBERT SERVICE WAY

Schwatka
Lake

CHADBURN LAKE RD.

HIGH
COUNTRY
RV PARK

Ear Lake

0   1 mi

0   1 km

SUSPENSION
BRIDGE

CANYON
CITY

To Carcross and
Watson Lake

PIONEER
RV PARK

Miles Canyon

© AVALON TRAVEL

Downtown Whitehorse

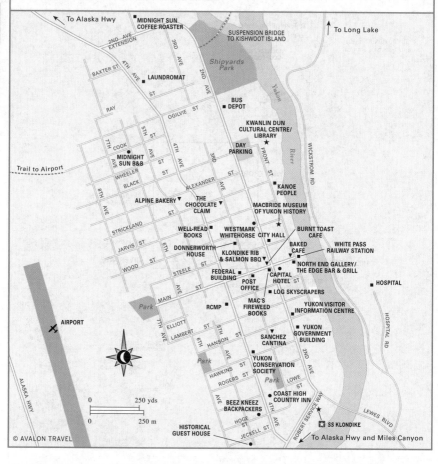

Museum (1124 Front St., at Wood St., 867/667-2709, 9:30am-5pm daily mid-May-Aug., 10am-4pm Tues.-Sat. Sept.-mid-May, adults $10, seniors $9, children $5). The main building is a sod-roofed log cabin filled with historical items, including taxidermied Yukon wildlife and hundreds of gold rush photographs. Surrounding it are other buildings and equipment: the old government telegraph office, engine No. 51 from the White Pass & Yukon Route, Sam McGee's cabin, and even a one-ton copper nugget.

Kwanlin Dun Cultural Centre

Continuing north two blocks from the MacBride Museum, it's difficult to miss the architecturally striking **Kwanlin Dun Cultural Centre** (1171 Front St., 867/456-5322, 9am-5pm daily June-early Sept., 9am-5pm Mon.-Fri. Sept.-May, free). Built entirely of local wood and providing a place for the Kwanlin Dun First Nation to showcase their art and culture, the hallways are filled with First Nations art and sculptures while other rooms are dedicating to changing exhibits.

Whitehorse Rapids Fishladder

Cross the bridge beside the *Klondike* and take Lewis Boulevard south or walk along the riverside Millennium Trail south toward the **Whitehorse Dam,** which created **Schwatka Lake,** tamed the once-feared White Horse Rapids, and now provides electricity for the city. Here, **Whitehorse Rapids Fishladder** (867/633-5965, 8:30am-8:30pm daily June-early Sept., donation), the world's longest wooden fish ladder at 366 meters (1,200 feet), allows fish to get around the dam and up to their spawning grounds upriver. Three underwater windows and TV monitors within the reception center give you a good look at the chinook (king) salmon (best in late July-early Sept.). You can also watch the salmon from a path that leads along the fishway to a riverfront viewing platform.

Miles Canyon

From the fishway, continue south on unpaved Chadburn Lake Road to the head of Schwatka Lake, where the Yukon River flows through spectacular Miles Canyon. Originating in town, the Millennium Trail leads along both sides of the canyon, crossing it at distinctive **Robert Lowe Suspension Bridge,** which spans the canyon at its high point.

Yukon Beringia Interpretive Centre

Named for the landmass that once linked Asia and North America, the dramatic **Yukon Beringia Interpretive Centre** (Km 1,423, Alaska Hwy., 867/667-8855, 9am-6pm daily mid-May-Sept., noon-5pm Sun.-Mon. Oct.-mid-May, adults $6, seniors $5, children $4), out by the airport, contains life-size exhibits of animals from the last ice age, including a spectacular 12,000-year-old, four-meter-tall (12-foot) woolly mammoth skeleton. Visitors will learn about the prehistoric animals that once roamed the north through exhibits, computer kiosks, dioramas, and a fascinating 30-minute film.

Yukon Transportation Museum

Located next to the Beringia Interpretive Centre, one of the finest museums in the north is the **Yukon Transportation Museum** (30 Electra Cres., 867/668-4792, 10am-6pm daily May-Aug., noon-5pm Sun.-Mon. Sept.-Apr., adults $10, seniors $8, children $5). You could easily spend a few hours examining the many excellent displays and watching the long historical videos: look up to view *Queen of the Yukon,* the first commercial aircraft in the territory, hanging from the ceiling; take the

Kwanlin Dun Cultural Centre

Floating the Yukon

Every year, hardy souls recreate the 742-kilometer (464-mile) route taken by stampeders heading to the Klondike goldfields by floating the Yukon River from Whitehorse to Dawson City. The most authentic way to travel is by canoe, which takes 14 to 16 days. While this is a trip for experienced wilderness travelers only, two Whitehorse companies make organization easy by providing rentals and transfers. Both companies also offer the option of floating the river as part of a guided tour.

Kanoe People (1147 Front St., 867/668-4899, www.kanoepeople.com) has been around the longest (since 1974), and rents canoes for $40 per day. They specialize in one-way rentals to Carmacks ($60 drop-off fee) or Dawson City ($75) and guided tours, such as a two-day river trip with meals and accommodations ($495). **Up North Adventures** (103 Strickland St., 867/667-7035, www.upnorthadventures.com) also offers canoe rentals (as well as bike and kayak rentals) with a local drop-off and pick-up service perfect for a single day on the Yukon River. For example, pay $70 pp for a rental and return transportation from the Takhini River Bridge. Their 19-day Whitehorse to Dawson float ($3,000 pp) includes Whitehorse and Dawson City accommodations.

Golden Stairs up to the second floor, where murals and artifacts recreate the gold rush from Skagway to Dawson; and check out the Alcan room, with a fascinating video on the highway's construction. Out front is a DC-3 that acts as the world's largest weathervane.

Takhini Hot Pools

The odorless (no sulfur) **Takhini Hot Pools** (867/456-8000, 8am-10pm daily mid-June-mid-Sept., noon-10pm daily mid-Sept.-mid-June, adults $12, seniors $11, children $9) bubble out of the ground at 36°C (96°F) north of Whitehorse. They have been developed and are as popular with locals as they are with visitors. The attached café has some of the best chicken soup north of Vancouver. Get to Takhini by driving 18 kilometers (11 miles) north from Whitehorse toward Dawson City, then take the 10-kilometer (6-mile) side road to the west (it's well signed).

Yukon Beringia Interpretive Centre

RECREATION

Whitehorse is small enough that you can cover downtown by foot. A pleasant paved walkway follows the Yukon River from the SS *Klondike* north to Shipyards Park.

★ Dog-Mushing

Also known as dog-sledding, sled-dogging, or simply mushing, what was once a form of transportation has grown into a major winter pastime, both as a recreational activity and as a competitive sport. One of the legends of the mushing world is Frank Turner, who owns and operates **Muktuk Adventures** (west of Whitehorse toward Haines Junction, 867/668-3647, www.muktuk.com), which is a place of work for Turner and his team of handlers, but also a bona fide tourist attraction. Through summer and fall, visitors are invited to take a look around for $18, but much more informative is the three-hour tour of the kennels (1pm daily, $40), or a full day with the dogs ($105). In fall (Sept.-Nov.), you can join a half-day training run with the dogs ($99). As you'd expect, it is in winter that the action really cranks up, with options that range from a full-day mushing trip ($279) to attending a weeklong Rookie Ranch ($1,800), including accommodations and meals.

Walking Tours

The **Yukon Conservation Society** (302 Hawkins St., 867/668-5678, 10am-4pm Mon.-Fri.) leads a two-hour hike through Miles Canyon (10am and 2pm daily mid-June-mid-Aug.). If the family is with you, the kids may enjoy joining the association's Kid Ed-Ventures program for a morning. The hikes are free; bring bug spray, wear sturdy boots, and bring lunch for the longer excursions. You can also buy self-guided trail booklets at the society's office and set out on your own.

SHOPPING

A number of fine galleries are scattered around town. Well worth a visit are the **North End Gallery** (1116 Front St., 867/393-3590, 10am-6pm Mon.-Sat., 11am-5pm Sun.), for its showcases of northern artists, and **Midnight Sun Emporium** (205 Main St., 867/668-4350, 10am-6pm Mon.-Sat.), with a wide range of Yukon souvenirs, including the brightly colored northern-themed paintings of Ted Harrison.

Across from the information center, **Folknits** (3123 3rd Ave., 867/456-4192, 10am-5:30pm Mon.-Fri., 10am-5pm Sat.) sells spinning fiber and finished knitwear made from *qiviuq*, the fine underhair of the musk ox.

Mac's Fireweed Books (203 Main St., 867/668-6104, 8am-9pm daily) is the biggest and most complete bookstore in the Yukon, with a large selection of local- and general-interest books and a basement filled with antiquarian books and maps. If you can't find what you're looking for using the in-store searchable database at **Well-Read Books** (4137 4th Ave., 867/393-2987, 10am-6pm Mon.-Fri., 10am-5pm Sat., noon-5pm Sun.), the knowledgeable staff will lead you in the right direction when it comes to looking through their extensive used book collection.

ENTERTAINMENT AND EVENTS

Whitehorse has no lack of rowdy bars, and none are as popular as **"The Cap"** (in the Capital Hotel, 103 Main St., 867/667-2565), which is music central, with rock bands seven nights a week. **Yukon Brewing Company** (102 Copper Rd., 867/668-4183, 10am-8pm Mon.-Sat., 11am-6pm Sun.) is the only brewery in the territory. Tours (noon, 2pm, and 4pm Mon.-Sat. summer, 2pm Mon.-Sat. fall-spring, $10 pp) include samples. These brews are available throughout Canada, but they are also available in the brewery shop, along with many beer-themed souvenirs.

Festivals and Events

One of the Yukon's biggest events is the **Yukon Quest** (www.yukonquest.com) a 1,600-kilometer (1,000-mile) dog-mushing race between Whitehorse and Fairbanks held each February. In early April, Whitehorse spins into action with the **Frostbite Festival**

(867/668-4921, www.frostbitefest.ca), featuring an eclectic mix of music and outdoor hockey games. Throughout winter up at Takhini Hot Pools, the completely unofficial **International Hair Freezing Contest** takes place whenever it's cold enough. The Saturday closest to summer solstice (June 21) is the **Midnight Sun Golf Tournament** at Mountain View Golf Course (867/633-6020, www.mountainviewgolf.ca).

FOOD

It's hard to go past **Baked Café** (100 Main St., 867/633-6291, 7am-7pm Mon.-Fri., 7am-6pm Sat., 8am-5pm Sun., lunch $7-11) as a recommendation for a centrally located café offering a familiar range of coffee concoctions, salads, soups, paninis, and baked goods.

Even though chains such as Starbucks have made an appearance in Whitehorse, go beyond what you know and search out **Midnight Sun Coffee Roaster** (9002 Quartz Rd., 867/633-4563, 8am-6pm Mon.-Fri., 10am-5pm Sat.), with coffee that is as good as you'll find anywhere. It's located in a bike shop, where bags of coffee beans are spread throughout. Flavors come with locally inspired monikers like Sam McGee's Black.

Also well worth a visit is **The Chocolate Claim** (305 Strickland St., 867/667-2202, 7:30am-6pm Mon.-Fri., 9:30am-5pm Sat., lunch $7-10), an arty space with handmade chocolates, freshly baked sunflower bread, sandwiches, savory soups, cappuccino, and a few outdoor tables.

In a two-story log building just off 4th Avenue on the north side of downtown, ★ **Alpine Bakery** (411 Alexander St., 867/668-6871, 8am-6pm Mon.-Fri., 8am-4pm Sat.) bakes wholesome European-style breads with organic ingredients, but they aren't cheap. A specialty is Expedition Bread, which stays edible for up to a month. The bakery is also part deli and has a few tables for dining in, with a lunch menu that includes soup, pizza, and sandwiches.

At street level of a 100-year-old hotel directly across from the railway station, **The**

Edge Bar & Grill (Edgewater Hotel, 101 Main St., 867/667-2572, 7am-9pm daily, $22-30) is a more welcoming room than you may image from the outside. It's a good choice for cooked breakfast, and with short but wide-ranging menus offered for lunch and dinner.

If you spend just one evening in Whitehorse and are looking for a tasty, fun northern experience, make reservations at ★ **Klondike Rib & Salmon BBQ** (2116 2nd Ave., 867/667-7554, 11am-10pm Mon.-Sat., 4pm-10pm Sun. mid-May-Sept., $18-36), which has a family-friendly atmosphere of long tables covered with checked tablecloths and a finger-lickin' menu. The house specialty is barbecued ribs, but you'll also find elk stroganoff, reindeer stew, smoked salmon, halibut fish-and-chips, and Alberta prime rib.

Do you have a second night in town? Head to the classy **Burnt Toast Café** (2112 2nd Ave., 867/393-2605, 8am-4:30pm Mon.-Fri., 9:30am-2pm Sat.-Sun., 4:30pm-9pm Wed.-Mon., $16-22), where the creative menu includes elk and blueberry sausages, lamb tacos, and a Kobe beef burger.

Right downtown, the city's best hotel dining is enjoyed at **The Deck** (Coast High Country Inn, 4051 4th Ave., 867/667-4471, 6am-2pm and 5pm-9pm daily, $15-32), which combines northern favorites with a clean, comfortable atmosphere and reasonable prices. The best choices focus on classic dishes with a northern twist, such as a caribou burger. As the name suggests, a large section of this restaurant is outside.

Away from the heart of downtown, **Sanchez Cantina** (211 Hanson St., 867/668-5858, 11:30am-2pm Mon.-Fri., 5pm-9pm Tues.-Sat., $13-19.50) is a casual, quiet place with familiar Mexican favorites and a small patio lined with flowers out front. Sides of salsa and guacamole are made in-house and are delicious.

ACCOMMODATIONS AND CAMPING

Whitehorse has a surprising number of motels and hotels for its size: around 1,000 guest rooms at last count. The competition, of course, works to the traveler's advantage, and some of the digs are actually affordable.

Under $50

Beez Kneez Bakpakers (408 Hoge St., 867/456-2333, www.bzkneez.com, dorm $30, $70 s or d) has dorm beds, private rooms with two single beds, and a couple of very basic cabins that sleep two. Other amenities include a living room, a communal kitchen, laundry facilities, and wireless Internet access.

If you have your own transportation, another option in this price range is **Hot Springs Campground and Hostel** (Takhini Hot Springs Rd., 867/456-8004, www.yukoncampground.com, dorm $35, private room $125), adjacent to the Takhini Hot Pools 18 kilometers (11 miles) north from Whitehorse toward Dawson City, then 10 kilometers (6 miles) west. This modern hostel has clean and comfortable rooms with two or four beds, a well-equipped kitchen, lots of outdoor space, wireless Internet, and discounted hot pools passes.

$100-150

★ **Historical Guest House** (5128 5th Ave., 867/668-3907, www.yukongold.com, $105-130 s, $115-130 d) is a comfortable downtown home that was built in 1907 for prospector Sam McGee, whose name was used by Robert Service in the poem "The Cremation of Sam McGee." The trim home has been extensively restored, exposing much of the original hand-hewn log work. Each of the two upstairs guest rooms has its own bath, while the basement holds a self-contained suite. Other amenities include a communal kitchen and living area, and out back is a garden and barbecue. Rates include a light self-serve breakfast.

If you're planning on traveling as far north as Whitehorse, you're more adventurous than most travelers, so why not do something really unique and stay on a ranch with 100 mushing dogs? You can at **Muktuk Adventures** (west of Whitehorse toward Haines Junction, 867/668-3647, www.muktuk.com, $109-169 s or d, includes breakfast), on the property of mushing legend Frank Turner. Lodging choices are wooden cabins or a room in the main lodge. Breakfast and dinner are provided at an extra charge. The property is right on the Takhini River, and in addition to tours of the facility, there are canoe rentals, hiking, and trail riding.

For modern, comfortable bed-and-breakfast accommodations within walking distance of downtown restaurants and shops, make reservations at **Midnight Sun B&B** (6188 6th Ave., 867/667-2255 or 866/284-4448, www.midnightsunbb.com, $109-199 s or d). Five of the six guest rooms are en suite, and one has a private bath down the hall. Each room also has a TV, a phone, and wireless Internet access. Guests have use of a lounge and kitchen.

$150-200

Sundog Retreat (Policeman's Point Rd., off the Klondike Hwy., 867/633-4183, www.sundogretreat.com, cabins $170-240) comprises six cabins spread over 60 hectares (160 acres) on a lightly treed property north of downtown. Each cabin has a kitchen and one or two bedrooms; some have decks, and all are very private.

My choice for a downtown hotel is the **Coast High Country Inn** (4051 4th Ave., 867/667-4471 or 800/716-6199, www.coasthotels.com, $169-259 s or d), a large and well-appointed hostelry with guest rooms in 15 configurations. The hotel has a fitness room, a business center with Internet access, and its own airport shuttle. Downstairs is a bistro-style restaurant with a large patio.

Camping

The prime choice for tenters (no RVs allowed) is ★ **Robert Service Campground** (S. Access Rd., 867/668-3721, www.robertservicecampground.com, mid-May-Sept., $20), a two-kilometer (1.2-mile) drive or 20-minute walk south of town along the riverside Millennium Trail. It has showers, an outdoor living room (complete with a TV), free firewood, and a small store and café that become a meeting point for travelers.

Near the south entrance to town, **Hi Country RV Park** (91374 Alaska Hwy., 867/667-7445, www.hicountryrv.com, tents $25, hookups $33-43) is one of a half-dozen private campgrounds spread along the Alaska Highway within a five-minute drive of downtown. It has 120 sites spread among the trees, modern shower facilities, laundry, an RV wash, a dump station, wireless Internet, and a convenience store. Farther south, **Pioneer RV Park** (91091 Alaska Hwy., 867/668-5944, www.pioneer-rv-park. com, May-Sept., tents $19, hookups $26-32) has cheaper sites but is not much more than a glorified parking lot.

Government-run **Wolf Creek Campground** (Km 1,408, Alaska Hwy., May-Sept., $12), 11 kilometers (7 miles) south of Whitehorse along the Alaska Highway, has campsites for tents and RVs (but no hookups), a short trail to a lookout above the Yukon River, a creek with spawning salmon (early Aug.), drinking water, and two cook shelters.

Finally, **Hot Springs Campground and Hostel** (Takhini Hot Springs Rd., 867/456-8004, www.yukoncampground.com, tents $20, hookups $30-37) is 28 kilometers (17 miles) north of town beside the territory's only commercial hot pools. It's a good place to spend the night, take an early dip, and then hit the road to Dawson.

INFORMATION

Taking up a full city block, the **Yukon Visitor Information Centre** (100 Hanson St., 867/667-3084, 8am-8pm daily May-Sept., 8:30am-5pm Mon.-Fri., 10am-2pm Sat. late Sept.-early Apr.) promotes both Whitehorse and the Yukon. The excellent **Whitehorse Public Library** (1171 Front St., 867/667-5239, 10am-9pm Mon.-Thurs., 10am-6pm Fri.-Sun.) is in the vicinity of the visitors center. It has a good selection of northern literature, newspapers from around the world, and both wireless Internet access and computer terminals.

The Yukon Visitor Information Centre is downtown.

GETTING THERE

Although Whitehorse is a bustling metropolis, it has a distinctive northern frontier vibe. You can't help but feel some kind of achievement in reaching the capital, especially if you've driven up from the south: It's 1,471 kilometers (914 miles) from Dawson Creek, 2,702 kilometers (1,663 miles) from Vancouver, or 2,054 kilometers (1,276 miles) from Edmonton, Alberta.

An easier way to reach Whitehorse is to fly. From its hub at **Whitehorse Airport** (YXY), local carrier **Air North** (800/661-0407, www.flyairnorth.com) has flights to and from the southern gateways of Edmonton, Calgary, and Vancouver, as well as onward flights to Dawson City and Inuvik. **Air Canada** (888/247-2262) has service to Whitehorse from both Vancouver and Calgary. **First Air** (800/267-1247, www. firstair.ca) has scheduled service between Whitehorse and Yellowknife (NWT) three times a week. The airport is right above town on the bluff beside the Alaska Highway. You can't miss the "world's largest weathervane" out front—the restored DC-3 (mounted on a moveable pedestal) that points its nose into the wind. Larger downtown hotels provide a shuttle, or you can catch a cab (around $15 to downtown).

Whitehorse Bus Depot (2191 2nd Ave., behind Qwanlin Mall, 867/668-2223) is the northern terminus for **Greyhound.** In summer, one bus a day heads south along the Alaska Highway. At the time of publication, the only bus service that continues to Alaska is provided by **Alaska/Yukon Trails** (800/770-7275, www.alaskashuttle.com, June-mid-Sept.), which charges US$375 for the shuttle trip between Whitehorse and Fairbanks (Alaska) via Dawson City.

GETTING AROUND

Whitehorse Transit (867/668-7433, 6am-7pm Mon.-Sat., $2.50 per ride) operates a citywide public bus service. Pick up a schedule at the visitors center or from the drivers. All routes begin and end beside Canadian Tire, opposite Qwanlin Mall. Local taxi companies are **5th Avenue Taxi** (867/667-4111), **Whitehorse Taxi** (867/393-6543), and **Yellow Cab** (867/668-4811).

If you need a rental vehicle, make reservations as far in advance as possible, since options are very limited. **Norcan** (867/668-2137, www.norcan.yk.ca) is the local franchisee for Driving Force, while **Budget** (867/667-6200) also maintains a fleet of vehicles in Whitehorse. If you're planning on renting a vehicle in Whitehorse, check mileage allowances. Unlike elsewhere in Canada, companies do not include unlimited travel.

Whitehorse to Beaver Creek

If Alaska is your final destination, you need to decide whether to take the Alaska Highway straight through to Alaska or continue north to Dawson City and then continue along the Top of the World Highway, which loops back down to the Alaska Highway at Tok (Alaska). The Top of the World Highway adds less than 200 kilometers (120 miles) to the distance between Whitehorse and Tok while taking in Dawson City, a must-stop on any northern itinerary. The entire loop, beginning and ending at Whitehorse, is 1,480 kilometers (920 miles).

This section covers the direct route to Alaska, along the Alaska Highway to Beaver Creek. The total distance to the border is 460 kilometers (187 miles). Haines Junction is the only town of any consequence en route, beyond which the highway parallels Kluane National Park.

Whitehorse to Haines Junction

It's an easy 160-kilometer (100-mile) drive to Haines Junction from the capital. The scenery doesn't really become memorable until the highway closes in on Haines Junction, when the Kluane Icefield Ranges and the foothills of the St. Elias Mountains start to dominate the view; when it's clear, Mount Hubbard (4,577 meters/15,000 feet) looms high and white straight ahead. Government **campgrounds** between Whitehorse and Haines Junction are located at Kilometer 1,543, Kilometer 1,602, and Kilometer 1,628.

HAINES JUNCTION

Established in 1942 as a base camp for Alaska Highway construction, this town of 800 is the largest between Whitehorse and Tok and is the gateway to Kluane National Park, the most accessible of the Yukon's three national parks. It's also the first town north of Haines (Alaska), and so sees a lot of traffic from the ferry passing through.

Sights

At the village square near the intersection of the Alaska and Haines Highways, a grotesque sculpture of mountains, mammals, and humans has been placed. Ironically, it's part of a

Yukon beautification program. It looks more like a misshapen cupcake with really ugly icing. Here you can also read the signboards describing the history and attractions of the Haines Junction area and sign your name in the gigantic guest book. Just up the road toward Whitehorse is **Our Lady of the Way Church,** built in 1954 by a Catholic priest who converted an old Quonset hut by adding a wooden front, a shrine on top, and a steeple with bell in back.

Practicalities

Several of the downtown hotels serve meals, including—most notably—the **Raven Hotel** (867/634-2500, 5:30pm-10pm daily May-Sept., $18-31). The menu here changes weekly, but the choices are always varied and thoughtful. Considering the remote location, the owners do a great job of sourcing fresh produce to go with lots of local game and seafood. Views of the snowcapped peaks of Kluane National Park are a bonus.

The best of the bunch when it comes to in-town lodging options is the **Raven Hotel** (181 Alaska Hwy., 867/634-2500, www.raven-hotelyukon.com, May-Sept., $135 s, $145 d), which has 12 comfortable motel rooms. You can't miss it: The Raven looks like a modular mansion, right in the middle of town. **The Cabin** (Hwy. 3, 867/634-2626, www.thecabi-nyukon.com, $115 s, $125 d), 27 kilometers (17 miles) south of Haines Junction, comprises six rustic cabins, each with a kitchenette and deck with views extending over Kluane National Park.

Right downtown, **Kluane RV Kampground** (Km 1,636, Alaska Hwy., 867/634-2709, www.kluanerv.ca, tents $25, hookups $34-43) separates tenters from RVers but offers lots of services for both. For in-town camping, the tent sites are pleasant, with lots of trees, and barbecues and firewood are supplied. Amenities include a shower block, laundry, a car and RV wash, a grocery store, and gas.

Haines Junction Visitor Information Centre (280 Alaska Hwy., 867/634-2345,

an abandoned vehicle alongside the Alaska Highway

8:30am-6pm daily mid-May-Aug., 8am-8pm daily July-Aug.) is a territorial government-operated facility within the Da Ku Cultural Centre, which is filled with artwork and sculptures created by the Champagne and Aishihik First Nations.

★ KLUANE NATIONAL PARK

The lofty ice-capped mountains of southwest Yukon, overflowing with glaciers and flanked by lower ranges rich in wildlife, have been set aside as 21,980-square-kilometer (8,490-square-mile) **Kluane National Park.** Although the Alaska and Haines Highways, which run along the fringe of the park, make it accessible, Kluane (kloo-AH-nee) is a wilderness hardly touched by human hands; once you leave the highways, you'll see few other people. No roads run into the park itself, so to experience the true magnificence of this wilderness, you must embark on an overnight hike or take a flightseeing trip.

The Land

The St. Elias Range, running from Alaska through the Yukon to British Columbia, is the highest mountain range in North America and the second-highest coastal range in the world (only the Andes are higher). Mount Logan, at 6,050 meters (19,850 feet), is the highest peak in Canada. The ranges you see from the Alaska Highway are impressive enough, but only through gaps can you glimpse the fantastic Icefield Ranges lying directly behind. These peaks are surrounded by a gigantic icefield plateau 2,500-3,000 meters (8,200-9,800 feet) high, the largest nonpolar ice field in the world, which occupies a little more than half the park. Radiating out from the icefield like spokes on a wheel are glaciers up to 60 kilometers (37 miles) long. Such is the importance of this area that—together with Wrangell-Saint Elias and Glacier Bay National Parks in Alaska, and Tatshenshini-Alsek Provincial Park in British Columbia—Kluane has been declared a World Heritage Site by UNESCO.

Although more than half of Kluane is ice, rock, and snow, the remainder includes habitat that holds large populations of wildlife. Some 4,000 Dall sheep—one of the world's largest populations—reside on the high open hillsides northwest of Kaskawulsh Glacier and elsewhere in the park. Many can be seen from the highway in the vicinity of Sheep Mountain. Kluane also has significant populations of moose, caribou, mountain goats, and grizzly bears.

Tours

If you're not comfortable exploring the backcountry without a local guide, consider using Kluane Ecotours (867/634-2600, www.kluaneco.com), which offers day and overnight trips on foot and in kayaks and canoes, including a paddling-hiking combo to King's Throne.

Flightseeing over the park is available from the Haines Junction Airport. The one-hour flight offered by Kluane Glacier Tours (867/634-2916, www.kluaneglacierairtours.com, $275) affords a spectacular view of Mount Logan plus several glaciers and is highly recommended if you happen to be there on a clear day.

Practicalities

Easily accessible 27 kilometers (17 miles) south of Haines Junction and within Kluane National Park is Kathleen Lake Campground (867/634-7250, mid-May-early Sept., $16), with 39 sites between the highway and the lake. Amenities are limited to firewood (fire permit $9), drinking water, and pit toilets, but it's a delightful spot that is a popular launching spot for kayaks and canoes. It also has a short interpretive trail and is the starting point for a five-kilometer (3-mile) trek up to the King's Throne, so named for its sweeping views across the park; allow four hours round-trip.

In Haines Junction, the Kluane National Park Visitor Centre (Da Ku Cultural Centre, 280 Alaska Hwy., 867/634-7207, www.pc.gc.ca, 9am-5pm daily mid-May-Aug.) has a relief map of the park and an excellent 20-minute sight-and-sound slide show presented every half hour. On the Alaska Highway 72 kilometers (45 miles) north of Haines Junction, Tachal Dhal Visitor Centre (867/734-7250, 9am-4:30pm daily June-Aug.) has a spotting scope to look for Dall sheep on nearby Sheep Mountain. Late August to mid-June is the best time of year for sheep-spotting.

HAINES JUNCTION TO BEAVER CREEK

For most of the 300 kilometers (186 miles) to Beaver Creek, the Alaska Highway parallels Kluane National Park or Kluane Wildlife Sanctuary—a comparatively well-populated, civilized, and stunningly scenic stretch of the road. Along the way are three government campgrounds (Km 1,725, Km 1,853, and Km 1,913), three little settlements, and a dozen lodges.

At Soldier's Summit, one kilometer (0.6 miles) north of the Tachal Dhal Visitor Information Centre, a sign commemorates the official opening of the Alaska Highway on November 20, 1942, a mere eight months after construction began; an interpretive trail from the parking area leads up to the site of the dedication ceremony.

Destruction Bay

This tiny town at Kilometer 1,685 (Mile 1,083) was named when the original road-construction camp was destroyed by a windstorm in 1942. The town hosts the 32-room Talbot Arm Motel (867/841-4461, www.talbotarm. com, $110-130 s or d). In addition to motel rooms, the roadside complex has a restaurant (7am-10pm daily, $15-25), showers, a general store, and gas pumps.

Burwash Landing

On Kluane Lake, 127 kilometers (79 miles) northwest of Haines Junction, is Burwash Landing, population 90. The fine Kluane Museum of History (867/841-5561, 9am-6:30pm daily mid-May-mid-Sept., adults $5, seniors $4, children $3) includes a wildlife exhibit, First Nations artifacts, a large model of the area, a theater where a wildlife documentary is shown, and some interesting fossils.

BEAVER CREEK

The last place with facilities in the Yukon, Beaver Creek is a tiny town (population 100) with a big travel-based economy.

Practicalities

On the west side of town, the 1202 Motor Inn (867/862-7600, www.1202motorinn. ca, $95-175 s or d, campsites $38) has motel rooms in an older wing, more modern units, large kitchen-equipped suites, and overnight parking for RVs. The complex also has a rustic log dining room, a lounge, public Internet access, and gas (which is cheaper on the U.S. side of the border). Beaver Creek Visitor Information Centre (867/862-7321, 8am-8pm daily May-Sept.) is operated by the Yukon government as an information resource for travelers entering the territory from Alaska.

Onward to Alaska

The Canada-U.S. border is 32 kilometers (20 miles) west of Beaver Creek and the U.S. Customs post is another one kilometer (0.6 miles) west. Heading into Alaska, be sure to turn your clocks back one hour to Alaska time. Traveling in the opposite direction, Canadian Customs is well inside Canada, just three kilometers (2 miles) northwest of Beaver Creek. Both posts are open 24 hours a day year-round, and you'll need a passport regardless of your citizenship or which direction you're headed.

If you're reading this before leaving home, begin planning your Alaska travels by visiting the official website of Alaska Tourism (www.travelalaska.com). The best guidebook out there is *Moon Alaska*. In Whitehorse, you'll find copies at Mac's Fireweed Books (203 Main St., 867/668-6104, 8am-9pm daily).

Whitehorse to Dawson City

It's 536 kilometers (333 miles) north from Whitehorse to Dawson City along Highway 2 (Klondike Hwy.). Allow six or seven hours nonstop driving, or stretch the trip out to a full day or two by stopping at the places detailed below.

LAKE LABERGE

Lake Laberge, 62 kilometers (39 miles) from Whitehorse, is famous primarily as the site of the burning of the corpse in Robert Service's immortal poem "The Cremation of Sam McGee." The excellent trout fishing here has also been well-known since stampeder days, when the fish were barged to Dawson by the ton. You get glimpses of the lake from Highway 2, but if you take Deep Creek Road three kilometers (2 miles) to the lakeshore, the views are much improved. Right on the lake is **Lake Laberge Campground** (mid-June-Aug., $12), with limited services but a priceless location.

CARMACKS

A little more than 180 kilometers (120 miles) from Whitehorse, Highway 2 cross the Yukon River at Carmacks (pop. 480). Named for George Carmack, who was credited with the Bonanza Creek strike that triggered the famous Klondike gold rush, Carmack established a trading post here in 1899.

Get the lay of town by driving down Three Gold Road (at the Carmacks Hotel) to the Yukon River. A two-kilometer (1.2-mile) **boardwalk** runs along the river from here to a park, complete with a gazebo. **Tage Cho Hudan Interpretive Centre** (867/863-5831, 9am-6pm daily mid-May-mid-Sept., donation) exhibits archaeological displays, a dugout canoe, a moose-skin boat, and a diorama of a mammoth snare.

Facing Highway 2 as it passes through town, **Hotel Carmacks** (867/863-5221, www.hotelcarmacks.com, from $95 s or d)

rents decent rooms (some with river views) and a few basic cabins. Here you'll find a large lounge sporting a couple of pool tables and an interesting brass railing along the bar, perfect for bellying up to. Occupying a 1903 log roadhouse, the hotel's **Goldpanner Restaurant** (6am-9:30pm daily July-Aug., 7am-9pm Sept.-June, $12-24) is a cozy dining room lined with northern memorabilia. The dinner menu includes halibut and chips, a bison burger, and a couple of pastas.

FIVE FINGER RAPIDS

North of Carmacks 25 kilometers (16 miles) is a pullout overlooking Five Finger Rapids, where four rock towers here choke the river, dividing it into five channels through which the current rips. Beside the highway, a wooden platform overlooks the river from afar, and stairs lead down to the river. Allow 20 minutes to reach the end of the trail, but longer to return, as there are a *lot* of stairs.

PELLY CROSSING

In another 108 kilometers (67 miles) you come to Pelly Crossing, roughly halfway between Whitehorse and Dawson. Beside the highway, interpretive panels describe how the settlement came to be and the story of its First Nations residents, who moved here from remote Fort Selkirk after the highway was completed in the 1950s.

SILVER TRAIL

The first settlement north of Pelly River is **Stewart Crossing,** the site of an 1883 trading post and the last gas stop before Dawson City, another 181 kilometers (112 miles) north. At Stewart Crossing, the Silver Trail (Hwy. 11) branches northeast through a heavily mined area of silver deposits. Two small towns and loads of history make a detour worthwhile.

Mayo (population 400), above a wide bend of the Stewart River, was once a bustling silver-mining center, with the ore transported out of the wilderness by stern-wheeler, eventually reaching smelters in San Francisco. Stop by the two-story **Binet House Museum** (304 2nd Ave., 867/996-2926, 10am-6pm daily late May-early Sept., donation) for a rundown of the Mayo District, including historical photos, displays on the Na-Cho Nyak First Nation, and locally mined geological samples. **Bedrock Motel** (north side of town, 867/996-2290, www.bedrockmotel.com, $115 s or d) is a modern wooden lodge with 12 clean, comfortable guest rooms, as well as RV parking ($35).

From Mayo, it's eight kilometers (5 miles) of paved road and then 51 kilometers (32 miles) on hard-packed gravel to **Keno City,** passing **Elsa,** the site of a silver mine that closed as recently as 1989, along the way. Once a booming silver town, Keno's population has dwindled to around 15. Its long and colorful history is cataloged at the **Keno City Mining Museum** (Main St., 867/995-3103, 10am-6pm daily late May-early Sept., donation), housed in a wooden 1920s community hall. The adjacent cabin has an interesting collection of locally collected fossils and mineral samples.

Dawson City

Of all the towns in Canada, Dawson City (not to be confused with Dawson Creek, British Columbia) has the widest fame and the wildest past. Although the Klondike gold rush was short-lived, tourists have rediscovered Dawson's charms in a big way. Many historic buildings have been given cheerful coats of paint, others have been built in the gold rush style, while many have very effectively been left to the ravages of Mother Nature.

The year-round population is around 1,300, but this more than doubles in summer. It's a long way north, some 536 kilometers (333 miles) from Whitehorse, but 60,000 visitors make the trek annually to this delightful salmagundi of colorful historic facades and abandoned buildings, tiny old cabins and huge new ones, rusted old stern-wheelers and touristy casinos.

HISTORY

The Klondike gold fields cover an area of 2,000 square kilometers (770 square miles) southeast of Dawson. It was in 1896 that Robert Henderson discovered the first gold—about 20 cents' worth per pan—in a creek he went ahead and named Gold-Bottom Creek. He spent the rest of the summer working the creek, while passing news of his find to fellow prospectors who were in the area. One

such man was George "Siwash" Washington Carmack, who with partners Tagish Charlie and Skookum Jim struck gold in extraordinary quantities—$3-4 a pan—on nearby Rabbit Creek (soon to be renamed Bonanza). They staked three claims before word began to spread. By fall, most of the richest ground had been claimed.

Gold Fever

News of the strike reached the outside world a year later, when a score of prospectors, so loaded down with gold that they couldn't handle it themselves, disembarked in San Francisco and Seattle. The spectacle triggered mass insanity across the continent, immediately launching a rush the likes of which the world had rarely seen before and has not seen since. Clerks, streetcar conductors, doctors, preachers, generals—even the mayor of Seattle—simply dropped what they were doing and started off "for the Klondike." City dwellers, factory workers, and men who had never climbed a mountain, handled a boat, or even worn a backpack were outfitted in San Francisco, Seattle, Vancouver, and Edmonton, and set out on an incredible journey through an uncharted wilderness with Dawson—a thousand miles from anywhere—as the imagined grand prize.

Dawson City

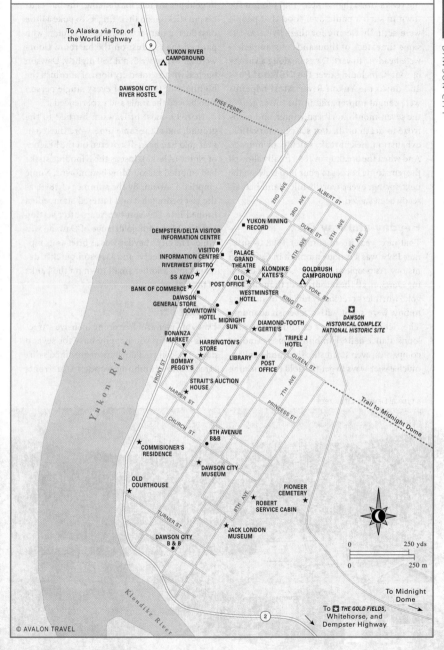

To Alaska via Top of the World Highway

9

YUKON RIVER CAMPGROUND

DAWSON CITY RIVER HOSTEL

FREE FERRY

Yukon River

2ND AVE
3RD AVE
ALBERT ST
DUKE ST
4TH AVE
5TH AVE
6TH AVE

YUKON MINING RECORD

DEMPSTER/DELTA VISITOR INFORMATION CENTRE

VISITOR INFORMATION CENTRE

PALACE GRAND THEATRE

RIVERWEST BISTRO

KLONDIKE KATES'S

GOLDRUSH CAMPGROUND

SS KENO

OLD POST OFFICE

BANK OF COMMERCE

WESTMINSTER HOTEL

DAWSON GENERAL STORE

KING ST

YORK ST

DOWNTOWN HOTEL

MIDNIGHT SUN

DIAMOND-TOOTH GERTIE'S

DAWSON HISTORICAL COMPLEX NATIONAL HISTORIC SITE

BONANZA MARKET

HARRINGTON'S STORE

TRIPLE J HOTEL

LIBRARY

QUEEN ST

FRONT ST

BOMBAY PEGGY'S

POST OFFICE

STRAIT'S AUCTION HOUSE

7TH AVE

HARPER ST

PRINCESS ST

Trail to Midnight Dome

CHURCH ST

5TH AVENUE B&B

COMMISIONER'S RESIDENCE

DAWSON CITY MUSEUM

OLD COURTHOUSE

PIONEER CEMETERY

8TH AVE

ROBERT SERVICE CABIN

TURNER ST

JACK LONDON MUSEUM

0   250 yds

DAWSON CITY B & B

0   250 m

Klondike River

2

To Midnight Dome

To ★ THE GOLD FIELDS, Whitehorse, and Dempster Highway

© AVALON TRAVEL

Meanwhile, the first few hundred lucky stampeders to actually reach Dawson before the rivers froze that winter (1897) found the town in such a panic over food that people were actually fleeing for their lives. At the same time, tens of thousands of stampeders were heading toward Dawson along a variety of routes, including over the **Chilkoot Pass** and down the Yukon River. Most hopefuls were caught unprepared in the bitter grip of the seven-month northern winter, and many froze to death or died of scurvy, starvation, exhaustion, heartbreak, suicide, or murder. And when the breakup in 1898 finally allowed the remaining hordes to pour into Dawson the next spring, every worthwhile claim had already been staked.

Heyday and Pay Dirt

That next year, from summer 1898 to summer 1899, was a unique moment in Canadian history. As people and supplies started deluging Dawson, all the hundreds of thousands in gold, worthless previously for lack of anything to buy, were spent with a feverish abandon. The richest stampeders established the saloons, dance halls, gambling houses, trading companies, even steamship lines and banks—much easier ways to get the gold than mining

it. The casinos and hotels were as opulent as any in Paris. The dance-hall girls charged $5 in gold per minute for dancing, the bartenders put stickum on their fingers to poke a little dust during transactions, and the janitors who panned the sawdust on the barroom floors were known to wash out $50 nightly. Dawson burned with an intensity born of pure lust, the highlight of the lives of every single person who braved the trails and experienced it.

In 1899, most of Dawson burned to the ground, and at the same time, word filtered in that gold had been discovered on the beaches of Nome (Alaska). Just as the Klondike strike had emptied surrounding boomtowns, Nome emptied Dawson. By the summer of 1899, as the last bedraggled and tattered stampeders limped into Dawson two years after setting out, the 12-month golden age of Dawson was done. The city's heyday was as brief as its reputation was beefy, and Dawson quickly declined into another small town on the banks of the Yukon.

SIGHTS

Dawson's plentiful free or inexpensive attractions can keep you happily busy for several days. The compact downtown area mixes dirt streets and crumbling wooden storefronts

a typical Dawson City street

Parks and Partner's Pass

The best way to enjoy all of Dawson's historic attractions at a reasonable price is by purchasing a **Parks and Partner's Pass** ($30.90 pp), which includes admission for one day to local attractions as well as a guided walking tour. Passes are also available to any three attractions ($13.70) or any five attractions ($22). They can be purchased from the **Visitor Information Centre** (Front St., 867/993-7200). For more information, go to www.pc.gc.ca and click through to the links for the Klondike National Historic Sites.

with faux gold rush-era buildings and bustling tourist businesses.

★ Dawson Historical Complex National Historic Site

The most historically important buildings dotted around Dawson City are protected as a national historic site. Combine these with the most picturesque ruins that have purposely been left to permafrost, gravity, and neglect, and you can plan on spending the best part of a day wandering around town. The following buildings are open mid-May to mid-September, with a variety interpretive programs offered at each.

Up a block from the visitors center, the **Palace Grand Theatre** (255 King St.) was built in 1899 from wood salvaged off sternwheelers by "Arizona Charlie" Meadows, the most famous bartender-gunslinger on the Trail of '98. At the time, the Grand was one of the most luxuriously appointed theaters in the west, hosting everything from Wild West shows to opera. The original horseshoe balcony, private box seats, and lavish interior have been lovingly restored. Take a tour (2pm daily, adults $7.50, seniors $6.50, children $4.50).

The beautifully restored **Commissioner's Residence** (Front St., near Church St.) was the official residence of the Commissioner of the Yukon from 1900 to 1916. Tours (adults $7.50, seniors $6.50, children $4.50) of the mansion and gardens are given daily by costumed interpreters. Along 3rd Avenue, beginning from behind the Commissioner's Residence, are many buildings with historic window displays, as well as the terribly slanted, oft-photographed **Strait's Auction House.**

SS Keno

The restored riverboat **SS Keno,** built in 1922 in Whitehorse, is beached on Front Street. It was used to transport ore from the mining area around Mayo down to the confluence of the Yukon River, from where larger riverboats transported it upriver to Whitehorse and the railhead. The *Keno* sailed under its own steam to its resting place here in 1960 but wasn't restored until 40 years later. Tours cost adults $7.50, seniors $6.50, children $4.50.

Dawson City Museum

The **Dawson City Museum** (595 5th Ave., 867/993-5291, 10am-6pm daily mid-May-Aug., 10am-2pm Tues.-Sat. Sept., adults $9, seniors and children $7), housed within the imposing 1901 Territorial Administration Building, is also well worth visiting. The south and north galleries present an enormous amount of history, from fossils and flora and fauna through lifestyles of the northern Athabascan people up to the gold rush and the subsequent developments. The mining-history displays alone, from hand mining to dredges, are worth the price of admission; also check out the display on law and order during the gold rush.

Robert Service Cabin

Stroll three blocks uphill from the museum to view the **Robert Service Cabin** (602 8th Ave., 9am-5pm daily summer, adults $7.50, seniors $6.50, children $4.50), which the poet called home from 1909 to 1912. Recitations of Service's best-known poems take place at 3pm daily. Service, who never took shovel nor pan to earth nor water, wound up as a troubadour-bank teller in Dawson and made his fame and fortune unexpectedly while living here, penning such classic poems as "The Cremation of Sam McGee" and "The Shooting of Dan McGrew." No one has lived in this cabin since Service left Dawson a celebrity in 1912, and people have been making pilgrimages to it ever since.

Jack London Museum

One block south of the Robert Service Cabin is the **Jack London Museum** (600 Firth St., 867/993-5575, 11am-6pm daily mid-May-late Sept., adults $7.50). Best known as the author *Call of the Wild* and *White Fang,* London came north searching for gold in 1897, but instead of striking it rich, established himself as a writer. His abandoned cabin was found south of Dawson City in 1936; today, the museum is a replica of his original cabin (although the adjacent food cache is original). It's worth timing your visit to coincide with the interpretive talks, held at noon and 3pm daily.

Midnight Dome

The 885-meter (2,900-foot) **Midnight Dome** provides a 360-degree view of the area. The Yukon River stretches out in both directions,

Dawson is right below you, to the west the Top of the World Highway winds away to Alaska, and to the south you look directly up Bonanza Creek, past the wavy tailings and hillsides pitted by hydraulic monitors that still bring pay dirt down for sluicing. The sign on top identifies all the topographic features. If you're driving, take King Street through downtown from Front Street and follow the signs; it's seven kilometers (4 miles) to the top. A steep hiking trail begins at the end of Queen Street (ask at the visitors center for a trail map).

★ The Gold Fields

For a close-up look at where the Klondike gold frenzy took place, head two kilometers (1.2 miles) back out of town and take Bonanza Creek Road south.

The highlight of the drive is a visit to **Dredge No. 4,** the largest wooden-hulled gold dredge in North America. Built in 1912, this massive machine scooped pay dirt from the creek beds right up until 1966, and is now protected as a National Historic Site. Tours (May-Aug., adults $7.50, seniors $5.50, children $4.50) are included in the Parks and Partner's Pass.

The Klondike Visitors Association owns **Claim 6** on the famous Bonanza Creek. You

the SS *Keno*

Try gold-panning in the Gold Fields.

4pm-midnight daily summer, 4pm-midnight Mon.-Sat. fall-spring), which is a low-key place with comfortable seating and a menu of Greek specialties prepared in the adjacent Greek restaurant.

Canada's first legal casino, **Diamond Tooth Gerties** (1001 4th Ave., 867/993-5525, 7pm-2am Sun.-Wed. and 2pm-2am Thurs.-Sat. early May-mid-Sept.), was named for a Dawson dance-hall queen with a diamond between her two front teeth. Though casinos were as common as sluice boxes and saloons at the height of the Dawson madness, gambling in the Yukon (and throughout Canada) wasn't formally legalized until 1971, the year this place opened. Games include slot machines, blackjack, poker, sic bo, and roulette, with odds that decidedly favor the house. Drinks are not free, even if you're dropping major-league cash. This sure isn't Vegas! The 30-minute floor show of Geritol oldies and cancan kicks is presented at 8:30pm, 10:30pm, and midnight daily. Cover charge is $12.

Gerties is run by the Klondike Visitors Association as a moneymaker to restore and promote Dawson City. Take a look around town and you'll see how much money they make at Gerties (or how much the tourists lose)—around $1 million annually. I'm not saying that you won't come out in front, but just approach this joint with the attitude that you're making a donation. And why not? It's for a very good cause.

can pan for gold free of charge mid-May to mid-September. Buy a pan from any one of many shops in Dawson or rent one from Claim 33 for $2. At Km 10 (Mile 7) of Bonanza Creek Road, **Claim 33** (867/993-6626, 10am-5pm daily mid-May-mid-Sept.) is a commercial panning operation where you pay $15 to pan for guaranteed "color." Hope I'm not giving away any secrets, but it's spiked. Still, it's good fun and a way to practice your technique. Claim 33 also has a great gift shop, light snacks, and a yard filled with mining artifacts.

A monument at **Discovery Claim,** 16 kilometers (10 miles) along Bonanza Creek Road, marks the spot where George Carmack made the strike in 1896 that set the rush into motion. A short interpretive trail winds through the site.

ENTERTAINMENT

Dawson City has a mix of rough bars filled with miners and hotel lounges filled with tourists. Somewhere in between is **Billy Goat's Pub** (952 2nd Ave., 867/993-6989,

FOOD

Your best bet for fresh meat, deli items, locally grown vegetables, and sandwiches made to order is the **Bonanza Market** (926 2nd Ave., 867/993-6567, 8:30am-7pm Mon.-Sat., 9am-6pm Sun.). You'll be amazed at the range and quality of vegetables and berries grown on local farms, and the best place to appreciate this fresh produce, along with baked and preserved goodies, is at the **Dawson City Farmers Market** (7:30am-5:30pm Sat. mid-May-mid-Sept.), which spreads out between Front Street and the Yukon River.

Riverwest Bistro (958 Front St., 867/993-6339, 7am-5pm Mon.-Fri., 8am-4pm Sat.-Sun., lunch $8-12) has good coffee plus a deli with the best sandwiches in town, and a delightful selection of baked goods.

The food at ★ Klondike Kate's (1102 3rd Ave., 867/993-6527, 4pm-10pm Mon.-Sat., 8am-3pm and 4pm-10pm Sun., $15-33) isn't as legendary as the restaurant's namesake was during the gold rush, but it's still mighty popular. On Sunday, bacon and eggs with baked beans and home fries will set you back $12, while at dinner, plan on starting with prawns in ouzo, and go on to alder-smoked elk meatloaf. This place has a warm ambience and Dawson's nicest patio.

The nationalistic exterior and brightly colored flowers make finding the Drunken Goat Taverna (950 2nd Ave., 867/993-5868, noon-9pm daily, $21-30) easy. Inside, you'll find a slightly overpriced menu of Greek specialties, but this far north, all is forgiven. The adjacent Billy Goat's Pub (952 2nd Ave., 867/993-6989, 4pm-midnight daily) shares the same kitchen and menu and is one of the best places in town to combine food and drink.

ACCOMMODATIONS AND CAMPING

Check the website of the Klondike Visitors Association (www.dawsoncity.ca) for a complete list of local lodgings and an online booking engine. If you arrive in Dawson without reservations, be sure to check out the lodging notebook in the Visitor Information Centre; often hotels, motels, and bed-and-breakfasts will advertise vacant rooms here.

Under $50

★ Dawson City River Hostel (Top of the World Hwy., 867/993-6823, www.yukonhostels.com, mid-May-Sept., camping $14 s, $24 d, dorm bed $22, private room $48 s or d) is Canada's northernmost hostel. Located on the west side of the Yukon River, it's a quick ferry ride from downtown. A back-to-the-land spirit infuses this friendly place with dorm-style lodging in cabins and a smattering of

---

Sourtoe Cocktails

Dawson's most infamous nightcap can be "enjoyed" at the Sourdough Saloon (Downtown Hotel, 1026 2nd Ave., 867/993-5346). It all began in 1973, when "Captain" Dick Stevenson was searching through an abandoned cabin and came across a pickle jar that held a toe that had been severed by an ax. Inspiration (if it could be called that) struck, and the toe landed in a drink. The original toe is long gone—it was swallowed by an overzealous patron—but at last check, the Sourdough Saloon has half a dozen toes to choose from, all looking ghastly at best. They're preserved in salt, and came from donations by folks who lost them in accidents or because of frostbite. It's pretty disgusting, but amazingly popular. Sourtoe cocktails are $6 (the toe can be included in any drink). There's just one rule: "You can drink it fast, you can drink it slow, but your lips have gotta touch the toe."

---

tent sites. The hostel doesn't have electricity (and therefore it's cash only, or pay online), but does have a cooking area with woodstove, canoe and mountain bike rentals, a communal cabin, plus the funkiest bathhouse going.

$50-100

The cheapest place right downtown is the shockingly pink Westminster Hotel (975 3rd Ave., 867/993-5463, $55-65 s, $65-75 d), where the very basic rooms all have shared baths. The Westminster is definitely not for everyone, and it helps to be a heavy sleeper, as the downstairs bar (known locally as "The Pit") gets noisy Friday-Saturday when the country house band gets going.

$100-150

In addition to having great food, ★ Klondike Kate's (1102 3rd Ave., 867/993-6527, www.klondikekates.ca, Apr.-Sept., $140-200 s or d) has 15 spacious wood cabins, each with a bath, cable TV, wireless Internet, and a private deck.

Next to the Dawson City Museum, 5th

Dawson City River Hostel

Avenue B&B (702 5th Ave., 867/993-5941 or 866/631-5237, www.5thavebandb.com, $105-135 s, $115-145 d) may have an uninspiring name, but the aquamarine exterior is impossible to miss. It features seven comfortable guest rooms with shared or private baths and a large sitting area. Rates include all-you-can-eat continental breakfast.

Fun and funky on the outside, the **Downtown Hotel** (1026 2nd Ave., 867/993-5346, www.downtownhotel.ca, $135 s, $145 d) is a modern building designed with a distinctive gold rush-era facade. Although the 59 guest rooms are somewhat clinical, it's close to everything, and the on-site bar has a rocking nighttime atmosphere.

Behind Diamond Tooth Gertie's is the **Triple J Hotel** (5th Ave. and Queen St., 867/993-5323 or 800/764-3555, www.triple-jhotel.com, mid-May-mid-Sept., rooms $149-199 s or d, cabins $189 s or d), similar to the Downtown Hotel in that beyond the brightly painted facade is a modern complex of motel rooms.

$150-200

On the outskirts of town and less than a block from the Klondike River, **Dawson City B&B** (451 Craig St., 867/993-5649, www.dawsoncitybnb.com, $165 s or d) is a neat two-story home with a pleasing blue and white exterior and guest rooms last renovated in 2017. Rates include a healthy and delicious cooked breakfast.

★ **Bombay Peggy's Inn & Pub** (corner 2nd Ave. and Princess St., 867/993-6969, www.bombaypeggys.com, Mar.-mid-Nov., $185-199 s, $195-219 d) is named for the former madam of a brothel that once operated in the building. Not only has it been totally renovated, it was moved from its original location. Most rooms are decorated in bold Victorian colors, with hardwood floors and lavish baths with antique tubs. You don't have to abandon modern comforts for the sake of atmosphere—there's also wireless Internet. Rates include a light breakfast. About the only reminders of the building's previous use are a racy cocktail list in the downstairs lounge and the phone number.

Camping

Directly across the Yukon River from town, **Yukon River Campground** (Top of the World Hwy., mid-May-mid-Sept., $16) is convenient but lacks amenities (drinking water, pit toilets, and firewood only). The free ferry from town runs 24 hours daily. Walk downstream from the campground to reach three rusting riverboats that are slowly disintegrating where they were beached many years ago.

RVers can circle their rigs at the **Goldrush Campground** (1207 5th Ave., 867/993-5247, www.goldrushcampground.com, mid-May-mid-Sept., $27-49), which is right downtown but doesn't offer much privacy between sites. Amenities include coin showers, laundry, and wireless Internet throughout. South of town at the turnoff to Bonanza Creek, **Bonanza Gold RV Park** (712 Klondike Hwy., 867/993-6789 or 888/993-6789, www.bonanzagold.ca, hookups $26-50) is a glorified parking lot with wireless Internet and cable TV.

Dempster Highway

Dawson is the jumping-off point for the 740-kilometer (460-mile) Dempster Highway, which leads across the **Arctic Circle** to **Inuvik** in the Northwest Territories. Unpaved all the way, it traverses endless tundra and snowcapped mountain ranges, crossing the migration path of the Porcupine caribou herd; in winter, you can drive clear through to the **Arctic Ocean** on the frozen Mackenzie River. But it's also one of the most remote public roads in North America, one for which you must be prepared with a full gas tank and spare tires. You also need to turn around at the end and return to Dawson along the same route.

DRIVING THE DEMPSTER

Request information packages from either of the territorial tourism bureaus before leaving home, then make a stop at the **Dempster-Delta Visitor Information Centre** (Front St., Dawson City, 867/993-6167, 9am-8pm daily mid-May-mid-Sept.). The ferry crossing of the Peel River operates mid-June to October. For a schedule and general highway conditions, call 800/661-0750 or go online to www.dot.gov.nt.ca.

Numerous campgrounds and three lodges dot the route. The **Arctic Circle** is reached at Km 403 (Mile 250) and the Yukon-Northwest Territories border at Km 471 (Mile 293). **Fort McPherson,** 550 kilometers (342 miles) from Dawson, is a Gwich'in Dene village of 800 people with a visitors center and other highway services.

INFORMATION AND SERVICES

Across the road from the Yukon River, **Dawson City Visitor Information Centre** (Front St. and King St., 867/993-5274, 8am-8pm daily mid-May-Sept.) is extremely well organized and prepared for the most common questions from the hordes of hopefuls that are, after all, Dawson's legacy.

Dawson City Community Library (894 5th Ave., 867/993-5571, noon-6:30pm Mon.-Fri.) is in the same building as the local public school. **Maximilian's Gold Rush Emporium** (Front St., 867/993-5486, 10am-6pm Mon.-Sat., noon-5pm Sun.) has a great selection of northern literature. One of the most unique souvenirs you can get in Dawson is an authentic **placer map** showing all the goldfields and claims. They are available along with topo maps at the **Dawson Mining Recorder** (1242 Front St., 867/993-5343, 8:30am-4:30pm Mon.-Fri.).

GETTING THERE

Dawson City is accessible from Whitehorse, 536 kilometers (333 miles) south along Highway 2, known locally as the **Klondike Highway.** Dawson's airport is 17 kilometers (11 miles) southeast of town beside Highway 2. **Air North** (867/668-2228) planes land on Dawson's unpaved runway daily from Inuvik and Whitehorse, with direct connections from Whitehorse to Vancouver, Calgary, and Edmonton. Taxis and a shuttle bus meet all flights.

CONTINUING WEST TO ALASKA

If you arrived in Dawson City by road from Whitehorse, you have the option of returning the way you came or continuing to Alaska along the **Top of the World Highway.** From downtown Dawson City, the highway crosses the Yukon River via a free **ferry,** with room for up to eight regular-size vehicles. Crossings are on demand 24 hours a day mid-May-mid-September.

From the west bank of the Yukon, the highway climbs out of Dawson into the alpine tundra of the lower White Mountains, with vast vistas in which you can see the road running along the ridgetops in the distance.

Civilization along the highway, however, is nonexistent until you reach **Poker Creek, Alaska,** at Km 106 (Mile 66). With a population of two, this is the northernmost border station in the United States. It's open 9am-9pm daily for as long as the Dawson car ferry operates (usually mid-May-mid-Sept.) After crossing into Alaska, you must also set your watch one hour earlier, to Alaska time. This means if you're traveling to Dawson from Alaska, the border station is open 8am-8pm daily.

Note: The Dawson ferry can get heavily backed up in midsummer, with delays of up to an hour at the busiest times (7am-11am and 4pm-7pm daily). Don't start too late in the day if you intend to make the border crossing before it closes.

Background

The Landscape

British Columbia is Canada's third-largest province, behind Ontario and Quebec. Covering 948,596 square kilometers (366,252 square miles), it's four times larger than Great Britain, two and a half times as large as Japan, larger than all U.S. states except Alaska, and larger than California, Oregon, and Washington combined. The province is long north to south, relatively narrow east to west, and lies between the 49th and 60th parallels. Its largest city, Vancouver, is on the same latitude as Paris and the same longitude as San Francisco. To the south are the U.S. states of Washington, Idaho, and Montana; to the west, the Pacific Ocean and the narrow panhandle of southeastern Alaska. To the north are Canada's Yukon Territory; to the east, across the Continental Divide, lies the Canadian province of Alberta. The land within those borders is dominated by mountain ranges, which trend northwest-southeast and are highest in the south.

MOUNTAINS

Mountains dominate British Columbia; half of its land area lies more than 1,000 meters (3,300 feet) above sea level. The province occupies part of the mountainous terrain that runs down the entire western margin of the Americas. It lies mainly in the Cordilleran Region, which is composed of Precambrian to Cenozoic rock formed into mountain ranges, deep intermountain troughs, and wide plateaus.

The landscape is defined by parallel north-south mountain ranges and a series of parallel valleys. The steep **Coast Mountains,** an unbroken chain extending for 1,500 kilometers (930 miles), rise abruptly from the Pacific Ocean. Their high point, and the highest peak

completely in British Columbia, is 4,016-meter-high (13,180-foot) **Mount Waddington.** The province's highest point is shared with Alaska; 4,663-meter (15,300-foot) **Mount Fairweather** (sixth highest in Canada) is part of the **St. Elias Range,** a northern extension of the Coast Mountains that straddles the BC-Alaska border in the extreme northwest corner of the province. The province's eastern border is defined by the **Continental Divide** of the **Rocky Mountains,** which reach a high point north of the 49th parallel at 3,954-meter (13,000-foot) **Mount Robson.** In the south of the province between the Coast Mountains and the Rockies lie the **Columbia Mountains,** the collective name for the **Cariboo, Monashee, Selkirk,** and **Purcell Ranges.** These ranges rise to peak elevations of just over 3,000 meters (9,900 feet) and are separated by deep valleys and long, narrow lake systems. Only the highest of the Columbia Mountains—including some glaciated peaks in the Selkirks and Purcells—are snow-covered year-round. In the northern half of the province, the ranges are lower, wider, and less well-defined, rising to vast plateaus that extend hundreds of kilometers in all directions. The least obvious of the province's mountain ranges lies mostly underwater, off the west coast. The range rises above sea level at thousands of points, forming a string of islands, including Vancouver Island, whose high point is 2,200-meter (7,200-foot) **Mount Golden Hinde.**

WATERWAYS

The province enjoys more than its share of waterways. Some 24,000 lakes, rivers, and streams contribute to British Columbia's two million hectares of freshwater surface area

Previous: bull elk; Moyie Lake.

(approximately 2 percent of the province's landmass). The largest watershed is drained by the **Fraser River.** With its headwaters around Mount Robson, this mighty river drains 233,000 square kilometers (90,000 square miles), almost 25 percent of the province, on its 1,368-kilometer (850-mile) journey to the Pacific Ocean at Vancouver. The Fraser is not the province's longest river; that title belongs to the 2,000-kilometer (1,240-mile) **Columbia River,** which follows a convoluted course through southeastern British Columbia before crossing the U.S. border and draining into the Pacific Ocean in Oregon.

The northern half of British Columbia comprises three major drainage basins: The 580-kilometer (360-mile) **Skeena River** flows westward through the heart of the province to the Pacific Ocean at Prince Rupert; the 1,900-kilometer (1,180-mile) **Peace River,** the only river system to cut across the Rocky Mountains, flows in a northeasterly direction into the Mackenzie River System, whose waters eventually flow into the Arctic Ocean; and in the far north, the **Liard River** drains a vast area of remote wilderness, also to join the Mackenzie River.

ISLANDS

British Columbia's deeply indented coastline comprises 6,500 islands. While most of these are uninhabited and many unexplored, the largest, 31,284-square-kilometer (12,100-square-mile) **Vancouver Island,** is home to over 500,000 people and holds the provincial capital. This island confusingly shares its name with the province's largest city, which lies on the mainland 50 kilometers (31 miles) to the east. Between the mainland and Vancouver Island, 200 islands dot the Strait of Georgia, some of which are populated and all of which are protected from the wind- and wave-battering action of the Pacific Ocean by Vancouver Island. The other major island group is **Haida Gwaii,** a remote archipelago linked geologically to Vancouver Island but with its own unique natural and human history.

CLIMATE

British Columbia's varied topography makes for radically varying **temperatures,** which rise or fall with changes in elevation, latitude, slope aspect, and distance from the ocean. The coastal region boasts the mildest climate in all of Canada, but this comes with one drawback: It rains a lot. The two main cities, Vancouver and Victoria, lie within this zone. Most of the interior is influenced by both continental and maritime air, resulting in colder, relatively dry winters and hot dry summers. Meanwhile, the northern latitudes are influenced by polar continental and arctic air masses, making for extremely cold snowy winters and short, cool, wet summers.

Precipitation in British Columbia is strongly influenced by the lay of the land and the waft of the wind, resulting in an astonishing variation in rainfall from place to place. For example, Lillooet, in the sheltered Fraser River Valley, is Canada's driest community, whereas Port Renfrew on Vancouver Island's west coast averages 4,000 millimeters (157 inches) of precipitation annually. The amount of precipitation any given area receives is greatly determined by its location on the windward or lee side of the major mountain ranges—the windward side usually cops most of the downpour. Hence, the western side of the Coast Range is wet, the Interior Plateau on the east side of the Coast Range is relatively dry, and the western, windward side of the Rockies along the Alberta border is once again wet.

ENVIRONMENTAL ISSUES

Humans have been exploiting British Columbia's abundant natural resources for thousands of years. Indigenous people hunting and fishing obviously had little effect on ecological integrity, but over time, the clearing of land for agriculture and development did. Today, the province is minimizing the effects of logging operations, global warming, fish farming, and offshore oil and gas exploration that are hot-button environmental issues in the region.

As rising population numbers have put ever-increasing demands on the region's plentiful natural resources, conservation measures have become necessary. The province has imposed fishing and hunting seasons and limits, a freeze on rezoning agricultural land, and mandatory reforestation regulations, and has restrained hydroelectric development to protect salmon runs. By preserving its superb physical environment, the province will continue to attract outdoors enthusiasts and visitors from around the world, ensuring a steady stream of tourism revenues. But the ongoing battle between concerned conservationists and profit-motivated developers continues.

Forestry

The issue of forestry management in British Columbia, and most notably on Vancouver Island, is very complex, and beyond the scope of a guidebook. In British Columbia, where a couple of mega-companies control an industry worth $17 billion annually to the local economy, many forestry decisions have as much to do with politics as they do with good management of natural resources. The most talked-about issue is **clear-cutting,** where entire forests are stripped down to bare earth, with the practice in old-growth forests especially contentious. The effect of this type of logging goes beyond just the removal of ancient trees—often salmon-bearing streams are affected. Clayoquot Sound, on the west coast of Vancouver Island, is synonymous with environmentalists' fight against the logging industry. The sound is home to the world's largest remaining coastal temperate forest. Environmentally friendly options are practiced, with companies such as the Eco-Lumber Co-op selling wood that is certified as being from responsibly managed forests.

You can see the extent of logging through British Columbia when you arrive, but visit Google Maps (http://maps.google.com) and click on the "Satellite" link. Then zoom into British Columbia—northern Vancouver Island is a good example—to see just how extensive the clear-cut logging is.

Contacts

For more information on any of these issues, contact the following local environmental organizations: **Canadian Parks and Wilderness Society** (www.cpaws.org), **Greenpeace** (www.greenpeace.ca), **British Columbia Environmental Network** (www.ecobc.org), **Society Promoting Environmental Conservation** (www.spec.bc.ca), and **Valhalla Wilderness Society** (www.vws.org).

Plants and Animals

PLANTS

Two colors invariably jump to mind when you say "British Columbia": green and blue. Just about everywhere you travel in British Columbia, you see trees, trees, and more trees—around two-thirds of the province is forested. But the types of trees differ in each geographic and climatic region. Coastal regions are dominated by temperate rainforest, which requires at least 1,000 millimeters (40 inches) of rain annually and is predominantly evergreen. This biome is extremely rare: it is estimated that at the end of the last ice age, 0.2 percent of the world's land area was temperate rainforest. Only 10 percent of such forests remain, 25 percent in British Columbia, where they are made up of mostly hemlock, western red cedar, and Sitka spruce.

Arbutus (known as Pacific madrone in the United States) is an evergreen hardwood distinctive for its red bark and glossy oval-shaped leaves. It grows near saltwater at the southern end of Vancouver Island and on the Southern Gulf Islands. Forests of Douglas fir thrive in drier areas of the coast. Engelmann

Wildlife and You

British Columbia's abundance of wildlife is one of its biggest draws. To help preserve this unique resource, obey fishing and hunting regulations and use common sense.

- **Do not feed the animals.** Many animals may seem tame, but feeding them endangers you, the animal, and other visitors. Animals become aggressive when looking for handouts.

- **Store food safely.** When camping, keep food in your vehicle or out of reach of animals. Just leaving it in a cooler isn't good enough.

- **Keep your distance.** Although it's tempting to get close to animals for a better look or a photograph, it disturbs the animal and, in many cases, can be dangerous.

- **Drive carefully.** The most common cause of premature death for larger mammals is being hit by cars.

BEARS

Bears are dangerous, and while bear-human encounters happen regularly, their infamous reputation far exceeds the actual number of attacks that occur (in the last 20 years, black bears have accounted for 12 fatalities, and grizzly bears for 5, within British Columbia). That said, common sense is your best weapon against an attack. First and foremost, **keep a safe distance,** particularly if cubs are present—the protective mother will not be far away. **Never harass** or attempt to **feed a bear,** and resist the temptation to move in for an award-winning close-up photo; they are wild animals and are totally unpredictable.

Before heading out on a hike, ask local park or forest-service staff about the likelihood of encountering bears in the area, and heed their advice. **Travel in groups,** never by yourself. Out on the trail, **watch for signs** of recent bear activity, such as fresh footprints or scat. **Make noise** when traveling through dense woods. Take a noisemaker—a few rocks in a soft-drink can or a bell—or let out a loud yell every now and again to let wildlife know you're coming. **Bear spray** has become popular in recent years, but don't trust your life to it by taking unnecessary risks.

Bears will usually avoid you; however, you may come across the odd bruin. Bear talk is a favorite

spruce is common throughout the interior at subalpine elevations. The interior also supports a mixture of Douglas fir and ponderosa pine in the south; interior western hemlock in the southeast; aspen and lodgepole pine in the central reaches; subboreal spruce, birch, and willow in the north; Sitka spruce in the west; and white spruce and black spruce in the northeast. The Haida Gwaii rainforest is thickly covered in spongy pale green moss, which grows alongside coastal Douglas fir. In the region's subalpine areas, you'll find mountain hemlock.

The official provincial floral emblem is the **Pacific dogwood,** a small tree sporting huge clusters of cream-colored flowers in spring and bright foliage and red berries in autumn. The tree is a protected plant in British Columbia; it's a punishable offense to pick from it or destroy it.

In summer, British Columbia turns on a really magnificent floral display. Wildflowers every color of the rainbow pop up on the roadsides: white and yellow daisies, purple lupines, pale pink and dark pink wild roses, blood-red Indian paintbrush, orange and black lilies, red and white clover, and yellow buttercups, to name but a handful. And if you venture off the beaten track and up into the alpine meadows, the floral beauty is hard to believe. You can pick up a wildflower guide at most any local bookshop, and most of the national park visitor centres stock brochures on wildflower identification.

Be very careful when driving, as animals can seemingly appear out of nowhere.

topic in the north, and everyone who has ever spent time in the wilderness has his or her own theory about the best course of action in the event of an encounter or an unlikely attack. On a few things, everyone agrees: **Stay in a group** and **back away slowly,** talking firmly the whole time. **Do not run**—a bear can easily outrun a human. Black bears can climb trees but grizzlies can't. If an attack seems imminent and it's a black bear, the general consensus is to try to fight the animal off; if it's a grizzly, drop to the ground in a hunched-up position, covering your neck, and play dead.

Park staff can supply you with bear-aware literature, and many books have been written on the subject. One of the best is *Bear Attacks: Their Causes and Avoidance* (Lyons Press, 2002) by Canadian bear expert Stephen Herrero.

MAMMALS

British Columbia is one of the best provinces in Canada for wildlife-watching. Thanks to a diverse topography that provides a wide variety of habitat, more species of mammals are found here than in any other province or territory in the country.

Bears

Two species of bears—black bears and grizzlies—are present in British Columbia. Both species are widespread and abundant across the province. The two can be differentiated by size and shape. Grizzlies are larger than black bears and have a flatter, dish-shaped face and a distinctive hump of muscle behind the neck. Color is not a reliable way to tell them apart.

Black bears are not always black. They can be brown or cinnamon, causing them to be confused with the brown grizzly.

If you spot a bear feeding beside the road, chances are it's a **black bear.** These are the most common of all large mammals in British Columbia, estimated to number between 120,000 and 150,000, with the highest concentrations on Vancouver Island and Haida Gwaii. Their weight varies considerably (the larger ones are found in coastal areas), but males average 150 kilograms (330 pounds), females 100 kilograms (220 pounds). Their diet is omnivorous, consisting primarily of grasses and berries but supplemented by small mammals. They are not true hibernators, but in winter they can sleep for up to a month at a time before changing position. Young are born in late winter, while the mother is still asleep.

British Columbia's estimated 15,000 **grizzlies** are widespread in all mainland areas of the province but are only occasionally seen by casual observers. Most sightings occur along coastal areas (where they are generally called **brown bears**) during salmon runs (the Khutzeymateen Grizzly Bear Sanctuary, near Prince Rupert, is world-renowned as a grizzly viewing spot) and in spring and fall in alpine and subalpine zones. The bears' color ranges from light brown to almost black, with dark tan being the most common. On average, males weigh 250-350 kilograms (550-770 pounds). The bears eat small- and medium-size mammals, and salmon and berries in fall. Like black bears, they sleep through most of the winter. When they emerge in early spring, the bears scavenge carcasses of animals that succumbed to the winter until the new spring vegetation becomes sufficiently plentiful.

The Deer Family

Mule deer and **white-tailed deer** are similar in size and appearance. Their color varies with the season but is generally light brown in summer, turning dirty gray in winter. While both species are considerably smaller than elk, the mule deer is a little stockier than the white-tailed deer. The mule deer has a white rump, a white tail with a dark tip, and large mule-like ears. It inhabits open forests along valley floors. The white-tailed deer's tail is dark on top, but when the animal runs, it holds its tail erect, revealing an all-white underside. White-tailed are common along valleys throughout British Columbia but especially prevalent on Vancouver Island. **Sitka** deer, a subspecies, inhabit Haida Gwaii.

The giant of the deer family, the **moose,** has a population in British Columbia estimated at around 170,000. It is an awkward-looking mammal that appears to have been designed by a cartoonist. It has the largest antlers of any animal in the world, stands up to 1.8 meters (6 feet) at the shoulder, and weighs up to 500 kilograms (1,100 pounds). Its body is dark brown, and it has a prominent nose, long spindly legs, small eyes, big ears, and an odd flap of skin called a bell dangling beneath its chin. Apart from all that, it's good-looking. Each spring the bull begins to grow palm-shaped antlers that by August will be fully grown. Moose are solitary animals, preferring marshy areas and weedy lakes, but they are known to wander to higher elevations searching out open spaces in summer. They forage in and around ponds on willows, aspen, birch, grasses, and all aquatic vegetation. They are most common in northern British Columbia.

The **elk** (also known as wapiti) has a tan body with a dark-brown neck, dark-brown legs, and a white rump. This second-largest member of the deer family weighs 250-450 kilograms (550-990 pounds) and stands 1.5 meters (5 feet) at the shoulder. Pockets of elk inhabit valleys in the east of the province, but the animals are not particularly common.

Small populations of **woodland caribou** are restricted to the far north of the province. You may see them feeding in open areas at higher elevations along the Alaska Highway. First Nations people named the animal *caribou* (hoof scraper) for the way in which they feed in winter, scraping away snow with their hooves. Caribou are smaller than elk and have a dark-brown coat with creamy patches on the neck and rump.

Wild Dogs and Cats

After being hunted to near extinction, **wolf** numbers have rebounded across the continent, including in British Columbia, where the vast wilderness is home to a widespread and stable population that numbers between 6,000 and 10,000 and is distributed across the province everywhere except the lower mainland and coastal islands. Wolves weigh up to 65 kilograms (145 pounds), stand one meter (3.3 feet) high at the shoulder, and resemble large huskies or German shepherds. Their color ranges from snow white to brown or black; those in British Columbia are most often shades of gray or brown. Unlike other predators, they are not solitary but are intriguing animals that adhere to a complex social order, living in packs of 5 to 10 animals and roaming over hundreds of kilometers in search of prey.

The **coyote** is often confused for a wolf, when in fact it is much smaller, weighing up to only 15 kilograms (33 pounds). It has a pointed nose and long bushy tail. Its coloring is a mottled mix of brown and gray, with lighter-colored legs and belly. The coyote is a skillful and crafty hunter preying mainly on rodents. They are common and widespread at lower elevations throughout British Columbia, often patrolling the edges of highways and crossing open meadows in low-lying valleys.

Cougars (also called mountain lions, Mexican lions, pumas, and catamounts) are relatively plentiful in British Columbia, especially on Vancouver Island, where it is estimated the population numbers around 800 (total British Columbia population is estimated to be around 3,500). Adult males can grow to over two meters (6.5 feet) in length and weigh up to 90 kilograms (200 pounds). The fur generally ranges in color from light brown to a reddish-tinged gray, but occasionally black cougars are reported. Their athletic prowess puts Olympians to shame. They can spring forward more than eight meters

(26 feet) from a standstill, leap four meters (13 feet) into the air, and safely jump from a height of 20 meters (66 feet). These solitary animals are versatile hunters whose acute vision takes in a peripheral span in excess of 200 degrees.

The elusive **lynx** is identifiable by its pointy black ear tufts and an oversize tabby-cat appearance. The animal has broad, padded paws that distribute its weight, allowing it to "float" on the surface of snow. It weighs up to 10 kilograms (22 pounds) but appears much larger because of its coat of long, thick fur. The lynx, uncommon but widespread throughout the interior, is a solitary creature that prefers the cover of subalpine forests, feeding mostly at night on snowshoe hares and other small mammals.

Sheep and Goats

Dall's sheep (also known as Rocky Mountain or bighorn sheep) are one of the most distinctive mammals of Canada. Easily recognized by their impressive horns, they are often seen grazing on grassy mountain slopes or at salt licks beside the road. The color of their coat varies with the season; in summer it's a brownish gray with a cream-colored belly and rump, turning lighter in winter. Bighorn

black bear

Whales of British Columbia

Whale-watching has gained great popularity off the BC coast in recent years. Most towns along the Vancouver Island coast offer trips out in various watercraft, many staying in sheltered waters where the whales are resting on migratory routes between Mexico and Alaska.

Once nearly extinct, today an estimated 20,000 **gray whales** swim the length of the BC coast twice annually between Baja Mexico and the Bering Sea. The spring migration (Mar.-Apr.) is close to the shore, with whales stopping to rest and feed in places such as Clayoquot Sound and Haida Gwaii.

Orcas, best known as killer whales, are the largest member of the dolphin family. Adult males can reach 10 meters (about 33 feet) in length and up to 10 tons in weight, but their most distinctive feature is a dorsal fin that protrudes more than 1.5 meters (five feet) from the back. Orcas are widespread in oceans around the world, but especially common along the BC coast, including Robson Bight, the world's only sanctuary established especially for the protection of the species. Three distinct populations live in BC waters: resident orcas feed primarily on salmon and travel in pods of up to 50; transients travel by themselves or in very small groups, feeding on marine mammals such as seals and whales; and offshore orcas live in the open ocean, traveling in pods and feeding only on fish. In total, they number around 500, of which about 300 are residents living in 15 pods.

Local waters are home to an abundance of other marine mammals. **Porpoises, dolphins,** and **humpback whales** frolic in coastal waters, and colonies of **seals** and **sea lions** can be viewed by boat or kayak.

---

sheep are particularly tolerant of humans and often approach parked vehicles; although they are not especially dangerous, you should not approach or feed them (as with all mammals).

The remarkable rock-climbing ability of nimble **mountain goats** allows them to live high in the mountains, retreating to rocky ledges or near-vertical slopes when threatened by predators.

Small Mammals

One of the animal kingdom's most industrious mammals is the **beaver.** Growing to a length of 50 centimeters (20 inches) and tipping the scales at around 20 kilograms (44 pounds), it has a flat, rudder-like tail and webbed back feet that enable it to swim at speeds up to 10 km/h (6 mph). The exploration of western Canada can be directly attributed to the beaver, whose pelt was in high demand in fashion-conscious Europe in the early 1800s. The beaver was never entirely wiped out from the mountains, and today the animals inhabit almost any forested valley with flowing water. Beavers build their dam walls and lodges of twigs, branches, sticks of

felled trees, and mud. They eat the bark and smaller twigs of deciduous plants and store branches underwater, near the lodge, as a winter food supply.

Several species of **squirrel** are common in British Columbia, including the golden-mantled ground, Columbian, and red squirrels. **Marmots** are common and widespread, with various species living in different habitats. They are stocky creatures, weighing 4-9 kilograms (9-20 pounds). The **porcupine,** a small, squat animal, is easily recognized by its thick coat of quills. It eats roots and leaves but is also known for being destructive around wooden buildings and vehicle tires.

REPTILES

Reptiles don't like cold climates, and therefore they don't like Canada. British Columbia is home to just 17 of the world's 10,000-odd reptile species. All 17 inhabit dry, hot valleys of grassland, such as the Okanagan Valley. The breakdown includes nine species of snakes, five turtles, two lizards, and one species of skink. The province's only poisonous snake is the extremely rare **western rattlesnake,** which lives in the southern interior. Like other rattlers, it waits for prey rather than actively hunting and won't bite unless provoked.

BIRDS

Of the 550 bird species recorded in British Columbia, 300 breed within the province (the most of any province or territory), and of these, 35 species nest nowhere else in Canada. The lower mainland is a migration stop for the million-odd birds that travel the Pacific Flyway each year. Huge populations of waterfowl winter at Boundary Bay near Vancouver, and large concentrations can also be seen around Fort St. James, Cranbrook, Prince George, and Lac La Hache. The province is home to half of the world's populations of both **trumpeter swans** and **blue grouse,** as well as a quarter of the world's **bald eagles.** You'll see beautiful **snow** and **Canada geese, herons, ospreys,** and all kinds of **ducks.**

British Columbia's official bird is the often cheeky, vibrant blue-and-black **Steller's jay,** found throughout the province.

FISH

Of the 72 species of fish in British Columbia, 22 are considered sport fish. The two varieties most sought after by anglers are salmon, found in tidal waters along the coast, and trout, inhabiting the freshwater lakes and rivers of interior British Columbia.

Salmon

Five species of salmon are native to the tidal waters of British Columbia. All are anadromous—that is, they spend their time in both freshwater and saltwater. The life cycle of these creatures is truly amazing. Hatching from small red eggs often hundreds of miles upriver from the ocean, the fry find their way to the ocean, undergoing massive internal changes along the way that allow them to survive in saltwater. Depending on the species, they then spend two to six years in the open water, traveling as far as the Bering Sea. After reaching maturity, they begin the epic

journey back to their birthplace, to the exact patch of gravel on the same river from where they emerged. Their navigation system has evolved over a million years—relying on, it is believed, a sensory system that uses measurements of sunlight, the earth's magnetic field, and atmospheric pressure to find their home rivers. Once the salmon are in range of their home river, scent takes over, returning them to the exact spot where they were born. Once the salmon reach freshwater, they stop eating. Unlike other species of fish (including Atlantic salmon), Pacific salmon die immediately after spawning; hence the importance of returning to their birthplace, a spot the salmon instinctively know gives them the best opportunity for their one chance to reproduce successfully.

The largest of the five salmon species is the **chinook,** which grows to 30 kilograms (66 pounds) in BC waters. Known as king salmon in the United States, chinooks are a prized sport fish most recognizable by their size but also by black gums and silver-spotted tails.

Averaging 2-3 kilograms (4.4-6.6 pounds), **sockeye** (red salmon) are the most streamlined of the Pacific salmon. They are distinguished from other species by a silvery-blue skin and prominent eyes. While other species swim into the ocean after hatching, the sockeye remain inland, in freshwater lakes and rivers, for at least a year before migrating into the Pacific. When it's ready to spawn, the body of the sockeye turns bright red and the head a dark green.

Chum (dog) salmon are very similar in appearance to sockeye, and the bodies also change dramatically when spawning; a white tip on the anal fin is the best form of identification. Bright, silver-colored **coho** (silver) average 1.5-3 kilograms (3.3-6.6 pounds). This species can be recognized by white gums and spots on the upper portion of the tail.

Smallest of the Pacific salmon are the **pinks,** which rarely weigh over 4 kilograms (9 pounds) and usually average around 2 kilograms (4.4 pounds). Their most dominant feature is a tail covered in large oval spots.

They are most abundant in northern waters in even-numbered years and in southern waters in odd-numbered years.

Freshwater Fish

Trout are part of the same fish family as salmon, but, with one or two exceptions, they live in freshwater their entire lives. Interestingly, the trout of British Columbia are more closely related to Atlantic salmon than to any of the species of Pacific salmon detailed here. The predominant species is the rainbow trout, common in lakes and rivers throughout the province. It has an olive-green back and a red strip running along the center of its body. Many subspecies exist, such as the large Gerrard rainbow trout of the southern interior; the steelhead, an oceangoing rainbow, inhabits rivers flowing into the Pacific Ocean.

Other trout species present include the bull trout, which struggles to survive through high levels of fishing and a low reproductive rate. Cutthroat trout, found in high-elevation lakes, are named for a bright red dash of color that runs from below the mouth almost to the gills. Colorful brook trout can be identified by their dark-green backs with pale splotches and purple-sheened sides. Brown trout are the only trout with both black and red spots.

The lake trout, which grows to 20 kilograms (44 pounds), is native to large, deep lakes throughout the province, but it is technically a member of the char family. The kokanee is a freshwater salmon native to major lakes and rivers of the southern interior. They are directly related to sockeye salmon and look similar in all aspects but size; kokanee rarely grow to over 30 centimeters (12 inches) in length, spawning in the same freshwater range as sockeye.

The whitefish, a light gray fish, is native to lower-elevation lakes and rivers across the province. Arctic grayling and Dolly Varden trout (named for a colorful character in a Charles Dickens story) inhabit northern waters. Walleye (also called pickerel) grow to 4.5 kilograms (10 pounds) and are common in sandy-bottomed areas of lakes in northeastern British Columbia. The monster freshwater fish of British Columbia is the sturgeon, growing to over 100 kilograms (220 pounds) in size and living for upward of 100 years.

History

THE EARLIEST INHABITANTS

Human habitation of what is now British Columbia began around 15,000 years ago, when *Homo sapiens* migrated from northeast Asia across a land bridge spanning the Bering Strait. During this time, the northern latitudes of North America were covered by an ice cap, forcing these people to travel south down the west coast before fanning out across the ice-free southern latitudes. As the ice cap receded northward, the people drifted north also, perhaps only a few kilometers in an entire generation, and began crossing the 49th parallel about 12,000 years ago. By the time the ice cap had receded from all but the far north and the highest mountain peaks, two distinct cultures had formed: one along the coast and one in the interior. Within these two broad groups, many tribes formed, developing distinct cultures and languages.

The Northwest Coast

Around 12,000 years ago, Canada's west coast had become ice-free, and humans had begun settling along its entire length. Over time they had broken into distinct linguistic groups, including the Coast Salish, Kwagiulth, Tsimshian, Gitxsan, Nisga'a, Haida, and Tlingit, but all had two things in common: their reliance on cedar and on salmon. They lived a very different lifestyle from the stereotypical plains dwellers—they had no bison to depend on, they didn't ride horses, nor did they live in tepees, but instead developed a unique and intriguing culture that remains in place in small pockets along the west coast. These coastal bands lived comfortably off the land and the sea, hunting deer, beavers, bears, and sea otters; fishing for salmon, cod, and halibut; and harvesting edible kelp. They built huge 90-meter-long (295-foot) cedar houses and 20-meter-long (65-foot) dugout cedar canoes, and developed a distinctive and highly decorative arts style featuring animals, mythical creatures, and oddly shaped human forms believed to be supernatural ancestors.

West coast First Nations society emphasized the material wealth of each chief and community, displayed to others during special events called potlatches. The potlatch ceremonies marked important moments in society, such as marriages, puberty celebrations, deaths, or totem-pole raisings. The wealth of a community became obvious when the chief gave away enormous quantities of gifts to his guests—the nobler the guest, the better the gift. The potlatch exchange was accompanied by much feasting, speech-making, dancing, and entertainment, all of which could last many days. Stories performed by hosts garbed in elaborate costumes and masks educated, entertained, and affirmed each clan's historical continuity.

The Interior Salish

Moving north with the receding ice cap around 10,000 years ago, the Salish people fanned out across most of southwestern and interior British Columbia. After spending summers in the mountains hunting and gathering, they would move to lower elevations to harvest their most precious natural resource: salmon. At narrow canyons along the Fraser River and its tributaries, the Salish put their fishing skills to the test, netting, trapping, and spearing salmon as the fish traveled upstream to spawn. Much of the catch was preserved by drying or roasting, then pounded into a powder known as pemmican for later use or to be traded. The Salish wintered in earth-covered log structures known as pit houses. Depressions left by these ancient structures can still be seen in places such as Keatley Creek, alongside the Fraser River. Within the Salish Nation, four distinct tribes have been identified: the Lillooet, the Thompson (Nlaka'pamux), the Okanagan, and the Shuswap. The Shuswap people occupied the largest area, with a territory that extended from the Fraser River to the Rocky Mountains; they were the only Salish who crossed the Rockies to hunt buffalo on the plains.

The Kootenay

The Kootenay people (other common spellings include Kootenai, Kootenae, and Kutenai) were once hunters of buffalo on the great American plains, but they were pushed westward by fierce enemies. Like the Salish people did farther west, they then moved north with the receding ice cap. They crossed the 49th parallel around 10,000 years ago, settling in the Columbia River Valley along the western edge of the Canadian Rockies. Like the Salish, they were hunters and gatherers and came to rely on salmon. The Kootenay were generally friendly, mixing freely with the Salish and treating the earliest explorers, such as David Thompson, with respect. They regularly traveled east over the Rockies to hunt—to the wildlife-rich Kootenay Plains or farther south to the Great Plains in search of bison.

The Athabascans

Athabascan (often spelled Athapaskan) is the most widely spread of all North American linguistic groups, extending from the Rio Grande to Alaska. In 1793, when Alexander Mackenzie made his historic journey across the continent, he spent the last summer before reaching the west coast in Athabascan territory, which at that time included most of what is now northern British Columbia. The largest division of the Athabascans within this area was the **Carrier** group, so named for

Totem Poles

Traveling through British Columbia, you can't help but notice all the totem poles decorating the landscape. Totem poles are made of red (or occasionally yellow) cedar painted black, red, blue, yellow, and white, with colored pigment derived from minerals, plants, and salmon roe. They are erected as validation or public record or documentation of an important event. Six types of poles are believed to have evolved in the following order: house posts (an integral part of the house structure), mortuary posts (erected as a chief's or shaman's grave, often with the bones or ashes in a box at the top), memorial posts (commemorating special events), frontal posts (a memorial or heraldic pole), welcome posts, and shame posts. None is an object of worship; each tells a story or history of a person's clan or family. The figures on the pole represent family lineage, animals, or a mythical character.

Since 1951, when a government ban on potlatch ceremonies (of which the raising of totem poles is an integral part) was lifted, the art form has been revived. Over the years, many totem poles have been moved from their original locations. Both historic and more modern poles can be viewed in British Columbia. The Haida people were renowned for their totem poles; many totem villages, long since abandoned, remain on the remote southern tip of the archipelago. Of these, **Ninstints** is regarded as the world's best example of an ancient Haida totem village. More modern totems can be found at **Stanley Park,** Vancouver; **Thunderbird Park,** Victoria; **Alert Bay,** Cormorant Island; and **Gitanyow,** at the south end of the Stewart-Cassiar Highway. The **Museum of Anthropology** in Vancouver also has an excellent collection.

their custom requiring a widowed woman to carry the ashes of her husband with her for at least a year. Aside from the fact that they cremated their dead, the Carrier people had similar traits to those found throughout the Athabascan peoples—they lived simply and were generally friendly toward each other and neighboring groups. They lived throughout the northern reaches of the Fraser River basin and along the Skeena River watershed. The Carrier, along with Athabascan tribes that lived farther north (including the Chilcotin, Tahltan, and Inland Tlingit), adopted many traits of their coastal neighbors, such as potlatch ceremonies and raising totem poles. Another Athabascan group inhabiting British Columbia was the **Beaver** people, who were forced westward, up the Peace River watershed, by the warlike Cree (the name Peace River originated after the two groups eventually made peace). With no access to salmon-rich waters west of the Rocky Mountains, the Beaver hunted bison, moose, and caribou and were strongly influenced by the fur trade. Over the subcontinental divide to the north is the upper watershed of the mighty

Mackenzie River; extending into the northeast corner of the province, this area was the traditional home of the **Slavey,** one of seven groups of the Dene (DEN-eh) people. Like the Beaver, they were nomadic hunters and gatherers but also relied heavily on fishing.

EUROPEAN EXPLORATION AND COLONIZATION

It was only a little more than 200 years ago that the first European explorers began to chart the northwest corner of North America. The area's geography presented formidable natural barriers to the east (the lofty Rocky Mountains) and the west (long stretches of ocean away from other landmasses).

By Sea

In the second half of the 18th century, curiosity about a western approach to the fabled Northwest Passage and a common desire to discover rich natural resources lured Russian, Spanish, British, and American explorers and fur traders along the coastline that is now British Columbia. In 1774, the ship of Mexican **Juan Pérez** was the first vessel to explore the coastline and trade with First Nations people. He was quickly followed by Spaniard **Juan Francisco Bodega y Quadra,** who took possession of the coast of Alaska for Spain. England's **Captain James Cook** arrived in 1778 to spend some time at Nootka, becoming the first European to actually come ashore, trading with the First Nations while he overhauled his ship. Cook received a number of luxuriantly soft sea otter furs, which he later sold at a huge profit in China. This news spawned a fur-trading rush that began in 1785 and continued for 25 years. Ship after loaded ship called in along the coast, trading iron, brass, copper, muskets, cloth, jewelry, and rum to First Nations people in exchange for furs. The indigenous people were eager to obtain the foreign goods, but they were also known for driving a hard bargain. The traders took the furs directly to China to trade for silk, tea, spices, ginger, and other luxuries. In 1789, Bodega y Quadra established a settlement at Nootka, but after ongoing problems with the British, who also claimed the area, he gave it up. In 1792, **Captain George Vancouver,** who had been the navigator on Cook's 1778 expedition, returned to the area and sailed into Burrard Inlet, claiming the land for Great Britain.

By Land

In the meantime, adventurous North West Company fur traders were crossing the Rockies in search of waterways to the coast. The first European to reach the coast was **Alexander Mackenzie,** who traveled via the Peace, Fraser, and West Road Rivers—you can still see the rock in the Dean Channel (off Bella Coola) where he inscribed "Alexander Mackenzie from Canada by land 22nd July 1793." Not far behind came other explorers, including **Simon Fraser,** who followed the Fraser River to the sea in 1808, and **David Thompson,** who followed the Columbia River to its mouth in 1811. Today the names of these men grace everything from rivers to

motels. In the early 19th century, the North West Company established trading posts in **New Caledonia** (the name Simon Fraser gave to the northern interior). These posts were taken over by Hudson's Bay Company after amalgamation of the two companies in 1821.

The First Nations Response

The fur trade brought prosperity to the indigenous society, which was organized around wealth, possessions, and potlatches. The Hudson's Bay Company had no interest in interfering with the First Nations and, in general, treated them fairly. This early contact with Europeans resulted in expanded trade patterns and increased commerce between coastal and interior tribes. It also spurred the production of indigenous arts and crafts to new heights, as chiefs required more carved headgear, masks, costumes, feast dishes, and the like for the increasingly frequent ceremonial occasions that came with increased wealth.

However, commerce between the Europeans and locals also caused the indigenous communities to abandon their traditional home sites and instead to cluster around the forts for trading and protection. In addition, the Europeans introduced muskets, alcohol, and disease (most significantly smallpox), all of which took their toll on the First Nations population, which stood at around 60,000 in 1850. Christian missionaries soon arrived and tried to ban the traditional potlatches, but not until land-hungry colonists showed up did major conflicts arise between First Nations peoples and Europeans. Those land-ownership conflicts proved tenacious, continuing to this day.

Vancouver Island

The British government decided in 1849 that Vancouver Island should be colonized to confirm British sovereignty in the area and forestall any American expansion. Though mostly content to leave the island in the hands of the Hudson's Bay Company, the Brits nevertheless sent **Richard Blanshard** out from England to become the island colony's first governor. Blanshard soon resigned and was replaced in 1851 by **James Douglas,** head of the Hudson's Bay Company. Douglas had long been in control of the island, and his main concerns were to maintain law and order and to purchase the land. He made treaties with the First Nations in which the land became the "entire property of the white people forever." In return, the indigenous people retained use of their village sites and enclosed fields, and could hunt and fish on unoccupied lands. Each indigenous family was paid a pitiful compensation.

In 1852, coal was discovered near Nanaimo, and English miners were imported to develop the deposits. Around the same time, loggers began felling the enormous timber stands along the Alberni Canal, and the Puget Sound Agricultural Association (a subsidiary of Hudson's Bay Company) developed several large farms in the Victoria region. By the 1850s, the town of Victoria, with its moderate climate and fertile soil, had developed into an agreeable settlement.

LAW, ORDER, AND GOLD
Firsts

In 1856 the first parliament west of the Great Lakes was elected, and Dr. J. S. Helmcken became speaker. (Today you can still see his house in Victoria.) Only two years later, this still relatively unexplored and quiet part of the world was turned upside down with the first whispers of "gold" on the mainland, along the banks of the Fraser River. As the news spread, miners—mostly Americans—arrived by the shipload at Victoria, increasing the town's population from several hundred to more than 5,000. Fur trading faded as gold mining jumped to the forefront. Realizing that enormous wealth could be buried on the mainland, the British government quickly responded by creating a mainland colony that at first was named New Caledonia. Because France possessed a colony of the same name in the South Pacific, Queen Victoria was

asked to change the name, which she did, using "Columbia," which appeared on local maps, and adding "British," making the name distinct from the Columbia River district across the border. In 1858, Governor James Douglas of Vancouver Island also became governor of British Columbia, giving up his Hudson's Bay Company position to serve both colonies. In 1866, the two colonies were combined into one.

Cariboo Gold

The lucrative Cariboo gold rush resulted in construction of the Cariboo Wagon Road (also called the Gold Rush Trail), an amazing engineering feat that opened up British Columbia's interior. Completed in 1865, the road connected Yale with Barkerville, one of the richest and wildest gold towns in North America. Mule trains and stagecoaches plied the route, and roadhouses and boomtowns dotted its entire length. Among the colorful characters of this era was Judge Matthew Baillie Begbie, an effective chief of law and order during a time when law and order might easily have been nonexistent.

In addition to the gold miners, groups of settlers soon began arriving in the Cariboo. One such group, a horde known as the **Overlanders,** left Ontario and Quebec with carts, horses, and oxen in summer 1862, intent on crossing the vast plains and the Rockies to British Columbia. One detachment rafted down the Fraser River, the other down the North Thompson. Both arrived in Kamloops in autumn that same year. Some continued north up the Cariboo Gold Rush Trail, but others headed for the coast, having had more than their fill of adventure on the trip across.

Rapid Development

In addition to the Cariboo Wagon Road, other trails opened up more of the province in the early 1860s. The Hope-Princeton and Dewdney Trails into the Kootenays led to settlement in British Columbia's eastern regions. Salmon canning was also developed in the 1860s, and several canneries on both the lower Fraser and Skeena Rivers had the world market in their pockets. (You can still see one of the old canneries near Prince Rupert today.)

It wasn't until 1862 that Burrard Inlet—site of today's city of Vancouver—sprang onto the map with the building of a small lumber mill on the north shore. The region's tall, straight trees became much in demand. More lumber mills started up, and a healthy export market developed in only a few years. Farmers began to move into the area, and by the end of the 1860s a small town had been established. "Gassy Jack" Deighton started a very popular saloon on the south shore of Burrard Inlet near a lumber camp, and for some time the settlement was locally called Gastown. After the town site was surveyed in 1870, the name was changed to Granville. Then, in 1886, the town was officially renamed Vancouver, in honor of Captain George Vancouver. At this time, New Westminster was the official capital of the colony of British Columbia, much to the concern and disbelief of Vancouver Islanders, who strongly believed Victoria should have retained the position. Two years later, with the mainland gold rushes over, the capital reverted to Victoria, where it has remained ever since.

Confederation and Beyond

The next big issue to concern British Columbia was confederation. The eastern colonies had become one large dominion, and BC residents were invited to join. London and Ottawa both wanted British Columbia to join, to assist in counterbalancing the mighty U.S. power to the south. After much public debate, the southwesternmost colony entered the Confederation as the Province of British Columbia in July 1871—on the condition that the west coast be connected to the east by railway. Many roads were built during the 1870s, but it was the completion of the transcontinental railway in 1885 that really opened up British Columbia to the rest of the country. Other railways followed, steamships plied the lakes and rivers, more roads were built, and industries—including logging, mining, farming, fishing, and tourism—started to develop.

During the 20th century, British Columbia moved from roads to major multilane highways, from horses to ferries, and from gold mining to sportfishing. Yet it still attracts explorers—backcountry hikers and mountain climbers in search of untrammeled wilderness, plenty of which remains.

Government and Economy

GOVERNMENT

Canada is a constitutional monarchy. Its system of government is based on England's, and the British monarch is also king or queen of Canada. However, because Canada is an independent nation, the British monarchy and government have no control over the political affairs of Canada. An appointed **governor general** based in Ottawa represents the Crown, as does a **lieutenant governor** in each province. Both roles are mainly ceremonial, but their "royal assent" is required to make any bill passed by parliament into law.

Elected representatives debate and enact laws affecting their constituents. The head of the federal government is the **prime minister,** and the head of each provincial government is its **premier.** The **speaker** is elected at the first session of each parliament to make sure parliamentary rules are followed. A bill goes through three grueling sessions in the legislature—a reading, a debate, and a second reading. When all the fine print has been given the royal nod, the bill then becomes a law.

Provincial Politics

In the BC legislature, the lieutenant governor is at the top of the ladder. Under him are the members of the **Legislative Assembly** (MLAs). Assembly members are elected for a period of up to five years, though an election for a new assembly can be called at any time by the lieutenant governor or on the advice of the premier. In the Legislative Assembly are the premier, the cabinet ministers and backbenchers, the leader of the official opposition, other parties, and independent members. All Canadian citizens who are BC residents age 19 and over can vote, providing they've lived in the province for at least six months.

In recent decades, provincial politics in British Columbia have been a three-party struggle. The province was the first in Canada to hold elections on a fixed date, with the next election scheduled for 2021. In the most recent election (May 9, 2017), the **New Democrats** (NDP) defeated the **Liberals** for the first time since 1996. The NDP first came to prominence in the late 1960s as the official opposition to the **Social Credit Party** (the Socreds, who had ruled the province for two decades), advocating free enterprise and government restraint.

The laws of British Columbia are administered by the cabinet, premier, and lieutenant governor; they are interpreted by a **judiciary** made up of the Supreme Court of BC, the Court of Appeal, and county or provincial courts. For information on the provincial government, its ministries, and current issues, surf the web to www.gov.bc.ca.

ECONOMY

British Columbia's economy has always relied on resource-based activities. The first indigenous people hunted the region's abundant wildlife and fished in its trout- and salmon-filled rivers. Then Europeans arrived on the scene, reaping a bounty by cutting down forests for timber and slaughtering the wildlife for its fur. Luckily, the province is blessed with a wealth of natural resources. In addition to timber and wildlife, British Columbia holds rich reserves of minerals, petroleum, natural gas, and coal, and water for hydroelectric power is plentiful.

Forestry

Almost two-thirds of British Columbia—some 60 million hectares (148 million acres)—is forested, primarily in coniferous softwood (fir, hemlock, spruce, and pine). These forests provide about half the country's marketable wood and about 25 percent of the North American inventory. On Vancouver Island, the hemlock species is dominant. Douglas fir, balsam, and western red cedar are other valuable commercial trees in the region. The provincial government owns 94 percent of the forestland, private companies own 5 percent, and the national government owns the remaining 1 percent. Private companies log much of the provincially owned forest under license from the government. Around 75 million cubic meters of lumber are harvested annually, employing 120,000 workers. The forestry industry generates $13 billion annually in exports, more than all other industries combined.

Tourism

Tourism has rapidly ascended in economic importance, with an annual value of $7.5 billion to the provincial economy; it's now the second-largest industry and the province's largest employer (more than 220,000 are directly employed in the industry). Vancouver and Victoria are the province's two major destinations, with Whistler one of North America's most visited ski resorts.

The tourism segment continues to grow, as more and more people become aware of outstanding scenery; numerous national, provincial, historic, and regional parks; and the bountiful outdoor recreation activities available year-round. **Tourism BC** promotes British Columbia to the world; latest figures record 26 million annual "visitor nights" (the number of visitors multiplied by the number of nights they stayed in British Columbia). Official visitor numbers are broken down to show that four million visitors were Canadians from outside British Columbia, four million were from the United States, while one million visitors originated from outside North America (Japan, Great Britain, and Germany provided most of these).

Mining

British Columbia is a mineral-rich province, and historically mining has been an important part of the economy. Since the first Cariboo gold rush in the late 1850s, the face of the industry has changed dramatically. Until the mid-1900s, most mining was underground, but today open-pit mining is the preferred method of mineral extraction. The province is home to over 25 major mines and three mineral processing plants that produce $2.8 billion worth of exports. Coal is the most valuable sector of the mining industry, accounting for $800 million of exports (most to Japan and other Asian markets). Other mining is for metals (such as copper, gold, zinc, silver, molybdenum, and lead), industrial minerals (sulfur, asbestos, limestone, gypsum, and others), and structural materials (sand, gravel, dimension stone, and cement). In northeastern British Columbia, drilling for petroleum and natural gas also helps fuel the economy.

Agriculture

Cultivated land is sparse in mountainous British Columbia—only 4 percent of the province is arable, with just 25 percent of this land regarded as prime for agriculture. Nevertheless, agriculture is an important part of the provincial economy; 18,000 farms growing 200 different crops contribute $1.5 billion annually. The most valuable sector of the industry is dairy farming, which is worth $260 million; that works out to an output of 650 million liters (169 million gallons) of milk per year. The best land for dairy cattle is found in the lower Fraser Valley and on southern Vancouver Island. Poultry farms, vegetables, bulbs, and ornamental shrubs are also found mostly in the Fraser River Valley and the southern end of Vancouver Island.

Fishing

Commercial fishing, one of British Columbia's principal industries, is worth $1 billion annually and comes almost entirely from species that inhabit tidal waters around Vancouver Island. The province has over 5,000 registered fishing boats. The industry concentrates on salmon (60 percent of total fishing revenues come from six species of salmon), with boats harvesting the five species indigenous to the Pacific Ocean. Other species harvested include herring, halibut, cod, sole, and shellfish, such as crabs. The province is also home to over 500 fish farms, with the aquaculture industry revolving around Atlantic salmon and adding $1 billion annually to the provincial economy. Canned and fresh fish are exported to markets all over the world—the province is considered the most productive fishing region in Canada. Japan is the largest export market, followed by Europe and the United States.

Film Industry

The value of the film industry in British Columbia has more than tripled since 1997 to be worth $1 billion annually; it directly employs 25,000 locals. The province is ideal both as a location for shooting and as a production center (Vancouver ranks third behind only Los Angeles and New York as a production center, with 70 post-production facilities). Since the late 1970s, more and more Hollywood production companies have discovered the beauty of Vancouver, its studio facilities, on-site production crews, and support services, as well as more recently a favorable exchange rate. The industry is overseen by the **BC Film Commission** (604/660-2732, www.bcfilmcommission.com).

Shipping and Maritime Commerce

The province boasts year-round ports, deep-sea international shipping lanes, log-towing vessels, specialized freight and passenger steamers, and all the requisite marine facilities. The United States and Japan are British Columbia's main export and import trading partners.

People and Culture

When British Columbia joined the confederation to become a Canadian province in 1871, its population was only 36,000, and 27,000 of the residents were First Nations people. With the completion of the Canadian Pacific Railway in 1885, immigration during the early 20th century, and rapid industrial development after World War II, the provincial population burgeoned. Between 1951 and 1971 alone, it doubled. Today 4.6 million people live in British Columbia (12 percent of Canada's total). The population is concentrated in the southwest, namely in Vancouver, on the south end of Vancouver Island, and in the Okanagan Valley. These three areas make up less than 1 percent of the province but account for 80 percent of the population. The overall population density is just 3.9 people per square kilometer.

British Columbia's annual population growth has been averaging 4 percent over the last decade. Around 70 percent of this population growth can be attributed to westward migration across the country. Retirees make up a large percentage of these new arrivals, as do, to a lesser extent, young professionals.

Around 40 percent of British Columbians are of British origin, followed by 30 percent of other European lineage, mostly French and German. To really get the British feeling, spend some time in Victoria—a city that has retained its original English customs and traditions from days gone by. First Nations people make up 3.7 percent of the population. While the First Nations peoples of British Columbia have adopted the technology and the ways of Europeans, they still remain a distinct group, contributing to and enriching the culture of the province. Asians have made up a significant percentage of the population since the mid-1800s, when they came in search of gold. More recently, the province saw an influx of settlers from Hong Kong prior to the 1997 transfer of control of that city from Britain to China.

LANGUAGE

The main language spoken throughout the province is English, though almost 6 percent of the population also speaks French, Canada's second official language. All federal government information is written in both English and French throughout Canada.

The indigenous people of British Columbia fall into 10 major ethnic groups by language: Nootka (west Vancouver Island), Coast Salish (southwest BC), Interior Salish (southern interior), Kootenay (in the Kootenay region), Athabascan (in the central and northeastern regions), Bella Coola and Northern Kwakiutl (along the central west coast), Tsimshian (in the northwest), Haida (on Haida Gwaii), and Inland Tlingit (in the far northwest corner of the province). However, most First Nations people still speak English more than their indigenous tongue.

INDIGENOUS ARTS AND CRAFTS

Indigenous artistry tends to fall into one of two categories: "arts," such as woodcarving and painting, argillite carving, jade- and silverwork, and totem restoration (all generally attended to by men), and "handicrafts," such as basketry, weaving, beadwork, skin work, sewing, and knitting (generally created by women). Today, all of these arts and crafts contribute significant income to First Nations communities.

Painting and **woodcarving** are probably the most recognized art forms of the northern west coast indigenous people. Throughout British Columbia—in museums and people's homes, outdoors, and of course in all the shops—you can see brightly colored carved totems, canoes, paddles, fantastic masks, ceremonial rattles, feast dishes, bowls, and spoons. Fabulous designs, many featuring animals or mythical legends, are also painstakingly painted in bright primary colors on paper. You can buy limited-edition, high-quality prints of these paintings at many indigenous crafts outlets. They are more reasonable in cost than carvings, yet just as stunning when effectively framed.

Basketry comes in a variety of styles and materials. Watch for decorative cedar-root (fairly rare) and cedar-bark baskets, still made on the west coast of Vancouver Island; spruce-root baskets from Haida Gwaii; and beautiful, functional birch-bark baskets from the Hazelton area, between Prince George and Prince Rupert.

Beaded and fringed **moccasins, jackets, vests,** and **gloves** are available at most craft outlets. And all outdoor types should consider forking out for a heavy, water-resistant, raw-sheep-wool sweater; they're generally white or gray with a black design, much in demand because they're warm, good in the rain, rugged, and last longer than one lifetime. One of the best places to get your hands on one is the Cowichan Valley on Vancouver Island, although you can also find them in the Fraser Valley from Vancouver to Lytton and in First Nations craft outlets. Expect to pay around $120-220 for the real thing, more in tourist shops.

Carved argillite (black slate) miniature totem poles, brooches, ashtrays, and other small items, highly decorated with geometric and animal designs, are created exclusively by the Haida on Haida Gwaii; the argillite comes from a quarry near Skidegate and can only be used by the Skidegate people. You can find argillite carvings in Skidegate and in craft shops in Prince Rupert, Victoria, and Vancouver. Silverwork is also popular, and some of the best is created by the Haida. Particularly notable is the work of Bill Reid, a Haida artist living in Vancouver. Jade jewelry can be seen in the Lillooet and Lytton areas.

Essentials

Getting There

The vast majority of North American visitors to British Columbia arrive by driving or flying, although you can also reach the province by bus, train, or ferry. Vancouver, in the southwest corner, is the main gateway. It is 225 kilometers (140 miles) north of Seattle and 1,060 kilometers (653 miles) west of Calgary along the **Trans-Canada Highway.** From farther afield, Vancouver is 2,055 kilometers (1,277 miles) north of Los Angeles, 4,530 kilometers (2,807 miles) west of Toronto, and 4,785 kilometers (2,973 miles) west of New York.

AIR

Vancouver International Airport (YVR, www.yvr.ca) is British Columbia's main gateway and Canada's second-busiest airport. Regularly scheduled service to and from Vancouver is offered by major airlines around the world. Victoria may be the capital, but it comes in a distant second when it comes to international flights; the only destinations served from its airport are major Canadian cities and Seattle.

From Canada

Air Canada (604/688-5515 or 888/247-2262, www.aircanada.com) is one of the world's largest airlines, serving five continents. It offers direct flights to Vancouver from across the country and to Victoria from Calgary and Edmonton. Canada's second-largest airline is **WestJet** (604/606-5525 or 800/538-5696, www.westjet.com). The least expensive flights land at Abbotsford, 72 kilometers (45 miles) east of downtown Vancouver. Flights also terminate at Vancouver's main airport and in Victoria. These three airports receive WestJet flights from Calgary, Edmonton, Hamilton, Ottawa, Regina, Saskatoon, Thunder Bay, and as far east as St. John's, Newfoundland. **Central Mountain Air** (250/877-5000 or 888/865-8585, www.flycma.com) flies from Calgary to Prince George and Edmonton to Fort St. John.

From the United States

Air Canada offers direct flights to Vancouver from the following U.S. cities: Chicago, Honolulu, Las Vegas, Los Angeles, Maui, Phoenix, Portland, San Francisco, and Seattle. Vancouver is also served by the following U.S. carriers: **Alaska Airlines** (800/252-7522, www.alaskaair.com) from Los Angeles, Portland, and Seattle; **American Airlines** (800/433-7300, www.aa.com) from Los Angeles, Las Vegas, and Dallas; **Delta** (800/221-1212, www.delta.com) from Seattle, Salt Lake City, and Los Angeles; and **United Airlines** (800/241-6522, www.united.com) from Denver and Los Angeles.

The easiest way to travel between Seattle and Vancouver Island is with **Kenmore Air** (425/486-1257 or 866/435-9524, www.kenmoreair.com), which has scheduled floatplane flights between the north end of Lake Washington and Victoria's Inner Harbour.

From Outside North America

From the South Pacific, **Air Canada** operates nonstop flights from Sydney, taking around 14 hours. **Air New Zealand** (800/663-5494, www.airnewzealand.com) offers nonstop flights between Vancouver and Auckland. This airline also has flights with stops throughout the South Pacific, including Nadi, Fiji.

Vancouver is the closest west coast

Air Taxes

The actual airfare is only a portion of the cost of flying—there are a raft of fees and taxes collected by numerous government agencies, as well as fuel surcharges. On domestic flights within Canada, expect to pay around $80-100 in additional charges. This includes an **Air Travellers Security Tax** ($5-10 one-way for flights within North America and $25 round-trip for international flights), an insurance surcharge of $3 one-way, and a fee of $9-20 one-way that goes to **NAV Canada** for the operation of the federal navigation system. Advertised domestic fares are inclusive of **fuel surcharges,** but on international flights expect to pay up to $200 extra. All major Canadian airports charge an **Airport Improvement Fee** to all departing passengers, with Victoria charging just $10; other British Columbia airports charge up to $21. You'll also need to pay this fee from your original departure point, and if connecting through Toronto another $8 is collected. And, of course, the above taxes are taxable, with the Canadian government collecting the 5 percent goods and services tax. Paying these taxes is made easy for consumers, with airlines lumping all the charges together in the ticket price.

gateway from Asia, being more than 1,200 kilometers (750 miles) closer to Tokyo than Los Angeles is. The city is well served by carriers from across the Pacific, in addition to Air Canada's Asian destinations. Vancouver is served by **Air China** (800/685-0921, www.airchina.com) from Beijing; **All Nippon Airways** (888/422-7533, www.ana.co.jp) from Osaka and Tokyo in affiliation with Air Canada; **Cathay Pacific** (604/606-8888, www.cathaypacific.com) twice daily from Hong Kong; **Eva Air** (800/695-1188, www.evaair.com) from Taipei; **Japan Airlines** (800/525-3663, www.jal.com) from Tokyo; **Korean Air** (800/438-5000, www.koreanair.com) from Seoul; **Philippine Airlines** (800/435-9725, www.philippineairlines.com) from Manila; and **Singapore Airlines** (604/689-1223, www.singaporeair.com) from Singapore via Seoul.

In addition to Air Canada's daily London-Vancouver flight, **British Airways** (800/247-9297, www.britishairways.com) also flies this route daily. Air Canada flights between Vancouver and continental Europe are routed through Toronto, but **KLM** (800/447-4747, www.klm.com) has a daily nonstop flight to Vancouver from Amsterdam, and **Lufthansa** (800/563-5954, www.lufthansa.com) flies from Frankfurt.

RAIL
VIA Rail

Government-run **VIA Rail** (416/366-8411 or 888/842-7245, www.viarail.ca) provides passenger-train service across Canada, with western terminuses at Vancouver and Prince Rupert. The *Canadian* is a thrice-weekly service between Toronto and Vancouver via Edmonton, Jasper, Kamloops, Saskatoon, and Winnipeg. Service is provided in two classes of travel: **Economy** features lots of legroom, reading lights, pillows and blankets, and a Skyline Car complete with bar service, while **Silver and Blue** is more luxurious, featuring sleeping rooms, daytime seating, all meals, a lounge and dining car, and shower kits for passengers.

PASSES AND PRACTICALITIES

If you're traveling to Vancouver from any eastern province, the least expensive way to travel is on a **Canrailpass,** which allows seven trips within a 21-day period anywhere on the VIA Rail system. During high season (June 1-Oct. 15), the pass is adults $899, over age 60 and children $849 for travel on 10 one-way trips.

On regular fares, discounts of 25-40 percent apply to travel in all classes October-June. Those over 60 and under 25 receive a 10 percent discount that can be combined with other seasonal fares. Check for advance-purchase restrictions on all discount tickets. The VIA Rail website (www.viarail.ca) provides route, schedule, and fare information, takes reservations, and offers links to towns and sights en route. Or pick up a train schedule at any VIA Rail station.

Rocky Mountaineer

Rocky Mountaineer Vacations (604/606-7245 or 877/460-3200, www.rockymountaineer.com) runs a luxurious rail trip between Vancouver and Banff or Jasper, through the spectacular interior mountain ranges of British Columbia. Travel is during daylight hours only, so you don't miss anything. Trains depart in either direction in the morning (every second or third day), overnighting at Kamloops. One-way travel in RedLeaf Service, which includes light meals, nonalcoholic drinks, and Kamloops accommodations, costs $1,399 pp d from Vancouver to either Banff or Jasper and $1,549 from Vancouver to Calgary. SilverLeaf is a step up in quality, with a glass-domed car allowing a wide range of viewing opportunities. Prices in SilverLeaf are $1,899 pp d from Vancouver to either Banff or Jasper and $2,059 from Vancouver to Calgary. GoldLeaf Service is the ultimate in luxury. Passengers ride in a two-story glass-domed car, eat in a separate dining area, and stay in Kamloops's most luxurious accommodations. GoldLeaf costs $2,499 pp d from Vancouver to Banff or Jasper and $2,549 to Calgary. Outside of high season (mid-Apr.-May and the first two weeks of Oct.), all fares are reduced a few hundred dollars. Trains terminate in Vancouver off Terminal Avenue at 1755 Cottrell Street, behind Pacific Central Station.

BUS

Bus travel throughout Canada is easy with **Greyhound** (604/482-8747 or 800/661-8747, www.greyhound.ca). The company offers Trans-Canada Highway service from Toronto, Winnipeg, Regina, and Calgary through Kamloops to Vancouver, as well as

a more southerly route from Calgary through Cranbrook and the Kootenays to Vancouver. Among the northern routes: Edmonton and Jasper southwest to Vancouver or west to Prince Rupert; and Grande Prairie northwest through Dawson Creek to Whitehorse (Yukon). Reservations are not necessary—just turn up when you want to go, buy your ticket, and kick back. As long as you use your ticket within 30 days, you can stop over wherever the bus stops and stay as long as you want. For those that have traveled extensively with Greyhound in the past, be aware that the Discovery Pass has been discontinued.

FERRY

One of the most pleasurable ways to get your first view of British Columbia is from sea level. Many scheduled ferry services cross from Washington state to Victoria, on Vancouver Island, but no ferries run to Vancouver from south of the border.

Three companies provide a ferry link between Washington State and Vancouver Island. **Clipper Navigation** (250/382-8110 or 800/888-2535, www.clippervacations.com, adults US$109 one-way, US$185 round-trip) has a passenger-only service departing Seattle's Pier 69 for Victoria's Inner Harbour up to five times daily in summer and less frequently the rest of the year. A daily, year-round link between Port Angeles and Victoria is made by the **MV Coho** (250/386-2202 or 360/457-4491, www.cohoferry.com, adults US$18.50, children US$9.25, vehicles and driver US$64), which has been sailing this route since 1959. Onboard the 1,000-passenger ship is a café, a gift shop, and a variety of indoor and outdoor observation decks for viewing the journey. **Washington State Ferries** (206/464-6400, 250/381-1551, or 888/808-7977, www.wsdot.wa.gov/ferries, adults US$19.45, seniors and children US$9.70, vehicles and driver US$53.65) link Anacortes, north of Seattle, with Sidney, 32 kilometers (20 miles) north of Victoria.

Getting Around

The best way to get around British Columbia is via your own vehicle—be it a car, RV, motorbike, or bicycle. It's easy to get around by bus, but you can't get off the beaten track and, let's face it, that's exactly where most of British Columbia is. It's also easy to get around by air—all the larger airports are served by scheduled intraprovincial flights, and charter services fly out of many of the smaller ones.

AIR

For travel connections throughout British Columbia, **Air Canada** (604/688-5515 or 888/247-2262, www.aircanada.ca), serves most major BC cities from both Vancouver and Victoria international airports.

Harbour Air (604/274-1277 or 800/665-0212, www.harbour-air.com) has scheduled floatplane flights between downtown Vancouver (the terminal is beside Canada Place) and Victoria's Inner Harbour. Expect to pay around $120 pp one-way for any of these flights. **Pacific Coastal** (604/273-8666 or 800/663-2872, www.pacificcoastal.com) has flights to Vancouver's South Terminal (connected to the main terminals by shuttle) and Victoria International Airport from Campbell River, Comox, Cranbrook, Kelowna, Port Hardy, Powell River, Williams Lake, and many remote coastal towns farther north, including Masset on Haida Gwaii. **Central Mountain Air** (250/877-5000 or 888/865-8585, www.fly-cma.com) is a Smithers-based airline with flights throughout the province, including central and northern British Columbia. **Hawk Air** (250/635-4295 or 800/487-1216, www.hawkair.ca) offers scheduled flights between Vancouver's South Terminal and Terrace, Prince Rupert, and Smithers. Also from the South Terminal, **KD Air** (604/688-9957 or 800/665-4244, www.kdair.com) flies up to five times daily to Qualicum Beach (Vancouver Island), with a connecting ground shuttle to Port Alberni. **Orca Airways** (604/270-6722 or 888/359-6722, www.flyorcaair.com) flies from the South Terminal to Qualicum Beach and Tofino/Ucluelet.

Air Canada and WestJet both serve Whitehorse, but with more options is the local carrier **Air North** (800/661-0407, www.flyairnorth.com), which has daily flights to Whitehorse from Vancouver, Kelowna, Edmonton, Calgary, and Yellowknife.

BUS

British Columbia by bus is a snap. Just about all the cities have local bus companies providing transportation in town and, in many cases, throughout their local region—check the transportation sections of each individual chapter for more details. **Greyhound** operates daily bus service to just about anywhere in the province. You don't need to make reservations—just buy your ticket and go. All scheduled services are nonsmoking. The bus depot in Vancouver is **Pacific Central Station** (1150 Station St., 604/482-8747 or 800/661-8747).

FERRY
BC Ferries

Chances are, at some stage of your British Columbia adventure, you'll use the services of **BC Ferries** (250/386-3431 or 888/223-3779, www.bcferries.com), which serves 46 ports with a fleet of 40 vessels. All fares listed for "vehicles" in this book cover cars and trucks up to 6.1 meters (20 feet) long and under 2.1 meters (7 feet) high (or under 2 meters/6 feet, 8 inches high on a few routes). Larger vehicles such as RVs pay more. Also note that prices listed for all types of vehicles are in addition to the passenger price; the vehicle's driver, rider, or porter is not included in the vehicle fare.

Vancouver has two major ferry terminals. From **Tsawwassen,** south of downtown, ferries run regularly across the Strait of Georgia to the Vancouver Island centers of Swartz Bay (32 kilometers/20 miles north of Victoria) and Nanaimo. From **Horseshoe Bay,** west of downtown Vancouver, ferries ply the strait to Nanaimo. Also from Horseshoe Bay, ferries run across Howe Sound to **Langdale,** gateway to the Sunshine Coast. From **Powell River,** at the north end of the Sunshine Coast, ferries depart for **Comox** (Vancouver Island), making it possible to visit both the island and the Sunshine Coast without returning to Vancouver.

BC Ferries also provides regular services from Vancouver Island and the mainland to the **Southern Gulf Islands.** Other islands in the Strait of Georgia linked to Vancouver Island by ferry include: Thetis (from Chemainus), Gabriola (from Nanaimo), Denman and Hornby (from Buckley Bay), Quadra and Cortes (from Campbell River), Malcolm and Cormorant (from Port McNeil), and Texada (from Powell River).

From **Port Hardy** at the northern tip of Vancouver Island, a ferry runs north up the coast to **Prince Rupert.** From the end of May through September, the ferry goes every other day; from October through April, once a week; and during May, twice a week. The trip takes 15 hours and links up with the **Alaska Marine Highway.** Also from Prince Rupert, ferries run to **Haida Gwaii;** these longer sailings require reservations, which should be made as far in advance as possible.

Inland Ferries

Many interior lakes and rivers are crossed by ferries owned and operated by the government. Of course, no service is available between freeze-up and breakup, but the rest of the year, expect service from 6am until at least 10pm daily. Some of the ferries are small, capable of carrying just 2 vehicles, while others can transport up to 50. Passage is free on all these ferries, including the 45-minute sailing across Kootenay Lake between Balfour and Kootenay Bay— the world's longest free ferry trip.

DRIVING IN CANADA

U.S. driver's licenses and International Driving Permits are valid in Canada. All highway signs give distances in kilometers and speeds in kilometers per hour. Unless otherwise posted, the maximum speed limit on the highways is 100 km/h (62 mph).

Use of safety belts is mandatory, and motorcyclists must wear helmets. Infants and toddlers weighing up to nine kilograms (20 pounds) must be strapped into an appropriate child's car seat. Use of a child car seat for larger children weighing 9-18 kilograms (20-40 pounds) is required of British Columbia residents and recommended for nonresidents. Before venturing north of the 49th parallel, U.S. residents should ask their vehicle insurance company for a Canadian Nonresident Interprovincial Motor Vehicle Liability Insurance Card. You may also be asked to prove vehicle ownership, so carry your vehicle registration form. If you're involved in an accident with a BC vehicle, contact the nearest Insurance Corporation of British Columbia office (800/663-3051).

If you're a member in good standing of an automobile association, take your membership card—the Canadian Automobile Association provides members of related associations full services, including free maps, itineraries, excellent tour books, road and weather condition information, accommodations reservations, travel agency services, and emergency road services. For more information, contact the **British Columbia Automobile Association** (604/268-5555 or 800/564-6222, www.bcaa.com).

Drinking and driving (with a blood-alcohol level of 0.08 percent or higher) in British Columbia can get you imprisoned for up to five years on a first offense and will cost you your license for at least 12 months.

Car Rental

All major car-rental companies have outlets at Vancouver International Airport, in downtown Vancouver, and in Victoria. Many companies also have cars available in towns and cities throughout the province. Try to book in advance, especially in summer. Expect to pay from $50 per day, $250 per week for a small economy car with unlimited kilometers in the off-season and from $80 per day and $400 per week in summer.

Vehicles can be booked for Canadian pickup through parent companies in the United States or elsewhere using the Internet or toll-free numbers. **Discount** (604/207-8140 or 800/263-2355, www.discountcar.com) is a Canadian company with 300 rental outlets across the country. Its vehicles are kept in service a little longer than those at the other major companies, but rates are excellent—even through summer—especially if booked in advance. Other major rental companies with outlets in Calgary, Edmonton, and Vancouver are **Avis** (800/974-0808, www.avis.ca), **Budget** (800/268-8900, www.budget.com), **Dollar** (800/800-4000, www.dollar.com), **Enterprise** (800/325-8007, www.enterprise.com), **Hertz** (800/263-0600, www.hertz.ca), **National** (800/227-7368, www.nationalcar.com), and **Rent-A-Wreck** (800/327-0116, www.rentawreck.ca).

RV and Camper Rental

You might consider renting a camper-van or other recreational vehicle for your British Columbia vacation. With one of these apartments-on-wheels, you won't need to worry about finding accommodations each night. Even the smallest units aren't cheap, but they can be a good deal for longer-term travel or for families or two couples traveling together. The smallest vans, capable of sleeping two people, start at $200 per day with 100 kilometers (62 miles) per day included. Standard extra charges include insurance, a preparation fee (usually around $60 per rental), a linen and cutlery charge (around $80 pp per trip), and taxes. Major Vancouver companies include **Canadream** (604/527-1102 or 866/412-8308, www.canadream.com) **Cruise Canada** (480/464-7300 or 800/671-8042, www.cruisecanada.com) and **Fraserway RV** (604/527-1102 or 800/661-2441, www.fraserway.com). In summer, expect to pay from $200 per day for your own home-on-wheels. Remember to figure in higher ferry charges for crossing to Vancouver Island with an RV.

Recreation

The great outdoors: British Columbia certainly has plenty of it. The province encompasses some 948,600 square kilometers (366,250 square miles) of land area and a convoluted coastline totaling 25,000 kilometers (15,500 miles). With spectacular scenery around every bend, millions of hectares of parkland, and an abundance of wildlife, the province is an outdoors lover's fantasy come true.

PARKS AND PROTECTED AREAS

Visitors and locals alike enjoy over 800 protected areas totaling 12 million hectares (29 million acres) throughout British Columbia.

From old-growth coastal rainforests to glaciated peaks, and ranging in size from less than one hectare (2.5 acres) to over a million hectares (2.5 million acres), these parks provide almost unlimited recreation opportunities.

National Parks

British Columbia holds 7 of Canada's 44 national parks. The most accessible is also the newest, **Southern Gulf Islands National Park,** which was created in 2003 by piecing together existing provincial and marine parks scattered throughout the archipelago. **Pacific Rim National Park** protects a stretch of Vancouver Island's rugged west coast, offering long beaches, remote islands, and the

National Park Passes

Permits are required for entry into all Canadian national parks. A **National Parks Day Pass** costs up to adults $10, seniors $8, children $5, up to a maximum of $20 per vehicle. It is interchangeable among parks and is valid until 4pm the day following its purchase. An annual **Discovery Pass**, good for entry into all of Canada's national parks and national historic sites (five of which are in British Columbia) for one year from the date of purchase, is adults $68, seniors $58, children $33, up to a maximum of $136 per vehicle.

Annual and day passes are available at park gates, at all park information centers, and at campground fee stations. Day passes are also available from automated ticket machines at popular stopping points in Pacific Rim National Park. For more information, check the Parks Canada website (www.pc.gc.ca).

famous West Coast Trail to explore. In the east of the province, **Kootenay** and **Yoho National Parks** form a part of the UNESCO Canadian Rocky Mountains Parks World Heritage Site; the two spectacular parks lie just across the Continental Divide from the more famous Banff and Jasper National Parks in neighboring Alberta. Also protecting a mountainous landscape are **Glacier** and **Mount Revelstoke National Parks** along the Trans-Canada Highway. The most remote of British Columbia's national parks is **Gwaii Haanas** on Haida Gwaii. No roads access this park, which encompasses the southern half of an archipelago renowned the world over for abandoned Haida villages. For information on all these parks, as well as **Kluane National Park** in the Yukon, contact **Parks Canada** (www.pc.gc.ca).

Provincial Parks

BC Parks manages more than 800 protected areas, including over 600 provincial parks. Many are day-use areas, others have campgrounds (11,000 campsites in over 340 campgrounds), but all have one thing in common: They protect a particularly scenic area, a unique natural feature, a wildlife habitat, or maybe a fish-filled lake.

Among these are **Cypress Provincial Park,** on Vancouver's city limits and offering great views; **Carmanah Walbran Provincial Park,** protecting a magnificent old-growth forest on Vancouver Island; **Manning Provincial Park,** a high-alpine area of snowcapped peaks and colorful flower-filled meadows; **Kokanee Glacier Provincial Park,** named for its spectacular ice field; **Mount Assiniboine Provincial Park,** a rugged Rocky Mountain wilderness perfect for extended hiking trips; **Mount Robson Provincial Park,** protecting the Canadian Rockies' highest peak; **Bowron Lake Provincial Park,** famous for its wilderness canoe route; and **Naikoon Provincial Park,** on Haida Gwaii.

Major new parks added in the last three decades include **Valhalla Provincial Park,** a remote wilderness area in the heart of the Kootenays; **Khutzeymateen Provincial Park,** an important coastal grizzly bear habitat; the 6.5-million-hectare (16-million-acre) **Muskwa-Kechika Management Area** of the northern Canadian Rockies; and, in the province's extreme northwest corner, **Tatshenshini-Alsek Provincial Park,** part of the world's largest UNESCO World Heritage Site.

For information on provincial parks, contact **BC Parks** (www.bcparks.ca).

Forest Service Lands

Over half of British Columbia—59 million hectares (146 million acres)—is forested and under the control of the Ministry of Forests, which manages the land for timber harvesting, recreational activities, and just plain wilderness. Many recreation areas have been provided on forest land, but facilities are often limited. Get more information on recreation areas, forest roads, safety, and possible fire closures from the **Ministry of Forests, Lands, Natural Resource Operations & Rural Development** (www.gov.bc.ca), regional offices, information centers throughout the province, or the interactive government website www.sitesandtrailsbc.ca.

HIKING

Just about everywhere you go in British Columbia you'll find good hiking opportunities, from short, easy walks in city and regional parks to long, strenuous hikes in wilderness parks.

The mountains are great places to hike. Short trails lead to waterfalls, lakes, rock formations, and viewpoints, and longer trails wander high into alpine meadows tangled with wildflowers, past turquoise lakes, and up to snow-dusted peaks providing breathtaking views. Rustic huts are provided at regular intervals along wilderness trails. Perhaps the best known of British Columbia's hikes lies not in the Rockies but along the wild and remote west shore of Vancouver Island; backpackers return time and again to the **West Coast Trail,** an unforgettable 75-kilometer (47-mile) trek along the remote coastline of Pacific Rim National Park.

To get the most out of a hiking trip, peruse the hiking section of any major bookstore—many books have been written on BC hiking trails. The **Don't Waste Your Time** series (www.hikingcamping.com) covers interior regions while the *Canadian Rockies Trail Guide* (www.summerthought.com) is the book of choice for Kootenay and Yoho National Parks. Before setting off on a longer hike, study the trail guides and a topographical map of the area. Leave details of your intended route and itinerary with a relative or friend. And try to travel in groups of at least two in the backcountry.

CYCLING AND MOUNTAIN BIKING

Cycling is a great way to explore British Columbia. The casual pace allows riders time to stop and appreciate the scenery, wildlife, and flowers that can easily be overlooked at high speeds. Some of the most popular areas for cycling trips are the **Southern Gulf Islands** between Vancouver Island and the mainland (quiet, laid-back, loads of sunshine, rural scenery, and lots of artists), the **east coast of Vancouver Island** (following the Strait of Georgia past lazy beaches and bustling towns), the **Kootenays** (forest-clad mountains, deep lakes, curious old gold- and silver-mining communities, and ghost towns—good mountain-bike country), and the **Rockies** (outstanding mountain scenery second to none, abundant wildlife often right beside the highways, hot springs, and hiking trails). Rocky Mountain routes suit the intermediate to advanced cyclist.

For information on touring, tour operators, bicycle routes, rental shops, and handy tips, visit the website of **Cycling BC** (604/737-3034, www.cyclingbc.net) or go to the **British Columbia Mountain Bike Guide** (www.bcmbg.com). The **Backroad Mapbook** series (available at most outdoor retailers and island gas stations) have sections dedicated to bike-accessible trails.

WATER SPORTS
Canoeing, Kayaking, and Stand-Up Paddleboarding

Canoes are a traditional form of transportation along British Columbia's numerous lakes and rivers. You can rent one at many of the more popular lakes, but if you bring your own you can slip into any body of water whenever you please, taking in the scenery and viewing wildlife from water level. One of the most popular canoe routes is in **Bowron Lake Provincial Park,** where a 117-kilometer (73-mile) circuit leads through a chain of lakes in the Cariboo Mountains. Shorter but no less challenging is the **Powell Forest**

Canoe Route, on the Sunshine Coast. Other, less-traveled destinations include **Slocan Lake** and **Wells Gray Provincial Park.** For information on canoe routes, courses, and clubs, contact the **Outdoor Recreation Council of BC** (604/873-5546, www.orcbc.ca).

Anywhere suitable for canoeing is also prime kayaking territory, although most keen kayakers look for white-water excitement. The best wilderness kayaking experiences are in the north, where access can be difficult but crowds are minimal. The **Stikine River** is challenging, with one stretch—the Grand Canyon of the Stikine—successfully run only a handful of times.

The province's long coastline is great for sea kayaking, and rentals are available in most coastal communities. The **Southern Gulf Islands** are ideal for kayakers of all experience levels, while destinations such as **Desolation Sound,** the **Broken Group Islands,** and **Gwaii Haanas National Park** are the domain of experienced paddlers. Most companies offering kayak rentals also provide stand-up paddleboard rentals, lessons, and often tours. One such Vancouver operation is the **Ecomarine Paddlesports Centres** (604/689-7575, www.ecomarine.com) based on Granville Island. Tofino, on Vancouver Island's west coast, is another hub for sea kayakers. **Tofino Sea Kayaking Company** (250/725-4222 or 800/863-4664, www.tofinoseakayaking.com) rents kayaks and leads tours through local waterways.

White-Water Rafting

The best and easiest way to experience a white-water rafting trip is on a half-day or full-day trip with a qualified guide. Close to Vancouver, the **Green, Fraser, Nahatlatch,** and **Thompson Rivers** are run commercially. In the Canadian Rockies, the **Kicking Horse River** provides the thrills. Expect to pay $120-175 for a full day's excitement, land transfers, and lunch.

Boating

British Columbia's 25,000 kilometers (15,500 miles) of coastline, in particular the sheltered, island-dotted Strait of Georgia between Vancouver Island and the mainland, is a boater's paradise. Along it are sheltered coves, sandy beaches, beautiful marine parks, and facilities specifically designed for boaters—many accessible only by water. One of the most beautiful marine parks is **Desolation Sound,** north of Powell River; locals claim it's one of the world's best cruising grounds. Many of the enormous freshwater lakes inland are also excellent places for boating.

Yachties and yachties-to-be should head for **Cooper Boating** (1832 Mast Tower Rd., Granville Island, 604/687-4110 or 888/999-6419, www.cooperboating.com), which boasts Canada's largest sailing school and also holds the country's biggest fleet for charters. For those with experience, Cooper's rents yachts (from $410 per day for a Catalina 32) for a day's local sailing, or take to the waters of the Strait of Georgia on a bareboat charter (from $2,100 per week for a Catalina 27).

Scuba Diving

Some of the world's most varied and spectacular cold-water diving lies off the coast of British Columbia. Diving is best in winter, when you can expect up to 40 meters of visibility. The diverse marinelife includes sponges, anemones, soft corals, rockfish (china, vermilion, and canary), rock scallops, and cukes. Plenty of shipwrecks also dot the underwater terrain. The most popular dive sites are off the Southern Gulf Islands, Ogden Point in Victoria, Nanaimo (for wreck diving), Telegraph Cove, Port Hardy, and Powell River (the scuba diving capital of Canada). Many of the coastal communities along Vancouver Island and the Sunshine Coast have dive shops with gear rentals and air tanks, and many can put you in touch with charter dive boats and guides.

A quick flip through the Vancouver Yellow Pages lets you know that scuba diving is alive and well north of the 49th parallel. The city's many scuba shops have everything you need, and they're excellent sources of information on all the best local spots. Coming highly recommended are **Rowand's Reef Scuba Shop** (1731 West 4th Ave., Vancouver, 604/669-3483, www.rowandsreef.com) and **Ogden Point Dive Centre** (199 Dallas Rd., 250/380-9119, www.divevictoria.com), both full-service dive shops offering rentals, sales, organized diving trips, and PADI dive-certification courses. The local *Diver* magazine (www.divermag.com) is another good source of information; its scuba directory lists retail stores, resorts, charter boats, and other services.

FISHING
Freshwater

The province's freshwater anglers fish primarily for trout—mostly rainbow trout, but also Dolly Varden, lake, brook, brown, and cutthroat trout. One particular type of rainbow trout, the large anadromous **steelhead,** is renowned as a fighting fish and considered by locals to be the ultimate fishing challenge. Salmon are also abundant in the province; several seagoing species come up British Columbia's rivers to spawn. **Kokanee** rarely grow over one kilogram (2.2 pounds), but this freshwater salmon is an excellent sport fish inhabiting lakes of the southern interior. Feeding near the surface and caught on wet or dry artificial flies, they taste great, especially when smoked.

Fishing guides, tours, lodges (from rustic to luxurious), and packages are available throughout the province; one is sure to suit you. Expect to pay $250-600 a day for a guide, and up to several thousand dollars for several days at a luxury lodge with all meals and guided fishing included.

Fishing licenses are required for freshwater fishing, and prices vary according to your age and place of residence. British Columbia residents pay $36 for an adult license, good for one year. All other Canadians pay $20 for a one-day license, $36 for an eight-day license,

or $55 for a one-year. Nonresidents pay $20, $50, and $80, respectively.

For more information, contact the **Ministry of Environment** (www.gov.bc.ca) and download the *British Columbia Freshwater Fishing Regulations Synopsis.* The nonprofit **Freshwater Fisheries Society of BC** website (www.gofishbc.com) is a good source of freshwater fishing information, and including reports for which lakes have been stocked with which species.

Tidal

The tidal waters of British Columbia offer some of the world's best fishing, with remote lodges scattered along the coast catering to all budgets. And although most keen anglers will want to head farther afield for the best fishing opportunities, many top fishing spots can be accessed on a day trip from Vancouver. The five species of Pacific salmon are most highly prized by anglers. The chinook (king) salmon in particular is the trophy fish of choice. They commonly weigh over 10 kilograms (22 pounds) and are occasionally caught at over 20 kilograms (44 pounds); those weighing over 12 kilograms (26.5 pounds) are often known as "tyee." Other salmon present are coho (silver), pink (humpback), sockeye (red), and chum (dog). Other species sought by local recreational anglers include halibut, lingcod, rockfish, cod, perch, and snapper.

A tidal-water sportfishing license for residents of Canada, good for one year from March 31, costs $22.05 ($11.55 for those 65 and over); for nonresidents, the same annual license costs $106, or $7.35 for a single-day license, $19.95 for three days, and $32.55 for five days. A **salmon conservation stamp** is an additional $6.30. Licenses are available from sporting stores, gas stations, marinas, and charter operators. When fish-tagging programs are on, you may be required to make a note of the date, location, and method of capture, or to record on the back of your license statistical information on the fish you catch. Read the current rules and regulations.

For further information, contact **Fisheries and Oceans Canada** (604/664-9250, www.pac.dfo-mpo.gc.ca).

The **Sport Fishing Institute of British Columbia** (604/270-3439, www.sportfishing.bc.ca) has an online database of charter operators and fishing lodges, and details license requirements.

GOLFING

Relative to the rest of Canada, British Columbia's climate is ideal for golfing, especially on Vancouver Island, where the sport can be enjoyed year-round. Many of the province's 280 courses are in spectacular mountain, ocean, or lake settings. Municipal courses offer the lowest greens fees, generally $20-70, but the semiprivate, private, and resort courses usually boast the most spectacular locations. At these courses, greens fees can be as high as $200. At all but the smallest municipal courses, club rentals, power carts, and lessons are available, and at all but the most exclusive city courses, nonmembers are welcomed with open arms. The mild climate and abundance of water create ideal conditions for the upkeep of golf courses in the south of the province—you'll be surprised at how immaculately manicured most are.

SKIING AND SNOWBOARDING

Most of the developed winter recreation areas are in the southern third of the province. Whether you're a total beginner or an advanced daredevil, BC resorts have a slope to suit you. The price of lift tickets is generally reasonable, and at most resorts, you don't have to spend half your day lining up for the lifts.

The best known of all Canadian winter resorts is **Whistler Blackcomb,** north of Vancouver, but others scattered through the southern interior provide world-class skiing and boarding on just-as-challenging slopes. The best of these include: **Big White** and **Silver Star** in the Okanagan Valley; **Red Mountain** and **Whitewater** near Nelson; **Fernie Alpine Resort** near Fernie;

Panorama near Invermere; and **Sun Peaks** north of Kamloops. In the north, **Powder King,** north of Prince George, lives up to its name with an average annual snowfall around 12 meters (39 feet)—among the highest of any North American resort. You can even go skiing and boarding out on Vancouver Island at **Mt. Washington.**

Heli- and Sno-Cat Skiing and Boarding

Alternatives to resorts are also available. If you're an intermediate or advanced skier or snowboarder, you can go heli-skiing and heli-boarding in the mind-boggling scenery and deep, untracked powder of the Coast and Chilcotin Ranges, the central Cariboo Mountains, the Bugaboos, and the BC Rockies. The world's largest heli-ski operation is **Canadian Mountain Holidays** (403/762-7100 or 844/862-7108, www.canadianmountainholidays.com), founded by Austrian mountain guide Hans Gmoser in the Bugaboos in 1965. Today the operation has grown to include almost limitless terrain over five mountain ranges accessed from 11 lodges. **Mike Wiegele Helicopter Skiing** (250/673-8381 or 800/661-9170, www.wiegele.com) offers heli-skiing and heli-boarding in the Monashee and Cariboo Mountains from a luxurious lodge at Blue River.

Another, less-expensive alternative is to hook up with one of the many Sno-Cat operations in the province. Sno-Cats are tracked all-terrain vehicles, similar to snow groomers but capable of carrying passengers, that can transport skiers and boarders up through the snow to virgin slopes in high-country wilderness. British Columbia has been a world leader in this type of skiing, and many operators are scattered through the province. Through its location amid some of the continent's most consistent powder snow and because of its luxurious lodgings, **Island Lake Catskiing** (250/423-3700 or 888/422-8754, www.islandlakecatskiing.com) near Fernie has gained a reputation for both its Sno-Cat skiing and its upscale backcountry lodge.

Accommodations and Camping

Over the last two decades, I've visited as many British Columbia and Yukon accommodations as possible, and my top choices in all price ranges are detailed in the travel chapters of this book. Destination British Columbia maintains the official government website, **www.hellobc.com,** which has a lodging search engine and booking system. You can also order a printed accommodations guide through this website or by calling 250/387-1642 or 800/435-5622. For Yukon lodging, check the website **www.travelyukon.com** or call 800/661-0494 to have an accommodations guide sent out.

Rates quoted in this book are for a standard double room through the high season, which generally runs June to early September (except in alpine resort towns such as Whistler, where December to March is the most expensive time to visit). Almost all accommodations are less expensive outside these busy months, some cutting their rates by as much as 50 percent. You'll enjoy the biggest seasonal discounts at properties that rely on summer tourists, such as those in Vancouver, on Vancouver Island, and in the Okanagan Valley. The same applies in Vancouver and to a lesser extent Victoria on weekends—many of the big downtown hotels rely on business and convention travelers to fill the bulk of their rooms; when the end of the week rolls down, the hotels are left with rooms to fill at discounted rates Friday, Saturday, and Sunday nights.

HOTELS AND MOTELS

Prices for a basic motel room in a small town start at $60 s, $65 d. In Vancouver and Victoria expect to pay at least double this amount for the least expensive rooms. The most luxurious lodgings in the province—Vancouver's Pan Pacific Hotel, Victoria's grand old Fairmont Empress, or any one of Whistler's resort hotels, for example—charge over $300 for a basic

room. Room rates outside the two major cities fluctuate greatly. For example, few lodgings on Vancouver Island charge less than $100, but along the Trans-Canada Highway, in places like Kamloops and Revelstoke, you can pay as little as $80 for a room. Try to plan ahead for summer travel and book as far in advance as possible, especially for accommodations in Vancouver and Prince Rupert, on Vancouver Island, and on Haida Gwaii.

Making Reservations

While you have no influence over the seasonal and weekday-weekend pricing differences, *how* you reserve a room *can* make a difference in how much you pay. First and foremost, when it comes to searching out actual rates, the Internet is an invaluable tool. Most accommodations websites listed in *Moon British Columbia* show rates, and many have online reservation forms. Use these websites to search out specials, many of which are available only on the Internet.

Don't be afraid to negotiate during slower times. Even if the desk clerk has no control over rates, there's no harm in asking for a bigger room or one with a better view. Just look for a "Vacancy" sign hanging out front.

Most hotels offer auto association members an automatic 10 percent discount, and whereas senior discounts apply only to those over 60 or 65 on public transportation and at attractions, most hotels offer discounts to those over 50, with chains such as Best Western also allowing senior travelers a late checkout. "Corporate Rates" are a lot more flexible than in years past; some hotels require nothing more than the flash of a business card for a 10-20 percent discount.

When it comes to frequent flyer programs, you really do need to be a frequent flyer to achieve free flights, but the various loyalty programs offered by hotels often provide benefits simply for signing up.

BED-AND-BREAKFASTS

Bed-and-breakfast accommodations are found throughout British Columbia. Styles run the gamut from restored heritage homes to modern townhouses. They are usually private residences, with up to four guest rooms, and as the name suggests, breakfast is included. Rates fluctuate enormously. In Vancouver and Victoria, for example, they range $60-180 s, $70-210 d. Amenities also vary greatly—the "bed-and-breakfast" may be a single spare room in an otherwise regular family home or a full-time business in a purpose-built home. Regardless, guests can expect hearty home cooking, a peaceful atmosphere, personal service, knowledgeable hosts, and conversation with like-minded travelers.

Reservation Agencies

The **British Columbia Bed & Breakfast Innkeepers Guild** (www.bcsbestbnbs.com) represents over 100 bed-and-breakfasts across the province. The association produces an informative brochure with simple descriptions and a color photo of each property, and manages an easily navigable website. This association doesn't take bookings—they must be made directly. **Bed and Breakfast Online** (www.bbcanada.com) doesn't take bookings either, but links are provided and an ingenious search engine helps you find the accommodations that best fit your needs.

BACKPACKER ACCOMMODATIONS

Budget travelers are enjoying more and more options in British Columbia, ranging from a renovated downtown Vancouver hotel to a remote backcountry lodge in Yoho National Park., all for around $25-54 pp. All backpacker lodges have shared living and dining facilities, most have wireless Internet access, and some have extras such as bike rentals.

Hostelling International

You don't *have* to be a member to stay in an affiliated hostel of Hostelling International (HI), but membership pays for itself after only a few nights of discounted lodging. Aside from lower rates, benefits of membership vary from country to country but often include discounted air, rail, and bus travel; discounts on car rental; and discounts on some attractions and commercial activities.

For Canadians, the membership charge is $35 annually or $175 for a lifetime membership. For more information, contact **HI-Canada** (800/663-5777, www.hihostels.ca). Joining the HI affiliate of your home country entitles you to reciprocal rights in Canada, as well as around the world. In the United States, the contact address is **Hostelling International USA** (301/495-1240, www. hiusa.org); annual membership is adults US$28 and seniors US$18, or become a lifetime member for US$250.

Other contact addresses include **YHA England and Wales** (0800/0191-700, www. yha.org.uk), **YHA Australia** (02/9261-1111, www.yha.com.au), and **YHA New Zealand** (03/379-9970, www.yha.org.nz). Otherwise, click through the links on the HI website (www.hihostels.com) to your country of choice.

CAMPING

Almost every town in British Columbia and the Yukon has at least one campground, often with showers and water, electricity, and sewer hookups. Prices range $15-30 in smaller towns, up to $60 in the cities and more popular destinations such as Tofino and the Okanagan Valley. If you're planning a summer trip to Vancouver, Vancouver Island, the Sunshine Coast, Whistler, or the Okanagan Valley, try to book in advance. At other times and places, advance reservations aren't usually necessary.

National parks provide some of the nicest campgrounds. All have picnic tables, fire grates, toilets, and fresh drinking water, although only some provide showers. Prices range $14-28 depending on facilities and services. They are all open through summer, with some parks having one area designated for winter camping. Sites at the most popular campgrounds can be reserved through the **Parks Canada Campground Reservation Service** (877/737-3783, www.pccamping.ca). Backcountry camping in a national park costs $8 pp per night.

Nearly 14,000 campsites lie scattered through 11,000 campgrounds in 300 provincial parks. Rates range $16-38 per night, depending on facilities, most of which are basic (only a very few provincial park campgrounds have hookups). Reserve a spot at most popular provincial parks through BC Parks' **Discover Camping** (519/826-6850 or 800/689-9025, www.discovercamping.ca) reservation system.

Reservations are taken between March 15 and September 15 for dates up to three months in advance. The reservation fee is $6 per night, to a maximum of $19 per stay, and is in addition to applicable camping fees.

Camping in the province's over 1,400 **Forest Service Campgrounds** costs $8-10 per site per night, which is collected on-site. For a list of site locations, visit www.sitesandtrailsbc.ca. Commercial and provincial park campgrounds are listed in Tourism BC's invaluable *Accommodations* guide, available online at www.hellobc.com or at all official visitors centers.

Travel Tips

VISAS AND OFFICIALDOM
Entry into Canada

To enter Canada, a **passport, passport card,** or **NEXUS card** is required by citizens and permanent residents of the United States. For further information, see the website http://travel.state.gov. For current entry requirements to Canada, check the Citizenship and Immigration Canada website (www.cic.gc.ca).

All other **foreign visitors** entering Canada must have a valid passport and may need a visitor permit or Temporary Resident Visa, depending on their country of residence and the vagaries of international politics. At present, visas are not required for citizens of Commonwealth nations or Western Europe. The standard entry permit is for six months, and you may be asked to show onward tickets or proof of sufficient funds to last you through your intended stay. Extensions are available from the Citizenship and Immigration Canada office in Vancouver. This department's website (www.cic.gc.ca) is the best source of the latest entry requirements.

Clearing Customs

You can take the following into Canada duty-free: reasonable quantities of clothes and personal effects, 50 cigars and 200 cigarettes, 200 grams of tobacco, 1.14 liters of spirits or wine, food for personal use, and gas (normal tank capacity). Pets from the United States can generally be brought into Canada, with certain caveats. Dogs and cats must be more than three months old and have a rabies certificate showing date of vaccination. Birds can be brought in only if they have not been mixing with other birds, and parrots need an export permit because they're on the endangered species list.

Handguns, automatic and semiautomatic weapons, and sawn-off rifles and shotguns are not allowed into Canada. Visitors with firearms must declare them at the border; restricted weapons will be held by Customs and can be picked up on exit from the country. Those not declared will be seized and charges may be laid. It is illegal to possess any firearm in a national park unless it is dismantled or carried in an enclosed case. Up to 5,000 rounds of ammunition may be imported but should be declared on entry.

On reentering the United States, if you've been in Canada more than 48 hours you can bring back up to US$400 worth of household and personal items, excluding alcohol and tobacco, duty-free. If you've been in Canada fewer than 48 hours, you may bring in only up to US$200 worth of such items duty-free.

For further information on all customs regulations contact **Canada Border Services Agency** (204/983-3500 or 800/461-9999, www.cbsa-asfc.gc.ca).

LIQUOR LAWS

Liquor laws in Canada are enacted on a provincial level. The minimum age for alcohol consumption in British Columbia is 19.

Like the rest of North America, driving in Vancouver and Victoria under the influence of alcohol or drugs is a criminal offense. Those convicted of driving with a blood alcohol concentration above 0.08 face big fines and an automatic one-year license suspension. Second convictions (even if the first was out of province) lead to a three-year suspension. Note that in British Columbia drivers below the limit can be charged with impaired driving. It is also illegal to have open alcohol in a vehicle or in public places.

SMOKING

Smoking is banned in virtually all public places across Canada. Most provinces have enacted province-wide bans on smoking in public places (including restaurants and bars), including British Columbia, where a blanket law went into effect in 2008. The ban does not include hotel rooms, although most lodgings do ban the practice. Smoking and vaping is also banned within six meters (20 feet) of all windows and doors. Additionally in British Columbia, smoking and vaping is prohibited in motor vehicles when a passenger age 16 or younger is present.

TIPPING

Gratuities are not usually added to the bill. In restaurants and bars, around 15-18 percent of the total amount is expected. But you should tip according to how good (or bad) the service was, as low as 10 percent or up to and over 20 percent for exceptional service. The exception to this rule is groups of eight or more, when it is standard for restaurants to add 15-20 percent as a gratuity. Tips are sometimes added to tour packages, so check this in advance, but you can also tip guides on stand-alone tours. Tips are also given to bartenders, taxi drivers, porters, and hairdressers.

EMPLOYMENT AND STUDY

Whistler and the resort towns are especially popular with young workers from across Canada and beyond. Aside from Help Wanted ads in local papers, a good place to start looking for work is the Whistler Employment Resource Centre (www.whistlerchamber.com).

International visitors wishing to work or study in Canada must obtain authorization *before* entering the country. Authorization to work will only be granted if no qualified Canadians are available for the work in question. Applications for work and study are available from all Canadian embassies and must be submitted with a nonrefundable processing fee. The Canadian government has a reciprocal agreement with Australia for a limited number of **holiday work visas** to be issued each year. Australian citizens ages 30 and under are eligible; contact your nearest Canadian embassy or consulate. For general information on immigrating to Canada, contact **Citizenship and Immigration Canada** (www.cic.gc.ca).

VISITORS WITH DISABILITIES

A lack of mobility should not deter you from traveling to Vancouver and Victoria, but you should definitely do some research before leaving home.

If you haven't traveled extensively, start by doing some online research. **Flying Wheels Travel** (507/451-5005 or 877/451-5006, www.flyingwheelstravel.com) caters solely to the needs of travelers with disabilities. The **Society for Accessible Travel and Hospitality** (212/447-7284, www.sath.org) supplies information on tour operators, vehicle rentals, specific destinations, and companion services. For frequent travelers, the annual membership fee (adults US$49, seniors US$29) is well worthwhile. *Emerging Horizons* (www.emerginghorizons.com) is a U.S. quarterly online magazine dedicated to travelers with special needs.

Access to Travel (800/465-7735, www.accesstotravel.gc.ca) is an initiative of the Canadian government that includes information on travel within and between Canadian cities, including Victoria. The website also has a lot of general travel information for those with disabilities. The **Canadian National Institute for the Blind** (800/563-2642, www.cnib.ca) offers a wide range of services from its Vancouver office (604/431-2121). Finally, click on the Resource Centre link at the **Spinal Cord Injury BC** (604/324-3611, www.sci-bc.ca) website, which is another good source of information.

TRAVELING WITH CHILDREN

Regardless of whether you're traveling with toddlers or teens, you will come upon decisions affecting everything from where you stay to your choice of activities. Luckily for you, Vancouver and Victoria are very family-friendly, with a variety of indoor and outdoor attractions aimed specifically at the younger generation.

Admission and tour prices for children are included throughout the destination chapters of this book. As a general rule, these reduced prices are for children ages 6-16. For two adults and two or more children, always ask about family tickets. Children under 6 nearly always get in free. Most hotels and motels will happily accommodate children, but always try to reserve your room in advance and let the reservations desk know the ages of your kids. Often, children stay free in major hotels, and in the case of some major chains—such as Holiday Inn—eat free also. Generally, bed-and-breakfasts aren't suitable for children and in some cases don't accept kids at all. Ask ahead.

As a general rule when it comes to traveling with children, let them help you plan the trip, looking at websites and reading up on the province together. To make your vacation more enjoyable if you'll be spending a lot of time on the road, rent a minivan (major rental agencies usually have a limited supply). Don't forget to bring along favorite toys and games from home—whatever you think will keep your kids entertained when the joys of sightseeing wear off.

The websites of **Destination British Columbia** (www.hellobc.com) and **Tourism Vancouver** (www.tourismvancouver.com) have sections devoted to children's activities. Another useful online tool is **Traveling Internationally with Your Kids** (www.travelwithyourkids.com).

Health and Safety

Compared to other parts of the world, Canada is a relatively safe place to visit. Vaccinations are required only if coming from an endemic area. That said, wherever you are traveling, carry a medical kit that includes bandages, insect repellent, sunscreen, antiseptic, antibiotics, and water-purification tablets. Good first-aid kits are available at most camping shops. Health care in Canada is mostly dealt with at the provincial level.

Taking out a travel-insurance policy is a sensible precaution because hospital and medical charges start at around $1,000 per day. Copies of prescriptions should be brought to Canada for any medicines already prescribed.

GIARDIA

Giardiasis, also known as beaver fever, is a real concern for those heading into the backcountry of British Columbia. It's caused by an intestinal parasite, *Giardia lamblia,* that lives in lakes, rivers, and streams. Once the parasite is ingested, its effects, although not instantaneous, can be dramatic: Severe diarrhea, cramps, and nausea are the most common symptoms. Preventive measures should always be taken, including boiling all water for at least 10 minutes, treating all water with iodine, or filtering all water using a filter with a pore size small enough to block the giardia cysts.

WINTER TRAVEL

Travel to Vancouver and Vancouver Island in winter is relatively easy, with snowfall only rarely falling in these regions. Traveling beyond the coast during winter months should not be undertaken lightly. Before setting out in a vehicle, check antifreeze levels, and always carry a spare tire and blankets or sleeping bags. **Frostbite** is a potential hazard, especially when cold temperatures are combined with high winds (a combination known as **wind chill**). Most often, frostbite leaves a numbing, bruised sensation, and the skin turns white. Exposed areas of skin, especially the nose and ears, are most susceptible.

Hypothermia occurs when the body fails to produce heat as fast as it loses it. It can strike at any time of the year but is more common during cooler months. Cold weather, combined with hunger, fatigue, and dampness, creates a recipe for disaster. Symptoms are not always apparent to the victim. The early signs are numbness, shivering, slurring of words, dizzy spells, and, in extreme cases, violent behavior, unconsciousness, and even death. The best way to dress for the cold is in layers, including a waterproof outer layer. Most important, wear headgear. The best treatment is to get the victim out of the cold, replace wet clothing with dry, slowly give hot liquids and sugary foods, and place the victim in a sleeping bag. Warming too quickly can lead to heart attacks.

CRIME

Although Vancouver and Victoria are generally safer than U.S. cities of the same size, the same safety tips apply there as elsewhere in the world. Visitors, unused to their surroundings and generally carrying valuables such as cameras and credit cards, tend to be easy targets for thieves. You can reduce the risk of being robbed by using common sense. First and foremost in Vancouver, avoid East Hastings Street, especially at night. It is known as one of the seediest areas in all of Canada, so you should catch a bus or cab between downtown and Chinatown to avoid this area. Wherever you are, avoid traveling or using ATMs at night, try to blend in with the crowd by walking with a purpose, be discreet if reading a map out in public, and don't wear expensive jewelry.

Information and Services

MONEY

As in the United States, Canadian currency is based on dollars and cents. Coins come in denominations of 5, 10, and 25 cents, and 1 and 2 dollars. The one-dollar coin is the gold-colored "loonie," named for the bird featured on it. The unique two-dollar coin is silver with a gold-colored insert. Notes come in $5, $10, $20, $50, and $100 denominations. **All prices quoted in this book are in Canadian dollars, unless noted.** American dollars are accepted at many tourist areas, but the exchange rate is more favorable at banks. Currency other than U.S. dollars can be exchanged at most banks, airport money-changing facilities, and foreign exchange brokers in Vancouver, Victoria, and Whistler. Travelers checks are the safest way to carry money, but a fee is often charged to cash them if they're in a currency other than Canadian dollars. All major credit and charge cards are honored at Canadian banks, gas stations, and most commercial establishments. Automatic teller machines (ATMs) can be found in almost every town.

Costs

The cost of living in British Columbia is similar to that of all other Canadian provinces, but higher than in the United States. If you will be staying in hotels or motels, accommodations will be your biggest expense. Gasoline is sold in liters (3.78 liters equals 1 U.S. gallon) and is generally $1.20-1.50 per liter for regular unleaded.

Taxes

A seven percent **Provincial Sales Tax** is applied to almost all purchases made within British Columbia (basic groceries are exempt), and a five percent **goods and services tax (GST)** is applied across Canada.

MAPS AND INFORMATION
Maps

Driving maps are available at bookstores, gas stations, and gift shops throughout the province. In Vancouver, pick up maps at these specialty bookstores: **International Travel Maps and Books** (12300 Bridgeport Rd., Richmond, 604/273-1400, www.itmb.com), **The Travel Bug** (2865 W. Broadway, 604/737-1122, www.travelbugbooks.ca), or **Wanderlust** (1929 W. 4th Ave., Kitsilano, www.wanderlustore.com, 604/739-2182). These stores stock many topographical maps and can order specific maps and marine charts for you.

If you're heading to the BC Rockies, look for **Gem Trek** (www.gemtrek.com) maps, which use GPS to plot hiking trails. The backs of the maps are filled with trail information and tidbits of history.

Tourism Information

Begin planning your trip by contacting the government tourist office: **Destination BC** (250/387-1642 or 800/435-5622, www.hellobc.com). The literature and maps can be downloaded from the website or ordered by phone.

Currency Exchange

Through 2017, the Canadian dollar held steady in value against the U.S. dollar after a number of years of decreasing value.

At press time, exchange rates (into Canadian dollars) for major currencies are:

- US$1 = $1.24
- AUS$1 = $0.97
- €1 = $1.50
- HK$10 = $1.62
- NZ$1 = $0.87
- GBP£1 = $1.69
- ¥100 = $1.13

On the Internet, check current exchange rates at www.xe.com/ucc.

All major currency can be exchanged at banks in British Columbia or at most airports. Many Canadian businesses will accept U.S. currency, but you will get a better exchange rate from the banks.

As well as being a great source of tourism information, the agency produces the invaluable *Accommodations* guide and a road map.

Each town of any size in British Columbia has a **visitor centre,** including the **Vancouver Visitor Centre** (200 Burrard St., 604/683-2000). Hours vary, but most are open June-August. When these are closed, head to the local chamber of commerce for information. Most chamber offices are open Monday-Friday year-round.

COMMUNICATIONS
Postal Services

Canada Post (www.canadapost.ca) issues postage stamps that must be used on all mail posted in Canada. First-class letters and postcards sent within Canada are $1, to the United States $1.20, to other international destinations $1.85. Prices increase along with the weight of the mailing. You can buy stamps at post offices, automatic vending machines, most hotel lobbies, airports, Pacific Central Station in Vancouver, many retail outlets, and some newsstands.

Phones and Cell Reception

The **area code** for Vancouver and the lower mainland, including the Sunshine Coast, as far north as Whistler, and east to Hope, is **604**. The area code for the rest of the province, including Victoria and all of Vancouver Island, is **250**. The area code **778** and **236** applies to new numbers. The area code for all of the Yukon is **867**. You must add the relevant area code to all numbers, even when dialed locally.

The country code for Canada is 1, the same as the United States. Toll-free numbers have the 800, 888, or 877 prefix, and may be good within British Columbia, in Canada, throughout North America, or, in the case of major hotel chains and car-rental companies, worldwide.

To make an international call from Canada, dial the prefix 011 before the country code or dial 0 for operator assistance.

Cell phone reception is good in populated areas, but you may lose reception quickly beyond town boundaries. For example, there is no reception along sections of the Trans-Canada Highway between Revelstoke and Golden.

Internet Access

Internet providers allow you to access your email away from your home computer, or open an email account with Outlook (www.live.com) or Gmail (www.gmail.com). Although there are restrictions to the size and number of emails you can store, these services are handy and, best of all, free.

Public Internet access is available throughout British Columbia. Nearly all lodgings have Wi-Fi access from guest rooms (the exceptions are lodges in remote locations), and it's usually free (the exceptions are larger hotels like the Fairmont chain). Except for wilderness hostels, backpacker lodges also provide free Internet access. You'll also find Internet cafés as well as free wireless Internet in cafés and public areas throughout the province.

WEIGHTS AND MEASURES

Canada officially adopted the **metric system** back in 1975, though you still hear grocers talking in ounces and pounds, golfers talking in yards, and seafarers talking in nautical miles. Metric is the primary unit used in this book, but we've added conversions for readers from the United States, Liberia, and Myanmar, the only countries that have not adopted the metric system. You can also refer to the metric conversion chart in the back of this book.

Electricity

Electrical voltage is 120 volts, 60 hertz, the same as in the United States.

Time Zones

Most of British Columbia and all of the Yukon are in the **Pacific time zone** (PST and PDT), the same as Los Angeles and three hours earlier than eastern time. The **mountain time zone** (MST and MDT) extends west into southern British Columbia, which includes Yoho and Kootenay National Parks as well as the towns of Golden and Radium Hot Springs.

Resources

Suggested Reading

NATURAL HISTORY

Cannings, Richard, and Russell Cannings. *Birdfinding in British Columbia.* Vancouver: Greystone Books, 2013. Written by a local expert and his son, this field guide covers all of the province, as well providing detailed directions to the best viewing spots.

Cannings, Richard and Sydney. *British Columbia: A Natural History.* Vancouver: Greystone Books, 2015. The natural history of the province divided into 10 chapters, including "Forests of Rain," "Mountaintops," and "The World of Fresh Water." A beautiful book with lots of color maps.

Cannings, Sydney, and Richard Cannings. *Geology of British Columbia.* Vancouver: Greystone Books, 2011. In the same format as their other books, the Cannings present a comprehensive guide to the geology of the province through easy-to-read text, diagrams, and an abundance of color photography.

Fischer, George (photographer). *Haida Gwaii Queen Charlotte Islands: Land of Mountains, Mystery, and Myth.* Halifax: Nimbus Publishing, 2006. A magnificent coffee table book that depicts the unique and intriguing natural and human history of these remote islands.

Folkens, Peter. *Marine Mammals of British Columbia and the Pacific Northwest.* Vancouver: Harbour Publishing, 2001. In a waterproof fold-away format, this booklet provides vital identification tips and habitat maps for 50 marine mammals, including all species of whales present in local waters.

Gadd, Ben. *Handbook of the Canadian Rockies.* Canmore, Alberta: Corax Press, 2009. Although bulky for backpackers, this classic field guide is a must-read for anyone interested in the natural history of the Canadian Rockies.

Gill, Ian. *Haida Gwaii: Journeys through the Queen Charlotte Islands.* Vancouver: Raincoast Books, 1997. A personal and touching view of the Queen Charlottes complemented by the stunning color photography of David Nunuk.

Haig-Brown, Roderick. *Return to the River.* Vancouver: Douglas & McIntyre, 1997. Although fictional, this story of the life of one salmon and its struggle through life is based on fact, and is a classic read for both anglers and naturalists. It was originally published in 1946 but has recently been reprinted and is available at most bookstores.

Herrero, Stephen. *Bear Attacks: Their Causes and Avoidances.* New York: Nick Lyons Books, 2018. Through a series of gruesome stories, the newest edition of this book catalogs the stormy relationship between people and bruins, provides hints on avoiding attacks, and tells what to do if you're attacked.

Mathews, Bill. *Roadside Geology of Southern British Columbia*. Victoria: Heritage House, 2010. This useful field guide uses natural landmarks to explain the geological history of the province's southern reaches.

Parfit, Michael, and Suzanne Chisholm. *The Lost Whale: The True Story of an Orca Named Luna*. New York: St. Martin's Press, 2013. In 2001, a young orca whale was separated from his family and found a new home in Nootka Sound (Vancouver Island), much to the delight of visitors and the consternation of conservationists. This is his story.

Pyne, Stephen J. *Awful Splendor*. Vancouver: University of British Columbia Press, 2007. This big, beautiful book tells the story of wildfires in Canada, both through specific fires and the effects on the environment and humans.

HUMAN HISTORY

Barman, Jean. *The West Beyond the West: A History of British Columbia*. Toronto: University of Toronto Press, 2007. Authored by a local university professor, this book makes interesting reading for its exploration of the province's lesser-known history.

Bosher, J. F. *Vancouver Island in the Empire*. Self-published, 2012. Don't be put off by this book being self-published—this extensive tome is the best historical reference to the island's European history currently in print.

Budd, Robert. *Voices of British Columbia: Stories from Our Frontier*. Vancouver: Douglas & McIntyre, 2010. This large volume puts into print the stories of people and places throughout British Columbia collected by journalist Imbert Orchard through the 1960s.

Coupland, Douglas. *City of Glass: Douglas Coupland's Vancouver*. Vancouver: Douglas & McIntyre, 2000. Best known for coining the term *Generation X* in his 1991 novel of the same name, local author Coupland delves deep into the cultural heart of Vancouver.

Johnson, Pauline. *Legends of Vancouver*. Vancouver: Douglas & McIntyre, 1998. First published in 1911, this small book contains the writings of Pauline Johnson, a well-known writer and poet in the early part of the 1900s. She spent much of her time with First Nations peoples, and this is her version of myths related to her by Joe Capilano, chief of the Squamish people. This most recent edition is the latest of many reprints over the years; search out others at Vancouver's many secondhand bookstores.

King, Thomas. *The Inconvenient Indian: A Curious Account of Native People in North America*. Toronto: Anchor Canada, 2013. One of Canada's preeminent novelists, King delves into what it means to be of First Nations descent through historical research and his own experiences.

Luxton, Donald. *Building the West: The Early Architects of British Columbia*. Vancouver: Talonbooks, 2007. Printed in two-tone, this beautiful reference book delves into the lives and work of prominent early architects, many of whom are represented by buildings that still stand today.

Mallory, Enid. *Robert Service: Under the Spell of the Yukon*. Vancouver: Heritage House, 2006. Follows the life of Robert Service, best known for poems such as "The Cremation of Sam McGee," from the time he stepped off a ship in Vancouver to his wildly successful change of careers in Dawson City.

Mather, Ken. *Buckaroos and Mud Pups: The Early Days of Ranching in British Columbia*. Victoria: Heritage House, 2010. Tells the story of the earliest days of ranching, beginning with an 1858 cattle drive through the Cariboo region.

Mather, Ken. *Frontier Cowboys and the Great Divide*. Victoria: Heritage House, 2013. Mather's most recent look at the province's cowboy history and how it differed from the culture in neighboring Alberta.

Murray, Tom. *Canadian Pacific Railway*. Osceola, Wisconsin: Zenith Press, 2006. Railway buffs are spoiled for choice when it comes to reading about the history of Canada's transcontinental railway, but this large-format book stands apart for its presentation of historic images and coverage of the railway industry today.

Nicol, Eric. *Vancouver*. Toronto: Doubleday Canada, 1970. An often humorous look at Vancouver and its colorful past through the eyes of Eric Nicol, one of Vancouver's favorite columnists of the 1960s. The book has been reprinted a few times, and although it has been out of print for many years, Vancouver's secondhand bookstores usually have multiple copies in stock.

Pepper, Don. *Fishing the Coast: A Life on the Water*. Madeira Park, BC: Harbour Publishing, 2013. Lifelong commercial fisherman and now industry analyst Pepper explore the history of one of the world's most dangerous occupations from a British Columbia perspective.

Thorburn, Mark. *British Columbia Place Names*. Edmonton: Dragon Hill, 2010. From the intriguing to the wacky, the meaning of place-names across the province is presented in a fun, easy-to-read format.

Valliant, John. *The Golden Spruce*. Toronto: Vintage Canada, 2006. The gripping true story of a man who chopped down one of the world's only golden spruce trees, then disappeared to leave many questions unanswered.

Varney, Philip. *Ghost Towns of the Pacific Northwest*. Minneapolis: Voyageur Press, 2013. Using color maps, stunning images, and detailed descriptions, Varney brings to life British Columbia boomtowns such as Sandon and Fort Steele, as well as many in Oregon and Washington.

RECREATION

Danehower, Cole. *Essential Wines and Wineries of the Pacific Northwest: A Guide to the Wine Countries of Washington, Oregon, British Columbia, and Idaho*. Portland, Oregon: Timber Press, 2010. Wine journalist Danehower takes readers on a journey through local wine regions in this stunning coffee-table book that catalogs the recent growth of the local wine industry.

Kimantas, John. *BC Coastal Recreation Kayaking and Small Boat Atlas*. Vancouver: Whitecap Books, 2012. A detailed guide to coastal waterways, with an excellent map list. Although primarily designed for maritime users, the maps and text are also relevant for those traveling the coastal areas by road.

Lewis, Jim, and Susan Campany. *Gold Panning in British Columbia*. Victoria: Heritage House, 2013. Lewis has written extensively on gold panning in British Columbia, and this is his most recent guide, which comes complete with detailed descriptions of mining sites.

Nature Vancouver. *The Birder's Guide to Vancouver and the Lower Mainland*. Vancouver: Harbour Publishing, 2016. This colorful field guide details 350 species recorded in the region and provides detailed directions to the best viewing spots.

Padmore, Christabel. *On the Flavour Trail*. Victoria: TouchWood Editions, 2013. A recipe book filled with dishes created by Vancouver Island's best-known chefs and culinary experts.

Patton, Brian, and Bart Robinson. *Canadian Rockies Trail Guide*. Banff, Alberta: Summerthought Publishing, 2017. This regularly updated guide, first published in 1971, covers 230 hiking trails and 3,400 kilometers (2,100 miles) in the Canadian Rockies, including Kootenay and Yoho National Parks.

Pratt-Johnson, Betty. *151 Dives in the Protected Waters of British Columbia and Washington State*. Seattle: Mountaineers Books, 2007. This book is the best source of detailed information on diving in British Columbia.

Scott, Chic. *Summits & Icefields 2: Alpine Ski Tours in the Columbia Mountains*. Victoria: Heritage House, 2012. The first edition covered the Canadian Rockies while the second is the most comprehensive guide to skiing in the backcountry of the nearby Columbia Mountains. Includes detailed maps.

Shewchuk, Murphy, and Judie Steeves. *Okanagan Trips and Trails*. Toronto: Fitzhenry and Whiteside, 2013. Perfectly described by its subtitle—A Guide to the Backroads and Hiking Trails of British Columbia's Okanagan-Similkameen Region—this locally written guide is the best resource I have found to Okanagan hiking trails.

GUIDEBOOKS AND MAPS

Backroad Mapbooks. Vancouver: Mussio Ventures, www.backroadmapbooks.com. This atlas series is perfect for outdoors enthusiasts, with detailed maps, and highlights such as campgrounds, fishing spots, and swimming holes.

Crockford, Ross. *Victoria: The Unknown City*. Vancouver: Arsenal Pulp Press, 2006. Filled with little-known facts and interesting tales, this book describes how to get the best seats on BC Ferries, where to shop for the funkiest used clothing, the history of local churches, and more.

Mackie, John. *Vancouver: The Unknown City*. Vancouver: Arsenal Pulp Press, 2003. Compiled from the author's many years uncovering city secrets revealed in his magazine writing, this book delves into the darkest corners of the city.

MapArt, www.mapart.com. Driving maps for all of Canada, including provinces and cities. Maps are published as old-fashioned fold-out versions, as well as laminated and in atlas form.

Wiebe, Joe. *Craft Beer Revolution*. Vancouver: Douglas & McIntyre, 2015. British Columbia was home to Canada's first brewpub, which this book catalogs, along with over 50 other brewpubs and microbreweries across the province.

MAGAZINES

British Columbia. Vancouver. Since 1959, this quarterly magazine has been depicting the beauty of the province through stunning color photography and informative prose (www.bcmag.ca).

Canadian Geographic. Ottawa: Royal Canadian Geographical Society. Bimonthly publication pertaining to Canada's natural and human histories and resources (www.canadiangeographic.ca).

Explore. Vancouver. Bimonthly publication of adventure travel throughout Canada (www.explore-mag.com).

Western Living. Vancouver. Lifestyle magazine for western Canada. Includes travel, history, homes, and cooking (www.westernliving.ca).

Internet Resources

TRAVEL PLANNING

Canadian Tourism Commission
www.canadatourism.com
Official tourism website for all of Canada.

Destination British Columbia
www.hellobc.com
Learn more about the province, plan your travels, and order tourism literature.

Tourism Vancouver
www.tourismvancouver.com
An excellent resource for planning your time in Vancouver.

Tourism Victoria
www.tourismvictoria.com
The official site for British Columbia's capital.

PARKS

BC Parks
www.bcparks.ca
A division of the government's Ministry of Environment, this office is responsible for British Columbia's provincial parks. Website includes details of each park, as well as recreation and camping information.

Canadian Parks and Wilderness Society
www.cpaws.org
Nonprofit organization that is instrumental in highlighting conservation issues throughout Canada. The link to the British Columbia chapter provides local information and a schedule of guided walks.

Parks Canada
www.pc.gc.ca
Official website of the agency that manages Canada's national parks and national historic sites. Website has information on each of western Canada's national parks (fees, camping, and wildlife) and national historic sites.

Parks Canada Campground Reservation Service
www.pccamping.ca
Online reservation service for national park campgrounds.

Yellowstone to Yukon Conservation Initiative
www.y2y.net
Network of 800 groups working on conservation issues along the Canadian Rockies from the United States north to the Yukon.

Yukon Conservation Society
www.yukonconservation.org
This Whitehorse-based organization is active in a variety of natural resources issues, but also offers public programs of hikes and lectures.

GOVERNMENT

Citizenship and Immigration Canada
www.cic.gc.ca
Check this government website for anything related to entry into Canada.

Environment Canada
www.weather.gc.ca
Seven-day forecasts from across Canada, including over 100 locations throughout British Columbia. Includes weather archives such as seasonal trends and snowfall history.

Government of British Columbia
www.gov.bc.ca
The official website of the BC government.

Government of Canada
www.gc.ca
The official website of the Canadian government.

TRANSPORTATION AND TOURS

Air Canada
www.aircanada.ca
Canada's largest airline.

BC Ferries
www.bcferries.com
Providing a link between Vancouver and Vancouver Island.

Rocky Mountaineer Vacations
www.rockymountaineer.com
Luxurious rail service to and from Vancouver to Banff and Jasper, including via Whistler.

WestJet
www.westjet.com
A western Canada-based Canadian airline.

VIA Rail
www.viarail.ca
Passenger rail service across Canada.

PUBLISHERS

Arsenal Pulp Press
www.arsenalpulp.com
A backstreet in Chinatown is the perfect location for this fiercely independent publisher with a title list stacked with urban literature.

Harbour Publishing
www.harbourpublishing.com
This Sunshine Coast publisher specializes in British Columbia history.

Heritage House
www.heritagehouse.ca
With over 700 nonfiction books in print, this large Victoria publisher is known for its historical and recreation titles covering all of western Canada.

Orca Book Publishing
www.orcabook.com
This Victoria publisher specializes in children's books.

Summerthought Publishing
www.summerthought.com
Publisher of Canadian Rockies books, including the *Canadian Rockies Trail Guide*.

Whitecap
www.whitecap.ca
Best known for its Canadian coffee-table books, this Vancouver publisher also produces respected cooking titles.

Index

XYZ

List of Maps

Photo Credits

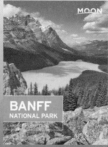

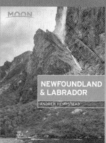
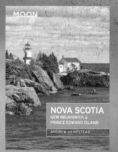

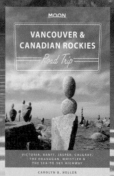

MONTRÉAL
ANDREA BENNETT

QUÉBEC CITY
SACHA JACKSON

VANCOUVER
Including Victoria, Vancouver Island, and Whistler
CAROLYN B. HELLER

MAINE, VERMONT & NEW HAMPSHIRE
JEN ROSE SMITH

NEW ENGLAND
JEN ROSE SMITH

NEW YORK STATE
JULIE SCHWIETERT COLLAZO

NIAGARA FALLS
Including the Canadian & U.S. Sides
JOEL A. DOMBROWSKI

SEATTLE
ALLISON WILLIAMS

WASHINGTON
MATTHEW LOMBARDI

Pack up the pemmican, grab a guide,
and find your next Canadian adventure!

MOON NATIONAL PARKS

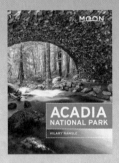

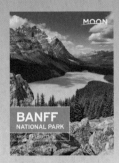

ACADIA
NATIONAL PARK
HILARY NANGLE

**ARCHES &
CANYONLANDS**
NATIONAL PARKS
W. C. MCRAE & JUDY JEWELL

BANFF
NATIONAL PARK

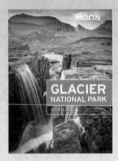

DEATH VALLEY
NATIONAL PARK
JENNA BLOUGH

GLACIER
NATIONAL PARK
BECKY LOMAX

**GRAND
CANYON**
KATHLEEN BRYANT

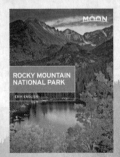

**GREAT SMOKY
MOUNTAINS**
NATIONAL PARK
JASON FRYE

**MOUNT RUSHMORE
& THE BLACK HILLS**
Including the Badlands
LAURAL A. BIDWELL

**ROCKY MOUNTAIN
NATIONAL PARK**
ERIN ENGLISH

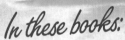

In these books:

- Full coverage of gateway cities and towns
- Itineraries from one day to multiple weeks
- Advice on where to stay (or camp) in and around the parks

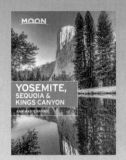

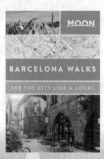

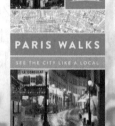

MAP SYMBOLS

▦	Expressway	○	City/Town	✈	Airport	⚲	Golf Course
▦	Primary Road	◉	State Capital	✗	Airfield	℗	Parking Area
▤	Secondary Road	⊛	National Capital	▲	Mountain	⬛	Archaeological Site
- - - -	Unpaved Road	★	Point of Interest	✛	Unique Natural Feature	✝	Church
———	Feature Trail	•	Accommodation			⛽	Gas Station
- - - -	Other Trail	▾	Restaurant/Bar	≈	Waterfall	◠	Glacier
··········	Ferry	■	Other Location	▲	Park		Mangrove
▦	Pedestrian Walkway	Δ	Campground	▣	Trailhead		Reef
▥	Stairs			✗	Skiing Area		Swamp

CONVERSION TABLES

°C = (°F − 32) / 1.8
°F = (°C × 1.8) + 32
1 inch = 2.54 centimeters (cm)
1 foot = 0.304 meters (m)
1 yard = 0.914 meters
1 mile = 1.6093 kilometers (km)
1 km = 0.6214 miles
1 fathom = 1.8288 m
1 chain = 20.1168 m
1 furlong = 201.168 m
1 acre = 0.4047 hectares
1 sq km = 100 hectares
1 sq mile = 2.59 square km
1 ounce = 28.35 grams
1 pound = 0.4536 kilograms
1 short ton = 0.90718 metric ton
1 short ton = 2,000 pounds
1 long ton = 1.016 metric tons
1 long ton = 2,240 pounds
1 metric ton = 1,000 kilograms
1 quart = 0.94635 liters
1 US gallon = 3.7854 liters
1 Imperial gallon = 4.5459 liters
1 nautical mile = 1.852 km

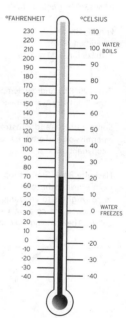

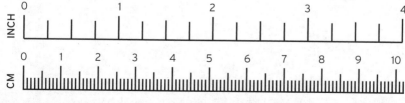

MOON BRITISH COLUMBIA

Avalon Travel
Hachette Book Group
1700 Fourth Street
Berkeley, CA 94710, USA
www.moon.com

Editor: Kimberly Ehart
Series Manager: Kathryn Ettinger
Copy Editor: Linda Cabasin
Graphics and Production Coordinator:
  Lucie Ericksen
Cover Design: Faceout Studios, Charles Brock
Interior Design: Domini Dragoone
Moon Logo: Tim McGrath
Map Editor: Albert Angulo
Cartographers: Brian Shotwell, Larissa Gatt
Indexer: Greg Jewett

ISBN-13: 978-1-64049-187-8

Printing History
1st Edition —1989
11th Edition — May 2018
5 4 3 2 1

Text © 2018 by Andrew Hempstead.
Maps © 2018 by Avalon Travel.

Front cover photo: Pacific Rim National Park, Vancouver Island © David Kleyn/Alamy Stock Photo
Back cover photo: boats on Lake O'Hara © LNelugo | Dreamstime.com

Printed in China by RR Donnelley

Avalon Travel is a division of Hachette Book Group, Inc. Moon and the Moon logo are trademarks of Hachette Book Group, Inc. All other marks and logos depicted are the property of the original owners.